The
COBOL
Environment

PRENTICE-HALL SOFTWARE SERIES
Brian Kernighan, advisor

The COBOL Environment

ROBERT T. GRAUER

Associate Professor
Management Science
University of Miami

MARSHAL A. CRAWFORD

Consultant
CGA Computer Associates
Rockville, Md.

PRENTICE-HALL, INC., Englewood Cliffs, New Jersey 07632

Library of Congress Cataloging in Publication Data

Grauer, Robert T   (date)
    The COBOL environment.

    (Prentice-Hall software series)
    Includes index.
    1. COBOL (Computer program language)
I. Crawford, Marshal A.,   (date)   joint author.
II. Title.   III. Series.
QA76.73.C25G73   001.6'424   78-25631
ISBN   0-13-139394-4

COBOL is an industry language and is not the property of any company or group of companies, or of any organization or group of organizations.

No warranty, expressed or implied, is made by any contributor or by the CODASYL Programming Language Committee as to the accuracy and functioning of the programming system and language. Moreover, no responsibility is assumed by any contributor, or by the committee, in connection therewith.

The authors and copyright holders of the copyrighted material used herein

FLOW-MATIC (trademark of Sperry Rand Corporation), Programming for the UNIVAC® I and II, Data Automation Systems copyrighted 1958, 1959, by Sperry Rand Corporation; IBM Commercial Translator Form No. F 28-8013, copyrighted 1959 by IBM; FACT, DSI 27A5260-2760, copyrighted 1960 by Minneapolis-Honeywell

have specifically authorized the use of this material in whole or in part, in the COBOL specifications. Such authorization extends to the reproduction and use of COBOL specifications in programming manuals or similar publications.

Editorial/Production Supervision by Lynn S. Frankel
Cover Design by Jorge Hernandez
Manufacturing Buyer: Gordon Osbourne

Printed in the United States of America
10   9   8

Prentice-Hall International, Inc., *London*
Prentice-Hall of Australia Pty. Limited, *Sydney*
Prentice-Hall of Canada, Ltd., *Toronto*
Prentice-Hall of India Private Limited, *New Delhi*
Prentice-Hall of Japan, Inc., *Tokyo*
Prentice-Hall of Southeast Asia Pte. Ltd., *Singapore*
Whitehall Books Limited, *Wellington, New Zealand*

To Benjy, Jessica, Marion, Michael,
Sherry, and Stacy

Contents

Section II. Debugging

Section III. JCL and Utilities for the COBOL Programmer

Appendices   369

Index   459

Preface

The professional COBOL programmer cannot exist with a knowledge of COBOL alone. Instead, he must be able to interact with the operating system, he must be able to debug his programs, and he must leave well written programs for those who follow. In short, he has need for several skills which are used in conjunction with COBOL; hence, the name *The COBOL Environment*. This book is designed to teach and/or to refresh these skills for the practitioner. In addition it presents newer concepts of vital importance including: VSAM, MVS differences, and new features in the ANSI 74 standard (As implemented by IBM in Release 2 of OS/VS COBOL).

The COBOL Environment is intended as a textbook for a *second* course in COBOL. Accordingly, it does not teach the rudiments of COBOL, but concentrates on advanced COBOL elements such as indexing, sorting, file maintenance, etc. Of greater importance, it covers subjects which are omitted entirely or at best covered only briefly, in elementary courses and books. In particular:

1. Introductory COBOL texts must necessarily concentrate on teaching the language. As such, little space is left to discuss the concepts of a well written program. Emphasis is justifiably placed on continued introduction of COBOL features and their incorporation into (often contrived) programs. A student is successful if his program works, regardless of how difficult that program may be to follow for a person other

than the original author. In short there is little, if any, discussion of programming style. Further, there is virtually no coverage of program development with the disastrous consequence that most students subsequently regard this activity as a waste of time.

2. Introductory texts are deficient in their coverage of debugging. Although there are many excellent treatments of compilation errors, few COBOL books go into ABEND debugging or debugging at the source level. There is a definite need for greater treatment of this subject.

3. Introductory texts often omit JCL entirely or include it only as an appendix. Even when the material is covered in the body of the text, it is insufficient for both the practicing programmer and the advanced student. Advanced COBOL features such as SORT and COPY are always presented in the body of the text, but rarely is there coverage of supporting JCL. We have yet to see an adequate discussion of the linkage editor and/or utilities.

We do not intend the above as an indictment of all COBOL books. Indeed there have been many excellent elementary texts, but these were primarily concerned with teaching language. Hence they could not cover additional topics, or if they attempted to do so, the presentation was of necessity on an introductory level. Alternatively, there have been entire books devoted to individual treatments of programming style, debugging, JCL, etc. However, most of these addressed only one subject and that with respect to several programming languages; hence the relationship with COBOL is lost. We believe therefore that there is a definite need for an intermediate COBOL text which covers the above areas from the exclusive viewpoint of COBOL. This book is intended for both a one semester course at the junior or senior level and/or for the practicing programmer. We require thorough familiarity with COBOL.

The text is composed of three sections, each aimed at a particular shortcoming of basic books. A consistent feature throughout the text, and a major strength, are the many COBOL listings. The authors strongly believe in 'learning by doing' and provide immediate entry into sample programs in Chapter 1.

Section I discusses programming style. Chapters 1 and 2 cover top down programming and related topics including: structured programming, stepwise refinement, pseudocode, and hierarchy charts. Chapter 3 discusses COBOL implementation and coding standards. Chapter 4 covers advanced features of the language; e.g. indexing, subprograms, sorting, etc., with attention to Release 2 of OS/VS COBOL; i.e. ANSI 74 standard. Chapter 5 compares the ISAM and VSAM access methods and develops programs for nonsequential file maintenance.

Section II is a meaningful treatment of COBOL debugging. Chapter 6 discusses debugging at the source level focusing on common misinterpretations of the language. Chapter 7 develops the necessary assembly background for ABEND debugging and hints at efficiency considerations. Chapter 8 is a sound introduction into dumps, and it covers the data exception, BL and BLL cells, the SAVE AREA TRACE, and the STATE and FLOW options. MVS differences are discussed. Chapter 9 covers data management ABENDs, and gives several hints on debugging over fifteen of the most common ABENDs.

Section III covers JCL (both OS and DOS), with substantial discussion of IBM system utilities. Chapter 10 is a thorough introduction to OS JCL, with specific attention to MVS differences. Chapter 11 discusses OS utilities and the linkage editor. Chapter 12 contains parallel material for DOS. The appendices contain material of special interest to the practitioner. Appendix A discusses multiprogramming and 'spooling'. Appendix B focuses on achieving standards in existing programs. Report Writer is presented in Appendix C. Appendices D through G contain various IBM references for OS/VS COBOL, MVS JCL, and Assembler. Answers to selected exercises are given in Appendix H.

In conclusion, knowledge of COBOL in and of itself, does not necessarily yield a competent COBOL programmer. Our aim is to produce a complete individual; i.e. one who can function independently on the job, and one who is looked upon as an expert by his peers.

The authors wish to thank Karl Karlstrom of Prentice-Hall for making this project possible, and also Cathy Van Yperen, Lynn Frankel, and Nancy Milnamow, all of Prentice-Hall for making it so pleasant. We want to express special appreciation to Stuart Meisel, Director of Technical Training for American Express, for inspiring many of our examples. We thank our reviewers: Thomas G. DeLutis, Brian W. Kernighan, Donald A. Sordillo, Ralph E. Szweda, and Richard J. Weiland for their many constructive suggestions. We thank our colleagues, Paul Aron, Pete Baday, Art Cooper, Al Savin, Steve Shatz, and Liana Stanton for their help and encouragement. Finally we thank our excellent typist, 'Kricket' Miller.

Robert T. Grauer

Marshal A. Crawford

Program Development

Structured Programming

OVERVIEW

Structured programming, whatever it is, occupies much of the current literature on programming technique. Proponents claim it to be the most significant development since that of the digital computer itself. Detractors say it is nothing special, that good programs have always been structured, and that PERFORM is a fancy way of saying GO TO. Management is anxious to try it, but often does not know where to begin. Programmer reaction has run the gamut from fear of the unknown to unbridled enthusiasm. One thing seems certain—structured programming is here to stay.

Any discussion of the topic should logically begin with a definition of structured programming. Unfortunately, this is not easily accomplished, because there is no clear agreement on what structured programming is. There is, however, universal agreement on a primary goal of structured programming: *to produce working programs which are easily read and maintained by someone other than the original author.*

The chapter begins with a statement of the "structured theorem," from the Bohm and Jacopini† paper, which forms the basis for structured programming. Next, we briefly consider implementation of structured programming in COBOL. We conclude with two COBOL listings to provide specific illustrations of structured programming in COBOL.

THE BASIS FOR STRUCTURED PROGRAMMING

In a now-classical paper, Bohm and Jacopini proved that any "proper" program can be solved using only the three *logic structures* of Figure 1.1:

1. Sequence.

2. Selection.

3. Iteration.

Conspicuous by its absence in Figure 1.1 is the GO TO statement, giving rise to the term *"GO TO less" programming* as being synonymous with *structured programming*. Although any program may be written *without* the GO TO, we will see in subsequent chapters that limited use of a forward GO TO under tight restrictions may, in the opinion of the authors, actually further the goals of structured programming. For the time being however, we will require that for a program to be considered structured, it must use only the logic structures of Figure 1.1.

The *sequence structure* formally specifies that program statements are executed sequentially, in the order in which they appear unless otherwise specified. The two blocks, A and B, may denote anything from single statements to complete programs.

Selection is the choice between two actions. A condition (known as a predicate) is tested. If the predicate is true, block A is executed; if it is false, block B is executed. A and B join in a single exit point from the structure. The predicate itself is the single entry point.

Iteration calls for repeated execution of code while a condition is true. The condition (predicate) is tested. If it holds true, block A is executed; if false, the structure relinquishes control to the next sequential statement. Again, there is exactly one entry point and exit point from the structure.

The logic structures of Figure 1.1 can be combined in a limitless variety of ways to produce any required logic. This is possible because an entire structure may be substituted anywhere block A or B appears. Figure 1.2 contains two such combinations.

The entry point to Figure 1.2(a) is a selection structure to evaluate predicate$_1$. If predicate$_1$ is true, an iteration structure is entered. If predicate$_1$ is false, a sequence structure is executed instead. Both the iteration and sequence structures meet at a single point, which in turn becomes the exit point for the initial selection structure.

In Figure 1.2(b) the entry point is again a selection structure. If predicate$_1$ is true, a second selection structure for predicate$_2$ is entered. If this is also true, a third

---

†Bohm and Jacopini, "Flow Diagrams, Turing Machines and Languages with only two Formation Rules," *Communications of the ACM*, Vol. 9, May 1966.

(a) SEQUENCE

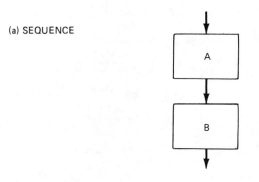

(b) SELECTION (IF THEN ELSE)

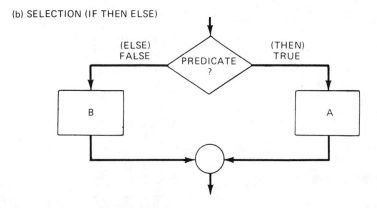

(c) ITERATION (DO WHILE)

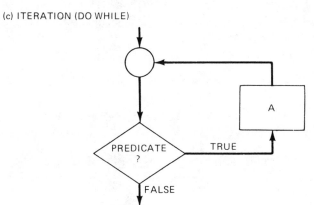

Figure 1.1 Logic Structures of a "Proper" Program

selection structure for predicate₃ is entered. Note that the alternate paths for each selection structure always meet in a single exit point for that structure. Note also that the entire logic structure of Figure 1.2(b) has a single entry, and also a single exit point.

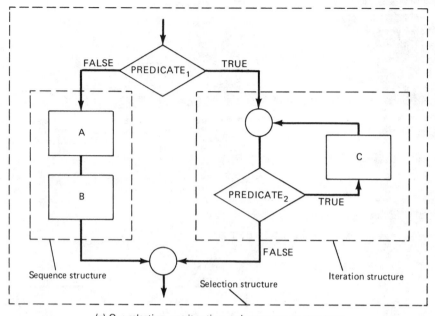

FALSE PREDICATE₁ TRUE

(a) One selection, one iteration, and one sequence structures

Figure 1.2 Combinations of Logic Structures

IMPLEMENTATION IN COBOL

The sequence structure is implemented by coding statements sequentially. Iteration is implemented by a PERFORM/UNTIL statement while selection is implemented by an IF/ELSE statement. Additional explanation is provided for the iteration and selection structures.

Iteration

The PERFORM verb is associated with the iteration structure. A simplified format is

> PERFORM procedure-name-1   [THRU procedure-name-2]
>   [UNTIL condition]

The PERFORM statement causes a portion of code to be executed. It transfers control to the procedure specified (e.g., a paragraph), continues execution from that point until another paragraph is encountered, and then returns control to the statement immediately following the PERFORM.

If the UNTIL clause is specified, the condition in the UNTIL clause is tested *prior* to any transfer of control. If the UNTIL condition is not satisfied, transfer takes place as described above; when the UNTIL condition is satisfied, control passes to the statement following the PERFORM.

6

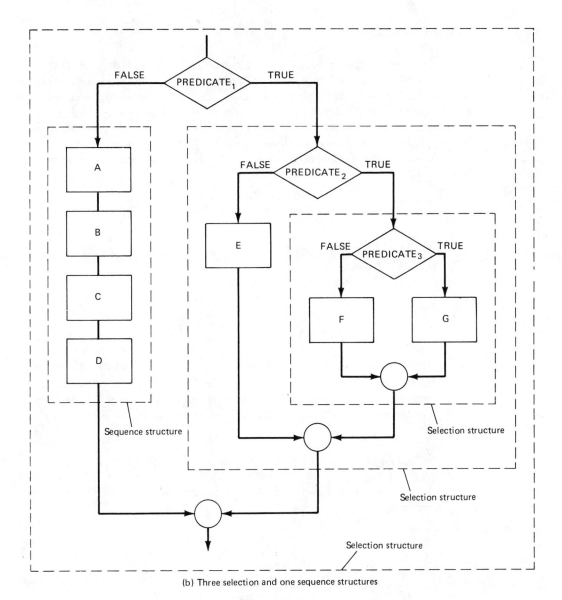

(b) Three selection and one sequence structures

Figure 1.2 Combinations of Logic Structures (continued)

Iteration is accomplished by using the UNTIL clause, specifying a condition, and modifying that condition during execution of the performed procedure. For example:

```
MOVE 'NO' TO END-OF-FILE-SWITCH.
PERFORM READ-A-CARD
    UNTIL END-OF-FILE-SWITCH = 'YES'.
    .
    .
    .
READ-A-CARD.
    READ CARD-FILE AT END MOVE 'YES' TO END-OF-FILE-SWITCH.
```

7

The paragraph READ-A-CARD will be performed until END-OF-FILE-SWITCH equals YES (i.e., until there are no more data cards). When the end of file is reached, the END-OF-FILE-SWITCH is set to YES. This causes the next test of the UNTIL condition to be met and prevents the READ-A-CARD paragraph from further execution. (*Care must be taken in using this technique, for it is quite easy to process the last card twice.* This point is made clearer in Figure 1.3, later in the chapter.)

A second example of iteration involves the establishment of a counter:

```
MOVE 1 TO COUNTER.
PERFORM PARAGRAPH-A UNTIL COUNTER > 20.
       .
          .
             .

    PARAGRAPH-A.
       ADD 1 TO COUNTER.
          .
             .
                .
```

PARAGRAPH-A will be executed 20 times as a result of the PERFORM statement. Since the UNTIL condition is tested *prior* to performing the specified paragraph, a greater-than condition is specified. Indeed, if the UNTIL clause were rewritten with an equal to 20 condition instead, the paragraph would only be executed 19 times.

Selection

The Selection structure is implemented by an IF/ELSE statement, having the general form

```
IF condition
   statement₁
ELSE
   statement₂
```

The condition tests the relationship between two items (i.e., equal, less than, etc.). Statements 1 and 2 denote any COBOL statements which are to be executed if the condition is true or false, respectively. In the general form of the IF statement, statements 1 and 2 can each denote a series of statements. [For example, the ELSE portion of Figure 1.2(a) calls for execution of two statements, A and B.]

Statements 1 and 2 can also denote additional IF statements giving rise to the "infamous" nested IF. In Figure 1.2(b) for example, if predicate₁ is true, a second predicate is tested, and if this is also true, a third predicate is also tested. COBOL implementation for Figure 1.2(b) would take the form

```
IF predicate₁
    IF predicate₂
        IF predicate₃
            statement G
        ELSE
            statement F
    ELSE
        statement E
ELSE
    statement A
    statement B
    statement C
    statement D
```

EXAMPLE 1: TWO-FILE MERGE

A primary goal of structured programming is to produce programs that are easily read and maintained by someone other than the author. The fact that structured programming can accomplish this rather lofty goal is best demonstrated by example. Consider two sequential files. We are to create a third file which merges the two. If duplicate IDs appear (i.e., the same ID number occurs on both files), a warning message is to be printed, but neither record should appear on the merged file. Figure 1.3 contains a structured COBOL program to merge the two files. There is nothing unusual about the Identification, Environment, or Data Divisions of Figure 1.3, although the latter contains two switches in Working-Storage, about which we say more later.

The Procedure Division consists essentially of two paragraphs, 005-MAIN-LINE and 010-PROCESS-FILES. The flowchart for 005-MAINLINE is quite simple and is shown in Figure 1.4. It has a rectangular block with two vertical lines indicating that the procedure 010-PROCESS-FILES is a performed routine. The iteration structure of Figure 1.1 is embedded in Figure 1.4 (i.e., 010-PROCESS-FILES is performed until there are no more data on either file.)

The COBOL program of Figure 1.3 revolves about the 010-PROCESS-FILES routine, in particular the nested IF of lines 70-80. If the current ID from the first file is less than the current ID from the second file, the merged record is written from the first file. If, however, the current ID from the second file is less than the current ID from the first file, the merged record is written from the second file. If the IDs are equal (i.e., if there are duplicate records), neither record is written and an appropriate error message is displayed.

The program makes use of two switches, WS-READ-INPUT-ONE-SWITCH and WS-READ-INPUT-TWO-SWITCH, to indicate from where the next record is to be taken. If, for example, a merged record is written from the first file (i.e., if INPUT-ONE-ID is less than INPUT-TWO-ID), the next record would come from the first file; hence, YES is moved to the switch controlling the first file (COBOL line 72). COBOL lines 82 and 87 test the switches associated with the first and second file, respectively.

```
00001          IDENTIFICATION DIVISION.
00002          PROGRAM-ID.   TWOFILES.
00003          AUTHOR.    R. GRAUER.
00004          ENVIRONMENT DIVISION.
00005          CONFIGURATION SECTION.
00006          SOURCE-COMPUTER.  IBM-370.
00007          OBJECT-COMPUTER.  IBM-370.
00008          INPUT-OUTPUT SECTION.
00009          FILE-CONTROL.
00010              SELECT INPUT-FILE-ONE ASSIGN TO UT-S-FILEONE.
00011              SELECT INPUT-FILE-TWO ASSIGN TO UT-S-FILETWO.
00012              SELECT MERGED-FILE ASSIGN TO UT-S-MERGED.
00013          DATA DIVISION.
00014          FILE SECTION.
00015          FD  INPUT-FILE-ONE
00016              LABEL RECORDS ARE STANDARD
00017              BLOCK CONTAINS 0 RECORDS
00018              RECORD CONTAINS 80 CHARACTERS
00019              DATA RECORD IS INPUT-RECORD-ONE.
00020          01  INPUT-RECORD-ONE.
00021              05  FILLER                              PIC X(9).
00022              05  INPUT-ONE-ID                        PIC X(9).
00023              05  INPUT-ONE-NAME                      PIC X(20).
00024              05  INPUT-ONE-SALARY                    PIC 9(6).
00025              05  INPUT-ONE-DEPARTMENT                PIC 9(4).
00026              05  INPUT-ONE-LOCATION                  PIC X(10).
00027              05  FILLER                              PIC X(22).
00028          FD  INPUT-FILE-TWO
00029              LABEL RECORDS ARE STANDARD
00030              BLOCK CONTAINS 0 RECORDS
00031              RECORD CONTAINS 80 CHARACTERS
00032              DATA RECORD IS INPUT-RECORD-TWO.
00033          01  INPUT-RECORD-TWO.
00034              05  FILLER                              PIC X(9).
00035              05  INPUT-TWO-ID                        PIC X(9).
00036              05  INPUT-TWO-NAME                      PIC X(20).
00037              05  INPUT-TWO-SALARY                    PIC 9(6).
00038              05  INPUT-TWO-DEPARTMENT                PIC 9(4).
00039              05  INPUT-TWO-LOCATION                  PIC X(10).
00040              05  FILLER                              PIC X(22).
00041          FD  MERGED-FILE
00042              LABEL RECORDS ARE STANDARD
00043              RECORD CONTAINS 80 CHARACTERS
00044              BLOCK CONTAINS 0 RECORDS
00045              DATA RECORD IS MERGED-RECORD.
00046          01  MERGED-RECORD                           PIC X(80).
00047          WORKING-STORAGE SECTION.
00048          77  WS-READ-INPUT-ONE-SWITCH    VALUE SPACES  PIC X(3).
00049          77  WS-READ-INPUT-TWO-SWITCH    VALUE SPACES  PIC X(3).
00050          PROCEDURE DIVISION.
00051
00052          005-MAINLINE.
00053              OPEN INPUT INPUT-FILE-ONE
00054                         INPUT-FILE-TWO
00055                  OUTPUT MERGED-FILE.
00056          READ INPUT-FILE-ONE
00057              AT END MOVE HIGH-VALUES TO INPUT-ONE-ID.
00058          READ INPUT-FILE-TWO
00059              AT END MOVE HIGH-VALUES TO INPUT-TWO-ID.
```

Definition of switches (lines 00048–00049)

Initial READS (lines 00056–00059)

Figure 1.3 COBOL Listing for a Two-File Merge

10

```
000ε0              PERFORM 010-PROCESS-FILES THRU 020-PROCESS-FILES-EXIT
00061                  UNTIL INPUT-ONE-ID = HIGH-VALUES
00062                    AND INPUT-TWO-ID = HIGH-VALUES.
00063              CLOSE INPUT-FILE-ONE
00064                    INPUT-FILE-TWO
00065                    MERGED-FILE.
00066              STOP RUN.
00067
00068          010-PROCESS-FILES.                          Nested IF statement
00069
00070          IF INPUT-ONE-ID LESS THAN INPUT-TWO-ID
00071              WRITE MERGED-RECORD FROM INPUT-RECORD-ONE
00072              MOVE 'YES' TO WS-READ-INPUT-ONE-SWITCH
00073          ELSE
00074              IF INPUT-TWO-ID LESS THAN INPUT-ONE-ID
00075                  WRITE MERGED-RECORD FROM INPUT-RECORD-TWO
00076                  MOVE 'YES' TO WS-READ-INPUT-TWO-SWITCH
00077              ELSE
00078                  DISPLAY 'DUPLICATE IDS ' INPUT-ONE-ID
00079                  MOVE 'YES' TO WS-READ-INPUT-ONE-SWITCH
00080                  MOVE 'YES' TO WS-READ-INPUT-TWO-SWITCH.
00081
00082          IF WS-READ-INPUT-ONE-SWITCH = 'YES'
00083              MOVE 'NO' TO WS-READ-INPUT-ONE-SWITCH    Resetting input switch
00084              READ INPUT-FILE-ONE                      for first file
00085                  AT END MOVE HIGH-VALUES TO INPUT-ONE-ID.
00086
00087          IF WS-READ-INPUT-TWO-SWITCH = 'YES'          Testing input switch
00088              MOVE 'NO' TO WS-READ-INPUT-TWO-SWITCH    for second file
00089              READ INPUT-FILE-TWO
00090                  AT END MOVE HIGH-VALUES TO INPUT-TWO-ID.
00091
00092          020-PROCESS-FILES-EXIT.
00093              EXIT.
```

Figure 1.3 COBOL Listing for a Two-File Merge (continued)

Note that if action is taken because a switch is found to be on (i.e., its value is YES), the switch is turned off (i.e., set to NO prior to the action being taken).

The two READ statements associated with each file (lines 56, 57 and 84, 85 for the first file; lines 58, 59 and 89, 90 for the second) are cause for potential objection by those who insist on only "one read per file." We address this question further in Figure 1.4. For the time being, however, let us say that all four statements are required, and must be included for the program to execute correctly as a structured program. Explanation is facilitated by the assumption of only one record in each file containing identical IDs. The READS of lines 56-59 are part of housekeeping and are done once. When 010-PROCESS-FILES is initially entered via the PERFORM of line 60, the first record on each file is processed. Since the IDs are the same, both switches are set to YES and each file is read again in lines 84, 85 and 89, 90. The end-of-file condition is hit and both IDs are set to HIGH-VALUES. This causes the next test of the UNTIL condition in line 61 to be met and control passes to line 63. The reasoning is easily extended to *n* data cards.

11

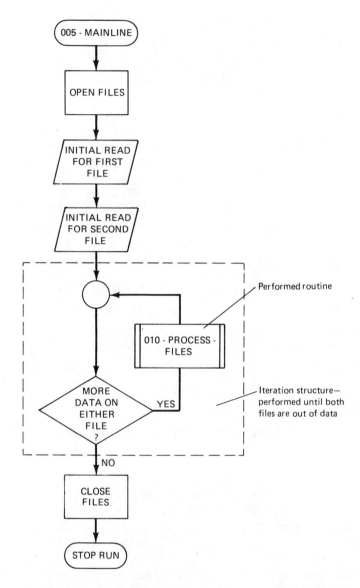

Figure 1.4 Flowchart for Mainline Routine of Two-File Merge

ADVANTAGES OF STRUCTURED PROGRAMMING

Let us make two rather important observations concerning structured programming in general, and Figure 1.3 in particular. The first is simply that the program in Figure 1.3 works; further, it works under *all* conditions. The second is that structured programs are easily changed to accommodate the inevitable modifications to problem specifications.

Consider the first statement—program validity. File processing programs in

12

Set 1: Records are interspersed among the two files

Input File 1	Input File 2	Merged File
100000000	111111111	100000000
200000000	222222222	111111111
300000000	333333333	200000000
400000000	444444444	222222222
500000000	555555555	300000000
		333333333
		400000000
		444444444
		500000000
		555555555

Set 2: All records in file 1 precede all records in file 2

Input File 1	Input File 2	Merged File
100000000	600000000	100000000
200000000	700000000	200000000
300000000	800000000	300000000
400000000	900000000	400000000
500000000		500000000
		600000000
		700000000
		800000000
		900000000

Set 3: File 2 is empty

Input File 1	Input File 2	Merged File
100000000		100000000
200000000		200000000
300000000	Empty	300000000
400000000		400000000
500000000		500000000

Figure 1.5 Test Data for the Merge Program

general are error-prone on end-of-file or "unusual" conditions. The reader should be made aware that the program in Figure 1.3 has been tested with the three distinct sets of input data shown in Figure 1.5 and found to be correct each time. We do not mean to say that a conventional (i.e., a nonstructured) program could not also be written to work with the data of Figure 1.5. We do believe, however, that the resulting program would probably take longer to write, and that it would be much more difficult to follow.

As to the second statement—program modification—despite the best intentions of users, supervisors, and so on, program specs are forever changing. In commercial situations it is the maintenance programmer who bears the brunt of this task, and indeed he/she is often justifiably in dire fear of playing with someone else's program. One of the strongest arguments for structured programming is that it simplifies program maintenance.

Assume, for example, that the specification on duplicate IDs is altered. Under the new specs, if duplicate IDs are detected (i.e., the same ID number appears in both files), the record with the higher salary is to be written to the merged file. If, however, both records have the same salary, then neither record is to be written and the error message is to be printed.

As Figure 1.3 now stands, COBOL lines 78-80 accommodate duplicate IDs. To affect the modification, these lines can be replaced by a single statement, PERFORM 030-PROCESS-DUPLICATES. The maintenance programmer then develops his/her own routine, 030-PROCESS-DUPLICATES, to handle the change. The suggested code is

```
030-PROCESS-DUPLICATES.
    IF INPUT-ONE-SALARY > INPUT-TWO-SALARY
        WRITE MERGED-RECORD FROM INPUT-RECORD-ONE

ELSE
    IF INPUT-TWO-SALARY > INPUT-ONE-SALARY
        WRITE MERGED-RECORD FROM INPUT-RECORD-TWO

ELSE
    DISPLAY 'DUPLICATE IDS' INPUT-ONE-ID.
MOVE 'YES' TO WS-READ-INPUT-ONE-SWITCH.
MOVE 'YES' TO WS-READ-INPUT-TWO-SWITCH.
```

THE MERGE PROGRAM REWRITTEN

Contrary to any impression we have conveyed to date, the authors were initially skeptical of the structured dogma, which often meant strict, sometimes blind, adherence to the logic structures of Figure 1.1. Our skepticism, however, has vanished with time; to paraphrase a rather worn commercial: "the more we tried it, the more we liked it." The authors are now firmly entrenched in the structured camp (nested IFs and all) and have become rather intolerant of the indiscriminate GO TO. We do, however, recognize a rather wide latitude associated with the COBOL implementation of structured concepts. For example, there may be objection to the two distinct read statements for the same file in Figure 1.3. This is not an objection to structured programming per se, but rather to a particular implementation of structured programming in COBOL. The latter is easily circumvented, by a perform to a read routine, which simultaneously eliminates the need for the two switches.

Figure 1.6 is a different COBOL implementation of the two-file merge. The logic is identical to that of Figure 1.3. There is a mainline routine which in turn performs a process-files routine until both files run out of data. The main difference between the two programs is that in Figure 1.6 the read for an input file is accomplished by a perform statement rather than by "in-line" code. There are two other minor differences. Figure 1.6 uses a READ INTO statement, whereas Figure 1.3 used a simple READ.

```
00001          IDENTIFICATION DIVISION.
00002          PROGRAM-ID.   TWOFILES.
00003          AUTHOR.     R. GRAUER.
00004          ENVIRONMENT DIVISION.
00005          CONFIGURATION SECTION.
00006          SOURCE-COMPUTER.  IBM-370.
00007          OBJECT-COMPUTER.  IBM-370.
00008          INPUT-OUTPUT SECTION.
00009          FILE-CONTROL.
00010              SELECT INPUT-FILE-ONE ASSIGN TO UT-S-FILEONE.
00011              SELECT INPUT-FILE-TWO ASSIGN TO UT-S-FILETWO.
00012              SELECT MERGED-FILE ASSIGN TO UT-S-MERGED.
00013          DATA DIVISION.
00014          FILE SECTION.
00015          FD  INPUT-FILE-ONE
00016              LABEL RECORDS ARE STANDARD
00017              BLOCK CONTAINS 0 RECORDS
00018              RECORD CONTAINS 80 CHARACTERS
00019              DATA RECORD IS INPUT-RECORD-ONE.
00020          01  INPUT-RECORD-ONE                      PIC X(80).
00021          FD  INPUT-FILE-TWO
00022              LABEL RECORDS ARE STANDARD
00023              BLOCK CONTAINS 0 RECORDS
00024              RECORD CONTAINS 80 CHARACTERS
00025              DATA RECORD IS INPUT-RECORD-TWO.
00026          01  INPUT-RECORD-TWO                      PIC X(80).
00027          FD  MERGED-FILE
00028              LABEL RECORDS ARE STANDARD
00029              RECORD CONTAINS 80 CHARACTERS
00030              BLOCK CONTAINS 0 RECORDS
00031              DATA RECORD IS MERGED-RECORD.
00032          01  MERGED-RECORD                         PIC X(80).
00033          WORKING-STORAGE SECTION.
00034          01  WS-RECORD-ONE.
00035              05  FILLER                            PIC X(9).
00036              05  WS-REC-ONE-ID                     PIC X(9).
00037              05  WS-REC-ONE-NAME                   PIC X(20).
00038              05  WS-REC-ONE-SALARY                 PIC 9(6).
00039              05  WS-REC-ONE-DEPARTMENT             PIC 9(4).
00040              05  WS-REC-ONE-LOCATION               PIC X(10).
00041              05  FILLER                            PIC X(22).
00042          01  WS-RECORD-TWO.
00043              05  FILLER                            PIC X(9).
00044              05  WS-REC-TWO-ID                     PIC X(9).
00045              05  WS-REC-TWO-NAME                   PIC X(20).
00046              05  WS-REC-TWO-SALARY                 PIC 9(6).
00047              05  WS-REC-TWO-DEPARTMENT             PIC 9(4).
00048              05  WS-REC-TWO-LOCATION               PIC X(10).
00049              05  FILLER                            PIC X(22).
00050          PROCEDURE DIVISION.
00051
00052          005-MAINLINE.
00053              OPEN INPUT INPUT-FILE-ONE
00054                         INPUT-FILE-TWO
00055                    OUTPUT MERGED-FILE.
00056              PERFORM 020-READ-FIRST-FILE.         ─Initial READS
00057              PERFORM 030-READ-SECOND-FILE.
00058              PERFORM 010-PROCESS-FILES
00059                  UNTIL WS-REC-ONE-ID = HIGH-VALUES
00060                     AND WS-REC-TWO-ID = HIGH-VALUES.
```

15   **Figure 1.6** Merge Program Rewritten

```
00061            CLOSE INPUT-FILE-ONE
00062                  INPUT-FILE-TWO
00063                  MERGED-FILE.
00064            STOP RUN.
00065
00066        010-PROCESS-FILES.                           Nested IF statement
00067
00068        IF WS-REC-ONE-ID LESS THAN WS-REC-TWO-ID
00069            WRITE MERGED-RECORD FROM INPUT-RECORD-ONE
00070            PERFORM 020-READ-FIRST-FILE
00071        ELSE
00072            IF WS-REC-TWO-ID LESS THAN WS-REC-ONE-ID
00073                WRITE MERGED-RECORD FROM INPUT-RECORD-TWO
00074                PERFORM 030-READ-SECOND-FILE
00075            ELSE
00076                DISPLAY 'DUPLICATE IDS ' WS-REC-ONE-ID
00077                PERFORM 020-READ-FIRST-FILE
00078                PERFORM 030-READ-SECOND-FILE.
00079
00080
00081        020-READ-FIRST-FILE.
00082            READ INPUT-FILE-ONE INTO WS-RECORD-ONE
00083                AT END MOVE HIGH-VALUES TO WS-REC-ONE-ID.
00084
00085        030-READ-SECOND-FILE.
00086            READ INPUT-FILE-TWO INTO WS-RECORD-TWO
00087                AT END MOVE HIGH-VALUES TO WS-REC-TWO-ID.
```

Read routine for second file

Figure 1.6 Merge Program Rewritten (continued)

Figure 1.6 performs only single paragraphs, whereas Figure 1.3 used a PERFORM THRU. Realize, however, that these represent variations in COBOL technique rather than "structured" versus "nonstructured" logic.

  We *do not* wish to debate the relative merits of one COBOL technique versus another as concerns Figures 1.3 and 1.6. What is important are the structural similarities between the two: both programs consist entirely of the basic logic structures of Figure 1.1. As such, both are structured programs, both are easily read and modified, and both are correct. The issue of whether duplicate in-line code is superior to performing single-statement paragraphs is *not* central to the issue of structured versus nonstructured programming.

SUMMARY

It is possible to develop any program with only three logic structures: sequence, selection, and iteration. Programs written in this manner are said to be structured, and are easier to read and maintain than conventional or nonstructured programs. COBOL implementation of these logic structures was discussed.

  Two distinct versions of a merge program were developed in COBOL. Both programs were structured in that they used only the three

16

basic logic forms. They differed in the COBOL implementation: two READs for one file versus PERFORM; READ versus READ INTO, PERFORM versus PERFORM THRU, and so on. However, such differences are of little importance in comparison to the structured versus nonstructured question, and the authors have no preference for one listing to another.

What is important is that the structured umbrella is large enough to encompass a wide variety of COBOL techniques. Thus, it would be presumptuous, and foolhardy, for the authors to argue for duplicate read statements versus performing a one-line read routine, or vice versa. It is really immaterial which approach you select. We do argue, and rather vociferously, for restricting programs to the basic building blocks of sequence, selection, and iteration. We believe that the relative ease with which modifications can be implemented in structured programs is a powerful endorsement of the approach.

As a final example, consider this change in the specifications for the two-file merge. A sequence check is now required; if either incoming file is found out of sequence, processing is to terminate immediately. The incorporation of this nontrivial change is easily accomplished in Figure 1.6. All that is necessary is modification of the performed read routine for each file. The routine 020-READ-FIRST-FILE is expanded to include an IF statement for the sequence check, as follows:

```
020-READ-FIRST-FILE.
    READ INPUT-FILE-ONE INTO WS-RECORD-ONE
        AT END MOVE HIGH-VALUES TO WS-REC-ONE-ID.
    IF WS-REC-ONE-ID < PREVIOUS-REC-ONE-ID
        DISPLAY 'FILE ONE OUT OF SEQUENCE'
        MOVE HIGH-VALUES TO WS-REC-ONE-ID, WS-REC-TWO-ID
    ELSE
        MOVE WS-REC-ONE-ID TO PREVIOUS-REC-ONE-ID.
```

As can be seen from the additional code, HIGH-VALUES are moved to each ID if a record is out of sequence. This will cause the next test of the PERFORM UNTIL to be met and thereby terminate processing. (This approach is followed because a program should end from its mainline routine; hence STOP RUN never appears in a performed procedure.) Parallel code would be added to the read routine for the second file. The modification also requires that two data names, PREVIOUS-REC-ONE-ID and PREVIOUS-REC-TWO-ID, be established in Working-Storage; both data names should be initialized to LOW-VALUES.

PROBLEMS

1. Can you venture a definition of structured programming? Would you say that structured programming *must be* "GO TO less" programming?

2. Write a structured COBOL program to accomplish a three-file merge. Assume that the ID numbers on each file are unique; duplicate IDs should not appear in the same file, nor should the same ID be contained in more than one file. Terminate the program if any file is out of sequence.

3. Do you think the program in Figure 1.3 is more structured than the program in Figure 1.6? Why or why not? Which COBOL implementation do you prefer and why?

4. Discuss the importance of testing under a variety of conditions. Do you believe the data of Figure 1.5 are a sufficient test of Figure 1.3? Why or why not?

Top-Down Program Development

Individuals are taught the elements of a programming language; *unfortunately they are not taught how to program.* The situation is somewhat analogous to teaching a foreign language by providing only a dictionary. The would-be linguist has all the language elements at his disposal, but lacks the grammar to construct proper sentences. He could hardly be said to be fluent in the language. Since this approach to teaching a foreign language is obviously infeasible, we structure courses covering grammar, idiomatic expressions, and so on.

Why, therefore, should individuals be expected to program well merely because they know the elements of a programming language? Is it not logical to argue that programmers should also be taught a method of programming? The objective of this chapter is to teach such a method, commonly known as *top-down program development.* We also cover the associated techniques of stepwise refinement, pseudocode, and hierarchy charts. Presentation is facilitated by development of a COBOL program, which is done in the context of a case study. The chapter concludes with discussion of two associated management techniques: the chief programmer team and the structured walkthrough.

TOP-DOWN VERSUS BOTTOM-UP PROGRAMMING

Simply stated, top-down program development concentrates on the highest levels of logic first and leaves the details for later. While this may sound reasonable, it is typically the opposite of what many programmers are used to: they usually begin, or are told to begin, with the detail and proceed from the bottom up.

To amplify the distinction, let us consider a problem requiring two control breaks. Specifications are as follows: World Wide Widgets has offices in several cities. Each month management requires reports on sales activity. Detailed information on every salesman is to be provided, showing all transactions for that salesman during the month. The reports on individual salesmen are to be sorted on location first, and alphabetically within location. In addition, summary totals for each location are to appear on a separate report. Examples of the two kinds of required reports are shown in Figure 2.1.

Input consists of transaction records, one card per transaction. Each transaction card contains the name of the salesman responsible, his location, the transaction type (sale or credit), date, and amount. Transaction records are validated and sorted in a previous run. Thus, we may accept input to the two-level control program as being in sequence by location, and by salesman within location. Further, each transaction record can be assumed to contain complete and valid data.

Peter Programmer has just been put on special assignment and now reports to the Director of Marketing. The Director has supplied copies of the individual salesman and location summary reports, and requests that Peter begin work. Naturally, the Director would like to see sample reports as soon as they are available. Accordingly, Peter begins coding immediately and develops the sample reports. The Director is generally satisfied but would like column headings altered, notes added, and so on. These modifications continue for several weeks before the Director is satisfied. Meanwhile the deadline is drawing near and Peter has yet to concern himself with the substantial logic of the problem (i.e., the control breaks). In all likelihood he will go into production with "beautiful" reports but inaccurate salesmen and location totals. Errors will be discovered with an abundance of panic, overtime, etc. This is the *bottom-up* approach.

By contrast, *top-down* development recognizes that the actual report formating is *trivial* in comparison to the overall program logic. The discipline requires that one *defer coding and concentrate instead on program development*, beginning with the highest level of logic. This concept of deferred coding is particularly difficult to get across. Management, even DP management, often refuses to believe that a programmer is productive if he is not coding. Even programmers themselves do not like to defer coding, because for many "eager beavers" coding is synonymous with programming. To them, the idea of taking hours, days, or even weeks to organize one's thoughts before coding is a distinct waste of time.

Unfortunately, such prevailing attitudes make a move away from the traditional bottom-up approach difficult to achieve. Successful implementation of the top-down philosophy requires both an enlightened management and willingness on the part

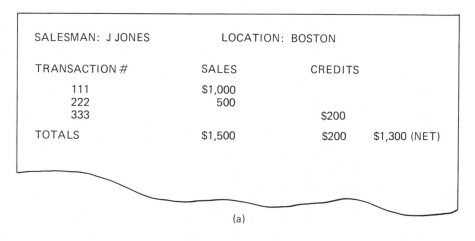

Figure 2.1(a) Individual Salesman Report (One report for each salesman in company)

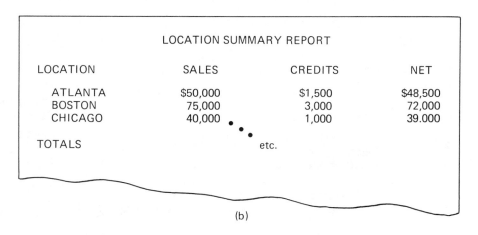

Figure 2.1(b) Location Summary Report (One report for entire company)

of the programmers to try something new. It has been our experience, however, that when both management and programmer make a definite commitment to objectively evaluate the top-down approach, they invariably accept it.

CASE STUDY

This chapter is devoted to top-down development of a program for the World Wide Widgets problem. (The reader is referred to Appendix C, Report Writer, for an alternative approach.) We begin with a discussion of stepwise refinement, a technique that continually divides the logic of a program into smaller pieces. Next, we discuss pseudocode and hierarchy charts, two ways of communicating a program's structure. Finally, we present the completed COBOL program.

Stepwise Refinement

The ideal, and strictly hypothetical solution would be a program consisting of a single instruction, PROCESS-TWO-CONTROL-BREAKS. Not only would that program be complete, but since it consists of only one instruction, it must be correct. Unfortunately, since the necessary instruction does not exist on available hardware, the solution must be broken into smaller pieces.

The procedure whereby a problem is continually broken into smaller pieces is known as *stepwise refinement*. We begin by breaking the problem into three steps: initialization, processing, and termination. These three instructions are also too comprehensive, and they in turn are further decomposed. Figure 2.2 shows the first real attempt to structure the Widgets problem.

In Figure 2.2, initialization consists of opening files and housekeeping. Processing involves a repetitive set of instructions for each location. The totals for each location are initialized, all salesmen in one location are processed, and the computed location totals are stored in a table. Termination causes the location summary report to be written and the files closed.

Figure 2.3 amplifies the processing segment of Figure 2.2. Totals for each salesman in a given location are initialized, and transactions are processed. There is a loop associated with all transactions of one salesman. (Incoming data are sorted by location and by salesman, so all transactions for one salesman appear together.) Figure 2.3 also shows further development of the location summary report of Figure 2.1(b). There is initialization—a heading line, processing—a detail line for each location, and termination—a total line.

Figure 2.4 further divides the processing function associated with each salesman. Individual totals are zeroed out and a heading line is written. Every transaction for the same salesman is processed to (1) determine transaction type, (2) increment individual salesman totals, and (3) write a detail line. When all transactions for one salesman are processed, a total line for that salesman is written, and location totals are incremented.

Figures 2.2, 2.3, and 2.4 are successive iterations in the stepwise refinement

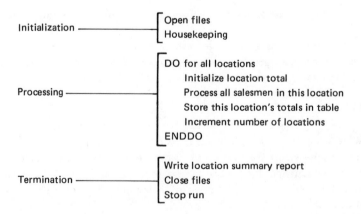

Figure 2.2 Two-Level Control-Break Program—Step 1

of a double-control-break problem. The earliest attempt (Figure 2.2) is the most general and consequently closest to the original problem specifications. Successive iterations (Figures 2.3 and 2.4) describe the problem in finer detail, until entries in the last iteration (Figure 2.4) are easily translated into program statements.

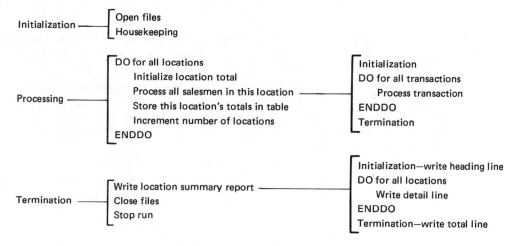

Figure 2.3 Two-Level Control-Break Program—Step 2

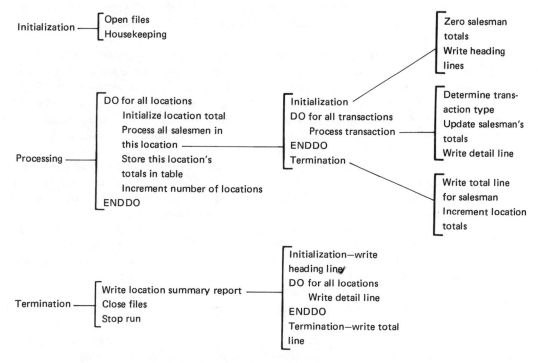

Figure 2.4 Two-Level Control-Break Program—Step 3

Documentation

The use of the traditional flowchart as a design aid and/or documentation technique has been in a steady decline for several years. Programmers have, almost universally, written the program first, then drawn the flowchart only to satisfy their manager. Hence, the main use for which the flowchart was intended (i.e., as a guide in writing the program) was destroyed. Moreover, its usefulness as documentation is practically nil, particularly as problems become larger and more complex. Structured programming therefore has given rise to its own documentation techniques. Two of the more common are pseudocode and HIPO (Hierarchy plus Input Process Output).

Pseudocode is a convenient way of expressing a program's logic *before* coding is started. It is similar to a programming language, but is not bound by syntactical rules or preciseness of instructions. Pseudocode uses indentation for clarity and is best restricted to the basic logic structures (i.e., sequence, selection, and iteration). Everything else is at the discretion of the programmer.

Figure 2.5 has expanded the pseudocode inherent in Figure 2.4 to indicate how the control breaks on location and salesman will be detected. Moreover, whereas Figure 2.4 was quite removed from an actual program, Figure 2.5 has been slanted toward COBOL by substitution of PERFORM for DO, and by a vertical ordering of the statements themselves.

HIPO is useful in both the design aid and documentation phases (see IBM Publication, GC20-1851-1, *HIPO—A Design Aid and Documentation Technique*). The hierarchy chart, or visual table of contents, is central to the HIPO approach. An example of a completed chart which could be used to write the double-control-break program is shown in Figure 2.6.

A *hierarchy chart* is developed from the top down. One module is always required to control the other modules on a program. This module sits at the top of the structure chart with the overall function of the program (e.g., CREATE-REPORTS). The next level breaks the main function into logical subfunctions (e.g., PROCESS-ALL-LOCATIONS and GENERATE-LOCATION-SUMMARY). Lower levels break these functions into further subfunctions as necessary. The process continues until the designer can fully understand the functions being described.

Each module in a hierarchy chart must be *independent* of all others. This means that a module can be modified without affecting any others in the program. Further, a module can be entered only from the module immediately above it and must return control to that module. There is one entry and exit point.

Second, the function of each module must be readily identifiable. Each module should be restricted to a single function. One way of verifying function is the name of the module; use only a single verb, two or three adjectives, and a one-word object (e.g., GENERATE-LOCATION-SUMMARY). If you cannot name modules in this way, they are probably not functional.

There are also attempts at quantitative definition; for example, a module should not contain more than 50 statements. Thus, if a module cannot be made to fit on a single page of a program listing, it is probably programming more than one function, in which case it should be divided into more than one module. Since many programmers welcome quantitative guidelines, we endorse the 50-line restriction.

24

```
Initialize
Open files
Read SALES-FILE at end indicate no more data
PERFORM until no more data
     Move TR-SALESMAN-LOCATION to WS-PREVIOUS-LOCATION
     Zero this location's totals
     PERFORM until TR-SALESMAN-LOCATION ≠ WS-PREVIOUS-LOCATION
     or no more data
          Move TR-SALESMAN-NAME to WS-PREVIOUS-SALESMAN
          Zero salesman totals
          Write salesman heading line
          PERFORM until TR-SALESMAN-NAME, ≠ WS-PREVIOUS-SALESMAN
          or no more data
               Determine transaction type
               Increment salesman totals
               Write detail line
               Read SALES-FILE at end indicate no more data
          ENDPERFORM
               Write salesman total line
               Increment this location's totals
     ENDPERFORM
          Store this location's totals in location table
          Increment number of locations
ENDPERFORM
     Write heading line for location summary report
PERFORM for all locations
     Write location detail line
     Increment grand total
ENDPERFORM
Write total line for location summary report
Close files
Stop run
```

Figure 2.5 Pseudocode for Double-Control-Break Program

Testing

Proper testing of a program is like motherhood and apple pie. Everyone agrees it should be done, yet testing is the one activity which is too often haphazard. One of the associated benefits of structured programming is the increased emphasis given to testing, in particular to top-down testing.

Top-down testing requires that modules in a hierarchy chart be tested in the order in which they are developed; i.e., from the top down. It requires that testing begin well in advance of the entire program being completed and causes testing and coding to become parallel activities. Top-down testing ensures that the higher-level modules, which typically contain the most complex logic, are tested earlier and more often than lower-level routines. It is far more important, for example, to establish the mechanism for control breaks than to perfect the exact format for heading lines.

25

In practice, there are often deviations from a complete top-down approach. Thus, the left side of Figure 2.6 is likely to be tested before the right. Realize, however, that PROCESS-ALL-LOCATIONS is developed and tested prior to PROCESS-ONE-LOCATION, which is tested prior to PROCESS-ONE-SALESMAN. Testing of the crucial interfaces between these modules does not require that all three routines be completely coded. Rather, the lower-level routine(s), such as PROCESS-ONE-SALESMAN, exist initially as program stubs. A stub, in turn, contains only a DISPLAY statement, indicating that the module was called, thereby allowing a test of the relationship between modules.

Top-down testing has several advantages, the foremost being that major bugs are discovered earlier and easier than with the bottom-up approach. Second, since testing is an ongoing activity, there is less need for large amounts of machine time as a project nears completion. Finally, successful tests in the early phases of program development provide a strong, and often necessary, boost to programmer confidence.

The concept of top-down testing can and should be extended from the unit to the system and even acceptance levels. (The unit test verifies the results of an individual program, the system test checks the interfaces between programs, and the acceptance test determines if the documentation is sufficient to enable the system to be run without help from its developers.) In other words, acceptance testing of a major system can start perhaps as soon as one month (as opposed to one year) after coding has begun. Obviously, the system will not do very much in its early stages. However, early testing at the acceptance level has the same benefits as the unit level, and in addition brings the user in from the beginning. Early feedback is invaluable in improving the quality of, and satisfaction with, the end product.

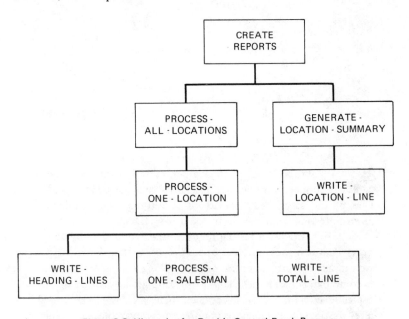

Figure 2.6 Hierarchy for Double-Control-Break Program

The Completed Program

The chapter began with specification of a program involving two control breaks. The logic has been developed via stepwise refinement and conveniently expressed in pseudocode. The relationships between the necessary COBOL modules were defined in a hierarchy chart. All that remains is the actual coding, which has been reduced to a relatively easy task. The completed COBOL program is shown in Figure 2.7

The program itself is unremarkable. Figure 2.7 is, however, a structured program as per the guidelines of Chapter 1. Thus, the Procedure Division consists entirely of the sequence, selection, and iteration structures. GO TO statements are conspicuously absent.

Figure 2.7 is a well-written program primarily because it is easy to follow. The logic is made clear through both the program's structure and associated documentation (i.e., pseudocode and hierarchy chart). Moreover, the use of COBOL standards—vertical alignment of PICTURE clauses, prefixing of data names, paragraph sequencing, and so on—improve appearance and overall legibility. These techniques have become so important that much of Chapter 3 is devoted to their discussion.

The reader is assumed to be familiar with the COBOL language, including subtleties such as indexing and variable-length tables. Such features are employed in Figure 2.7 and are covered pedagogically in Chapter 4.

ASSOCIATED MANAGEMENT TECHNIQUES

The COBOL programmer is concerned with programming, not management. However, it is certainly beneficial to prepare our audience for potential management changes which may accompany a conversion to structured programming. Two of the more common are the chief programmer team and structured walkthrough.

The chief programmer team involves complete reorganization of the data-processing function, and as such is the more radical change. Many shops have totally converted to structured programming, design, etc. *without* adopting the chief programmer team. The structured walkthrough on the other hand, almost universally accompanies structured programming. A *structured walkthrough* is a group review of an individual's work and is intended to catch errors as early as possible in the development cycle. The ensuing discussion is intended to capture the flavor of each technique and is intended only as an introduction to the programmer of what may be in store for him.

Structured Walkthroughs

Continuous evaluation of progress is essential to the successful completion of any project. The structured walkthrough brings this evaluation into the open. It requires a programmer to formally, and periodically, have his work reviewed by a peer group. Management's motivation is simple; a programmer is too close to his work to adequately see, and objectively evaluate, potential problems. Hence, the purpose of a walkthrough is to ensure that all specifications are met, that logic is correct, and that standards are observed.

While the term itself is new, the concept of program review is not. Program-

```
00001              IDENTIFICATION DIVISION.
00002              PROGRAM-ID.    TWOLEVEL.
00003              AUTHOR.       R GRAUER.


00005              ENVIRONMENT DIVISION.
00006              CONFIGURATION SECTION.
00007              SOURCE-COMPUTER.       IBM-370.
00008              OBJECT-COMPUTER.       IBM-370.
00009              SPECIAL-NAMES.
00010                  C01 IS TOP-OF-PAGE.


00012              INPUT-OUTPUT SECTION.
00013              FILE-CONTROL.
00014                  SELECT SALES-FILE ASSIGN TO UT-S-SYSIN.
00015                  SELECT PRINT-FILE ASSIGN TO UT-S-SYSOUT.


00017              DATA DIVISION.
00018              FILE SECTION.


00020              FD  SALES-FILE
00021                  RECORDING MODE IS F
00022                  LABEL RECORDS ARE OMITTED
00023                  RECORD CONTAINS 80 CHARACTERS
00024                  DATA RECORD IS TRANSACTION-RECORD.

00026              01  TRANSACTION-RECORD        PIC X(80).


00028              FD  PRINT-FILE
00029                  RECORDING MODE IS F
00030                  LABEL RECORDS ARE OMITTED
00031                  RECORD CONTAINS 133 CHARACTERS
00032                  DATA RECORD IS PRINT-LINE.

00034              01  PRINT-LINE               PIC X(133).

00036              WORKING-STORAGE SECTION.
00037              77  FILLER                   PIC X(14)
00038                      VALUE 'WS BEGINS HERE'.
00039              77  WS-PREVIOUS-SALESMAN     PIC X(20) VALUE SPACES.
00040              77  WS-PREVIOUS-LOCATION     PIC X(20) VALUE SPACES.
00041              77  WS-DATA-FLAG             PIC X(3)  VALUE SPACES.
00042                  88  NO-MORE-DATA                   VALUE 'NO'.
00043              77  WS-NUMBER-LOCATIONS      PIC 99    VALUE ZEROS.

00045              01  FINAL-TOTALS.
00046                  05  FINAL-SALES-TOTAL    PIC S9(6) VALUE ZEROS.
00047                  05  FINAL-CREDITS-TOTAL  PIC S9(6) VALUE ZEROS.
00048                  05  FINAL-NET-TOTAL      PIC S9(6) VALUE ZEROS.

00050              01  TOTALS-FOR-ONE-LOCATION
```

Figure 2.7 COBOL Program for Two Control Breaks

```
00051              05   THIS-LOCATION-SALES     PIC S9(6) VALUE ZEROS.
00052              05   THIS-LOCATION-CREDITS   PIC S9(6) VALUE ZEROS.
00053              05   THIS-LOCATION-NET       PIC S9(6) VALUE ZEROS.

00055   01   LOCATION-TABLE.
00056        05   LOCATION-TABLE-ENTRIES OCCURS 1 TO 50 TIMES
00057        DEPENDING ON WS-NUMBER-LOCATIONS
00058        INDEXED BY LOC-INDEX.
00059              10   LOCATION-NAME           PIC X(20).
00060              10   LOCATION-SALES          PIC S9(6).
00061              10   LOCATION-CREDITS        PIC S9(6).
00062              10   LOCATION-NET            PIC S9(6).

00064   01   TOTALS-FOR-ONE-SALESMAN.                        Variable-
00065        05   SALESMAN-TOTAL-SALES     PIC S9(4).        length table
00066        05   SALESMAN-TOTAL-CREDITS   PIC S9(4).
00067        05   SALESMAN-TOTAL-NET       PIC S9(4).

00069   01   SALESMAN-HEADING-LINE-ONE.
00070        05   FILLER                   PIC X(60) VALUE SPACES.
00071        05   FILLER       Vertical    PIC X(5)  VALUE 'PAGE '.
00072        05   PAGE-NUMBER  alignment of PIC 9(4)  VALUE ZEROS.
00073        05   FILLER       picture clause PIC X(64) VALUE SPACES.

00075   01   SALESMAN-HEADING-LINE-TWO.
00076        05   FILLER                   PIC X(10) VALUE SPACES.
00077        05   SHL-SALESMAN             PIC X(20)
00078        05   FILLER                   PIC X(10) VALUE SPACES.
00079        05   SHL-LOCATION             PIC X(15).
00080        05   FILLER                   PIC X(78) VALUE SPACES.

00082   01   SALESMAN-HEADING-LINE-THREE.
00083        05   FILLER                   PIC X(10) VALUE SPACES.
00084        05   FILLER                   PIC X(13) VALUE 'TRANSACTION #'.
00085        05   FILLER                   PIC X(5)  VALUE SPACES.
00086        05   FILLER                   PIC X(4)  VALUE 'SALE'.
00087        05   FILLER                   PIC X(5)  VALUE SPACES.
00088        05   FILLER                   PIC X(6)  VALUE 'CREDIT'.
00089        05   FILLER                   PIC X(90) VALUE SPACES.

00091   01   TRANSACTION-AREA.
00092        05   TR-SALESMAN-NAME         PIC X(20).
00093        05   TR-AMOUNT                PIC S9(4).
00094        05   FILLER                   PIC XX.
00095        05   TR-NUMBER                PIC X(6).
00096        05   TR-TYPE                  PIC X(1).
00097             88   SALE                          VALUE 'S'.
00098             88   CREDIT                        VALUE 'C'.
00099        05   FILLER                   PIC X(17).
00100        05   TR-SALESMAN-LOCATION     PIC X(20).
00101        05   FILLER                   PIC X(10).

00103   01   SALESMAN-DETAIL-LINE.
00104        05   FILLER                   PIC X(12).
00105        05   DETAIL-TRANSACTION       PIC X(6).
00106        05   FILLER                   PIC X(8).
00107        05   DETAIL-SALES             PIC $Z,ZZ9.
```

Figure 2.7 COBOL Program for Two Control Breaks (continued)

29

```
00108              05   FILLER              PIC X(4).
00109              05   DETAIL-CREDITS      PIC $Z,ZZ9.
00110              05   FILLER              PIC X(91).

00112          01  SALESMAN-TOTAL-LINE.
00113              05   FILLER              PIC X(16) VALUE SPACES.
00114              05   FILLER              PIC X(6)   VALUE 'TOTALS'.
00115              05   FILLER              PIC X(4)   VALUE SPACES.
00116              05   TOTAL-LINE-SALES    PIC $Z,ZZ9.
00117              05   FILLER              PIC X(4)   VALUE SPACES.
00118              05   TOTAL-LINE-CREDITS  PIC $Z,ZZ9.
00119              05   FILLER              PIC X(4)   VALUE SPACES.
00120              05   TOTAL-LINE-NET      PIC $Z,ZZ9CR.
00121              05   FILLER              PIC X(5)   VALUE ' NET'.
00122              05   FILLER              PIC X(74) VALUE SPACES.

00124          01  LOCATION-HEADING-LINE-ONE.
00125              05   FILLER              PIC X(20) VALUE SPACES.
00126              05   FILLER              PIC X(23)
00127                   VALUE 'LOCATION SUMMARY REPORT'.
00128              05   FILLER              PIC X(90) VALUE SPACES.

00130          01  LOCATION-HEADING-LINE-TWO.
00131              05   FILLER              PIC X(6)   VALUE SPACES.
00132              05   FILLER              PIC X(8)   VALUE 'LOCATION'
00133              05   FILLER              PIC X(13) VALUE SPACES.
00134              05   FILLER              PIC X(5)   VALUE 'SALES'.
00135              05   FILLER              PIC X(8)   VALUE SPACES.
00136              05   FILLER              PIC X(7)   VALUE 'CREDITS'.
00137              05   FILLER              PIC X(5)   VALUE SPACES.
00138              05   FILLER              PIC X(3)   VALUE 'NET'.
00139              05   FILLER              PIC X(78) VALUE SPACES.

00141          01  LOCATION-DETAIL-LINE.
00142              05   FILLER              PIC X(7)   VALUE SPACES.
00143              05   LOC-DET-NAME        PIC X(15).
00144              05   FILLER              PIC XX    VALUE SPACES.
00145              05   LOC-DET-SALE        PIC $$$$,$$9.
00146              05   FILLER              PIC X(5)   VALUE SPACES.
00147              05   LOC-DET-CREDIT      PIC $$$$,$$9.
00148              05   FILLER              PIC X(5)   VALUE SPACES.
00149              05   LOC-DET-NET         PIC $$$$,$$9CR.
00150              05   FILLER              PIC X(73) VALUE SPACES.
                                            Prefixed data names
00152          01  FINAL-TOTAL-LINE.
00153              05   FILLER              PIC X(9)   VALUE SPACES.
00154              05   FILLER              PIC X(6)   VALUE 'TOTALS'
00155              05   FILLER              PIC X(9)   VALUE SPACES.
00156              05   PRINT-FINAL-SALES   PIC $$$$,999.
00157              05   FILLER              PIC X(5)   VALUE SPACES.
00158              05   PRINT-FINAL-CREDITS PIC $$$$,999
00159              05   FILLER              PIC X(5)   VALUE SPACES.
00160              05   PRINT-FINAL-NET     PIC $$$$,999.
00161              05   FILLER              PIC X(75) VALUE SPACES.
00163          01  FILLER                   PIC X(12)
```

Figure 2.7 COBOL Program for Two Control Breaks (continued)

30

```
00164                   VALUE 'WS ENDS HERE'.

00166          PROCEDURE DIVISION.                    MAINLINE
00167          0010-CREATE-REPORTS.
00168              OPEN INPUT SALES-FILE
00169                   OUTPUT PRINT-FILE.
00170              READ SALES-FILE INTO TRANSACTION-AREA
00171                   AT END MOVE 'NO' TO WS-DATA-FLAG.
00172              SET LOC-INDEX TO 1.
00173              PERFORM A000-PROCESS-ALL-LOCATIONS UNTIL NO-MORE-DATA.
00174              PERFORM B000-GENERATE-LOCATION-SUMMARY.
00175              CLOSE SALES-FILE
00176                    PRINT-FILE.
00177              STOP RUN.

00179          A000-PROCESS-ALL-LOCATIONS.
00180              MOVE TR-SALESMAN-LOCATION TO WS-PREVIOUS-LOCATION.
00181              MOVE ZEROS TO THIS-LOCATION-SALES.
00182              MOVE ZEROS TO THIS-LOCATION-CREDITS.
00183              ADD 1 TO WS-NUMBER-LOCATIONS.
00184              PERFORM A100-PROCESS-ONE-LOCATION
00185                   UNTIL TR-SALESMAN-LOCATION NOT = WS-PREVIOUS-LOCATION
00186                        OR NO-MORE-DATA.
00187              MOVE WS-PREVIOUS-LOCATION TO LOCATION-NAME (LOC-INDEX).
00188
00189
00190              MOVE THIS-LOCATION-SALES TO LOCATION-SALES (LOC-INDEX).
00191              MOVE THIS-LOCATION-CREDITS TO LOCATION-CREDITS (LOC-INDEX).
00192              MOVE THIS-LOCATION-NET TO LOCATION-NET (LOC-INDEX).
00193              SET LOC-INDEX UP BY 1.
00194                                          Use of an index
00195          A100-PROCESS-ONE-LOCATION.
00196              MOVE TR-SALESMAN-NAME TO WS-PREVIOUS-SALESMAN.
00197              MOVE ZEROS TO TOTALS-FOR-ONE-SALESMAN.
00198              PERFORM A300-WRITE-HEADING-LINE.
00199              PERFORM A310-PROCESS-ONE-SALESMAN
00200                   UNTIL TR-SALESMAN-NAME NOT = WS-PREVIOUS-SALESMAN
00201                        OR NO-MORE-DATA.
00202              PERFORM A320-WRITE-TOTAL-LINE.
00203              ADD SALESMAN-TOTAL-SALES TO THIS-LOCATION-SALES.
00204              ADD SALESMAN-TOTAL-CREDITS TO THIS-LOCATION-CREDITS.
00205              ADD SALESMAN-TOTAL-NET TO THIS-LOCATION-NET.
00206
00207          A300-WRITE-HEADING-LINE.
00208              ADD 1 TO PAGE-NUMBER.
00209              WRITE PRINT-LINE FROM SALESMAN-HEADING-LINE-ONE
00210                   AFTER ADVANCING TOP-OF-PAGE LINES.
00211              MOVE TR-SALESMAN-NAME TO SHL-SALESMAN.
00212              MOVE TR-SALESMAN-LOCATION TO SHL-LOCATION.
00213              WRITE PRINT-LINE FROM SALESMAN-HEADING-LINE-TWO
00214                   AFTER ADVANCING 2 LINES.
00215              WRITE PRINT-LINE FROM SALESMAN-HEADING-LINE-THREE
00216                   AFTER ADVANCING 2 LINES.
00217
00218          A310-PROCESS-ONE-SALESMAN.
00219              MOVE SPACES TO SALESMAN-DETAIL-LINE.
```

Figure 2.7 COBOL Program for Two Control Breaks (continued)

31

```
00220
00221              IF SALE
00222                  ADD TR-AMOUNT TO SALESMAN-TOTAL-SALES
00223                  ADD TR-AMOUNT TO SALESMAN-TOTAL-NET
00224                  MOVE TR-AMOUNT TO DETAIL-SALES
00225              ELSE
00226                  IF CREDIT
00227                      ADD TR-AMOUNT TO SALESMAN-TOTAL-CREDITS
00228                      SUBTRACT TR-AMOUNT FROM SALESMAN-TOTAL-NET
00229                      MOVE TR-AMOUNT TO DETAIL-CREDITS
00230                  ELSE
00231                      DISPLAY 'TRANSACTION TYPE IN ERROR' TR-SALESMAN-NAME.
00232
00233              MOVE TR-NUMBER TO DETAIL-TRANSACTION.
00234              WRITE PRINT-LINE FROM SALESMAN-DETAIL-LINE
00235                  AFTER ADVANCING 2 LINES.
00236              READ SALES-FILE INTO TRANSACTION-AREA
00237                  AT END MOVE 'NO' TO WS-DATA-FLAG.
00238
00239          A320-WRITE-TOTAL-LINE.
00240              MOVE SALESMAN-TOTAL-SALES TO TOTAL-LINE-SALES.
00241              MOVE SALESMAN-TOTAL-CREDITS TO TOTAL-LINE-CREDITS.
00242              MOVE SALESMAN-TOTAL-NET TO TOTAL-LINE-NET.
00243              WRITE PRINT-LINE FROM SALESMAN-TOTAL-LINE
00244                  AFTER ADVANCING 2 LINES.


00246          B000-GENERATE-LOCATION-SUMMARY.
00247              WRITE PRINT-LINE FROM LOCATION-HEADING-LINE-ONE
00248                  AFTER ADVANCING TOP-OF-PAGE LINES.
00249              WRITE PRINT-LINE FROM LOCATION-HEADING-LINE-TWO
00250                  AFTER ADVANCING 2 LINES.
00251              PERFORM B100-WRITE-LOCATION-LINE
00252                  VARYING LOC-INDEX FROM 1 BY 1
00253                  UNTIL LOC-INDEX > WS-NUMBER-LOCATIONS.
00254              MOVE FINAL-SALES-TOTAL TO PRINT-FINAL-SALES.
00255              MOVE FINAL-CREDITS-TOTAL TO PRINT-FINAL-CREDITS.
00256              MOVE FINAL-NET-TOTAL TO PRINT-FINAL-NET.
00257              WRITE PRINT-LINE FROM FINAL-TOTAL-LINE
00258                  AFTER ADVANCING 2 LINES.
00259
00260          B100-WRITE-LOCATION-LINE.
00261              MOVE LOCATION-NAME (LOC-INDEX) TO LOC-DET-NAME.
00262              MOVE LOCATION-SALES (LOC-INDEX) TO LOC-DET-SALE.
00263              MOVE LOCATION-CREDITS (LOC-INDEX) TO LOC-DET-CREDIT.
00264              MOVE LOCATION-NET (LOC-INDEX) TO LOC-DET-NET.
00265              WRITE PRINT-LINE FROM LOCATION-DETAIL-LINE
00266                  AFTER ADVANCING 2 LINES.
00267              ADD LOCATION-SALES (LOC-INDEX) TO FINAL-SALES-TOTAL.
00268              ADD LOCATION-CREDITS (LOC-INDEX) TO FINAL-CREDITS-TOTAL.
00269              ADD LOCATION-NET (LOC-INDEX) TO FINAL-NET-TOTAL.
```

Nested IF statement

Figure 2.7 COBOL Program for Two Control Breaks (continued)

32

mers have always been urged to desk-check. There are, however, two essential differences. First, a walkthrough is held before a group, whereas desk checking is an individual effort. Second, a walkthrough emphasizes design considerations, whereas desk checking is primarily concerned with code.

Generally, walkthroughs are scheduled by the programmer, who also selects his reviewers. This is not to say that walkthroughs just happen. Rather, there is usually some attempt by management at the start of a project to establish a tentative schedule with realistic dates. As the individual being reviewed, you are responsible for distributing copies of your work prior to the session. Attendees study this material in advance. Their role is one of preparation; their function is to question, to explore inconsistencies, and to resolve ambiguities. Your role is to present your work, objectively, concisely, and dispassionately. You should encourage discussion and be genuinely glad when (not if) errors are discovered. (After all, better now than later.) At the start of the meeting you appoint a secretary to make an "action list" of items for you to correct later. You also appoint a moderator to keep the discussion on track and impersonal. In no event should you consider yourself as secretary or moderator.

We, as programmers, often profess a dislike for the walkthrough concept. Our stated reason is a waste of time: it is far too expensive for highly paid technical people to pass the time of day reviewing someone else's work. Our unstated, and probably truer reason, is that we dislike having our work reviewed, and regard criticism of our code, intended or otherwise, as a personal affront. This attitude is natural and stems from years of working as individuals. Management will therefore attempt to sell us on the benefits of teamwork and open review. They are not wrong. It is up to us to make the concept work.

Walkthroughs can and have become unpleasant and ego-deflating experiences. On the other hand, when the atmosphere is kept open and nondefensive, when discussion is restricted to major problems rather than trivial errors, and when personality clashes are avoided, the walkthrough is an extremely effective check on program development. Believe it or not a problem-solving atmosphere in which everyone, especially the individual being reviewed, is eager to find potential errors can be established. To achieve this, we as programmers, who function as both reviewer and reviewed, should keep the following in mind:

1. The program and *not* the programmer is reviewed. Structured walkthroughs are intended to find programming problems; they will not be used by management as an evaluation tool. No one keeps count of how many errors are found in your work or how many errors you find in someone else's. It is quite logical, therefore, to exclude the project manager (i.e., the individual in charge of salaries, promotions, etc.) from review sessions.

2. Emphasis is on error detection, *not* correction. It is simply assumed that the individual being reviewed will take the necessary corrective action. Reviewers should

not harp on errors by discussing how to correct them; indeed, *no* corrections whatsoever are made during a walkthrough. Finally, reviewers should focus on major problems and omit trivial errors entirely.

3. Everyone, from senior analyst to trainee, has his work reviewed. This avoids singling out an individual and further removes any stigma from having one's work reviewed. It also promotes the give-and-take atmosphere that is so vital to making the concept work.

Chief Programmer Teams

The authors have long believed in a fundamental inequality of data processing—that a single gifted programmer can have the impact of 5, 10, 20 or even 50 average programmers. This theory was put to the test by IBM, in an experiment known as "the super programmer project."† In this experiment, a single programmer, Harlan Mills, was to complete an estimated 30-man-year undertaking in 6 months. The project eventually took 6-man-years, but the still rather substantial increase in productivity over a parallel control group gave rise to new ideas in project organization. The two most important findings were the success of the top-down approach and the necessary assistance required by a top-level programmer to perform optimally (i.e., the chief programmer team).

Mills formulated the chief programmer team (CPT) concept, which states simply that the *programming activity should be rigidly separated from the associated clerical tasks.* Separation is achieved by having the programmer indicate whatever changes are necessary directly on current listings (or on coding sheets). Another team member, the librarian, implements these changes and places corrected versions in a binder for programmer review. Thus, the programmer is presumably freed of routine obligations and can make more effective use of his time.

A chief programmer team has three permanent members: chief programmer, backup programmer, and librarian; and several temporary members, additional programmers, analysts, and so on. Each permanent member has a well-defined function, as follows:

Chief programmer: Has complete technical responsibility for the project. Writes the mainline and critical routines and the system interfaces (i.e., JCL). Defines the modules to be coded by other team members and is responsible for their interface. May arrange for additional team members when necessary. Oversees all testing. Finally, reports to management on the project's status.

Backup programmer: Also a senior-level programmer; could assume the chief's duties, if necessary. Active in the technical design and supervision aspects.

Librarian: Full-time member of the team with sufficient administrative skill to implement maintenance procedures associated with the

---

†J. D. Aron. "The Super-programmer Project," *Software Engineering Techniques*, NATO Scientific Affairs Division, Brussels, Belgium, 1970, pp. 50-52.

program library. Arranges for program compilations and/or tests requested by team members. Is responsible for all input preparation and for the filing of all output.

The advantages of the CPT approach stem from a program central library. In the traditional structure, one without a central library, each programmer uniquely maintains his own libraries. Each individual spends large amounts of time on library maintenance, leading to considerable variation from programmer to programmer in both quality and reliability. The CPT structure frees the programmer from clerical details of library maintenance and allows him to concentrate on the more important functions of design, coding, and testing. However, in spite of the apparent advantages of the CPT approach, it has yet to gain widespread acceptance in the programming community.

SUMMARY

Recent developments in programming have emphasized the importance of well-written programs. Such programs do not happen by chance but are the result of careful thought and planning by the programmer. This chapter has concentrated on developing a methodology for achieving such programs.

Fundamental to this philosophy is the top-down approach, in which the highest levels of logic are developed, coded, and tested first. Stepwise refinement is used to continually refine program logic. Subsequent coding must be structured—limited to the basic building blocks of sequence, selection, and iteration. Pseudocode and hierarchy charts are used to communicate a program's logic.

Two new management techniques are often, but not necessarily, associated with structured programming. The chief programmer team relieves top programmers of clerical activity. It is a radical departure from traditional management and is not an integral part of structured programming. The structured walkthrough is a less severe change and almost always accompanies a conversion to the structured discipline. The walkthrough is a group review of an individual's work designed to catch errors, at the earliest possible time in the development cycle, when their impact is least.

PROBLEMS

1. The documentation of structured programs often consists entirely of pseudocode and hierarchy charts. Conspicuous by its absence is the conventional flowchart. Discuss whether or not flowcharts should be included in a program's documentation.

2. Unlike conventional flowcharts, hierarchy charts do not show logical decisions in a program. Nor do they indicate how often a particular segment is executed. Consequently, they are not worth much as a design aid. Discuss.

3. Do you write programs from the top down, the bottom up, or somewhere in the middle? Discuss the pros and cons of each approach.

4. A programmer should not write a single line of code until a minimum of 3 days have passed after he has received the program specifications. Do you agree or disagree? Comment on the rigid specification of 3 days.

5. It is impossible to test half a program. Consequently, testing should not begin until a program has been completely coded. Do you agree or disagree?

6. Develop pseudocode and a hierarchy chart for the two-file merge of Chapter One.

7. Expand the World Wide Widgets problem to three control breaks from two. Locations are grouped into regions (e.g., New York, Boston, and Philadelphia may be considered the northeast region). Totals are required by salesman, by location, and by region. Implement the expansion in all phases of program development: stepwise refinement, pseudocode, and the hierarchy chart.

8. Are you comfortable with the structured walkthrough; do you think it is possible to put personalities aside and develop the necessary atmosphere? Would it bother you to have your code reviewed by your peers in open discussion?

9. This problem, a project really, focuses on control breaks. We Sell Everything, Inc. (WSE), is a large national corporation with offices in several cities. Personnel has requested information from data processing on salary distributions; specifically, they need to know the total salaries in each location. There is already a file of employee records with the following information: name, social security number, location, department, date of hire, and salary. Incoming records have been sorted by location and by department within location. Write a COBOL program that will:

(a) Produce a separate report for each location, showing the salaries of all individuals in that location.
(b) Each report under item (a) is to begin on a separate page (use page numbers). Develop an appropriate heading line(s).
(c) Print complete information for each individual: name, social security number, location, department, date of hire, and salary. Use editing where appropriate.
(d) Print a single summary report (i.e., one page) showing total salaries for each location.

Suggested extra:
(e) Use two control breaks (e.g., location and department) rather than one. Thus, each report under item (a) will have a subtotal for each department.

COBOL
Implementation

OVERVIEW

The preceding chapters have dealt with program development on a fairly general level. This chapter moves to specifics of COBOL programming. We begin with a discussion of coding standards. Next, we cover COBOL implementation of the selection and iteration structures via the IF and PERFORM statements. These are two of the more powerful verbs in COBOL and are presented in great detail. We introduce the case structure and discuss its implementation via the COBOL GO TO DEPENDING statement. The chapter concludes with a sequential maintenance application to summarize the material on structured programming.

CODING STANDARDS

In spite of what you may think of the COBOL compiler, COBOL is a relatively free-form language. There is considerable flexibility as to starting column for most entries (i.e., in or beyond column 12). The rules for paragraph and data names are equally lenient. Notes are permitted but are not required. These aspects make programs easy to write, but not necessarily easy to read.

In a commercial installation, it is absolutely essential that programs be well documented, as the person who writes a program today may not be here tomorrow. Indeed, continuing success depends on someone other than the author being able to maintain a program. Accordingly, most installations impose a set of coding standards, such as those described herein, which go beyond the requirements of COBOL. Such standards are optional for the student. However, they are typical of what is, or should be, required in the real world.

Data Division

1. *Begin all PICTURE clauses in the same column*, usually between columns 36 and 52, but the choice is arbitrary. Further, choose one form of the PICTURE clause (PIC, PIC IS, PICTURE, or PICTURE IS) and follow it consistently. The actual starting column and form chosen are immaterial, but consistency is essential. Vertical alignment of the PICTURE clause greatly improves the overall appearance of a COBOL program. (Similar guidelines apply to the VALUE and USAGE clauses.)

2. *Prefix all data names within the same 01 record* (e.g., two characters unique to the FD, such as *CD*-LAST-NAME, *CD*-FIRST-NAME, *CD*-ADDRESS, etc.). The utility of this guideline becomes apparent in the Procedure Division, when it becomes necessary to refer back to the definition of a data name. The prefix points you immediately to the proper FD. Note that adherence to this guideline precludes the CORRESPONDING option in MOVE and/or arithmetic statements. We believe, however, that the additional program clarity provided by the prefix is well worth any additional Procedure Division statements.

3. *Prefix all 77 level entries by WS- and list them in alphabetical order.* The reasoning here is similar to the previous suggestion. WS- in front of a data name indicates that its definition occurred in the Working-Storage Section. Alphabetical listing speeds references, particularly in long application programs.

4. *Indent successive-level numbers in an FD or 01 by a consistent amount* (e.g., two or four columns). Use the same level numbers from FD to FD (or 01 to 01) and leave numerical gaps between successive levels: 05, 10, 15, 20 or 03, 07, 11, 15, etc.

5. *Choose mnemonically significant data names.* Although COBOL allows data names up to 30 characters, two- and three-character cryptic names are used too frequently. It is impossible for a maintenance programmer, or even the original author, to determine the significance of CDX, RF-P, and the like. Moreover, *meaningful* names should be chosen; END-OF-FIRST-FILE-SWITCH is far superior to SWITCH-1.

6. *Indent successive lines of the same entry.* If a given statement contains several clauses, it is usually not possible to fit the entire entry on one line. In those instances the continued line should be indented. Further, a clause should not be split over two lines (not always possible with VALUE clauses).

The following code summarizes these suggestions:

```
01     EMPLOYEE-INPUT-RECORD.
       05   EM-EMPLOYEE-NAME.
            10    EM-EMPLOYEE-LAST-NAME          PIC A(20).
            10    EM-EMPLOYEE-FIRST-NAME         PIC A(10).
       05   EM-BIRTH-DATE.
            10    EM-BIRTH-MONTH                 PIC 99.
            10    EM-BIRTH-YEAR                  PIC 99.
                •
                  •
                •

WORKING-STORAGE SECTION.
77     WS-EMPLOYEE-COUNT                         PIC 9(4)
            VALUE IS ZERO.
77     WS-TOTAL-TUITION                          PIC 9(6)
            VALUE IS ZERO.
```

Procedure Division

1. *Do not put more than one statement on a line.* The COBOL compiler accepts a period as the delimiter between statements, but a new line is much easier for the eye to follow. Further, if a sentence extends past column 72, continued lines should be indented by a consistent amount (e.g., four columns).

2. *Paragraph and section headers should be the only entries on a line.* The first statement in a section or paragraph should always begin a new line. In addition, a blank line before each paragraph or section name helps the entry to stand out further. IBM compilers permit SKIP1, SKIP2, and SKIP3 (beginning in or past column 12) to skip one, two, or three lines, respectively.

3. *Sequence all section and paragraph names.* Virtually everyone agrees on the importance of this technique to quickly locate paragraph and/or section headers. There is considerable disagreement, however, on exactly how to apply this technique; just what should the sequence consist of? The simplest approach is a strict numeric sequence: for example, 0010-MAINLINE, 0020-HOUSEKEEPING, 0030-PROCESS-TRANSAC-TIONS, and so on. A slight variation is to prefix each section with a letter, then apply sequencing to the paragraphs within that section: for example, A SECTION, A0010-FIRST-PARAGRAPH-IN-A, A0020-SECOND-PARAGRAPH-IN-A, B SECTION, B0010-FIRST-PARAGRAPH-IN-B, and so on.

There are untold variations of sequencing with both letters and numbers. Almost any commonsense approach will do and we will not make a case for any one scheme in particular. We do, however, urge consistency from program to program. We also believe strongly in the sequencing concept in general and frown upon programs in which no attempt is made in this direction.

A parallel question to sequencing is that of procedure placement in the COBOL program. (The reader is referred to Yourdon's excellent book, *Techniques of Program Structure and Design*, Prentice-Hall, 1975, for additional discussion.) Figure

3.1(a) contains a hierarchy chart with modules numbered according to a simple, and hopefully obvious, scheme utilizing both letters and numbers. Two approaches for ordering these procedures in a COBOL program are shown in Figure 3.1(b) and (c).

Figure 3.1(b) groups the modules in a *horizontal* manner. Modules are listed in the program as they appear in the hierarchy chart, one row at a time, from left to right. Figure 3.1(c) on the other hand, is known as a *vertical* arrangement. It groups modules in the listing as they appear in the hierarchy chart, from the top down, and then from left to right. The vertical arrangement appears to offer a better view of program flow, but either technique is quite proper and common.

4. *Indent IF/ELSE statements with the ELSE portion under the relevant IF.* This can be tricky, particularly with nested IFs, but it is absolutely essential. The compiler does not interpret ELSE clauses as the programmer writes them, but *associates the ELSE clause with the closest unpaired previous IF.* Incorrect indentation in a listing conveys a programmer's intention, which is not recognized by the compiler. Consider the *misleading* example:

```
IF CD-SEX IS EQUAL TO 'M'
    IF CD-AGE IS GREATER THAN 30
        MOVE CD-NAME TO MALE-OVER-30
ELSE MOVE CD-NAME TO REJECT.
```

The indentation implies that CD-NAME be moved to REJECT if CD-SEX is not equal to 'M'. This is *not* the compiler interpretation. *The ELSE clause is associated with the closest previous IF which is not already paired with another ELSE.* Therefore, the

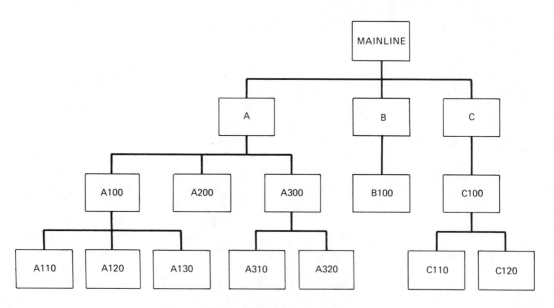

Figure 3.1(a) Hierarchy Chart

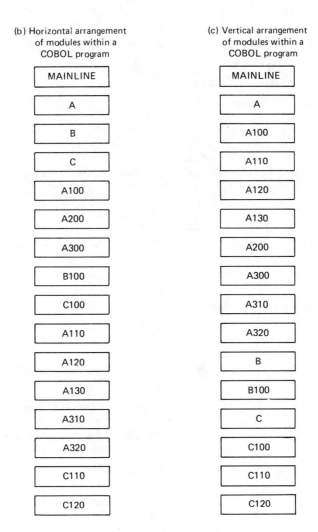

(b) Horizontal arrangement
of modules within a
COBOL program

MAINLINE
A
B
C
A100
A200
A300
B100
C100
A110
A120
A130
A310
A320
C110
C120

(c) Vertical arrangement
of modules within a
COBOL program

MAINLINE
A
A100
A110
A120
A130
A200
A300
A310
A320
B
B100
C
C100
C110
C120

Figures 3.1(b) and (c)

compiler will move CD-NAME to REJECT if CD-SEX equals 'M' but CD-AGE is not greater than 30.

5. *Indent subservient clauses under the associated verb.* Thus, AT END should be indented under READ, INVALID KEY under WRITE, SIZE ERROR under COMPUTE, etc. The following are examples of good indentation:

41

```
READ MASTER-FILE
    AT END PERFORM END-OF-JOB-ROUTINE.

WRITE NEW-MASTER-RECORD
    INVALID KEY
        MOVE 'YES' TO INVALID-SWITCH
        PERFORM INVALID-ROUTINE
        PERFORM ERROR-ROUTINE.
```

Note that in the second example, the INVALID KEY condition causes three specific actions. Indentation of the MOVE and PERFORM clauses under INVALID KEY further clarifies intent. The reader is referred to Chapter 6 for additional examples of good indentation.

6. *Strive to make the PERFORM statements legible.* The COBOL PERFORM is vital to the implementation of the iteration structure and, as such, appears frequently in most programs. The statement is one of the more flexible in COBOL and has a host of associated options. The variety is so great that we do not issue explicit guidelines; rather, we urge the reader to be especially conscientious in coding. The following examples can form the basis for lively discussion; note also the use of condition names in the third PERFORM statement.

```
PERFORM PARAGRAPH-A THRU PARAGRAPH-C
    UNTIL EOF-SWITCH = 'YES'.

PERFORM SECTION-B
    VARYING LOCATION-SUB FROM 1 BY 1
        UNTIL LOCATION-SUB > 3
    AFTER DEPARTMENT-SUB FROM 1 BY 1
        UNTIL DEPARTMENT-SUB > 5.

PERFORM SECTION-C
    UNTIL END-OF-FIRST-FILE
        OR END-OF-SECOND-FILE
        OR END-OF-THIRD-FILE.
```

7. *Stack (i.e., vertically align) similar portions of a statement or group of statements.* The MOVE statement provides a good example:

```
MOVE CD-NAME            TO PR-NAME.
MOVE CD-STUDENT-ID      TO PR-STUDENT-ID.
MOVE CD-AGE             TO PR-AGE.
MOVE CD-ADDRESS         TO PR-ADDRESS.
                                        etc.
```

Stacking can also be applied to OPEN and/or CLOSE statements:

```
OPEN INPUT    FIRST-FILE
              SECOND-FILE
              THIRD-FILE
      OUTPUT  FOURTH-FILE
              FIFTH-FILE.
```

8. *Code in a straightforward manner.* This guideline is more stylistic in nature, but of such concern that we include it anyway. Procedure Division code should be kept as straightforward as possible and efforts at being cute or fancy should be discouraged. Beginning programmers, especially, are notorious for trying to impress their peers with "clever" code. Compare, for example, the following IF statements, which are logically equivalent:

```
IF    HOURS-WORKED > 48
      COMPUTE GROSS-PAY
          = 40 * HOURLY-RATE
          +  8 * HOURLY-RATE * 1.5
          + (HOURS-WORKED — 48) * HOURLY-RATE * 2.

IF    HOURS-WORKED > 48
      COMPUTE GROSS-PAY
          = 52 * HOURLY-RATE
          + (HOURS-WORKED — 48) * HOURLY-RATE * 2.
```

It is fairly easy to determine the method of payment from the first statement. Individuals working more than 48 hours receive straight time for the first 40 hours, time and a half for the next 8 hours, and double time for any hours over 48. The second statement produces equivalent results for GROSS-PAY and is a line shorter. It is however, decidedly *poorer* code because it deviates significantly from the physical situation. A maintenance programmer would be hard-pressed to understand the meaning of the constant 52. Lest the reader think that this a concocted example, we credit it to a math major in "COBOL 1." The student was an accomplished mathematician and FORTRAN programmer. His solution may be elegant in a mathematical sense, but it is certainly undesirable in a commercial environment.

Both Divisions

1. *Use blank lines, SKIPs, and EJECTs freely.* EJECT (restricted to IBM systems) causes the next statement in a COBOL listing to begin on top of a new page. SKIP1, SKIP2, and SKIP3 (also restricted to IBM) cause the listing to space one, two, or three lines, respectively, before the next statement. (Although there is no explicit mention of SKIP and EJECT in OS/VS COBOL, both features are supported. A slash in column 7 will also eject to a new page under this compiler.) Blank lines, SKIPs, and EJECTs should be freely used prior to section and division headers, FDs, 01s, and so on.

2. *Make use of columns 73-80.* Columns 73-80 are optional in COBOL but can be put to good use (e.g., to indicate program corrections). Any statement which is added or altered could contain the modifier's initials, and date of modification. Thus, RTG08/78, appearing in columns 73-80, would indicate that programmer RTG modified (or added) this statement in August 1978.

3. *Use appropriate comments.* Although there is growing disillusionment with comments in structured COBOL programs, good code does *not* eliminate their necessity. As Yourdon has so eloquently stated: "No programmer, no matter how wise, no matter how experienced, no matter how hard pressed for time, no matter how well intentioned, should be forgiven an uncommented and undocumented program." The mere presence of comments however, does not ensure a well-documented program, and poor comments are sometimes worse than no comments at all. The most common fault is redundancy with the source code. For example, in the code

```
*    CALCULATE NET PAY
     COMPUTE NET-PAY = GROSS-PAY − FEDERAL-TAX − VOLUNTARY-DEDUCTION.
```

the comment does not add to the readability of the program. It might even be said to detract from legibility because it breaks the logical flow as one is reading. Worse than redundant, comments may be obsolete or incorrect (i.e., inconsistent with the associated code). This happens if program statements are changed during debugging or maintenance and the comments are not correspondingly altered. The compiler, unfortunately, does not validate comments. Comments may also be correct, but incomplete and hence misleading. In sum, the presence of comments is essential, but great care, *more than is commonly exercised*, should be applied to developing and maintaining comments in a program.

As a general rule, comments should be provided whenever you are doing something which is not immediately obvious to another person. When considering a comment, imagine that you are turning the program over for maintenance, and insert comments whenever you would pause to explain a feature in your program. Do assume, however, that the maintenance programmer is as competent in COBOL as you are. Thus, your comments should be directed to *why* you are doing something, rather than to what you are doing.

4. *Avoid commas.* The compiler treats a comma as "noise"—that is, a comma has no effect on the generated object code. Many programmers, the authors included, have acquired the habit of inserting commas to increase legibility. While this works rather well with prose, it can have just the opposite effect in COBOL. This is because of blurred print chains, which make it difficult to distinguish a comma from a period. As we will learn in Chapter Six, the presence or absence of a period is critical. Hence, the inability to distinguish a period from a comma becomes rather annoying; consequently, we suggest avoiding commas altogether.

COBOL IMPLEMENTATION OF STRUCTURED PROGRAMMING

This section discusses COBOL implementation of the logic structures presented in Chapter One. In addition, the case structure is presented.

The Iteration Structure

The PERFORM verb is the primary means for implementing the iteration structure. The verb is one of the most powerful in COBOL and enables transfer of control to and from a procedure elsewhere in the program. Four distinct formats are possible, as shown in Figure 3.2.

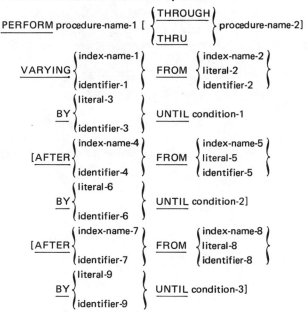

#1   **PERFORM Statement—Basic PERFORM**

$$\text{PERFORM } \underline{\text{procedure-name-1}} \left[\begin{Bmatrix} \underline{\text{THROUGH}} \\ \underline{\text{THRU}} \end{Bmatrix} \text{procedure-name-2} \right]$$

#2   **PERFORM Statement—TIMES Option**

$$\text{PERFORM } \underline{\text{procedure-name-1}} \left[\begin{Bmatrix} \underline{\text{THROUGH}} \\ \underline{\text{THRU}} \end{Bmatrix} \text{procedure-name-2} \right]$$

$$\begin{Bmatrix} \text{identifier-1} \\ \text{integer-1} \end{Bmatrix} \underline{\text{TIMES}}$$

#3   **PERFORM Statement—Conditional PERFORM**

$$\text{PERFORM } \underline{\text{procedure-name-1}} \left[\begin{Bmatrix} \underline{\text{THROUGH}} \\ \underline{\text{THRU}} \end{Bmatrix} \text{procedure-name-2} \right]$$

$$\underline{\text{UNTIL}} \text{ condition-1}$$

#4   **PERFORM Statement—VARYING Option**

$$\text{PERFORM } \underline{\text{procedure-name-1}} \left[\begin{Bmatrix} \underline{\text{THROUGH}} \\ \underline{\text{THRU}} \end{Bmatrix} \text{procedure-name-2} \right]$$

$$\underline{\text{VARYING}} \begin{Bmatrix} \text{index-name-1} \\ \text{identifier-1} \end{Bmatrix} \underline{\text{FROM}} \begin{Bmatrix} \text{index-name-2} \\ \text{literal-2} \\ \text{identifier-2} \end{Bmatrix}$$

$$\underline{\text{BY}} \begin{Bmatrix} \text{literal-3} \\ \text{identifier-3} \end{Bmatrix} \underline{\text{UNTIL}} \text{ condition-1}$$

$$\left[\underline{\text{AFTER}} \begin{Bmatrix} \text{index-name-4} \\ \text{identifier-4} \end{Bmatrix} \underline{\text{FROM}} \begin{Bmatrix} \text{index-name-5} \\ \text{literal-5} \\ \text{identifier-5} \end{Bmatrix} \right.$$

$$\underline{\text{BY}} \begin{Bmatrix} \text{literal-6} \\ \text{identifier-6} \end{Bmatrix} \underline{\text{UNTIL}} \text{ condition-2}]$$

$$\left[\underline{\text{AFTER}} \begin{Bmatrix} \text{index-name-7} \\ \text{identifier-7} \end{Bmatrix} \underline{\text{FROM}} \begin{Bmatrix} \text{index-name-8} \\ \text{literal-8} \\ \text{identifier-8} \end{Bmatrix} \right.$$

$$\underline{\text{BY}} \begin{Bmatrix} \text{literal-9} \\ \text{identifier-9} \end{Bmatrix} \underline{\text{UNTIL}} \text{ condition-3}]$$

Figure 3.2 Permissible Forms of the PERFORM Verb

45

All forms cause a portion of code, appearing elsewhere in the program, to be executed. The executed code may consist of a single paragraph or section, or multiple paragraphs and sections if the THRU clause is included. Execution of the designated code may occur once (as in Format 1), a specified number of times (as in Format 2), or a non-specified number of times—until a specified condition occurs (as in Formats 3 and 4).

The simplest form, Format 1, calls for execution of a designated procedure (i.e., either a paragraph or section) one time. Consider Figure 3.3, which illustrates functional representation of the PERFORM verb.

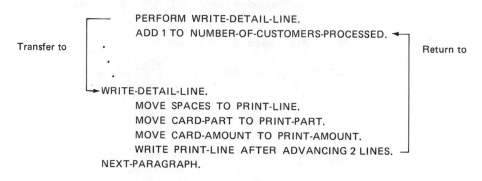

Figure 3.3 Functional Representation of the PERFORM Verb

The statement PERFORM WRITE-DETAIL-LINE transfers control to the first statement in the paragraph WRITE-DETAIL-LINE. When every statement in WRITE-DETAIL-LINE has been executed (i.e., when the next paragraph is encountered), control returns to the statement immediately after the PERFORM (i.e., to the ADD statement).

Format 2 allows for performance of a routine a predetermined number of times. Figure 3.4 is a modified version of Figure 3.3 to illustrate the TIMES option. It accommodates a situation in which multiple detail lines are written for the same customer.

```
        MOVE 1 TO WS-SUBSCRIPT.
        PERFORM WRITE-DETAIL-LINE NUMBER-OF-ITEMS TIMES.
        ADD 1 TO NUMBER-OF-CUSTOMERS-PROCESSED.
            .
            .
            .
    WRITE-DETAIL-LINE.
        MOVE SPACES TO PRINT-LINE.
        MOVE CARD-PART (WS-SUBSCRIPT) TO PRINT-PART.
        MOVE CARD-AMOUNT (WS-SUBSCRIPT) TO PRINT-AMOUNT.
        WRITE PRINT-LINE AFTER ADVANCING 2 LINES.
        ADD 1 TO WS-SUBSCRIPT.
    NEXT-PARAGRAPH.
```

Figure 3.4 Illustration of the TIMES Option

A performed procedure can be either a paragraph or a section. If the procedure is a section, as in Figure 3.5, every paragraph in that section will be executed prior to returning control.

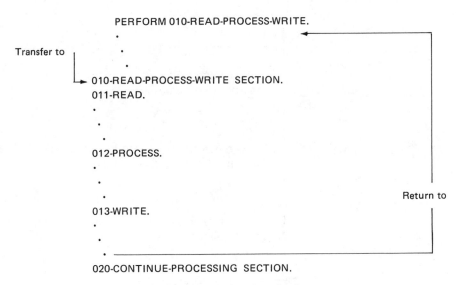

Figure 3.5 Performing a Section

Control is transferred to the first sentence in the section. Control does not return to the sentence after the PERFORM, until the last statement in the performed section is executed. Thus, performing a section typically results in the execution of several paragraphs.

Inclusion of the THRU option in any of the four formats causes execution of all statements between the designated procedure names. A suggested practice is to make the second procedure contain only a single sentence, EXIT. The EXIT statement causes no explicit action per se, but delineates the end of the perform. Use of PERFORM THRU nominally causes execution of all statements within the designated procedures. There are, however, times when it is necessary to exit immediately from a performed routine, and this is readily accomplished by the THRU option and EXIT paragraph, as shown in Figure 3.6.

Figure 3.6 contains the statement GO TO 020-READ-EXIT in several places. The GO TO does *not* leave the PERFORM, but jumps forward to the end of the PER-FORM (i.e., to the EXIT statement). The PERFORM is terminated and control returns to the statement after the PERFORM. *Although the strictest definition of structured programming does not permit the use of GO TO, we believe its use in this fashion is completely permissible and indeed consistent with the overall goal of structured programming, which is greater legibility. We permit, and sometimes even encourage, the use of GO TO provided that it is a forward branch to an exit paragraph.*

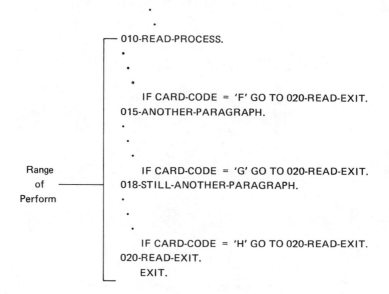

Figure 3.6 The THRU Option of the PERFORM Verb

Note well that it is extremely important to exit properly from performed routines. Indeed, improper exits are the cause of many subtle and hard-to-detect execution errors. Programmers who learn COBOL as a second language, after being proficient in either FORTRAN or PL/I, are particularly prone to such errors. Consequences of improper exits are shown in Figures 6.3 and 6.4.

Formats 3 and 4 contain an UNTIL option, which accommodates the DO WHILE logic of structured programming. If the UNTIL clause is specified, the condition in the UNTIL clause is tested prior to any transfer of control. *The performed paragraph is executed until the condition is met: that is, if the condition is not satisfied, transfer of control takes place.* When the condition is satisfied, the PERFORM is finished and control passes to the statement following the PERFORM.

Iteration is accomplished by using the UNTIL clause, specifying a condition, and modifying that condition during execution of the performed paragraph, as shown in Figure 3.7.

The paragraph READ-A-CARD is performed until END-OF-FILE-SWITCH equals YES (i.e., until there are no more data cards). When the end of file is reached, the END-OF-FILE-SWITCH is set to YES. This causes the next test of the UNTIL condition to be met and prevents the READ-A-CARD paragraph from further execution. Use of this technique to process a file also requires an "initial read," as was shown in the two-file merge program of Figure 1.3.

```
MOVE 'NO' TO END-OF-FILE-SWITCH.
PERFORM  READ-A-CARD
    UNTIL END-OF-FILE-SWITCH = 'YES'.
    .

    .

    .

READ-A-CARD.
    .

    .

    .

READ CARD-FILE, AT END MOVE 'YES' TO END-OF-FILE-SWITCH.
```

Figure 3.7 Illustration of the UNTIL Option

It is important to emphasize that the procedure is performed until the condition is satisfied, and that *the condition is tested prior to performing the procedure.* Thus, if the condition is satisfied initially, the procedure is never performed. For example, the statements

```
            MOVE 10 TO N.
and     PERFORM PARAGRAPH-A UNTIL N = 10.
```

will *not* cause a perform because the condition is satisfied immediately (i.e., N = 10). Consider the example in Figure 3.8.

```
            MOVE 1 TO N.
            PERFORM PARAGRAPH-A UNTIL N = 5.
            .

            .

            .

PARAGRAPH-A.
            ADD 1 TO  N.
            .

            .

            .

NEXT-PARAGRAPH.
```

Figure 3.8 Illustration of the UNTIL Option/II

PARAGRAPH-A will be performed four times, not five. After the fourth time through PARAGRAPH-A, N = 5. Thus, when the condition is next tested, N = 5 and PARAGRAPH-A is not performed. (If the paragraph is to be performed five times, change the condition to N $>$ 5. An alternative way to accomplish this is to retain N = 5, but MOVE ZERO TO N initially.)

The VARYING option of Format 4 is used to manipulate subscripts and/or indexes in one, two, or three dimensions. Consider

```
PERFORM 010-READ-CARDS
     VARYING COLLEGE-SUB
          FROM 1 BY 1 UNTIL COLLEGE-SUB > 3
     AFTER SCHOOL-SUB
          FROM 1 BY 1 UNTIL SCHOOL-SUB > 5
     AFTER YEAR-SUB
          FROM 1 BY 1 UNTIL YEAR-SUB > 4.
```

The procedure 010-READ-CARDS will be performed a total of 60 times. Initially, COLLEGE-SUB, SCHOOL-SUB, and YEAR-SUB are all set to 1 and the first perform is done. Then YEAR-SUB is incremented by 1 and becomes 2 (COLLEGE-SUB and SCHOOL-SUB remain at 1), and a second perform is done. YEAR-SUB is incremented to 3, then to 4 resulting in two additional performs. YEAR-SUB temporarily becomes 5 but no perform is realized, since YEAR-SUB > 4. SCHOOL-SUB is then incremented to 2, YEAR-SUB drops to 1, and we go merrily on our way.

The Selection Structure

The IF statement is the means for COBOL implementation of the selection structure. Syntactically, the format of the IF is remarkably simple:

$$\underline{\text{IF}} \text{ condition } \left[\text{THEN}\right] \left\{ \frac{\text{NEXT SENTENCE}}{\text{Statement-1}} \right\}$$

$$\left[\left\{ \frac{\text{OTHERWISE}}{\underline{\text{ELSE}}} \right\} \left\{ \frac{\text{NEXT SENTENCE}}{\text{Statement-2}} \right\} \right]$$

In practice, the statement acquires varying degrees of complexity. First, the condition itself can assume several forms. It may be a simple relational test, a class test, a sign test, a condition name, or compound combinations (i.e., OR, AND, or NOT) of any or all of the various tests. Second, either Statement-1 or Statement-2 may contain several clauses, including another IF, giving rise to the infamous nested IF, which is actually prohibited in some shops. In this section the IF statement is covered in detail, beginning with the condition portion.

Class Tests

These tests are an excellent means of detecting improper data, which are a frequent cause of a program's failure to execute. It is critical that a numeric field contain only the digits 0-9 (a sign is optional), while an alphabetic field contain only the letters A-Z and/or blanks. Alphanumeric fields can contain anything: letters, numbers, or special characters, (e.g., +, &, etc.).

The presence of nonnumeric data in a numeric field, used for computation, will cause rather unpleasant results (see the discussion in Chapter 8 on the data exception). Class tests will ensure that numeric data are numeric, alphabetic data are alphabetic, and so on. The general format is

$$\text{IF identifier IS} \begin{bmatrix} \underline{\text{NOT}} \end{bmatrix} \begin{Bmatrix} \underline{\text{NUMERIC}} \\ \underline{\text{ALPHABETIC}} \end{Bmatrix}$$

Caution must be used in applying the class test. Specifically, a numeric test is valid only on data names defined with a numeric picture (i.e., a picture of 9's). An alphabetic test is valid only on data names defined with a picture of A. Either test may be performed on alphanumeric items, as shown in Table 3.1 and Figure 3.9.

Table 3.1 Valid Forms of Class Test

Data Type and Pictures	Valid Tests
Numeric (9)	NUMERIC, NOT NUMERIC
Alphabetic (A)	ALPHABETIC, NOT ALPHABETIC
Alphanumeric (X)	NUMERIC, NOT NUMERIC, ALPHABETIC, NOT ALPHABETIC

```
           05    NUMERIC-FIELD          PIC 9(5).
           05    ALPHABETIC-FIELD       PIC A(5).
           05    ALPHANUMERIC-FIELD     PIC X(5).
(valid)          IF NUMERIC-FIELD IS NUMERIC.....
(valid)          IF NUMERIC-FIELD IS NOT NUMERIC.....
(invalid)        IF NUMERIC-FIELD IS NOT ALPHABETIC.....
(invalid)        IF ALPHABETIC-FIELD IS NOT NUMERIC.....
(valid)          IF ALPHANUMERIC-FIELD IS NOT NUMERIC.....
(valid)          IF ALPHANUMERIC-FIELD IS NOT ALPHABETIC.....
```

Figure 3.9 Example of Class Test

Relational Tests

The general form of the relational test is

$$\text{IF} \begin{Bmatrix} \text{identifier} \\ \text{literal} \\ \text{expression} \end{Bmatrix} \begin{Bmatrix} \text{IS} & [\underline{\text{NOT}}] & \underline{\text{LESS THAN}} \\ \text{IS} & [\underline{\text{NOT}}] & < \\ \text{IS} & [\underline{\text{NOT}}] & \underline{\text{EQUAL}} \text{ TO} \\ \text{IS} & [\underline{\text{NOT}}] & = \\ \text{IS} & [\underline{\text{NOT}}] & \underline{\text{GREATER THAN}} \\ \text{IS} & [\underline{\text{NOT}}] & > \end{Bmatrix} \quad \ldots\ldots$$

The action of this test is easily predictable when only numeric quantities are involved, but more explanation is required concerning alphabetic or alphanumeric items. Assume that BAKER is compared to BROWN. BAKER is considered smaller, since it is alphabetically before BROWN. Comparison proceeds from left to right one letter at a time. Both names begin with B, but the A in BAKER precedes the R in BROWN.

Now, compare GREEN to GREENFIELD. GREEN is considered smaller. Comparison again proceeds from left to right. The first five characters, G, R, E, E, and N, are the same in both names. The shorter field, GREEN, is extended with blanks so that comparison may continue. A blank, however, is always considered smaller than any other letter, so GREEN is the smaller of the two names.

Comparison is possible on alphanumeric fields as well as alphabetic fields. In this instance, determination of the smaller field depends on the collating sequence of the machine. Collating sequence is defined as the ordered list (from low to high) of all valid characters. Collating sequence is a function of manufacturer; IBM uses EBCDIC and most others use ASCII. Selected characters in both sequences are shown in Figure 3.10.

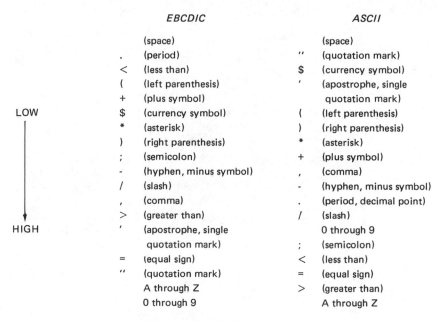

Figure 3.10 Collating Sequences

As can be seen from Figure 3.10, 1 is greater than A for EBCDIC. Under ASCII, however, 1 is less than A. It is certainly not necessary for you to memorize either collating sequence. Simply learn which one applies to your machine and be aware of the conceptual significance.

Sign Test

The *sign test* determines the sign of a numeric data field:

$$IF \left\{ \begin{array}{c} \text{identifier} \\ \text{arithmetic expression} \end{array} \right\} \quad IS \quad \left[\underline{NOT} \right] \quad \left\{ \begin{array}{c} \text{POSITIVE} \\ \text{NEGATIVE} \\ \text{ZERO} \end{array} \right\}$$

A value is positive if it is greater than zero and negative if it is less than zero. This test may validate incoming data or verify the results of a calculation. For example:

```
IF NET-PAY IS NOT POSITIVE PERFORM TOO-MUCH-TAXES.
IF CHECK-BALANCE IS NEGATIVE PERFORM OVERDRAWN.
```

Condition Name Tests

The condition portion of the IF statement often tests the value of an incoming code (e.g., IF YEAR-CODE = 1. . .). While such coding is quite permissible, and indeed commonplace, the meaning of YEAR-CODE is not immediately apparent in the Procedure Division. An alternative form of coding, condition names (88-level entries), provides superior documentation; 88-level entries appear in the Data Division and can only be applied to elementary items. Consider:

```
05   YEAR-CODE              PIC 9.
     88 FRESHMAN            VALUE 1.
     88 SOPHOMORE           VALUE 2.
     88 JUNIOR              VALUE 3.
     88 SENIOR              VALUE 4.
     88 UNDER-CLASSMAN      VALUES ARE 1  2.
     88 ERROR-CODES         VALUES ARE 0, 5 THRU 9.
```

If these entries were made in the Data Division, we can code

```
IF FRESHMAN
```

as equivalent to

```
IF YEAR-CODE = 1
```

The advantage of condition names is threefold. First, they provide improved documentation (i.e., FRESHMAN is inherently clearer than YEAR-CODE = 1). Second, they facilitate maintenance in that additions and/or changes to existing codes need to be made in only one place (i.e., the Data Division). Finally, they provide for convenient grouping of codes, *without* resorting to compound conditions in the IF statement itself. Thus,

```
IF ERROR-CODES
```

is equivalent to

```
IF YEAR-CODE = 0 OR YEAR-CODE > 4 AND YEAR-CODE NOT > 9
```

Indeed, the latter is an example of a compound condition which can rapidly become extremely difficult to follow.

Compound Tests

Any two "simple" tests (i.e., relational, class, condition name, or sign) may be combined to form a compound test. This is accomplished through the logical operators AND and OR. *AND means both; two conditions must be satisfied for the IF to be considered true. OR means either; only one of the two conditions needs to be satisfied for the IF to be considered true.*

Compound conditions can become rather complex, as shown by the following example:

```
IF   SALARY > 30000 AND SALARY < 40000
     OR DEPARTMENT = 10 OR DEPARTMENT = 20
     PERFORM QUALIFIED-EMPLOYEE.
```

To perform the routine QUALIFIED-EMPLOYEE, only one of three conditions has to hold: *either* salary is between $30,000 and $40,000, *or* department = 10, *or* department = 20. Unequivocal interpretation of this, or any compound condition, is provided by the COBOL hierarchy:

1. Arithmetic expressions.

2. Relational operators.

3. NOT condition.

4. AND (from left to right if more than one).

5. OR (from left to right if more than one).

However parentheses, can, and should, be used to clarify the intent of compound conditions, just as they clarify intent in a COMPUTE statement.

Implied Conditions

The compound condition can be further clouded by the use of implied subjects; that is, if a compound condition has the same subject immediately before each relation, only the first occurrence of the subject need to be written. In other words,

```
IF SALARY > 30000 AND < 40000
```

is equivalent to

```
IF SALARY > 30000 AND SALARY < 40000
```

If both the subject and relational operator of the simple conditions within a compound condition are the same, only the first occurrence of both need be written:

IF DEPARTMENT = 10 OR 20

is equivalent to

IF DEPARTMENT = 10 OR DEPARTMENT = 20

Since implied conditions are often confusing, the following are provided as additional examples:

X = Y OR Z	is equivalent to	X = Y OR X = Z
A = B OR C OR D	is equivalent to	A = B OR A = C OR A = D
A = B AND > C	is equivalent to	A = B AND A > C

Significance of the Period

In a simple IF statement, i.e. one without an ELSE clause or a second IF, statement-1 is terminated by a period. Thus, a simple IF statement could cause one or several actions to be performed depending on where the period is located. Consider

```
IF   SALARY > 10000
     PERFORM EXEMPT-ROUTINE
     PERFORM PRINT-ROUTINE
     ADD 1 TO HIGH-SALARIED-EMPLOYEES.
```

If salary is greater than $10,000, EXEMPT-ROUTINE will be performed, after which PRINT-ROUTINE will be performed, after which one will be added to a counter. *Note well* that the action of the IF would be radically altered if an additional period were inserted after the clause, PERFORM EXEMPT-ROUTINE.

In a simple IF/ELSE statement, statement-1 is terminated by the ELSE verb itself and statement-2 by the period. Consider

```
IF      EXEMPT-EMPLOYEE
        PERFORM FIRST-ROUTINE
        PERFORM SECOND-ROUTINE
        PERFORM THIRD-ROUTINE
ELSE    PERFORM FOURTH-ROUTINE
        PERFORM FIFTH-ROUTINE
        PERFORM SIXTH-ROUTINE.
```

First realize that for the IF statement to make sense, EXEMPT-EMPLOYEE must be a condition name (i.e., an 88-level entry). If the condition is met, three routines will be performed; if it is not met, three other routines will be performed. The significance of the period in an IF statement is further discussed through additional examples in Chapter Six.

Nested IFs

Advocates of structured programming use nested IFs extensively, whereas other installations discourage (and even prohibit) their use. We like the capability, but suggest *strict* attention to proper indentation. Nested IFs stem from the fact that in the syntactical format of the IF statement itself, either Statement-1 or Statement-2 may in turn be another IF statement. Consider Figure 3.11, which shows a flowchart and corresponding COBOL code to determine the largest of three quantities A, B, and C. (They are assumed to be unequal numbers.)

Compiler interpretation of nested IFs is as follows: *The ELSE clause is associated with the closest previous IF which is not already paired with another ELSE.* Thus, the code in Figure 3.11 is consistent with the flowchart and compiler interpretation. Consider a second example

```
IF   LOCATION = 'NEW YORK'
   IF   SALARY > 10000
        ADD 1 TO QUALIFIED-EMPLOYEES
   ELSE
        PERFORM NOT-QUALIFIED.
```

Interpretation is as follows: If the first condition fails, (i.e., if the location is not New York), control passes to the next sentence. The routine NOT-QUALIFIED is performed only if location is New York *and* salary is not greater than $10,000. Nested IF statements should always be indented in a manner consistent with compiler interpretation. This can be achieved through the LISTER option of VS COBOL (see the IBM Programmer's Guide), or through various commercial aids, as described in Appendix B.

Case Structure (GO TO DEPENDING)

Structured programming is often referred to as GO TO less programming, which is, in fact, a slight misrepresentation. No special effort is made to avoid the GO TO, even if there are valid reasons for not using it. The GO TO statement just never occurs if the three standard logic structures are adhered to. However, situations can occur in which the GO TO may actually improve clarity. We are referring to a fourth logic structure, the case structure, and a *forward* branch to an EXIT paragraph. Although the strictest advocates of structured programming may not approve of these statements, we believe they can be used to good advantage and in a manner consistent with the spirit of structured programming. Indeed, it is our opinion that anyone who would prohibit a forward GO TO is simply not a COBOL programmer.

The case structure expresses a multibranch situation by testing the value of a variable to determine which of several routines is to be executed. Its flowchart is shown in Figure. 3.12. As with the other building blocks of structured programming, there is

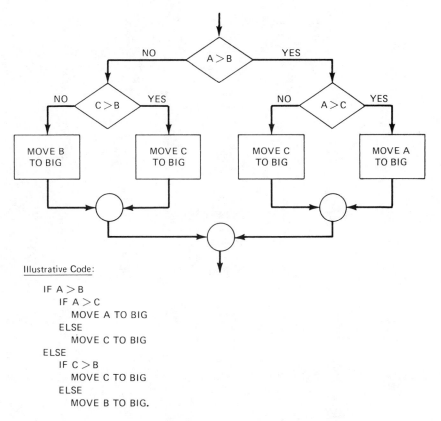

Illustrative Code:

```
IF A > B
    IF A > C
        MOVE A TO BIG
    ELSE
        MOVE C TO BIG
ELSE
    IF C > B
        MOVE C TO BIG
    ELSE
        MOVE B TO BIG.
```

Figure 3.11 Flowchart and COBOL Code for Nested IFs

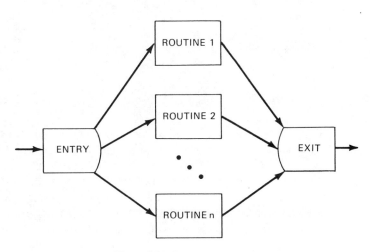

Figure 3.12 The Case Structure

57

exactly one entry and one exit point. Implementation is through the GO TO DEPEND-
ING statement and is illustrated in Figure 3.13.

```
            PERFORM YEAR-IN-COLLEGE THRU YEAR-IN-COLLEGE-EXIT.
                .
                .
                .
    YEAR-IN-COLLEGE.
        GO TO
            FRESHMAN
            SOPHOMORE
            JUNIOR
            SENIOR
            GRAD-SCHOOL
            GRAD-SCHOOL
        DEPENDING ON INCOMING-YEAR-CODE.
        · · · process error · · ·
        GO TO YEAR-IN-COLLEGE-EXIT.
    FRESHMAN.
        · · · process · · ·
        GO TO YEAR-IN-COLLEGE-EXIT.
    SOPHOMORE.
        · · · process · · ·
        GO TO YEAR-IN-COLLEGE-EXIT.
    JUNIOR.
        · · · process · · ·
        GO TO YEAR-IN-COLLEGE-EXIT.
    SENIOR.
        · · · process · · ·
        GO TO YEAR-IN-COLLEGE-EXIT.
    GRAD-SCHOOL.
        · · · process · · ·
    YEAR-IN-COLLEGE-EXIT.
        EXIT.
```

Figure 3.13 COBOL Implementation of the Case Structure

The GO TO DEPENDING statement tests the value of a code, in this instance
INCOMING-YEAR-CODE. If it is equal to 1, control passes to the first procedure specified
after GO TO (i.e., FRESHMAN). If INCOMING-YEAR-CODE is equal to 2, control
passes to the second paragraph (i.e., SOPHOMORE) and so on. If the code has any value
other than 1, 2, 3, 4, 5, or 6 (since six procedures were specified), control passes to the
statement immediately following the GO TO DEPENDING, which should be an error
routine. Note that two values of INCOMING-YEAR-CODE, either 5 or 6, will transfer
control to GRAD-SCHOOL. Indentation in the GO TO DEPENDING is strictly for
legibility; it is not required by COBOL.

Figure 3.13 also contains five "villainous" GO TO statements, but their use is completely acceptable (to us, if not to the most rigid advocate of structured programming). If the GO TO statement is used in a structured program, it should appear only in conjunction with GO TO DEPENDING or within the range of a PERFORM sttatement, and should always branch forward to the end of the routine. This, in turn, is a "dummy" paragraph consisting of a single statement EXIT. We believe that such usage adds to, rather than detracts from, clarity.

Of course, the GO TO DEPENDING may be omitted entirely in favor of a series of IF THEN ELSE statements, but we opt for the case structure. Indeed, the larger the number of acceptable codes, the clearer the GO TO DEPENDING becomes, particularly if paragraphs are stacked and an EXIT paragraph is used, as in Figure 3.13.

SUMMARY

This chapter contained little that is truly new to the practitioner. However, the relationship of the IF and PERFORM statements to implementation of structured programming in COBOL is of vital importance. Hence, the COBOL practitioner who is first embarking on structured programming should thoroughly review this chapter, paying particular attention to the flexibility of both verbs.

The material on structured programming can best be summarized by a complete program. We have chosen a sequential maintenance application with the following specifications:

1. There are two input files, an old master file and a transaction file. Both are in ascending sequence by social security numbers. Every record in both files contains three fields; name, social security number, and salary. In addition, each transaction record contains a transaction code (A for addition, D for deletion, C for salary change).

2. Output consists of a new master file reflecting additions, deletions, and salary changes.

3. The incoming files have been "scrubbed" via a separate edit program. Thus, the transaction file is assumed to be in order, to contain valid data in all fields, and to contain a valid transaction code.

4. The edit program did not, and could not, check for two types of errors; (a) no matches in which a salary change is indicated for a record not present in the master file, and (b) a duplicate addition for a record already in the master file. Both of these conditions are to be checked in the maintenance program.

Sequential file maintenance is one of the most common, yet logically difficult, applications. It is still somewhat remarkable to us how the top-down structured approach facilitates development of this problem and, more importantly, reduces logic errors. The COBOL program is shown in Figure 3.14. (This listing is taken from Grauer and Crawford, *COBOL: A Pragmatic Approach*, Prentice-Hall, 1978. However, it has been slightly altered to reflect variations in COBOL technique. These include performed READ routines as opposed to duplicate READ statements, and greater use of nested IFs.)

The mainline routine of Figure 3.14 opens all files and performs initial reads for the transaction and old master files. It performs the COM-PARE-IDS routine until both files are out of data, after which all files are closed and processing is terminated.

```
00001          IDENTIFICATION DIVISION.
00002          PROGRAM-ID.        UPDATE.
00003          AUTHOR.            GRAUER.
00004          ENVIRONMENT DIVISION.
00005          CONFIGURATION SECTION.
00006          SOURCE-COMPUTER.   IBM-370.
00007          OBJECT-COMPUTER.   IBM-370.
00008          INPUT-OUTPUT SECTION.
00009          FILE-CONTROL.
00010              SELECT TRANSACTION-FILE ASSIGN TO UT-S-TRANS.
00011              SELECT ERROR-FILE ASSIGN TO UT-S-PRINT.
00012              SELECT OLD-MASTER-FILE ASSIGN TO UT-S-OLD.
00013              SELECT NEW-MASTER-FILE ASSIGN TO UT-S-NEW.
00014          DATA DIVISION.
00015          FILE SECTION.
00016          FD  OLD-MASTER-FILE
00017              LABEL RECORDS ARE STANDARD
00018              RECORDING MODE IS F
00019              BLOCK CONTAINS 0 RECORDS
00020              RECORD CONTAINS 40 CHARACTERS
00021              DATA RECORD IS OLD-MAST-RECORD.
00022          01  OLD-MAST-RECORD          PIC X(40).
00023          FD  NEW-MASTER-FILE
00024              LABEL RECORDS ARE STANDARD
00025              RECORDING MODE IS F
00026              BLOCK CONTAINS 0 RECORDS
00027              RECORD CONTAINS 40 CHARACTERS
00028              DATA RECORD IS NEW-MAST-RECORD.
00029          01  NEW-MAST-RECORD          PIC X(40).
00030          FD  TRANSACTION-FILE
00031              LABEL RECORDS ARE OMITTED
00032              RECORDING MODE IS F
00033              RECORD CONTAINS 80 CHARACTERS
00034              DATA RECORD IS TRANS-RECORD.
00035          01  TRANS-RECORD             PIC X(80).
00036          FD  ERROR-FILE
00037              LABEL RECORDS ARE OMITTED
00038              RECORDING MODE IS F
00039              RECORD CONTAINS 132 CHARACTERS
00040              DATA RECORD IS ERROR-RECORD.
00041          01  ERROR-RECORD             PIC X(132).
00042          WORKING-STORAGE SECTION.
00043          77  FILLER                   PIC X(14)  VALUE 'WS BEGINS HERE'.
00044          77  WS-OLD-MAST-READ-SWITCH  PIC X(3)   VALUE 'NO'.
```

Device-independent SELECT statements

OS feature to indicate that block size is entered in JCL

Literal to facilitate subsequent debugging

Figure 3.14 Sequential File Maintenance

```
00045      77  WS-TRANS-READ-SWITCH      PIC X(3)    VALUE 'NO'.
00046      01  WS-OLD-MAST-RECORD.
00047          05  WS-OLDMAST-ID         PIC X(9).
00048          05  WS-OLDMAST-NAME       PIC X(25).
00049          05  WS-OLDMAST-SALARY     PIC 9(6).
00050      01  WS-NEW-MAST-RECORD.
00051          05  WS-NEWMAST-ID         PIC X(9).
00052          05  WS-NEWMAST-NAME       PIC X(25).
00053          05  WS-NEWMAST-SALARY     PIC 9(6).
00054      01  WS-TRANS-RECORD.
00055          05  WS-TRANS-ID           PIC X(9).
00056          05  WS-TRANS-NAME         PIC X(25).
00057          05  WS-TRANS-SALARY       PIC 9(6).
00058          05  WS-TRANS-CODE         PIC X.
00059              88  ADDITION                      VALUE 'A'.
00060              88  DELETION                      VALUE 'D'.
00061              88  SALARY-CHANGE                 VALUE 'C'.
00062          05  FILLER                PIC X(39).
00063      01  WS-PRINT-RECORD.
00064          05  WS-PRINT-MESSAGE      PIC X(40).
00065          05  WS-PRINT-ID           PIC X(9).
00066          05  FILLER                PIC X(5)    VALUE SPACES.
00067          05  WS-PRINT-NAME         PIC X(25).
00068          05  FILLER                PIC X(53)   VALUE SPACES.
00069      PROCEDURE DIVISION.
00070      005-MAINLINE.
00071          OPEN INPUT TRANSACTION-FILE
00072                     OLD-MASTER-FILE
00073               OUTPUT NEW-MASTER-FILE
00074                      ERROR-FILE.
00075          PERFORM 080-READ-TRANSACTION.
00076          PERFORM 090-READ-OLD-MASTER.
00077          PERFORM 010-COMPARE-IDS
00078              UNTIL WS-TRANS-ID = HIGH-VALUES
00079              AND WS-OLDMAST-ID = HIGH-VALUES.
00080          CLOSE TRANSACTION-FILE
00081                OLD-MASTER-FILE
00082                NEW-MASTER-FILE
00083                ERROR-FILE.
00084          STOP RUN.
00085
00086      010-COMPARE-IDS.
00087          IF WS-OLDMAST-ID < WS-TRANS-ID
00088              PERFORM 050-COPY-OLD-REC
00089          ELSE
00090              IF WS-OLDMAST-ID = WS-TRANS-ID
00091                  PERFORM 060-MATCH-ROUTINE
00092              ELSE
00093                  PERFORM 070-NEW-RECORD.
00094
00095          IF WS-TRANS-READ-SWITCH = 'YES'
00096              MOVE 'NO ' TO WS-TRANS-READ-SWITCH
00097              PERFORM 080-READ-TRANSACTION.
00098
00099          IF WS-OLD-MAST-READ-SWITCH = 'YES'
00100              MOVE 'NO ' TO WS-OLD-MAST-READ-SWITCH
00101              PERFORM 090-READ-OLD-MASTER.
00102
```

Indicates whether to read from transaction file

Use of condition names

Stacked OPEN statement

Use of compound condition in PERFORM

Nested IF which drives the program

Figure 3.14 Sequential File Maintenance (continued)

61

```
00103
00104            050-COPY-OLD-REC.
00105                WRITE NEW-MAST-RECORD FROM WS-OLD-MAST-RECORD.
00106                MOVE 'YES' TO WS-OLD-MAST-READ-SWITCH.
00107                                                  Nested IF to control matching
00108            060-MATCH-ROUTINE.                    old master and transaction
00109                IF ADDITION
00110                    MOVE WS-TRANS-NAME                TO WS-PRINT-NAME
00111                    MOVE WS-TRANS-ID                  TO WS-PRINT-ID
00112                    MOVE 'ERROR - RECORD IN FILE' TO WS-PRINT-MESSAGE
00113                    WRITE ERROR-RECORD FROM WS-PRINT-RECORD
00114                    WRITE NEW-MAST-RECORD FROM WS-OLD-MAST-RECORD
00115                ELSE
00116                    IF SALARY-CHANGE
00117                        MOVE WS-TRANS-SALARY TO WS-OLDMAST-SALARY
00118                        WRITE NEW-MAST-RECORD FROM WS-OLD-MAST-RECORD
00119                    ELSE
00120                        IF DELETION
00121                            NEXT SENTENCE.
00122
00123                MOVE 'YES' TO WS-TRANS-READ-SWITCH.      Switches set to read
00124                MOVE 'YES' TO WS-OLD-MAST-READ-SWITCH.   from both files
00125
00126            070-NEW-RECORD.
00127                IF ADDITION
00128                    WRITE NEW-MAST-RECORD FROM WS-TRANS-RECORD
00129                ELSE
00130                    MOVE WS-TRANS-NAME                TO WS-PRINT-NAME
00131                    MOVE WS-TRANS-ID                  TO WS-PRINT-ID
00132                    MOVE 'ERROR - NO MATCH'           TO WS-PRINT-MESSAGE
00133                    WRITE ERROR-RECORD FROM WS-PRINT-RECORD.
00134                MOVE 'YES' TO WS-TRANS-READ-SWITCH.
00135
00136            080-READ-TRANSACTION.
00137                READ TRANSACTION-FILE INTO WS-TRANS-RECORD
00138                    AT END MOVE HIGH-VALUES TO WS-TRANS-RECORD.
00139
00140            090-READ-OLD-MASTER.
00141                READ OLD-MASTER-FILE INTO WS-OLD-MAST-RECORD
00142                    AT END MOVE HIGH-VALUES TO WS-OLD-MAST-RECORD.
```

Figure 3.14 Sequential File Maintenance (continued)

The COMPARE-IDS routine drives the entire program. The social security number from the current old master record is compared to the social security number from the current transaction. If the former is less, the current old master record is copied to the new master via the COPY routine. If the numbers are equal, the MATCH routine is performed; otherwise, the NEW RECORD routine called. After control returns from either the COPY, MATCH, or NEW RECORD routines, two switches are tested to determine from which file or files another record should be read.

The MATCH routine is itself driven by a nested IF. An attempted addition here is an error and flagged accordingly. A salary change causes the transaction salary to be moved to the old master salary, after which the new master record is written from the old. A deletion is accomplished by not writing the current master record on the new master file. Finally, note that the MATCH routine sets switches to read from both files.

The NEW RECORD routine writes a record in the new master file provided that the transaction code indicates an addition. Otherwise, a no-match condition is flagged, meaning that the social security number in the transaction file did not exist in the old master file.

Some COBOL techniques in Figure 3.14 are worth mentioning. The SELECT statements are device-independent, meaning that the old master, new master and transaction files could be contained on either tape or disk (see Chapter Ten). BLOCK CONTAINS 0 RECORDS, COBOL lines 19 and 26, is an OS feature to indicate that block size will be entered in the JCL. The literal, WS BEGINS HERE, is used in conjunction with READ INTO and WRITE FROM to facilitate ABEND debugging (see Chapter Eight). Nested IFs are used to good advantage and scrupulously indented. Condition names are used for the transaction types. Note also, the use of a compound condition in the PERFORM statement of lines 77-79.

PROBLEMS

1. Write out the 12 pairs of values that will be assumed by FIRST-SUBSCRIPT and SECOND-SUBSCRIPT as a result of the statement

```
PERFORM 10-READ-CARDS
    VARYING FIRST-SUBSCRIPT FROM 1 BY 1
        UNTIL FIRST-SUBSCRIPT > 6
    AFTER SECOND-SUBSCRIPT FROM 1 BY 1
        UNTIL SECOND-SUBSCRIPT > 2.
```

2. Write out the 24 pairs of values that will be assumed by FIRST-SUBSCRIPT, SECOND-SUBSCRIPT, and THIRD-SUBSCRIPT as a result of the statement

```
PERFORM 10-READ-CARDS
    VARYING THIRD-SUBSCRIPT FROM 1 BY 1
        UNTIL THIRD-SUBSCRIPT > 4
    AFTER SECOND-SUBSCRIPT FROM 1 BY 1
        UNTIL SECOND-SUBSCRIPT > 3
    AFTER FIRST-SUBSCRIPT FROM 1 BY 1
        UNTIL FIRST-SUBSCRIPT > 2.
```

3. Given the following pairs of IF statements, indicate whether the statements in each pair have the same effect:

(a) IF A $>$ B OR C $>$ D AND E $=$ F $\cdot\cdot\cdot$
    IF A $>$ B OR (C $>$ D AND E $=$ F) $\cdot\cdot\cdot$

(b) IF A $>$ B OR C $>$ D AND E $=$ F $\cdot\cdot\cdot$
    IF (A $>$ B OR C $>$ D) AND E $=$ F $\ldots$

(c) IF A $>$ B OR A $>$ C OR A $>$ D $\cdot\cdot\cdot$
    IF A $>$ B OR C OR D $\cdot\cdot\cdot$

(d) IF A $>$ B $\cdot\cdot\cdot$
    IF A NOT $<$ B OR A NOT $=$ B $\cdot\cdot\cdot$

4. Given the IF statement

```
IF A = B OR A = C
   PERFORM FIRST-ROUTINE
ELSE
   IF A > 10 AND B > 10 OR C = 10
      PERFORM SECOND-ROUTINE
   ELSE
      PERFORM THIRD-ROUTINE.
```

Indicate, for each set of values, which routine will be performed.

(a) A $=$ 50, B $=$ 5, C $=$ 5
(b) A $=$ 50, B $=$ 40, C $=$ 40
(c) A $=$ 50, B $=$ 50, C $=$ 50
(d) A $=$ 50, B $=$ 5, C $=$ 10
(e) A $=$ 0, B $=$ 0, C $=$ 0
(f) A $=$ 1, B $=$ 2, C $=$ 3

5. Recode the following statements to show the ELSE indented under the relevant IF. Draw appropriate flowcharts.

(a) IF A $>$ B, IF C $>$ D, MOVE E TO F,
    ELSE MOVE G TO H.

(b) IF A $>$ B, IF C $>$ D, MOVE E TO F
    ELSE MOVE G TO H, ELSE MOVE X TO Y.

(c) IF A $>$ B, IF C $>$ D, MOVE E TO F
    ADD 1 TO E, ELSE MOVE G TO H,
    ADD 1 TO G.

(d) IF A $>$ B, MOVE X TO Y, MOVE Z TO W,
    ELSE IF C $>$ D MOVE 1 TO N,
    ELSE MOVE 2 TO Y, ADD 3 TO Z.

6. How many times will PARAGRAPH-A be performed, given the following statements?

(a) PERFORM PARAGRAPH-A.

    (b) PERFORM PARAGRAPH-A
          VARYING SUBSCRIPT FROM 1 BY 1
             UNTIL SUBSCRIPT > 5.
    (c) PERFORM PARAGRAPH-A
          VARYING SUBSCRIPT FROM 1 BY 1
             UNTIL SUBSCRIPT = 5.
    (d) PERFORM PARAGRAPH-A
          VARYING SUBSCRIPT FROM 1 BY 1
             UNTIL SUBSCRIPT < 5.

7. Given Figure 3.13, illustrating the use of GO TO DEPENDING:

    (a) What would happen if all the GO TO statements were removed and INCOMING-YEAR-CODE were equal to 1?

    (b) What would happen if INCOMING-YEAR-CODE were equal to 6?

    (c) Suppose that the codes of interest were 10, 20, 30, 40, 50, and 60 rather than 1, 2, 3, 4, 5, or 6. Explain how the GO TO DEPENDING construct could still be used.

    (d) Assume that the codes of importance were 11, 17, 23, 46, 59, and 65, which would preclude use of GO TO DEPENDING. Develop alternative code (i.e., a nested IF) to accommodate the logic of Figure 3.13.

8. Modify the COBOL program of Figure 3.14 to accommodate:

    (a) New fields for LOCATION-CODE (PIC 99) and TITLE-CODE (PIC 999) in the old master, new master, and transaction records.

    (b) Flag as an error any attempted addition which does not have all of the following: name, salary, location and title codes.

    (c) Process two additional transaction codes, L and T, to process location and title changes respectively. These should function in a manner analogous to a salary change.

    (d) Flag as an error any transaction record with a code other than A, C, D, L, or T.

A Potpourri of
Advanced Features

OVERVIEW

This chapter might well have been taken from a basic book on COBOL, and indeed much of it was (Grauer and Crawford, *COBOL: A Pragmatic Approach*, Prentice-Hall, 1978). It covers several elements of the language, none of which is unique to structured programming. It is included, however, because these topics are gaining increased use in structured shops (e.g., subprograms) and because many programmers are still uncomfortable with some of the newer techniques (e.g., indexing).

The chapter begins with a thorough discussion of subprograms and associated language elements (i.e., CALL, USING, EXIT PROGRAM, GOBACK, LINKAGE SECTION, etc.). We discuss the COPY clause and the SORT and MERGE verbs in detail. Finally, we discuss table processing, subscripting and indexing, two- and three-dimension tables, and the SEARCH verb. Moreover, the discussion is for IBM OS/VS COBOL, Release 2, which may include features not present in your compiler. This release complies with the ANSI 74 standards.

SUBPROGRAMS

The essence of structured programming is the division of a complex program into a series of smaller, easier-to-code, independent modules. When these modules are entirely contained within one program, the perform statement divides the program into a series of routines called by the mainline segment. In effect, the perform invokes a kind of subprogram which is wholly contained in the COBOL program. As such the called (i.e., performed) routine must be coded, compiled and debugged *within* the main program. An alternative technique is to make the called routine an entirely separate and independent entity. This is accomplished by creating a subprogram.

A *subprogram* (i.e., one that is independent of any other program) contains the four divisions of a regular program. In addition, it contains a LINKAGE SECTION in its Data Division that passes information to and from the main program. The same program may call several subprograms, and a subprogram may in turn call other subprograms.

Consider Figure 4.1, which depicts skeletal code illustrating the linkage between a main and a subprogram. (Figure 8.1 contains complete COBOL programs to further illustrate these points.) The main program contains a CALL statement somewhere in its Procedure Division. When the CALL is executed, control is transferred to the subprogram. The point in the subprogram which receives control depends on the entry immediately after CALL. In the first CALL statement of Figure 4.1, CALL 'SUBRTN' . . ., SUBRTN appears in the PROGRAM-ID paragraph of the subprogram. In this instance control will pass to the first executable statement in the Procedure Division of the subprogram. The latter will continue executing until it encounters either a GOBACK or EXIT PROGRAM statement, at which point control returns to the main program to the statement immediately following the initial CALL.

The second CALL statement has 'INMIDDLE' appearing immediately after the word CALL. This name corresponds to an ENTRY statement in the subprogram, ENTRY 'INMIDDLE' USING FIELD-C FIELD-D. Control passes to the subprogram, but this time to the first executable statement after the entry point INMIDDLE rather than the first statement in the Procedure Division as was the case previously. Control returns to the main program when the GOBACK statement is executed.

Data are passed between the main and subprogram via USING clauses which appear in the CALL statement of the main program, in the Procedure Division header of the subprogram, and in ENTRY statements in the subprogram. In addition, data names which are passed as arguments must be defined in the LINKAGE SECTION of the subprogram. Any CALL statement in the main program contains a USING clause which specifies the data on which the subprogram is to operate (e.g., CALL 'SUBRTN' USING FIELD-A FIELD-B). The subprogram, in turn, contains a USING clause in either (or both) its Procedure Division header or ENTRY statement(s) (e.g., PROCEDURE DIVISION USING FIELD-C FIELD-D). The data names in the main and subprogram USING clauses are different, but the *order* of data names within these clauses is critical. The first item in the USING clause of the main program, FIELD-A, corresponds to the first item in the USING clause of the subprogram, FIELD-C. Both are defined as three-byte numeric fields. In similar fashion, FIELD-B of the main program corresponds to FIELD-D of the subprogram. Note well that when either program changes the value of a passed parameter,

67

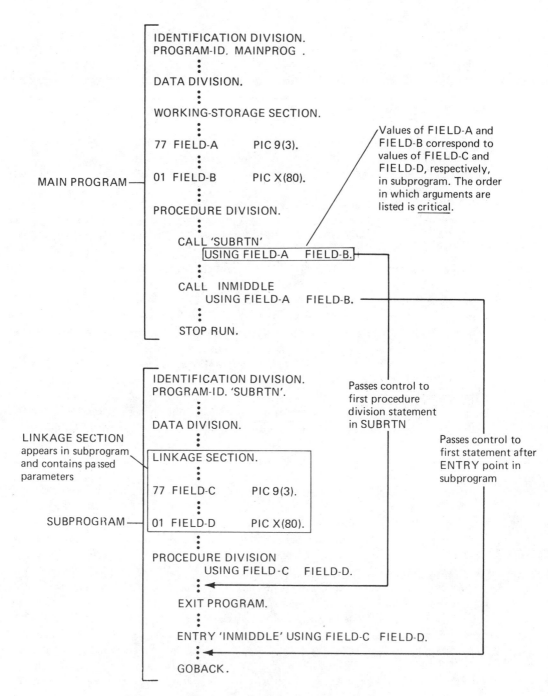

Figure 4.1 Skeletal COBOL Code for Calling a Subprogram

that value changes simultaneously in both programs. This is because only a single storage location is assigned to both data names (e.g., the *same* location is assigned to FIELD-A from the main program *and* FIELD-C from the subprogram). At the risk of repeating ourselves, the order in which arguments are listed is *critical*. Passing parameters in the wrong order is one of the most frequent problems in modular systems consisting of several programs.

Execution of a subprogram will terminate upon encountering either an EXIT PROGRAM or a GOBACK statement. If either is reached when operating under control of a CALL statement, control will return to the statement in the calling program immediately after the CALL. The difference between the statements is subtle and occurs if no CALL is active. If EXIT PROGRAM is reached in this instance, control remains in that program and passes to the first statement in the next paragraph. If, however, GOBACK is reached and no CALL is active, control returns to the calling program, which may be the supervisor and terminate the job; hence, GOBACK is often used in lieu of STOP RUN in a main program.

Although a subprogram may contain a STOP RUN statement, this is decidedly poor practice, particularly in a structured environment. Insertion of STOP RUN in a subprogram obscures program flow and makes it difficult to determine when processing should cease. Similar reasoning would preclude placing the STOP RUN statement in a performed routine of the calling program. Hence, STOP RUN should always appear in the mainline portion of the main program. Moreover, there should only be a single STOP RUN statement; else the program would have two exit points.

SORTING

The COBOL programmer can include a sort directly in his/her program. He/she will, however, need command of the SORT, RELEASE, RETURN, and SD statements. The SORT verb has the following format:

<u>SORT</u> file-name-1

ON $\left\{ \begin{array}{l} \underline{ASCENDING} \\ \underline{DESCENDING} \end{array} \right\}$ KEY data-name-1 [data-name-2] . . .

[ON $\left\{ \begin{array}{l} \underline{ASCENDING} \\ \underline{DESCENDING} \end{array} \right\}$ KEY data-name-3 [data-name-4] . . .] . . .

[<u>COLLATING SEQUENCE</u> IS alphabet-name]

$\left\{ \begin{array}{l} \underline{USING} \text{ file-name-2 [file-name-3] . . .} \\ \underline{INPUT} \text{ PROCEDURE} \\ \quad \text{IS section-name-1 } [\left\{ \begin{array}{l} \underline{THROUGH} \\ \underline{THRU} \end{array} \right\} \text{ section-name-2]} \end{array} \right\}$

$\left\{ \begin{array}{l} \underline{GIVING} \text{ file-name-4} \\ \underline{OUTPUT} \underline{PROCEDURE} \\ \quad \text{IS section-name-3 } [\left\{ \begin{array}{l} \underline{THROUGH} \\ \underline{THRU} \end{array} \right\} \text{ section-name-4]} \end{array} \right\}$

As can be seen, several forms are possible. One can use INPUT PROCEDURE in combination with OUTPUT PROCEDURE or USING in conjunction with GIVING (INPUT PROCEDURE can also be used with GIVING or USING with OUTPUT PRO-CEDURE). *However, INPUT PROCEDURE is a more general technique than USING in that it permits sorting on a calculated field, bypassing records, combining matching records from two files into a single record for the sort, and so on.* Assume, for example, that an incoming record has both an employee's present and previous salary. USING permits a sort on either field, but not on percent salary increase because the latter is a calculated field (i.e., it is not contained in an incoming record per se but is calculated from two fields which are). The INPUT PROCEDURE option is required if sorting is on percent salary increase or, for that matter, on any other calculated field. Our discussion focuses on this option in conjunction with OUTPUT PROCEDURE.

When the SORT verb is encountered in a COBOL program, control passes to the section (or sections) specified as the INPUT PROCEDURE. The primary function of the INPUT PROCEDURE is to process incoming records and write them to the sort file. When the INPUT PROCEDURE has concluded, a utility sort program takes control and sorts the file. After sorting, control is passed to the section (or sections) in the OUTPUT PROCEDURE, which read records from the sorted file, prepare reports, and so on. At the conclusion of the OUTPUT PROCEDURE, control returns to the statement immediately under the SORT verb.

Note the optional presence of COLLATING SEQUENCE in the SORT statement. Omission of this clause defaults to EBCDIC. Its inclusion, together with appropriate entries in the SPECIAL-NAMES paragraph, permits a different sort sequence [e.g., ASCII (see Figure 3.10)]. COLLATING SEQUENCE is present under Release 2 of the OS/VS compiler. Another subtle extension of this compiler is the use of THROUGH as synonymous with THRU.

Within the SORT verb, multiple sort keys are listed in order of importance. (A maximum of 12 sort keys is permitted.) The statement

```
SORT EMPLOYEE-FILE    ASCENDING KEY EMPLOYEE-LOCATION
                      DESCENDING KEY EMPLOYEE-SERVICE
                      ASCENDING EMPLOYEE-NAME . . .
```

has EMPLOYEE-LOCATION as the major (primary) key and EMPLOYEE-NAME as the minor (tertiary) key. The word KEY is an optional reserved word in the SORT statement and need not appear (e.g., ASCENDING EMPLOYEE-NAME). In this example, EMPLOYEE-FILE is the file to be sorted, hence it must be designated in an SD in the Data Division. An SD is analogous to an FD, except that it relates to a file that is sorted. Syntactically, the SD appears as follows:

$$
\text{SD file-name} \left[\underline{\text{DATA}} \left\{ \begin{array}{l} \underline{\text{RECORD}} \text{ IS} \\ \underline{\text{RECORDS}} \text{ ARE} \end{array} \right\} \text{data-name-1 \quad data-name-2} \right]
$$

$$
\left[\underline{\text{RECORD}} \text{ CONTAINS} \quad [\text{integer-1} \underline{\text{TO}}] \quad \text{integer-2 CHARACTERS} \right]
$$

The RELEASE and RETURN verbs are required with the INPUT PROCEDURE/OUTPUT PROCEDURE format. The RELEASE verb appears in the INPUT PROCEDURE and has the format

RELEASE record-name   [FROM identifier]

The effect of the RELEASE verb is to *write* a record to the sort file. It provides the capability of passing only selected records to the sort program and/or to calculate new fields in selected records.

The RETURN statement appears in the OUTPUT PROCEDURE and has the form

RETURN file-name   [INTO identifier]   AT END statement

The RETURN verb *reads* a record from the sorted file.

Use of the SORT verb and related statements is shown in the skeletal outline of Figure 4.2. (See also Figure 4.12, a complete COBOL program illustrating the SORT.)

Several features in Figure 4.2 are worthy of mention. First, note that the SORT verb itself is typically contained in the MAINLINE portion of a structured program. The file name mentioned in the SORT verb appears in a SELECT statement in the Environment Division and has an SD in the Data Division. The programmer does not open or close this file.

When the SORT verb is encountered, control passes to the section specified as the INPUT PROCEDURE. This section processes incoming records from an input file and passes only *selected* records to the sort program via the RELEASE verb. (The incoming file itself is opened and closed in the INPUT PROCEDURE.) Note well that the record length of an incoming record (80 characters in Figure 4.2) can be different from the record length of a sort record (90 characters in Figure 4.2). Thus, the INPUT PROCEDURE allows one to pass only selected records to sort, to sort on a calculated field, and to fully control the length of a sort record.

The sort program takes control after the INPUT PROCEDURE has concluded. (As of this writing, approximately one half of OS installations use SYNCSORT as the utility program rather than IBM's utility sort.) However, the utility sort program called by the COBOL verb is transparent to the programmer and should pose no concern whatsoever. Figure 4.2 has FIELD-ONE as its major key and FIELD-TWO as its minor key. Both FIELD-ONE and FIELD-TWO are defined in the SD for SORT-FILE. The sort sequences are ascending and descending, respectively.

After the sort has taken place, control passes to the OUTPUT PROCEDURE. This section reads (i.e., RETURNs) records from the sorted file and prepares reports. Output files are usually opened and closed in this section. At the conclusion of the OUTPUT PROCEDURE, control passes to the statement immediately under the SORT verb. The STOP RUN statement to terminate the COBOL program *must* appear in the mainline section rather than in the OUTPUT PROCEDURE. Inclusion of STOP RUN in the latter will invariably result in an ABEND.

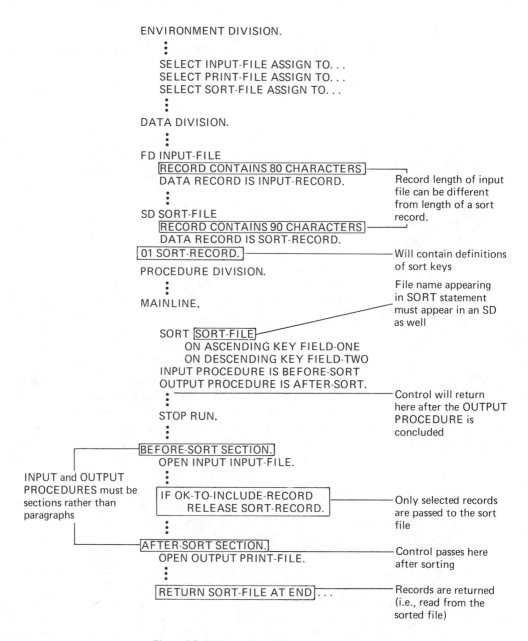

ENVIRONMENT DIVISION.
⋮

  SELECT INPUT-FILE ASSIGN TO. . .
  SELECT PRINT-FILE ASSIGN TO. . .
  SELECT SORT-FILE ASSIGN TO. . .
  ⋮

DATA DIVISION.
⋮

FD INPUT-FILE
  RECORD CONTAINS 80 CHARACTERS
  DATA RECORD IS INPUT-RECORD.   Record length of input
  ⋮   file can be different
                                         from length of a sort
SD SORT-FILE   record.
  RECORD CONTAINS 90 CHARACTERS
  DATA RECORD IS SORT-RECORD.
01 SORT-RECORD.   Will contain definitions
                                         of sort keys
PROCEDURE DIVISION.
⋮   File name appearing
                                         in SORT statement
MAINLINE.   must appear in an SD
                                         as well

  SORT SORT-FILE
    ON ASCENDING KEY FIELD-ONE
    ON DESCENDING KEY FIELD-TWO
    INPUT PROCEDURE IS BEFORE-SORT
    OUTPUT PROCEDURE IS AFTER-SORT.
    ⋮   Control will return
                                         here after the OUTPUT
  STOP RUN.   PROCEDURE is
  ⋮   concluded

BEFORE-SORT SECTION.
  OPEN INPUT INPUT-FILE.

INPUT and OUTPUT   ⋮
PROCEDURES must be
sections rather than   IF OK-TO-INCLUDE-RECORD
paragraphs   RELEASE SORT-RECORD.   Only selected records
                                                       are passed to the sort
                      ⋮   file

AFTER-SORT SECTION.   Control passes here
  OPEN OUTPUT PRINT-FILE.   after sorting

  ⋮

  RETURN SORT-FILE AT END . . .   Records are returned
                                         (i.e., read from the
                                         sorted file)

Figure 4.2 Skeleton Outline for Use of Sort Verb

MERGE STATEMENT

The MERGE verb takes several input files, with identical record formats sorted in the same sequence, and combines them into a single output file (device type and blocking may differ for the various files). A merge achieves the same results as sorting,

72

but more efficiently. In other words, the several input files to a merge could be concatenated as a single input file to a sort which would also produce a single output file. The advantage of the merge over a sort is in execution speed (i.e., a merge will execute faster because its logic realizes that the several input files are already in order).

Release 2 of IBM OS/VS COBOL incorporates a MERGE verb that conforms to the ANSI 74 standard. Its format is as follows:

MERGE file-name-1

$$\text{ON} \left\{ \frac{\text{ASCENDING}}{\text{DESCENDING}} \right\} \text{KEY data-name-1} \quad [\text{data-name-2}] \dots$$

$$[\text{ON} \left\{ \frac{\text{ASCENDING}}{\text{DESCENDING}} \right\} \text{KEY data-name-3} \quad [\text{data-name-4}] \dots] \dots$$

[COLLATING SEQUENCE IS alphabet-name]
USING file-name-2 file-name-3 [file-name-4] ...

$$\left\{ \begin{array}{l} \text{GIVING file-name-5} \\ \text{OUTPUT PROCEDURE} \\ \quad \text{IS section-name-1} \; [\left\{ \begin{array}{l} \text{THROUGH} \\ \text{THRU} \end{array} \right\} \; \text{section-name-2}] \end{array} \right\}$$

File-name-1 must be specified in an SD. Rules for ASCENDING/DESCENDING KEY, COLLATING SEQUENCE, USING/GIVING, and OUTPUT PROCEDURE are identical to the SORT verb.

Unlike the SORT verb, there is no INPUT PROCEDURE option. The programmer must specify USING and list all files from which incoming records will be chosen. Hence, *every* record in *every* file specified in USING will appear in the merged file. The user does, however, have a choice between GIVING and OUTPUT PROCEDURE.

All files specified in a MERGE statement cannot be open when the statement is executed, as the MERGE operation implicitly opens them. In similar fashion, the files will be automatically closed by the MERGE.

An example of a MERGE statement is as follows:

```
MERGE WORK-FILE
    ON ASCENDING CUSTOMER-ACCOUNT-NUMBER
        DESCENDING AMOUNT-OF-SALE
    USING
        MONDAY-SALES-FILE
        TUESDAY-SALES-FILE
        WEDNESDAY-SALES-FILE
        THURSDAY-SALES-FILE
        FRIDAY-SALES-FILE
    GIVING
        WEEKLY-SALES-FILE.
```

WORK-FILE is defined in a COBOL SD. WEEKLY-SALES-FILE, MONDAY-SALES-FILE, TUESDAY-SALES-FILE, and so on, are each specified in both FD and SELECT statements. These files must all be sequential and are both opened and closed by the merge operation.

The primary key is CUSTOMER-ACCOUNT-NUMBER (ascending) and the secondary key is AMOUNT-OF-SALE (descending). All records with the same account number will be grouped together with the highest sale for each account number listed first. Records with identical keys in one or more input files will be listed in the order in which the files appear in the MERGE statement itself. Hence, in the event of a tie on *both* account number and amount of sale, Monday's transactions will appear before Tuesday's, and so on.

COPY STATEMENT

The COPY verb eliminates the need for several programmers having to code and recode identical program segments. Instead, the segment is coded once and entered into a library. Any programmer needing the segment uses a COPY statement and the desired code is brought into the particular program. The programmer can then access any line in the copied module as though he had coded it himself. Advantages of this technique are as follows:

1. Programming errors are reduced and standardization is promoted. For example, if the COPY clause is used for record descriptions, all fields within a record will be defined consistently. There is no chance of omitting an existing field or erroneously creating a new one. All picture, usage, and value clauses will be correct. This is particularly important in modular programming or with subprograms where the *identical* record layout must be available to more than one program. (See Figure 8.1 for the COPY statement in both a main program and a subprogram.)

2. Changes to copied modules are made in only one place, the library version. Although changes to file and/or record descriptions occur infrequently, they do happen. If COPY is used exclusively (e.g., every program needing a given record description contains a COPY rather than longhand coding), only the library version need be altered. Individual programs will automatically bring in the most current, and also consistent, version of the record description during compilation.

3. Writer's cramp is significantly reduced, as individual programmers need not code the extensive Data Division entries, which can make COBOL so tedious. This is especially helpful when record descriptions run into hundreds of lines.

It is, of course, necessary to initially enter the copied module into a system library, and the procedure for accomplishing this is discussed in Chapter Eleven.

The general form of the COPY statement is as follows:

$$\underline{\text{COPY}} \text{ text-name } [\left\{ \begin{array}{c} \underline{\text{OF}} \\ \underline{\text{IN}} \end{array} \right\} \text{ library-name}]$$

$$\boxed{[\text{SUPPRESS}]}$$

$$[\underline{\text{REPLACING}} \ (\left\{ \begin{array}{l} \text{==pseudo-text-1==} \\ \text{identifier-1} \\ \text{literal-1} \\ \text{word-1} \end{array} \right\}$$

$$\underline{\text{BY}} \left\{ \begin{array}{l} \text{==pseudo-text-2==} \\ \text{identifier-2} \\ \text{literal-2} \\ \text{word-2} \end{array} \right\} \ ) \ \dots].$$

The SUPPRESS option is restricted to IBM. It suppresses printing of the text and is used to condense the size of program listings. The REPLACING option allows the programmer to substitute his data names for those in the library.

The most common use of a COPY clause is to bring in FDs and record descriptions in the Data Division. However, it can also be used in the Environment Division (in both the Configuration and Input-Output Sections) and in the Procedure Division to bring in entire sections and/or paragraphs. ANSI 74 COBOL, and consequently Release 2 of VS COBOL, permits a COPY statement to appear *anywhere* in a source program, wherever a character string or separator is allowed. The only exception is that a COPY clause is *not* permitted within another COPY statement. Other IBM compilers limit the use of COPY to situations shown in Figure 4.3, which in practice is hardly any limitation at all.

Note the repeated use of the phrase "COPY member" in Figure 4.3. The copy library is always a partitioned data set (PDS) and the COPY statement brings in a member of the PDS. A SYSLIB statement is required in the JCL, and the LIB option must be specified (see Table 10.1 and discussion regarding Figure 11.12).

Brief mention will be made of the REPLACING option, which allows substitution of elements in the copied text. As can be seen from the general format of the copy, one may replace identifiers (e.g., data names), literals, COBOL reserved words, and/or pseudotext. The latter is a sequence of character strings and/or separators bounded by, but not including, the pseudotext delimiters, ==. Consider the following COPY statement:

```
COPY LIBMEM
    REPLACING == + == BY == — ==
                    PENALTY-AMOUNT BY DISCOUNT.
```

Let us assume that the member, LIBMEM, consists of the following code:

```
PARAGRAPH-A.
    COMPUTE AMOUNT-DUE =
    BASIC-ORDER + PENALTY-AMOUNT.
```

The copy statement indicates that both the plus sign and data name PENALTY-AMOUNT are to be replaced. Thus the library entry would be copied and treated as though it had been coded as

```
PARAGRAPH-A.
    COMPUTE AMOUNT-DUE =
    BASIC-ORDER — DISCOUNT.
```

Note well that while the REPLACING clause existed under other compilers, the pseudo-text option is new to Release 2.

Environment Division:

SOURCE-COMPUTER.	COPY member.
OBJECT-COMPUTER.	COPY member.
SPECIAL-NAMES.	COPY member.
FILE-CONTROL.	COPY member.
I-O-CONTROL.	COPY member.
SELECT file-name	COPY member.

Data Division:

FD file-name	COPY member.
SD file-name	COPY member.
RD file-name	COPY member.
CD cd-name	COPY member.
01 data-name	COPY member.
77 data-name	COPY member.

Procedure Division:

section-name SECTION.	COPY member.
paragraph-name.	COPY member.

Figure 4.3   Limitations of the COPY Verb Prior to OS/VS COBOL

TABLE PROCESSING

Table processing is hardly restricted to structured programming. However, the authors view the subject with such importance that it is covered anyway. We hope this material is useful to the practitioner who is expected to know anything and everything about tables, but who somehow may never have acquired complete understanding. We include in our discussion indexing, the SEARCH and SET verbs, variable-length tables, and multidimension tables.

Establishment of a table (i.e., the allocation of space) requires an OCCURS clause in the Data Division, with the general format

$$\underline{\text{OCCURS}} \quad \left\{ \begin{array}{ll} \text{integer-1} \ \underline{\text{TO}} \ \text{integer-2 TIMES} & \underline{\text{DEPENDING}} \ \text{ON data-name-3} \\ \text{integer-2} & \text{TIMES} \end{array} \right\}$$

$$\left[\left\{ \begin{array}{l} \underline{\text{ASCENDING}} \\ \underline{\text{DESCENDING}} \end{array} \right\} \ \text{KEY IS data-name-1} \quad [\text{data-name-2}] \quad \ldots \right]$$

$$\left[\underline{\text{INDEXED}} \ \text{BY index-name-1} \quad [\text{, index-name-2}] \quad \ldots \right]$$

As can be seen, there are several options within an OCCURS. The DEPENDING ON clause is used with variable-length tables and enjoys frequent application. INDEXED BY is required if either indexing or a SEARCH verb is to be used in processing the table. The ASCENDING (or DESCENDING) KEY clause is necessary if a binary search is to be implemented.

Subscripts versus Indexes

Subscripts and indexes are both used in table processing. Indexing, however, is more efficient and for that reason the practitioner is well advised to use the technique. In addition, indexing is required for the SEARCH statement, a powerful means of table processing.

A subscript and an index are conceptually the same, in that both reference an entry in a table. A subscript, however, represents an *occurrence*, whereas an index is a *displacement* within a table. Consider the following COBOL entries:

```
05   LOCATION-TABLE   OCCURS 10 TIMES
                      INDEXED BY LOCATION-INDEX.
     10   LOC-CODE    PIC X(3).
     10   LOC-NAME    PIC X(12).
```

The OCCURS clause establishes a table with 10 entries, LOCATION-TABLE, occupying a total of 150 bytes. Valid subscripts for LOC-CODE are 1,2,3,...,10 (i.e., LOC-CODE can occur 10 times). Valid displacements for LOC-CODE are 0, 15, 30, ..., 135. For example, the second value of LOC-CODE begins in the sixteenth byte of the table, or a displacement of 15 bytes from the table's origin. The first element in the table is referenced by a subscript of 1 or a displacement of 0; the second element by a subscript of 2 or a displacement of 15; the tenth element by a subscript of 10 or a displacement of 135.

In practice, the COBOL programmer is not concerned with the actual value of an index. Instead, he/she simply regards an index as a subscript and trusts in compiler-generated instructions to calculate the proper displacement. This is accomplished through

the SET verb, whose only purpose is to manipulate indexes. The SET verb has two forms:
Format 1:

$$\underline{SET} \quad \begin{Bmatrix} \text{index-name-1} \\ \text{identifier-1} \end{Bmatrix} \quad \begin{matrix} [\text{index-name-2}] \\ [\text{identifier-2}] \end{matrix} \quad \dots \quad \underline{TO} \quad \begin{Bmatrix} \text{index-name-3} \\ \text{identifier-3} \\ \text{literal-1} \end{Bmatrix}$$

Format 2:

$$\underline{SET} \quad \text{index-name-1} \quad [\text{index-name-2}] \quad \dots \quad \begin{Bmatrix} \underline{UP}\ \underline{BY} \\ \underline{DOWN}\ \underline{BY} \end{Bmatrix} \quad \begin{Bmatrix} \text{identifier-1} \\ \text{literal-1} \end{Bmatrix}$$

Figure 4.4 illustrates the use of a SET verb to initialize and increment an index. A variable-length table is established, whose length depends on the number of checks written. It varies from 11 to 1100 bytes (i.e., there are 11 bytes per entry and the number of entries ranges from 1 to 100). In the Procedure Division, the SET verb is used to both initialize and increment the index, CHECK-INDEX.

```
    DATA DIVISION.
      .
      .
      .
    05   CHECKS-PROCESSED
         OCCURS 1 TO 100 TIMES DEPENDING ON NUMBER-OF-CHECKS
         INDEXED BY CHECK-INDEX.
         10   CHECK-NUMBER          PIC 9(4).
         10   CHECK-AMOUNT          PIC 9(5)V99.
      .
      .
      .
 PROCEDURE DIVISION.
      SET CHECK-INDEX TO 1.
      PERFORM COMPUTE-CHECKBOOK-BALANCE NUMBER-OF-CHECKS TIMES.
      .
      .
      .
 COMPUTE-CHECKBOOK-BALANCE.
      SUBTRACT CHECK-AMOUNT (CHECK-INDEX) FROM INITIAL-BALANCE.
      SET CHECK-INDEX UP BY 1.
```

Figure 4.4 Illustration of SET Verb with Variable-Length Table

Note well that indexing is *not* required in COBOL; it is preferred because it generates more efficient object code. Thus, it is syntactically correct in Figure 4.4 to add a 77-level entry for CHECK-SUBSCRIPT, remove the INDEXED BY clause, substitute CHECK-SUBSCRIPT for CHECK-INDEX in the SUBTRACT statement, and change the two SET statements to MOVE 1 TO CHECK-SUBSCRIPT and ADD 1 TO CHECK-SUBSCRIPT, respectively. Such changes have no effect on the complexity of the source code. Indeed, their impact can only be measured by examining procedure division maps and generated object code.

Table Initialization

Tables are initialized in one of two ways: through a REDEFINES clause in the Data Division, or by reading values from a file. Figure 4.5 illustrates the latter technique for a one-dimension variable-length table. The authors view this technique as the more preferable way of table initialization. This is because table values can be changed without requiring recompilation of a program. Moreover, if several programs utilize the same table, changes need be made in only one place (i.e., the input file).

Several features of Figure 4.5 deserve mention. Note the INDEXED BY clause in the definition of the table. As previously stated, indexing is not a requirement of COBOL but rather a means of achieving more efficient object code. Consequently, Figure 4.5 could be easily modified to employ subscripts rather than indexes, but this would not be desirable. Note also that the LOCATION-INDEX is initialized and incremented in a PERFORM statement, as contrasted to the use of SET statements in Figure 4.4. Figure 4.5 also contains two checks for potential errors. The initial read assures that the location file is not empty. The IF statement verifies that the number of entries in the file does not exceed the allocated storage space. The latter check is particularly important to prevent subscript (index) errors, which can cause a variety of perplexing ABENDs and wasted programmer time.

Storage Organization

The OCCURS clause can appear with either a group or an elementary item. Figure 4.6 shows the OCCURS clause with a group item and the associated storage layout. (The presence of the INDEXED BY clause does *not* affect storage layout.)

A total of 150 bytes are set aside in storage for LOCATION-TABLE. The first three bytes are for LOC-CODE (1), the next 12 for LOC-NAME (1). Bytes 16-18 are for LOC-CODE (2), bytes 19-30 for LOC-NAME (2), and so on.

Figure 4.7 also defines a 150-byte table, LOCATION-TABLE, but uses two OCCURS clauses on the elementary level. Accordingly, the 30 bytes for the location codes are assigned contiguous locations and appear before the 120 bytes for the location names. Thus, bytes 1, 2, and 3 are for LOC-CODE (1); bytes 4, 5, and 6 for LOC-CODE (2); bytes 28, 29, and 30 for LOC-CODE (10); bytes 31-42 for LOC-NAME (1); and bytes 139-150 for LOC-NAME (10).

LOC-CODE (1) and LOC-NAME (1) are valid COBOL entries in both Figures 4.6 and 4.7, denoting the code and name of the first location, respectively. Figure 4.6 also permits a reference to LOCATION-TABLE (1) to refer to the 15 bytes for code and name of the first location. The latter is not permitted in Figure 4.7.

```
      DATA DIVISION.
         •
           •
             •

      77  NUMBER-OF-LOCATIONS              PIC 9(3)    VALUE ZEROS.
      77  LOCATION-FILE-SWITCH             PIC X(3)    VALUE 'NO'.
          88   END-OF-LOCATION-FILE                    VALUE 'YES'.
             •
               •
                 •

      01  LOCATION-TABLE.
          05   LOCATION-AND-CODES
               OCCURS 1 TO 500 TIMES DEPENDING ON NUMBER-OF-LOCATIONS
               INDEXED BY LOCATION-INDEX.
               10   LOC-CODE               PIC X(3).
               10   LOC-NAME               PIC X(12).
             •
               •
                 •

      PROCEDURE DIVISION.
          READ LOCATION-FILE
              AT END DISPLAY 'LOCATION FILE EMPTY'
                  MOVE 'YES' TO LOCATION-FILE-SWITCH.
          PERFORM INITIALIZE-LOCATION-TABLE
              VARYING LOCATION-INDEX FROM 1 BY 1
              UNTIL END-OF-LOCATION-FILE.
             •
               •
                 •

      INITIALIZE-LOCATION-TABLE.
          ADD 1 TO NUMBER-OF-LOCATIONS.
          IF NUMBER-OF-LOCATIONS > 500
              DISPLAY 'LOCATION TABLE TOO SMALL'
              MOVE 'YES' TO LOCATION-FILE-SWITCH
          ELSE
              MOVE INCOMING-FILE-CODE TO LOC-CODE (LOCATION-INDEX)
              MOVE INCOMING-FILE-NAME TO LOC-NAME (LOCATION-INDEX).
          READ LOCATION-FILE
              AT END MOVE 'YES' TO LOCATION-FILE-SWITCH.
```

Figure 4.5 Initialization of a One-Dimension Table by Reading from a File

TWO-DIMENSION TABLES

Figure 4.8 shows a two-dimension table to determine entry-level salaries in Company X. The personnel department has established a policy that starting salary is a function of both responsibility level (values 1-10) and experience (values 1-5). For example, an employee with responsibility level of 4 and experience level of 1 receives $10,000. An employee with responsibility of 1 and experience of 4 would receive $9,000.

80

```
05  LOCATION-TABLE OCCURS 10 TIMES
                INDEXED BY LOCATION-INDEX.

    10    LOC-CODE    PIC X(3).
    10    LOC-NAME    PIC X(12).
```

LOCATION-TABLE							
LOCATION-TABLE (1)		LOCATION-TABLE (2)			LOCATION-TABLE (10)		
CODE (1)	NAME (1)	CODE (2)	NAME (2)	•••	CODE (10)	NAME (10)	

Figure 4.6 OCCURS Clause with a Group Item

```
05  LOCATION-TABLE.

    10  LOC-CODE OCCURS 10 TIMES      PIC X(3).
    10  LOC-NAME OCCURS 10 TIMES      PIC X(12).
```

LOCATION-TABLE							
CODE (1)	CODE (2)	••• CODE (10)	NAME (1)	NAME (2)	•••	NAME (10)	

Figure 4.7 OCCURS Clause with Elementary Item

Establishment of space for the table in Figure 4.8 requires Data Division entries as follows:

```
01    SALARY-TABLE.
      05    SALARY-RESPONSIBILITY OCCURS 10 TIMES.
            10    SALARY-EXPERIENCE OCCURS 5 TIMES      PIC 9(5).
```

These entries cause a total of 250 consecutive storage positions to be allocated (10 X 5 X 5) as shown:

SALARY-TABLE										
SALARY-RESPONSIBILITY (1)					SALARY-RESPONSIBILITY (2)					
Exp 1	Exp 2	Exp 3	Exp 4	Exp 5	Exp 1	Exp 2	Exp 3	Exp 4	Exp 5	

81

Experience

	1	2	3	4	5
1	6,000	7,000	8,000	9,000	10,000
2	7,000	8,000	9,000	10,000	11,000
3	8,000	9,000	10,000	11,000	12,000
4	10,000	12,000	14,000	16,000	18,000
5	12,000	14,000	16,000	18,000	20,000
6	14,000	16,000	18,000	20,000	22,000
7	16,000	19,000	22,000	25,000	28,000
8	19,000	22,000	25,000	28,000	31,000
9	22,000	25,000	28,000	31,000	34,000
10	26,000	30,000	34,000	38,000	42,000

Responsibility

{ Responsibility level = 4
{ Experience level = 1

{ Responsibility level = 1
{ Experience level = 4

Figure 4.8 Entry-Level Salary (Illustration of Two-Dimension Table)

The first 25 bytes in storage refer to the five experience levels for the first responsibility level. Bytes 1-5 refer to experience level 1, responsibility level 1; bytes 6-10 refer to experience level 2, responsibility level 1; and so on. In similar fashion, bytes 26-50 refer to the experience levels for responsibility level 2; bytes 51-75 to the experience levels for responsibility level 3; and so on.

COBOL provides additional flexibility to reference data at different hierarchical levels. Definition of a two-dimension table automatically allows reference to other one-dimension tables as well. However, the order of the subscripts and level of reference is absolutely critical. Some examples:

SALARY-TABLE: Refers to the entire table of 50 elements (250 bytes). SALARY-TABLE may *not* be used with any subscripts

SALARY-RESPONSIBILITY (1):   Refers collectively to the five experience levels associated with the first level of salary responsibility; SALARY-RESPONSIBILITY must always appear with a single subscript

SALARY-EXPERIENCE (10, 5):   Refers to salary responsibility level 10, experience level 5; note well, however, that SALARY-EXPER-IENCE (5,10), referring to responsibility and experience levels of 5 and 10, respectively, is invalid according to the given OCCURS clause

Figure 4.9 illustrates the use of REDEFINES to initialize the two-dimension table of Figure 4.8. This apparently cumbersome technique is made necessary because the definition of a table which contains an OCCURS clause cannot also have a VALUE clause, hence the need for REDEFINES.

```
01  SALARY-TABLE.
    05   FILLER  PIC X(25)    VALUE '06000070000080000900010000'.
    05   FILLER  PIC X(25)    VALUE '07000080000090001000011000'.
    05   FILLER  PIC X(25)    VALUE '08000090001000011000012000'.
    05   FILLER  PIC X(25)    VALUE '10000120001400016000018000'.
    05   FILLER  PIC X(25)    VALUE '12000140001600018000020000'.
    05   FILLER  PIC X(25)    VALUE '14000160001800020000022000'.
    05   FILLER  PIC X(25)    VALUE '16000190002200025000028000'.
    05   FILLER  PIC X(25)    VALUE '19000220002500028000031000'.
    05   FILLER  PIC X(25)    VALUE '22000250002800031000034000'.
    05   FILLER  PIC X(25)    VALUE '26000300003400038000042000'.

01  SALARY-MIDPOINTS REDEFINES SALARY-TABLE.
    05    SALARY-RESPONSIBILITY OCCURS 10 TIMES.
        10    SALARY-EXPERIENCE OCCURS 5 TIMES     PIC 9(5).
```

Figure 4.9   Initialization of a Two-Dimension Table via REDEFINES

The statement SALARY-MIDPOINTS REDEFINES SALARY-TABLE gives another name to SALARY-TABLE and, consequently, places specified values in subscripted entries. The first VALUE clause fills the first 25 bytes in storage, the second VALUE clause fills bytes 26-50, and so on. The order of the VALUE clauses is critical and coincides with Figure 4.8.

THREE-DIMENSION TABLES

Three-dimension tables require three subscripts (indexes) to identify an elementary item. Consider a corporation with four sales regions, three states in each region, and five salesmen in each state. A three-dimension table is defined as follows:

```
01   CORPORATION.
    05    REGION OCCURS 4 TIMES
                INDEXED BY REGION-INDEX.
        10    STATE OCCURS 3 TIMES
                    INDEXED BY STATE-INDEX.
            15    SALESMAN OCCURS 5 TIMES
                        INDEXED BY SALESMAN-INDEX    PIC 9(5).
```

There are 60 (4 X 3 X 5) elements in the table. SALESMAN is the only elementary item, hence the only entry with a picture clause. The value contained in each elementary item (i.e., the value in SALESMAN) might be an individual's sales to date. A total of 300 bytes (60 elements X 5 bytes per element) will be allocated, as shown in Figure 4.10. The presence of three index clauses does nothing to affect the storage layouts, but speeds subsequent processing.

As can be implied from Figure 4.10, bytes 1-75 refer to the first region, bytes 76-150 to the second region, bytes 151-225 to the third region, and bytes 226-300 to the fourth region. Positions 1-25 refer to the first state in the first region and positions 1-5 to the first salesman in the first state in the first region.

Some additional examples reflect the flexibility of references at different hierarchical levels, as discussed under two-dimension tables. In particular:

SALESMAN (1,2,3): Refers to sales of the third salesman, in the second state, of the first region

SALESMAN (3,4,5): Is incorrect, since there are only three states per region (not 4) (i.e., STATE OCCURS 3 TIMES and hence the second subscript should not exceed 3)

CORPORATION: Refers to the entire table of 60 elements and may *not* be referenced with a subscript

REGION (1): Refers collectively to the 15 entries in the first region

STATE (1,2): Refers collectively to the five entries (i.e., salesmen) in the second state of the first region

It should be noted that the COBOL community is not unanimous in endorsing the use of three-level tables. Some installations maintain that three subscripts are too confusing and discourage their use. Others argue that if the situation fits, three subscripts will clarify program logic. The authors are of the latter opinion but will not proselytize in this area.

Once a three-level table has been established, processing is straightforward and best accomplished through the PERFORM verb. The following code calculates total corporate sales:

```
MOVE ZERO TO TOTAL-CORPORATE-SALES.
PERFORM CALCULATE-TOTAL-SALES
    VARYING REGION-INDEX
        FROM 1 BY 1 UNTIL REGION-INDEX > 4
    AFTER STATE-INDEX
        FROM 1 BY 1 UNTIL STATE-INDEX > 3
    AFTER SALESMAN-INDEX
        FROM 1 BY 1 UNTIL SALESMAN-INDEX > 5.



    .

    .

    .

CALCULATE-TOTAL-SALES.
    ADD SALESMAN (REGION-INDEX, STATE-INDEX, SALESMAN-INDEX)
        TO TOTAL-CORPORATE-SALES.
```

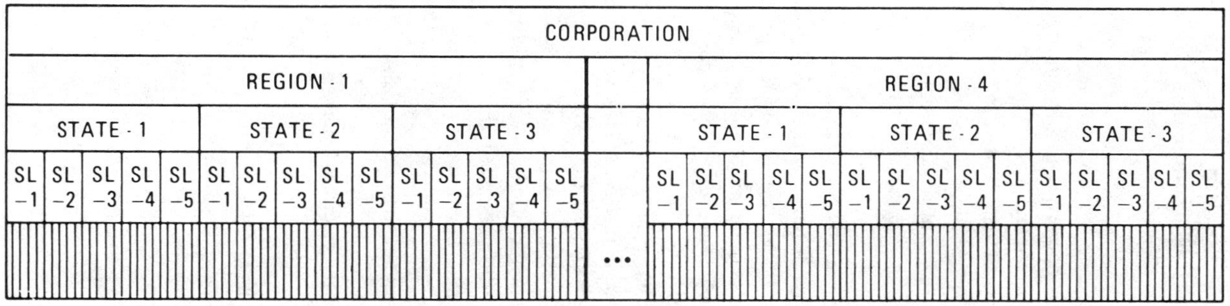

Figure 4.10 Storage Allocation for a Three-Dimension Table

85

The use of perform was thoroughly discussed in Chapter Three and the reader is referred there for a discussion of the order in which the indexes are varied. As in previous examples, subscripts could be used in lieu of indexes with little change in source code, but with significant loss of efficiency in the object code.

THE SEARCH VERB

Data are invariably stored in *coded* rather than in expanded format. The obvious advantage is that less space is required in the storage medium. However, since printed reports rarely contain coded information, a conversion from one form to the other has to take place. This is best accomplished by using a subscript or index to address the table directly. For example, Location (99) would refer to the ninety-ninth element in a table. In many instances, however, this is not possible (e.g., nonnumeric codes). When this happens the conversion is accomplished through a table-lookup or search routine.

A *linear search* examines entries in a table sequentially. A *binary search* begins in the middle of a table, and then with each successive search eliminates half the remaining entries. A linear search works regardless of how table elements are arranged; a binary search requires table entries to be in sequence; either ascending or descending.

To illustrate the difference, consider the following example. Assume that one is trying to guess a number from 1 to 1000, and further that the number is 327. A linear search would begin at 1 and progress in sequential fashion. Next guess would be 2, then 3, 4, 5 . . ., and finally 327, a total of 327 guesses. The binary search would start at 500, then 250 (since the number is less than 500), then 375, 313, and so on, until the number is found. A maximum of only 10 tries would be required for a binary search, regardless of what number was chosen. The linear (or sequential) search could require as many as 1000 guesses (if the number picked was 1000). Thus, a binary search is more efficient than a linear search for large tables; indeed, the larger the table, the greater the advantage.

The syntax for the COBOL SEARCH verb follows:

SEARCH Statement—Sequential Search

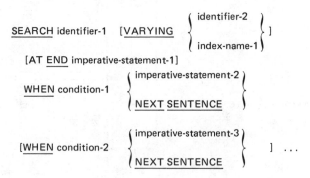

SEARCH Statement—Binary Search

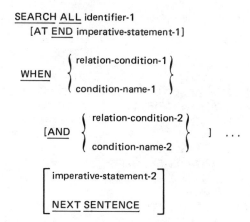

SEARCH <u>ALL</u> identifier-1
 [AT <u>END</u> imperative-statement-1]

<u>WHEN</u>   { relation-condition-1 }
             { condition-name-1 }

[<u>AND</u>   { relation-condition-2 }   ] ...
             { condition-name-2 }

[imperative-statement-2]
[<u>NEXT</u> <u>SENTENCE</u>]

Note: In Format 2, each relation-condition must be an
EQUAL TO (=) condition with an ASCENDING/DESCENDING
KEY data item for this table element as the subject.

SEARCH ALL denotes a binary search; SEARCH by itself specifies a linear search. Identifier-1, in both formats, designates a table defined in the Data Division containing OCCURS and INDEXED BY clauses. If a binary search is specified (i.e., SEARCH ALL), identifier-1 must also contain an ASCENDING (DESCENDING) KEY clause.

The AT END clause is optional in both formats. If omitted, control passes to the next sentence following the search if the end of the table has been reached and no match was found. If the AT END clause is supplied but does not contain a GO TO, control also passes to the next sentence at the end of the search.

The WHEN clause specifies a condition and imperative sentence. Note that more than one of these clauses may be contained in a linear search (e.g., searching a table for one of two keys and the required action depends on which key is matched). If the WHEN clause does not contain a GO TO statement, control passes to the statement immediately following the search whenever the WHEN condition is satisfied.

A VARYING option is also possible with a linear search, but is not discussed here.

Figure 4.11 illustrates use of the SEARCH verb. Definition of the table requires an INDEXED BY clause for either SEARCH or SEARCH ALL; however, the ASCENDING KEY clause is necessary only if a binary search is used. A SET statement is required prior to a linear search, to initiate where in the table the search is to begin (i.e., the search need not start at the first entry). The SET statement is *not* used in conjunction with a binary search, as the SEARCH verb will always calculate its starting position.

```
01  TABLE-VALUES.
    05  FILLER                          PIC X(15)    VALUE '1234ACCOUNTING'.
    05  FILLER                          PIC X(15)    VALUE '2000ADVERTISING'.
      °
      .
      .
    05  FILLER                          PIC X(15)    VALUE '9800WAREHOUSE'.
01  TABLE-VALUE-WITH-INDEXES REDEFINES TABLE-VALUES.
    05  TABLE-ENTRIES OCCURS 100 TIMES
                      ASCENDING KEY IS TABLE-CODE
                      INDEXED BY TABLE-INDEX.
        10  TABLE-CODE        PIC X(4).
        10  TABLE-EXPANSION   PIC X(11).

*LINEAR SEARCH
    SET TABLE-INDEX TO 1.
    SEARCH TABLE-ENTRIES
        AT END MOVE 'NO MATCH' TO OUTPUT-FIELD
        WHEN INCOMING-CODE = TABLE-CODE (TABLE-INDEX)
            MOVE TABLE-EXPANSION (TABLE-INDEX) TO OUTPUT-FIELD.
*BINARY SEARCH
    SEARCH ALL TABLE-ENTRIES
        AT END MOVE 'NO MATCH' TO OUTPUT-FIELD
        WHEN INCOMING-CODE = TABLE-CODE (TABLE-INDEX)
            MOVE TABLE-EXPANSION (TABLE-INDEX) TO OUTPUT-FIELD.
```

Figure 4.11 Illustration of the SEARCH Verb

SUMMARY

Chapter Four is entitled "A Potpourri of Advanced Features." As such it contains several elements of COBOL, none of which are unique to structured programming, but all of which are very useful to the practitioner. Accordingly, the chapter is best reviewed through presentation of a COBOL program. Specifications are as follows.

Input is a file of personnel records containing typical employee information (e.g., historical salary data, education code, location code, etc.). The incoming coded data are to be transformed into expanded format for inclusion in a report, which lists employees in alphabetical order. However, employees with a salary grade of 99 are *not* to appear in the printed report.

The COBOL program to accomplish this is shown in Figure 4.12. It encompasses all the features discussed in the chapter, with the exception of subprograms. Use of the latter is illustrated in Figure 8.1(a) and (b).

The Data Division of Figure 4.12 is rather lengthy in that it contains several print lines. It also defines three tables for job title, education, and location (COBOL lines 151-188). Incoming records contain a code for each of these functions, which is subsequently expanded through various table-lookup techniques in the Procedure Division. The layout of incoming records is described in a COPY clause (COBOL lines 191-208). Note well that the record description appears in the Working-Storage rather than the File Section. This permits the use of READ INTO (COBOL line 276), which in conjunction with the literal WS BEGINS HERE (COBOL lines 82 and 83) is a valuable technique for debugging. (See the discussion in Chapter Eight describing Figure 8.17.)

The Procedure Division begins by initializing the JB-TITLE-TABLE. This is a variable-length table per the OCCURS DEPENDING clause in line 154. Note well that the table is initialized by reading values from a file. The advantage of this technique over that of specifying a fixed set of codes via VALUE clauses is that additional entries may be added to the table without recompiling the program. Observe the use of a PERFORM VARYING to alter an index value and of the check in line 240 to avoid exceeding the table limit of 200 entries. Note also that the AT END condition in the initial read for the table (line 217) is different from the AT END condition in the performed routine. We like this technique of checking for an empty file and thereby justify two reads for the same file. Others will disagree, stating cogent arguments for a single read in a performed routine. So be it; as stated in Chapter One, two reads for the same file versus a single read in a performed routine is not a major concern to the authors, although it might be to others. Let us return therefore to the business at hand, reviewing Figure 4.12.

The SORT statement, lines 227-230, calls for an ascending sort on SR-LAST-AND-FIRST-NAME, a field defined in the SD for SORT-FILE. Control passes from the sort verb to the *section* specified in the INPUT PROCEDURE. The INPUT PROCEDURE opens the PERSONNEL-FILE and RELEASEs selected records (i.e., those with a SALARY-GRADE other than 99) to the SORT-FILE. Accordingly, the sort file contains only a subset of the records in the input file. When all records in PERSONNEL-FILE have been processed, the file is closed and control goes to the sort utility. After sorting, control passes to the *section* specified in the OUTPUT PROCEDURE of the SORT verb.

The OUTPUT PROCEDURE opens the PRINT-FILE and RETURNs (i.e., reads) records from SORT-FILE until none are left. Three codes (PR-JOB-CODE, PR-CURR-LOCATION-CODE, and PR-EDUCATION-CODE) in each returned record are expanded. SEARCH ALL (lines 307-311) illustrates a binary search. Use of SEARCH ALL requires both INDEXED BY and ASCENDING KEY clauses in the definition of the job table (lines 152-156). The table lookup of PR-EDUCATION-CODE (lines 328-332) illustrates a sequential search. An INDEXED BY clause is required in the table definition (lines 169 and 170), but the ASCENDING (DESCENDING) KEY clause is not. Observe also how an index must be initialized prior to a linear search (line 327), but *not* before a binary search.

Expansion of PR-CURR-LOCATION-CODE is accomplished by direct access to the table element rather than a table lookup (i.e., the value of location code itself indicates the appropriate location name). The table was defined with an index, although "old-fashioned" subscripting could be used as easily (i.e., an index is required in a table definition only if the SEARCH verb is used). An index was defined, for illustrative purposes only, to show how an incoming code can be converted to an index via a SET statement (COBOL line 323).

Figure 4.12 also illustrates a heading routine with a page and line counter. Pagination is accomplished through the AFTER POSITIONING rather than the AFTER ADVANCING option (other listings in the book use the latter). Observe that *all* lines are printed from the paragraph C310-PRINT-LINE, and that either 1, 2, or 3 is added to the line counter depending on the value of the carriage control character. Finally, note the use of INSPECT, lines 313 and 367, as an editing technique. (INSPECT is used rather than EXAMINE to support the ANSI 74 standard, although Version 2 of IBM/VS COBOL supports both.)

```
00001          IDENTIFICATION DIVISION.
00002
00003          PROGRAM-ID.
00004              TESTPROG.
00005
00006          AUTHOR.
00007              MARSHAL CRAWFORD.
00008
00009          DATE-WRITTEN.
00010              NOVEMBER, 1977.



00012          ENVIRONMENT DIVISION.
00013          CONFIGURATION SECTION.
00014
00015          SOURCE-COMPUTER.
00016              IBM-370.
00017
00018          OBJECT-COMPUTER.
00019              IBM-370.


00021          INPUT-OUTPUT SECTION.
00022
00023          FILE-CONTROL.
00024
00025              SELECT JOB-TITLE-FILE
00026                  ASSIGN TO UT-S-JOBS.
00027
00028              SELECT PERSONNEL-FILE
00029                  ASSIGN TO UT-S-PERSONS.
```

Figure 4.12 "A Potpourri of COBOL Techniques"

```
00030
00031            SELECT PRINT-FILE
00032                ASSIGN TO UT-S-REPORT.
00033
00034            SELECT SORT-FILE
00035                ASSIGN TO UT-S-SORTOUT.


00037        DATA DIVISION.
00038        FILE SECTION.
00039
00040        FD   JOB-TITLE-FILE
00041                RECORDING MODE IS F
00042                BLOCK CONTAINS Q RECORDS
00043                LABEL RECORDS ARE STANDARD
00044                RECORD CONTAINS 18 CHARACTERS
00045                DATA RECORD IS JOB-TITLE-RECORD.
00046
00047        01   JOB-TITLE-RECORD.
00048             05   JOB-NUMBER                PIC 999.
00049             05   JOB-TITLE                 PIC X(15).
00050
00051        FD   PERSONNEL-FILE
00052                RECORDING MODE IS F
00053                LABEL RECORDS ARE OMITTED
00054                RECORD CONTAINS 80 CHARACTERS
00055                DATA RECORD IS PR-RECORD.
00056
00057        01   PR-RECORD                      PIC X(80).
00058
00059        FD   PRINT-FILE
00060                RECORDING MODE IS F
00061                LABEL RECORDS ARE OMITTED
00062                RECORD CONTAINS 80 CHARACTERS
00063                DATA RECORD IS PRINT-RECORD.
00064
00065        01   PRINT-RECORD.
00066             05   PR-CARRIAGE-CTL           PIC X.
00067                 88   PR-START-NEW-PAGE                      VALUE '1'.
00068                 88   PR-TRIPLE-SPACE                        VALUE '-'.
00069                 88   PR-DOUBLE-SPACE                        VALUE '0'.
00070                 88   PR-SINGLE-SPACE                        VALUE ' '.
00071             05   PR-REST-RECORD            PIC X(79).
00072
00073        SD   SORT-FILE
00074                RECORDING MODE IS F
00075                RECORD CONTAINS 80 CHARACTERS
00076                DATA RECORD IS SORT-RECORD.
00077
00078        01   SORT-RECORD.
00079             05   SR-LAST-AND-FIRST-NAME   PIC X(19).
00080             05   FILLER                   PIC X(61).
00081        WORKING-STORAGE SECTION.
00082        77   FILLER                        PIC X(14)
00083                    VALUE 'WS BEGINS HERE'.
```

Appears as a key in SORT verb

Facilitates ABEND debugging

Figure 4.12 "A Potpourri of COBOL Techniques" (continued)

91

```
00084    77  WS-END-OF-FILE-SWITCH          PIC XXX      VALUE SPACES.
00085        88  WS-END-OF-PERSONNEL-FILE                VALUE 'YES'.
00086    77  END-OF-SORT-SWITCH             PIC XXX      VALUE SPACES.
00087        88  END-OF-SORT-FILE                        VALUE 'YES'.
00088    77  WS-JOB-FILE-SWITCH             PIC XXX      VALUE SPACES.
00089        88  WS-END-OF-JOB-FILE                      VALUE 'YES'.
00090    77  WS-LINE-COUNT                  PIC S9(3)
00091            COMP-3                                  VALUE ZEROS.
00092    77  WS-NUMBER-JOB-ENTRIES          PIC S9(3)
00093            COMP-3                                  VALUE ZEROS.
00094    77  WS-PAG-NUMBER                  PIC S9(3)
00095            COMP-3                                  VALUE ZEROS.
00096
00097    01  H1-TOP-HEADING.
00098        05  H1-CARR-CTL                PIC X        VALUE '1'.
00099        05  FILLER                     PIC X(59)    VALUE SPACES.
00100        05  FILLER                     PIC X(5)
00101                                                    VALUE 'PAGE '
00102        05  H1-PAGE-NUMBER             PIC ZZZ9.
00103        05  FILLER                     PIC X(11)
00104                                                    VALUE SPACES.
00105
00106    01  H3-SECOND-HEADING.
00107        05  H3-CARR-CTL                PIC X        VALUE '0'.
00108        05  H3-CURR-DATE               PIC X(8).
00109        05  FILLER                     PIC X(71)    VALUE SPACES.
00110
00111    01  D1-FIRST-DETL-LINE.
00112        05  D1-CARR-CTL                PIC X        VALUE '-'.
00113        05  D1-NAME-CONST              PIC X(5)     VALUE 'NAME:'.
00114        05  D1-LAST-NAME               PIC X(10).
00115        05  FILLER                     PIC X        VALUE SPACES.
00116        05  D1-FIRST-NAME              PIC X(9).
00117        05  FILLER                     PIC XXX      VALUE SPACES.
00118        05  D1-TITLE-CONST             PIC X(6)     VALUE 'TITLE:'.
00119        05  D1-TITLE                   PIC X(15).
00120        05  FILLER                     PIC XXX      VALUE SPACES.
00121        05  D1-EMPL-NUMB-CONST         PIC X(11)    VALUE 'EMPLOYEE #:'.
00122        05  D1-EMPL-NUMBER             PIC 999B99B9999.
00123        05  FILLER                     PIC X(5)     VALUE SPACES.
00124
00125    01  D2-SECOND-DETAIL-LINE.
00126        05  D2-CARR-CTL                PIC X        VALUE '0'.
00127        05  D2-LOC-CONST               PIC X(9)     VALUE 'LOCATION:'.
00128        05  D2-LOCATION                PIC X(10)
00129        05  FILLER                     PIC XXX      VALUE SPACES.
00130        05  D2-ADDR-CONST              PIC X(5)     VALUE 'ADDR:'.
00131        05  D2-ADDRESS                 PIC X(22).
00132        05  FILLER                     PIC XXX      VALUE SPACES.
00133        05  D2-EDUCATION-CONST         PIC X(5)     VALUE 'EDUC:'.
00134        05  D2-EDUCATION               PIC X(10).
00135        05  FILLER                     PIC X(12)    VALUE SPACES.
00136
00137    01  D3-THIRD-DETAIL-LINE.
```

Figure 4.12 "A Potpourri of COBOL Techniques" (continued)

92

```
00138          05  D3-CARR-CTL              PIC X          VALUE '0'.
00139          05  FILLER                   PIC X(20)      VALUE SPACES.
00140          05  D3-SAL-CONSTANT-ONE      PIC X(8)       VALUE 'SALARY'.
00141          05  D3-SAL-CONSTANT-TWO      PIC X(14)      VALUE 'HISTORY'.
00142
00143      01  D4-FOURTH-DETAIL-LINE.
00144          05  D4-CARR-CTL              PIC X          VALUE ' '.
00145          05  FILLER                   PIC X(10)      VALUE SPACES.
00146          05  D4-SALARY                PIC $$$,$$$.$$.
00147          05  FILLER                   PIC X(5)       VALUE SPACES.
00148          05  D4-DATE                  PIC 99B99B99.
00149          05  FILLER                   PIC X(47)      VALUE SPACES.
00150
00151      01  JB-TITLE-TABLE.
00152          05  JB-TITLE-ENTRIES                             Variable-length table
00153              OCCURS 1 TO 200 TIMES
00154              DEPENDING ON WS-NUMBER-JOB-ENTRIES
00155              ASCENDING KEY IS JB-NUMBER
00156              INDEXED BY JOB-INDEX.                    Required for binary
00157          10  JB-NUMBER                PIC 999.        search
00158          10  JB-TITLE                 PIC X(15).
00159
00160      01  EDUCATION-TABLE.
00161          05  FILLER                   PIC X(10)      VALUE 'AHIGH SCH'.
00162          05  FILLER                   PIC X(10)      VALUE 'BASSOC DEG'.
00163          05  FILLER                   PIC X(10)      VALUE 'C4 YR DEG'.
00164          05  FILLER                   PIC X(10)      VALUE 'DMS/MA'.
00165          05  FILLER                   PIC X(10)      VALUE 'EMBA'.
00166          05  FILLER                   PIC X(10)      VALUE 'FPH. D.'.
00167          05  FILLER                   PIC X(10)      VALUE 'XOTHER'.
00168      01  EDUCATION-TBL REDEFINES EDUCATION-TABLE.
00169          05  EDUCATION OCCURS 7 TIMES
00170              INDEXED BY EDUC-INDEX.                  Required for search
00171          10  EDUC-CODE                PIC X.         verb
00172          10  EDUC-VALUE               PIC X(9).
00173
00174      01  LOCATION-TABLE.
00175          05  LOCATION-1               PIC X(33)
00176              VALUE 'CHICAGO      1234 NORTH STREET'.
00177          05  LOCATION-2               PIC X(33)
00178              VALUE 'NEW YORK     42 9TH STREET FLUSING'.
00179          05  LOCATION-3               PIC X(33)
00180              VALUE 'MONTREAL     87 ALBERT AVENUE'.
00181          05  LOCATION-4               PIC X(33)
00182              VALUE 'ATLANTA      4 ROSE LANE'.
00183
00184      01  LOCATION-TBL REDEFINES LOCATION-TABLE.
00185          05  LOCATION OCCURS 4 TIMES INDEXED BY LOCATION-INDEX.
00186          10  LOCATION-CITY            PIC X(10).
00187          10  FILLER                   PIC X.
00188          10  LOCATION-ADDRESS         PIC X(22).
00189
00190
```

Figure 4.12 "A Potpourri of COBOL Techniques" (continued)

93

```
00191        COPY PERSON.
00192 C      01   PERSONNEL-RECORD.
00193 C           05   PR-NAME.
00194 C                10   PR-LAST-NAM          PIC X(10).
00195 C                10   PR-FIRST-NAM         PIC X(9).
00196 C           05   PR-EMPL-NUMBER           PIC 9(9).
00197 C           05   PR-CURR-LOCATION-CODE    PIC 9.
00198 C           05   PR-SALARY-GRADE          PIC 99.
00199 C           05   PR-JOB-CODE              PIC 999.
00200 C           05   PR-EDUCATION-CODE        PIC X.
00201 C           05   FILLER                   PIC X(2).
00202 C           05   PR-NUMBER-OF-SALARIES    PIC 99.
00203 C           05   PR-HISTORICAL-DATA.
00204 C                10   PR-OLD-SALARY-DATA OCCURS 3 TIMES
00205 C                     INDEXED BY PR-SALARY-INDEX.
00206 C                     15   PR-REVIEW-DATE  PIC 9(6).
00207 C                     15   PR-SALARY       PIC S9(5)V99.
00208 C           05   FILLER                   PIC X(2).
```

— Copy clause describing incoming records

```
00210        PROCEDURE DIVISION.
00211
00212        010-HSKPG.
00213            OPEN INPUT JOB-TITLE-FILE.
00214
00215        020-READ-1ST-JOB-RECD.
00216            READ JOB-TITLE-FILE
00217                AT END DISPLAY 'EMPTY TITLE FILE'
00218                     STOP RUN.
00219
00220        030-LOAD-JOB-TABLE.
00221            PERFORM A-LOAD-JOB-TABLE
00222                VARYING JOB-INDEX FROM 1 BY 1
00223                UNTIL WS-END-OF-JOB-FILE.
00224            CLOSE JOB-TITLE-FILE.
00225
00226        040-SORT-PERSONNEL-FILE.
00227            SORT SORT-FILE
00228                ASCENDING KEY SR-LAST-AND-FIRST-NAME
00229                INPUT PROCEDURE B-INPUT-PROCEDURE
00230                OUTPUT PROCEDURE C-OUTPUT-PROCEDURE.
00231
00232        050-EOJ-PROCESSING.
00233            GOBACK.
00235        A-LOAD-JOB-TABLE SECTION.
00236
00237        A010-KEEP-COUNT.
00238            ADD 1 TO WS-NUMBER-JOB-ENTRIES.
00239
00240            IF WS-NUMBER-JOB-ENTRIES IS GREATER THAN 200
00241                DISPLAY 'JOB TABLE TOO SMALL'
00242                MOVE 'YES' TO WS-JOB-FILE-SWITCH
```

Check for an "empty" file

Defined in an SD

Both input and output procedures must be sections

Check that table limit is not exceeded

Figure 4.12 "A Potpourri of COBOL Techniques" (continued)

94

```
00243              ELSE
00244                  MOVE JOB-NUMBER TO JB-NUMBER (JOB-INDEX)
00245                  MOVE JOB-TITLE TO JB-TITLE (JOB-INDEX).
00246
00247        A030-READ.
00248            READ JOB-TITLE-FILE
00249                AT END MOVE 'YES' TO WS-JOB-FILE-SWITCH.
00250
00251        A999-EXIT.
00252            EXIT.
00254        B-INPUT-PROCEDURE SECTION.
00255
00256        B010-OPEN.
00257            OPEN INPUT PERSONNEL-FILE.
00258
00259        B020-READ-FIRST-RECD.
00260            READ PERSONNEL-FILE INTO PERSONNEL-RECORD
00261                AT END DISPLAY 'NO INPUT RECS'
00262                    MOVE 'YES' TO WS-END-OF-FILE-SWITCH.
00263
00264        B030-RELEASE-RECORDS.
00265            PERFORM B100-SELECT-AND-READ
00266                UNTIL WS-END-OF-PERSONNEL-FILE.
00267            CLOSE PERSONNEL-FILE.
00268            GO TO B999-EXIT-SECTION.
00269
00270        B100-SELECT-AND-READ.
00271            IF PR-SALARY-GRADE IS EQUAL TO 99
00272                NEXT SENTENCE
00273            ELSE
00274                MOVE PERSONNEL-RECORD TO SORT-RECORD
00275                RELEASE SORT-RECORD.
00276            READ PERSONNEL-FILE INTO PERSONNEL-RECORD
00277                AT END MOVE 'YES' TO WS-END-OF-FILE-SWITCH.
00278
00279        B999-EXIT-SECTION.
00280            EXIT.


00282        C-OUTPUT-PROCEDURE SECTION.
00283
00284        C010-OPEN.
00285            OPEN OUTPUT PRINT-FILE.
00286            MOVE 60 TO WS-LINE-COUNT.
00287            PERFORM C030-PROCESS-RECORD UNTIL END-OF-SORT-FILE.
00288
00289        C030-PROCESS-RECORD.
00290            RETURN SORT-FILE INTO PERSONNEL-RECORD
00291                AT END MOVE 'YES' TO END-OF-SORT-SWITCH.
00292            IF NOT END-OF-SORT-FILE
00293                PERFORM C100-PRINT-DETAIL-LINES
00294            ELSE
00295                CLOSE PRINT-FILE
00296                GO TO C999-EXIT-SECTION.
00297
```

Prevents specified records from being passed to sort

Use of READ INTO

Figure 4.12 "A Potpourri of COBOL Techniques" (continued)

95

```
00298              C100-PRINT-DETAIL-LINES.
00299
00300                  IF WS-LINE-COUNT IS GREATER THAN 54
00301                      PERFORM C250-HEADING-ROUTINE.
00302
00303          *  PRINT D1 LINE
00304                  MOVE PR-LAST-NAM TO D1-LAST-NAME.
00305                  MOVE PR-FIRST-NAM TO D1-FIRST-NAME.                Binary search

00307                  SEARCH ALL JB-TITLE-ENTRIES
00308                      AT END
00309                          MOVE SPACES TO D1-TITLE
00310                      WHEN JB-NUMBER (JOB-INDEX) IS EQUAL TO PR-JOB-CODE
00311                          MOVE JB-TITLE (JOB-INDEX) TO D1-TITLE.
00312                  MOVE PR-EMPL-NUMBER TO D1-EMPL-NUMBER.
00313                  INSPECT D1-EMPL-NUMBER REPLACING ALL ' ' BY '-'.
00314                  MOVE D1-FIRST-DETL-LINE TO PRINT-RECORD.
00315                  PERFORM C310-PRINT-LINE.                          Use of INSPECT
00316
00317          *  PRINT D2 LINE
00318                  IF PR-CURR-LOCATION-CODE IS EQUAL TO ZERO
00319                      OR PR-CURR-LOCATION-CODE IS GREATER THAN 4
00320                          MOVE 'UNKNOWN' TO D2-LOCATION
00321                          MOVE SPACES TO D2-ADDRESS          Conversion of a data
00322                  ELSE                                      name to an index value
00323                      SET LOCATION-INDEX TO PR-CURR-LOCATION-CODE
00324                      MOVE LOCATION-CITY (LOCATION-INDEX) TO D2-LOCATION
00325                      MOVE LOCATION-ADDRESS (LOCATION-INDEX) TO D2-ADDRESS.
00326                                          Initializing an index prior to
00327                  SET EDUC-INDEX TO 1.    sequential search
00328                  SEARCH EDUCATION
00329                      AT END
00330                          MOVE 'UNKNOWN' TO D2-EDUCATION
00331                      WHEN PR-EDUCATION-CODE = EDUC-CODE (EDUC-INDEX)
00332                          MOVE EDUC-VALUE (EDUC-INDEX) TO D2-EDUCATION.
00333
00334                  MOVE D2-SECOND-DETAIL-LINE TO PRINT-RECORD.    Sequential search
00335                  PERFORM C310-PRINT-LINE.
00336
00337          *  PRINT-D3-LINE
00338                  MOVE D3-THIRD-DETAIL-LINE TO PRINT-RECORD.
00339                  PERFORM C310-PRINT-LINE.
00340
00341          *  PRINT SALARY DETAIL LINES
00342                  SET PR-SALARY-INDEX TO 1.
00343                  PERFORM C400-PRINT-SALARY-LINE PR-NUMBER-OF-SALARIES TIMES.
00344
00345              C250-HEADING-ROUTINE.
00346                  ADD 1 TO WS-PAG-NUMBER.
00347                  MOVE WS-PAG-NUMBER TO H1-PAGE-NUMBER.
00348                  MOVE H1-TOP-HEADING TO PRINT-RECORD.
00349                  PERFORM C310-PRINT-LINE.
00350                  MOVE CURRENT-DATE TO H3-CURR-DATE.
00351                  MOVE H3-SECOND-HEADING TO PRINT-RECORD.
00352                  PERFORM C310-PRINT-LINE.
00353
00354              C310-PRINT-LINE.
00355                  IF PR-CARRIAGE-CTL IS EQUAL TO '1'
00356                      MQVE 1 TO WS-LINE-COUNT.
```

Figure 4.12 "A Potpourri of COBOL Techniques" (continued)

```
00357                    IF PR-CARRIAGE-CTL IS EQUAL TO '0'
00358                        ADD 2 TO WS-LINE-COUNT.
00359                    IF PR-CARRIAGE-CTL IS EQUAL TO '-'
00360                        ADD 3 TO WS-LINE-COUNT.
00361                    WRITE PRINT-RECORD
00362                        AFTER POSITIONING PR-CARRIAGE-CTL LINES.
00363
00364                C400-PRINT-SALARY-LINE.
00365                    MOVE PR-SALARY (PR-SALARY-INDEX) TO D4-SALARY.
00366                    MOVE PR-REVIEW-DATE (PR-SALARY-INDEX) TO D4-DATE.
00367                    INSPECT D4-DATE REPLACING ALL ' ' BY '/'.
00368                    MOVE D4-FOURTH-DETAIL-LINE TO PRINT-RECORD.
00369                    PERFORM C310-PRINT-LINE.
00370                    SET PR-SALARY-INDEX UP BY 1.
00371
00372
00373                C999-EXIT-SECTION.
00374                    EXIT.
```

Figure 4.12 A Potpourri of COBOL Techniques (continued)

REVIEW EXERCISES

true   *false*   1. The COPY clause is not permitted in the Procedure Division.

true   *false*   2. A given entry cannot contain both an OCCURS clause and a PICTURE clause.

true   *false*   3. The LINKAGE SECTION appears in the calling program.

true   *false*   4. GOBACK and EXIT PROGRAM are completely interchangeable.

true   *false*   5. A called program must have only one entry point.

true   *false*   6. The order of parameters in a USING clause is unimportant.

true   *false*   7. A given program cannot contain more than a single CALL statement.

true   *false*   8. A subprogram consists of only the Data and Procedure Divisions.

true   *false*   9. Subscripting is more efficient than indexing.

true   *false*   10. A subscript of 1 refers to the first element in a table.

true   *false*   11. An index whose value (i.e., displacement) is zero refers to the first element in a table.

true   *false*   12. SEARCH and SEARCH ALL are interchangeable.

true   *false*   13. Indexes can be manipulated in a PERFORM statement.

true   *false*   14. Subscripts can be manipulated in a PERFORM statement.

true   *false*   15. ASCENDING (DESCENDING) KEY is required in an OCCURS clause if the SEARCH verb is used.

true   *false*   16. A binary search could be applied to a table if the elements were arranged in descending sequence.

97

true	*false*	**17.** A linear search over a table of 500 elements requires 10 or fewer comparisons.
true	*false*	**18.** A binary search over a table of 500 elements requires 10 or fewer comparisons.
true	*false*	**19.** The SORT verb cannot be used on a calculated field.
true	*false*	**20.** The SORT verb can use INPUT PROCEDURE in conjunction with GIVING.
true	*false*	**21.** The SORT verb can use OUTPUT PROCEDURE in conjunction with USING.
true	*false*	**22.** RELEASE is present in the INPUT PROCEDURE.
true	*false*	**23.** RETURN is present in the OUTPUT PROCEDURE.
true	*false*	**24.** The SORT verb can contain no more than two sort keys.
true	*false*	**25.** The MERGE verb can specify INPUT PROCEDURE/OUTPUT PROCEDURE.
true	*false*	**26.** The MERGE verb can specify USING/GIVING.
true	*false*	**27.** In OS/VS COBOL, the collating sequence used in a merge or sort can be other than EBCDIC.
true	*false*	**28.** The file specified immediately after the word MERGE must be specified in an MD.
true	*false*	**29.** In OS/VS COBOL, a COPY clause may appear within a COPY.

PROBLEMS

1. How many storage positions are allocated for each of the following table definitions? Show an appropriate schematic indicating storage assignment for each table.

```
(a)  01  STATE-TABLE.
         05  STATE-NAME OCCURS 50 TIMES          PIC A(15).
         05  STATE-POPULATION OCCURS 50 TIMES    PIC 9(8).
(b)  01  STATE-TABLE.
         05  NAME-POPULATION OCCURS 50 TIMES.
             10  STATE-NAME                       PIC A(15).
             10  STATE-POPULATION                 PIC 9(8).
(c)  01  ENROLLMENTS.
         05  COLLEGE OCCURS 4 TIMES.
             10  SCHOOL OCCURS 5 TIMES.
                 15  YEAR OCCURS 4 TIMES          PIC 9(4).
(d)  01  ENROLLMENTS.
         05  COLLEGE OCCURS 4 TIMES.
             10  SCHOOL  OCCURS 5 TIMES           PIC 9(4).
             10  YEAR OCCURS 4 TIMES              PIC 9(4).
```

2. Use the COBOL language manual to determine how the USING/GIVING option of the SORT verb works. Then, given the COBOL statement

```
SORT SORT-FILE
    ASCENDING KEY EMPLOYEE-LOCATION
    DESCENDING KEY EMPLOYEE-DEPARTMENT
    ASCENDING KEY EMPLOYEE-NAME
USING FILE-ONE
GIVING FILE-TWO.
```

answer the following:

(a) What is the major key?
(b) What is the minor key?
(c) Which file is specified in a COBOL SD?
(d) Which file contains the sorted output?
(e) Which file(s) will be specified in a SELECT?
(f) Which file must contain the data names EMPLOYEE-LOCATION, EMPLOYEE-DEPARTMENT, and EMPLOYEE-NAME?

3. Given the statement

```
MERGE WORKFILE
    ASCENDING ACCOUNT-NUMBER
    DESCENDING AMOUNT-OF-SALE
USING
    JANUARY-SALES
    FEBRUARY-SALES
    MARCH-SALES
GIVING
    FIRST-QUARTER-SALES.
```

(a) Which file(s) is specified in an SD?
(b) Which file(s) is specified in an FD?
(c) Which file(s) contains the key ACCOUNT-NUMBER?
(d) What is the primary key?
(e) What is the secondary key?
(f) If a record on the JANUARY-SALES file has the identical ACCOUNT-NUMBER as a record on the FEBRUARY-SALES file, which record would come first on the merged file?
(g) If a record on the JANUARY-SALES file has the identical AMOUNT-OF-SALE as a record on the FEBRUARY-SALES file, which record would come first on the merged file?
(h) If a record on the JANUARY-SALES file has the identical AMOUNT-OF-SALE and ACCOUNT-NUMBER as a record on the FEBRUARY-SALES file, which record would come first on the merged file?

4. Discuss why a COPY clause is often used to establish values for a table. Would reading values from a file be preferable to using a COPY?

5. This problem, really a project, develops an appreciation for sorting, subprograms, and table processing. Write a COBOL program(s) to read a file containing employee name, present salary, previous salary, location code, department code, education code, and job title code. Then list employees in order of increasing salary percentage. Print complete information for each employee. In addition:

(a) Use a *binary* search on employee location. Establish the table of location codes by *reading* values from a file and *subscripting.*

(b) Use a *linear* search on employee department. Establish the table of department codes via a REDEFINES clause. This routine is to be contained in a *subprogram.*

(c) Do a "direct" lookup on the education code.

(d) Code a table-lookup routine "longhand" for job title. Establish the table of title codes by *reading* values from a file and *indexing.*

Indexed Files

This chapter covers indexed files. This type of file organization is particularly important because it permits both random and sequential access. We begin with a conceptual discussion of ISAM and VSAM. Next we present a COBOL program for creating an ISAM file and discuss the differences for VSAM.

The logic for nonsequential file maintenance is developed in pseudocode. Two programs, for ISAM and VSAM, are presented. Differences and similarities are discussed in detail. The chapter concludes with presentation of new features for VSAM processing. These include: ALTERNATE KEY, FILE STATUS, and DYNAMIC ACCESS.

ISAM (INDEXED SEQUENTIAL ACCESS METHOD)

The *indexed sequential access method*, ISAM as it is commonly known, permits both sequential and direct access. It requires that records be loaded sequentially so that indexes can be established for direct access of individual records. In the simplest form there is one cylinder index for the entire file, and many track indexes, one for each

Cylinder Number	Highest Key
100	130
101	249
102	800
103	1240
104	1410
105	1811
106	2069
107	2410
108	2811
109	3040
110	3400
111	3619
112	4511
113	4900
114	5213
115	6874

Figure 5.1 Cylinder Index

cylinder in the file. (Very large files may also have a third level of indexing. A single master index points to one of several cylinder indexes, which in turn points to a track index.) The cylinder index contains the key of the highest record contained in every cylinder in the file. The track index (for a given cylinder) contains the key of the highest record for every track in that cylinder. As an illustration, assume that an ISAM file was loaded on cylinders 100-115 of a disk device. A hypothetical cylinder index (Figure 5.1) for this file contains 16 entries (one for each cylinder in the file).

Let us further assume that there are 10 tracks per cylinder on our device, that the first track (i.e., track 0), contains the track index itself, and that the last two tracks, tracks 8 and 9, are reserved for a cylinder overflow area. Thus, each cylinder will have only seven tracks for data, and each track index will have seven entries. A hypothetical track index for cylinder 102 is shown in Figure 5.2.

Suppose that we seek the record whose key is 430. The record key, 430, is first compared to entries in the cylinder index. Since an ISAM file is loaded sequentially, we conclude that record 430 is on cylinder 102. (The highest key in cylinder 101 is 249, the highest key in cylinder 102 is 800; therefore, key 430, if it is present, must be contained in cylinder 102.) Next, we examine the track index for cylinder 102 (Figure 5.2). Each entry in the track index contains the highest key for that track. (Observe that the last entry in the track index has a key of 800, which matches the entry in the cylinder index for cylinder 102). The highest keys on tracks 2 and 3 are 346 and 449, respectively; hence key 430 is contained on track 3 of cylinder 102. We now know both the cylinder and track on which the record, if it is present, may reside and can proceed directly to it.

When an ISAM file is accessed in a COBOL program, the I/O routines of the operating system perform the preceding search for the programmer. The cylinder and track indices are established automatically by the system when the file is loaded. The

Track Number	Highest Key
1	312
2	346
3	449
4	598
5	642
6	717
7	800

Note: *Track 0 contains the track index.*
        Tracks 8 and 9 contain the cylinder overflow area.

Figure 5.2 Track Index for Cylinder 102

COBOL necessary to create and access ISAM files is straightforward and should present little difficulty when introduced.

Let us consider what happens when a new record is added to an existing ISAM file. A major disadvantage of sequential organization is that the entire file has to be rewritten if even a single record is added. One might logically ask if ISAM files are loaded sequentially, shouldn't a similar requirement pertain. Fortunately, the answer is no. ISAM solves the problem by establishing an overflow area and appropriate linkages. When an ISAM file is initially loaded, the programmer provides, through the JCL, a prime data area and an overflow area. (Usually, two or more tracks of every cylinder are reserved as a cylinder overflow area, as was done in Figure 5.2. It is also possible to designate entire cylinders as an independent overflow area.)

Figure 5.3 is an expanded version of Figure 5.2, to reflect both prime and overflow area for cylinder 102. In addition, we have appended the hypothetical record keys of every record in every track (assume four records per track).

The track index of Figure 5.3 reflects the file immediately after creation; all records are stored in the prime data area and the overflow area is entirely empty. This is denoted by identical entries in the overflow and prime portions of the track index.

What happens when a new record with key 410 is added to the file? The existing indices indicate that this record belongs in cylinder 102, track 3. ISAM places

Prime		Overflow		Actual Record Keys			
Track	Key	Track	Key				
1	312	1	312	251	269	280	312
2	346	2	346	318	327	345	346
3	449	3	449	377	394	400	449
4	598	4	598	469	500	502	598
5	642	5	642	617	619	627	642
6	717	6	717	658	675	700	717
7	800	7	800	722	746	748	800

Figure 5.3 Track Index plus Record Keys

103

Prime		Overflow		Actual Record Keys			
Track	*Key*	*Track*	*Key*				
1	289	T8,R3	312	251	269	280	289
2	346	2	346	318	327	345	346
3	410	T8,R1	449	377	394	400	410
4	598	4	598	469	500	502	598
5	642	5	642	617	619	627	642
6	717	6	717	658	675	700	717
7	748	T8,R2	800	722	730	746	748
Overflow 8	No entries			449	800	312	
9	No entries			No entries			

Figure 5.4 Track Index of Figure 5.3 with Three Additions

the new record with key 410 in its proper place and "bumps" record 449 to an overflow area. No change is required in the cylinder index, for the highest key in cylinder 102 is still 800. However, changes are made in the track index for cylinder 102. The highest record in the prime area of track 3 is no longer 449, but 410; the overflow area is no longer empty but contains record 449. The overflow entries for track 3 are adjusted to contain a key of 449 and a pointer to the overflow area: track 8, record 1.

Figure 5.4 reflects the track index of Figure 5.3 after three new records with keys 410, 730, and 289 were added (in that order). The cylinder overflow area (tracks 8 and 9) contains the three bumped records in the order in which they were bumped. Thus, the first record in track 8 is 449, the second is 800, and the last is 312.

Suppose another record, with key 380, is added to the file. Logically, 380 belongs in track 3, and, as in the previous example, it will bump a record in the prime area to overflow. The prime area for track 3 now consists of records 377, 380, 394, and 400. The bumped record, key 410, is written in the first available space in overflow (i.e., track 8, record 4). Consider carefully the contents of the overflow area—records 449, 800, 312, and 410. Both 449 and 410 logically belong to track 3. They are physically separated from track 3 and from each other. They must be logically reconnected, and this is done via link fields in the overflow area. Each record in overflow has an associated link field which points to the next logical record in the track. Figure 5.5 is an updated version of Figure 5.4, to reflect the addition of record 380 to track 3 and the linkage fields in overflow. (Figure 5.5 also contains three new additions, records 316, 618, and 680, as additional examples.)

Let us trace through track 3 in Figure 5.5. The prime area contains keys 377, 380, 394, and 400. The overflow area begins on track 8, record 4 (i.e., key 410). This, in turn, has a link field to track 8, record 1, key 449. The link associated with key 449 is ★★★, indicating the logical end of the chain.

As more and more records are added to the file, the overflow area becomes increasingly full and processing necessarily slows. Periodically, the file will be reorganized. It is read sequentially (i.e., via overflow linkages), then rewritten to a work file. Finally, the work file is reloaded as a new ISAM file with all records in strict physical order and overflow areas empty.

Prime		Overflow		Actual Record Keys			
Track	Key	Track	Key				
1	289	T8,R3	312	251	269	280	289
2	345	T9,R1	346	316	318	327	345
3	400	T8,R4	449	377	380	394	400
4	598	4	598	469	500	502	598
5	627	T9,R2	642	617	618	619	627
6	700	T9,R3	717	658	675	680	700
7	748	T8,R2	800	722	730	746	748

		Key	Link	Key	Link	Key	Link	Key	Link
Overflow	8	449	★★★	800	★★★	312	★★★	410	T8,R1
	9	346	★★★	642	★★★	717	★★★		

Figure 5.5 Track Index plus Overflow Linkages

VSAM (VIRTUAL STORAGE ACCESS METHOD)

The *virtual storage access method* (VSAM), like ISAM, permits direct access to any record, as well as sequential access to records following one another. VSAM data sets are of two types: key-sequenced or entry-sequenced. A *key-sequenced* data set has its records in order, according to a unique field in each record (e.g., employee number, invoice number, etc.). *Entry-sequenced* data sets store records in the order in which they are loaded, without regard to record content.

A VSAM data set is divided into *control intervals*, which are continuous areas of auxiliary storage. A control interval is *independent* of the physical device on which it resides (i.e., a control interval which fits exactly on one track of a given DASD may require more or less than one track if the data set were moved to another type of device). That situation is of no concern to the user.

The length of a control interval is fixed, either by VSAM or the user. VSAM will determine an optimum length based on record size, type of DASD, and the amount of space required for an I/O buffer. All control intervals in a given data set are the same length and cannot be changed without creating an entirely new data set.

The balance of this discussion pertains only to key-sequenced data sets, by far the more common organization. A key-sequenced data set is defined with an index so that individual records may be located on a random basis. Entries in an index are known as index records. The lowest-level index is called the *sequence set*. Records in all higher levels are collectively called the *index set*. (Our discussion of ISAM contained two levels of indexes, track and cylinder, which correspond to the sequence and index sets for VSAM. Large ISAM files can also contain a higher level of index, the master index. In this instance, the track index would still correspond to the sequence set, but the master and cylinder indexes would collectively correspond to the index set.)

An entry in a sequence set contains the *highest* key in a control interval and a vertical pointer to that interval. An entry in an index set contains the highest key in the index record at the next lower level and a vertical pointer to that index record. These concepts are made clearer by examination of Figure 5.6.

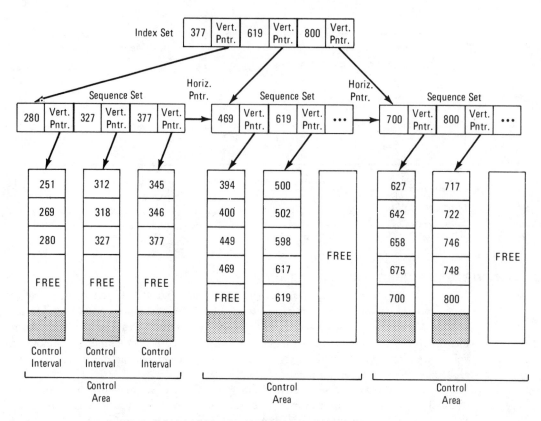

Figure 5.6 Initial Distribution of Records in a VSAM Data Set

Figure 5.6 shows the 28 records of Figure 5.3 hypothetically distributed in a key-sequenced data set. The entire data set consists of three control areas; each area in turn contains three control intervals. The shaded areas shown at the end of each control interval contain information required by VSAM. The index set has only one level of indexing. There are three entries in the index set, one for each control area. Each entry in the index set contains the highest key in the corresponding control area; thus, 377, 619, and 800 are the highest keys in the first, second, and third control areas, respectively. Each control area has its own sequence set. The entries in the first sequence set show the highest keys of the control intervals in the first control area to be 280, 327, and 377, respectively. Note that the highest entry in the third control interval, 377, corresponds to the highest entry in the first control area of the index set.

Figure 5.6 alludes to two kinds of pointers, vertical and horizontal. Vertical pointers are used for direct access to an individual record. For example, assume that the record with a key of 449 is to be retrieved. VSAM begins at the highest level of index (i.e., at the index set). It concludes that record key 449 is in the second control area (377 is the highest key in the first area, whereas 619 is the highest key in the second control area). VSAM follows the vertical pointer to the sequence set for the second area and

106

draws its final conclusion: record key 449, if it exists, will be in the first control interval of the second control area.

Horizontal pointers are used for sequential access only. In this instance, VSAM begins at the sequence set and uses the horizontal pointer in a sequence set record to get from that sequence set record to the one containing the next highest key. Put another way, the vertical pointer in a sequence set record points to data; the horizontal pointer in a sequence set record points to the sequence set record containing the next highest record.

Figure 5.6 contains several allocations of free space, which is distributed in one of two ways: as free space within a control interval, or as a free control interval within a control area. In other words, as VSAM loads a file, empty space is deliberately left throughout the file. This is done to facilitate subsequent insertion of new records. By employing this technique, VSAM eliminates the need for the overflow areas of ISAM. Retrieval of records is generally faster under VSAM because there is no need to chain through the overflow areas as in ISAM.

The discussion so far has assumed that sufficient space exists in a control interval for new records; when this is not the case, a control interval split results, as illustrated in Figure 5.7.

Figure 5.7 shows the changes brought about by the addition of three new records, with keys of 410, 730, and 289, to the file of Figure 5.6. Addition of the first record, key 410, poses no problem, as free space is available in the control interval where the record belongs. Record 410 is inserted into its proper place and the other records in that control interval are moved down.

The addition of record key 730 requires different action. The control interval that should contain this record is full. Consequently, VSAM causes a *control interval split*, in which some of the records in the previously filled control interval are moved to an empty control interval in the same control area. Entries in the sequence data set for the third control area will change, as shown in Figure 5.7. This makes considerable sense when we realize that each record in a sequence data set contains the key of the highest record in the corresponding control interval. Thus, the records in the sequence data set must reflect the control interval split. Note that after a control interval split, subsequent additions are facilitated, as free space is again readily available. Figure 5.8 shows the results of including four additional records, with keys of 316, 380, 618, and 680.

Record 316 is inserted into free space in the second control interval of the first control area, with the other records initially in this interval shifted down. Record 380 is inserted at the end of the third control interval in the first control area. Record 618 causes a control interval split in the second control area.

Record 680 also requires a control interval split except there are no longer any free control intervals in the third control area. Accordingly, a *control area split* is initiated, in which some of the records in the old control area are moved into a new control area at the end of the data set. Both the old and the new control areas will have free control intervals as a result of the split. In addition, the index set has a fourth entry, indicating the presence of a new control area. The sequence set is also expanded to allow for the fourth control area.

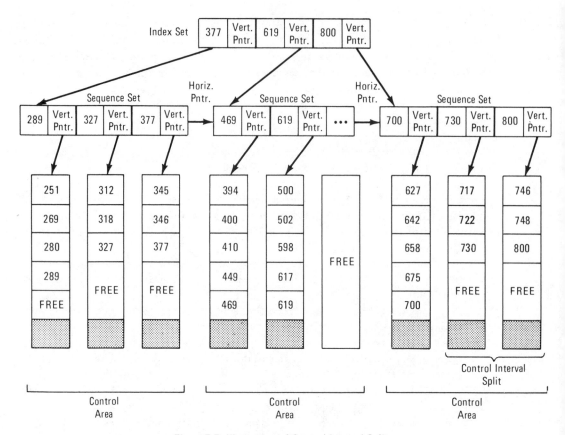

Figure 5.7 Illustration of Control Interval Split

CREATING AN INDEXED FILE

Figure 5.9 contains a COBOL program to create an ISAM file. The program reads records from an incoming transaction file and creates an ISAM file as output. *The incoming file must be in sequential order.*

The SELECT statement for the ISAM file, line 11, contains the clause ACCESS IS SEQUENTIAL, indicating that, in this particular run, we are accessing the file sequentially. It also contains a RECORD KEY clause (line 13), which specifies the field *within* the record that serves as the key. Note that the RECORD-KEY, ISAM-ID-NUMBER, *must* be defined within the ISAM record itself.

ISAM does not physically delete inactive records. Instead, a one-byte field is established at the beginning of each record (line 22), with the convention that LOW-VALUES denotes an active record and HIGH-VALUES an inactive record. When a file is created, all records are initially active, hence the MOVE statement of line 49. Subsequent processing (e.g., file maintenance) may "delete" specified records by moving HIGH-VALUES to this field. Note well, however, that logically deleted records in an ISAM file are physically present. They are removed only when the file is reorganized (i.e., read

108

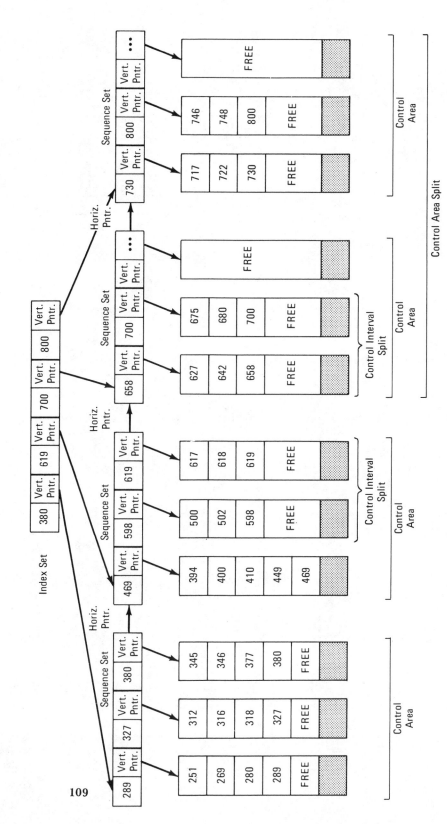

Figure 5.8 Illustration of Control Area Split

109

```
00001          IDENTIFICATION DIVISION.
00002          PROGRAM-ID.    CREATE.
00003          AUTHOR.        GRAUER.
00004          ENVIRONMENT DIVISION.
00005          CONFIGURATION SECTION.
00006          SOURCE-COMPUTER.    IBM-370.
00007          OBJECT-COMPUTER.    IBM-370.
00008          INPUT-OUTPUT SECTION.
00009          FILE-CONTROL.
00010              SELECT TRANSACTION-FILE ASSIGN TO UT-S-SYSIN.
00011              SELECT ISAM-FILE ASSIGN TO DA-I-NEWMAST
00012                  ACCESS IS SEQUENTIAL
00013                  RECORD KEY IS ISAM-ID-NUMBER.
00014          DATA DIVISION.                              SELECT statement
00015          FILE SECTION.
00016          FD  ISAM-FILE
00017              LABEL RECORDS ARE STANDARD
00018              RECORDING MODE IS F
00019              RECORD CONTAINS 41 CHARACTERS
00020              DATA RECORD IS ISAM-MASTER-RECORD.    One-byte field to indicate
00021          01  ISAM-MASTER-RECORD.                   active records
00022              05  ISAM-DELETE-CODE        PIC X.
00023              05  ISAM-ID-NUMBER          PIC X(9).
00024              05  ISAM-NAME               PIC X(25).
00025              05  ISAM-SALARY             PIC X(6).
00026          FD  TRANSACTION-FILE
00027              LABEL RECORDS ARE OMITTED
00028              RECORDING MODE IS F
00029              RECORD CONTAINS 80 CHARACTERS
00030              DATA RECORD IS TRANSACTION-RECORD.
00031          01  TRANSACTION-RECORD.
00032              05  TR-ID-NUMBER            PIC X(9).
00033              05  TR-NAME                 PIC X(25).
00034              05  TR-SALARY               PIC X(6).
00035              05  FILLER                  PIC X(40).
00036          WORKING-STORAGE SECTION.
00037          77  WS-TRANSACTION-SWITCH       PIC X(3)    VALUE 'NO'.
00038          PROCEDURE DIVISION.
00039              OPEN INPUT TRANSACTION-FILE
00040                   OUTPUT ISAM-FILE.
00041              READ TRANSACTION-FILE
00042                  AT END MOVE 'YES' TO WS-TRANSACTION-SWITCH.
00043              PERFORM 010-READ-TRANSACTION
00044                  UNTIL WS-TRANSACTION-SWITCH = 'YES'.
00045              CLOSE TRANSACTION-FILE
00046                    ISAM-FILE.
00047              STOP RUN.
00048          010-READ-TRANSACTION.
00049              MOVE LOW-VALUES    TO ISAM-DELETE-CODE.   Denotes an active record
00050              MOVE TR-ID-NUMBER TO ISAM-ID-NUMBER.
00051              MOVE TR-NAME      TO ISAM-NAME.
00052              MOVE TR-SALARY    TO ISAM-SALARY.
00053              WRITE ISAM-MASTER-RECORD
00054                  INVALID KEY DISPLAY 'RECORD OUT OF SEQUENCE OR '
00055                      'DUPLICATE' TR-ID-NUMBER.
00056              READ TRANSACTION-FILE
00057                  AT END MOVE 'YES' TO WS-TRANSACTION-SWITCH.
00058                                              INVALID KEY clause in
                                                    WRITE statement
```

Figure 5.9 Creation of an ISAM File

110

sequentially to a work file and then reloaded from the work file). Under OS, this process is best accomplished by the utility, IEBISAM (see Chapter Eleven).

The WRITE statement of line 53 contains an INVALID KEY clause which checks two conditions. It ensures that each ISAM record has a unique key (i.e., that the RECORD KEY of the present record is not a duplicate). It also assures that the keys of incoming records are in ascending order. Failure to meet either of these conditions activates the INVALID KEY clause.

Figure 5.9 would require only slight modification to create a VSAM, rather than an ISAM, file. First a new clause, ORGANIZATION IS INDEXED, is required in the SELECT statement. Second, the ASSIGN clause is altered to remove the organization (e.g., DA-VSAMMAST as opposed to DA-I-ISAMMAST). Finally, the RECORDING MODE clause in the FD is not permitted for VSAM.

COBOL line 22 defines a one-byte field to denote active and inactive records in an ISAM file. COBOL line 49 moves LOW-VALUES to this field for every record. These entries are required for ISAM and should be removed for VSAM. Failure to do so would not cause errors but is a waste of space and processing time.

RANDOM ACCESS OF INDEXED FILES

The summary in Chapter Three presented a COBOL program for sequential file maintenance. In particular, Figure 3.14 represented the traditional update program: a transaction file and old master as input, creating a new master file as output. Since processing was strictly sequential, every record in the old master had to be read and rewritten, regardless of whether or not it was changed. Needless to say, if only a small percentage of records are changed, sequential access is rather inefficient.

Indexed files, both ISAM and VSAM, provide the capability to do file maintenance on a random basis (i.e., only new or changed records are written and unchanged records are left alone). Thus, while sequential maintenance requires two distinct master files, an old and a new, random access uses only a single master file, from which records are both read and written.

Figure 5.10 contains the logic for random maintenance expressed in pseudocode. As in the sequential example of Chapter Three, three types of transactions are possible. A transaction specified as an addition is to be added to the file, a deletion is to be removed from the file, and a salary change is to alter the salary field of an existing record. Incoming transactions have been scrubbed in a prior run and can be assumed to contain valid data. However, the random maintenance program will still check for two types of errors, which could not be caught in the stand-alone edit program:

1. No matches—in which deletions or salary changes are attempted for records not in the master file.

2. Duplicate additions—in which an addition is specified for a record already in the file.

The logic inherent in Figure 5.10 conforms to these specifications and should be readily apparent.

```
  Initialize
  Open files
  READ TRANSACTION-FILE at end indicate no more data
 ┌PERFORM until no more data
 │      MOVE TRANSACTION-ID to nominal-key
 │      READ INDEXED-FILE
 │          INVALID KEY means transaction record does not exist
 │   ┌IF transaction record does not exist
 │   │   ┌PERFORM new record routine
 │   │   │    IF TRANSACTION-CODE is addition
 │   │   │        WRITE new record on INDEXED-FILE
 │   │   │    ELSE write error message
 │   │   └ENDPERFORM
 │   │ ELSE
 │   │   ┌PERFORM match routine
 │   │   │    IF TRANSACTION-CODE is addition
 │   │   │        WRITE error message
 │   │   │    ELSE
 │   │   │        IF TRANSACTION-CODE is deletion
 │   │   │           Remove record
 │   │   │        ELSE do salary update
 │   │   └ENDPERFORM
 │   └ENDIF
 │      READ TRANSACTION-FILE at end indicate no more data
 └ENDPERFORM
  Close files
  Stop run
```

Figure 5.10 Pseudocode for Random Update

Figures 5.11 and 5.12 contain COBOL programs for random updating of an ISAM and VSAM file, respectively. Although the programs are remarkably similar, there are some specific differences. These include:

1. The ASSIGN clauses of the SELECT statement. The organization field must *not* be specified for VSAM [e.g., ASSIGN TO DA-VSAMMAST (line 12 in Figure 5.12)]. It is specified for ISAM [e.g., DA-I-ISAMMAST (line 12 in Figure 5.11)].

2. ORGANIZATION IS INDEXED is required for VSAM files (line 14 of Figure 5.12) but is not used with ISAM.

3. NOMINAL KEY is used with ISAM (line 14 of Figure 5.11) but not with VSAM. Further, the data name specified as the NOMINAL KEY is defined in Working-Storage (line 43 of Figure 5.11). To retrieve a record on a random basis from an ISAM file, the transaction key is moved to the NOMINAL KEY (line 91 in Figure 5.11). The ISAM file is accessed by the READ statement in line 92. INVALID KEY is activated if the file does not contain a record with the value of NOMINAL KEY. Random retrieval in VSAM is accomplished in much the same way, except that the transaction key is moved to RECORD KEY (line 89 in Figure 5.12). Hence, the SELECT statement for

112

```
00001          IDENTIFICATION DIVISION.
00002          PROGRAM-ID.    UPDATE2.
00003          AUTHOR.         GRAUER.
00004          ENVIRONMENT DIVISION.
00005          CONFIGURATION SECTION.
00006          SOURCE-COMPUTER.    IBM-370.
00007          OBJECT-COMPUTER.    IBM-370.
00008          INPUT-OUTPUT SECTION.
00009          FILE-CONTROL.
00010              SELECT TRANSACTION-FILE ASSIGN TO UT-S-TRANS.
00011              SELECT ERROR-FILE ASSIGN TO UT-S-SYSOUT.
00012              SELECT ISAM-FILE ASSIGN TO DA-I-ISAMMAST
00013                  ACCESS IS RANDOM
00014                  NOMINAL KEY IS WS-MATCH-NUMBER
00015                  RECORD KEY IS ISAM-ID-NUMBER.
00016          DATA DIVISION.
00017          FILE SECTION.                      SELECT statement
00018          FD   ISAM-FILE                     for ISAM file
00019              LABEL RECORDS ARE STANDARD
00020              RECORDING MODE IS F               RECORDING MODE clause
00021              RECORD CONTAINS 41 CHARACTERS
00022              DATA RECORD IS ISAM-RECORD.    RECORD KEY
00023          01   ISAM-RECORD.
00024              05 ISAM-DELETE-CODE            PIC X.
00025              05 ISAM-ID-NUMBER              PIC X(9).
00026              05 ISAM-NAME                   PIC X(25).
00027              05 ISAM-SALARY                 PIC X(6).
00028          FD   TRANSACTION-FILE
00029              LABEL RECORDS ARE OMITTED
00030              RECORDING MODE IS F
00031              RECORD CONTAINS 80 CHARACTERS
00032              DATA RECORD IS TRANS-RECORD.
00033          01   TRANS-RECORD                  PIC X(80).
00034          FD   ERROR-FILE
00035              LABEL RECORDS ARE OMITTED
00036              RECORDING MODE IS F
00037              RECORD CONTAINS 133 CHARACTERS
00038              DATA RECORD IS ERROR-RECORD.
00039          01   ERROR-RECORD                  PIC X(133).
00040          WORKING-STORAGE SECTION.
00041          77   FILLER                        PIC X(14)
00042                                        VALUE 'WS BEGINS HERE'.
00043          77   WS-MATCH-NUMBER               PIC X(9).    Definition of NOMINAL KEY
00044          77   WS-EOF-INDICATOR              PIC X(3)     in Working-Storage
00045                                        VALUE 'NO '.
00046          77   WS-INVALID-SWITCH             PIC X(3).
00047              88 NO-MATCH-OR-NEW-RECORD          VALUE 'YES'.
00048          01   WS-TRANS-RECORD.
00049              05 WS-TRANS-ID                 PIC X(9).
00050              05 WS-TRANS-NAME               PIC X(25).
00051              05 WS-TRANS-SALARY             PIC 9(6).
00052              05 FILLER                      PIC X(39).
00053              05 WS-TRANS-CODE               PIC X.
00054                  88 ADDITION            VALUE 'A'.
00055                  88 DELETION            VALUE 'D'.
00056                  88 SALARY-CHANGE       VALUE 'C'.
00057          01   WS-ERROR-MESSAGE-1            PIC X(40)
00058                                        VALUE ' RECORD ALREADY IN FILE '.
00059          01   WS-ERROR-MESSAGE-2            PIC X(40)
00060                                        VALUE ' NO MATCH '.
```

Figure 5.11 Random Access of ISAM File

113

```
00061          01  WS-PRINT-RECORD.
00062              05 WS-PRINT-MESSAGE          PIC X(40).
00063              05 WS-PRINT-ID               PIC X(9).
00064              05 FILLER                    PIC X(5)
00065                                      VALUE SPACES.
00066              05 WS-PRINT-NAME             PIC X(25).
00067              05 FILLER                    PIC X(53)
00068                                      VALUE SPACES.
00069          01  WS-ISAM-RECORD.
00070              05 WS-ISAM-DELETE-CODE       PIC X.
00071              05 WS-ISAM-ID                PIC X(9).
00072              05 WS-ISAM-NAME              PIC X(25).
00073              05 WS-ISAM-SALARY            PIC X(6).
00074          01  FILLER                       PIC X(12)
00075                                      VALUE 'WS ENDS HERE'.
00076          PROCEDURE DIVISION.
00077              MOVE 'NO ' TO WS-INVALID-SWITCH.
00078              OPEN INPUT TRANSACTION-FILE
00079                   I-O ISAM-FILE          ──ISAM file opened as I-O
00080                   OUTPUT ERROR-FILE.
00081              READ TRANSACTION-FILE INTO WS-TRANS-RECORD
00082                   AT END MOVE 'YES' TO WS-EOF-INDICATOR.
00083              PERFORM 010-READ-ISAM-FILE THRU 010-READ-ISAM-FILE-EXIT
00084                   UNTIL WS-EOF-INDICATOR = 'YES'.
00085              CLOSE TRANSACTION-FILE
00086                    ISAM-FILE
00087                    ERROR-FILE.
00088              STOP RUN.                      Transaction key moved
00089                                             to NOMINAL KEY
00090          010-READ-ISAM-FILE.                          INVALID KEY clause
00091              MOVE WS-TRANS-ID TO WS-MATCH-NUMBER.      in ISAM READ
00092              READ ISAM-FILE INTO WS-ISAM-RECORD
00093                   INVALID KEY MOVE 'YES' TO WS-INVALID-SWITCH.
00094              IF NO-MATCH-OR-NEW-RECORD
00095                   PERFORM 070-NEW-RECORD THRU 070-NEW-RECORD-EXIT
00096              ELSE
00097                   PERFORM 060-MATCH-ROUTINE THRU 060-MATCH-ROUTINE-EXIT.
00098              READ TRANSACTION-FILE INTO WS-TRANS-RECORD
00099                   AT END MOVE 'YES' TO WS-EOF-INDICATOR.
00100
00101          010-READ-ISAM-FILE-EXIT.
00102              EXIT.
00103
00104          060-MATCH-ROUTINE.
00105              IF ADDITION
00106                   MOVE WS-TRANS-NAME       TO WS-PRINT-NAME
00107                   MOVE WS-TRANS-ID         TO WS-PRINT-ID
00108                   MOVE WS-ERROR-MESSAGE-1 TO WS-PRINT-MESSAGE
00109                   WRITE ERROR-RECORD FROM WS-PRINT-RECORD
00110                   GO TO 060-MATCH-ROUTINE-EXIT.
00111              IF DELETION
00112                   MOVE HIGH-VALUES TO WS-ISAM-DELETE-CODE ── Logical deletion
00113                   REWRITE ISAM-RECORD FROM WS-ISAM-RECORD    of inactive records
00114                   GO TO 060-MATCH-ROUTINE-EXIT.
00115              IF SALARY-CHANGE
00116                   MOVE WS-TRANS-SALARY TO WS-ISAM-SALARY
00117                   REWRITE ISAM-RECORD FROM WS-ISAM-RECORD.
00118
00119          060-MATCH-ROUTINE-EXIT.            REWRITE statement
00120              EXIT.
```

Figure 5.11 Random Access of ISAM File (continued)

```
00121
00122        070-NEW-RECORD.
00123            MOVE 'NO ' TO WS-INVALID-SWITCH.
00124            IF ADDITION
00125                MOVE LOW-VALUES          TO WS-ISAM-DELETE-CODE
00126                MOVE WS-TRANS-ID         TO WS-ISAM-ID
00127                MOVE WS-TRANS-NAME       TO WS-ISAM-NAME
00128                MOVE WS-TRANS-SALARY     TO WS-ISAM-SALARY
00129                WRITE ISAM-RECORD FROM WS-ISAM-RECORD
00130            ELSE
00131                MOVE WS-TRANS-NAME       TO WS-PRINT-NAME
00132                MOVE WS-TRANS-ID         TO WS-PRINT-ID
00133                MOVE WS-ERROR-MESSAGE-2 TO WS-PRINT-MESSAGE
00134                WRITE ERROR-RECORD FROM WS-PRINT-RECORD.
00135
00136        070-NEW-RECORD-EXIT.
00137            EXIT.
```

Routine to process new records
or no matches

Figure 5.11 Random Access of ISAM File (continued)

VSAM contains *only* a RECORD KEY clause, whereas ISAM requires both RECORD *and* NOMINAL KEY.

4. RECORDING MODE is specified in the FD for an ISAM file (line 20 in Figure 5.11). It is *not* allowed for VSAM.

5. The first byte of an ISAM record indicates active or inactive status via LOW and HIGH VALUES, respectively (i.e., logically inactive records in ISAM are physically present in the file with HIGH-VALUES in the first byte). VSAM, however, physically deletes inactive records, hence the first byte in the VSAM records of Figure 5.12 is extraneous. (The reader may wonder, then, why it is there. Our answer is that we used the program of Figure 5.10 to initially create an ISAM file. We then used Access Methods Services to convert this "existing" ISAM file to a VSAM file. The conversion changed the file organization, but did not eliminate the first byte, which no longer has meaning under VSAM.)

6. Inactive records are physically deleted from the VSAM file by a DELETE statement (line 110 of Figure 5.12). They are logically deleted in the ISAM file by moving HIGH-VALUES to the first byte in the record (line 112 in Figure 5.11).

In spite of these differences, there is a good deal of commonality between the two listings. Several statements merit attention. Both files are opened as I-O (line 79 in Figure 5.11 and line 77 in Figure 5.12) rather than INPUT or OUTPUT. This means that in a random update, the master file is both read from and written to. Second, changed records are rewritten rather than simply written to the indexed file (line 117 in Figure 5.11 and line 114 in Figure 5.12). Next the READ and WRITE statements for both files (lines 92 and 129 in Figure 5.11; lines 90 and 126 in Figure 5.12) are virtually identical. Finally, and most important, the overall processing logic is the same. Hence, the similarities far outweigh the differences, so one should experience little difficulty in converting to VSAM.

115

```
00001              IDENTIFICATION DIVISION.
00002              PROGRAM-ID.   UPDATE.
00003              AUTHOR.        GRAUER.
00004              ENVIRONMENT DIVISION.
00005              CONFIGURATION SECTION.
00006              SOURCE-COMPUTER.   IBM-370.
00007              OBJECT-COMPUTER.   IBM-370.              Organization must not be specified
00008              INPUT-OUTPUT SECTION.                    for key-sequenced VSAM data set
00009              FILE-CONTROL.      ⟋NOMINAL KEY is not specified
00010                  SELECT TRANSACTION-FILE ASSIGN TO UT-S⟋TRANS.
00011                  SELECT ERROR⟋FILE ASSIGN TO UT-S-SYSOUT.
00012                  SELECT VSAM-FILE ASSIGN TO DA-VSAMMAST
00013                      ACCESS IS RANDOM
00014                      ORGANIZATION IS INDEXED————————Required entry for key-sequenced
00015                      RECORD KEY IS VSAM-ID-NUMBER.  VSAM data sets
00016              DATA DIVISION.
00017              FILE SECTION.    Recording mode is not
00018              FD   VSAM-FILE   specified
00019                   LABEL RECORDS ARE STANDARD
00020                   RECORD CONTAINS 41 CHARACTERS
00021                   DATA RECORD IS VSAM-RECORD.         First-byte delete code
00022              01   VSAM-RECORD.                        has no meaning under
00023                   05 VSAM-DELETE-CODE          PIC X. VSAM
00024                   05 VSAM-ID-NUMBER            PIC X(9).
00025                   05 VSAM-NAME                 PIC X(25).
00026                   05 VSAM-SALARY               PIC X(6).
00027              FD   TRANSACTION-FILE
00028                   LABEL RECORDS ARE OMITTED
00029                   RECORDING MODE IS F
00030                   RECORD CONTAINS 80 CHARACTERS
00031                   DATA RECORD IS TRANS-RECORD.
00032              01   TRANS-RECORD                 PIC X(80).
00033              FD   ERROR-FILE
00034                   LABEL RECORDS ARE OMITTED
00035                   RECORDING MODE IS F
00036                   RECORD CONTAINS 133 CHARACTERS
00037                   DATA RECORD IS ERROR-RECORD.
00038              01   ERROR-RECORD                 PIC X(133).
00039              WORKING-STORAGE SECTION.
00040              77   FILLER                       PIC X(14)
00041                                                VALUE 'WS BEGINS HERE'.
00042              77   WS-EOF-INDICATOR             PIC X(3)
00043                                                VALUE 'NO '.
00044              77   WS-INVALID-SWITCH            PIC X(3).
00045                   88 NO-MATCH-OR-NEW-RECORD        VALUE 'YES'.
00046              01   WS-TRANS-RECORD.
00047                   05 WS-TRANS-ID               PIC X(9).
00048                   05 WS-TRANS-NAME             PIC X(25).
00049                   05 WS-TRANS-SALARY           PIC 9(6).
00050                   05 FILLER                    PIC X(39).
00051                   05 WS-TRANS-CODE             PIC X.
00052                      88 ADDITION           VALUE 'A'.
00053                      88 DELETION           VALUE 'D'.
00054                      88 SALARY-CHANGE      VALUE 'C'.
00055              01   WS-ERROR-MESSAGE-1           PIC X(40)
00056                                                VALUE ' RECORD ALREADY IN FILE '.
00057              01   WS-ERROR-MESSAGE-2  ·         PIC X(40)
00058                                                VALUE ' NO MATCH '.
00059              01   WS-PRINT-RECORD.
00060                   05 WS-PRINT-MESSAGE          PIC X(40).
00061                   05 WS-PRINT-ID               PIC X(9).
```

Figure 5.12 Random Access of a VSAM File

116

```
00062              05 FILLER                    PIC X(5)
00063                                     VALUE SPACES.
00064              05 WS-PRINT-NAME             PIC X(25).
00065              05 FILLER                    PIC X(53)
00066                                     VALUE SPACES.
00067         01  WS-VSAM-RECORD.
00068              05 WS-VSAM-DELETE-CODE       PIC X.
00069              05 WS-VSAM-ID                PIC X(9).
00070              05 WS-VSAM-NAME              PIC X(25).
00071              05 WS-VSAM-SALARY            PIC X(6).
00072         01  FILLER                        PIC X(12)
00073                                     VALUE 'WS ENDS HERE'.
00074         PROCEDURE DIVISION.
00075             MOVE 'NO ' TO WS-INVALID-SWITCH.
00076             OPEN INPUT TRANSACTION-FILE
00077                  I-O VSAM-FILE          ──────OPEN statement
00078                  OUTPUT ERROR-FILE.   identical to ISAM
00079             READ TRANSACTION-FILE INTO WS-TRANS-RECORD
00080                  AT END MOVE 'YES' TO WS-EOF-INDICATOR.
00081             PERFORM 010-READ-VSAM-FILE THRU 010-READ-VSAM-FILE-EXIT
00082                  UNTIL WS-EOF-INDICATOR = 'YES'.
00083             CLOSE TRANSACTION-FILE
00084                  VSAM-FILE
00085                  ERROR-FILE.
00086             STOP RUN.              Transaction key moved to
00087                                    RECORD KEY
00088         010-READ-VSAM-FILE.                        VSAM READ identical to
00089             MOVE WS-TRANS-ID TO VSAM-ID-NUMBER.    ISAM READ
00090             READ VSAM-FILE INTO WS-VSAM-RECORD
00091                  INVALID KEY MOVE 'YES' TO WS-INVALID-SWITCH.
00092             IF NO-MATCH-OR-NEW-RECORD
00093                  PERFORM 070-NEW-RECORD THRU 070-NEW-RECORD-EXIT
00094             ELSE
00095                  PERFORM 060-MATCH-ROUTINE THRU 060-MATCH-ROUTINE-EXIT.
00096             READ TRANSACTION-FILE INTO WS-TRANS-RECORD
00097                  AT END MOVE 'YES' TO WS-EOF-INDICATOR.
00098
00099         010-READ-VSAM-FILE-EXIT.
00100             EXIT.
00101
00102         060-MATCH-ROUTINE.
00103             IF ADDITION
00104                  MOVE WS-TRANS-NAME        TO WS-PRINT-NAME
00105                  MOVE WS-TRANS-ID          TO WS-PRINT-ID
00106                  MOVE WS-ERROR-MESSAGE-1 TO WS-PRINT-MESSAGE
00107                  WRITE ERROR-RECORD FROM WS-PRINT-RECORD
00108                  GO TO 060-MATCH-ROUTINE-EXIT.
00109             IF DELETION
00110                  DELETE VSAM-FILE      ──Removal of inactive record
00111                  GO TO 060-MATCH-ROUTINE-EXIT.
00112             IF SALARY-CHANGE
00113                  MOVE WS-TRANS-SALARY TO WS-VSAM-SALARY
00114                  REWRITE VSAM-RECORD FROM WS-VSAM-RECORD.
00115                                        REWRITE statement identical
00116         060-MATCH-ROUTINE-EXIT.        to ISAM
00117             EXIT.
00118
00119         070-NEW-RECORD.
00120             MOVE 'NO ' TO WS-INVALID-SWITCH.
```

Figure 5.12 Random Access of a VSAM File (continued)

117

```
                                              First byte has no meaning under VSAM
00121          IF ADDITION
00122              MOVE LOW-VALUES          TO WS-VSAM-DELETE-CODE
00123              MOVE WS-TRANS-ID         TO WS-VSAM-ID
00124              MOVE WS-TRANS-NAME       TO WS-VSAM-NAME
00125              MOVE WS-TRANS-SALARY     TO WS-VSAM-SALARY
00126              WRITE VSAM-RECORD FROM WS-VSAM-RECORD
00127          ELSE
00128              MOVE WS-TRANS-NAME       TO WS-PRINT-NAME
00129              MOVE WS-TRANS-ID         TO WS-PRINT-ID
00130              MOVE WS-ERROR-MESSAGE-2 TO WS-PRINT-MESSAGE
00131              WRITE ERROR-RECORD FROM WS-PRINT-RECORD.
00132
00133      070-NEW-RECORD-EXIT.
00134          EXIT.
```

Figure 5.12 Random Access of a VSAM File (continued)

ADDITIONAL COBOL ELEMENTS

Release 2 of OS/VS COBOL conforms to the ANSI 74 standard. As such, several facilities are available which were absent in other compilers. The biggest change is in the SELECT statement, which now has the following format:

SELECT file-name

ASSIGN TO assignment-name-1 [assignment-name-2] . . .

[RESERVE integer
$$\begin{bmatrix} \text{AREA} \\ \text{AREAS} \end{bmatrix}$$
]

ORGANIZATION IS INDEXED

[ACCESS MODE IS
$$\left\{ \begin{array}{l} \text{SEQUENTIAL} \\ \text{RANDOM} \\ \text{DYNAMIC} \end{array} \right\}$$
]

RECORD KEY IS data-name-3

[PASSWORD IS data-name-1]

[ALTERNATE RECORD KEY IS data-name-4

[PASSWORD IS data-name-5]

[WITH DUPLICATES]] . . .

[FILE STATUS IS data-name-2].

118

Note well that this SELECT statement applies to VSAM only. ISAM requires a NOMINAL KEY for random access, which is not used for VSAM. VSAM requires ORGANIZATION IS INDEXED, which is not used for ISAM. In addition, ISAM files cannot specify ACCESS IS DYNAMIC, ALTERNATE RECORD, or FILE STATUS.

The ALTERNATE RECORD KEY provides a second direct path into a file. However, unlike the RECORD KEY, which must be unique for each record, the ALTERNATE KEY need not be unique. This capability is extremely powerful and gives COBOL some limited facility for data-base management. Thus, it is possible to retrieve not only individual records, but also groups of records. Consider, for example:

```
SELECT EMPLOYEE-FILE
    .

    .

    .
    RECORD KEY IS EMPLOYEE-NUMBER
    ALTERNATE RECORD KEY IS LOCATION WITH DUPLICATES.
```

This statement permits us to access *directly* the first employee with a given location, and then all the rest of the employees in the same location.

FILE STATUS defines a two-byte area which indicates results of each I/O operation. Its use is optional. Status keys and their meanings for VSAM files are shown in Table 5.1.

FILE STATUS is commonly used in conjunction with DECLARATIVES to facilitate the processing of I/O errors. DECLARATIVES must immediately follow the Procedure Division and must end with the sentence END DECLARATIVES. This is illustrated in Figure 5.13.

Table 5.1   I/O Status Codes

Key 1	Key 2	Cause	
0	0	Successful completion	
1	0	End of file	
2	1	Invalid key:	Sequence error
	2		Duplicate key
	3		No record found
	4		Boundary violation
3	0	Permanent I/O error:	No further information
	4		Boundary violation
9	1	Other error:	Password failure
	2		Logic error
	3		Resource not available
	4		Sequential record not available
	5		Invalid or incomplete file information
	6		No DD statement

```
SELECT VSAM-FILE
     ASSIGN TO DA-VSAMMAST
     ORGANIZATION IS INDEXED
     RECORD KEY IS VSAM-KEY
     STATUS IS STATUS-FILE-ONE.
          .
          .
          .

WORKING-STORAGE SECTION.
01   STATUS-FILE-ONE.
     05   FIRST-KEY          PIC X.
     05   SECOND-KEY         PIC X.
          .
          .
          .

PROCEDURE DIVISION.
DECLARATIVES.
D010-INVALID-KEY SECTION.
   USE AFTER ERROR PROCEDURE ON VSAM-FILE.
   IF  FIRST-KEY = '2' AND SECOND-KEY = '1'
       DISPLAY 'SEQUENCE ERROR — VSAM-FILE'.
   IF  FIRST-KEY = '2' AND SECOND-KEY = '2'
       DISPLAY 'DUPLICATE KEY — VSAM-FILE'.
          .
          .
          .

END DECLARATIVES.
REST-OF-PROCEDURE-DIVISION SECTION.
          .
          .
          .

WRITE VSAM-FILE.
     .
     .
     .
```

Figure 5.13 Use of FILE STATUS and DECLARATIVES

Consider the action taken on an INVALID KEY condition. If FILE STATUS is specified in the SELECT statement for a file, a value is placed into the designated two-byte area after every I/O operation for that file. If the INVALID KEY option is specified in the statement causing the condition, control is transferred to the imperative statement following INVALID KEY. Any declarative procedure for this file is *not* executed.

If, however, INVALID KEY is not specified and the condition occurs (see Figure 5.13), control passes to the declarative procedure for that file. Control returns to the statement immediately following the one causing the error after the action specified in DECLARATIVES has been taken. Thus, if an INVALID KEY condition was raised as a consequence of the WRITE in Figure 5.13, control would pass to the DECLARATIVES SECTION and return to the statement immediately under WRITE.

VSAM files can specify ACCESS IS DYNAMIC in lieu of RANDOM or SEQUENTIAL. This permits records to be accessed both sequentially and/or randomly in the same program. The form of the READ statement determines the access method. For sequential access, READ file-name NEXT . . . must be specified; for random access, NEXT is omitted.

The START statement causes the file to be positioned to the first record whose value is equal to, greater than, or not less than the value contained in the identifier. INVALID KEY is raised if no record is found that meets the specified criterion. Syntactically, the START statement has the form

$$\underline{\text{START}} \text{ file-name} \left[\text{KEY IS} \left\{ \begin{array}{l} \underline{\text{EQUAL}} \text{ TO} \\ = \\ \underline{\text{GREATER}} \text{ THAN} \\ > \\ \underline{\text{NOT}} \underline{\text{ LESS}} \text{ THAN} \\ \underline{\text{NOT}} < \end{array} \right\} \text{identifier} \right]$$

[INVALID KEY imperative statement]

START is also permitted for ISAM, but *only* for an equal condition.

SUMMARY

This chapter dealt exclusively with indexed files, ISAM and VSAM. Both access methods were discussed from a conceptual viewpoint. The cylinder and track indexes for ISAM were illustrated in detail, as were the index and sequence sets for VSAM. Retrieval of VSAM records is said to be from 1½ to 3 times faster than ISAM, owing to the more efficient index structure.

The COBOL requirements for creating an indexed file were demonstrated in a complete COBOL program (Figure 5.9). The logic for a random update was developed in pseudocode. Next, two programs, for ISAM and VSAM, were presented to implement the pseudocode. COBOL differences between the two were emphasized.

The chapter closed with a discussion of new and/or modified capabilities of OS/VS COBOL. These included ALTERNATE RECORD KEY, FILE STATUS, DYNAMIC ACCESS, and START.

In conclusion, the differences between ISAM and VSAM processing are, for the most part, minor. However, differences do exist and the reader must pay strict attention to the IBM reference manual in order to realize the subtleties involved. Our discussion reflects Release 2 of IBM VS COBOL for OS/VS (GC26-3857-0).

REVIEW EXERCISES

true   *false*   **1.** Inactive records in an ISAM file are physically deleted.

true   *false*   **2.** Inactive records in a VSAM file are physically deleted.

true   *false*   **3.** Records in an ISAM file are physically in sequential order.

true   *false*   **4.** Records in an ISAM file are logically in sequential order.

true   *false*   **5.** Records in a control interval are physically in sequential order.

true   *false*   **6.** Records in a control area are logically in sequential order.

true   *false*   **7.** LOW-VALUES denote active records for ISAM files.

true   *false*   **8.** HIGH-VALUES denote inactive records for VSAM files.

true   *false*   **9.** A given READ statement can contain both the INVALID KEY and AT END clauses.

true   *false*   **10.** WRITE and REWRITE may be used interchangeably.

true   *false*   **11.** An ISAM file can be accessed either sequentially or nonsequentially.

true   *false*   **12.** A VSAM file can be accessed either sequentially or nonsequentially.

true   *false*   **13.** NOMINAL KEY is required for sequential access of an ISAM file.

true   *false*   **14.** An ISAM file has more than one track index.

true   *false*   **15.** An ISAM file has at least two, and possibly three, levels of indexing.

true   *false*   **16.** REWRITE can be specified for a file opened as input.

true   *false*   **17.** The index set is a higher-level index than the sequence set.

true   *false*   **18.** ISAM processing is not possible with a "virtual" system.

true   *false*   **19.** A key-sequenced data set is a VSAM data set.

true   *false*   **20.** When creating an ISAM (or VSAM) file, the incoming records need not be in order.

PROBLEMS

1. Modify Figure 5.5 to show the addition of record keys 412 and 750. Indicate the changes, if any, if record key 269 were deleted.

2. Modify Figure 5.8 to show the addition of record keys 412 and 750. Indicate the changes, if any, if record key 269 were deleted.

3. Explain the statement "Records in an ISAM file are in *logically sequential*, but not *physically sequential* order." Are ISAM records ever in physically sequential order? What is meant by reorganization of an ISAM file?

Debugging

Use and Abuse of COBOL

OVERVIEW

Any programmer is realistically expected to make mistakes and a test of a good programmer is not whether he/she makes mistakes, but how quickly he/she can correct the errors that invariably occur. Virtually all textbooks and/or lectures begin the treatment of debugging by saying that it is an art; what is really meant is that debugging per se cannot be taught; or at best that debugging is extremely difficult to teach. There is hope, however. Debugging skills improve with time, if only because one tries to avoid making the same mistakes. If a bug does reoccur, one may remember what was done last time and can usually proceed from there with little difficulty. Our approach to debugging therefore accepts as fundamental the premise that the same errors continually occur, albeit in differing disguises. Thus, the thrust of this chapter is first to develop an appreciation for the different kinds of errors that occur, to discuss reasons why they occur, and finally to find ways in which they may be prevented.

Execution errors are broadly classified into two types:

1. Those errors which find the computer unable to execute a particular instruction, resulting in an ABEND (*AB*normal *END* of job) and dump.

2. Those errors which allow the entire program to execute, but which produce calculated results that are different from those the programmer expected or intended. These errors are further divided into two subclasses:

   a. Those due to an incorrect algorithm, flowchart, and so on, all of which are euphemisms for a logic error.
   b. Those caused by incorrect implementation in COBOL of a correct algorithm.

Errors of the first kind are discussed in Chapters Eight and Nine. In spite of any preconceived ideas about dump reading, execution errors of this type are generally easier to find than those which do not ABEND. This is because a dump invariably provides a hint of where to look. The computer has been instructed to do something it could not do; hence, it objects and gives a reason for its objection. Analysis of the subsequent dump may be trivial, or even unduly complicated, but in any event one knows that a bug exists, and there is a lead as to its nature and location.

Errors of the second kind are more difficult to locate and definitely more harmful. In some instances, there is no evidence of a bug until the comptroller realizes he/she is a few million dollars short, and by then it is too late. Discussion of logic errors of type 2a is avoided entirely, as algorithmic development is well beyond our present scope. We suggest, however, that the techniques of program design from Section I are pertinent to this area and can reduce the errors that do occur. Errors of type 2b can be due to simple carelessness (e.g., using an asterisk for a plus sign, forgetting to code a portion of the flowchart, etc.). More often, however, these errors are due to a misunderstanding about the language: the programmer codes exactly what he intended to code, but his/her interpretation of the action taken by COBOL is different from what actually happens.

Given this brief discussion of error classification, let us proceed to the business at hand, debugging at the source level. The most important quality of the competent debugger is the ability to understand one's self, to know the types of errors most likely to occur. To that end this chapter concentrates on errors in COBOL implementation, those instances where programmer interpretation of particular statements is frequently erroneous. We focus on common abuses of the COBOL language and discuss:

1. Significance of the period.

2. Importance of indentation.

3. Improper transfer from a performed routine.

4. Accessing an FD area after a WRITE statement.

5. Misuse of signed numbers.

6. Misuse of the SEARCH verb.

ERRORS DUE TO COBOL MISINTERPRETATION

Significance of the Period

The presence or absence of a period can have tremendous impact on program execution. Consider the flowcharts and corresponding code shown in Figures 6.1(a) and (b). The flowcharts are significantly different in their intended logic, yet the COBOL is remarkably similar; indeed, the only significant difference between the two sets of COBOL code is an extra period in Figure 6.1(b).

The difference in logical intent between the two flowcharts is enormous. The routine MAIL-COMPANY is to be performed *only* for nonunion members in Figure 6.1(a), but for everyone in Figure 6.1(b). The period in COBOL is quite important in that it ends a statement; that is, if an ELSE branch is taken, every statement between the word ELSE and the next period is executed. Hence, in the code for Figure 6.1(a), *both* ADD and PERFORM are executed after the ELSE, whereas in Figure 6.1(b), *only* the ADD is executed after the ELSE, while the PERFORM is always done.

The presence or absence of a period also affects AT END, INVALID KEY, and SIZE ERROR clauses. Consider the difference between

```
READ TRANSACTION-FILE                                        No period
    AT END MOVE HIGH-VALUES TO TRANSACTION-ID
        MOVE 'NO' TO TRANSACTION-SWITCH.
```

and

```
READ TRANSACTION-FILE                                        Extra period
    AT END MOVE HIGH-VALUES TO TRANSACTION-ID.
        MOVE 'NO' TO TRANSACTION-SWITCH.
```

The addition of the second period causes the value of TRANSACTION-SWITCH to be set to NO after *every* read. Omission of the period (i.e., the first example) changes the value of TRANSACTION-SWITCH only after the end-of-file condition has been reached.

The "missing" period can cause significant frustration in debugging. Consider the code in Figure 6.2, which produces the results shown. Again, this is not a concocted example but rather the work of a frustrated student in "COBOL 1" who could not understand why the NET was consistently wrong for orders less than 2000.

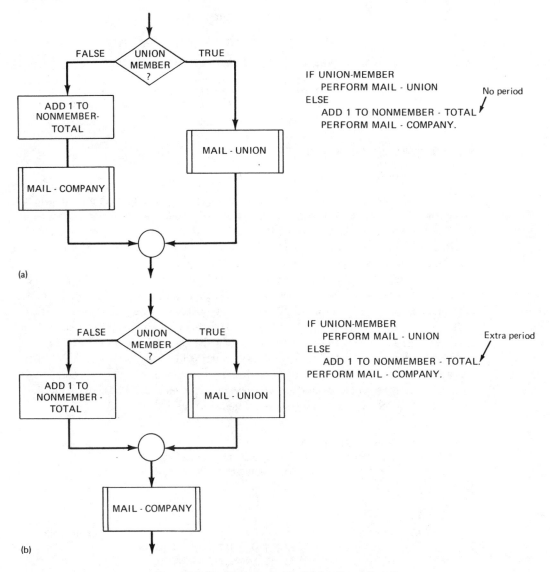

IF UNION-MEMBER
    PERFORM MAIL - UNION   No period
ELSE
    ADD 1 TO NONMEMBER - TOTAL
    PERFORM MAIL - COMPANY.

(a)

IF UNION-MEMBER
    PERFORM MAIL - UNION   Extra period
ELSE
    ADD 1 TO NONMEMBER - TOTAL.
PERFORM MAIL - COMPANY.

(b)

Figure 6.1 Significance of a Missing (or Extra) Period

The logic is apparently straightforward. An order of $2000 or more receives a discount of 2% on the entire order. The amount due (i.e., NET) is equal to the amount ordered minus the discount. The code seems correct, yet the calculated net amounts are wrong for any order less than 2000. Notice that the net amount printed for these orders equals the net for the previous order (i.e., the net for an order of 1000 is *incorrectly* printed as 3920, which was the correct net for the preceding order of 4000). The net amount for an order of 1500 was printed as 4900, and so on. Why?

128

```
COBOL code:      IF   AMOUNT-ORDERED-THISWEEK < 2000              Period terminating
                      MOVE ZEROS TO CUSTOMER-DISCOUNT            compute is in
                 ELSE                                            column 73
                      COMPUTE CUSTOMER-DISCOUNT = AMOUNT-ORDERED-THISWEEK * .02
                 COMPUTE NET = AMOUNT-ORDERED-THISWEEK − CUSTOMER-DISCOUNT.
                 DISPLAY AMOUNT-ORDERED-THISWEEK '      '
                         CUSTOMER-DISCOUNT '      ' NET '         '.      Inadvertently taken as
                                                                          part of ELSE clause
```

Output:	Amount Ordered	Discount	Net
	3000	60	2940
	4000	80	3920
	1000	0	3920
	5000	100	4900
	1500	0	4900

Correct calculation

Net is incorrect and equal to value of previous order

Figure 6.2 The "Missing" Period

The only possible explanation is that the COMPUTE NET statement is not executed for net amounts less than 2000. The only way that can happen is if the COMPUTE NET statement is taken as part of the ELSE clause, and that can happen only if the ELSE is not terminated by a period. The period is "present," however, so we are back at ground zero—or are we? The period is present, but in *column 73*, which is *ignored* by the compiler. Hence, the visual code does not match the compiler interpretation and, hence the bug.

This kind of bug is extremely difficult to detect. The only effective way of eliminating such a problem is through a formatting package which realigns COBOL code according to compiler rather than programmer interpretation. A good package will indent the COMPUTE statement as a detail line under the ELSE (see Appendix B), and thereby highlight the error. The solution is to make the first COMPUTE stretch over two lines.

Importance of Indentation

COBOL programs should always be indented in a manner consistent with compiler interpretation. Although this makes no difference to the compiler, proper indentation is critical for anyone reading the program. It is our unfortunate experience, however, that too many programmers pay too little attention to formatting. Contrary to what others may think, this is not nit-picking but is absolutely essential to a well-written program. We maintain that it is virtually impossible to comprehend the logic of even simple COBOL programs if they are improperly indented. Consider the following pairs of "poor" and "proper" indentation:

129

EXAMPLE 1

Poor indentation:

```
WRITE ISAM-RECORD
    INVALID KEY MOVE 'YES' TO INVALID-SWITCH
PERFORM INVALID-ROUTINE.
```

Proper indentation:

```
WRITE ISAM-RECORD
    INVALID KEY
        MOVE 'YES' TO INVALID-SWITCH
        PERFORM INVALID-ROUTINE.
```

EXAMPLE 2

Poor indentation:

```
READ ISAM-FILE
    INVALID KEY MOVE 'YES' TO INVALID-SWITCH.
    PERFORM PROCESS-TRANSACTIONS-ROUTINE.
```

Proper indentation:

```
READ ISAM-FILE
    INVALID KEY MOVE 'YES' TO INVALID-SWITCH.
PERFORM PROCESS-TRANSACTIONS-ROUTINE.
```

EXAMPLE 3

Poor indentation:

```
COMPUTE GROSS-PAY = HOURS-WORKED * HOURLY-RATE
    ON SIZE ERROR MOVE 'YES' TO ERROR-SWITCH
PERFORM ERROR-ROUTINE-ONE
PERFORM ERROR-ROUTINE-TWO.
```

Proper indentation:

```
COMPUTE GROSS-PAY = HOURS-WORKED * HOURLY-RATE
    ON SIZE ERROR
        MOVE 'YES' TO ERROR-SWITCH
        PERFORM ERROR-ROUTINE-ONE
        PERFORM ERROR-ROUTINE-TWO.
```

Example 1 focuses on the INVALID KEY clause of the WRITE statement. If the invalid condition is raised, all clauses between INVALID KEY and the first period are executed. Thus, in this example, both the MOVE and PERFORM statements will be executed after an invalid key is sensed; hence, both clauses should be indented as shown under proper indentation.

Example 2 also deals with the INVALID KEY clause. This time, however, a period follows the MOVE, hence *only* the MOVE will be executed after an invalid key.

Example 3 illustrates the SIZE ERROR clause of the COMPUTE statement. All clauses between SIZE ERROR and the first period will be executed when the condition is raised, and the indentation should reflect this.

Proper indentation is necessary because the human eye is generally "uncritical" and sees what it wants or expects to see. If you are skeptical, and believe your eye is more discerning than most, try this simple exercise. Read the sentence in the box below, once and only once, and as you do count the number of F's appearing in the box.

> Finished Files are the result of years
> of scientific study combined with
> the experience of years.

There are six F's in the sentence and if you got all six you are good. The average person spots only three and you can feel reasonably proud if you got four or five. Our point in this seemingly trivial example is that our eyes are less discriminating than we would like to believe. Accordingly, we must consciously slow down when reading COBOL. Further, one can use all available help and it is vital that programs are indented properly. An easy and effective way of matching indentation on a source listing and compiler interpretation is through COBOL-compatible products which realign existing COBOL programs (see Appendix B).

Improper exit from a PERFORM

A major difficulty in the implementation of the PERFORM verb stems from improper exit out of a performed procedure. Simply stated, *one must never branch out of a performed routine without returning.* It is perfectly permissible, and often desirable, to "perform out of a perform." It is not acceptable, and in fact disastrous, to exit a PERFORM via a GO TO. However, it is allowable to GO TO an exit paragraph within a PERFORM. Consider the following examples.

Examples 1 and 2 are commonly used and accepted techniques. Example 3 may appear harmless, but its effects can be devastating, as will be shown. Consider the COBOL listing of Figure 6.3 and resultant output in Figure 6.4.

EXAMPLE 1
"Perform out of a Perform" (Acceptable)

PERFORM PAR-A.
.

.

.

PAR-A.
.

.

.

PERFORM PAR-B.
.

.

.

PAR-B.
.

.

.

PAR-C.
.

.

.

EXAMPLE 2
"GO TO within a Perform" (Acceptable)

PERFORM PAR-A THRU PAR-A-EXIT.
.

.

.

PAR-A.
.

.

.

IF N > 50, GO TO PAR-A-EXIT.
.

.

.

PAR-A-EXIT.
EXIT.

EXAMPLE 3
"GO TO out of a Perform" (Totally Unacceptable)

```
                    PERFORM PAR-A.
                        .
                        .
                        .
        PAR-A.
                        .
                        .
                    IF  N > 50, GO TO PAR-B.
                        .
                        .
                        .
        PAR-B.
                        .
                        .
                        .
```

The intended logic of Figure 6.3 is simple. A file is to be processed with each card containing a sales table of 12 monthly entries. The objective is to determine how many months it took to exceed $50,000 in total sales for each record. The PERFORM statement of COBOL line 43 causes the paragraph ANNUAL-TOTAL to be executed 11 times unless YEAR-TOTAL exceeds 50,000. If YEAR-TOTAL is less than 50,000, ANNUAL-TOTAL is executed a twelfth time upon completion of the PERFORM. Regardless of how often ANNUAL-TOTAL is executed, an appropriate message is printed indicating either that total sales did not exceed $50,000, or the number of months it took to reach that figure.

Consider the output of Figure 6.4, which includes both DISPLAY messages and results of the READY TRACE of line 34. The first record for John Smith contained all zeros. Hence, the paragraph ANNUAL-TOTAL (line 45) was executed 12 times, the paragraph NOT-OVER-50000 (line 52) was executed once, and an appropriate message was printed for Mr. Smith stating that his sales did not exceed 50,000. The second record was for Peter Brown, who had sales of $7,000 a month. ANNUAL-TOTAL was executed eight times and Brown's sales exceeded $50,000 after 8 months. In a similar fashion, Henry Jones exceeded $50,000 after 7 months.

Now consider John Johnson, with sales of $1,000 a month. One would

```
00001          IDENTIFICATION DIVISION.
00002          PROGRAM-ID. ERROR3.
00003          AUTHOR.
00004              GRAUER.
00005          DATE-WRITTEN.
00006              DECEMBER 1976.
00007          ENVIRONMENT DIVISION.
00008          CONFIGURATION SECTION.
00009          SOURCE-COMPUTER.
00010              IBM-370.
00011          OBJECT-COMPUTER.
00012              IBM-370.
00013          INPUT-OUTPUT SECTION.
00014          FILE-CONTROL.
00015              SELECT CARD-FILE
00016                  ASSIGN TO UT-S-SYSIN.
00017          DATA DIVISION.
00018          FILE SECTION.
00019          FD  CARD-FILE
00020              RECORDING MODE IS F
00021              LABEL RECORDS ARE OMITTED
00022              RECORD CONTAINS 80 CHARACTERS
00023              DATA RECORD IS CARD-RECORD.
00024          01  CARD-RECORD.
00025              05  CARD-NAME                    PICTURE X(20).
00026              05  SALES          OCCURS 12 TIMES  PICTURE 9(4).
00027              05  FILLER                       PICTURE X(12).
00028          WORKING-STORAGE SECTION.
00029          77  SUB                          PICTURE IS S9(4)
00030              USAGE IS COMPUTATIONAL    SYNC         VALUE IS ZEROS.
00031          77  YEAR-TOTAL                   PICTURE IS S9(5)
00032              USAGE IS COMPUTATIONAL-3              VALUE IS ZEROS.
00033          PROCEDURE DIVISION.
00034              READY TRACE.
00035              OPEN INPUT CARD-FILE.
00036
00037          READ-A-CARD.
00038              READ CARD-FILE
00039                  AT END STOP RUN.
00040              DISPLAY '    INPUT RECORD ' CARD-RECORD.
00041              MOVE 1 TO SUB.
00042              MOVE ZEROS TO YEAR-TOTAL.
00043              PERFORM ANNUAL-TOTAL 11 TIMES.
00044
00045          ANNUAL-TOTAL.
00046              ADD SALES (SUB) TO YEAR-TOTAL.
00047
00048              IF YEAR-TOTAL > 50000
00049                  GO TO OVER-50000.
00050              ADD 1 TO SUB.
00051
00052          NOT-OVER-50000.
00053              DISPLAY '    SALES FOR ' CARD-NAME ' DID NOT EXCEED 50000'.
00054              GO TO READ-A-CARD.
00055
00056          OVER-50000.
00057              DISPLAY '    SALES FOR ' CARD-NAME   ' EXCEEDED 50000 AFTER '
00058                  SUB ' MONTHS'.
00059              GO TO READ-A-CARD.
```

Line number 45 appears in output of READY TRACE to indicate execution of the paragraph ANNUAL-TOTAL.

GO TO out of a PERFORM— totally unacceptable

Figure 6.3 Improper Exit from a PERFORM

134

Paragraph at line 45
was executed 12 times

Execution associated with John Smith

```
37   INPUT RECORD JOHN SMITH        0000000000000000000000000000000000000000000000000000
45   (00000012),52 ,
     SALES FOR JOHN SMITH           DID NOT EXCEED 50000

37   ,                              7000700070007000700070007000700070007000700070007000
45   (00000008),56 ,
     SALES FOR PETER BROWN          EXCEEDED 50000 AFTER 0008 MONTHS

37   INPUT RECORD HENRY JONES        8000800080008000800080008000800080008000800080008000
45   (00000007),56 ,
     SALES FOR HENRY JONES          EXCEEDED 50000 AFTER 0007 MONTHS

37   INPUT RECORD JOHN JOHNSON       1000100010001000100010001000100010001000100010001000
45   (00000013)
```

Execution for John Johnson

Figure 6.4 Output from Figure 6.3

expect ANNUAL-TOTAL to execute 12 times followed by the paragraph NOT-OVER-50000. In actuality, ANNUAL-TOTAL was executed 13 times, followed by a dump! This unhappy situation is caused by the GO TO statement of line 49 and is explained as follows: The PERFORM of line 43 established a linkage to and from the paragraph ANNUAL-TOTAL. Thus, after ANNUAL-TOTAL has executed 11 times, control is to return to the statement immediately following the PERFORM. Then, since ANNUAL-TOTAL is immediately under the PERFORM, it is executed a twelfth time, and if YEAR-TOTAL still does not exceed $50,000, control falls through to NOT-OVER-50000. This is exactly what happened for John Smith, the first record. (In effect, there is a "pointer" at the end of ANNUAL-TOTAL, directing flow to the paragraph NOT-OVER-50000.)

The second record executed ANNUAL-TOTAL only eight times, not 11, and then transferred control to the paragraph OVER-50000. Hence, the pointer at the end of the ANNUAL-TOTAL paragraph is caught in the middle of the PERFORM and still points back to logic in the Perform statement (i.e., control will no longer fall through to NOT-OVER-50000). There is no problem as long as YEAR-TOTAL exceeds $50,000 as was the case for Henry James. However, if YEAR-TOTAL fails to exceed $50,000, it will be impossible to "fall through" to NOT-OVER-50000, as was originally the case. Hence, John Johnson caused ANNUAL-TOTAL to be executed 13 times, at which point there is a data exception when SALES(13) is referenced.

Improper transfer out of performed routines is particularly difficult to debug in that the object code has actually been altered during execution of the program; in effect, the COBOL source program no longer represents the executed instructions. Adoption of structured programming conventions should eliminate this problem entirely; indeed, if one codes according to the principles of the discipline, one never encounters this situation. However, it is included in our list of common errors because there is inevitably at least one program in every shop with such a bug.

Access of an FD Area After a Write Statement

This is a mistake that every beginner makes at least once. Figure 6.5 is a COBOL program to read a card file and write a disk file. The records are read in line 58, moved in line 61, and written in line 63. Lines 62 and 64 display the contents of the output FD area before and after writing to the disk. What could be easier?

Figure 6.6 contains the display messages produced by Figure 6.5. Peter Jones is the first record shown. However, when the output FD area is displayed immediately after writing, we see John Smith rather than Peter Jones. Then Henry Brown is the next input record, and when the FD area is displayed after writing, Peter Jones reappears.

```
00001          IDENTIFICATION DIVISION.
00002          PROGRAM-ID.  ERRORS.
00003          AUTHOR.
00004             GRAUER.
00005          DATE-WRITTEN.
00006             DECEMBER 1976.
```

Figure 6.5 Access of an FD Area After a WRITE

```
00008          ENVIRONMENT DIVISION.
00009          CONFIGURATION SECTION.
00010          SOURCE-COMPUTER.
00011              IBM-370.
00012          OBJECT-COMPUTER.
00013              IBM-370.


00015          INPUT-OUTPUT SECTION.
00016          FILE-CONTROL.
00017              SELECT CARD-FILE
00018                  ASSIGN TO UT-S-SYSIN.
00019              SELECT DISK-FILE                    ┌ Establishes two
00020                  ASSIGN TO UT-S-DISKOUT          │ output buffers
00021                  RESERVE 1 ALTERNATE AREA.



00023          DATA DIVISION.
00024          FILE SECTION.


00026          FD  CARD-FILE
00027              RECORDING MODE IS F
00028              LABEL RECORDS ARE OMITTED
00029              RECORD CONTAINS 80 CHARACTERS
00030              DATA RECORD IS CARD-RECORD.

00032          01  CARD-RECORD                     PICTURE IS X(80).


00034          FD  DISK-FILE
00035              RECORDING MODE IS F
00036              LABEL RECORDS ARE OMITTED
00037              RECORD CONTAINS 80 CHARACTERS
00038              DATA RECORD IS DISK-RECORD.

00040          01  DISK-RECORD.
00041              05  DISK-NAME                   PICTURE IS X(20).
00042              05  FILLER                      PICTURE IS X(60).

00044          WORKING-STORAGE SECTION.
00045          77  WS-END-OF-FILE                  PICTURE IS X(3)
00046                              VALUE IS SPACES.



00048          PROCEDURE DIVISION.
00049              OPEN INPUT CARD-FILE
00050                   OUTPUT DISK-FILE.
00051              PERFORM READ-AND-WRITE THRU READ-AND-WRITE-EXIT
00052                  UNTIL WS-END-OF-FILE = 'YES'.
00053              CLOSE CARD-FILE
00054                    DISK-FILE.
00055              STOP RUN.
```

Figure 6.5 Access of an FD Area After a WRITE (continued)

137

```
00056
00057            READ-AND-WRITE.
00058               READ CARD-FILE
00059                  AT END MOVE 'YES' TO WS-END-OF-FILE
00060                     GO TO READ-AND-WRITE-EXIT.
00061               MOVE CARD-RECORD TO DISK-RECORD.
00062               DISPLAY DISK-NAME 'DISK-NAME BEFORE WRITING'.
00063               WRITE DISK-RECORD.
00064               DISPLAY DISK-NAME 'DISK-NAME AFTER WRITING'.
00065
00066            READ-AND-WRITE-EXIT.           Cannot reference record
00067               EXIT.                        after writing
```

Figure 6.5 Access of an FD Area After a WRITE (continued)

The explanation is quite simple. There are two output areas (i.e., output buffers), per the RESERVE 1 ALTERNATE AREA clause in line 21. One alternate area is also the default for most compilers, and the presence of an alternate area speeds I/O processing.)

Execution of a WRITE automatically causes a "pointer" to switch to the alternate area. The situation is shown schematically below:

Step 1: PETER JONES has been read and moved to I/O area. Line 62 executes: PETER JONES DISK-NAME BEFORE WRITING.

Step 2: PETER JONES has been written in line 63, causing I/O pointer to move. Line 64 executes: JOHN SMITH DISK-NAME AFTER WRITING.

Step 3: HENRY BROWN has been read as next record and moved to I/O area replacing JOHN SMITH. Line 62 executes: HENRY BROWN DISK-NAME BEFORE WRITING.

Step 4: HENRY BROWN has been written in line 63, causing I/O pointer to move. Line 64 executes: PETER JONES DISK-NAME AFTER WRITING.

138

```
PETER JONES          DISK-NAME BEFORE WRITING
JOHN SMITH           DISK-NAME AFTER WRITING
HENRY BROWN          DISK-NAME BEFORE WRITING
PETER JONES          DISK-NAME AFTER WRITING
MARION MILGROM       DISK-NAME BEFORE WRITING
HENRY BROWN          DISK-NAME AFTER WRITING
CHANDLER LAVOR       DISK-NAME BEFORE WRITING
MARION MILGROM       DISK-NAME AFTER WRITING
BENJAMIN LEE         DISK-NAME BEFORE WRITING
CHANDLER LAVOR       DISK-NAME AFTER WRITING
JOHN HENRY           DISK-NAME BEFORE WRITING
```

Figure 6.6 Output Produced by Figure 6.5

Misuse of Signed Numbers

EXAMPLE 1

The inclusion of an S in a numeric picture clause significantly affects the way in which the numeric field is subsequently manipulated. Inclusion of the S generally results in more efficient object code but can produce "strange" output if signed fields are printed directly. Omission of the S will produce incorrect algebraic results when negative numbers are expected.

Consider Figure 6.7, a COBOL program for a simplistic inventory system. Customer orders are always shipped if the remaining quantity on hand (i.e., after subtraction of the current order) is greater than zero (see COBOL lines 63 and 64). Processing is terminated when the remaining stock falls below zero. Initial stock is set at 100 via the VALUE clause in COBOL line 39.

Output for six customers is shown in Figure 6.8. Note well that the total amount shipped is 250, which is 150 units more than the initial allocation! The problem stems from the COBOL definition of WS-QUANTITY-ON-HAND as PIC 9(3) in line 39. *Simply stated, COBOL does not allow an unsigned numeric field to assume a negative value*; hence, the remaining stock on hand will never fall below zero. Subtraction is done according to regular algebraic rules in line 61, but any time the result of the subtraction becomes negative, the answer is automatically made positive.

John Jones is the first customer processed. After his order of 55 is taken, WS-QUANTITY-ON-HAND is equal to 45 (100 - 55). Next the 30 units of PETER SMITH are subtracted, leaving 15 as the value of WS-QUANTITY-ON-HAND. At this point, Jeff Borow enters the system, with an order of 40 units. We would expect the subtraction to yield a result of -25 (15 - 40). However, since WS-QUANTITY-ON-HAND was defined as an unsigned number, its value is always made positive. Consequently, the expected -25 is converted to +25 and processing continues.

139

```
00001          IDENTIFICATION DIVISION.
00002          PROGRAM-ID.  SIGNED.
00003          AUTHOR.      R. GRAUER.
00004          ENVIRONMENT DIVISION.
00005          CONFIGURATION SECTION.
00006          SOURCE-COMPUTER.
00007              IBM-370.
00008          OBJECT-COMPUTER.
00009              IBM-370.
00010          INPUT-OUTPUT SECTION.
00011          FILE-CONTROL.
00012              SELECT ORDER-FILE ASSIGN TO UT-S-SYSIN.
00013              SELECT PRINT-FILE ASSIGN TO UT-S-SYSOUT.
00014          DATA DIVISION.
00015          FILE SECTION.
00016          FD  ORDER-FILE
00017              RECORDING MODE IS F
00018              LABEL RECORDS ARE OMITTED
00019              RECORD CONTAINS 80 CHARACTERS
00020              DATA RECORD IS CARD.
00021          01  CARD.
00022              05  CUSTOMER-NAME         PIC X(20).
00023              05  CUSTOMER-ORDER        PIC 9(2).
00024              05  FILLER                PIC X(58).
00025          FD  PRINT-FILE
00026              RECORDING MODE IS F
00027              LABEL RECORDS ARE OMITTED
00028              RECORD CONTAINS 133 CHARACTERS
00029              DATA RECORD IS PRINT-LINE.
00030          01  PRINT-LINE.
00031              05  FILLER                PIC X(4).
00032              05  PRT-NAME              PIC X(20).
00033              05  FILLER                PIC X.
00034              05  PRT-CUSTOMER-AMOUNT   PIC 9(3).
00035              05  FILLER                PIC X(8).     Should be
00036              05  PRT-QUANTITY-LEFT     PIC 9(3).     defined with
00037              05  FILLER                PIC X(94).    a signed
00038          WORKING-STORAGE SECTION.                    picture
00039          77  WS-QUANTITY-ON-HAND       PIC 9(3)      VALUE 100.
00040          77  WS-EOF-SWITCH             PIC X(3)      VALUE SPACES.
00041          01  HDG-LINE.
00042              05  FILLER                PIC X(8)      VALUE SPACES.
00043              05  FILLER                PIC X(8)      VALUE 'CUSTOMER'.
00044              05  FILLER                PIC X(7)      VALUE SPACES.
00045              05  FILLER                PIC X(6)      VALUE 'AMOUNT'.
00046              05  FILLER                PIC X(3)      VALUE SPACES.
00047              05  FILLER                PIC X(10)     VALUE 'STOCK LEFT'.
00048              05  FILLER                PIC X(91)     VALUE SPACES.
00049          PROCEDURE DIVISION.
00050              OPEN INPUT ORDER-FILE
00051                  OUTPUT PRINT-FILE.
00052              WRITE PRINT-LINE FROM HDG-LINE.
00053              READ ORDER-FILE AT END MOVE 'YES' TO WS-EOF-SWITCH.
00054              PERFORM 010-PROCESS-ORDERS
00055                  UNTIL WS-EOF-SWITCH = 'YES' OR WS-QUANTITY-ON-HAND < 0.
00056              CLOSE ORDER-FILE
00057                  PRINT-FILE.
00058              STOP RUN.
00059
```

Figure 6.7 Misuse of Signed Numbers in Algebraic Calculations

```
00060                010-PROCESS-ORDERS.
00061                   SUBTRACT CUSTOMER-ORDER FROM WS-QUANTITY-ON-HAND.
00062
00063                   IF WS-QUANTITY-ON-HAND > 0        Result of subtraction can
00064                       PERFORM 020-SHIP-ORDER        never be negative
00065                   ELSE
00066                       DISPLAY 'STOCK SLIPPING BELOW 0 ' CUSTOMER-NAME.
00067                   READ ORDER-FILE AT END MOVE 'YES' TO WS-EOF-SWITCH.
00068
00069                020-SHIP-ORDER.
00070                   MOVE SPACES TO PRINT-LINE.
00071                   MOVE CUSTOMER-NAME TO PRT-NAME.
00072                   MOVE CUSTOMER-ORDER TO PRT-CUSTOMER-AMOUNT.
00073                   MOVE WS-QUANTITY-ON-HAND TO PRT-QUANTITY-LEFT.
00074                   WRITE PRINT-LINE.
```

Figure 6.7 Misuse of Signed Numbers in Algebraic Calculations (continued)

CUSTOMER	AMOUNT	STOCK LEFT
JOHN JONES	055	045
PETER SMITH	030	015
JEFF BOROW	040	025
STEVE BLOCK	020	005
RICH JAFFE	040	035
HENRY JAMES	065	030

Total quantity shipped = 250

Figure 6.8 Output from Figure 6.7

EXAMPLE 2

Although signed numeric pictures are essential to ensure correct algebraic results, a different problem can occur if signed numbers are printed directly via an EXHIBIT statement. Consider Figure 6.9 and its associated output (Figure 6.10). We would expect the results of both FIELD-B and FIELD-D to be 5. Unfortunately, the latter shows as E. Complete explanation requires knowledge of internal representation of data and the assembler OI (Or Immediate) instruction. Suffice it to say that signed numbers are necessary to ensure algebraic correctness but should not be used for printed output. (Instead, the results in a signed field should be moved to an edit field containing the symbols DB, CR, or —).

Misuse of the SEARCH Verb

SEARCH and SEARCH ALL, denoting a linear and a binary search, respectively, are available with most compilers. A binary search requires the table to be searched to have its keys in sequence (either ascending or descending), whereas no special order is necessary for a linear search. Essentially, the binary procedure eliminates "half a table" in each attempt at finding a match. A linear search, on the other hand, looks at one element at a time. Obviously, the larger the table, the more advantageous the binary search becomes. For example, in a table of 100 elements, the binary approach would

141

```
00001               IDENTIFICATION DIVISION.
00002               PROGRAM-ID.    SIGNED2.
00003               AUTHOR.  GRAUER AND CRAWFORD.
00004               ENVIRONMENT DIVISION.
00005               CONFIGURATION SECTION.
00006               SOURCE-COMPUTER.    IBM-370.
00007               OBJECT-COMPUTER.    IBM-370.
00008               DATA DIVISION.
00009               WORKING-STORAGE SECTION.
00010               77  FIELD-A                    PIC S9   VALUE +2.
00011               77  FIELD-B                    PIC 9    VALUE 3.
00012               77  FIELD-C                    PIC 9    VALUE 3.
00013               77  FIELD-D                    PIC S9   VALUE +2.

00015               PROCEDURE DIVISION.

00017                   ADD FIELD-A TO FIELD-B.
00018                   EXHIBIT NAMED FIELD-B.

00020                   ADD FIELD-C TO FIELD-D.
00021                   EXHIBIT NAMED FIELD-D.

00023                   STOP RUN.
```

Figure 6.9 Misuse of Signed Numbers via EXHIBIT Statement

```
FIELD-B = 5
FIELD-D = E
```

Figure 6.10 Output of Figure 6.9

require no more than seven comparisons, whereas a linear search could take as many as 100. In a 1000-element table, the corresponding numbers are 10 and 1000.

The key to implementing a binary search is that the incoming table have its keys in sequence. Failure to do this could cause the binary search to fail. Consider the COBOL program of Figure 6.11 and its associated output in Figure 6.12. In the COBOL program a table of location codes has been established in lines 20-29. The ASCENDING KEY clause of line 32 requires that the codes be in ascending order. The first nine codes are fine, but the tenth code (045 for DENVER) is out of sequence. SEARCH ALL is implemented in COBOL line 38 for New York, and again in line 43 for Denver. The first search is successful, the second is not, even though a linear search for Denver in COBOL line 49 was successful.

Admittedly, this particular example is contrived, in that a cursory examination of Figure 6.11 quickly reveals that the location codes are out of sequence. However, we have seen countless instances where a binary search fails because the table is not in order. This is particularly true in fluid situations where additional codes are constantly added to existing tables. The solution is obvious and easy to implement. We advocate that a housekeeping routine, to verify proper sequence of table codes, be incorporated into any and all programs utilizing a binary search.

Figure 6.11 also contains a common error in relation to the linear search— failure to initialize the associated index. A linear search is initiated in COBOL lines 49

142

```
00001          IDENTIFICATION DIVISION.
00002          PROGRAM-ID.
00003             ERRORS.
00004          AUTHOR.
00005             GRAUER.
00006          INSTALLATION.
00007             CITY UNIVERSITY OF NEW YORK
00008          DATE-WRITTEN.
00009             DECEMBER, 1976.
00010          ENVIRONMENT DIVISION.
00011          CONFIGURATION SECTION.
00012          SOURCE-COMPUTER.
00013             IBM-370.
00014          OBJECT-COMPUTER.
00015             IBM-370.
00016
00017          DATA DIVISION.
00018          WORKING-STORAGE SECTION.
00019          01   LOCATION-VALUE.
00020               05   FILLER               PIC X(16) VALUE '010ATLANTA       '.
00021               05   FILLER               PIC X(16) VALUE '020BOSTON        '.
00022               05   FILLER               PIC X(16) VALUE '030CHICAGO       '.
00023               05   FILLER               PIC X(16) VALUE '040DETROIT       '.
00024               05   FILLER               PIC X(16) VALUE '050KANSAS CITY   '.
00025               05   FILLER               PIC X(16) VALUE '060LOS ANGELES   '.
00026               05   FILLER               PIC X(16) VALUE '070NEW YORK      '.
00027               05   FILLER               PIC X(16) VALUE '080PHILADELPHIA  '.
00028               05   FILLER               PIC X(16) VALUE '090SAN FRANCISCO'.
00029               05   FILLER               PIC X(16) VALUE '045DENVER        '.
00030          01   LOCATION-TABLE REDEFINES LOCATION-VALUE.
00031               05   LOCATION OCCURS 10 TIMES
00032                    ASCENDING KEY IS LOCATION-CODE
00033                      INDEXED BY LOCATION-INDEX.
00034                    10   LOCATION-CODE   PIC X(3).
00035                    10   LOCATION-NAME   PIC X(13).
00036          PROCEDURE DIVISION.
00037          *SHOW BINARY SEARCH WORKS FOR NEW YORK
00038               SEARCH ALL LOCATION,
00039                    AT END DISPLAY '*ERROR FOR NY IN BINARY SEARCH'
00040                    WHEN LOCATION-CODE (LOCATION-INDEX) = '070'
00041                    DISPLAY 'BINARY SEARCH OK FOR NEW YORK'.
00042          * SHOW BINARY SEARCH FAILS FOR DENVER
00043               SEARCH ALL LOCATION,
00044                    AT END DISPLAY  '*ERROR FOR DENVER IN BINARY SEARCH'
00045                    WHEN LOCATION-CODE (LOCATION-INDEX) = '045'
00046                    DISPLAY 'BINARY SEARCH OK FOR DENVER'.
00047          *SHOW LINEAR SEARCH WORKS FOR DENVER
00048               SET LOCATION-INDEX TO 1.
00049               SEARCH LOCATION,
00050                    AT END DISPLAY  '*ERROR IN LINEAR SEARCH FOR DENVER'
00051                    WHEN LOCATION-CODE (LOCATION-INDEX) = '045'
00052                    DISPLAY 'LINEAR SEARCH OK FOR DENVER'.
00053          *SHOW LINEAR SEARCH FAILS FOR BOSTON IF INDEX NOT RESET
00054               SEARCH LOCATION,
00055                    AT END DISPLAY  '*ERROR IN LINEAR SEARCH FOR BOSTON'
00056                    WHEN LOCATION-CODE (LOCATION-INDEX) = '020'
00057                    DISPLAY 'LINEAR SEARCH OK FOR BOSTON'.
00058               STOP RUN.
```

Code is out
of sequence

Requires codes to be in
ascending sequence

SET statement missing

Figure 6.11 SEARCH Program

143

```
BINARY SEARCH OK FOR NEW YORK
*ERROR FOR DENVER IN BINARY SEARCH
LINEAR SEARCH OK FOR DENVER
*ERROR IN LINEAR SEARCH FOR BOSTON
```

Figure 6.12 Output of SEARCH Program

and 54 for Denver and Boston, respectively. As can be seen from Figure 6.12, the linear search for Denver was successful, whereas the search for Boston failed. It is the responsibility of the programmer to establish an entry point within the table for a linear search. This was done for Denver, by the SET statement in line 48. It was *not* done for Boston; thus, the search of line 54 begins with whatever value happens to be in LOCATION-INDEX. LOCATION-INDEX was last affected by the linear search for Denver. Hence, since Denver is past Boston in the table, a match is not found and the AT END condition is reached.

SUMMARY

Debugging is a fact of life, so much so that the average programmer probably spends as much time on debugging as on initial coding. Unlike the COBOL language, however, debugging per se cannot be taught explicitly. A bug is found in much the same way as a detective solves a crime, by trial and error, and by perseverance. The criminal is always said to make a fatal mistake; so it is with bugs, because the same errors occur continually albeit in different disguises.

We reemphasize that a most important part of debugging is knowing what to look for. This chapter dealt with errors in COBOL implementation and common misconceptions about the operation of basic COBOL elements. Additional bugs, which appear constantly in one form or another at the source level, are listed below. We firmly believe that a conscious awareness of these kinds of errors will improve the reader's debugging skill.

1. *Failure to initialize (reinitialize) a counter.* All programmers have at one time forgotten to initialize a 77-level entry used as a counter. The usual result is a 0C7 ABEND (data exception), which is relatively easy to find and is discussed in Chapter Eight. A more subtle error is the failure to *reinitialize* counters when control breaks are called for. Consider the sales report below, sorted by location first, then salesperson within location.

```
LOCATION:  ATLANTA
                SALESPERSON          YEAR-TO-DATE-SALES
                ADAMS                      $10,000
                BAKER                      $50,000
                SMITH                      $40,000
                      TOTAL SALES FOR ATLANTA = $100,000
```

```
LOCATION:  BOSTON
           SALESPERSON          YEAR-TO-DATE-SALES
             BROWN                   $15,000
             JONES                   $20,000
             TURNER                  $ 8,000
             YOUNG                   $60,000
           TOTAL SALES FOR BOSTON = $203,000
```

The correct total for Boston should be $103,000, not $203,000. The problem is caused by failure to reinitialize the district sales total when a new location was encountered. Problems involving control breaks are often best solved using Report Writer (see Appendix C).

2. *Invalid subscript or index*. One of the most common errors and very difficult to find, because the result can take many forms. For example, one can exceed the bounds of a table during a table lookup. One can also exceed the declared size of a table during its initialization and thereby overlay a portion of code. Both problems stem from the freedom permitted by the compiler-generated instructions. Consider

```
05   TABLE-ENTRY OCCURS 20 TIMES      PIC X(10).
```

This OCCURS clause sets aside a 200 (20 X 10) byte table in storage. Logically, we should be permitted to reference only entries with subscripts of 1 to 20. Most compilers, however, *do not* insert machine code to check on the validity of a subscript. Thus, if we tried to reference TABLE-ENTRY (21), we would access the first 10 bytes past the table. In similar fashion, TABLE-ENTRY (0) would point to the 10 bytes immediately before the actual table. The best defense against errors of this sort is for the programmer to insert his own Procedure Division code to check on the validity of subscripts, with appropriate error messages.

3. *Errors in looping*. The establishment and execution of a loop requires four basic steps:

    a. Initialization of a counter.
    b. Incrementing a counter.
    c. Comparison of the counter to a predetermined value.
    d. An appropriate branch.

Regardless of whether the programmer establishes his own loop or utilizes various features of COBOL to do it for him, these four basic steps must be accomplished in one way or another. A frequent error occurs when a loop is executed an improper number of times, often one too many or too few. Consider the following PERFORM statement

145

```
PERFORM  COMPUTE-YEAR-TOTAL
    VARYING  MONTH-SUB  FROM  1  BY  1  UNTIL  MONTH-SUB = 12.
```

The routine COMPUTE-YEAR-TOTAL will be performed 11 times, not 12, because COBOL does the comparison *before* the branch. Thus, after the routine has been performed 11 times, MONTH-SUB is incremented from 11 to 12. Then since MONTH-SUB = 12, the perform is terminated.

4. *Errors in COBOL implementation.* Misconception about the operation of basic COBOL verbs is one of the more difficult problems to solve. We summarize the errors discussed in this chapter and add a few more:

    a. Missing and/or extra period.
    b. Access of an FD area after a WRITE statement.
    c. Improper exit from a performed routine.
    d. Improper use of the SEARCH verb.
    e. Incorrect use of a GROUP MOVE (see Figures 7.4 and 7.5).
    f. Difficulty with signed numbers.
    g. Improper use of nested IF statements.
    h. Misuse of Boolean functions in an IF statement.

5. *Failure to set/reset switches.* This is a difficulty usually prevalent in structured programs since these are heavily dependent on logic switches. Errors of this type are usually difficult to find, because their effects can take many forms. There is not much we can offer in the way of advice except a rule of thumb: whenever specific action is taken because a switch is turned on, the switch should be immediately turned off. We repeat, this is only a rule of thumb and undoubtedly has many exceptions.

6. *Improper linkage to a subroutine.* Although the COBOL statement to call a subprogram presents no great difficulty in and of itself, improper linkage often leads to trouble. Specifically, the arguments in both the calling and called program must appear in the same order and should usually have identical pictures. Moreover, if a group item (e.g., an 01 record) is passed as a parameter, it is often essential that the elementary items in the group item be defined identically in both programs. We suggest, therefore, that any group item used as a parameter be defined in the Data Division via a COPY statement.

7. *End and/or beginning file conditions.* These "logic" errors are usually prevalent in file maintenance applications, particularly where multiple files are concerned. We have seen untold examples of complex maintenance programs which "work" 99 percent of the time, but fail if a unique combination of events occurs (e.g., the key of the last record on the transaction

file is higher than the last record in the old master file, etc.). The structured approach should minimize these errors.

As a parting word of advice, *if all else fails, know when to stop.* Everyone reaches a point where the coffee tastes bitter, the cigarettes are lousy, and no further productive thinking is possible. Stop! Put the problem away! Go home, get a good night's sleep or whatever, and get a fresh start in the morning. You'll be surprised at what a difference a few hours can make. Moreover, the mind is funny in that the subconscious continues to work at a problem, and as often as not, the solution will come when you least expect it.

PROBLEMS

1. Insert or remove a period(s) so that the given alignment will correspond with the COBOL interpretation:

(a) IF A > B
      MOVE C TO D
      MOVE E TO F
  MOVE G TO H.

(b) READ TRANSACTION-FILE
      AT END MOVE 'YES' TO READ-SWITCH.
          MOVE 'YES' TO EOF-SWITCH.

(c) IF A > B
      ADD 1 TO COUNT-FIELD.
      IF C > D
        ADD 1 TO SECOND-FIELD.
  MOVE X TO Y.

(d) IF A > B
      MOVE C TO D.
      MOVE E TO F.

(e) IF WRITE-SWITCH = 'YES'
    WRITE ISAM-RECORD
        INVALID KEY MOVE 'YES' TO INVALID-SWITCH.
         MOVE 'NO' TO WRITE-SWITCH.

2. Realign the following statements so that your indentation matches the compiler interpretation. Also, align the ELSE clause under its associated IF. Retain all periods.

(a) READ CARD-FILE
      AT END MOVE 'YES' TO END-OF-FILE.
        ADD 1 TO RECORDS-READ.

(b) IF A > B
       IF C > D
          ADD 1 TO X
       ELSE
          IF E > F
             ADD 1 TO Y
     ELSE
       ADD 1 TO Z.

(c) IF A > B, IF C > D, MOVE 1 TO X,
    ELSE MOVE 1 TO Y, ELSE MOVE 1 TO Z.

(d) IF A > B
       MOVE X TO Y.
       MOVE A TO B.
       MOVE C TO D.
       MOVE E TO F.

(e) COMPUTE AA = BB + CC
         ON SIZE ERROR ADD 1 TO ERROR-COUNTER.
         PERFORM ERROR-ROUTINE.

(f) WRITE ISAM-RECORD
         INVALID KEY PERFORM ERROR-ROUTINE.
         PERFORM PROCESS-TRANSACTION.
         PERFORM WRITE-EXCEPTION-REPORT.

3. Given the Data Division entries

```
01   FIRST-SET-OF-COUNTERS.
     05   COUNTER-A    DISPLAY    PIC 9(3).
     05   COUNTER-B    DISPLAY    PIC 9(3).
     05   COUNTER-C    DISPLAY    PIC 9(3).


01   SECOND-SET-OF-COUNTERS.
     05   COUNTER-D    COMP       PIC S9(4).
     05   COUNTER-E    COMP       PIC S9(4).
     05   COUNTER-F    COMP       PIC S9(4).


01   THIRD-SET-OF-COUNTERS.
     05   COUNTER-G    COMP-3     PIC 9(5).
     05   COUNTER-H    COMP-3     PIC 9(5).
     05   COUNTER-I    COMP-3     PIC 9(5).
```

is there anything wrong with the following?

(a) MOVE ZEROS TO FIRST-SET-OF-COUNTERS.

(b) MOVE ZEROS TO SECOND-SET-OF-COUNTERS.

(c) MOVE ZEROS TO THIRD-SET-OF-COUNTERS.

4. The following is *not* a typographical error but rather an example of the importance of a missing period. The EXHIBIT statement below shows both switches to contain spaces. Why? (*Hint*: Count the columns.)

```
WORKING-STORAGE SECTION.
77   FIRST-FILE-SWITCH                     PIC X(3) VALUE SPACES.
77   SECOND-FILE-SWITCH                    PIC X(3) VALUE SPACES.


PROCEDURE DIVISION.
        OPEN INPUT CARD-FILE.
        READ CARD-FILE,
            AT END MOVE 'NO' TO FIRST-FILE-SWITCH, SECOND-FILE-SWITCH.
        MOVE 'YES' TO FIRST-FILE-SWITCH, SECOND-FILE-SWITCH.
        EXHIBIT NAMED FIRST-FILE-SWITCH SECOND-FILE-SWITCH.
```

5. Do you think that debugging is a skill which can be easily taught? If so, how would you go about teaching it?

6. Do you think that debugging is better accomplished at the source level or by reading a dump? Give specific examples from your own experience to support your conclusion.

7. Select an error from our summary list, then take an existing program and insert the bug. Have a colleague do the same, then exchange programs and find each other's bugs. Do this several times.

Assembler Fundamentals

OVERVIEW

Chapter Six dealt exclusively with debugging at the source level. There are times, however, when the most expeditious way to debug a program is to begin from a dump. This type of debugging relies heavily on concepts of number systems, internal data representation, base displacement addressing, and instruction formats. The reader is assumed to be familiar with the binary and hexadecimal number systems. All other topics will be covered in this chapter.

As the reader may guess, we are progressing toward a discussion of basic assembler concepts. Indeed, the question of whether the COBOL applications programmer should have a knowledge of assembler language is open to debate. We answer with an emphatic yes, but there are those who would disagree, reasoning that one can invariably find someone to debug a program. The authors, however, are of the firm belief that even a superficial knowledge of the machine on which one is working greatly enhances the capabilities of the individual with respect to both debugging and efficiency considerations. This is readily appreciated when one realizes that the computer does not execute COBOL instructions per se, but rather the machine language statements generated by the COBOL compiler.

The chapter begins with discussion of internal data representation. Packed, binary, zoned-decimal, and floating-point numbers are covered, as is the COBOL USAGE clause. The relevance of this material to debugging is established through a COBOL example. Base displacement addressing and instruction formats are presented next. The chapter concludes with a series of guidelines for efficient COBOL coding.

INTERNAL REPRESENTATION OF DATA

The smallest addressable unit of storage is the *byte*. Each byte consists of 9 *bits* (binary digits), 8 of which are used to represent data and a ninth bit, known as the *parity bit*, which is used for internal checking of data. The parity bit is of little concern to the programmer and is not discussed.

Three formats are commonly used by the IBM COBOL programmer. These are DISPLAY, packed (or internal decimal), and binary. A fourth form, floating point, is also available and is used in special instances.

EBCDIC

Data represented according to EBCDIC (Extended Binary Coded Decimal Interchange Code) use specific bit combinations of 0's and 1's to denote different characters. Since a byte contains 8 data bits, each of which can assume either a 0 or 1, there are 2^8 = 256 different combinations for a given byte. Table 7.1 displays the bit combinations for letters, numbers, and some special characters.

Table 7.1 shows both binary and hexadecimal representation. In actuality, all internal workings of a computer are in binary. For human convenience, as well as for paper conservation, internal representations are shown in hex, and the reader is assumed to be familiar with hexadecimal notation and arithmetic. Hexadecimal is chosen as a shorthand over decimal because exactly 4 binary digits equal 1 hex digit. Thus, conversion between the two bases (i.e., binary and hex) is immediate since 16 is an exact power of 2 (i.e., 2^4 = 16). The reader should realize that octal (base 8) would also be a suitable shorthand; indeed, there are several octal machines on the market.

Yes, reader, there is rhyme and reason to Table 7.1, at least where the letters and numbers are concerned. The 8 bits of a byte are divided into a zone and numeric portion as follows:

The four leftmost bits constitute the zone portion, the four rightmost bits make up the digit portion. Notice from Table 7.1 that the letters A through I all have the same zone (1100 in binary or C in hex). Note further that the letters J through R,

Table 7.1   EBCDIC Configuration for Letters, Numbers, and Some Special Characters

Letters:

Character	EBCDIC Binary	EBCDIC Hex
A	1100 0001	C1
B	1100 0010	C2
C	1100 0011	C3
D	1100 0100	C4
E	1100 0101	C5
F	1100 0110	C6
G	1100 0111	C7
H	1100 1000	C8
I	1100 1001	C9
J	1101 0001	D1
K	1101 0010	D2
L	1101 0011	D3
M	1101 0100	D4
N	1101 0101	D5
O	1101 0110	D6
P	1101 0111	D7
Q	1101 1000	D8
R	1101 1001	D9
S	1110 0010	E2
T	1110 0011	E3
U	1110 0100	E4
V	1110 0101	E5
W	1110 0110	E6
X	1110 0111	E7
Y	1110 1000	E8
Z	1110 1001	E9

Numbers:

Character	EBCDIC Binary	EBCDIC Hex
0	1111 0000	F0
1	1111 0001	F1
2	1111 0010	F2
3	1111 0011	F3
4	1111 0100	F4
5	1111 0101	F5
6	1111 0110	F6
7	1111 0111	F7
8	1111 1000	F8
9	1111 1001	F9

Special Characters:

Character	EBCDIC Binary	EBCDIC Hex
Blank	0100 0000	40
.	0100 1011	4B
(	0100 1101	4D
+	0100 1110	4E
$	0101 1011	5B
*	0101 1100	5C
)	0101 1101	5D
—	0110 0000	60
/	0110 0001	61
,	0110 1011	6B
'	0111 1101	7D
=	0111 1110	7E

S through Z, and the digits 0 through 9 also have the same zones: D, E, and F, respectively.

Consider the word 'COBOL' in EBCDIC. Since COBOL contains five characters, five bytes of storage are required. Using Table 7.1, COBOL would appear internally as shown in Figure 7.1.

(Binary)	11000011	11010110	11000010	11010110	11010011
(Hex)	C3	D6	C2	D6	D3

Figure 7.1 EBCDIC Representation of "COBOL"

Now suppose that we wanted to represent the number 678 in EBCDIC. This time, three bytes are required and, again using Table 7.1, we get Figure 7.2.

(Binary)	11110110	11110111	11111000
(Hex)	F6	F7	F8

Figure 7.2 EBCDIC Representation of "678"

152

The zone portion of each byte is the same in Figure 7.2, and does it not seem inherently wasteful to use half of each byte for the zone, when, in a numeric field, that zone is always 1111? The solution is an alternative form of data representation, known as packed format.

Packed Format

The *packed format* is used to represent numeric data more concisely. Essentially, it stores two numeric digits in one byte by eliminating the zone. This is done throughout except in the rightmost byte, which contains a numeric digit in the zone portion and the sign of the entire number in the digit portion. The letters C or F denote a positive number, and the letter D represents a negative number. Figure 7.3 shows both positive and negative packed representations of the numbers 678 and 112233. Only two bytes are required to represent the number 678 in packed format, compared to three bytes in EBCDIC (Figure 7.2). Note, however, that the packed representation of numbers with an even number of digits (e.g., 112233) always contains an extra half-byte of zeros.

Both the EBCDIC and packed formats are said to represent variable-length fields in that the number of bytes required depends on the data that are stored. "COBOL" requires five bytes for EBCDIC representation, "IBM" only three. "112233" takes four bytes in packed format, "678" only two.

```
(a)   Positive configuration (112233):
00000001   00010010   00100011   00111100   (Binary)
   01         12         23         3C       (Hex)

(b)   Negative configuration (112233):
00000001   00010010   00100011   00111101   (Binary)
   01         12         23         3D       (Hex)

(c)   Positive configuration (678):
            01100111   10001100   (Binary)
               67         8C       (Hex)

(d)   Negative configuration (678):
            01100111   10001101   (Binary)
               67         8D       (Hex)
```

Figure 7.3 Packed Representation

Binary Format

Numeric data can also be stored in fixed-length units as binary numbers. Two bytes (half-word), four bytes (full-word), or eight bytes (double-word) are used depending on the size of a decimal number according to the rule:

$$
\begin{array}{ll}
\text{Up to 4 decimal digits:} & \text{2 bytes} \\
\text{5 to 9 decimal digits:} & \text{4 bytes} \\
\text{10 to 18 decimal digits:} & \text{8 bytes}
\end{array}
$$

Some explanation is in order. Consider a half-word (16 bits). The largest positive number that can be represented is a 0 and fifteen 1's (the high-order zero indicates a positive number), which equals $2^{15} - 1$, or 32,767. Any four-digit decimal number will fit in a half-word, since the largest four-digit decimal number is only 9999. However, not all five-digit numbers will fit, hence the limitation to four digits in a half-word.

The largest binary number that can be stored in a full-word is $2^{31} - 1$, or 2,147,483,647 in decimal, hence the limit of nine decimal digits in a full-word. In similar fashion, a limit of 18 decimal digits is obtained for a double-word.

Two's-Complement Notation

The sign of a binary number is indicated by its leftmost (high-order) bit. This is true regardless of whether the number occupies a half-word, word, or double-word. *A 0 in the sign bit indicates a positive number; a 1 means that the number is negative and stored in two's-complement notation.*

The two's-complement of a number is obtained in two steps:

1. Reverse all bits; wherever there is a 0, make it 1, and wherever a 1 occurs, make it 0.

2. Add 1 to your answer from step 1.

For example, suppose that we want the two's complement of 01101111:

Step 1:   Reverse all bits   10010000
Step 2:   Add 1 to answer from step 1 +   1
                                                   ―――――――
                                                  10010001

Thus, the two's-complement of 01101111 is 10010001. As a check on the answer, simply add the original number and its calculated complement. The result should be all 0's and a high-order carry of 1:

Check: 01101111
                              +10010001
                            ――――――――――――
high-order carry ────▸ 1 00000000

Now that we can determine the sign of a number in storage and calculate its two's-complement if necessary, consider the following half-words in storage:

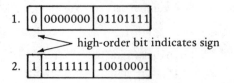

1. | 0 | 0000000 | 01101111 |

                └──▸ high-order bit indicates sign

2. | 1 | 1111111 | 10010001 |

In the first example, the number is positive, as indicated by the high-order bit. Accordingly, its decimal value is simply +111. The second example, however, has a high-order bit of 1, indicating a negative number, and further that the number itself is stored in two's-complement. In order to get its decimal value, we must first get the two's-complement of the number, then put a minus sign in front of the answer. You should get −111.

The importance of two's-complement representation will be made evident in the discussion of the Group Move example, which follows shortly.

Floating Point

Many excellent COBOL programmers go through entire careers without encountering floating-point data. However, this feature is useful in applications requiring either very large or very small quantities; hence, we present some introductory material. There are two kinds of floating-point numbers, denoted as COMPUTATIONAL-1 (short precision) and COMPUTATIONAL-2 (long precision). Both forms consist of a sign bit, a characteristic (exponent), and a mantissa (the digits in the number itself). Short-precision floating-point numbers (COMP-1) are assigned a full-word in storage; long-precision numbers (COMP-2) occupy a double-word. Consider the COMP-1 representation for the decimal number 133 shown below in both hex and binary.

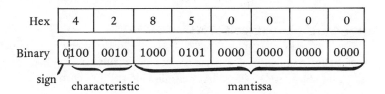

The first bit represents the sign of the entire number; a 0 indicates a positive number, and a 1 denotes a negative number. Unlike binary numbers, negative numbers are *not* stored in their two's-complement. The characteristic (or exponent) consists of the next 7 bits and is 66 in this example. Exponents are stored with a bias of 64, so the true exponent is always obtained by subtracting 64 from the stored exponent. Thus, the true exponent in this example is 2 (66 − 64). The remaining 24 bits are the mantissa, the actual digits of the number, expressed as a hexadecimal fraction. To obtain the value of the number, we take the mantissa (a fraction in base 16) and raise it to the appropriate power (i.e., shift the decimal point the number of places equal to the exponent). The example above has a mantissa of .850000 and an exponent of 2; hence, the true number is $(85.0000)_{16} = (133)_{10}$.

Consider some additional examples:

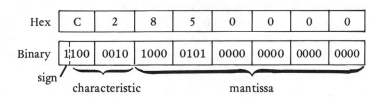

This example is exactly like the first, except that the sign bit is 1, meaning a negative number of $(-85.0000)_{16}$ or $(-133)_{10}$.

Now consider a negative exponent (i.e., a negative number results after subtraction of 64):

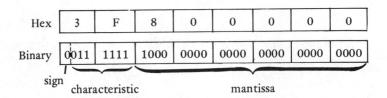

The sign bit is 0; thus, the entire number is positive. The stored characteristic is 63; hence, the true exponent is -1 ($63 - 64$). A negative exponent means that the decimal point is moved to the left instead of to the right. Thus, the actual number is $(.080)_{16} = (.03125)_{10}$.

Long-precision floating-point numbers (COMP-2) are stored in a double-word (64 bits). The allocation for the sign bit and characteristic is exactly as with short precision; the difference is in the mantissa. Long-precision floating-point numbers use the extra 32 bits for the mantissa, making a total of 56 bits for the mantissa. The other 8 bits are used for the sign and characteristic, as described previously.

THE COBOL USAGE CLAUSE AND DATA FORMATS

The COBOL USAGE clause explicitly specifies how data are to be stored internally. (Omission of the clause causes default to DISPLAY, which can result in inefficient object code.) Consider the following COBOL entries:

```
77 FIELD-A      PICTURE IS 9(4)
                USAGE IS DISPLAY           VALUE IS 1.

77 FIELD-B      PICTURE IS 9(4)
                USAGE IS COMPUTATIONAL-3   VALUE IS 1.

77 FIELD-C      PICTURE IS 9(4)
                USAGE IS COMPUTATIONAL     VALUE IS 1.

77 FIELD-D      PICTURE IS 9(4)
                USAGE IS COMPUTATIONAL-1   VALUE IS 1.

77 FIELD-E      PICTURE IS 9(4)
                USAGE IS COMPUTATIONAL-2   VALUE IS 1.
```

A numeric constant of 1 is defined in every instance. However, each entry has a different usage specified, hence the fields will have very different internal formats. In particular, USAGE IS DISPLAY indicates storage in zoned-decimal (EBCDIC) format, COMPUTATIONAL-3 packed format, COMPUTATIONAL binary format, COMPUTATIONAL-1 short precision floating point, and COMPUTATIONAL-2 long precision floating point.

FIELD-A occupies four bytes of storage and stores the constant 1 in zoned decimal format, with high-order zeros. The internal representation of FIELD-A, shown in hex, is as follows:

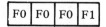

FIELD-B occupies three bytes of storage and stores the constant 1 in packed format, again with high-order zeroes. Internal representation of FIELD-B, shown in hex, is as follows:

FIELD-C is stored as a binary number with the number of bytes determined as per previous discussion. Thus, FIELD-C will occupy two bytes of storage as follows:

in binary: | 00000000 | 00000001 |

in hex: | 00 | 01 |

FIELD-D and FIELD-E are both stored as floating-point numbers, requiring four and eight bytes, respectively. The sign bit and exponent are the same for both fields, but FIELD-E has an additional 32 bits allocated to the mantissa. Hex representations for each field are as follows:

FIELD-D: | 41 | 10 | 00 | 00 |

FIELD-E: | 41 | 10 | 00 | 00 | 00 | 00 | 00 | 00 |

COBOL IMPLICATIONS—DEBUGGING

We have established several distinct forms of internal data representation—further that the COBOL USAGE clause determines actual storage allocation. This limited knowledge of assembler considerations is immediately applicable to COBOL debugging. Consider Figure 7.4, a COBOL listing which illustrates both *correct* and *incorrect* ways of initializing group fields. The output produced by Figure 7.4 is shown in Figure 7.5. The values of FIRST-BINARY, FIRST-DISPLAY, and FIRST-PACKED are all 1, as expected. The value of SECOND-DISPLAY is also 1, but the value of SECOND-BINARY is 3855, and attempted execution of statement 47 (to calculate SECOND-PACKED) resulted in job termination and subsequent dump. Why? Simply stated, the difficulties with SECOND-BINARY and SECOND-PACKED are caused by the group move of line 40. *All group moves are treated as alphanumeric moves.* Hence, the "wrong" kind of zeros are moved to SECOND-BINARY and SECOND-PACKED; in effect, these fields are not initialized to zero at all.

```
00001          IDENTIFICATION DIVISION.
00002          PROGRAM-ID.   GROUPMV.
00003          AUTHOR.     R GRAUER.


00006          ENVIRONMENT DIVISION.
00007          CONFIGURATION SECTION.
00008          SOURCE-COMPUTER.      IBM-370.
00009          OBJECT-COMPUTER.      IBM-370.


00012          DATA DIVISION.
00013          WORKING-STORAGE SECTION.
00014          77  FILLER              PIC X(14)   VALUE 'WS BEGINS HERE'.
00015          01  FIRST-GROUP-FIELD.
00016              05  FIRST-DISPLAY   PIC 9(4).
00017              05  FIRST-BINARY    PIC 9(4)    COMP.
00018              05  FIRST-PACKED    PIC 9(4)    COMP-3.

00020          01  SECOND-GROUP-FIELD.
00021              05  SECOND-DISPLAY  PIC 9(4).
00022              05  SECOND-BINARY   PIC 9(4)    COMP.
00023              05  SECOND-PACKED   PIC 9(4)    COMP-3.


00025          PROCEDURE DIVISION.
00026        * CORRECT INITIALIZATION
00027            MOVE ZEROS TO FIRST-BINARY.
00028            ADD 1 TO FIRST-BINARY.
00029            DISPLAY 'FIRST-BINARY = ' FIRST-BINARY.

00031            MOVE ZEROS TO FIRST-DISPLAY.
00032            ADD 1 TO FIRST-DISPLAY.
00033            DISPLAY 'FIRST-DISPLAY = ' FIRST-DISPLAY.

00035            MOVE ZEROS TO FIRST-PACKED.
00036            ADD 1 TO FIRST-PACKED.
00037            DISPLAY 'FIRST-PACKED = ' FIRST-PACKED.

00039        *INCORRECT INITIALIZATION
00040            MOVE ZEROS TO SECOND-GROUP-FIELD.
00041            ADD 1 TO SECOND-BINARY.
00042            DISPLAY 'SECOND-BINARY = ' SECOND-BINARY.

00044            ADD 1 TO SECOND-DISPLAY.
00045            DISPLAY 'SECOND-DISPLAY = ' SECOND-DISPLAY.

00047            ADD 1 TO SECOND-PACKED.
00048            DISPLAY 'SECOND-PACKED = ' SECOND-PACKED.
00049            STOP RUN.
```

Figure 7.4 Example of a Group Move

The preceding discussion provides a technically correct, albeit unsatisfying, explanation of the problem. Nevertheless, it is typical of the wording found in COBOL manuals, where discussion contains examples of valid and invalid moves, padding, truncation, and so on. This is followed by a one-sentence disclaimer stating that the rules

158

```
FIRST-BINARY    =   0001
FIRST-DISPLAY   =   0001
FIRST-PACKED    =   0001
SECOND-BINARY   =   3855
SECOND-DISPLAY  =   0001
```

Figure 7.5 Output of Figure 7.4

above apply only to elementary moves and that group moves are considered as alphanumeric.

The net effect is to leave the student with a correct, but thoroughly incomplete, understanding of the COBOL language. He goes merrily on his way, until one day he runs into trouble and indubitably feels betrayed by the machine. He will look everywhere, usually to no avail. In reality, the explanation is right under his nose, if only he knew how to find it. All that is required are some very basic assembler concepts, which have already been covered in this chapter. Unfortunately, many programmers never obtain the total picture because they learned COBOL as a high-level language and never studied assembler at all, or because COBOL and assembler were covered in separate courses and no one ever linked the two.

The Binary Problem

Given the knowledge of internal data representation, we can intuitively explain the "strange" output associated with Figure 7.5. From previous discussion we expect SECOND-DISPLAY, SECOND-BINARY, and SECOND-PACKED to have lengths of four, two, and three bytes, respectively. The MOVE ZEROS statement of line 40 in Figure 7.4 is a group move; hence, alphanumeric (i.e., EBCDIC) zeros are moved to the three fields as follows:

SECOND-DISPLAY: | F0 | F0 | F0 | F0 |

SECOND-BINARY: | F0 | F0 |

SECOND-PACKED: | F0 | F0 | F0 |

Now consider COBOL statement 41, ADD 1 TO SECOND-BINARY. The compiler generates the instructions to do binary addition and the contents of SECOND-BINARY, before and after, are shown in binary:

SECOND-BINARY (before):   1111 0000 1111 0000
                          +0000 0000 0000 0001
                          ─────────────────────
SECOND-BINARY (after):   1111 0000 1111 0001

159

Since the high-order bit in the sum is a 1, the sum is negative and stored in two's-complement form. However, since SECOND-BINARY is defined as an unsigned field (COBOL line 22), the minus sign is dropped after the two's-complement is obtained.

SECOND-BINARY (after addition):	1111 0000 1111 0001
Reverse 0's and 1's:	0000 1111 0000 1110
Add 1:	+ 1
Two's-complement:	0000 1111 0000 1111

The two's-complement is converted to a hex 0F0F, then to its decimal value of 3855; the latter is the displayed value.

The Packed Problem

Packed fields *must always* have a sign as the low-order hex digit. Valid signs are a hex C or F for positive numbers, and a hex D for negative numbers. Anything else is invalid as a sign and will cause problems in subsequent execution. *Specifically, any attempt to do arithmetic on a packed field with an invalid sign will invariably fail and produce a data exception.*

The field SECOND-PACKED has been initialized by the group move to contain F0F0F0. The low-order hex digit is 0, which is invalid as a sign. Hence, attempted execution of the COBOL ADD in statement 47 failed. Complete explanation requires knowledge of base/displacement addressing and BAL instruction formats, topics to be covered next. In addition, one must be familiar with various compiler aids, such as the core dump, and Data and Procedure Division maps. The latter are presented in Chapter Eight in a complete treatment of the data exception.

BASE/DISPLACEMENT ADDRESSING

Since the byte is the smallest addressable unit of storage, every byte in main storage is assigned an address. System 360/370 is designed to reach a maximum address of 16,776,216, the equivalent of a 24-bit binary number. This implies that an instruction referencing two addresses in storage would require six bytes (48 bits) for the addresses alone, and clearly this is far too costly in terms of storage requirements. The solution is known as *base/displacement addressing.*

The addressing scheme uses the CPU's general-purpose registers (GPRs) to reduce storage requirements. A GPR is a hardware device capable of holding information during processing. Information is transferred to or from a register much faster than from main storage. There are 16 GPRs numbered from hex 0 to F; each contains 32 bits.

In the base/displacement method, a 24-bit base address is loaded into a register which is then designated as a base register. A 12-bit displacement is calculated for each location. [The displacement of a location is defined as the number of bytes higher (i.e., greater) than the base address.] The address of a particular location is determined by specifying a base register and displacement from that base. Since it takes only 4 bits to designate a base register (0 through F) and 12 bits for a displacement, we are effectively providing a 24-bit address in only 16 bits.

Consider the following example. GPR 9 has been designated as the base register. A program is to be stored beginning at core location $(8800)_{16}$, which is loaded into the 24 low-order bits of register 9 as the base address. It is required to reference core location $(8950)_{16}$. Given a base address of $(8800)_{16}$, the displacement for location $(8950)_{16}$ is calculated to be $(150)_{16}$. Now we have the 16 bits to specify the address of core location $(8950)_{16}$, as shown in Figure 7.6. Four are used to designate GPR 9, and 12 bits are used for the hex displacement 150.

Assumptions:

1. GPR 9 is the base register.
2. $(8800)_{16}$ is the base address, which is loaded into register 9.
3. $(150)_{16}$ is the calculated displacement.

	Base	Displacement		
(Binary)	1001	0001	0101	0000
(Hex)	9	1	5	0

Figure 7.6 Base/Displacement Representation of Address $(8950)_{16}$

There is another major advantage to the base/displacement method, in addition to economy of space. All programs are easily relocatable; that is, all addresses in a given program are easily changed by altering only the contents of the base register(s).

INSTRUCTION FORMATS

System 360/370 has different, but parallel, instructions for different data types. The instruction to add two packed numbers is different from the instruction to add two binary numbers; indeed, the instruction to add binary half-words is different from that for binary full-words. The instruction set is designed in such a way that the instruction's length and format are dependent on the type and location of data on which the instruction is to operate. Specifically, there are five types of instructions:

RR: Register to Register (two bytes long)

RX: Register and Indexed Storage (four bytes long)

RS: Register to Storage (four bytes long)

SI: Storage Immediate (four bytes long)

SS: Storage to Storage (six bytes long)

Any of these instruction types provides the following information to the computer:

1. The operation to be performed (e.g., addition, subtraction, etc.).

2. The location of the operands [e.g., in registers, storage, or immediate (i.e., in the instruction)].

3. The nature of the data [i.e., fixed or variable in length, and if the latter, then the length of the data field(s)].

Machine instruction formats are displayed in Figure 7.7 Although Figure 7.7 may not make much sense now, it will assume greater importance in Chapters Eight and Nine when dump reading is studied. An explanation of the notation of Figure 7.7 is helpful:

OP: Operation code

B: Base register

D: Displacement

X: Register designated as an index register (RX only)

R: Register designated as an operand

I: Immediate data [i.e., the operand is contained in the instruction itself (SI only)]

L: Length used only for variable-length operands in SS format

In later chapters, it becomes necessary to dissect a machine instruction into its component parts. Consider the instruction D208B0156250. Using Figure 7.7, we must somehow decipher this cryptic combination of characters. The key is the first byte of the instruction, which contains the op code D2. Armed with this essential piece of information, we go to Appendix F and find that D2 is the machine op code for MVC (move characters), an SS instruction. We are therefore able to separate the essential components of the instruction according to Figure 7.7.

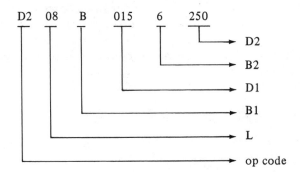

Essentially, the instruction is moving nine bytes (always one more than the length code) beginning at the address specified in the second operand to the address specified in the first operand. Both addresses are derived according to the base/displacement scheme. Thus, the address of the first operand is obtained by taking the base address contained in register 11, plus a hex displacement of 015. The address of the second operand is found by taking the base address in register 6 and adding a hex displacement of 250.

Appreciation for the different instruction formats comes from the realization that data are stored internally in varying formats, as explained further in the next section.

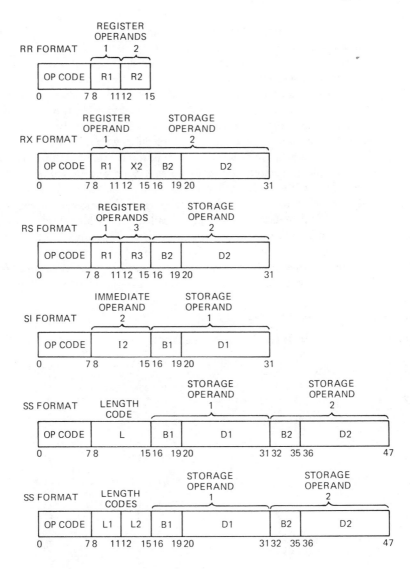

Figure 7.7 Instruction Formats

COBOL IMPLICATIONS—EFFICIENCY

The compiler-generated instructions to add two COMPUTATIONAL fields are necessarily different from those which add two COMPUTATIONAL-3 or DISPLAY fields. Further, if the COBOL operands in the same instruction are of different data types, decimal alignments, and so on, additional machine instructions are required to convert and/or shift the data prior to arithmetic. Since the COBOL programmer is permitted to mix data types and/or decimal alignments in the same instruction, he may unwisely conclude that the internal manipulations are not his concern. This attitude is most unfortunate.

We are not suggesting that the applications programmer spend inordinate amounts of time analyzing every COBOL statement. We are saying, however, that there are often several ways to accomplish the same task and that some ways are better than others. The COBOL programmer should, at the very least, be conscious that additional instructions are required to convert and/or shift numeric data. Consequently, he should make some attempt to reduce the need for these extra instructions.

As a simple illustration, consider the COBOL program in Figure 7.8. (A more complete example can be found in Grauer and Crawford, *COBOL: A Pragmatic Approach*, Prentice-Hall, 1978, pages 259-267). The Procedure Division is straightforward and consists entirely of addition statements. The interest in this example does not concern the COBOL program itself, but rather the machine language statements generated by the compiler. Figure 7.9 shows the generated machine code with explanation added for the convenience of the reader. While complete understanding of Figure 7.9 requires a greater knowledge of Assembler than is assumed at this point, the concepts covered to date (i.e., internal representation, instruction formats, and base/displacement addressing)

```
00021          DATA DIVISION.

00023          WORKING-STORAGE SECTION.
00024          77  BINARY-FIELD-ONE            PIC S9(5)
00025                  USAGE IS COMPUTATIONAL       VALUE IS ZEROS.
00026          77  BINARY-FIELD-TWO            PIC S9(5)
00027                  USAGE IS COMPUTATIONAL       VALUE IS ZEROS.
00028          77  DISPLAY-FIELD-ONE           PIC S9(5)
00029                                               VALUE IS ZEROS.
00030          77  DISPLAY-FIELD-TWO           PIC S9(5)
00031                                               VALUE IS ZEROS.
00032          77  PACKED-FIELD-ONE            PIC S9(5)
00033                  USAGE IS COMPUTATIONAL-3     VALUE IS ZEROS.
00034          77  PACKED-FIELD-TWO            PIC S9(5)
00035                  USAGE IS COMPUTATIONAL-3     VALUE IS ZEROS.
00036          77  PACKED-FIELD-WITH-DECIMAL   PIC S9(5)V9(2)
00037                  USAGE IS COMPUTATIONAL-3     VALUE IS ZEROS.
00038          77  PACKED-FIELD-UNSIGNED       PIC 9(5)
00039                  USAGE IS COMPUTATIONAL-3     VALUE IS ZEROS.

00041          PROCEDURE DIVISION.

00043              ADD BINARY-FIELD-ONE TO BINARY-FIELD-TWO.
00044              ADD PACKED-FIELD-ONE TO PACKED-FIELD-TWO.
00045              ADD DISPLAY-FIELD-ONE TO DISPLAY-FIELD-TWO.

00047              ADD BINARY-FIELD-ONE TO PACKED-FIELD-ONE.

00049              ADD PACKED-FIELD-ONE TO PACKED-FIELD-UNSIGNED.

00051              ADD PACKED-FIELD-ONE TO PACKED-FIELD-WITH-DECIMAL.

00053              STOP RUN.
```

Figure 7.8 COBOL Listing for Efficiency Considerations

provide sufficient background for meaningful discussion. Thus, Figures 7.8 and 7.9 will be used to provide intuitive justification for some rather commonplace COBOL guidelines. These include:

1. Where possible, arithmetic should be performed on packed fields (i.e., those defined as COMPUTATIONAL-3). Arithmetic should not be performed on zoned-decimal fields (i.e., those with no USAGE clause or with USAGE IS DISPLAY), as additional instructions are required to convert these fields to packed data prior to arithmetic. With respect to Figure 7.9, the statement

ADD PACKED-FIELD-ONE TO PACKED-FIELD-TWO

is preferable to

ADD DISPLAY-FIELD-ONE TO DISPLAY-FIELD-TWO.

As can be seen from Figure 7.9, addition of packed fields requires one instruction, addition of binary fields takes three instructions, and addition of zoned-decimal fields takes four instructions.

2. Regardless of what usage is specified, all data names in the same instruction should contain the same number of decimal places. Thus, the statement

ADD PACKED-FIELD-ONE TO PACKED-FIELD-TWO

is preferable to

ADD PACKED-FIELD-ONE TO PACKED-FIELD-WITH-DECIMAL.

The second statement, involving addition of two operands with different numbers of decimal places, requires two additional machine instructions to align the data prior to the arithmetic.

3. The receiving operand, whether packed, binary, or display, should always be signed. Omission of the sign in the PICTURE clause causes an extra instruction, which removes the sign generated as the result of the arithmetic operation. Further, omission of a sign in the PICTURE clause of the receiving data name could cause algebraic errors in cases where negative numbers could legitimately be present (see Figures 6.7 and 6.8). Thus, the statement

ADD PACKED-FIELD-ONE TO PACKED-FIELD-TWO

is preferable to

ADD PACKED-FIELD-ONE TO PACKED-FIELD-UNSIGNED.

Statement Number	COBOL	Generated Machine Instructions	Comments
43	ADD BINARY-FIELD-ONE TO BINARY-FIELD-TWO	58 30 6 000 5A 30 6 004 50 30 6 004	Three machine language statements are generally required to add two binary fields. These are (1) a load instruction to bring the first operand into a register, (2) an add instruction, and (3) a store instruction to place the result of the addition in the appropriate storage location.
44	ADD PACKED-FIELD-ONE TO PACKED-FIELD-TWO	FA 22 6 015 6 012	Only a single add packed instruction is required to add two packed fields, if the receiving field is signed (see Guideline 1).
45	ADD DISPLAY-FIELD-ONE TO DISPLAY-FIELD-TWO	F2 74 D 1F8 6 008 F2 74 D 200 6 00D FA 32 D 1FC D 205 F3 43 6 00D D 1FC	Four statements are generally required to add two DISPLAY fields. These are Pack, Pack, Add Packed, and Unpack. The pack instructions convert the two operands to packed fields suitable for addition; the unpack instruction restores the packed sum to a display field. A fifth instruction, Or Immediate, is needed if the sum is unsigned (see COBOL Statement #49).

Figure 7.9 Annotated Machine Instructions for Figure 7.8

166

47	ADD BINARY-FIELD-ONE TO PACKED-FIELD-ONE	58 30 6 000 4E 30 D 200 FA 22 6 012 D 205	Additional machine instructions are required to convert dissimilar data types (e.g., binary and packed) to like forms prior to addition. In this instance, the binary field is loaded into an accumulator, converted to decimal, then the two operands are added via an add packed instruction (see Guideline 4).
49	ADD PACKED-FIELD-ONE TO PACKED-FIELD-UNSIGNED	FA 22 6 01C 6 012 96 0F 6 01E	An additional machine instruction is required whenever the result of an arithmetic operation is unsigned. The extra instruction is apparent if COBOL statements 44 and 49 are compared (see Guideline 3). Further, unsigned numbers may lead to unexpected results, as was explained in Chapter Six.
51	ADD PACKED-FIELD-ONE TO PACKED-FIELD-WITH-DECIMAL	F8 72 D 200 6 012 FC 41 D 203 C 008 FA 33 6 018 D 204	Additional machine instructions are always required if the two operands are nonaligned. There is great variety as to the actual instructions generated, depending on data type, the number of extra decimal places, etc.

Figure 7.9 Annotated Machine Instructions for Figure 7.8 (continued)

167

4. Arithmetic should be performed on fields with like usage clauses, to avoid conversion from one format to another; thus, the statement

ADD PACKED-FIELD-ONE TO PACKED-FIELD-TWO

is superior to

ADD PACKED-FIELD-ONE TO BINARY-FIELD-ONE.

In reviewing these suggestions, the reader must remember that they are only guidelines and consequently cannot be implemented 100% of the time. The problem specifications may, in and of themselves, prohibit implementation and consequently the guidelines must be subservient to the problem itself.

SUMMARY

Much of the material in this chapter may seem somewhat removed from COBOL. However, the groundwork developed here is essential to a deeper understanding of COBOL, especially since the computer does not execute COBOL instructions as such, but the machine instructions generated by the COBOL compiler. It is imperative that the reader be familiar with the material on base/displacement addressing and instruction formats before proceeding to the chapters on ABEND debugging. Moreover, these concepts are also helpful in writing efficient programs. We do not mean that the applications programmer should spend entire days scrutinizing his work to save a few nanoseconds or bytes of storage. We are saying that he should at least be aware of what the compiler is doing.

In conclusion, the COBOL programmer can and does function with no knowledge of the machine on which he is working. However, a little information in this area goes a long way toward genuine understanding of debugging and efficiency considerations. We hope this point has been made effectively. We firmly believe the best COBOL programmers are those who know, or at least have a fundamental understanding of, Assembler as well.

PROBLEMS

1. Can you think of any peculiar output you may have seen where a knowledge of Assembler would have been helpful?

2. Show internal representation for the following COBOL entries:

(a) 77 FIELD-A PIC 9(4) DISPLAY VALUE 20.
(b) 77 FIELD-B PIC 9(4) VALUE 20.
(c) 77 FIELD-C PIC 9(4) COMP VALUE 20.
(d) 77 FIELD-D PIC 9(3) COMP VALUE 20.
(e) 77 FIELD-E PIC 9(5) COMP VALUE 20.
(f) 77 FIELD-F PIC 9(10) COMP VALUE 20.
(g) 77 FIELD-G PIC 9(10) COMP-3 VALUE 20.
(h) 77 FIELD-H PIC 9(5) COMP-3 VALUE 20.
(i) 77 FIELD-I PIC 9(9) COMP-3 VALUE 20.

3. (a) Express the decimal equivalents of the following halfwords, all of which represent binary numbers:

(1) | 0000 0101 | 1101 0010 |

(2) | 1111 1111 | 1111 1111 |

(3) | 0111 1111 | 1111 1111 |

(4) | 1000 0000 | 0000 0000 |

(b) Show the hex representations for each of the fields above.

4. Express the decimal equivalents of the following, all of which represent packed numbers:

(a) | 12 | 34 | 5F |

(b) | 12 | 34 | 5C |

(c) | 54 | 32 | 1D |

5. The largest positive binary number that can be stored in a half-word is 32,767. The largest (in magnitude) negative number that can be stored in the same space is −32,768. Explain why there is a difference.

6. Is it efficient (or possible) to use packed fields on card input to a COBOL program? Discuss. What about binary input?

7. Show the internal representation of the largest number that can be stored as a single-precision floating-point number; show the internal representation for the smallest (in magnitude) single-precision floating-point number. What are the approximate decimal values?

8. How many places of decimal accuracy can be achieved with a single-precision floating-point number? How many places of decimal accuracy can be achieved with a double-precision number?

9. Although hexadecimal arithmetic was not covered explicitly in this chapter, the reader will need these concepts in the following chapters. Accordingly, try the following:

(a) $(1\ 2\ 34)_{16}$
     $+ (ABCD)_{16}$
     _____

(b) $(ABCD)_{16}$
     $+ (FACE)_{16}$
     _____

(c) $(ABCD)_{16}$
     $- (1\ 2\ 34)_{16}$
     _____

(d) $(FACE)_{16}$
     $- (ABCD)_{16}$
     _____

10. Indicate the instruction type which:

(a) Has an operand contained in the instruction itself.
(b) Uses two registers to calculate a storage address.
(c) References two storage locations.
(d) Is six bytes long.
(e) Does not reference a storage location.
(f) Is two bytes long.
(g) Contains one length code.
(h) Contains two length codes.

11. Assume that the contents of register 4 is $(00001234)_{16}$ and the contents of register 11 is $(00005678)_{16}$.

Given the instruction F2124123B500:

(a) What is the effective address of the second operand?
(b) What is the effective address of the first operand?
(c) What is the nature of the instruction?

12. Consider the COBOL statement

ADD COMP3-DATA-NAME TO DISPLAY-DATA-NAME.

where

77 COMP3-DATA-NAME PICTURE IS S9(4)
USAGE IS COMPUTATIONAL-3.

and

77 DISPLAY-DATA-NAME PICTURE IS S9(4)

are the definitions for the respective data names. The following statements were found in a Procedure Division map corresponding to the above:

```
F2   F3 3168 A009    (PACK)
FA   F2 3168 A021    (AP)
F3   3F A009 3168    (UNPK)
```

(a) Where is the compiler work area? How many bytes does it contain?

(b) What is the location associated with each COBOL data name? (*Do not guess*, but explain how the structure of the COBOL and BAL ADD statements provides an unambiguous answer.)

13. Why should binary data names be specified with a picture of 9(4) rather than 9, 99, or 999?

Introduction to
ABEND Debugging

OVERVIEW

This is the first of two chapters on ABEND debugging. It begins with a presentation of two compiler aids, the Data and Procedure Division maps. Next a working COBOL program is "ABENDed" in three distinct places and the resulting dumps are utilized to determine the cause of each error. Substantial material is presented in conjunction with the dump analyses. We cover both BL and BLL cells, the SAVE AREA TRACE, occurrence in a COBOL subprogram, and use of the link edit map. In addition, the STATE and FLOW options are discussed.

It should be emphasized that while a dump may yield the technical cause of an ABEND, it is up to the programmer to relate this information to the source program. Thus a dump will not, in and of itself, pinpoint an error. It is only a tool, and like all tools, it must be used properly; else it is worthless.

Unfortunately, too many COBOL programmers give up almost immediately upon encountering a dump. We attempt, therefore, in this chapter and the next, to provide some insight into dump reading. We assume elementary knowledge of some assembler concepts, specifically: internal data representation (i.e., packed versus display fields), base/displacement addressing, and instruction formats.

There is one final point before we begin: the best way to debug a program is to avoid bugs altogether. While bugs are invariably present in the initial and even revised versions of most programs, many bugs can be eliminated by sound programming design and prudent error checks. Indeed, each of the three ABENDs considered in this chapter *should* have been prevented by defensive programming. In other words, any debugging procedure suffers from the fact that it is applied *after* a bug has occurred. It is, however, inherently easier to insert defensive checks at the source level before problems arise. In spite of this rather lofty advice, dumps can, do, and probably will always happen—hence, the reason for this chapter and the next.

THE PROBLEM AT HAND

A COBOL program and subprogram have been written to calculate and print student transcripts. Specifications are as follows:

Input

Read a file of student records containing name, major code, number of courses taken in the last semester, and for each course—number, credits, and grade.

Processing

Calculate a grade-point average for each student. A four-point system is used in which A, B, C, D, and F are worth 4, 3, 2, 1, and 0, respectively. The quality points for each course are equal to the numerical value of the grade times the number of credits. Thus, an A in a three-credit course is worth 12 quality points; a D in a two-credit course, 2 points; and so on. The grade-point average is equal to the total number of quality points divided by the total number of credits.

Output

Print a separate transcript for each student as shown. Also, calculate and print the total number of transcripts processed.

```
┌────────────────────────────────────────────┐
│                 TRANSCRIPT                   │
│                                              │
│  NAME:BENJAMIN, L           MAJOR:BIOLOGY    │
│                                              │
│         COURSE#   CREDITS   GRADE            │
│            111       3        A              │
│            222       3        B              │
│            333       3        C              │
│            444       3        B              │
│            555       3        B              │
│           AVERAGE: 3.00                      │
│                                              │
└────────────────────────────────────────────┘
```

The COBOL program to accomplish these specifications is shown in Figure 8.1(a) and (b). Figure 8.1(a) consists of a main program which reads the student file, determines the student's major from the incoming code, and prints the transcript. Figure 8.1(b) consists of a COBOL subroutine to calculate the grade-point average. Note well the use of the same copy entry in both programs to obtain the incoming record layouts. This is good technique to ensure that both the main and subprograms are working on identical record descriptions. The logic in Figure 8.1(a) and (b) is straightforward and will not be discussed further.

COMPILER AIDS

A compiler translates a source program into an object program, and it is the latter which is eventually executed. The COBOL compiler can supply both Data and Procedure Division maps as debugging aids. Figure 8.2 is a truncated Data Division map for the COBOL program of Figure 8.1(a). It lists the data names in a program and ties them to internal addresses by specifying a base locator (later tied to a base register) and a displacement. Reading from left to right in Figure 8.2, the seven columns denote:

1. The internal data name.

2. The COBOL level number.

3. The COBOL data name.

4. The base locator.

5. Displacement.

6. The internal name repeated.

7. The length of the data name, as in an assembler DS or DC statement.

All data names within the same file are assigned the same base locator. Thus, in Figure 8.2, BL = 1 for the entry(s) in CARD-FILE and BL = 2 for the entry(s) in PRINT-FILE. All entries in Working-Storage are assigned BL = 3.

The base locators are tied to specific base registers by a table of register assignments shown in Figure 8.3. BL = 1 points to register 7, BL = 2 to register 8, and BL = 3 to register 6.

Figure 8.4 is a truncated Procedure Division map corresponding to Figure 8.1(a). It contains information about the machine language instructions generated by the compiler. Reading from left to right in Figure 8.4, the five columns denote:

1. The computer-generated COBOL statement number.

2. The COBOL verb referenced in the statement number.

3. The relative location, in hex, of the machine instruction.

4. The actual machine instruction.

5. The symbolic instruction format.

Recall that the "instruction-explosion" effect causes a single COBOL instruction to generate one or more machine language statements [e.g., COBOL statement 147 (IF) spawned 10 machine language statements; statement 148 (MOVE) 2 statements, etc.].

```
00001              IDENTIFICATION DIVISION.
00002              PROGRAM-ID.  'MAINPROG'.
00003              AUTHOR.      GRAUER.
00004
00005
00006              ENVIRONMENT DIVISION.
00007
00008              CONFIGURATION SECTION.
00009              SOURCE-COMPUTER.  IBM-370.
00010              OBJECT-COMPUTER.  IBM-370.
00011              SPECIAL-NAMES.
00012                  C01 IS TOP-OF-PAGE.
00013
00014              INPUT-OUTPUT SECTION.
00015              FILE-CONTROL.
00016                  SELECT CARD-FILE ASSIGN TO UT-S-CARDS.
00017                  SELECT PRINT-FILE ASSIGN TO UT-S-SYSOUT.
00018
00019
00020              DATA DIVISION.
00021              FILE SECTION.
00022              FD   CARD-FILE
00023                   RECORDING MODE IS F
00024                   LABEL RECORDS ARE OMITTED
00025                   RECORD CONTAINS 80 CHARACTERS
00026                   DATA RECORD IS STUDENT-RECORD.
00027              01   STUDENT-RECORD          PIC X(80).
00028              FD   PRINT-FILE
00029                   RECORDING MODE IS F
00030                   LABEL RECORDS ARE OMITTED
00031                   RECORD CONTAINS 133 CHARACTERS
00032                   DATA RECORD IS PRINT-LINE.
00033              01   PRINT-LINE              PIC X(133).          ⎫ Literal to facilitate
00034              WORKING-STORAGE SECTION.                          ⎭ ABEND debugging
00035              77   FILLER                  PIC X(14)
00036                            VALUE 'WS BEGINS HERE'.
00037              77   WS-SUB                  PIC S9(4)      COMP.
00038              77   WS-END-OF-FILE          PIC X(3)   VALUE 'NO '.
00039              77   WS-FOUND-MAJOR-SWITCH   PIC X(3)   VALUE 'NO '.
00040              77   WS-GRADE-AVERAGE        PIC S9V99.
00041              77   WS-TOTAL-STUDENTS       PIC 999        COMP-3.   ⎤ Data name was
00042              01   WS-STUDENT-RECORD    COPY STUDREC.               ⎦ never initialized
00043   C          01   WS-STUDENT-RECORD.
00044   C              05   ST-NAME               PIC A(15).      ⎫Copied entry
00045   C              05   ST-MAJOR-CODE         PIC 9(4).
00046   C              05   ST-NUMBER-OF-COURSES  PIC 99.
00047   C              05   ST-COURSE-TABLE OCCURS 8 TIMES.
00048   C                  10   ST-COURSE-NUMBER  PIC X(3).
00049   C                  10   ST-COURSE-GRADE   PIC A.
00050   C                  10   ST-COURSE-CREDITS PIC 9.
00051              01   HEADING-LINE-ONE.
00052                  05   FILLER               PIC X(20)   VALUE SPACES.
00053                  05   FILLER               PIC X(10)   VALUE 'TRANSCRIPT'.
00054                  05   FILLER               PIC X(103)  VALUE SPACES.
00055              01   HEADING-LINE-TWO.
00056                  05   FILLER               PIC X(6)    VALUE ' NAME:'.
00057                  05   HDG-NAME             PIC A(15).
00058                  05   FILLER               PIC X(5)    VALUE SPACES.
00059                  05   FILLER               PIC X(6)    VALUE 'MAJOR:'.
00060                  05   HDG-MAJOR            PIC X(10).
```

Figure 8.1a Main Program for Transcript Problem

175

```
00061              05  FILLER                 PIC X(91)   VALUE SPACES.
00062         01  HEADING-LINE-THREE.
00063              05  FILLER                 PIC X(10)   VALUE SPACES.
00064              05  FILLER                 PIC X(9)    VALUE 'COURSE#  '.
00065              05  FILLER                 PIC X(9)    VALUE 'CREDITS  '.
00066              05  FILLER                 PIC X(5)    VALUE 'GRADE'.
00067              05  FILLER                 PIC X(100)  VALUE SPACES.
00068         01  DETAIL-LINE.
00069              05  FILLER                 PIC X(13)   VALUE SPACES.
00070              05  DET-COURSE             PIC X(3).
00071              05  FILLER                 PIC X(9)    VALUE SPACES.
00072              05  DET-CREDITS            PIC 9.
00073              05  FILLER                 PIC X(5)    VALUE SPACES.
00074              05  DET-GRADE              PIC A.
00075              05  FILLER                 PIC X(101)  VALUE SPACES.
00076         01  TOTAL-LINE.
00077              05  FILLER                 PIC X(16)   VALUE SPACES.
00078              05  FILLER                 PIC X(9)    VALUE 'AVERAGE: '.
00079              05  TOT-GPA                PIC 9.99.
00080              05  FILLER                 PIC X(104)  VALUE SPACES.
00081         01  MAJOR-VALUE.
00082              05  FILLER                 PIC X(14)   VALUE '1234ACCOUNTING'.
00083              05  FILLER                 PIC X(14)   VALUE '1400BIOLOGY    '.
00084              05  FILLER                 PIC X(14)   VALUE '1976CHEMISTRY '.
00085              05  FILLER                 PIC X(14)   VALUE '2100CIVIL ENG '.
00086              05  FILLER                 PIC X(14)   VALUE '2458E. D. P.  '.
00087              05  FILLER                 PIC X(14)   VALUE '3245ECONOMICS '.
00088              05  FILLER                 PIC X(14)   VALUE '3960FINANCE   '.
00089              05  FILLER                 PIC X(14)   VALUE '4321MANAGEMENT'.
00090              05  FILLER                 PIC X(14)   VALUE '4999MARKETING '.
00091              05  FILLER                 PIC X(14)   VALUE '5400STATISTICS'.
00092         01  MAJOR-TABLE REDEFINES MAJOR-VALUE.
00093              05  MAJORS      OCCURS 10 TIMES.
00094                  10  MAJOR-CODE         PIC 9(4).
00095                  10  MAJOR-NAME         PIC X(10).
00096         01  FILLER                      PIC X(12)
00097                  VALUE 'WS ENDS HERE'.
00098         PROCEDURE DIVISION.
00099         001-MAINLINE.
00100              OPEN INPUT CARD-FILE,
00101                   OUTPUT PRINT-FILE.
00102              READ CARD-FILE INTO WS-STUDENT-RECORD,
00103                   AT END MOVE 'YES' TO WS-END-OF-FILE.
00104              PERFORM 020-PROCESS-CARDS THRU 025-PROCESS-CARDS-EXIT
00105                   UNTIL WS-END-OF-FILE = 'YES'.
00106              DISPLAY 'TOTAL PROCESSED = ' WS-TOTAL-STUDENTS.
00107              CLOSE CARD-FILE, PRINT-FILE.
00108              STOP RUN.
00109
00110         020-PROCESS-CARDS.
00111              ADD 1 TO WS-TOTAL-STUDENTS.
00112              CALL 'SUBRTN'
00113                   USING WS-STUDENT-RECORD
00114                         WS-GRADE-AVERAGE.
```

Table of major codes

Call to subprogram

Figure 8.1a Main Program for Transcript Problem (continued)

```
00116          *DETERMINE MAJOR
00117              MOVE 1 TO WS-SUB.
00118              MOVE 'NO ' TO WS-FOUND-MAJOR-SWITCH.
00119              PERFORM 030-FIND-MAJOR THRU 030-FIND-MAJOR-EXIT
00120                  UNTIL WS-FOUND-MAJOR-SWITCH = 'YES'.

00122          *WRITE HEADING LINES
00123              WRITE PRINT-LINE FROM HEADING-LINE-ONE
00124                  AFTER ADVANCING TOP-OF-PAGE LINES.
00125              MOVE ST-NAME TO HDG-NAME.
00126              WRITE PRINT-LINE FROM HEADING-LINE-TWO
00127                  AFTER ADVANCING 2 LINES.
00128              WRITE PRINT-LINE FROM HEADING-LINE-THREE
00129                  AFTER ADVANCING 2 LINES.

00131          *WRITE DETAIL LINES - 1 PER COURSE
00132              PERFORM 040-WRITE-DETAIL-LINE THRU 040-WRITE-DETAIL-EXIT
00133                  VARYING WS-SUB FROM 1 BY 1
00134                  UNTIL WS-SUB > ST-NUMBER-OF-COURSES.

00136          *WRITE GRADE POINT AVERAGE
00137              MOVE WS-GRADE-AVERAGE TO TOT-GPA.
00138              WRITE PRINT-LINE FROM TOTAL-LINE
00139                  AFTER ADVANCING 2 LINES.
00140              READ CARD-FILE INTO WS-STUDENT-RECORD,
00141                  AT END MOVE 'YES' TO WS-END-OF-FILE.
00142
00143        025-PROCESS-CARDS-EXIT.
00144            EXIT.
00145
00146        030-FIND-MAJOR.
00147            IF ST-MAJOR-CODE = MAJOR-CODE (WS-SUB)
00148                MOVE 'YES' TO WS-FOUND-MAJOR-SWITCH
00149                MOVE MAJOR-NAME (WS-SUB) TO HDG-MAJOR
00150
00151            ELSE
00152                ADD 1 TO WS-SUB.
00153
00154        030-FIND-MAJOR-EXIT.
00155            EXIT.
00156
00157        040-WRITE-DETAIL-LINE.
00158            MOVE ST-COURSE-NUMBER (WS-SUB) TO DET-COURSE.
00159            MOVE ST-COURSE-CREDITS (WS-SUB) TO DET-CREDITS.
00160            MOVE ST-COURSE-GRADE (WS-SUB) TO DET-GRADE.
00161            WRITE PRINT-LINE FROM DETAIL-LINE
00162                AFTER ADVANCING 1 LINES.
00163
00164        040-WRITE-DETAIL-EXIT.
00165            EXIT.
```

Figure 8.1a Main Program for Transcript Problem (continued)

```
00001           IDENTIFICATION DIVISION.
00002           PROGRAM-ID.  'SUBRTN'.
00003           AUTHOR.        GRAUER.
00004
00005
00006           ENVIRONMENT DIVISION.
00007
00008           CONFIGURATION SECTION.
00009           SOURCE-COMPUTER.   IBM-370.
00010           OBJECT-COMPUTER.   IBM-370.
00011
00012
00013           DATA DIVISION.
00014           WORKING-STORAGE SECTION.
00015           77   WS-TOTAL-CREDITS                PIC 999.
00016           77   WS-QUALITY-POINTS               PIC 999.
00017           77   WS-MULTIPLIER                   PIC 9.
00018           77   WS-SUB                          PIC S9(4)      COMP.

00020           *************************************************
00021           LINKAGE SECTION.
00022           77   LS-CALCULATED-AVERAGE               PIC S9V99.
00023           01   DATA-PASSED-FROM-MAIN       COPY STUDREC.
00024  C        01   DATA-PASSED-FROM-MAIN.
00025  C             05   ST-NAME                   PIC A(15).
00026  C             05   ST-MAJOR-CODE             PIC 9(4).          Copied entry
00027  C             05   ST-NUMBER-OF-COURSES      PIC 99.
00028  C             05   ST-COURSE-TABLE OCCURS 8 TIMES.
00029  C                  10   ST-COURSE-NUMBER     PIC X(3).
00030  C                  10   ST-COURSE-GRADE      PIC A.
00031  C                  10   ST-COURSE-CREDITS    PIC 9.
00032           *************************************************

00034           PROCEDURE DIVISION                      Arguments passed
00035                USING DATA-PASSED-FROM-MAIN          from main program
00036                      LS-CALCULATED-AVERAGE.
00037           *************************************************
00038           * ROUTINE TO COMPUTE GRADE POINT AVERAGE
00039           * WEIGHTS:  A=4, B=3, C=2, D=1, F=0
00040           * NO PLUS OR MINUS GRADES
00041           * QUALITY POINTS FOR A GIVEN COURSE = WEIGHT X CREDITS
00042           * GRADE POINT AVERAGE = TOTAL QUALITY POINTS / TOTAL CREDITS
00043           *************************************************
00044           001-MAINLINE.
00045                MOVE ZERO TO WS-QUALITY-POINTS.
00046                MOVE ZERO TO WS-TOTAL-CREDITS.
00047                PERFORM 010-COMPUTE-QUALITY-POINTS
00048                    VARYING WS-SUB FROM 1 BY 1
00049                    UNTIL WS-SUB > ST-NUMBER-OF-COURSES.
00050                COMPUTE LS-CALCULATED-AVERAGE ROUNDED
00051                    = WS-QUALITY-POINTS / WS-TOTAL-CREDITS.
00052           005-RETURN-TO-MAIN.
00053                EXIT PROGRAM.
00054
00055           010-COMPUTE-QUALITY-POINTS.
00056                MOVE ZERO TO WS-MULTIPLIER.
00057           * NESTED IF COULD BE USED, BUT ISN'T IN ORDER TO OBTAIN
00058           * GREATER CLARITY.
00059                IF ST-COURSE-GRADE (WS-SUB) = 'A', MOVE 4 TO WS-MULTIPLIER.
00060                IF ST-COURSE-GRADE (WS-SUB) = 'B', MOVE 3 TO WS-MULTIPLIER.
00061                IF ST-COURSE-GRADE (WS-SUB) = 'C', MOVE 2 TO WS-MULTIPLIER.
00062                IF ST-COURSE-GRADE (WS-SUB) = 'D', MOVE 1 TO WS-MULTIPLIER.
00063                COMPUTE WS-QUALITY-POINTS =  WS-QUALITY-POINTS
00064                    + ST-COURSE-CREDITS (WS-SUB) * WS-MULTIPLIER.
00065                ADD ST-COURSE-CREDITS (WS-SUB) TO WS-TOTAL-CREDITS.
```

Figure 8.1b Subprogram for Transcript Problem

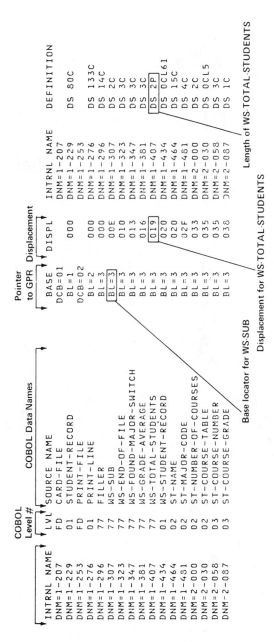

Figure 8.2 Truncated Data Division Map for Figure 8.1a

COBOL Data Names

INTRNL NAME	COBOL Level# LVL	SOURCE NAME	BASE (Pointer to GPR)	DISPL (Displacement)	INTRNL NAME	DEFINITION
DNM=1-207	FD	CARD-FILE	DCB=01		DNM=1-207	
DNM=1-229	01	STUDENT-RECORD	BL=1	000	DNM=1-229	DS 80C
DNM=1-253	FD	PRINT-FILE	DCB=02		DNM=1-253	
DNM=1-276	01	PRINT-LINE	BL=2	000	DNM=1-276	DS 133C
DNM=1-296	77	FILLER	BL=3	000	DNM=1-296	DS 14C
DNM=1-307	77	WS-SUB	BL=3	00E	DNM=1-307	DS 2C
DNM=1-323	77	WS-END-OF-FILE	BL=3	010	DNM=1-323	DS 3C
DNM=1-347	77	WS-FOUND-MAJOR-SWITCH	BL=3	013	DNM=1-347	DS 3C
DNM=1-381	77	WS-GRADE-AVERAGE	BL=3	016	DNM=1-381	DS 3C
DNM=1-407	77	WS-TOTAL-STUDENTS	BL=3	019	DNM=1-407	DS 2P
DNM=1-434	01	WS-STUDENT-RECORD	BL=3	020	DNM=1-434	DS 0CL61
DNM=1-464	02	ST-NAME	BL=3	020	DNM=1-464	DS 15C
DNM=1-481	02	ST-MAJOR-CODE	BL=3	02F	DNM=1-481	DS 4C
DNM=2-000	02	ST-NUMBER-OF-COURSES	BL=3	033	DNM=2-000	DS 2C
DNM=2-030	02	ST-COURSE-TABLE	BL=3	035	DNM=2-030	DS 0CL5
DNM=2-058	03	ST-COURSE-NUMBER	BL=3	035	DNM=2-058	DS 3C
DNM=2-087	03	ST-COURSE-GRADE	BL=3	038	DNM=2-087	DS 1C

Base locator for WS-SUB

Displacement for WS-TOTAL-STUDENTS

Length of WS-TOTAL-STUDENTS

REGISTER ASSIGNMENT

REG 6	BL = 3
REG 7	BL = 1
REG 8	BL = 2

Base locator three is tied to register six

Figure 8.3 Table of Register Assignments

179

Figure 8.4 Truncated Procedure Division Map for Figure 8.1a

COBOL Card #	COBOL Verb	Relative Location	Machine Instruction		Symbolic Assembler Formats	
111	ADD	000B32	FA 10 6 019 C 0A8		AP	019(2,6),0A8(1,12)	DNM=1-407	L'IT+0
112	CALL	000B38	96 0F 6 01A		OI	01A(6),X'0F'	DNM=1-407+1
		000B3C	41 10 6 020		LA	1,020(0,6)	DNM=1-434
		000B40	50 10 D 250		ST	1,250(0,13)	PRM=1
		000B44	41 10 6 016		LA	1,016(0,6)	DNM=1-381
		000B48	50 10 D 254		ST	1,254(0,13)	PRM=2
		000B4C	96 80 D 254		OI	254(13),X'80'	PRM=2
		000B50	41 10 D 250		LA	1,250(0,13)	PRM=1
		000B54	58 F0 C 014		L	15,014(0,12)	V(ILBODBG4)
		000B58	05 EF		BALR	14,15
		000B5A	96 40 D 049		OI	049(13),X'40'
		000B5E	58 F0 C 024		L	15,024(0,12)	V(SUBRTN)
		000B62	05 EF		BALR	14,15
		000B64	94 BF D 049		NI	049(13),X'BF'
		000B68	40 F0 C 05C		STH	15,05C(0,13)
		000B6C	58 F0 D 1B8		L	15,1B8(0,13)
		000B70	50 D0 F 080		ST	13,080(0,15)
117	MOVE	000B74	D2 01 6 00E C 0A9		MVC	00E(2,6),0A9(12)	DNM=1-307	LIT+1
118	MOVE	000B7A	D2 02 6 013 C 0C6		MVC	013(3,6),0C6(12)	DNM=1-347	LIT+30
· · · · ·
144	EXIT	000D0A	58 10 D 238		L	1,238(0,13)	VN=01
		000D0E	07 F1		BCR	15,1
146	*030-FIND-MAJOR			PN=03
		000D10			EQU	*
		000D10	58 F0 C 010		L	15,010(0,12)	V(ILBOFLW1)
		000D14	05 1F		BALR	1,15
		000D16	00000092		DC	X'00000092'
147	IF	000D1A	41 40 6 308		LA	4,308(0,6)	DNM=3-366
		000D1E	48 30 6 00E		LH	3,00E(0,6)	DNM=1-307
		000D22	5C 20 C 0B4		M	2,0B4(0,12)	LIT+12
		000D26	1A 43		AR	4,3
		000D28	5B 40 C 0B4		S	4,0B4(0,12)	LIT+12
		000D2C	F2 73 D 200 6 02F		PACK	200(8,13),02F(4,6)	TS=01
		000D32	F2 73 D 208 4 000		PACK	208(8,13),000(4,4)	TS=09
		000D38	F9 22 D 205 D 20D		CP	205(3,13),20D(3,13)	TS=06
		000D3E	58 F0 C 084		L	15,084(0,12)	GN=016
				Instruction at D3E
		000D42	07 7F		BCR	7,15
148	MOVE	000D44	50 40 D 220		ST	4,220(0,13)	SBS=1
		000D48	D2 02 6 013 C 0C3		MVC	013(3,6),0C3(12)	DNM=1-347	DNM=1-481
149	MOVE	000D4E	41 40 6 30C		LA	4,30C(0,6)	DNM=3-389	TS=014

Location B38

180

A *core dump* is a picture of the computer's memory at an instant of time. Usually, dumps are taken only if an ABEND (ABnormal END of job) occurs. Realize that the contents of main storage are strictly binary, but that they are displayed in a dump in hexadecimal for conciseness. Dumps appear foreboding to the uninitiated, but, as with everything else, a little practice goes a long way.

Consider Figure 8.5, which contains a portion of a dump. The leftmost column indicates the internal location number. Subsequent digits are the contents of that location and others. Since the smallest addressable location is the byte (8 bits or two hex digits), every two hex digits indicate the contents of a particular byte.

Go down the first column in Figure 8.5 until you read "26CB20." The two hex digits immediately following are F5, indicating that the contents of byte 26CB20 are F5. The next two hex digits, F4, are the contents of the next sequential location, 26CB21. In similar fashion, F3 is the contents of 26CB22, F2 is the contents of 26CB23, and so on. There are a total of 64 hex digits on the line beginning with 26CB20. Accordingly, the contents of 32 bytes beginning at 26CB20 and continuing to 26CB3F are shown on the same line.

Immediately following the 64 hex digits on a given line is the corresponding alphabetic interpretation of those digits. According to the EBCDIC configurations of Table 7.1, F5 is the representation for 5, F4 for 4, and so forth. Many of the interpretation columns are blank because the contents of the corresponding locations are hex 40s, which is the internal representation of a blank.

Now that we are vaguely familiar with the basic debugging tools of the core dump and Procedure and Data Division maps, we are ready to try an actual problem.

EXAMPLE 1
Dump Reading

When execution of Figure 8.1(a) and (b) was attempted, the computer vehemently objected. We received a message 'COMPLETION CODE = 0C7' followed by pages of semi-intelligible data, culminating in a dump. Where do we go from here?

First, look up the meaning of an 0C7 in the IBM manual: *IBM System/360 (or 370) Operating System: Messages and Codes* and find that 0C7 is a data exception. Experience tells us (and will tell you shortly) that a data exception occurs when one attempts to use invalid decimal (i.e., packed) data. To debug the program, we have to determine where within the COBOL program the data exception occurred. To do this we have extracted some of the more relevant information associated with a dump and grouped it into Figure 8.6. Specifically, Figure 8.6 contains:

1. Job Identification (i.e., name, time, and date).

2. The completion code.

3. The contents of the *Program Status Word* (PSW) at the time of the ABEND.

4. The *Entry Point Address* (EPA) of the COBOL program.

5. The contents of the 16 registers at the time of the ABEND.

Core location   Internal contents (in hex)   Alphabetic interpretation of internal contents

PAGE 0014

```
3FD680   07FE0700 07000700                                                        *................*    *.............."...*
```

LOAD MODULE   IGG019AA

```
3FE0E0   47FF0010 00000000 D202104D 10490 7FF   90E8D014 188F1821 98362044 1B77437C   *................K..(....Y........*
3FE100   20424A50 20521945 4720807A 58FC205C   05EF58F0 203405EF 95503004 4780802C   *..ε.........:.0.*..0.....&.......*
3FE120   58573000 41550000 48673006 48630016   41456000 91082034 4780806E 95002051   *..........................>.....*
3FE140   4780806E 1B114310 20511B61 1A519190   20244710 807A4060 20521815 91082034   *...>.........../.........: -.....*
3FE160   47808090 18761B66 48802052           90352044 9828D024 58ED0014 07FE0700   *........................:........*
```

LOAD MODULE   IGG019AQ

```
3FD680   90EFD040 188F5833                     00004133 00001B77 43702042 917F3004   *.............................."..*
3FD6A0   47108070 4740802E 41130004 41000001   0A0147F0 80149550 30044780 80701812   *.........................0..ε....*
3FD6C0   18034111 00000A37 12FF4780 805A05EF   580D0028 581D0020 41110000 0A3747F0   *............................0.*..*
3FD6E0   80149120 20304780 80149 4DF 203058ED   00149808 D01C07FE 91082034 47808168   *................................*
3FD700   58573000 41550000 48673006 91042 03D   47108098 9101203C 471080AA 48630016   *................................*
3FD720   41173000 950C1000 477080AA 1B564155   00011815 18060A67 91202024 4780814E   *...............................+*
3FD740   1A659140 20504780 810245E0 80E61B61   1A654155 000445E0 80E61A51 19564780   *...ε......W./....εW.......&.1....*
3FD760   814E955F 50004780 814E47F0 80CED707   30103010 F2233015 50004F13 00104013   *..+ε....+.0..P.....2....ε.|......*
3FD780   00100203 50003010 07FE1B11 431C2051   1A519104 203D4780 81429110 20244710   *..K..ε.......0.+.............&...*
3FD7A0   812E45E0 80E61B65 1A615C5C 204C5060   204847F0 814E4110 00028910 000C4100   *...ε...W../&ε..<.&-...0.+........*
3FD7C0   00808900 00181610 0A0D5050 204C5060   204847F0 80CE4157 30009180 50044780   *....ε...ε.<.&-...0......&........*
3FD7E0   81624177 00084 7F0 60781B77 43702042   58ED0040 588D0018 50302044 07FE0700   *...........0.......ε.............*
```

SP 252

Figure 8.5 Illustrative Core Dump

Figure 8.5 Illustrative Core Dump (continued)

```
26D7FE0                                              0003DB50  403F2FD2   *......CS......M.......M...C&  ..K*

SP 000

26C8A0  4126C8A0 7F00065D 02000000 7F268F20  0026C8D0 0C000000 4026C8C8 0026C8D0  *...H.."..).....H......HH..H.*
26C8C0  00000000 00010000 0126B1A0 2000065D  00000000 00000000 00000000 00000033  *........................*
26C8E0  00818300 00000001 00004000 00000001  04000001 54000000 00A40020 0002E27C  *..c..........Sä..@*
26C900  923FC8E8 003FC688 06000001 00C00660  00000000 4126C8A0 013FCCF8 003FCCF8  *..HY..F.......--...H...8..8*
26C920  0000007D 00000001 4126C958 7F000000  7F26C92C 0C000000 0026C958 0C000000  *....I&..Q.......IO...I..I...*
26C940  4026C950 0024D8B0 00000000 00010000  20000085 0026C928 7F000000           *.....I*.....I0....I..I.....*
26C960  00000000 0026C95C 00000000 00000000  00000000 0024D8B0 00010000           *....I*........I...C........*
26C980  0126CA78 20000085 0126C9B8 7F000000  00000000 7F26C98C 0026C9B8 00C00000  *...I&........I*....I..I....*
26C9A0  4026C9B0 0024D7FC 00000000 00010000  00000000 0026C988 7F000000           *..I..P.......&..I.".....*
26C9C0  00000000 7F26C9BC 0026C9E8 0C000000  0226C9E0 0024D7FC 0024D7FC 00010000  *....."I...IY....I..P.........*
26C9E0  0226CB58 0K000050 00000000 0C000000  00000000 40D5C1D4 C5404040 C5404040  *......&....ISTUDENT NAME*
26CA00  40404040 40404040 40404040 D6C340E2  E4D44040 C3D9C5C4 C9E3E240 40E3E4C9  *         SCC SEC NUM CREDITS TUI*
26CA20  E3C9D6D5 4040E4D5 C9D6D540 C6C5C540  40C1C3E3 40C6C5C5 4040E2C3 C8D6D3C1  *TION UNION FEE ACT FEE  SCHOLA*
26CA40  D9E2C8C9 D74040E3 D6E3C1D3 40C2C9D3  D3404040 40404040 40000000 40404040  *RSHIP TOTAL BILL*
26CA60  60606060 60606060 60606060 60606060  60606060 60606060 60606060 60606060  *             ...  ------*
26CA80  60606060 60606060 60606060 60606060  60606060 60606060 60606060 60606060  *                        *

LINE 26CAA0 SAME AS ABOVE

26CAC0  60606060 60606060 60606060 60606060  60606060 60606060 60404040 40E8E2C9  *                        *
26CAE0  40404040 40404040 40404040 40404040  40404040 40404040 40E8E2C9           *                     YSI*
26CB00  00000000 00020050 C8C5D5D9 F0F5F0F0  D4C5E240 40404040 F9F8F7F6 40404040  *.....&HENRY JAMES      9876*
26CB20  F5F4F3F2 F1F1F5D5 F0F5F0F0 40404040  40404040 40404040 40404040 40404040  *5432[1]5N0500*
26CB40  4D404040 40404040 40404040 40404040  40404040 D1D6C8D5 40E2D4C9 40E2D4C9  *              JOHN SMI*
26CB60  E3C84040 40404040 F1F2F3F4 F1F2F3F4  F5F6F7F8 F9F1F5E8 F0F0F0F0 40404040  *TH         1234567891 5YO0C0*
26CB80  40404040 40404040 40404040 40404040  40404040 40404040 40404040 40404040  *                        *
```

Hex contents of location 26CB20

Hex contents of location 26CB24

EBCDIC equivalent for location 26CB24

EBCDIC equivalent for location 26CB20

```
JOB ARTJHM22           STEP GO                 TIME 141604  DATE 77340

COMPLETION CODE        SYSTEM = 0C7

PSW AT ENTRY TO ABEND   071D1000 001C1830          ILC 6    INTC 0007



CDE

    C4F140      ATR1 0B   NCDE 000000   ROC-RB 00C4ED10   NM GO         USE 01   EPA 1C0CF8   ATR2 20   XL/MJ C4F018
    FFE500      ATR1 B9   NCDE FFE4D8   ROC-RB 00000000   NM IGG019BA   USE 08   EPA F67480   ATR2 20   XL/MJ FFE518
    FFE4D8      ATR1 B8   NCDE FFA848   ROC-RB 00000000   NM IGG019BB   USE 08   EPA F67690   ATR2 20   XL/MJ FFE4F0
    FF9A18      ATR1 B1   NCDE FF97F0   ROC-RB 00000000   NM IGG019CF   USE 0C   EPA D4E618   ATR2 20   XL/MJ FF9A30
    FF97F0      ATR1 B0   NCDE FFE528   ROC-RB 00000000   NM IGG019CL   USE 0D   EPA F37938   ATR2 20   XL/MJ FF9808
    FFE460      ATR1 B8   NCDE FFE118   ROC-RB 00000000   NM IGG019AI   USE 14   EPA F67A90   ATR2 20   XL/MJ FFE478



REGS AT ENTRY TO ABEND

    FLTR 0-6      0000000000000000        0001E5E2F2F1F7F1          4040404040404040     4040404040404040

    REGS 0-7      001C172E   501C1826     001C1740   5CC4EB50       001C11F8   001C171E  001C0D98   001FEA58
    REGS 8-15     001C12B0   001C1B76     001C0CF8   001C0CF8       001C15B8   001C1338  001C182A   001C3D16
```

Job name — ARTJHM22

Time of day — TIME 141604

Date — DATE 77340

Completion code — SYSTEM = 0C7

Last three bytes of PSW — 1C1830

Entry point address — EPA 1C0CF8

Contents of register 12 — 001C15B8

Contents of register 6 — 001C0D98

Figure 8.6 Information Associated with Core Dump of Example 1

We now begin the analysis of a dump. The last three bytes (6 hex digits) of the PSW provide the location of the interrupt. Subtraction of the *Entry Point Address* (EPA) of the COBOL program from the three bytes in the PSW yields the relative address (i.e., the location within the COBOL program of the error). Thus, using numbers obtained from Figure 8.6:

Address from PSW	1C1830
− Entry point of COBOL Program	1C0CF8
Relative Address	B38

Since all addresses in a dump are specified in hexadecimal, the subtraction is in hex as well. Now take the relative address (B38) to the Procedure Division map of Figure 8.4 and find that B38 occurs within COBOL statement 111, indicating that program execution terminated within this COBOL statement. *The instruction at B38 is the next instruction that would have been executed had not the ABEND occurred; the instruction that caused the problem is the one immediately before at B32.* However, both machine instructions are contained within the COBOL ADD.

In order to determine the exact cause of the error, we examine the machine language instruction at B32 which failed to execute. It has an op code of FA, and from previous knowledge, or the material in Chapter Seven, we dissect the instructions as follows:

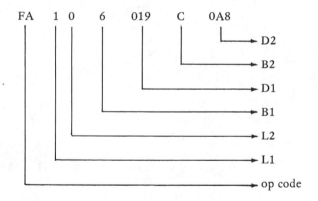

From Appendix F we learn that FA is the op code for Add Packed. The instruction at B32 will add the contents of the second operand to the contents of the first operand and store the results in the first operand. The addresses of both operands are calculated in accordance with the base/displacement addressing scheme discussed in Chapter Seven.

The first operand has a displacement of 019 (in hex) from the address in register 6; the second operand has a displacement of 0A8 (also in hex) from the address in register 12. Figure 8.6 shows the addresses (i.e., the three low-order bytes) in registers

6 and 12, respectively, to be 1C0D98 and 1C15B8. Thus, the actual addresses of both operands are calculated as follows:

Contents of register 6	=		1C0D98
+ 1st displacement	=	+	019
Location of 1st operand	=		1C0DB1
Contents of register C	=		1C15B8
+ 2nd displacement	=	+	0A8
Location of 2nd operand	=		1C1660

The first operand begins at location 1C0DB1. Its length code in the Add Packed instruction is one, so the first operand extends one byte past 1C0DB1 (i.e., the first operand is in locations 1C0DB1 and 1C0DB2). The actual number of bytes in the operand is always one more than the corresponding length code contained in the instruction. In similar fashion, the second operand is one byte long beginning at 1C1660.

Now we can use the dump produced by the ABEND, and shown in Figure 8.7 to determine the cause of the data exception. The value of the second operand, located in location 1C1660 is 1C, a packed one, and a valid decimal number. The value of the first operand, located in location 1C0DB1 and 1C0DB2, is 0000, an invalid packed number (the sign is missing) and hence the data exception. We have determined the cause of the data exception, invalid data in the first operand. Unfortunately, it seems to have little relation to the COBOL program. Let us therefore consider COBOL statement 111, which generated the machine language instruction in the first place to try for a more satisfying explanation. COBOL statement 111 is

ADD 1 TO WS-TOTAL-STUDENTS.

In effect, statement 111 is counting the number of records processed. WS-TOTAL-STUDENTS is defined as a 77-level entry in COBOL line 41, and therein lies the problem. Look carefully at statement 41

77   WS-TOTAL-STUDENTS   PIC 999   COMP-3.

WS-TOTAL-STUDENTS was never initialized. Hence, the computer uses whatever happens to be in WS-TOTAL-STUDENTS at the time the program is executed. Insertion of a VALUE ZEROS clause would initialize our counter and eliminate the data exception. Let us further analyze the machine language instruction that "blew up." It referenced WS-TOTAL-STUDENTS as being 19 displaced from register 6. How and why?

The answer lies in the Data Division map of Figure 8.2. WS-TOTAL-STU-DENTS is tied to BL = 3, which is subsequently linked to register 6 in Figure 8.3. Further, Figure 8.2 shows a displacement of 019 and a length of 2 for WS-TOTAL-STUDENTS. Indeed, these are the numbers appearing in the first operand of the Add Packed instruction. (Remember that a three-digit decimal number requires only two bytes if it is stored as a packed field. In addition, the length in the Add Packed instruction was 1, which

```
LOAD MODULE    GO

1C0CE0  4580F010  D4C1C9D5  D7D9D6C7  E5E2D9F1    0700989F  F02407FF  90ECD00C  185DD5F0   *..0.MAINPROGVSR1....0........0*
1C0D00  0001D7FE  001C1B76  001C0CF8              001C15B8  001C1333  96021034  07FE41F0  001C1B36   *............8..8.........0*
1C0D20  40614040  40404040  E2E3D6D7              4040F7F7  F3F4F04B  F1F4F1F3  40C3D7E4   *. .     STOP  77340.1413 CPU*
1C0D40  40404040  40406140  E2E3D6D7              40E2E3D6  D940E5C9  D9E340F1  00000000   *      OMIN 01.49SEC STOR VIRT 1.*
1C0D60  40404040  D4C9D540  F0F14BF4  F9E2C5C3    F1F9F7F7  00000000  C2C5C7C9  C1D4C9D5   *14.09.08DEC  6. 1977....WS BEGIN*
1C0D80  F1F44BF0  F94BF0F8  C4C5C340  40F66B40    00000000  C2C5C7C9  C2C5D5D1  C1D4C9D5   *S HERE..NO NO ......BENJAMIN*
1C0DA0  E240C8C5  D9C59500  D5D640D5  D6400000    C2C5D5D1  F2C2F3F3  F3C3F3F3  F4C2F4C2   *.L  14005111A3222B3333C3444B*
1C0DC0  6B40D340  404040F1  F4F0F0F0  F5F1F1F1    F3F3C3F3  F4F40000  40404040  40404040   *3555B3        TRANSCRIPT...*
1C0DE0  F3F5F5F5  C2F34040  40404040  E3D9C1D5    D7E34040  E2C9D7E3  40404040  40404040   *                         *
1C0E00  40404040  40404040  40404040  40404040    40404040  40404040  40404040  40404040
1C0E20  40404040  40404040  40404040  40404040    D7E34040  D9C9D7E3  40404040  40404040

   LINES 1C0E40-1C0E60 SAME AS ABOVE

1C0E80  40D5C1D4  C57A8902  04C7C1E8  E204F3F3    F2F20000  40404040  4040D4C1  D1D6D97A   *NAME....GAYS.3322...    MAJOR.*
1C0EA0  00000000  00000000  00004040  40404040    40404040  40404040  40404040  40404040   *..........               *
1C0EC0  40404040  40404040  40404040  40404040    40404040  40404040  40404040  40404040

   LINE 1C0EE0 SAME AS ABOVE

1C0F00  40404040  40000000  40404040  40404040    4040C3D6  E4D9E2C5  7B4040C3  D9C5C4C9   *TS  GRADE      COURSE.  CREDI*
1C0F20  E3E24040  C7D9C1C4  C5404040  40404040    40404040  40404040  40404040  40404040
1C0F40  40404040  40404040  40404040  40404040    40404040  40404040  40404040  40404040

   LINE 1C0F60 SAME AS ABOVE

1C0F80  40404040  40404040  40404040  40006DD4    40404040  40404040  40404040  40504FC9   *                     ..I*
1C0FA0  40404040  40404040  40C54040  40404040    40404040  40404040  40404040  40404040   * E           ..M         *
1C0FC0  40404040  40404040  40404040  40404040    40404040  40404040  40404040  40404040
```

Contents of locations
1C0DB1‑1C0DB2 = '0000',
an invalid packed number

Figure 8.7 Partial Core Dump for Example 1
(continued on next page)

Contents of location
1C1660 = '1C', a packed 1

```
1C15A0   001C1BEC  001C4672  001C1CBE  00000000   00000000  60000000  001C4672  001C2EFA   *................*
1C15C0   001C3D12  001C4672  001C3D16  001C2F0A   001C3C9A  001C1CF2  001C4676  001C26E8   *........Y......Y*
1C15E0   001C41E2  001C1820  001C19F8  001C1B08   001C1A78  001C1A88  001C1B20  001C1B30   *..S......8......*
1C1600   001C1718  001C171E  001C172E  001C1740   001C1888  001C189A  001C18CC  001C1900   *................*
1C1620   001C192E  001C194E  001C196A  001C1942   001C1978  001C19C6  001C19F2  001C1A6C   *..........F..2..*
1C1640   001C17EA  001C1814  001C181A  001C117C   001C1230  001C1A03  001C1A88  001C1B30   *................*
1C1660   1C000100  0001F021  4B202000  0000000E   00000005  48004805  EF0700E8  C5E2D5D6   *..........0..YESNO*
1C1680   40E3D6E3  C1D340D7  D9D6C3C5  E2E2C5C4   407E4029  58F0C010  051F0000  006358F0   * TOTAL PROCESSED ..0....0*

1C16A0   C01405EF  58100094  D2011032  C0BC5840   1024D202  4011C019  5010D244  9200D244   *.........K.....K.*
1C16C0   58100098  D2011032  C0BDD203  1060C0BF   58401024  D2024011  C0195010  D248920F   *.K....K....K....0*
1C16E0   D2489680  D2484110  D2440A13  58F0C014   05EF5810  C0941821  D2022021  C04958F0   *K...K...0...K...0*
1C1700   103005EF  5010D1F4  5870D1F4  D23C6020   70005850  C04C07F5  D2026010  C0C35800   *J4..J4K...5K...C..*
1C1720   D2385000  D22C5800  C0505000  D2385820   C054D502  6010C0C3  07825810  C02C07F1   *K...K...N...C...1*
1C1740   5800D22C  5000D238  58F0C014  05EF58F0   C01C051F  00011000  00120C00  00C90000   *K...0...0...I...*
1C1760   02020003  0DD001FC  0019FFFF  53F0C014   05EF5810  C0949110  10300550  4780500C   *K...0...0..*
1C1780   58301C2C  910F300C  0550C47E0 50105820   104C4B20  10525020  104C5010  D2449240   *0...0...*
1C17A0   D2445810  C0985010  D2489240  D2489680   D2484110  D2440A14  5850D1B0  5050D1F4   *K....K....K....K...*
1C17C0   5820C094  58400088  91012017  07145810   20149601  20177B44  43401005  4C401006   *K...K...K...K...J...J4*
1C17E0   41004008  41101000  0A0A5820  C0985340   C08C9101  20170714  58102014  96012017   *0...0...*
1C1800   1B444340  10054C40  10064100  40084110   10000A0A  58F0C014  05EF58F0  C02007FF   *0.....0...*
```

Figure 8.7 Partial Core Dump for Example 1 (continued)

is as it should be, since the length code in a machine instruction is always one less than the actual length of a field.)

The STATE Option

One might logically, or perhaps hopefully, ask: Is this really necessary to determine the cause of an ABEND? We answer with an equivocal "maybe" (i.e., there are other debugging aids which can sometimes lead to an answer more quickly). The most useful of these is the STATE option, which is requested at compile time. Specification of this option displays the last COBOL statement executed (i.e., the statement that probably caused the ABEND). Consider Figure 8.8.

As can be seen from Figure 8.8, COBOL statement 111 produced the ABEND. (This is the same conclusion that was reached by subtracting the Entry Point Address from the last 3 bytes in the PSW and relating the answer to the PMAP.) An experienced programmer would know immediately that an 0C7 can only be caused by an invalid packed field and conclude that one or both of the operands in the ADD statement was invalid. A quick inspection of the COBOL listing should immediately point to WS-TOTAL-STUDENTS. Thus, in this example at least, the detailed analysis of the dump is probably not necessary. There are, however, many situations where quick answers are not readily apparent, as shown in the next section.

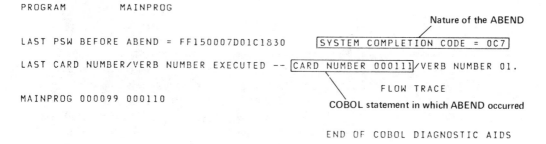

```
PROGRAM         MAINPROG
                                                          Nature of the ABEND
LAST PSW BEFORE ABEND = FF150007D01C1830    SYSTEM COMPLETION CODE = 0C7

LAST CARD NUMBER/VERB NUMBER EXECUTED --  CARD NUMBER 000111/VERB NUMBER 01.

                                                    FLOW TRACE
MAINPROG 000099 000110                      COBOL statement in which ABEND occurred


                                    END OF COBOL DIAGNOSTIC AIDS
```

Figure 8.8 Illustration of the STATE Option

EXAMPLE 2
Dump Reading

Figure 8.1(a) was revised to include a VALUE IS ZEROS clause for WS-TOTAL-STUDENTS in COBOL line 41. Insertion of this clause does not have any effect on either the Data or Procedure Division maps of Figures 8.2 and 8.4 A new run was made and the corrected program produced a transcript before another data exception occurred.

A good place to start is with the output of the STATE option shown in Figure 8.9. As can be seen, the data exception resulted during execution of the IF statement of COBOL line 147. At first glance, the computer seems to have erred (i.e., how can invalid decimal data occur during a comparison?) After some thought, and analysis

```
PROGRAM          MAINPROG                                COBOL statement in
                                                         which ABEND occurred

LAST PSW BEFORE ABEND = FF150007E01C1A36      SYSTEM/COMPLETION CODE = 0C7

LAST CARD NUMBER/VERB NUMBER EXECUTED --  CARD NUMBER 000147/VERB NUMBER 01.

                                                   ------ FLOW TRACE ------
MAINPROG 000154 000146 000154 000146 000154 000146 000154 000146 000154 000146
```

Statement number of last 10 paragraphs
immediately preceding the ABEND   END OF COBOL DIAGNOSTIC AIDS

Figure 8.9 Illustration of the FLOW Option

of the Procedure Division map in Figure 8.4, we realize that the IF statement involves two numeric fields, ST-MAJOR-CODE (PIC 9(4)) and MAJOR-CODE (PIC 9(4)), and that the generated instructions include a compare packed instruction. We conclude that one or both operands are invalid. Experience suggests (1) invalid incoming data (e.g., a blank field for ST-MAJOR-CODE), (2) an invalid code in the majors table itself, or (3) a valid ST-MAJOR-CODE in the sense that it is a proper decimal number but invalid in that the code is not contained in the major table. Any of these are possible, and the STATE option did little to find the bug.

The FLOW Option

There is, however, another aid to consider before the dump. The FLOW option specifies the last n paragraphs which were executed prior to the ABEND (the value of n is entered at compile time). Figure 8.9 shows the last 10 paragraphs executed alternated between statement 146, 030-FIND-MAJOR, and 154, 030-FIND-MAJOR-EXIT. We conclude, therefore, that the incoming value of ST-MAJOR-CODE was a valid decimal number. Further, after examining COBOL lines 82-91, we conclude that the code values in the table are all valid. Thus, the cause of the data exception was probably an incoming code, which is not present in the table. Analysis of the dump will confirm our conclusion and also identify the student causing the problem. Salient information is contained in Figures 8.10 and 8.11. We begin with the usual subtraction:

Last three bytes of PSW	=	1C1A36
− Entry Point Address	=	− 1C0CF8
Relative location	=	D3E

The Procedure Division map of Figure 8.4 is used to determine that D3E falls within the IF statement of COBOL line 147. This, in turn, is within the COBOL routine to find an expanded value for MAJOR-NAME, given a ST-MAJOR-CODE. D3E points to the instruction that would have been executed if the data exception had not occurred. The instruction which actually caused the data exception is immediately before. Let us analyze the instruction at D38 in depth:

190

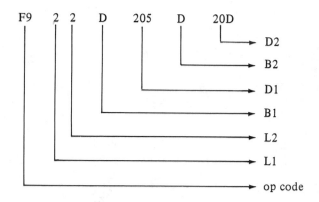

F9 is the op code for Compare Packed. This instruction compares the contents of two fields and establishes a condition code for a subsequent branch instruction. Both operands must be valid packed fields; else a data exception will occur.

The value of both operands is computed by adding the contents of register 13 and the appropriate displacements. Register 13 contains 1C1338. The displacements of the two operands are 205 and 20D, respectively. Thus, the first operand is contained in the three bytes beginning at location 1C153D. (*The length code in the machine instruction is always one less than the number of bytes in the field.*) In similar fashion, the second operand is contained in three bytes beginning at 1C1545 (1C1338 + 20D).

From the dump in Figure 8.11, the first operand is seen to contain 07 77 7F, a valid packed field. The second contains 000000, an *invalid* packed number. Unfortunately, neither appears to shed too much light on the situation. In effect, we have determined the technical reason for the dump, but have not yet related the information to the source program.

The chapter began by stating that a dump, in and of itself, reveals nothing. We cannot overemphasize that point! In order to properly analyze a dump, one must also play detective: *list the suspects and gather evidence.* Analysis of the PSW and entry point address has shown that a data exception occurred within the routine to find a major from an incoming code. The dump has confirmed the presence of the data exception. Now identify the prime suspect, which is the student in core at the time of the ABEND.

The Data Division map of Figure 8.2 shows that WS-STUDENT-RECORD is displaced 20 (in hex) bytes from Base Locator 3 (register 6). The incoming record begins therefore at location 1C0DB8 (1C0D98 + 20). Further analysis of Figure 8.11 shows the incoming student to be MILGROM, M and the incoming major code to be 7777.

The first operand (beginning at locations 1C153D) in the compare packed instruction was 07777F, which is nothing more than 7777 as a packed number. The program was able to find major codes for other students because transcripts have already printed, yet it could not find a major name corresponding to a code of 7777. *The only conclusion is that there is no major code of 7777!* [See COBOL lines 82-91 in Figure 8.1(a), or examine the table as it appears in the dump.]

```
JOB ARTJHM22              STEP GO           TIME 140717    DATE 77340

COMPLETION CODE           SYSTEM = 0C7

PSW AT ENTRY TO ABEND   071D2000  00 1C1A36           ILC 6    INTC 0007
                                     └─────┘
                                Last three bytes of PSW

CDE

                                                                            Entry point address
                                                                           ┌─────────┐
C9F020   ATR1 0B   NCDE 000000   RDC-RB 00C9EC38   NM GO        USE 01   EPA 1C0CF8  ATR2 20   XL/MJ C9EE30
FFE500   ATR1 B9   NCDE FFE4D8   RDC-RB 00000000   NM IGG019BA  USE 08   EPA F67480  ATR2 20   XL/MJ FFE518
FFE4D8   ATR1 B8   NCDE FFA848   RDC-RB 00000000   NM IGG019BB  USE 08   EPA F67690  ATR2 20   XL/MJ FFE4F0
FF9A18   ATR1 B1   NCDE FF97F0   RDC-RB 00000000   NM IGG019CF  USE 09   EPA D4E618  ATR2 20   XL/MJ FF9A30
FF97F0   ATR1 B0   NCDE FFE460   RDC-RB 00000000   NM IGG019CL  USE 0A   EPA F37938  ATR2 20   XL/MJ FF9808
FFE460   ATR1 B8   NCDE FFE488   RDC-RB 00000000   NM IGG019AI  USE 10   EPA F67A90  ATR2 20   XL/MJ FFE478


REGS AT ENTRY TO ABEND

                                                                                        Contents of
                                                                                        register 6
FLTR 0-6    0000000000000000   00D71D0000000000   0116320001210D00   0116730000D71B08
                                                                                          ┌────────┐
REGS 0-7    001C1868   50IC1A0E   00000000   000000B6   001C1148   001C19F8   001CD93  001FEA08
REGS 8-15   001C12B0   001C1B76   001C0CF8   001C0CF8   001C15B8   001C1338   001C1A12  001C3D16
                                                                        └────────┘
                                                                       Contents of
                                                                       register 13
```

Figure 8.10 Information Associated with Core Dump of Example 2

Core dump (Figure 8.11, Example 2):

Annotations on the dump:
- "Incoming major code" — arrow to location near 1C0CE0
- "WS BEGIN"
- box around `MILGROM.` / `77706123A256A3789A4012A` — "Student causing data exception"
- "Location 1C0DB8 — beginning of problem record" (pointing to `D4C9D3C7` region)
- "TRANSCRIPT"
- box around the major-code table — "Table of major codes and values"
- "ENDS HERE"
- "BY"

```
                        Incoming major code
1C0CE0  4580F010 D4C1C9D5 D7D9D6C7 E5E2D9F1   90ECD00C 185DD5F0  *...0.MAINPROGVSR1.....0*
1C0D00  000107FE 001C1B76 001C0CF8   0700989F F02407FF E5E2D9F1  *...0.........8...8....0*
1C0D20  40404040 40404040 40F1F9F4   001C15B8 001C1B36           *...........194.........*
1C0D40  40404040 40405C40 D9D5C4C5   40F1F9F4 001C1694 001C1B36  *........194...........*
1C0D60  D9D6E4E3 C9D5C540 E3D640C3   40D7D6C9 40405C40            *ROUTINE TO COMPUTE GRADE POI....*
                 E3C540C7 D9C1C4C5   40D7D6C9 40D7D6C9
1C0D80  F1F44BBF F6 C9D5C540 E3D640C3  E6E2F040 C5C7C9D5 00000000  *14.03.56DEC 6. 1977 .WS BEGIN*
        F1F9F7F7  E5E2F040  C5C7C9D5
1C0DA0  E240C8C5 D9C50040 40404040 D9D6D46B C5C7C9D5              *S HERE..NO NO 36G..GHTS.MILGROM.*
1C0DC0  40D4404040 40404040 F7F7F7F0  C8C5D9C5  C9D3C7D46B       *M  77706123A256A3789A4012A*
        40404040  F6F1F2F3
1C0DE0  F3F3F4F5 C2F3F6F7 F8C2F340   40404040 40404040           *3345B3678B3*
1C0E00  40404040 40404040 40404040   D7E34040 E2C3D9C9 E3D9C1D5  *.........TRANSCRIPT......*
1C0E20  E2C3D9C9 D7E34040             E3D9C1D5                    *TRANSCRIPT*
        ────────── Location 1C0DB8 – beginning of problem record

LINE 1C0E40  SAME AS ABOVE
1C0E60  40404040 40404040 40404040 40404040 40C3D9C5             *NAME.BENJAMIN. L        CRE*
1C0E80  40D5C1D4 C57AC2C5 D5D1C1D4 40404D4C1 D1D6D97A            *NAME.BENJAMIN. L     MAJOR.*
1C0EA0  C2C9D6D3 D6C7E840 40404040 40404040 40404040             *BIOLOGY*
1C0EC0  40404040 40404040 40404040 40404040 40404040             *                        *

LINE 1C0EE0  SAME AS ABOVE
1C0F00  40404040 405C5C5C 40404040 E4D9E2C5 7B40404C3 D9C5C4C9   *TS   GRADE        COURSE.  CREDI*
1C0F20  E3E24040 C7D9C1C4 C5404040 40404040 40404040 D9C1C4C5    *TS   GRADE*
1C0F40  40404040 40404040 40404040 40404040 40404040             *                        *

LINE 1C1060  SAME AS ABOVE
1C1080  40404040 40404040 40404040 40404040 40C2E840            *1234ACCOUNTINGI400BIOLOGY 1976  BY*
1C10A0  F1F2F3F4 C1C3C3D6 E4D5E3C9 D5C7F1F4 F0F0C2C9 D6D3D6C7 E8404040 F1F9F7F6
1C10C0  C3C8C5D4 C9E2E3D9 E840F2F1 F0F0C3C9 E5C9D340 C5D5C740 F2F4F5F8 C54B40C4  *CHEMISTRY 2100CIVIL ENG 2458E. D*
1C10E0  4B40D74B 4040F3F2 F4F5C3C3 F3F6F6F0 C6C9D5C1 D5C3C540 D5C3C540          *. P. 3245ECONOMICS 3960FINANCE D*
1C1100  4040F4F3 F2F1D4C1 D5C1C7C5 D4C5D5E3 F4F9F9D4 C1D9D2C5 E3C9D5C7 F5F4     *  4321MANAGEMENT499MARKETING 54*
1C1120  F0F0E2E3 C1E3C9E2 E3C9C3E2 E2604040 C3C1E6E2 C8C5D9C5 D9C1C7C5          *00STATISTICSS CAWS HEREAGE*
1C1140  40D9D6E4 40404040 00000000 051C3C9A 051C3C9A 40D9D6E4                   *ROU...*
1C1160  00000000 00000000 00000000 00000000 80000000 00000001                  * ........... codes and values .2*
1C1180  00000000 00000000 00C41000 021FEA00 00000001 461C19F2
1C11A0  801C1144 00C9E60C 00900050 28022828
1C11C0  001FE888 001FEA58 001FEA08 00F5E0C8 00000000
1C11E0  00000000 00000000 00000000 00800040 00000000
1C1200  00000000 051C3C9A 051C3C9A 001C0D1E 00000000
```

Figure 8.11 Partial Core Dump for Example 2
(continued on next page)

```
1C1400  001C6808 00010F8A 011C5810 401C122C   061C3568 001C2DA8 20000036 001C2270   *..............IZ....*
1C1420  401C11C6 001C16E8 00000002 601C298A   00C9EC60 00C9E978 001C287C 401C294A   *.F...Y....I...*
1C1440  00035000 00005CD8          00000063   9D6E0011 00060C40 E3000000 4040407B   *...Q....T..#*
1C1460  F5F7F4F0 60C3C2F1 40C3D6D7 E8D9C9C7   C8E340C9 C2D440C3 D6D9D74B 40F1F9F7   *5740.CB1 COPYRIGHT IBM CORP. 197*
1C1480  F56BF2F4 F0F3F7F7 C9D2C6C3 C2D3F0F0   C9D2C6C3 C2D3F0F0 E5E2D9F1 F1D7F0F7   *5.240377IKFCBL00IKFCBL00VSR11P07*
1C14A0  90ECD00C 055047F0 55700000 00000000   00000000 00000000 00200020 00000000   *......0...*
1C14C0  01900028 00000000 00000000 00000000   001C0003 00000000 0E100024 00000000   *......0.*
1C14E0  001C1852 401C09E0 001C0CF8 000008A0   001C2DA8 E2E8E2D6 E4E34040 E3000000   *.......8....SYSOUT T.*
1C1500  001C0D80 00000000 00080008 00000000   00280008 00000000 00140002 00000000   *.......8...*
1C1520  0C000180 00000000 00400008 001FEA08   001C12B0 001C0D98 00000000 0007777F   *...............*
1C1540  00000000 000000   F0F34BF0 F0000000   00000000 00000000 001C0DE1 001C0DE5   *......V.*
1C1560  001C0DE4 001C1A88 001C0DB8 801C0DAE   001C172E 001C1888 001C1B30 001C117C   *...U....03.00...*
1C1580  8F1C1230 00000000 801C0DB8 801C0DAE   801C1230 00000000 0A000E3E 00000000   *..........*
1C15A0  001C1BEC 001C1CB4 001C1CBE 00000000   00080022 00000000 001C4672 001C2EFA   *......*
1C15C0  001C3D12 001C4672 001C3D16 001C2F0A   001C3C9A 001C1CF2 001C4676 001C26E8   *......2......Y*
```

Value of second operand beginning at location 1C1545

Value of first operand beginning at location 1C153D

Figure 8.11 Partial Core Dump for Example 2 (continued)

Now let us recreate what happened. The COBOL routine to find a major from a major code, is reproduced from Figure 8.1(a):

```
MOVE 1 TO WS-SUB.
MOVE 'NO' TO WS-FOUND-MAJOR-SWITCH.
PERFORM 030-FIND-MAJOR THRU 030-FIND-MAJOR-EXIT
    UNTIL WS-FOUND-MAJOR-SWITCH = 'YES'.
    .
    .
    .
030-FIND-MAJOR.
    IF    ST-MAJOR-CODE = MAJOR-CODE (WS-SUB)
          MOVE 'YES' TO WS-FOUND-MAJOR-SWITCH
          MOVE MAJOR-NAME (WS-SUB) TO HDG-MAJOR
    ELSE
          ADD 1 TO WS-SUB.
030-FIND-MAJOR-EXIT.
    EXIT.
```

The table of major names has been established by VALUE clauses in COBOL lines 82-91. The table is 140 bytes long and is shown schematically as follows:

```
|1|2|3|4|A|C|C|O|U|N|T|I|N|G|1|4|0|0|B|I|O|L|O|G|Y| | | |1|9|7|6|C|H|E|M|
```

```
|.........|5|5|0|0|S|T|A|T|I|S|T|I|C|S|
```

The COBOL code begins by initializing WS-SUB to 1. It compares the incoming code of 7777 to the first code in the table, which is 1234. If no match is found, it then increments WS-SUB by one and looks at the second code, and so on. Now consider what happened to MILGROM. The incoming code of 7777 was not found in the table. After WS-SUB reached 10 without finding a match, WS-SUB was incremented to 11 to look at the next entry in the table. (*We know that the table only has 10 entries, but the computer does not.*) Hence, it goes past the table, takes whatever is there, and subsequently encounters a data exception.

EXAMPLE 3
Dump Reading

After Figure 8.1(a) was revised to include the VALUE clause for WS-TOTAL-STUDENTS and the invalid code for MILGROM was corrected, the program was rerun. Another data exception occurred, and the salient information is shown in Figure 8.12.

We begin as before; take the last three bytes of the PSW and subtract the Entry Point Address.

Last three bytes of PSW	=	292C0E
− Entry Point Address	=	− 290CF8
Relative location	=	1F16

JOB [ARTJHM22]   STEP GO   TIME 140238   DATE 77340
                 └─ Job name

COMPLETION CODE   [SYSTEM = 0C7] ── Completion code

PSW AT ENTRY TO ABEND   071D2000 00[292C0E]   ILC 6   INTC 0007
                                    └─ Last three bytes of PSW

CDE

								Entry point address		
C9F020	ATR1 0B	NCDE 000000	ROC-RB 00C9EC38	NM GO	USE 01	EPA 290CF8	ATR2 20	XL/MJ C9EE30
FFE500	ATR1 B9	NCDE FFE4D8	ROC-RB 00000000	NM IGG019BA	USE 06	EPA F67480	ATR2 20	XL/MJ FFE518
FFE4D8	ATR1 B8	NCDE FFA848	ROC-RB 00000000	NM IGG019BB	USE 06	EPA F67690	ATR2 20	XL/MJ FFE4F0
FF9A18	ATR1 B1	NCDE FF97F0	ROC-RB 00000000	NM IGG019CF	USE 04	EPA D4E618	ATR2 20	XL/MJ FF9A30
FF97F0	ATR1 B0	NCDE FFE460	ROC-RB 00000000	NM IGG019CL	USE 06	EPA F37938	ATR2 20	XL/MJ FF9808
FFE460	ATR1 B8	NCDE FFE488	ROC-RB 00000000	NM IGG019AI	USE 02	EPA F67A90	ATR2 20	XL/MJ FFE478

REGS AT ENTRY TO ABEND

FLTR 0-6   0000000000000000   00981D0000000000   00BD0E00009D0D00   00BD0F0000981B08

REGS 0-7   00292A7E   50292B2E   00000000   00000005   00290DD1   00000001   00292788   0029298F
REGS 8-15   00292990   00292CC2   002926E8   00292E8   002929E0   00292798   00290DB8   00293D16

Figure 8.12 Information Associated with Core Dump of Example 3

Next, take 1F16 as the relative location within the program and go to the Procedure Division map of Figure 8.4. Unfortunately the relative locations stop well below 1F16, and hence we cannot find where we are in our program. The procedure which worked so well only a short time ago, seems to have failed completely. Do not panic. The dump is still as useful as always; it must, however, be coaxed a little more to tell us what we need to know.

What should come immediately to mind is that we are executing a load module, comprised of two COBOL programs (a main program and a subprogram), which have been link-edited into a single executable program. Perhaps our problem lies in the subprogram and not in the main program. We can determine if this is the case by examining Figure 8.13.

Figure 8.13 is an OS linkage-editor map which lists all the Control Sections (CSECTs) comprising the load module. The first column lists the CSECT's name. The next column shows the origin (i.e., the relative location of each routine within the load module), and the last column shows the length of the routine in bytes (in hex). We can recognize MAINPROG and SUBRTN as the PROGRAM-ID's from Figure 8.1(a) and (b) (COBOL line 2 in each program). The remaining, rather strangely named routines are IBM subroutines required by our COBOL program for I/O and other functions.

Recall from Figure 8.12 that the main program had an EPA of 290CF8. The subroutine, in turn, has an origin of 19F0 bytes past MAINPROG, and the relationship between these modules is shown schematically in Figure 8.14.

Now reconsider 1F16 the relative address where our program blew out. We can verify that the error did occur somewhere in the link-edit map of Figure 8.13 since 1F16 is less than 41E0, the origin of ILBOMSG (the last module shown). We scan the origins of Figure 8.13 (which are listed in ascending order) and find that the problem occurred in SUBRTN (i.e., the highest origin that does not exceed 1F16). We find where within SUBRTN by subtraction:

Location in load module	=	1F16
− Origin of SUBRTN	=	− 19F0
Relative location	=	526

Next, consider a partial Procedure Division map for SUBRTN, shown in Figure 8.15. 526 is contained within the COMPUTE statement, COBOL line 63. A good intuitive conclusion is that the incoming course data for a particular student are in error. The question is: Which student and which data?

The Linkage Section of the subprogram contains the 01 record, DATA-PASSED-FROM-MAIN, which in turn has the student name and course data. The CALL statement of the main program [COBOL lines 112-114 in Figure 8.1(a)] shows that the 01 record, WS-STUDENT-RECORD, corresponds to DATA-PASSED-FROM-MAIN in the subprogram [i.e., *the two 01 records, WS-STUDENT-RECORD (main program) and DATA-PASSED-FROM-MAIN (subprogram), occupy a single area in core*]. Hence, if we can locate either 01 record, we automatically have the other! [This "single" area is always part of the *calling* program; in other words, data names, defined in the Linkage Section of a *called* program exist elsewhere (i.e., in the calling program).]

CROSS REFERENCE TABLE

CONTROL SECTION — PROGRAM-ID of main program / PROGRAM-ID of subprogram / Origin of subprogram

NAME	ORIGIN	LENGTH	ENTRY NAME	LOCATION	NAME	LOCATION	NAME	LOCATION	NAME	LOCATION
MAINPROG	00	FC6								
ILBODSP	FC8	A28	ILBODSS0	FFA	ILBODSP0	FFA				
SUBRTN	19F0	6BB								
ILBOCOM*	20B0	120	ILBOCOM	20B0						
ILBODBG *	21D0	DD0	ILBODBG0	2202	ILBODBG1	2202	ILBODBG2	220A	ILBODBG3	220E
			ILBODBG4	2212	ILBODBG5	2216	ILBODBG6	221A	ILBODBG7	221E
ILBOEXT *	2FA0	46	ILBOEXT0	2FA2						
ILBOFLW *	2FE8	500	ILBOFLW0	301A	ILBOFLW1	301E	ILBOFLW2	3022		
ILBOSPA *	34E8	454	ILBOSPA0	34EA	ILBOSPA1	34EE				
ILBOSRV *	3940	408	ILBOSRV0	397A	ILBOSR5	397A	ILBOSR3	397A	ILBOSR	397A
			ILBOSRV1	397E	ILBOSTP1	397E	ILBOST	397E	ILBOSTP0	3982
ILBOBEG *	3D48	C2	ILBOBEG0	3D7A						
ILBOCMM *	3E10	3CE	ILBOCMM0	3E42	ILBOCMM1	3E46				
ILBOMSG *	41E0	128	ILBOMSG0	4212						

LOCATION	REFERS TO SYMBOL	IN CONTROL SECTION	LOCATION	REFERS TO SYMBOL	IN CONTROL SECTION
8C0	ILBOSRV0	ILBOSRV	8C4	ILBODBG0	ILBODBG
8C8	ILBOFLW0	ILBOFLW	8CC	ILBOSR5	ILBOSRV
8D0	ILBOFLW1	ILBOFLW	8D4	ILBODBG4	ILBODBG
8D8	ILBOEXT0	ILBOEXT	8DC	ILBODSP0	ILBODBG
8E0	ILBOSRV1	ILBOSRV	8E4	SUBRTN	SUBRTN
8E8	ILBOSPA0	ILBOSPA	7F8	ILBOCOM0	ILBOCOMO
1CE8	ILBOSRV0	ILBOSRV	1CEC	ILBODBG0	ILBODBG
1CF0	ILBOFLW0	ILBOFLW	1CF4	ILBOSR5	ILBOSRV
1CF8	ILBOFLW1	ILBOFLW	1CFC	ILBODBG4	ILBODBG
1D00	ILBOSRV1	ILBOSRV	1C58	ILBOCOM0	ILBOCOMO
2E60	ILBOFLW0	ILBOFLW	2E64	ILBOFLW2	ILBOFLW
2E68	ILBOTEF3	$UNRESOLVED(W)	2E6C	ILBOSTN0	$UNRESOLVED(W)
2E74	ILBOTC00	$UNRESOLVED(W)	3C4C	ILBOCOM	ILBOCOMO
3C5C	ILBOSTT0	$UNRESOLVED(W)	3C50	ILBOCMM0	ILBOCMM
3C54	ILBOBEG0	ILBOBEG	3C58	ILBOMSG0	ILBOMSG

Figure 8.13 Linkage-Editor Map

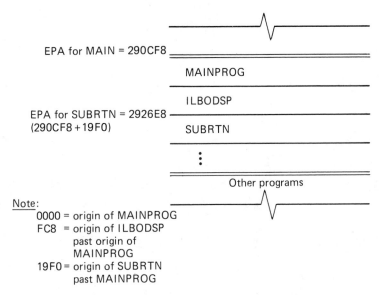

EPA for MAIN = 290CF8

MAINPROG

ILBODSP

EPA for SUBRTN = 2926E8
(290CF8 + 19F0)

SUBRTN

⋮

Other programs

Note:
    0000 = origin of MAINPROG
    FC8 = origin of ILBODSP
           past origin of
           MAINPROG
    19F0 = origin of SUBRTN
           past MAINPROG

Figure 8.14 Origins and Lengths of Main Programs and Subprogram

Figure 8.16 is the Data Division map of the subprogram, which is similar to Figure 8.2, which contained the Data Division map for the main program. There is one *significant* difference, however; the entires in the Linkage Section of the subprogram are tied to a Base Linkage Locator (BLL). The simple procedure we used in the other examples will *not* work because there is no direct tie from the BLL to a corresponding register. Nor can one take the contents of register 6 and assume they point to Working-Storage for the main program. The program blew out in SUBRTN, not in the main program; hence, the registers displayed in Figure 8.12 are those of the subprogram and go nowhere fast. Give up? Don't! We have another trick up our sleeve.

Notice COBOL lines 35 and 36 of the main program in Figure 8.1(a). We establish the literal WS BEGINS HERE at the start of Working-Storage for the main program and use this as a crutch (i.e., we begin at the start of the dump, Figure 8.17, and scan the alphabetic interpretation at the right-hand side of each line looking for WS BEGINS HERE. We then deduce that Working-Storage begins at hex location 290D98. Using the Data Division map for the main program, we see immediately that the student named BOROW, J had the incorrect data. Specifically credits were left blank for his first course, #666, in which he received a B, hence the data exception and ABEND. [The hex representation for a blank is 40, so that when credits is packed, the low-order digit (i.e., sign) of the resulting packed field will be 4. This is an invalid sign and will subsequently cause the ABEND.]

Before you object too strongly to the use of our crutch, consider the following:

1. It works, and consequently allows the reader to build confidence immediately. This is extremely important because dumps are often anathema even to the most ambitious applications programmer. Too often the response is a premature yell for help, which we are trying to avoid.

2. It substantiates more sophisticated means; obviously, there should be other ways to find Working-Storage, and indeed we proceed to cover both BL and BLL

199

```
COBOL  COBOL                        Relative   Machine              Assembler Formats
Card#  Verb                         Location   Instruction

50  COMPUTE                         0003D8  F2 72 D 1F8 6 000  PACK 1F8(8,13),000(3,6)   TS=01      DNM=1-109
                                    0003DE  F2 72 D 200 6 003  PACK 200(8,13),003(3,6)   TS=09      DNM=1-135
                                    0003E4  F0 30 D 204 0 003  SRP  204(4,13),003(0),0   TS=013
                                    0003EA  FD 51 D 202 D 1FE  DP   202(6,13),1FE(2,13)  TS=011     TS=07
                                    0003F0  F8 73 D 200 D 202  ZAP  200(8,13),202(4,13)  TS=09      TS=011
                                    0003F6  F0 35 D 204 0 03F  SRP  204(4,13),03F(0),5   TS=013
                                    0003FC  58 E0 D 210        L    14,210(0,13)         BLL=3
                                    000400  F3 22 E 000 D 205  UNPK 000(3,14),205(3,13)  DNM=1-201  TS=014

52  *005-RETURN-TO-MAIN                                                                  PN=01

55  *010-COMPUTE-QUALITY-POINTS
                                    000440  58 F0 C 010        L    15,010(0,12)         V(ILBOFLW1)
                                    000444  05 1F              BALR 1,15
                                    000446  00000037           DC   X'00000037'
56  MOVE                            00044A  92 F0 6 006        MVI  006(6),X'F0'         DNM=1-162
                                    00044E  58 E0 D 214        L    14,214(0,14)         BLL=4
                                    000452  41 40 E 018        LA   4,018(0,14)          DNM=1-393
                                    000456  48 30 6 007        LH   3,007(0,6)           DNM=1-185
59  IF                              00045A  5C 20 C 058        M    2,058(0,12)          LIT+8
                                    00045E  1A 43              AR   4,3

             . . . . .

62  MOVE                            0004FA  92 F1 6 006        MVI  006(6),X'F1'         DNM=1-162
63  COMPUTE                         0004FE                     EQU  *                                          GN=08
                                    000502  58 E0 D 214        L    14,214(0,13)         BLL=4
                                    000506  41 40 E 019        LA   4,019(0,14)          DNM=1-421
                                    00050A  48 30 6 007        LH   3,007(0,6)           DNM=1-185
                                    00050E  1A 43              AR   4,3
                                    000510  5B 40 C 058        S    4,058(0,12)          LIT+8
                                    000514  F2 70 D 200 6 006  PACK 200(8,13),006(1,6)   TS=09
                                    00051A  F2 70 D 1F8 6 000  PACK 1F8(8,13),000(1,4)   TS=01
                                    000520  FC 10 D 206 D 1FF  MP   206(2,13),1FF(1,13)  TS=015
                                    000526  F2 72 D 1F8 6 003  PACK 1F8(8,13),003(3,6)   TS=01      DNM=1-135
                                    00052C  FA 21 D 205 D 1FE  AP   205(3,13),1FE(2,13)  TS=014
                                    000532  F3 22 6 003 D 205  UNPK 003(3,6),205(3,13)   DNM=1-135  DNM=1-135+2
                                    000538  96 F0 6 005        OI   005(6),X'F0'         DNM=1-135+2
65  ADD                             00053C  F2 70 D 200 4 000  PACK 200(8,13),000(1,4)   TS=09      DNM=1-109
                                    000542  F2 72 D 1F8 6 000  PACK 1F8(8,13),000(3,6)   TS=01      TS=07
                                    000548  FA 22 D 205 D 1FE  AP   205(3,13),1FE(2,13)  TS=014
                                    00054E  F3 22 6 000 D 205  UNPK 000(3,6),205(3,13)   DNM=1-109  DNM=1-109+2
                                    000554  96 F0 6 002        OI   002(6),X'F0'         VN=01
                                    000558  58 10 D 224        L    1,224(0,13)
                                    00055C  07 F1              BCR  15,1
```

Instruction at location 526 (boxed: 000526 F2 72 D 1F8 6 003)

Figure 8.15 Truncated Procedure Division Map for SUBRTN

INTRNL NAME	LVL	SOURCE NAME	BASE	DISPL	INTRNL NAME	DEFINITION	USAGE
DNM=1-109	77	WS-TOTAL-CREDITS	BL=1	000	DNM=1-109	DS 3C	DISP-NM
DNM=1-135	77	WS-QUALITY-POINTS	BL=1	003	DNM=1-135	DS 3C	DISP-NM
DNM=1-162	77	WS-MULTIPLIER	BL=1	006	DNM=1-162	DS 1C	DISP-NM
DNM=1-185	77	WS-SUB	BL=1	007	DNM=1-185	DS 2C	COMP
DNM=1-201	77	LS-CALCULATED-AVERAGE	BLL=3	000	DNM=1-201	DS 3C	DISP-NM
DNM=1-232	01	DATA-PASSED-FROM-MAIN	BLL=4	000	DNM=1-232	DS 0CL61	GROUP
DNM=1-266	02	ST-NAME	BLL=4	000	DNM=1-266	DS 15C	DISP
DNM=1-283	02	ST-MAJOR-CODE	BLL=4	00F	DNM=1-283	DS 4C	DISP-NM
DNM=1-306	02	ST-NUMBER-OF-COURSES	BLL=4	013	DNM=1-306	DS 2C	DISP-NM
DNM=1-336	02	ST-COURSE-TABLE	BLL=4	015	DNM=1-336	DS 0CL5	GROUP
DNM=1-364	03	ST-COURSE-NUMBER	BLL=4	015	DNM=1-364	DS 3C	DISP
DNM=1-393	03	ST-COURSE-GRADE	BLL=4	018	DNM=1-393	DS 1C	DISP
DNM=1-421	03	ST-COURSE-CREDITS	BLL=4	019	DNM=1-421	DS 1C	DISP-NM

Base linkage locators

Figure 8.16 Data Division Map for SUBRTN

201

LOAD MODULE   GO

Start of working storage location 290D98   Working-storage begins here

```
290CE0                                                                              *...............0*
290D00  4580F010 D4C1C9D5 D7D9D6C7 E5E2D9F1    90ECD00C 185D05F0                    *...............0*
290D20  000107FE 00291B76 00290CF8 00290CF8    96021034 07FE41F0                    *..0.MAINPROGVSR1....0*
290D40  00000001 00000001 AC001001 05050000    00291338 00291B36                    *......8...8....*
290D60  922F5A53 40000008 062F5A98 60000104    0001AC00 00010505                    *..............*
290D80  F1F34BF5 F94BF5F2 C4C5C340 40F66B40    922F5A5F 06000000                    *13.59.52DEC  6. 1977...[WS BEGIN]*
290DA0  E240C8C5 D9C50006 D5D640E8 C5E2F3F0    F1F9F7F7 00000001                    *S HERE..NO YES30....[BOROW]. J*
290DC0  40404040 40404040 40404040 F9F6F0F0    C0002F00 0001AC00    E6E240C2 C5C7C9D5   *4        39004666B[ ]777B488C4999C*
290DE0  F4404040 40404040 40404040 40404040    C240F7F7 F7C2F4F8    F9F9F9C3           *4          TRANSCRIPT...*
290E00  40404040 40404040 40404040 E3D9C1D5    E2C3D9C9 D7E34040    40404040           *                    *
290E20  40404040 40404040 40404040 40404040    40404040 40404040    40404040           *                    *
```

ST-NAME begins here (290DB8)   Credits was left blank

```
LINE 290F60 SAME AS ABOVE
290F80  40404040 40404040 40404040 40000000    40404040 40404040 40F5F5F5            *              555*
290FA0  40404040 40404040 40F34040 404040C2    40404040 40F34040 404040C2            *        3    ..B*
290FC0  40404040 40404040 40404040 40404040    40404040 40404040 40404040            *              *
LINE 290FE0 SAME AS ABOVE
291000  40404040 40404040 40404040 40404040    40404040 4000002C 40404040            *              *
291020  40F34BF0 F0404040 C1E5C5D9 C1C7C57A    40F34BF0 F0404040 40404040            *AVERAGE. 3.00 ...*
291040  40404040 40404040 40404040 40404040    40404040 40404040 40404040            *              *
LINE 291060 SAME AS ABOVE
291080  40404040 40404040 40404040 40404040    40404040 40404040 40276000            *              *
2910A0  F1F2F3F4 C1C3C3D6 E4D5E3C9 D5C7F1F4    F0F0C2C9 D6D3D6C7 F1F9F7F6            *1234ACCOUNTING1400BIOLOGY  1976*
2910C0  C3C8C5D4 C9E2E3D9 E840F2F1 F0F0C3C9    E5C9D340 C5D5C740 F2F4F5F8 C54B40D4   *CHEMISTRY 2100CIVIL ENG 2458E. D*
2910E0  4B40D74B 404F3F2 F4F5C5C3 D6D5D6D4    C9C3E240 F3F9F6F0 C5C3D6D5 F3C9D5C1   *. P.  3245ECONOMICS 3960FINANCE *
```

Figure 8.17 Partial Core Dump for Example 3

Value of BL = 3 for main program

Value of BLL = 4 for the subprogram

Figure 8.17 Partial Core Dump for Example 3 (continued)

cells in the next section. When we do, however, the reader is often unsure of himself and our crutch is a valuable means to check on one's calculations.

Use of BL and BLL Cells

This section will corroborate conclusions drawn from WS BEGINS HERE. Figure 8.18 contains the memory map of the COBOL program, SUBRTN. It was produced by the compiler and contains displacements of work areas used by the compiler. One entry in Figure 8.18, the BLL cells, will help to identify the record in question.

Each BLL (Base Linkage Locator) cell contains an address that is used to locate entries in the Data Division map. BLL cells are analogous to BL cells except that they indicate parameters that were passed as arguments from another program. BL cells, on the other hand, are associated with data names originating in the program under consideration. In other words, any data name associated with a BLL cell was originally defined in *another* program, whereas any data name associated with a BL cell was defined in *this* program.

Figure 8.18 shows the displacement of the BLL cells to be 2B8. This means that the value of the first BLL cell will be found 2B8 bytes into the SUBRTN program. Recall that the entry point of the entire module was 290CF8 and the origin of SUBRTN was 19F0. Thus, the first BLL cell is at location 2929A0 (290CF8 + 19F0 + 2B8). Each Base Linkage Locator is one word (four bytes) long. The Data Division map of Figure 8.16 indicates that ST-NAME is associated with BLL = 4. Thus, its value will be found in the four bytes beginning at 2929AC, at the start of the fourth word from 2929A0.

The dump in Figure 8.17 shows the value of BLL = 4 to be 290DB8 (only the three low-order bytes are used). This is the exact location of ST-NAME (since ST-NAME has a displacement of 000 in Figure 8.16) and contains BOROW, J. Note that the address obtained from BLL cells substantiates the conclusion drawn from WS BEGINS HERE. Hopefully, this will make some sense to you. If so, you are well on your way towards a real understanding of program linkages. If not, you are not alone, as many programmers become confused on first encountering BLL cells. Try re-reading the material and discussing it with a colleague. Eventually, it will all come clear.

The data name DATA-PASSED-FROM-MAIN in the subprogram of Figure 8.1(b) occupies the identical storage locations as WS-STUDENT-RECORD in the main program of Figure 8.1(a). We have seen that the BLL cells are used to locate data names in the subprogram. We will now show how the BL cells can be used to identify data names in the main program. Recall that the Data Division map of the main program, Figure 8.2, showed that ST-NAME is displaced hex 20 bytes from BL = 3. To find the address of ST-NAME, we need the value of BL = 3. Figure 8.19 is a partial memory map of the main program. As can be seen, 834 is the displacement of the BL cells in the main program. The first BL cell for the main program is at location 29152C (290CF8 + 834). The value of the third BL cell is found in the four bytes beginning at location 291534 and is equal to 290D98. WS-STUDENT-RECORD begins therefore at location 290DB8 (290D98 + 20), which is the identical location of DATA-PASSED-FROM-MAIN in the subprogram. The circle of checks and double checks is complete.

TGT	000B0
SAVE AREA	000B0
SWITCH	000F8
TALLY	000FC
SORT SAVE	00100
ENTRY-SAVE	00104
SORT CORE SIZE	00108
RET CODE	0010C
SORT RET	0010E
WORKING CELLS	00110
SORT FILE SIZE	00240
SORT MODE SIZE	00244
PGT-VN TBL	00248
TGT-VN TBL	0024C
VCONPTR	00250
LENGTH OF VN TBL	00254
LABEL RET	00256
CURRENT PRIORITY	00257
DBG R14SAVE	00258
COBOL INDICATOR	0025C
A(INIT1)	00260
DEBUG TABLE PTR	00264
SUBCOM PTR	00268
SORT-MESSAGE	0026C
SYSOUT DDNAME	00274
RESERVED	00275
COBOL ID	00276
COMPILED POINTER	00278
COUNT TABLE ADDRESS	0027C
RESERVED	00280
DBG R11SAVE	00288
COUNT CHAIN ADDRESS	0028C
PRBL1 CELL PTR	00290
RESERVED	00294
TA LENGTH	00299
RESERVED	0029C
OVERFLOW CELLS	002A4
BL CELLS	002A4
DECBADR CELLS	002A8
FIB CELLS	002A8
TEMP STORAGE	002A8
TEMP STORAGE-2	002B8
TEMP STORAGE-3	002B8
TEMP STORAGE-4	002B8
BLL CELLS	002B8 |— Displacement of BLL cells in SUBRTN
VLC CELLS	002CC
SBL CELLS	002CC
INDEX CELLS	002CC
SUBADR CELLS	002CC
ONCTL CELLS	002D0
PFMCTL CELLS	002D0
PFMSAV CELLS	002D0
VN CELLS	002D4
SAVE AREA =2	002D8
SAVE AREA =3	002D8
XSASW CELLS	002D8
XSA CELLS	002D8
PARAM CELLS	002D8
RPTSAV AREA	002D8
CHECKPT CTR	002D8
VCON TBL	002D8
DEBUG TABLE	002D8

Figure 8.18 Memory Map of SUBRTN

```
                    MEMORY MAP

          TGT                        00640

      SAVE AREA                      00640
      SWITCH                         00688
      TALLY                          0068C
      SORT SAVE                      00690
      ENTRY-SAVE                     00694
      SORT CORE SIZE                 00698
            •
              •
                •
                  •

      TA LENGTH                      00829
      RESERVED                       0082C
      OVERFLOW CELLS                 00834    ⎫Location of
      BL CELLS                       00834    ⎭ BL cells
      DECBADR CELLS                  00840
      FIB CELLS                      00840
      TEMP STORAGE                   00840
      TEMP STORAGE-2                 00850
```

Figure 8.19 Partial Memory Map of Main Program

The SAVE AREA TRACE

At this point we have completely debugged three 0C7s using a variety of techniques. We now introduce one additional aid which, although not immediately necessary, may prove invaluable in the future. We are referring to the SAVE AREA TRACE and the method by which control is passed from one program to another.

As the reader is well aware, there are 16 general-purpose registers which are constantly used by any executing program. Any time a program is called by another program, the called program is expected to save the registers of the calling program in an area known as a *save area*. The called program is then free to use and alter the 16 registers. When the called program returns control to the calling program, it must first restore the contents of the calling program's registers.

All this sounds very complicated but is made easier in practice by the fact that the COBOL compiler automatically generates the necessary instructions. (Assembler programmers must, on the other hand, explicitly code these instructions themselves.) A brief knowledge of some of these linkage conventions may prove helpful in debugging. This is particularly true in modular systems where control is passed through several routines.

We will concern ourselves with only two conventions. Register 14 contains the return address [i.e., the place in the calling program (e.g., a COBOL main program) where the called program (e.g., a COBOL subprogram) is to return control]. Register 15 contains the entry point address (i.e., the place in the called program where execution is to begin). These points are clarified by Figure 8.20, which shows the SAVE AREA TRACE from the third 0C7.

206

```
SAVE AREA TRACE

GO      WAS ENTERED VIA LINK

                                                                Return point in supervisor     Entry point in the main
                                                                                                       program

SA  2CEF68  WD1 00000000   HSA 00000000   LSA 00291338   RET 00010F8A   EPA 01290CF8   R0  00C9EE38
            R1  002CEFF8    R2  00C9E758    R3  5CC9E840    R4  00C9F2E0    R5  00C9EEF0    R6  00C9EE24
            R7  00C9F118    R8  00C9E818    R9  00C9EC60    R10 00C9E840    R11 00000000    R12 40F582E2

GO      WAS ENTERED VIA CALL

                                           Return point in the                             Entry point in the
                                              main program                                    subprogram

SA  291338  WD1 0030C4C2   HSA 002CEF68   LSA 00292798   RET 5029185C   EPA 002926E8   R0  00C9E8B0
            R1  00291588    R2  00291740    R3  00000005    R4  00290DE5    R5  002919F8    R6  00290D98
            R7  002CEA08    R8  002C12B0    R9  00291576    R10 00290CF8    R11 002930CF8   R12 002921530

GO      WAS ENTERED VIA CALL

                                                                Return point in the
                                                                   subprogram

SA  292798  WD1 0030C4C2   HSA 00291338   LSA 002CEB48   RET 00292B32   EPA 00293D16   R0  00292A7E
            R1  50292B2E    R2  00000000    R3  00000004    R4  00291588    R5  00000001    R6  00292783
            R7  0029298F    R8  00292990    R9  00292CC2    R10 002926E8    R11 002926E8    R12 002929E0
```

Figure 8.20 The SAVE AREA TRACE

Figure 8.20 shows the flow between programs in effect at the time of the ABEND. The first line is *always* associated with the main (sometimes only) COBOL program. The low return address, 010F8A, indicates a return address in the supervisor which receives control when the COBOL program is finished executing. The entry point on the first line, 290CF8, is the entry point for the main COBOL program. The return address in the second save area, 29185C, is the place where control is to return in the main program after the subprogram has completed execution. Subtracting the entry point from the return address yields a relative address of B64, which can be found in the Procedure Division map of Figure 8.4.

Note well two instructions immediately above relative address B64. Location B5E contains a load instruction which places the address of SUBRTN into register 15. The next instruction at B62 is BALR 14,15, which puts the address of the next sequential instruction into register 14 and branches to the address contained in register 15. This demonstrates the linkage conventions exactly. Register 14 contains the return address (i.e., the first instruction to be executed when control is returned to the main program). Register 15 contains the first instruction in the called program (i.e., SUBRTN).

In similar fashion the subprogram itself is seen to call another program. Subtracting the EPA of the subprogram, 2926E8, from the return address of 292B32 yields a relative address of 44A in the subprogram. Consider the two instructions immediately above 44A in the Procedure Division map in Figure 8.15. The first, at 440, loads the address of ILB0FLW1, an IBM module associated with the FLOW option, into register 15. Recall that this option keeps track of the last n procedures executed prior to an ABEND, and evidently was called in this instance. The instruction at 444 is BALR 1,15, which branches to the address contained in register 15, and stores the address of the next sequential instruction in register 1. (The IBM routine will set register 14 to the return address which is four bytes past register 1. Register 1 therefore is seen to contain a parameter list.)

The SAVE AREA TRACE is always present in a dump and appears slightly before the registers at entry to ABEND. In our example it contained three levels of program flow, but it could contain many more! The trace is often used to determine program flow prior to an ABEND.

SUMMARY

This chapter introduces ABEND debugging for COBOL programs. Attempted execution of the same COBOL program causes a data exception for three distinct reasons. The rudiments of a debugging procedure were established. *One takes the address contained in the PSW at the time of the ABEND, subtracts the entry point address, and determines the relative location within the COBOL program of the instruction causing the problem.* There are, however, numerous subtleties associated with the subtraction. First and foremost, a dump may reveal the technical reason for an ABEND (e.g., invalid decimal data), but it is up to the programmer to relate this information to the source listing and/or to the data. Second, the contents of the registers at the time of the ABEND may not coincide with the BL cells and the latter must be determined. The SAVE AREA TRACE was introduced as an additional technique. We hope that we have not falsely represented debugging as a "cookbook" procedure. It is anything but! A dump is a valuable tool in determining the cause and location of a bug, but it is only a tool. In the final analysis it is the programmer who somehow, perhaps by divine inspiration, is able to interpret the dump and find the answer.

In conclusion, there are many ways to debug the same problem and this allows programmers to use a variety of techniques. For example, we have a colleague who uses the SAVE AREA TRACE to the exclusion of almost everything else. Another makes extensive use of the STATE and FLOW options and uses a dump only as a last resort. The method you choose is up to you. More than likely, however, you will use a collection of techniques, for no method seems to work every time.

PROBLEMS

1. Take a COBOL program of your own and cause a data exception. Do it two ways, first by failing to initialize a Working-Storage entry, then by improper input. Analyze the resulting dumps to pinpoint the errors. Better yet, exchange your dump with that of a partner and try to debug the other person's program.

2. Consider the COBOL programs of Figure 8.1(a) and (b). List at least three "defensive" checks that could be included. Show the necessary COBOL code.

3. Explain how a data exception need not occur, even though a 77-level entry used as a counter was not initialized; specifically, consider the first example in this chapter, in which WS-TOTAL-STUDENTS was not set to zero. What would be the consequences of *not* getting a data exception, even if WS-TOTAL-STUDENTS was not initialized?

4. (a) Example 3 showed that a blank in a one-position numeric field causes a data exception if arithmetic is performed on that field. Assume that we define a four-position numeric field that is also used in arithmetic calculations. Further, assume that this four-position field has a valid low-order digit but is punched with leading (high-order) blanks. Will a data exception result? Why or why not?

(b) Explain why an incoming numeric field (USAGE DISPLAY) will cause a data exception if a decimal point is actually punched in the field.

5. Consider the following COBOL entries:

```
77   TOTAL-COUNTER          PIC S9(4)   COMP.
```

and

```
ADD 1 TO TOTAL-COUNTER.
```

Explain why the ADD statement will *never* cause a data exception, even though TOTAL-COUNTER was never initialized. What can you say about the ultimate value of TOTAL-COUNTER (assuming that it was never initialized)?

6. (a) Consider COBOL line 41 of Figure 8.1(a), in which WS-TOTAL-STUDENTS is initialized to zero (i.e., after the error has been found in Example 1). Would there be any difference in substituting the statement MOVE ZEROS TO WS-TOTAL-STUDENTS in the MAINLINE paragraph of the Procedure Division? Why?

   (b) Would there be any difference if COBOL lines 45 and 46 were removed in the subprogram of Figure 8.1(b), provided that the clause VALUE IS ZEROS were added to COBOL lines 15 and 16? Why?

7. Use the COBOL listing, register assignments, and so on, from the chapter (Figures 8.1-8.4) to determine the cause of the ABEND in Figure 8.21. A series of leading questions is provided to help.

   (a) Analyze the completion code.
       (1) What is the completion code?
       (2) What does the completion code mean?
   (b) Determine where the ABEND occurred.
       (3) What address is contained in the PSW?
       (4) At what location was the program loaded?
       (5) Subtract the address in part 4 from the one in part 5.
       (6) Is the relative location obtained in part 5 contained in the main program?
       (7) What is the origin of the subroutine within the load module?
       (8) Subtract the address in part 7 from the one in part 5.
       (9) To which program does the relative location in part 8 refer?
       (10) What machine instruction is at that location?
       (11) What is the actual machine address of the instruction in part 10?
       (12) What is the corresponding COBOL instruction?
   (c) Examine the machine instruction that failed to execute. The instruction that actually produced the ABEND is the one immediately before the instruction determined in part 11.
       (13) What is the machine instruction that actually caused the ABEND?
       (14) What is its op code?
       (15) Which base register is associated with the first operand?
       (16) What is the displacement of the first operand?
       (17) What is the effective address of the first operand?
       (18) How many bytes are associated with the first operand? (Careful.)
       (19) What are the internal contents of the first operand? Are they valid as a decimal number?
       (20) Which base register is associated with the second operand?
       (21) What is the displacement of the second operand?
       (22) How many bytes are associated with the second operand?
       (23) What are the internal contents of the second operand? Are they valid as a decimal number?

(24) Technically, why did the ABEND occur?

(d) Relate the technical cause of the ABEND to the COBOL program.

(25) Which data name *in the main program* contains the description of the invalid student record?

(26) Which base locator is associated with that data name?

(27) What is the displacement of the BL cells in the main program?

(28) Add the entry point address of the main program to the answer to part 27.

(29) What is contained at the four bytes beginning at the address found in part 28?

(30) What is the value of Base Locator 3?

(31) Which student had the invalid data? Identify his record in core.

(e) Verify the solution using the BLL cells.

(32) Which data name in the subprogram contains the description of the invalid student record?

(33) Which Base Linkage Locator is associated with that data name?

(34) What is the displacement of the BLL cells in the subprogram?

(35) Add the Entry Point Address of the main program, plus the origin of the subprogram, plus the answer from question 34.

(36) What is contained at the 4 bytes beginning at the address found in part 35?

(37) What is the value of Base Linkage Locator 4?

(38) What is the relationship between the answers in questions 30 and 37?

(f) Using the SAVE AREA TRACE:

(39) What are the linkage conventions for registers 14 and 15?

(40) What is the entry point in the main program?

(41) What return address is specified in the first called program in the save area trace?

(42) Subtract the address in step 40 from that in step 41. Examine the assembler instruction in the main program immediately before this one and explain its significance.

```
JOB ARTJHM22              STEP GO          TIME 100751    DATE 77330

COMPLETION CODE           SYSTEM = 0CB

PSW AT ENTRY TO ABEND  ,071D0000 001D2AD8          ILC 6    INTC 000B

CDE

  CCF140   ATR1 0B   NCDE 000000   ROC-RB 00CCE930   NM GO       IGG019BA   USE 01   EPA 1D0CF8   ATR2 20   XL/MJ CCF018
  FFE500   ATR1 B9   NCDE FFE4D8   ROC-RB 00000000   NM          IGG019BB   USE 07   EPA F67480   ATR2 20   XL/MJ FFE518
  FFE4D8   ATR1 B8   NCDE FFA848   ROC-RB 00000000   NM          IGG019BC   USE 07   EPA F67690   ATR2 20   XL/MJ FFE4F0
  FF7620   ATR1 B1   NCDE FF7828   ROC-RB 00000000   NM          IGG019CL   USE 02   EPA D4E618   ATR2 20   XL/MJ FF7638
  FF7828   ATR1 B0   NCDE FFE460   ROC-RB 00000000   NM          IGG019AI   USE 02   EPA F37938   ATR2 20   XL/MJ FF7840
  FFE460   ATR1 B8   NCDE FFE488   ROC-RB 00000000                          USE 03   EPA F67A90   ATR2 20   XL/MJ FFE478


SAVE AREA TRACE

GO    WAS ENTERED VIA LINK

SA 20EF68   WD1 00000000   HSA 00000000   LSA 001D1338   RET 00010F8A   EPA 011D0CF8   R0 00CCF150
            R1  0020EFF8   R2  00CCE790   R3  5CCCEAB8   R4  00CCF2E0   R5  00CCEEF0   R6  00CCEBB4
            R7  00CCF118   R8  00CCEA90   R9  00CCEC60   R10 00CCEAB8   R11 00000000   R12 40F582E2

GO    WAS ENTERED VIA CALL

SA 1D1338   WD1 0030C4C2   HSA 0020EF68   LSA 001D2798   RET 501D185C   EPA 001D26E8   R0 00CCE5F8
            R1  001D1588   R2  001D1740   R3  00000005   R4  001D0DE5   R5  001D19F8   R6  001D0D98
            R7  0020EA08   R8  001D12B0   R9  001D1B76   R10 001D0CF8   R11 001D0CF8   R12 001D15B8

GO    WAS ENTERED VIA CALL

SA 1D2798   WD1 0030C4C2   HSA 001D1338   LSA 0020EB48   RET 001D2B32   EPA 001D3D16   R0 001D2A7E
            R1  401D2B2E   R2  00000000   R3  00000000   R4  001D0DDB   R5  00000004   R6  001D2788
            R7  001D298F   R8  001D2990   R9  001D2CC2   R10 001D26E8   R11 001D26E8   R12 001D29E0


REGS AT ENTRY TO ABEND

FLTR 0-6    0000000000000000   0000000000000000   0000000000000000   0000000000000000   0000000000000000

REGS 0-7    00000000   001D2C46   00000000   00000004   00000000   00000005   001DDDE0   001D2788
REGS 8-15   001D298F   001D2990   001D26E8   001D2CC2   001D2798   001D29E0   001D0DB8   001D2AB8
```

Figure 8.21 Material for Problem 7

```
1D0CE0  4580F010 D4C1C9D5 D7D9D6C7 E5E2D9F1 0700989F F02407FF 90ECD00C 185D05F0  *..0.MAINPROGVSR1....0..........0*
1D0D00  001107FE 001D1B76 001D0CF8 001D0CF8 001D15B8 001D1338 96021034 07FE41F0  *...........8...8..............0*
1D0D20  00000000 00000000 00000000 00000000 00000000 00000000 00000000 001D1B36  *...............................*
1D0D40  00000000 00000000 00000800 00000000 00C3FBE8 00000000 00C3F9C8 00000000  *..........C.Y.......C9H.........*
1D0D60  F1F04BF0 F54BF4F3 D5D6E540 F2F66B40 F1F9F7F7 00000390 E6E240C2 C5C7C9D5  *10.05.43NOV 26. 1977....WS BEGIN*
1D0D80  E240C8C5 D9C54B4B D5D640E8 C5E2F3F0 4B4B4B4B 4BE2D4C9 E3C86B40 D1404040  *S HERE..NO YES30.....SMITH. J   *
1D0DA0  D6C8D540 F3F9F6F0 F4F6F6F6 C2F0F7F7 F7C2F0F8 F8F8C3F0 F9F9F9C3 40404040  *OHN 39604666B0777B0888C0999C    *
1D0DC0  F0404040 40404040 E3D9C1D5 E2C3D9C9 D7E34040 40404040 40404040 40404040  *0       TRANSCRIPT              *
1D0DE0  40404040 40404040 40404040 40404040 40404040 40404040 40404040 40404040  *                                *
1D0E00  40404040 40404040 40404040 40404040 40404040 40404040 40404040 40404040  *                                *
1D0E20  40404040 40404040 40404040 40404040 40404040 40404040 40404040 40404040  *                                *
LINE 1D0E40 SAME AS ABOVE
1D0E60  40404040 40404040 40404040 40404040 40F59002 40404040 40404040 40F0F1F5  *                 5..         015*
1D0E80  40D5C1D4 C54BC2C5 D5D1C1D4 C9D54B40 D3404040 40404040 40D4C1D1 D6D97A40  * NAME.BENJAMIN. L       MAJOR.  *
1D0EA0  C2C9D6D3 D6C7E840 40404040 40404040 40404040 40404040 40404040 40404040  *BIOLOGY                         *
1D0EC0  40404040 40404040 40404040 40404040 40404040 40404040 40404040 40404040  *                                *
LINE 1D0F60 SAME AS ABOVE
1D0F80  40404040 40404040 40404040 40F59002 40404040 40404040 40404040 40F5F5F5  *             5..             555*
1D0FA0  40404040 40404040 40F34040 40404040 40404040 40404040 404040C2 40404040  *         3               B      *
1D0FC0  40404040 40404040 40404040 40404040 40404040 40404040 40404040 40404040  *                                *
LINE 1D0FE0 SAME AS ABOVE
1D1000  40404040 40404040 40404040 40CCDDCC 40404040 40404040 40404040 40404040  *                                *
1D1020  C1E5C5D9 C1C7C54B 40404040 40F34BF0 F0404040 40404040 40404040 40404040  *AVERAGE.    3.00                *
1D1040  40404040 40404040 40404040 40404040 40404040 40404040 40404040 40404040  *                                *
LINE 1D1060 SAME AS ABOVE
1D1080  40404040 40404040 40404040 40404040 40404040 40404040 40404040 40D6D7D4  *                             OPM*
1D10A0  F1F2F3F4 C1C3C3D6 E4D5E3C9 D5C7F1F4 F0F0C2C9 D6D3D6C7 E8404040 F1F9F7F6  *1234ACCOUNTING1400BIOLOGY   1976*
```

Figure 8.21 Material for Problem 7 (continued)

```
1D10C0  C3C8C5D4 C9E2E3D9 E840F2F1 F0F0C3C9  E5C9D340 C5D5C740 F2F4F5F8 C54B40C4  *CHEMISTRY 2100CIVIL ENG 2458E. D*
1D10E0  4B40D74B 40F3F2F4 F5C5C3D6 D5D6D4C9  C3E240F3 F9F6F0C6 C9D5C1D5 C3C54040  *. P. 3245ECONOMICS 3960FINANCE *
1D1100  4040F4F3 F2F1D4C1 D5C1C7C5 D4C5D5E3  F4F9F9F9 D4C1D9D2 C5E3C9D5 C740F5F4  *  4321MANAGEMENT4999MARKETING 54*
1D1120  F0F0E2E3 C1E3C9E2 E3C9C3E2 C5C2C1E3  E6E240C5 D5C4E240 C8C5D9C5 40404040  *00STATISTICSEBATWS ENDS HERE ....*
1D1140  87B287B4 00000000 00000000 00000000  00000000 051D3C9A 001D0D1E 00000001  *................................*

1D14C0  1000D49D 411E5B5C 00000000 1000D49A  41EE5B61 001FA300 5B5ED202 1000D49A  *....M...........K...M...........*
1D14E0  001D1852 601D3EBA 001D0CF8 00000000  E2E8E2D6 E4E34040 001D2DA8 E2E8E2D6  *.......8.......8...SYSOUT T.....*
1D1500  001D0D80 F322A7C3 D21595D5 000008A0  B3D0D200 E31F0008 B3CA92D5 001D12B0  *.....CK.N.......N...............*
1D1520  D201A7CB 771596F0 F322A7C3 001FA358  00000000 001FA368 F322A7C3 001D12B0  *K...0.K.........................*
1D1540  00000000 0001400F A7CCD201 0020EA08  00000000 0003300C 00000000 001D0DE5  *..........03.00.................*
1D1560  00000000 801D1A08 001D1A88 F0F34BF0  001D172E 001D1A88 001D1B30 001D0DE5  *.U.......03.00.................V*
1D1580  8F1D1230 D220D4B0 001D0DB8 801D0DAE  801D1230 F844A2B0 0A000E3E 00000000  *.K.M...8........................*
1D15A0  00000EF4 00000FBC 0000FC6 001D3D16   F311D220 A7AC96F0 001DCF2 001D4676   *.4...F..83.K...0................*
1D15C0  001D3D12 001D4672 001D3D16 001D41E2   001D1820 001D4672 001D4676 001D26E8  *.4.......2.....................*
1D15E0  001D41E2 001D1820 001D19F8 001D1A08   001DA78 001D1A88 001D1B20 001D1B30   *.S.......8.....................*
1D1600  001D1718 001D171E 001D172E 001D1740   001D1888 001D189A 001D18CC 001D1900  *.L.............................*

1D2900  00000000 00000000 0000D758 00C8EAB0   00000000 00000000 81D3F648 L6.*      *5U....P..H....L6...............*
1D2920  00000000 01F5E430 01F5E430 000011EE0  000010C 14200003 05C8E200              *.....SYSOUT..HS.................*
1D2940  10000000 401D09E0 001D26E8 001D2DA8   E2E8E2D6 E4E34040 E4E34040             *...Y...Q...SYSOUT T.............*
1D2960  001D2770 00110000 00150005 18000E0C   00000000 00160001 18000E0C             *................................*
1D2980  00000000 00170001 001D2788 00000000   0000000F 00000000 0000000C             *................................*
1D29A0  00000000 00000000 801D0DAE 001D0DDF   001D2C46 00000000 001D2C46             *................................*
1D29C0  0A00059A 00000000 001D2D30 001D2D99   001D2DA3 00C8D750 00C8D750 00000028    *............H.U.HP..............*
1D29E0  001D4672 001D2EFA 001D3D12 001D2F0A   001D3D16 001D4676 001D4676 001D2B28    *................................*
1D2A00  001D2C46 001D2A8A 001D3D12 001D2AAA   001D2AB8 001D2B62 001D2B8E 001D2BBA    *................................*
1D2A20  001D2BE6 001D2AF8 001D2C46 F6111DE8   F0F0F010 01000000 00000005 5840D004    *W..8..6.YOO0....................*
1D2A40  58404018 58504000 5050D214 58504004   5050D210 58F0C010 051F0000 05C2CD202   *K.O...K.........................*
```

Figure 8.21 Material for Problem 7 (continued)

ABEND Debugging, II

OVERVIEW

The subtraction technique of Chapter Eight to find the next sequential instruction works in only a limited number of instances, when the instruction causing the problem is contained within the COBOL program. As likely as not, an ABEND occurs during execution of a routine entirely outside the COBOL program (e.g., during an I/O operation). The linkage-editor map of Figure 8.13 indicates the large number of IBM-supplied routines necessary in the execution of a relatively simple COBOL program. Although the applications programmer has obviously not written any of these routines, he must nevertheless be responsible for debugging problems in their use. After all, it was his COBOL program in the first place that called the external routine. All these routines are part of the operating system.

Any operating system, be it MVS, SVS, MVT, or whatever, accomplishes its myriad functions by monitoring a set of tables, directories, lists, queues, and so on, which control execution of the COBOL program. These items are collectively known as control blocks, and their net effect is to provide the system with a complete description of the current program. The control blocks are routinely displayed in the first few pages of every dump and are usually avoided like the plague.

Most applications programmers know little more about control blocks other than the fact they exist. This is not a handicap in debugging if the ABEND is contained within the COBOL program (e.g., an 0C7). As Chapter Eight has shown, one can do a significant amount of debugging without ever referencing a control block. Lack of knowledge of control blocks may not even pose a handicap when debugging some external ABENDs (e.g., data management errors), for today's operating systems provide debugging messages far superior to those of a few years ago. Why, then, should one bother with control blocks?

There are several reasons. First and foremost, while such information is often not mandatory, it certainly is not a hindrance. Knowledge of control blocks provides another way of attacking a problem and confirms conclusions drawn from other means. Second, there are instances, if only infrequent instances, where control blocks may be the only means of finding a bug. Finally, there is the loftier reason that control blocks provide us with greater understanding of what an operating system is all about. Many of us could not care, but the truly competent professional always tries to broaden his horizons and we know of no better place than with the operating system itself. Given this bit of encouragement, we continue our treatment of ABEND debugging.

IDENTIFICATION OF I/O AREAS

Our treatment of control blocks centers on two blocks associated with data management, the DCB (Data Control Block) and the DEB (Data Extent Block). Every open data set has both. The DCB contains information about the logical attributes of a file (e.g., record length, block size, etc.). The DEB describes where the file is physically located. Both control blocks are constructed during an OPEN, and as the practitioner is well aware, a significant number of ABENDs results from unsuccessful attempts to open a file. These include conflict in block length between the COBOL FD and the file itself, missing data set, and so on.

A primary use of the DEB and DCB is to identify I/O areas in core. In Chapter Eight we recommended use of READ INTO and WRITE FROM to identify the current record being processed. This is sound technique because areas in Working-Storage are inherently easier to locate than I/O areas, since the latter are best found through the DEB and DCB. Identification of I/O areas may not be necessary in situations where READ INTO and WRITE FROM are utilized; however, location of I/O areas is certainly helpful in programs not using this technique.

Figure 9.1 shows additional portions of the dump associated with Example 3 in Chapter Eight. Recall that an 0C7 resulted during processing of the record for BOROW, J. and that this record was located in Working-Storage. We now proceed to identify the I/O area associated with CARD-FILE in Figure 8.1(a).

The first control block printed in a dump under MVT is the TCB (Task Control

Block). A task is the basic unit of work to the operating system, and execution of a program is considered by the system to be a task. The TCB contains all information about the task and serves as the starting point for locating other control blocks, in particular the DEB.

The address contained in the DEB field in the TCB of Figure 9.1 is C9E414. This is the address of the first DEB associated with our COBOL program. Every file open at the time of the ABEND has a DEB, and each DEB contains the address of another DEB until all DEBs have been located.

The first DEB in the chain is located at the address specified in the TCB (i.e., at C9E414). This DEB, in turn, contains the address of the next DEB in the chain, in the low-order three bytes of its second word (i.e., the second DEB begins at C9E58C). The location of the third DEB is found in the second word of the second DEB to be C9E60C. The location of the fourth DEB (if it existed) would be found in the second word of the third DEB, which in Figure 9.1 is all zeros, indicating the end of the chain.

The seventh word of each DEB points to the associated DCB. Thus, the addresses of the DCBs for three DEBs in question are 2CE680, 291230, and 29117C, respectively. The DCB, in turn, will be shown shortly to contain a wealth of information. Before leaving the DEB, we pause to mention that the first word of every DEB contains the address of the TCB (which pointed to the first DEB to begin with). Hence, the first word of every DEB in Figure 9.1 contains the hex address C9E8B0. This latter piece of information does not buy us very much other than to give a little bit of confidence that we have indeed located a DEB.

We now know the addresses of three DCBs from Figure 9.1. The next concern is to relate each DCB to its associated file in the COBOL program of Figure 8.1. In particular, we seek the DCB for CARD-FILE since our objective is to find the input record that caused the data exception. The relationship between DEBs and COBOL files is simple; the DEBs appear in the *inverse* order in which files were opened. In the OPEN statement of Figure 8.1, CARD-FILE was opened first and PRINT-FILE second. Thus, the last DEB is associated with CARD-FILE and the next-to-last DEB with PRINT-FILE. Hence, the DCB address of 29117C which is contained in the *last* DEB of Figure 9.1, is the DCB address for the *first* open file (i.e., CARD-FILE).

Considerable energy has been expended to arrive at the DCB for CARD-FILE, but the effort will be worthwhile. Table 9.1 contains the displacements within a DCB for several attributes. Using Table 9.1 in conjunction with the DCB address of 29117C, we may find any of the listed attributes. For example, the address of the current record in CARD-FILE (i.e., the record that caused the ABEND), is found in the three bytes beginning at 2911C9 (29117C + 4D). This address is 2CEA08. Using Figure 9.1, we see that the record for BOROW, J. is indeed found at location 2CEA08. Hence, the I/O area for CARD-FILE has been located in core. This substantiates the earlier conclusions from Example 3 in Chapter Eight, which were based on other techniques.

As can be seen from Table 9.1, the DCB contains other information which may be useful in debugging. The logical record length, for example, is found in the two bytes beginning at location 2911CE (29117C + 52). The record length is a hex 50, which corresponds to a decimal 80, which in turn matches the COBOL FD. Although the verification of record length does not shed any additional light for the problem at hand,

Table 9.1   Partial List of DCB Attributes (Displacements and Lengths)

DCB Attribute	Displacement (in Hex)	Length of Field (in Bytes)
Number of buffers	14	1
TIOT offset*	28	2
DEB address	2D	3
Maximum block size	3E	2
Address of current record	4D	3
Logical record length	52	2

Note: If the file in question is not open, then the DDname itself, rather than a TIOT offset, will be found. Further, DEBs do not exist for unopened files.

identification of fields in a DCB is valuable for debugging data management ABENDs, which are discussed later in the chapter.

USE OF THE TIOT

Every task has an associated TIOT (Task Input/Output Table), which contains information about all data sets in the task. The TIOT offset field in a data set's DCB can be used to determine the DDname associated with that DCB. From the previous example, we know that DEBs are listed in the opposite order in which files are opened; hence, the last DEB in Figure 9.1 is tied to the first file of the OPEN statement of Figure 8.1 (i.e., to CARD-FILE with the DDname of CARDS) (see SELECT statement in Figure 8.1). The TIOT will be used to verify this conclusion.

The address of the DCB of any DEB is found in the seventh word of the DEB; hence, the DCB of the third DEB in Figure 9.1 is at location 29117C. Table 9.1 shows that the TIOT offset is a two-byte field within the DCB, displaced hex 28 bytes from the beginning of the DCB. Thus, the TIOT offset for the third DEB is at 2911A4 (29117C + 28).

The value of the TIOT offset (i.e., the contents of the two bytes beginning at 2911A4) is 00A4 in hex or 164 in decimal. What this means is that the TIOT entry for the file in question begins 164 bytes in the TIOT. In order to reconcile this to a particular file, we need one last piece of magic—that the TIOT has a 24-byte header at its beginning and takes 20 bytes for each entry. Accordingly, take the TIOT offset of 164, subtract 24, and divide the remaining 140 by 20. The quotient is 7, indicating that seven entries were completed and that the table is pointing to the start of the eighth entry. The DDname in question is the eighth line down in the TIOT of Figure 9.1 and is found to be CARDS.

Although the determination of the DDname from the TIOT offset in the DCB was unnecessary in this instance (i.e., we began with the DEB and knew the file), there are many occasions where the preceding calculations are quite useful. For example, one may start with the DCB address of the problem file without knowing which file it is.

DATA MANAGEMENT ABENDs

Data management ABENDs occur when there is an error between a user's request for service and a data management routine. These errors are particularly irksome to the COBOL programmer because the "subtraction" method of Chapter Eight is of no

```
TCB  [C9E8B0]

      RBP    00C9FCF0    PIE    00000000    [DEB   00C9E414]   TIO  00C9ED68    CMP    300C7000    TRN   00000000
      MSS    00C9F5E8    PK-FLG 10850540     FLG   00003F3B    LLS  00C9F6A0    JLB    00C9ED28    JPQ   00C9F020
      FSA    012CEF68    TCB    00000000     TME   00000000    JST  00C9E8B0    NTC    00000000    OTC   00C9EEF0
      LTC    00000000    IQE    00000000     ECB   00C9E83C    TSF  20000000    D-PQE  00C9F760    AQE   00C9E100
      STAB   80C9ED00    TCT    80C9EC60     USER  00000000    SDF  00000000    MDID   00000000    JSCB  00C9ED8C
      RESV   00000000    IOBRC  00000000     DIAG  00000000    EXT  00000000    BITS   00000000    DAR   00000000
      EXT2   00C9E9B0    XTNT   002904C9     TIRB  00C9E670    BAK  00C6E8C0    LSQAP  00C9FFF8    IOTM  00000000
      TMSAV  00000000    ABCR   12000000     QECB  00000000    FOE  00000000    SWA    00C9FFE0    RESV  00000000
      GTF    00000000    RCMP   00C70000     RESV  00000000    RES  00000000
                                                    ↑
Address of TCB                                Address of first DEB
```

```
DEB
                 Address of associated DCB                  Beginning of first DEB   Address of second DEB
C9E3E0                                                    01F37938  00004FC0  00004FC0  00000000   *............3...*
C9E400   00000000  00000000  00002BE0                    04C9E8B0  C8000000  C3000000  00000000   *.........IY..IV.*
C9E420   8F000000  01000000  1F[2CE680]                  10[C9E58C] 00010001  0F000000  00000085   *.......W..ITO...*
C9E440   00000000  0000007D  C2C2C2C1  C3D3C3C6          02C9E3F0  33002A1C  00000000  00000000   *...BBBACLCF.....*
C9E460   00000000  00000000  00000000                    00000000  00000000  00000000  00000000   *.......H........*
```

```
DEB
         Address of associated DCB                          Beginning of second DEB   Address of third DEB
C9E560   00000000  00010BE0  1F[291230]                    01F37938  00004FC0  00004FC0  00000000   *............3...*
C9E580   0F200002  04C9E8B0  33002AAC                      10[C9E60C] C8000000  0F000000  01000000   *.........IY..IW.*
C9E5A0   02C9E568  33002AAC  00000000                      00010001  00000000  00000000  00000035   *.......IV.......*
C9E5C0   C1D9C1C9  C3D3C3C6                                00000000  00000000  00000000  00000000   *ARAICLCF........*
                                                                                                    *.......H........*
```

```
DEB
         Address of associated DCB              First word of DEB points back to TCB   End of DEB chain
C9E5E0   00000000  00010AE0  1F[29117C]                    00004FC0  00004FC0  00004FC0  00000000   *............3...*
C9E600   0F200001  03[C9E8B0]  33002271C  C3C30000         10000000  C8000000  0F000000  01000000   *.........IY...H.*
C9E620   02C9E5E8  33002271C                               00010001  C8000000  00000000  00000050   *.......IV.......*
C9E640   C1D8C1C1  C3C30000                                00000000  00000000  00000000  00000000   *AQAACC..........*
```

Figure 9.1 Control Blocks and Relevant Portions in Memory

```
TIOT
    JOB  ARTJHM22  STEP  GO
    DD              14040140   PGM=*.DD     008D2D00   80000E0C
    DD              14040140   SYSUDUMP     007C0400   80002A1C
    DD              14040140   SYSDBOUT     007C0B00   30002A34
    DD              14040140   STEPLIB      00930E00   80000E4C
    DD              14040100   SYSTERM      00981000   80002A64
    DD              14040140   SYSUDUMP     00981200   80002A94
    DD              14040140   SYSOUT       00981400   80002AAC
    DD              14040140   CARDS        00981600   8000271C
```
Eighth line of TIOT contains DDname of cards

```
291080  40404040 40404040 40404040 40404040   40404040 40404040 40276000 80000E0C   *                                *
2910A0  F1F2F3F4 C1C3C3D6 E4D5E3C9 D5C7F1F4   F0F0C2C9 D6D3D6C7 E8404040 F1F9F7F6   *1234ACCOUNTING1400BIOLOGY   1976*
2910C0  C3C8C5D4 C9E2E3D9 E840F2F1 F0F0C3C9   E5C9D340 C5D5C740 F2F4F5F8 C54B4CC4   *CHEMISTRY 2100CIVIL ENG 2458E. D*
2910E0  4B40D74B 4040F3F2 F4F5C5C3 D6D5D6D4   C9C3E240 F3F9F6F0 C6C9D5C1 D5C3C540   * P. 3245ECONOMICS 3960FINANCE 54*
291100  4040F4F3 F2F1D4C1 D5C1C7C5 D4C5D5E3   F4F9F9F9 D4C1D9D2 C5E3C9D5 C740F5F4   * 4321MANAGEMENT499MARKETING 54..*
291120  F0F0E2E3 C1E3C9E2 E3C9C3E2 0001856C   E6E240C5 D5C4E240 C3C5D9C5 00000000   *00STATISTICS....WS ENDS HERE....*
291140  00000000 00000000 00000000 00000000   00000000 05293C9A 00290D1E 00000000   *................................*
291160  00000001 00000000 00410000 00000000   00000000 00000001 00000001 462919F2   *.........................2..*
291180  00000000 00000000 00000000 12F545A8   022CEA00 00004000 00090050 28022828   *................................*
2911A0  80291144 00A24800 00C9E60C 00000050   00F54400 06000001 00FE0C8 00000000   *...Y......IW..5...5.....*
2911C0  002CE888 002CEA58 00000000 0290D1E    00000000 006000D3 00000000 00000000   *................5.H...*
2911E0  00000000 00000000 05293C9A 00290D1E   00000000 00000001 00000000 00000000   *...Y.........L.....*
291220  00000000 00000000 00000000 80000000   46000001 84291FF8 00900048 00C9E58C   *.........YY...........3...IV.*
291240  00480000 022CE8E8 00F67980 00000001   28022828 002CE818 002CE975 002CE975   *.6..6.........Y..Z...Z.*
291260  92F67A90 00F67980 07000001 00090065   05EF0700 00000000 00000000 00000000   *........MW........*
291280  00000065 00000001 00000000 00D4E618   404040 40 40404040 40404040 40404040   *..............6.....*
2912A0  00000000 00000000 00840010 B1F65811   B1F65811 40404040 40404040 40404040   *AVERAGE. 3.00..........*
2912C0  C1E5C5D9 C1C7C57A 40F34BF0 F0404040   00000000 00FE0C8 40404040 40404040   *                                *
2912E0  40404040 40404040 40404040 40404040   40404040 40404040 40404040 40404040   *                                *
LINE 291300   SAME AS ABOVE
291320  40404040 40404040 40404040 40404040   40404040 40404040 0030C4C2 002CEF68   *.............DB...*
291340  00292798 50291B5C 002926E8 00C9E8B0   00291588 00291740 00000005 00290DE5   *........8.....Y.IY.....V*
291360  00291BF8 002CEA0B 002CEA0B 00291B76   00291B76 002CF8 00290CF8 002915B8   *.8..........8..8..*
291380  3462804B 00000000 00000000 00291694   00000000 00000000 60291BC6 00294E2   *.....F..S*
2913A0  00291B30 00291588 002915B8 00290DE4   00000005 00290D98 00290D98 002CEA58   *....U....V....WCSVRI*
2913C0  00292B0  00291B76 002915B8 00290CF8   00290CF8 0001101F0 007CE6C3 E2E5D9C9   *.8...8...0...WCSVRI*
2913E0  D6400A09 947FB674 9140B674 4780C09C   4500C096 E6C3E2D7 D4C7D940 0A0994BF   *O......E.0....WCSPMGR*
291400  B6749200 A2AC9200 B6609FF8 B2614780   06293568 00292DA8 2009013D B2614780   *.........A...*
291420  C0C045E0 C51841F0 0008850F0 B43091FF   B2634780 C17E9102 B2604780 C0E09139   *.E.0.......A...*
```

TIOT offset (in hex)

Logical record length (in hex)

Address of record causing ABEND begins at 2911C9

Figure 9.1 Control Blocks and Relevant Portions in Memory (continued)

```
2CE880  012CE979 20000084 012CE8B8 7F000000   00000000 7F2CE88C 002CE8B8 0C000000   *...Z.......Y...Y.*
2CE8A0  002CE8B0 0029117C 002CE8B0 00000000   022CEA08 20000050 002CE888 7F000000   *...Y.....Y...Y.*
2CE8C0  00000000 7F2CE8BC 002CE8E8 0C000000   002CE8E0 0029117C 002CE8E0 00000000   *...Y....Y...Y.*
2CE8E0  022CEA58 00000000 00020088 F0404040   F0404040 40404040 40404040 40404040   *......0         *
2CE900  C1E5C5D9 C1C7C57A 40F34BF0 F0404040   40404040 40404040 40404040 40404040   *AVERAGE. 3.00   *
2CE920  40404040 40404040 40404040 40404040   40404040 40404040 40404040 40404040   *                *
        _LINE 2CE940 SAME AS ABOVE
2CE960  40404040 40404040 40404040 40000000   40404040 40404040 40404040 40002400   *                *
2CE980  40F5F5F5 40404040 40F34040 40404040   40F34040 40404040 40404040 40404040   * 555     3    3 *
2CE9A0  40404040 40404040 40404040 40904040   40404040 40404040 40404040 40404040   *          B     *
        _LINE 2CE9C0 SAME AS ABOVE
2CE9E0  40404040 40404040 40404040 40404040   40404040 40404040 40404040 40002400   *                *
2CEA00  00000000 00020050 C2D6D9D6 E66B40D1   40404040 40404040 F9F6F0F0 F4F6F6F6   *....BOROW, J    9600 4666*
2CEA20  C240F7F7 F7C2F4F8 F8C3F4F3 F9F9F9C3   F4404040 40404040 40404040 F9F6F0F6   *B 777B488C4999C4  39600 4666*
2CEA40  40404040 40404040 40404040 4B404040   40F2F3F2 4B404040 D4C9D3C7 D9D6D46B   * 777B488C4999C4  232. MILGROM.*
2CEA60  40D44040 404040F7 F7F7F7F6   F6C1F3F7 F8F9C1F4 F0F1F2C1   *M    777706123A2456A3789A4012A*
2CEA80  F3F3F4F5 C2F3F6F7 F8C2F340 40404040   40404040 002CEB28 D4C1C9D5   *3345B3678B3      .....MAIN*
2CEAA0  40F2F3F3 4B404040 002CEB34 00000090   002CEB28 D4C1C9D5 00000000   *233..............MAIN*
2CEAC0  D7D9D6C7 E2E4C2D9 E3D54040 00000100   04000000 03044001 008D2F00   *PROGSUBRTN      .....*
2CEAE0  0001F440 00006400 00000000 00000000   0100009D 0100008F 01000006E   *.4              *
2CEB00  003D2C03 00000E0C 00000000 010000A4   0100009D 008D2D00 01000070   *.4              *
2CEB20  02000002 02000000 01000000 010000A4   008D2D00 002CEBA3 00029374DC  *........U       *
2CEB40  0000006E 002CEDEC 0001B6E0 00000037   80294114 002932E4 802937DC   *...........8    *
2CEB60  00292798 002CEB28 00186E00 00000063   002CEE63 002CEAB0 002CEB24   *...8.8          *
2CEB80  00292798 002CEB28 00293CE0 00000055C  00000000 00000084 002CEAB0   *.8..8           *
2CEBA0  00028000 00000000 0003C0C0 0029383A   002CE768 002CEBF3 4029383A   *...X...8*
```

Beginning of current record → (points to BOROW, J at 2CEA00)

First byte of current record begins at 2CEA08

Figure 9.1 Control Blocks and Relevant Portions in Memory (continued)

help. Moreover, the problem may be due to the files given to the programmer rather than the program itself. Regardless of the reason for their occurrence, the good programmer should know how to proceed.

System Code 001

Figure 9.2 is a COBOL listing for a two-file merge, extremely similar to those of Chapter One. (A few statements have been altered from Figure 1.3 to produce an ABEND.) The program in Figure 9.2 was run and an ABEND, with a system completion code of 001, resulted.

An ABEND with a completion code that is neither in the 0C group nor a 322 is typically an external ABEND (i.e., it occurred in a routine outside the COBOL program), often in a data management routine—OPEN, READ, etc. The *best* place to begin debugging external ABENDs is not in the dump but in the JCL listing of system

```
00001              IDENTIFICATION DIVISION.
00002              PROGRAM-ID.    TWOFILES.
00003              AUTHOR.     R. GRAUER.
00004              ENVIRONMENT DIVISION.
00005              CONFIGURATION SECTION.
00006              SOURCE-COMPUTER.
00007                 IBM-370.
00008              OBJECT-COMPUTER.                   DDname of problem file
00009                 IBM-370.                        in 001 ABEND
00010              INPUT-OUTPUT SECTION.
00011              FILE-CONTROL.
00012                 SELECT INPUT-FILE-ONE ASSIGN TO UT-S-FILEONE.
00013                 SELECT INPUT-FILE-TWO ASSIGN TO UT-S-FILETWO.
00014                 SELECT MERGED-FILE ASSIGN TO UT-S-MERGED.
00015              DATA DIVISION.
00016              FILE SECTION.
00017              FD  INPUT-FILE-ONE
00018                  LABEL RECORDS ARE STANDARD
00019                  BLOCK CONTAINS 0 RECORDS
00020                  RECORD CONTAINS 80 CHARACTERS
00021                  DATA RECORD IS INPUT-RECORD-ONE.
00022              01  INPUT-RECORD-ONE.
00023                  05  FILLER                           PIC X(9).
00024                  05  INPUT-ONE-ID                     PIC X(9).
00025                  05  INPUT-ONE-NAME                   PIC X(20).
00026                  05  INPUT-ONE-SALARY                 PIC 9(6).
00027                  05  INPUT-ONE-DEPARTMENT             PIC 9(4).
00028                  05  INPUT-ONE-LOCATION               PIC X(10).
00029                  05  FILLER                           PIC X(22).
00030              FD  INPUT-FILE-TWO
00031                  LABEL RECORDS ARE STANDARD        Indicates block size will
00032                  BLOCK CONTAINS 0 RECORDS          be entered in JCL
00033                  RECORD CONTAINS 80 CHARACTERS
00034                  DATA RECORD IS INPUT-RECORD-TWO.
00035              01  INPUT-RECORD-TWO.
00036                  05  FILLER                           PIC X(9).
00037                  05  INPUT-TWO-ID                     PIC X(9).
```

Figure 9.2 COBOL Listing for a Two-File Merge

```
00038              05  INPUT-ONE-NAME                      PIC X(20).
00039              05  INPUT-ONE-SALARY                    PIC 9(6).
00040              05  INPUT-ONE-DEPARTMENT                PIC 9(4).
00041              05  INPUT-ONE-LOCATION                  PIC X(10).
00042              05  FILLER                              PIC X(22).
00043          FD  MERGED-FILE
00044              LABEL RECORDS ARE STANDARD
00045              RECORD CONTAINS 80 CHARACTERS
00046              BLOCK CONTAINS 0 RECORDS
00047              DATA RECORD IS MERGED-RECORD.
00048          01  MERGED-RECORD                           PIC X(80).
00049          WORKING-STORAGE SECTION.
00050          77  WS-READ-INPUT-ONE-SWITCH    VALUE SPACES  PIC X(3).
00051          77  WS-READ-INPUT-TWO-SWITCH    VALUE SPACES  PIC X(3).
00053          PROCEDURE DIVISION.                 Initialized to SPACES
00054
00055          005-MAINLINE.
00056              OPEN INPUT INPUT-FILE-ONE
00057                         INPUT-FILE-TWO
00058                   OUTPUT MERGED-FILE.
00059              READ INPUT-FILE-ONE
00060                  AT END MOVE LOW-VALUES TO INPUT-ONE-ID.
00061              READ INPUT-FILE-TWO
00062                  AT END MOVE HIGH-VALUES TO INPUT-TWO-ID.
00063              PERFORM 010-PROCESS-FILES THRU 020-PROCESS-FILES-EXIT,
00064                  UNTIL INPUT-ONE-ID = HIGH-VALUES
00065                    AND INPUT-TWO-ID = HIGH-VALUES.
00066              CLOSE INPUT-FILE-ONE
00067                    INPUT-FILE-TWO
00068                    MERGED-FILE.
00069              STOP RUN.
00070
00071          010-PROCESS-FILES.
00072
00073              IF INPUT-ONE-ID LESS THAN INPUT-TWO-ID,
00074                  WRITE MERGED-RECORD FROM INPUT-RECORD-ONE,
00075                  MOVE 'YES' TO WS-READ-INPUT-ONE-SWITCH,
00076              ELSE,
00077                  IF INPUT-TWO-ID LESS THAN INPUT-ONE-ID,
00078                      WRITE MERGED-RECORD FROM INPUT-RECORD-TWO,
00079                      MOVE 'YES' TO WS-READ-INPUT-TWO-SWITCH
00080                  ELSE
00081                      DISPLAY 'DUPLICATE IDS ' INPUT-ONE-ID
00082                      MOVE 'YES' TO WS-READ-INPUT-ONE-SWITCH
00083                      MOVE 'YES' TO WS-READ-INPUT-TWO-SWITCH.
00084
00085              IF WS-READ-INPUT-ONE-SWITCH = 'YES',   Statement causing 001 ABEND
00086                  MOVE 'NO' TO WS-READ-INPUT-ONE-SWITCH
00087                  READ INPUT-FILE-ONE
00088                      AT END MOVE LOW-VALUES TO INPUT-ONE-ID.
00089
00090              IF WS-READ-INPUT-TWO-SWITCH = 'YES',
00091                  MOVE 'NO' TO WS-READ-INPUT-TWO-SWITCH
00092                  READ INPUT-FILE-TWO
00093                      AT END MOVE HIGH-VALUES TO INPUT-TWO-ID.
00094
00095          020-PROCESS-FILES-EXIT.
00096              EXIT.                      HIGH-VALUES moved to INPUT-TWO-ID
                                              on end-of-file condition
```

Figure 9.2 COBOL Listing for a Two-File Merge (continued)

messages. Figure 9.3 shows a partial list of JCL messages for Figure 9.2 The reader is referred to Chapter Ten for a thorough discussion of OS JCL.

Figure 9.3 contains the statement // EXEC COBVCLG, which attempts to compile, link edit, and execute a COBOL program. The first two steps were successful, as indicated by condition codes of 0000, whereas the GO step resulted in a system completion code of 001. This, in turn, is accompanied by a message, IEC020I—GET ISSUED AFTER END-OF-FILE—which specifies the cause of the problem. Two lines above this message one finds the DDname of the problem file to be FILEONE.

It is now a simple matter to examine the COBOL program of Figure 9.2 to see why the problem occurred. First, inspect the SELECT statements and conclude that the DDname FILEONE is associated with the COBOL file INPUT-FILE-ONE. Next, see where in the Procedure Division the program reads from this file and determine why the READ was executed after the end-of-file condition was detected.

There are two READs for INPUT-FILE-ONE, COBOL lines 59 and 87, either of which could be in error. (The former is an initial read for the file, which was explained in Chapter One. The occurrence of multiple reads for the same file and an end-of-file error is a good argument for each file having only a single READ.) Examination of Figure 9.2 shows that 010-PROCESS-FILES will be performed until both IDs are equal to HIGH-VALUES. The READ statement(s), in turn, should move HIGH-VALUES to the appropriate ID when the end of file is reached. Closer inspection of Figure 9.2 shows that this is accomplished for INPUT-FILE-TWO (COBOL lines 62 and 93). It is *not* accomplished for INPUT-FILE-ONE, as LOW-VALUES are moved instead. Hence, the problem and solution: change LOW-VALUES to HIGH-VALUES in lines 60 and 88.

Note well that this problem was analyzed and solved *without* reference to a dump. This should not be construed to mean that dump reading is not essential but rather that *analysis of system messages is another tool in the arsenal of the debugger.* Further, it should be realized that a quick solution was obtained only because of the preciseness of the system message, which identified the problem file immediately. Earlier versions of OS did not give such specific messages, and more detailed analyses almost always were required. Since we are on the subject of dumps, a supporting analysis will be provided using Figure 9.4.

In many ABEND situations, register 2 will contain the address of the DCB last referenced (i.e., the one causing the problem. This address is 400D94 in Figure 9.4. To this, one adds the TIOT offset, hex 28 (see Table 9.1) and obtains an address of 400DBC. The two bytes beginning at 400DBC contain 0090 in hex, or 144 in decimal. Subtracting 24, dividing by 20, and adding 1 to the quotient points us to the seventh line in the TIOT, which identifies FILEONE as the DDname. At this point, one proceeds with analysis of the source program.

Figure 9.4 contains other information, affording the reader an opportunity for additional practice. He/she should be able to trace through the DEB chain and determine the address of the DCB for INPUT-FILE-ONE directly from its DEB.

Although the ABEND has effectively been solved, we have not as yet indicated which of the two READ statements for INPUT-FILE-ONE actually caused the problem. This is easily determined from Figure 9.5, which displays results from the STATE and FLOW options. (Note how these were requested in the JCL of Figure 9.3.) The STATE

```
//STEP3 EXEC COBVCLG,PARM.COB=(NOPT,PMAP,NOLIB,'FLOW=10',STATE)
    .                                          └──────────────────┘
    .                                          Specification of STATE
    .                                          and FLOW options
    .
IEF236I ALLOC. FOR SSTBERN1 COB          STEP3
IEF237I 12E    ALLOCATED TO STEPLIB
IEF237I 12D    ALLOCATED TO SYSIN1
IEF237I 12D    ALLOCATED TO SYSIN2
IEF237I 12D    ALLOCATED TO SYSUT1
IEF237I 12D    ALLOCATED TO SYSUT2
IEF237I 12D    ALLOCATED TO SYSUT3
IEF237I 12D    ALLOCATED TO SYSUT4
IEF237I 24F    ALLOCATED TO SYSUT5
IEF237I 24E    ALLOCATED TO SYSLIN
IEF237I 722    ALLOCATED TO SYSPRINT    Successful execution of compile step
IEF237I 702    ALLOCATED TO SYSIN
IEF142I - STEP WAS EXECUTED - COND CODE 0000
    .
    .
    .
    .
IEF236I ALLOC. FOR SSTBERN1 LKED          STEP3
IEF237I 12E    ALLOCATED TO SYSLIB
IEF237I 12E    ALLOCATED TO
IEF237I 24E    ALLOCATED TO SYSLMOD
IEF237I 24E    ALLOCATED TO SYSLIN
IEF237I 24F    ALLOCATED TO SYSUT1       Successful execution of link-
IEF237I 722    ALLOCATED TO SYSPRINT     edit step
IEF237I 134    ALLOCATED TO STEPLIB
IEF142I - STEP WAS EXECUTED - COND CODE 0000
    .
    .
    .
    .
//GO.STEPLIB DD DSN=SYS2.COBLIB,DISP=SHR
//GO.SYSOUT DD SYSOUT=T
//GO.SYSUDUMP DD SYSOUT=T
//GO.FILEONE DD UNIT=DISK,DISP=(OLD,PASS),DSN=&&TP1,
//    DCB=(RECFM=FB,BLKSIZE=640)
//GO.FILETWO DD UNIT=DISK,DISP=(OLD,PASS),DSN=&&TP2,
//    DCB=(RECFM=FB,BLKSIZE=640)
//GO.MERGED DD UNIT=DISK,DISP=(NEW,PASS),DSN=&&MERGED,
//    SPACE=(80,(5,1)),DCB=(BLKSIZE=80,RECFM=FB)
IEF236I ALLOC. FOR SSTBERN1 GO          STEP3
IEF237I 24E    ALLOCATED TO PGM=*.DD
IEF237I 722    ALLOCATED TO SYSUDUMP
IEF237I 727    ALLOCATED TO SYSDBOUT
IEF237I 12E    ALLOCATED TO STEPLIB
IEF237I 72A    ALLOCATED TO SYSOUT
IEF237I 72B    ALLOCATED TO SYSUDUMP
IEF237I 12D    ALLOCATED TO FILEONE
IEF237I 24E    ALLOCATED TO FILETWO   DDname of problem file
IEF237I 24F    ALLOCATED TO MERGED
IEC020I 001-5,SSTBERN1,GO,FILEONE,12D,AMX537,
IEC020I SYS78022.T235917.RV000.SSTBERN1.TP1      Completion code and message
IEC020I GET ISSUED AFTER END-OF-FILE             pertaining to ABEND
COMPLETION CODE - SYSTEM=001  USER=0000
IEF285I   SYS78022.T235917.RV000.SSTBERN1.GOSET          PASSED
```

Figure 9.3 Partial List of System Messages for 001 Dump

COMPLETION CODE   SYSTEM = 001

PSW AT ENTRY TO ABEND 070C1000 00DE9F14   ILC 2   INTC 000D   **Address of first DEB**

```
TCB  CBE610
 RBP   00CBFD88    PIE   00000000    DEB  [00CBE314]   TIO 00CBEBA0    CMP  80001000    TRN  00000000
 MSS   00CBF220    PK-FLG 10850540   FLG   00003F3B    LLS 00CBE2D8    JLB  00CBEB60    JPQ  00CBF140
 FSA   0143EF68    TCB   00000000    TME   00000000    JST 00CBE610    NTC  00000000    OTC  00CBEEF0
 LTC   00000000    IQE   00000000    ECB   00CBED64    TSF 20000000    D-PQE 00CBF760   AQE  00CBE200
 STAB  80CBEA18    TCT   80CBEC80    USER  00000000    SDF 00000000    MDID 00000000    JSCB 00CBED8C
 RESV  00000000    IOBRC 00000000    DIAG  00000000    EXT 00000000    BITS 00000000    DAR  00000000
 EXT2  00CBE710    XTNT  004004CB    TIRB  00CBE888    BAK 00C9E278    LSQAP 00CBFFF8   IOTM 00000000
 TMSAV 00000000    ABCR  12000000    QECB  00000000    FOE 00000000    SWA  00CBFFE0    RESV 00000000
 GTF   00000000    RCMP  00001000    RESV  00000000    RES 00000000
```

DEB   **Beginning of first DEB**   **Address of first DEB**   **Address of TCB**   **Address of next DEB**

```
CBE2E0  00004FC0 00000000 00000000 00002BE0    00004FC0 01E6BA50 04CBE610 00004FC0   *..............W.*
CBE300  8F000000 01000000 3B000000 1F43DA10    0F200004 [04CBE610] [10CBE464] C8000000  *..........W...U.H.*
CBE320  00000000 0000007D C2C2C2C1 C3D3C3C6    02CBE2F0 33002A34 00010001 00000000   *.......BBBACLCF...S0*
CBE340  00000000 00000000 00000000 00000000    00000000 00000000 00000000 00000000   *................*
CBE360  00000000
```

DEB   **Beginning of second DEB**

```
CBE440  00004FC0 00000000 00000000 01F5E430    00004FC0 81D3F648 00004FC0 01F5E430   *.....L6.....5U.*
CBE460  11200003 [05CBE610] 10CBE4F4 C8000000   11200002 06CBE610 10CBE584 68000000   *....W...U4H.*
CBE480  04CBE440 1800168C 00000000 00090000    04CBE4D0 5800164C 0000000A 001C000A   *...U.....*
CBE4A0  00000050 C1D9C1C9 C6D5C3C9 C3C40000    00000050 C1D8C1C1 C6D5C3C8 C3C9C3C3   *...ARAIFNCICD...AQAAFNCHCICC*
CBE4C0  00000000 0000E4C8                       00000000 0000E558                     *....UH*   *....V.*
```

DEB   **Beginning of third DEB**

```
CBE4C0  00004FC0 00000000 00000000 01F5E9B0    00004FC0 81D3F648 00004FC0 01F5E430   *.....5Z..L6.....5U.*
CBE4E0  00000000 01FFFFFF 3B000000 1F400E48    00000000 01000000 3B000000 1F400EFC   *.......W...V.*
CBE500  001C0001 00010001 00000000 00000000    04CBE4D0 5800164C 0000000A 001C000A   *.......U.....AQAAFNCICC*
CBE520  00000000 00000000 00000000 00000000    00000050 C1D8C1C1 C6D5C3C8 C3C9C3C3   *.......AQAAFNCHCICC*
CBE540  00000000 00000000                       0000E558                             *....V.*
```

Figure 9.4 Partial Dump for 001

DEB

Beginning of fourth DEB   End of DEB chain   DCB address for INPUT-FILE-ONE

```
CBE560  01F5E9B0  81D3F648  00004FC0  01F5E430  00004FC0  00000000  00000112  00011EE0  *.5Z..L6......5U........*
CBE580  11200001  06CBE610  10000000  68000000  00004000  01000000  3B000000  1F40D94   *.............W.........*
CBE5A0  04CBE560  58000E0C  00000000  001C0000  001C0001  00010001  00000000  00000000  *........V..............*
CBE5C0  00000050  C1D8C1C1  C6D5C3C8  C3C9C3C3  00000000  00000000  00000000  00000000  *......AQAAFNCHCICC.....*
CBE5E0  00000000  0000E5E8                                                              *..........VY...........*
```

CDE

```
CBF140  ATR1 0B  NCDE 000000  ROC-RB 00CBEA30  NM GO       ATR2 20  EPA 400CB0  USE 01  XL/MJ CBF4D8
FF4968  ATR1 B1  NCDE FF7D10  ROC-RB 00000000  NM IGG019CF  ATR2 20  EPA D4E618  USE 01  XL/MJ FF4980
FF7D10  ATR1 B0  NCDE FFE500  ROC-RB 00000000  NM IGG019CL  ATR2 20  EPA E6BA50  USE 01  XL/MJ FF7D28
FFE500  ATR1 B9  NCDE FFE4D8  ROC-RB 00000000  NM IGG019BA  ATR2 20  EPA F67480  USE 07  XL/MJ FFE518
FFE4D8  ATR1 B8  NCDE FFA848  ROC-RB 00000000  NM IGG019BB  ATR2 20  EPA F67690  USE 07  XL/MJ FFE4F0
FFD7D8  ATR1 B9  NCDE FFE460  ROC-RB 00000000  NM IGG019CD  ATR2 20  EPA F5E6A0  USE 06  XL/MJ FFD7F0
FFE460  ATR1 B0  NCDE FFE488  ROC-RB 00000000  NM IGG019AI  ATR2 20  EPA F67A90  USE 03  XL/MJ FFE478
FFE488  ATR1 B8  NCDE FFE118  ROC-RB 00000000  NM IGG019AR  ATR2 20  EPA F67980  USE 04  XL/MJ FFE4A0
FFE118  ATR1 B9  NCDE FFE0F0  ROC-RB 00000000  NM IGG019CC  ATR2 20  EPA F5E0C8  USE 07  XL/MJ FFE130
FFE0F0  ATR1 B0  NCDE FFD7B0  ROC-RB 00000000  NM IGG019CI  ATR2 20  EPA F5E430  USE 07  XL/MJ FFE108
FFD7B0  ATR1 B9  NCDE FFE060  ROC-RB 00000000  NM IGG019CH  ATR2 20  EPA F5E9B0  USE 04  XL/MJ FFD7C8
FFE060  ATR1 B9  NCDE FFD350  ROC-RB 00000000  NM IGG019FN  ATR2 20  EPA D3F648  USE 08  XL/MJ FFE078
FFD350  ATR1 B8  NCDE FFD378  ROC-RB 00000000  NM IGG019AA  ATR2 20  EPA F545A8  USE 05  XL/MJ FFD368
FFD378  ATR1 B8  NCDE FFD3A0  ROC-RB 00000000  NM IGG019AQ  ATR2 20  EPA F54400  USE 05  XL/MJ FFD390
```

TIOT   JOB SSTBERN1 STEP 14040140   PROC   STEP3
                               GO

```
DD  14040140    PGM=*.DD    01370E00   8000164C
DD  14040140    SYSUDUMP    01791800   80002A34
DD  14040140    SYSDBOUT    01791E00   80002AAC
DD  14040140    STEPLIB     01A01500   80000E4C
DD  14040140    SYSOUT      01A01700   80002AF4
DD  14040100    SYSUDUMP    01A01900   80002B0C
DD  14040140    FILEONE     01A01B00   8000E0C    ── TIOT entry for problem file
DD  14040140    FILETWO     01A01E00   8000164C
DD  14040140    MERGED      01A02000   8000168C
```

Figure 9.4 Partial Dump for 001 (continued)

```
SAVE AREA TRACE

GO      WAS ENTERED VIA LINK
                                                        Return address to supervisor
                                                        Entry point in COBOL program

SA  43EF68  WD1 00000000  HSA 00000000  RET 0001 0F8A  EPA 01400CB0  R0  00CBF4E0
            R1  0043EFF8  R2  00CBEB20  R4  00CBF2E0   R5  00CBEEF0   R6  00CBEC70
            R7  00CBF118  R8  00CBED40  R10 00CBED68   R11 00000000   R12 40F582F2
            LSA 00400F78
            R3  5CCBED68
            R9  00CBEC80

GO      WAS ENTERED VIA CALL
                                                        Return address in COBOL program

SA  400F78  WD1 0030C4C2  HSA 0043EF68  RET 004014E2  EPA 0040316E  R0  40401608
            R1  16F545A8  R2  90005D24  R4  00400D94   R5  5CCBED68   R6  90400EC4
            R7  0040153A  R8  00400D50  R10 0043E3C0   R11 40F545E0   R12 00F54400
            LSA 0043EB43
            R3  00400D94
            R9  0043E7D8


REGS AT ENTRY TO ABEND
                                                        DCB address of problem file

FLTR 0-6   0000000000000000   0000000000000000   0000000000000000   0000000000000000

REGS 0-7   80000000  80001000  00400D94  0043FDD8  0043FE08  0043FDE0  0043FD68
REGS 8-15  00CBFC58  0043FBD0  58000E0C  0043FF9C  00400F78  00000000  4001B172


                                                        WS-READ-INPUT-ONE-SWITCH

400CA0
400CC0  C9D3C5E2 E5E2D9F1 0700989F F02407FF  90ECD00C 185D05F0 4580F010 E3E6D6C6  *ILESVSR1....0......0.......TWOF*
400CE0  00400CB0 00400CB0 004011B8 00400F78  96021034 07FE41F0 0040167C 00000000  *................................*
400D00  00000000 00000000 00000000 00000000  00401268 00000000 00000000 00000000  *................................*
400D20  00000000 00000000 00000000 00000000  00000000 00000000 40F84BF2 F84BF5F2  *.............. ...8.28.52*
400D40  D1C1D540 F2F36B40 F1F9F7F8 00000000  D5D640D5 D6400000 00000000 00000000  *JAN 23, 1978....NO NO ....*
400D60  00000000 00000000 00000000 054030F2  00400CD6 00000001 00000000 00000000  *.......2.O....*
```

Figure 9.4 Partial Dump for 001 (continued)

```
400D80  00000000 00000000 00000000 00000000 00000000 00000000 80000000 0000001C  *....................*
400DA0  00028510 002B4B36 0243E5A0 00000000 00028510 46401616 90400D5C 00904800  *..e..,K6.ÃV......e...  .V..*
400DC0  COCBE584 16F545A8 00F54400 0E000001 16F545A8 00000000 0043DE70 0043E828  *.ÃEu.6Ey.5...6Ey.....V..5..5.*
400DE0  0043E7D8 00000050 00000001 00000000 00F5E0C8 00000000 0043DE70 0043E828  *.XQ....5.H....Y.*
400E00  00000000 00400CD6 00000000 00900000 00000000 00000000 00000000 00000000  *........*
400E20  054030F2 00000000 00000000 52000000 0000001C 00028510 002B4B36 0243E098  *.2..O.........*
400E40  00000000 80000000 00000000 00000000 00A44800 COCBE4F4 12F545A8 00F54400  *............*
400E60  00004000 00000001 4640165C 90400E10 00A44800 0043E3C0 00000050 00000001  *..........U4.5..5.*
400E80  00000001 10090280 00005800 0043DDF8 0043E410 0043E3C0 00000000 00000000  *.....8.U..T....5.*
400EA0  0E000000 00F5E0C8 00000000 00000000 00000000 054030F2 00400CD6 00000000  *..5.H.........8.U..T.*
400EC0  00900000 00000000 00000000 00000000 00000000 00400CD6 00000000 00000000  *.....2...O.*
400EE0  00000001 00000000 00000000 00000000 00000000 80000000 00000000 00000000  *............*
400F00  52000000 00000000 1D028510 0243DF58 00000001 0D000001 00090050 46000000  *..........*
400F20  90400EC4 00B80048 00CBE464 92F67A90 00000001 00F67980 00F5E6A0 30060050  *..D....U.6..6....5W.*
400F40  0043DD18 0043E000 0043E000 00000050 00000000 00F5E6A0 05EF0000 05EF68..  *..........DB.*
400F60  00000000 00000000 00000000 00000000 00000000 0030C4C2 0043EF68 0043EF68  *............*
400F80  0043EB48 004014E2 0040316E 40401608 90005D24 90400D94 90400D94 00400D94  *......S....5...*
400FA0  5CCBED68 90400EC4 0040015 3A 00400D50 0043E7D8 40F545E0 00F5 4400 00F54400  *..D......XQ..T..5..5.*
400FC0  3422804B 0043EBB0 0D0001F8 00401268 00000000 00000009 00000000 00000000  *..........*
400FE0  00000000 00000000 00000000 00000000 00000000 00000000 00000000 00000000  *.......8........*
401000  00000000 00000000 00000000 00000000 00000000 00000000 00000000 00000000  *........*
```

LINE 401020 SAME AS ABOVE

```
401040  00000000 00000000 00000000 064029C0 00402200 20000000 00000000 00000000  *..6....*
401060  00000000 00000000 00000000 004015AA 004015CC 004015AA 01000000 00000000  *........*
401080  004015B0 0040180A 00000001 004015AA 5CCBED68 90400EC4 00401666 004015CE  *........D..*
4010A0  00400D50 0043E6E8 0043E280 00400CB0 00400CB0 004011B8 004015CC 004015CE  *..WY.S.....*
4010C0  0040180A 00000001 8F43E010 00010000 00000000 004015CC 00000000 00000000  *........*
4010E0  00000000 0043EBB0 00000000 00000000 00000000 00000000 00000000 00000000  *........*
```

LINE 401100 SAME AS ABOVE

```
401120  004015F6 40400998 00400CB0 000004F0 00402200 E2E8E2D6 E4E34040 E3000008  *.6...0..SYSOUT T..*
401140  00400D38 00000000 00000000 00000000 00000000 00000000 00000000 00000000  *........*
401160  00000000 00000000 004011676 0043E7D8 0043E3C0 0043DFB0 00400D50  *...XQ.T..*
401180  00000000 00401360 004001360 00400D94 00400E48 8F400EFC 8F400EFC 00000000  *..........*
4011A0  004017676 004017736 004017D6 00437048 00403672 00402352  *..D....*
4011C0  0040316A 00403672 004 0316E 00030F2 00403676 004180A 004014D8  *..O..*
4011E0  00401666 00401676 00401316 004013 46 00401350 00401360 00401388  *..2..*
401200  00401138E 00401546 00401316 004015 9E 00401620 00401616  *..K..*
401220  004016 5C 00401468 004 0149A 004014 D2 0040153A 00401 59E 00400D94  *..K..*
401240  00400E48 0040 1676 0040 1676 48004805 EFE8C5E2 D5D6C4E4 D7D3C9C3  *..YESNODUPLIC*
```

TIOT offset (in hex) for FILE ONE

Value of BL = 4

Figure 9.4 Partial Dump for 001 (continued)

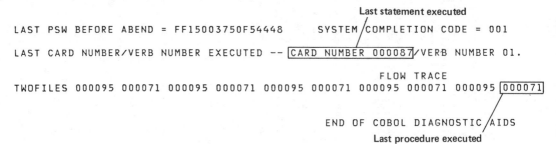

Figure 9.5 Compiler Aids for Debugging

option points directly to statement 87, whereas the FLOW option showed the ABEND occurred within the procedure beginning at line 71, (i.e., within 010-PROCESS-FILES).

Both options are very useful, but expensive (in terms of machine time) when large files are processed. Accordingly, many installations encourage their use in testing but distinctly discourage it during production. An indication of the expense can be seen by examining the SAVE AREA TRACE of Figure 9.4.

Recall from Chapter Eight that the SAVE AREA TRACE is a trace through a series of called programs. The very first line is always the COBOL program, and the low address indicates a return to the supervisor. The second line relates to a program called by COBOL. Subtracting the EPA address of the COBOL program, 400CB0, from the return address, 4014E2, yields a relative address of 832. This means that the called program returns control to the COBOL program at relative location 832. In order to determine the nature of the called program, we examine the Procedure Division map of Figure 9.6. The last executable statement immediately preceding the one at location 832 is a branch to an external subroutine, ILBOFLW1, mandated by the FLOW option. This makes considerable sense when we realize that the branch to ILBOFLW1 occurs immediately on encountering the paragraph name, 010-PROCESS-FILES in COBOL line 71. In other words, the FLOW option will specify the last n procedures if an ABEND occurs. However, this can happen only if the compiler generates instructions to keep track of procedures as they are executed, hence the function of the IBM routine, ILBOFLW1. This, in turn, requires insertion of two assembler instructions, a load and a branch after every procedure name. This could extort a heavy penalty in a virtual system (e.g., MVS) if continuous paging to and from virtual space were required to fetch the routine.

One last point—since the STATE and/or FLOW options may not be desirable from an efficiency viewpoint, how else can one determine which READ actually caused the problem? We suggest examination of various program switches, in particular WS-READ-INPUT-ONE-SWITCH. The switch is initialized to SPACES in line 50 of Figure 9.2 and reset to NO in line 86. If its value at the time of the ABEND is NO, then one can safely conclude that the READ in line 87 is the problem. Determination of the value requires use of Figures 9.7 and 9.8, the Data Division and Memory maps, respectively. The BL cells begin at location 401170 (EPA address of 400CB0 in Figure 9.4 plus BL displacement of 4C0). Our switch is associated with BL = 4 (Figure 9.7), which is located beginning at 40117C and contains the value 400D50. 400D50 is, in turn, added

230

Figure 9.6 Partial PMAP for a Two-File Merge

```
                                          Instruction to load address
                                          of external subroutine

71  *010-PROCESS-FILES          PN=01
    000828                      EQU    *
    000828  58 F0 C 010         L     15,010(0,12)          V(ILBOFLW1) ─── Name of subroutine
    00082C  05 1F               BALR  1,15
    00082E  00000047            DC    X'00000047'
73  IF
    000832  58 20 C 04C         L     2,04C(0,12)           GN=08
    000836  D5 08 7 009 8 009   CLC   009(9,7),009(8)       DNM=1-171    DNM=1-385
    00083C  07 B2               BCR   11,2
74  WRITE
    00083E  58 F0 C 014         L     15,014(0,12)          V(ILBODBG4)
    000842  05 EF               BALR  14,15
    000844  D2 4F 9 000 7 000   MVC   000(80,9),000(7)      DNM=2-69     DNM=1-131
    00084A  58 10 C 08C         L     1,08C(0,12)           DCB=3
    00084E  18 21               LR    2,1
    000850  92 00 2 07A         MVI   07A(2),X'00'                       Branch to external subroutine
    000854  58 40 2 024         L     4,024(0,2)
    000858  92 00 4 014         MVI   014(4),X'00'
    00085C  96 01 4 01B         OI    01B(4),X'01'
    000860  58 10 C 08C         L     1,08C(0,12)           DCB=3
    000864  58 00 1 04C         L     0,04C(0,1)
    000868  58 F0 1 030         L     15,030(0,1)
    00086C  44 00 1 060         EX    0,060(0,1)
    000870  58 20 C 08C         L     2,08C(0,12)           DCB=3
    000874  91 40 2 07A         TM    07A(2),X'40'
    000878  92 00 2 07A         MVI   07A(2),X'00'
    00087C  58 50 C 07C         L     5,07C(0,12)           GN=020
    000880  07 15               BCR   1,5
    000882  50 10 D 200         ST    1,200(0,13)           BL =3
    000886  58 90 D 200         L     9,200(0,13)           BL =3
    00088A          GN=020      EQU   *
    00088A          GN=09       EQU   *
75  MOVE
    00088A  D2 02 6 000 C 09D   MVC   000(3,6),09D(12)      DNM=2-92     LIT+5
    000890  58 10 C 054         L     1,054(0,12)           GN=010
```

231

INTRNL NAME	LVL	SOURCE NAME	BASE	DISPL	INTRNL NAME	DEFINITION	USAGE
DNM=1-104	FD	INPUT-FILE-ONE	DCB=01		DNM=1-104		QSAM
DNM=1-131	01	INPUT-RECORD-ONE	BL=1	000	DNM=1-131	DS 0CL80	GROUP
DNM=1-160	02	FILLER	BL=1	000	DNM=1-160	DS 9C	DISP
DNM=1-171	02	INPUT-ONE-ID	BL=1	009	DNM=1-171	DS 9C	DISP
DNM=1-193	02	INPUT-ONE-NAME	BL=1	012	DNM=1-193	DS 20C	DISP
DNM=1-217	02	INPUT-ONE-SALARY	BL=1	026	DNM=1-217	DS 6C	DISP-NM
DNM=1-243	02	INPUT-ONE-DEPARTMENT	BL=1	02C	DNM=1-243	DS 4C	DISP-NM
DNM=1-273	02	INPUT-ONE-LOCATION	BL=1	030	DNM=1-273	DS 10C	DISP
DNM=1-301	02	FILLER	BL=1	03A	DNM=1-301	DS 22C	DISP
DNM=1-315	FD	INPUT-FILE-TWO	DCB=02		DNM=1-315		QSAM
DNM=1-342	01	INPUT-RECORD-TWO	BL=2	000	DNM=1-342	DS 0CL80	GROUP
DNM=1-371	02	FILLER	BL=2	000	DNM=1-371	DS 9C	DISP
DNM=1-385	02	INPUT-TWO-ID	BL=2	009	DNM=1-385	DS 9C	DISP
DNM=1-407	02	INPUT-ONE-NAME	BL=2	012	DNM=1-407	DS 20C	DISP
DNM=1-434	02	INPUT-ONE-SALARY	BL=2	026	DNM=1-434	DS 6C	DISP-NM
DNM=1-463	02	INPUT-ONE-DEPARTMENT	BL=2	02C	DNM=1-463	DS 4C	DISP-NM
DNM=2-000	02	INPUT-ONE-LOCATION	BL=2	030	DNM=2-000	DS 10C	DISP
DNM=2-031	02	FILLER	BL=2	03A	DNM=2-031	DS 22C	DISP
DNM=2-045	FD	MERGED-FILE	DCB=03		DNM=2-045		QSAM
DNM=2-069	01	MERGED-RECORD	BL=3	000	DNM=2-069	DS 80C	DISP
DNM=2-092	77	WS-READ-INPUT-ONE-SWITCH	BL=4	000	DNM=2-092	DS 3C	DISP
DNM=2-126	77	WS-READ-INPUT-TWO-SWITCH	BL=4	003	DNM=2-126	DS 3C	DISP

Base locator and displacement for WS-READ-INPUT-ONE-SWITCH

Figure 9.7 Data Division Map for Figure 9.2

```
                    MEMORY  MAP

        TGT                             002C8

    SAVE  AREA                          002C8
    SWITCH                              00310
    TALLY                               00314
    SORT  SAVE                          00318
    ENTRY-SAVE                          0031C
    SORT  CORE  SIZE                    00320
    RET  CODE                           00324
    SORT  RET                           00326
    WORKING  CELLS                      00328
    SORT  FILE  SIZE                    00458
    SORT  MODE  SIZE                    0045C
    PGT-VN  TBL                         00460
                .
              .
            .
          .
        .                        Displacement of BL cells
      .
    COUNT  CHAIN  ADDRESS      /        004A4
    PRBL1  CELL  PTR          /         004A8
    RESERVED                /           004AC
    TA  LENGTH             /            004B1
    RESERVED             /             004B4
    OVERFLOW  CELLS    /                004C0
   | BL  CELLS       /         004C0 |
    DECBADR  CELLS                      004D0
    FIB  CELLS                          004D0
    TEMP  STORAGE                       004D0
```

Figure 9.8 Partial Memory Map for Figure 9.2

to the displacement of WS-READ-INPUT-ONE-SWITCH (000 in Figure 9.7) to provide the address of the switch. Looking at the three bytes beginning at 400D50 (400D50 + 000), we find the value of the switch to be NO, which supports our earlier conclusion.

System Code 013

The COBOL program of Figure 9.2 was rerun with a different jobstream, as shown in Figure 9.9. Figure 9.9 is longer than the listing in Figure 9.3 because it shows two additional steps to create temporary files to test the COBOL program. This is accomplished through the utility program, IEBGENER, and is fully explained in Chapter Eleven.

Analysis of Figure 9.9 shows that the steps to create the test files executed successfully, as did the compile and link edit steps of the proc COBVCLG. The job ABENDed during the GO step with a system code 013. This is accompanied by a message, IEC141I 013-20, and an indication of the problem DDname (FILETWO). Referring to the manual for System Messages and Codes, we get the following:

The error occurred during execution of an OPEN macro instruction. In the message text 013-rc associates this message with system completion code 013 and with return code rc.

```
//STEP1 EXEC PGM=IEBGENER          Step 1 — create the first test file
//SYSPRINT DD SYSOUT=T
//SYSUT1 DD *
//SYSUT2 DD DSN=&&TP1,UNIT=DISK,DCB=(LRECL=80,BLKSIZE=640),
//    DISP=(NEW,PASS),SPACE=(TRK,(1,1))
//SYSIN DD DUMMY
IEF236I ALLOC. FOR SSTBERN1 STEP1
IEF237I 727   ALLOCATED TO SYSPRINT
IEF237I 703   ALLOCATED TO SYSUT1         Successful creation of first test file
IEF237I 12D   ALLOCATED TO SYSUT2
IEF142I - STEP WAS EXECUTED - COND CODE 0000
IEF285I    SYS78022.T235917.RV000.SSTBERN1.TP1        PASSED
IEF285I    VOL SER NOS= AMX537.
IEF373I STEP /STEP1   / START 78023.0817
IEF374I STEP /STEP1   / STOP  78023.0817 CPU   0MIN 00.08SEC STOR VIRT  12K
//STEP2 EXEC PGM=IEBGENER          Step 2 — create the second test file
//SYSPRINT DD SYSOUT=T
//SYSUT1 DD *
//SYSUT2 DD DSN=&&TP2,UNIT=DISK,DCB=(LRECL=80,BLKSIZE=640),
//    DISP=(NEW,PASS),SPACE=(TRK,(1,1))
//SYSIN DD DUMMY                          DCB characteristics of second test file
IEF236I ALLOC. FOR SSTBERN1 STEP2
IEF237I 727   ALLOCATED TO SYSPRINT
IEF237I 703   ALLOCATED TO SYSUT1         Successful creation of second test file
IEF237I 12D   ALLOCATED TO SYSUT2
IEF142I - STEP WAS EXECUTED - COND CODE 0000
IEF285I    SYS78022.T235917.RV000.SSTBERN1.TP2        PASSED
IEF285I    VOL SER NOS= AMX537.
IEF373I STEP /STEP2   / START 78023.0817
IEF374I STEP /STEP2   / STOP  78023.0817 CPU   0MIN 00.08SEC STOR VIRT  12K
//STEP3 EXEC CQBVCLG,PARM.COB=(NOPT,PMAP,NOLIB,'FLOW=10',STATE)
  .
  .                                           Specification of STATE and FLOW
  .                                           options
IEF236I ALLOC. FOR SSTBERN1 COB       STEP3
IEF237I 12E   ALLOCATED TO STEPLIB
IEF237I 24E   ALLOCATED TO SYSIN1
IEF237I 24F   ALLOCATED TO SYSIN2
IEF237I 12D   ALLOCATED TO SYSUT1
IEF237I 24E   ALLOCATED TO SYSUT2
IEF237I 24F   ALLOCATED TO SYSUT3
IEF237I 12D   ALLOCATED TO SYSUT4
IEF237I 24E   ALLOCATED TO SYSUT5
IEF237I 24F   ALLOCATED TO SYSLIN
IEF237I 727   ALLOCATED TO SYSPRINT        Compilation step successful
IEF237I 703   ALLOCATED TO SYSIN
IEF142I - STEP WAS EXECUTED - COND CODE 0000
  .
  .
  .
IEF236I ALLOC. FOR SSTBERN1 LKED       STEP3
IEF237I 12E   ALLOCATED TO SYSLIB
IEF237I 12E   ALLOCATED TO
IEF237I 12D   ALLOCATED TO SYSLMOD
IEF237I 24F   ALLOCATED TO SYSLIN
IEF237I 24E   ALLOCATED TO SYSUT1
IEF237I 727   ALLOCATED TO SYSPRINT        Linkage-editor step successful
IEF237I 134   ALLOCATED TO STEPLIB
IEF142I - STEP WAS EXECUTED - COND CODE 0000
  .
  .
  .
```

Figure 9.9 Partial System Messages for 013 Dump

```
//GO.SYSOUT DD SYSOUT=T                          Invalid specification of
//GO.SYSUDUMP DD SYSOUT=T                         block size
//GO.FILEONE DD UNIT=DISK,DISP=(OLD,PASS),DSN=&&TP1,
//   DCB=(RECFM=FB,BLKSIZE=640)
//GO.FILETWO DD UNIT=DISK,DISP=(OLD,PASS),DSN=&&TP2,─DSN matches that of
//   DCB=(RECFM=FB,BLKSIZE=120)                            SYSUT2 in STEP2
//GO.MERGED DD UNIT=DISK,DISP=(NEW,PASS),DSN=&&MERGED,
//   SPACE=(80,(5,1)),DCB=(BLKSIZE=80,RECFM=FB)
IEF236I ALLOC. FOR SSTBERN1 GO          STEP3
IEF237I 12D    ALLOCATED TO PGM=*.DD
IEF237I 727    ALLOCATED TO SYSUDUMP
IEF237I 72A    ALLOCATED TO SYSDBOUT─Message explaining ABEND
IEF237I 12E    ALLOCATED TO STEPLIB
IEF237I 72B    ALLOCATED TO SYSOUT
IEF237I 72C    ALLOCATED TO SYSUDUMP
IEF237I 12D    ALLOCATED TO FILEONE    DDname of problem file
IEF237I 12D    ALLOCATED TO FILETWO
IEF237I 24E    ALLOCATED TO MERGED
IEC141I 013-20,SSTBERN1,GO,FILETWO,12D,AMX537, Completion code
IEC141I SYS78022.T235917.RV000.SSTBERN1.TP2
COMPLETION CODE - SYSTEM=013  USER=0000
IEF285I    SYS78022.T235917.RV000.SSTBERN1.GOSET        PASSED
```

Figure 9.9 Partial System Messages for 013 Dump (continued)

Reading further under a return code of 20, since 013-20 was specified in Figure 9.9:

An OPEN macro instruction was issued for a sequential data set using the queued access technique with RECFM = FB, but BLKSIZE is not a multiple of LRECL.

In other words, the program ABENDed because of an unsuccessful OPEN for FILETWO. Apparently, there was some kind of DCB conflict involving block size. Figure 9.9 shows that the test file corresponding to DDname FILETWO was created successfully in STEP2 with DCB characteristics LRECL = 80 and BLKSIZE = 640. The FD of the COBOL program indicates a record size of 80 and that blocksize will be entered at execution time (i.e., BLOCK CONTAINS 0 RECORDS). The DD statement, GO.FILETWO, specifies BLKSIZE = 120, which is not consistent with the physical characteristics of the file as created in STEP2. Hence, the problem and solution; change the BLKSIZE specification for GO.FILETWO to 640.

As with the previous example, an ABEND was corrected without referring to the dump, and in this case with no real reference even to the COBOL program. The process can be just as simple in practice if one approaches problems with a positive mental attitude and open mind. We do, however, include relevant portions of the 013 dump in Figure 9.10 for continued practice.

Register 2 will contain the DCB address of the last referenced file. Our immediate objective is to determine which file is related to this DCB. We must determine the TIOT offset for the DCB in question and tie this to a line in the TIOT table. Table 9.1 shows that the TIOT offset is displaced 28 (in hex) bytes from the DEB address and that the TIOT offset itself is two bytes. Hence, take the address in register 2 which is 540E48, add a hex 28 to obtain 540E70, and examine the contents of the two bytes beginning at

235

```
JOB SSTBERN1              STEP GO              TIME 081813    DATE 78023

COMPLETION CODE          SYSTEM = 013

PSW AT ENTRY TO ABEND    070C1000 00DEEECC    ILC 2    INTC 000D

TCB CAE680  RBP   00CAFD88   PIE    00000000   TIO  00CAE4FC   DEB  00CAE898   CMP   80013000   TRN  00000000
            MSS   00CAF220   PK-FLG 10850540   LLS  00CAF5E8   FLG  00003F3B   JLB   00CAEB30   JPQ  00CAF140
            FSA   0157EF68   TCB    00000000   JST  00000000   TME  00000000   NTC   00000000   QTC  00000000
            LTC   00000000   IQE    00000000   TSF  20000000   ECB  00CAED64   D-PQE 00CAF760   AQE  00CAE400
            STAB  80CAE9E8   TCT    80CAEC80   SDF  00000000   USER 00000000   MDID  00000000   JSCB 00CAED8C
            RESV  00000000   IOBRC  00000000   EXT  00000000   DIAG 00000000   BITS  00000000   DAR  00000000
            EXT2  00CAE780   XTNT   005404CA   BAK  00CAEB78   TIRB 00CBE710   LSQAP 00CAFFF8   IOTM 00000000
            TMSAV 00000000   ABCR   12000000   FOE  00000000   QECB 00000000   SWA   00CAFFE0   RESV 00000000
            GTF   00000000   RCMP   00013000   RES  00000000   RESV 00000000

CDE
CAF140  ATR1 0B   NCDE 000000   ROC-RB 00CAEA00   NM GO        USE 01   EPA 540CB0   ATR2 20   XL/MJ CAF4D8   *.........................W.*
FEF2E8  ATR1 B1   NCDE FF4968   ROC-RB 00000000   NM IGG019CF  USE 01   EPA D4E618   ATR2 20   XL/MJ FEF300   *.........................W.*
FF4968  ATR1 B0   NCDE FFE500   ROC-RB 00000000   NM IGG019CL  USE 01   EPA E6BA50   ATR2 20   XL/MJ FF4980   *.......H.............Y..UQ..*
FFE500  ATR1 B9   NCDE FFE4D8   ROC-RB 00000000   NM IGG019BA  USE 06   EPA F67480   ATR2 20   XL/MJ FFE518   *.................BBBACLCF...*
FFE4D8  ATR1 B8   NCDE FFA848   ROC-RB 00000000   NM IGG019BB  USE 06   EPA F67690   ATR2 20   XL/MJ FFE4F0   *.........................*,

DEB
                   End of DEB chain                                         Beginning of first DEB
CAE4C0  00004FC0   00004FC0   00004FC0   00000000   00000000   00002BE0   00004FC0 01E6BA50  *
CAE4E0  10000000   C8000000   8F000000   01000000   3B000000   1F57E840   0F200001 04CAE680  *
CAE500  00010001   00000000   00000000   0000007D   C2C2C2C1   C3D3C3C6   02CAE4D8 33002AAC  *
CAE520  00000000   00000000   00000000   00000000   00000000   00000000   00000000          *
CAE540  00000000

TIOT
JOB  SSTBERN1  14040140   STEP GO      PGM=*.DD    PROC STEP3
DD             14040140   SYSUDUMP     00F92800    80000E0C
DD             14040140   SYSDBOUT     00F91700    80002AAC
DD             14040140   STEPLIB      00F91D00    80002AF4
DD             14040100   SYSOUT       00FA2200    80002B0C
DD             14040100   SYSUDUMP     00FA2400    80002B24
DD             14040100   FILEONE      00FA2600    80000E0C
DD             14040100   FILETWO      00FA2800    80000E0C  ──── TIOT entry of problem file
DD             14040100   MERGED       00FB0200    8000164C
```

Figure 9.10 Partial Dump for 013

REGS AT ENTRY TO ABEND

FLTR 0-6   D9C9D5E300F91300   E2E3C5D7D3C9C240   00F915008000FCC

                                          DCB address of problem file
REGS 0-7   80000000 80013000 80002AAC →40040140   40DEACA   0057FFBD8 00541190   0057FFB8 00541194
REGS 8-15   0057FFE0 00CAE93C 00540E0C 00540D90   00540D90 00000028   00000001   00CAE680 00000020

LOAD MODULE   GO

Block size = (78)₁₆ = (120)₁₀   Record length = (50)₁₆ = (80)₁₀
```
540CA0  C9D3C5E2 E5E2D9F1 0700989F F02407FF  90ECD00C 185D05F0 4580F010 E3E6D6C6  *ILESVSR1....0.........0..0.TWOF*
540CC0  00540CB0 00540CB0 005411B8 00540F78  96021034 07FE41F0 000107FE 005416BC  *....0..........................*
540CE0  00000000 00540CB0 00900000 00000000  00541268 00541678 00000000 40000000  *...............................*
540D00  06172A98 60000104 92172A5F 40000008  06172F14 44002720 92172A53 40000008  *...............................*
540D20  D1C1D540 F2F36B40 F1F9F7F8 080066BD  08172CD0 00000000 40F84BF1 F74BF2F3  *JAN 23. 1978...4........8.17.23*
540D40  00000000 00000000 00000000 055430F2  40404040 404066F4 0000002E 00000000  *...............2..0............*
540D60  00000000 00000000 00000001 00000000  00540CD6 00000001 00000000 00000000  *...............................*
540D80  00000000 00000001 00000000 00000400  80000000 46000000 90540D5C 00704800  *...............................*
540DA0  0057FDC8 03004800 00000000 00000001  00010280 00000000 90540D5C 00704800  *...H...........................*
540DC0  00000000 00000000 00000000 00000001  00000000 00000000 00000000 00000000  *...............................*
540DE0  00000000 00000000 00000000 00000000  00000000 00000000 00000000 00000000  *...............................*
540E00  00000000 00000000 00000001 00000000  00000000 00000000 00000000 00000000  *...2..0........U...............*
540E20  055430F2 00540CD6 00000000 00000000  00000000 00540CD6 00000000 00000001  *...............................*
540E40  00000000 80000000 00000001 00000000  00000000 00000000 80000000 00000001  *...............................*
540E60  00000001 00010078 00000000 90540E10  0057FBD8 03004800 00000000 00000000  *...............Q...............*
540E80  00000000 00000000 00000000 00000000  00000000 00000000 000A4800 00000050  *...............................*
540EA0  00900000 00000000 00000000 00000000  00000000 00000000 00540CD6 00000001  *...............................*
540EC0  00000001 00000000 00000000 00000000  00000000 00000000 00000000 00000001  *...............2..0............*
540EE0  00000000 00000001 00000000 00000000  00000001 00000000 46000000 00000000  *...............................*
540F00  90540EC4 00B80048 0057F9E8 03000048  00000001 00000050 05EF0000 00000000  *....D.....9Y...................*
540F20  00000000 00000000 00000000 00000050  00000000 00000000 00000000 00000000  *...............................*
540F40  00000000 00000000 00000000 00000000  00900000 0030C4C2 0057EF68 00000000  *..........DB...................*
540F60  0057EB48 00541272 0054316E 00540D50  5054126E 00CAEAF0 5CCAED68 00540CB0  *....0..........0...............*
540F80  505416EE 00540D50 00000000 00000000  00000000 00540CB0 005411B8 00000000  *...............................*
540FA0  3422804B 00000000 00000000 00541268  00000000 00000000 00CADA20 00000000  *...............................*
540FC0  70E1319E 0057EBB0 00CADCE0 00020000  00000000 00575E88 00CADA20 00000000  *...............0...............*
540FE0  00000F2F 00575E98 00575E98 00000000  00000000 002A06E0 002A06E0 002A0F70  *...............................*
541000  002A7000 80CADBC8 0CADE28 80CADE2C  00CADE44 002A06E0 002A06E0 002A3F18  *...............................*
541020  00000000 002A7000 20CAF2C8 08CAF2D4  065429C0 00542200 20000000 002A3F18  *...H...2H..2M..................*
541040  00CADF3C 00575EF8 00000000 00000000  00172000 08CADBA0 002A3F18 00CADF14  *...8............Q..............*
541060  00000000 00065F18 00089000 00000000  0023D000 0023D800 001E0000 00000000  *...............................*
541080  00000000 00575F38 00000000 00000000  00000000 00575F48 00000000 00000000  *...............................*
```

TIOT offset (in hex) of problem file

Figure 9.10 Partial Dump for 013 (continued)

540E70. We find the value of the TIOT offset to be 00A4 in hex or 164 in decimal. Subtract 24 (for the header line of the TIOT) and divide the resulting 140 by 20 (each entry takes 20 bytes). The quotient is 7, which means that seven entries were fully processed and that our file is on the eighth line of the table (i.e., FILETWO is the DDname of the problem file). This substantiates the earlier conclusion drawn from analysis of the JCL.

Other DCB characteristics for FILETWO can be found by adding appropriate displacements from Table 9.1. For example, the maximum blocksize and record length are found at locations 540E86 and 540E9A, respectively.

MVS DIFFERENCES

Conversion to MVS is a *major* undertaking for the systems group, yet the impact of conversion on ABEND debugging is minor for the COBOL programmer, at least at our level of discussion. MVS dumps do contain more information. In addition, some of the existing information is formatted differently. These differences are slight, however, and the individual who has understood Chapters Eight and Nine should have little trouble in debugging COBOL ABENDs produced under MVS. We do include Figure 9.11 to provide specific illustrations. It contains portions of an MVS dump extracted from the transcript problem and corresponds to Figure 9.1

The first difference gleaned from Figure 9.11 is that the TCB (Task Control Block) is no longer the first control block printed. It is preceded by the ASCB (Address Space Control Block), which is seldom used in debugging COBOL programs. Recall that our only use for the TCB was to extract the address of the first DEB. This is done exactly as before (i.e., 979838 is the hex address of the first DEB).

The DEB chain is followed as under MVT. The first word of each DEB contains the address of the TCB; the second contains the address of the next DEB in the chain. MVS however formats the DEBs with key words (e.g., NEXTDEB), so that one need no longer remember what is found where. [The alert reader may have noticed that the TCB and DEB entries have offsets in their presentation. Notice, for example, that the TCBADR is at offset +0 (i.e., the first word in the DEB). The field NEXTDEB is at displacement +4 in a DEB (i.e., the second word).]

One field of particular interest in any DEB is the address of the corresponding DCB, which is 0849A8 for the last DEB in Figure 9.11. Recall from Figure 9.1 that the last DEB in the chain points to the first file open (i.e., CARD-FILE). We should therefore be able to verify this conclusion using information contained in the dump.

Table 9.1 states the TIOT offset is found in the two bytes displaced by hex 28 from the DCB. Hence, the value of the TIOT offset corresponding to the last DEB in Figure 9.11 will begin at location 849D0 (849A8 + 28) and is found to be 00B8. This is the offset into the TIOT, which is used to determine the DDname and hence the COBOL file. Note, however, that the offsets are printed alongside the TIOT in an MVS dump. Hence, it is no longer necessary to convert the hex value of the offset to a line in the TIOT. [Realize, however, that the method described earlier in the chapter still works (i.e., B8 in hex = 184 in decimal; subtract 24 to eliminate the TIOT header leaving 160; divide by 20, obtaining a quotient of 8, indicating that eight entries were completed and the file in question is on the ninth line.)]

```
JOB SGTDR                STEP GO            TIME 083539     DATE 78085     ID = 000

COMPLETION CODE          SYSTEM = 0CB

PSW AT ENTRY TO ABEND    078D0000 00087AD8     ILC 6     INTC 000B
```

New control block →
```
ASCB 00FE55E0
+0   ASCB  C1E2C3C2   FWDP  00000000   BWDP  00FEAB30   CMSF  00000000   SVRB  0099E7A8   SYNC  0001B23E
+18  IOSP  00000000   SPL   00FE56B0   CPUS  00000001   IDSQ  00000004   IODP  B8E20075   STOR  0F185C00
+30  LDA   0099F548   RSM   00FE54F0   CSCB  00FE56C8   TSB   00000000   EJST  00000000   XJST  33375000
+48  EWST  8C54DE3D   XWST  D7D6F000   JSTL  00000116   ECB   8099EE58   UBET  8C547CE0   RESV  00000000
+60  DUMP  0099E3A0   FW1   FFFF0000   TMCH  00000000   ASXB  0099F300   SWCT  E2650000   SSRB  00000000
+78  VSC   0000000E   TCBS  00000000   LOCK  00000001   LSQH  00000000   QECB  00000000   MECB  40000000
+90  OUCB  00FED540   OUXB  00FEC630   FMCT  002A0000   XMPQ  00000000   IQEA  00000000   RTWA  00000000
+A8  MCC   00000000   JBNI  00FF06E8   JBNS  00FE56D8   SRQ   00000000   VGTT  00000000   PCTT  00000000
+C0  SMCT  00000000   SWTL  00000478   SRBT  00000478   ATME  04309000
```

Address of first DEB →
```
TCB 970DD8
+0    RBP  0099E6E0   PIE    00000000   DEB  00979838   CMP   00000000   TIO  00971020   TRN  00000000
+18   MSS  0099C7B0   PK-FLG 80010000   FLG  0000FFFF   JLB   0099C118   LLS  0099C118   JPQ  0099C868
+70   FSA  01084FB0   TCB    00000000   TME  00000000   NTC   00970DD8   JST  00970DD8   OTC  00970070
+88   LTC  00000000   IQE    00000000   ECB  0099C04C   D-PQE 0099C04C   TSF  20000000   AQE  0099F548
+A0   STAB 0099CED0   TCT    8099CE58   USER 00000000   MDID  00000000   SDF  00000000   JSCB 00970B44
+B8   RESV 00000000   IOBRC  00000000   XCPD 00000000   BITS  00000000   EXT  00000000   DAR  00000000
+D0   EXT2 00970F00   AECB   00000000   TIRB 0099C9A8   RTMWA 00000000   BAK  0099C9A8   IOTM 00000000
+E8   TMSAV 00000000  ABCR   00000000   XSCT 80000000   SWA   0099C570   FOE  00000040   STAW 00000000
+100  BID  E3C3C240   RTM1   80000000   ESTA 80000000   CPVI  0099C770   UKY  0099C770   BYT1 08040000
+118  RPT  00000000   DBTB   00000000   SWAS 00969F48   RESV  00000000   SCB  00969F48   RESV 00000000
EXT2  GTF  00000000   SVAB   00000000   EVNT 00000000   RESV  00000000   RES  00000000   RESV 00000000
```

```
TIOT 971020
        JOB SGTDR
                      STEP
OFFSET  LN-STA        DDNAME      GO TTR-ST   STB-UC
 + 0018 14010100      PGM=*.DD       97D4C000 90001C30
 + 002C 14010102      SYSUDUMP       97CB8000 80001C30
 + 0040 14010102      SYSDBOUT       97C70000 80000000
 + 0054 14010100      STEPLIB        97C58000 80001CF0
 + 0068 14010100      SYS00050       96EB8000 80001C60
 + 007C 14010102      SYSTERM        97C34000 80000000
 + 0090 14010102      SYSUDUMP       97C1C000 80000000
 + 00A4 14010102      SYSOUT         97C04000 80000000
 + 00B8 14010102      CARDS          97BE8000 80000000
```
TIOT offsets appear with table

Figure 9.11 Selected Portions of MVS Dump

-DEB--AT LOCATION 00979838 ──── Address of first DEB

DEB is formatted with key words

```
-8   EXTNSION 00979820  LENGTH   10        AMTYPE 81        TBLOF  0003
+0   TCBADR   00970DD8  NEXTDEB  009790C8  IRBADR 0896DEE0  PATB   0F000900
+10  USRPG    00000000  RRQ      00240000  DCBADR 0096AE08  APPADR 8F08AEB8  00E6E57C
+20  000024A0' E2E2C9C2 00240000  D1C5E2F2  00000000
+30  00000000 00000000  00000000  E2E2D6C2  00140010
+40  00000000 00000000  0097985C  00979894  00979838
+50  0097985C 00000000  009799B4  00180000
+60  00000000 009799B4  009790C8  0096DEE0
+70  00000000 00000000
```

Hex offsets in the DEB

*** FOR THIS DEB THERE IS NO DCB, THE CONTROL BLOCK POINTED TO BY THE DEB IS AN ACB ***

-DEB--AT LOCATION 009790C8

DEB begins at displacement of 0;
TCB address is in the first word

```
-3   EXTNSION 009791C0  LENGTH   10        AMTYPE 81        TBLOF  0002
+0   TCBADR   00970DD8  NEXTDEB  00979148  IRBADR 0896DA60  PATB   0F000900
+10  USRPG    00000000  RRQ      00240000  DCBADR 00086230  APPADR 8F084840  00E6E57C
+20  000024A0 E2E2C9C2  00240000  D1C5E2F2  00000000
+30  00000000 00000000  00000000  00000000
+40  00000000 00000000  E2E2D6C2  00140010
+50  00979EC  00000000  00979124  00180000
+60  00000000 00979304  009790C8  0096DA60
+70  00000000 00000000
```

*** FOR THIS DEB THERE IS NO DCB, THE CONTROL BLOCK POINTED TO BY THE DEB IS AN ACB ***

-DEB--AT LOCATION 00979148

```
-8   EXTNSION 009791E0  LENGTH   10        AMTYPE 81        TBLOF  0001
+0   TCBADR   00970DD8  NEXTDEB  00000000  IRBADR 0896D940  PATB   00000900
+10  USRPG    00000000  RRQ      00240000  DCBADR 0008617C  APPADR 8F0849A8  00E6E57C
+20  000024A0 E2E2C9C2  00240000  D1C5E2F2  00000000
+30  00000000 00000000  00000000  E2E2D6C2  00140010
+40  00000000 00000000  00979916C 00180000
+50  0097916C 00000000  009791A4  00180000
+60  00000000 00000000  00979960  0096D940
+70  00000000 00000000
```

Address of associated DCB is in seventh word

Binary zeros indicate end of chain

*** FOR THIS DEB THERE IS NO DCB, THE CONTROL BLOCK POINTED TO BY THE DEB IS AN ACB ***

```
0848E0  0000014C  00000000  40000000  00000000    00000000  00000000  00000000  00000000    *................*
084900  000843E0  00000000  20002000  00084820    00000085  00000085  00000000  00000365    *................*
084920  01000008  00000000  0008493C  00000000    00000000  00000000  00000000  000843E0    *................*
084940  00000000  00000000  00000005  00000000    00000000  00000000  00000000  000843E0    *................*
084960  00000000  00000000  00000000  00084840    03000000  00000000  04000000  00000000    *................*
084980  00000000  00000000  00084988  40000000    00000000  0008498C  00000000  00000000    *................*
0849A0  00000000  0008617C  A000004C  00000000    00E6E57C  54000000  00000000  00000000    *....WV..........*
0849C0  48900008  00000000  00000000  00000000    00B80041  00779148  12000000  000846C0    *................*
0849E0  00000000  00500050  00000000  00000000    00000000  C9C7C7F0  F1F9C1C8  00000000    *......IGG019AH..*
084A00  00086338  00000006  40F88B00  00000000    00000000  00084A48  00084988  00084988    *......8.........*
084A20  0008617C  00000000  0008493C  00084690    000862B0  00084A48  00085CF8  12F88A6C    *......8......8.8*
084A40  000865B8  00000000  0000004C  00000000    40000000  00000200  00000000  00000000    *................*
084A60  000849A8  00000000  00084690  02000000    20000000  00000050  00000050  00000050    *................*
084A80  00000000  0000030E  02000002  00000000    00000000  00084988  00000000  00000000    *................*
084AA0  00000000  00000000  00000000  00000000    00000000  00000000  00000000  00000000    *................*
084AC0  00000000  00084690  00000000  00000000    00000000  000849A8  08000000  00000000    *................*
084AE0  04000000  00000000  00000000  00000000    00084B80  00000090  00084B7C  00084B54    *................*
084B00  00084B54  D4C1C9D5  D7D9D6C7  E2E4C2D9    E3D54040  00000000  00000000  00000000    *....MAINPROGSUBRTN..*
084B20  00000000  00000000  00000000  00000000    00000000  00000000  00000000  00000000    *................*
084B40  00000000  00000000  00000000  010000A3    00000000  00000000  010000A3  010000A3    *................*
084B60  0100008E  0100006D  0200002B  02000036    02000036  02000036  0100009C  02000036    *................*
```

TIOT offset

Dump index appearing at end of dump

Figure 9.11 Selected Portions of MVS Dump (continued)

Finally, note that Figure 9.11 includes a dump index, which appears at the end of each dump. It serves as a mini table of contents and is designed to facilitate location of various entries.

LIST OF COMMON ABENDs

This section contains a series of common ABENDs with possible causes. The list is by no means complete, nor is it the last word on debugging. Numerous codes have been omitted as well as reasons for ABENDing within a given code. We do hope, however, that our list provides a useful starting place.

0C1: Operation exception (i.e., an invalid operation code). Figure 7.7 on instruction formats shows that the first byte of any instruction is its op code. An operation exception results if this byte is unknown to the system.

Common causes:

1. A missing (or misspelled) DD statement. (Missing DD statements can sometimes be caused by an inadvertent duplication of an EXEC statement, where the duplicated statement would have no DD statements.)
2. Attempting to read from a data set that has not been opened (e.g., a misplaced OPEN statement).
3. A subscript or index error which caused a portion of code to be overlaid, resulting in an attempt to "execute" data.

Corrective action:

1. A very low address for the interrupt indicates that the error occurred in a data management routine rather than in the COBOL program per se. Check the JCL messages carefully for indication of missing DD statements.
2. If the JCL messages are not helpful, register 2 plus hex 28 should point to the TIOT offset of the DDname in question.
3. If the interrupt address is within the program (or close to it), chances are the 0C1 was caused by a subscript (or index) problem. A careful review of program logic is called for with particular attention to any routines which fill tables.

0C4: Protection exception—attempting to overwrite a protected area in storage.

Common causes:

1. Invalid subscript or index.
2. Inclusion of a STOP RUN statement in the INPUT or OUTPUT PROCEDURE of the SORT verb.
3. Missing or misspelled DD statement.
4. Block size and record size specified as equal in a variable length file.

Corrective action:

1. An interrupt at a low address indicates a missing DD statement or attempt to read an unopened file.
2. If the interrupt is within the COBOL program, it is probably a subscript (index) error. A *thorough* review of program logic is required. Subscript errors are often the most difficult to find.

0C5:   Addressing exception—an address has been calculated outside the bounds of available storage.

Common causes:

1. Invalid subscript or index.
2. Attempting to close an already closed file.
3. An attempt to reference an I/O area before READ or OPEN was issued.
4. Improper exit from a performed routine; remember that GO TO out of perform is strictly prohibited.
5. Invoking a subprogram with a Linkage Section but with no associated USING clause, or too few parameters, or parameters listed in the wrong order.

Corrective action:

1. Review program logic to determine if a subscript error exists.
2. Register 1 contains the DCB address of the last referenced file. Register 14 should contain the next sequential instruction in the COBOL program.

0C6:   Specification exception—an address was generated which does not fall on the proper boundary.

Common causes:

1. Invalid subscript or index.
2. Incorrect or missing DD statement.
3. Improper exit from a performed routine; remember that GO TO out of a perform is strictly prohibited.

Corrective action:

1. Register 2 contains the DCB address of the last file referenced prior to the ABEND.
2. Review program logic to determine if a subscript error exists.

0C7:   Data exception (i.e., invalid "decimal" data). This error can result only after attempted execution of an instruction to process packed data. Specifically, the sign or digits of an operand in a decimal arithmetic, editing, or CVB instruction are invalid.

Common causes:

1. Failure to initialize a counter.
2. Invalid incoming data (e.g., blanks, decimal points, or commas in a numeric field).

3. Exceeding a table via a subscript (index) error, causing a reference to invalid data. This can also result in an 0C4, 0C5, or 0C6.

4. Moving zeros or LOW-VALUES to a group field defined as numeric.

5. An omitted or erroneous USAGE clause.

6. Passing parameters between programs in the wrong order.

Corrective action:

1. The subtraction technique of Chapter Eight, or the STATE option will identify the COBOL statement causing the ABEND. The error may be immediately obvious, as in the case of an uninitialized counter or erroneous USAGE clause. If not, a check of the program's logic is necessary to determine if invalid data are referenced.

2. Register 2 will point to the DCB for the last referenced file.

0CB: Decimal Divide Exception (division by zero). This error results from attempted execution of a DP (Divide Packed) Assembler instruction where the divisor is zero.

Common causes:

1. A COBOL DIVIDE or COMPUTE statement has a divisor of zero.

Corrective action:

1. The STATE option can identify the COBOL statement in error. Review program logic to determine how the divisor is calculated.

001: An incorrectable input/output error which is sometimes attributable to DCB conflicts.

Common causes:

1. Attempting to read from a file after the AT END condition has been encountered.

2. A device malfunction, or a damaged (dirty) tape or disk.

3. Wrong-length record of physical block.

Corrective action:

1. Check the JCL messages for an indication of the file in question.

2. Register 2 points to the DCB.

013: Unsuccessful attempt to OPEN a file, usually due to a DCB conflict. An error message will appear in the JCL to indicate the exact nature of the error. The return code mentioned in the error message specifies the error.

Common causes (with return codes):

1. 18—System was unable to find specified member of a partitioned data set.

2. 20—BLKSIZE is not a multiple of LRECL.

3. 34—BLKSIZE not specified; the system knows it has to allocate buffers, but is unable to do so.

4. 60—BLKSIZE is not equal to LRECL for unblocked (i.e., RECFM = F) records.

5. 68—BLKSIZE specified as greater than 32, 767.

Corrective action:

1. Check the JCL messages to determine the file in question. Look for any immediately obvious inconsistencies.
2. Register 2 contains the DCB address of the file in question. Use the table of DCB offsets to determine DCB information.

122:   Job canceled by operator for unspecified reason.

Common causes:

1. Program in an apparent loop.
2. Program is producing an "abnormal" number of error messages.
3. Program requested an unavailable resource.
4. A "panic" job required immediate processing and needed resources assigned to your job.
5. A mistake on the part of operations.

Corrective action:

1. It is definitely possible that nothing is wrong with your job. Accordingly, find out why the operator canceled. Make the necessary corrections and resubmit.

213:   An error in opening a file on a direct-access device; specifically, the system cannot locate the data set specified in the DSNAME parameter.

Common causes:

1. The DSNAME parameter is misspelled.
2. The wrong volume was specified.
3. The data set no longer exists because it was accidentally scratched.
4. The DISP parameter specified OLD or SHR for an output data set.

Corrective action:

1. Register 2 contains the DCB address. Add hex 28 to locate the two-byte TIOT offset. Determine the DDname from the TIOT offset.
2. Register 4 plus hex 64 contains the DSNAME as specified in the JCL.
3. Register 4 plus hex DA contains the volume serial number as specified in the JCL or catalog.

322:   CPU time limit for a step or job was exceeded.

Common causes:

1. An error in program logic causing an endless loop.
2. A switch to a slower CPU.
3. A switch to a different operating system.
4. The time requested was insufficient.

Corrective action:

1. Check to see if a slower CPU was used. This can happen in large shops with multiple CPU's where for some reason your job was switched to a different CPU.
2. Review program logic to insure that no endless loops are present. Structured programs will not contain 'traditional' loops; i.e., those

induced by backward GO TO statements. However they can well contain problems brought about by improper setting (resetting) of switches. Some advice—do *not* use the same switch for more than one purpose, and do use meaningful names: e.g. TRANSACTION-FILE-SWITCH as opposed to SWITCH-1.

3. The subtraction technique can be used to determine the next sequential instruction. This may be useful in determining the endless loop if one exists.

4. The READY TRACE statement and/or FLOW option may be useful in identifying the loop. Use of READY TRACE should be carefully controlled with ON and RESET TRACE statements to avoid needless volumes of paper.

513:   An attempt was made to open more than one data set on the same tape volume.

Common causes:

1. Attempting to open a second file before closing the first.
2. Assignment of two data sets to the same tape device.
3. Transferring data sets from direct access devices which may have more than one data set open simultaneously.

Corrective action:

1. This type of error may be easily corrected at the source level. Examine all OPEN and associated CLOSE statements to determine where the problem exists.
2. The JCL allocation messages can also be studied to determine which devices are used for which files.
3. Register 2 contains the address of the DCB in question.

80A, 804:   More storage was requested than is currently available in the region.

Common causes:

1. The REGION parameter was omitted and the installation's default is too small.
2. The REGION parameter on the JOB or EXEC statement did not specify sufficient storage. Realize that if REGION is specified on the JOB card, it *overrides* any subsequent specification on EXEC cards (i.e., the REGION parameter of EXEC statements is ignored).
3. Blocking factors were increased without corresponding increase in REGION parameter.

Corrective action:

1. Review JCL to ensure that REGION parameters are not omitted and/or overridden.

806:   A requested program could not be found.

Common causes:

1. Missing JOBLIB or STEPLIB statements.
2. Misspelled module name.

Corrective action:

1. The system messages will typically contain the module name. (A list of commonly called I/O subroutines and their function can be found in the programmer's guide by looking under ILB subroutines in the index.)
2. The address in register 12 plus 4 may point to the missing module.
3. Register 15 will contain 00000004 if the requested module could not be found in the private, job, or link library. It will contain 00000008 if an I/O error occurred in searching the directory of the indicated libraries.

813: An error in label processing for tape; specifically, the data set name on the header label does not match the specification in the JCL.

Common causes:

1. The DSNAME parameter is misspelled.
2. The wrong volume was called for and mounted.
3. The data set no longer exists.

Corrective action:

1. Add 64 to the address contained in register 4 to determine the DSNAME parameter in storage obtained from the DD statement.
2. Add 4 to the address contained in register 4 to determine the data set name as it appears on the header label. Attempt to resolve the conflict between this and the JCL entry from step 1. If more than a misspelling, a review of file logs, etc., is probably called for.

B37, D37, E37: Space problems; insufficient space available for an output data set.

Common causes:

1. An infinite loop containing a WRITE statement.
2. The space requested was insufficient. This may happen if a secondary allocation was not specified in the SPACE parameter, or if specified, it was not large enough to accommodate the data set.
3. Sufficient space was requested but was not available on the volume specified.

Corrective action:

1. The possibility of an infinite loop should be eliminated through review of program logic.
2. Check the SPACE parameter for a secondary allocation on the file in question. Register 2 plus hex 28 will supply the TIOT offset from where the DDname can be determined.
3. The DCB/DEB relationship can be used to determine the number of extents (i.e., secondary allocations) actually made. Register 2 plus hex 2D contains the DEB address of the file in question. The first byte of the fifth word in the DEB contains the number of extents used. If this value is less than 15, the system did not have sufficient space.

SUMMARY

This chapter continued the discussion of ABEND debugging begun in Chapter Eight. Although the emphasis was on data management ABENDs, there was a reference to some techniques previously introduced. These included the use of BL cells to identify a data name in core, and the SAVE AREA TRACE to analyze the flow of control between programs. The latter technique is particularly useful with external ABENDs as simple subtraction (i.e., PSW − EPA) is useless when the ABEND is outside the COBOL program. The SAVE AREA TRACE will, however, point to the COBOL statement that called the external routine and may prove useful. The chapter called attention to the JCL listing as a useful tool in debugging, alluded to differences under MVS, and summarized a list of common ABENDs.

One should approach debugging with an open mind; suspect everything and eliminate nothing. The most difficult task is to maintain objectivity. Do not go in with preconceived ideas as to the problem. Know when you hit a dead end and avoid rehashing the same ground. If one technique fails, leave it and try another.

A dump reveals the technical cause of an ABEND, but the programmer must relate this information to the source program and/or data. Some individuals therefore prefer to debug at the source level, and contend dumps are rather useless. We certainly do not agree on the latter point, but readily concede the utility of the DEBUG packet and/or JCL messages. Indeed, we often drift between source code and the dump.

In conclusion, debugging is more art than science. There are no guaranteed debugging procedures, only debugging aids. A bug does not leap from the pages of a dump, but must be coaxed out by logic, perseverance, and even luck. In short, debugging is an incomparable source of both frustration and satisfaction.

PROBLEMS

1. Figure 9.12 supplements the dump of problem 7 in Chapter Eight. Answer the following:

(a) Locate the control blocks:
   (1) What is the address of the TCB?
   (2) What is the address of the first DEB in the chain?
   (3) What address is contained in the first word of the DEB from part 2?
   (4) What is the address of the second DEB?
   (5) What is the address of the third DEB?
   (6) How is the end of the DEB chain indicated?

(b) Supply DCB displacements for the following:
   (7) Address of the current record.
   (8) TIOT offset.
   (9) Logical record length.
   (10) Maximum block size.
   (11) Address of the associated DEB.

(c) Using the DCB for CARD-FILE:
   (12) Which DEB is associated with CARD-FILE?
   (13) What is the DCB address contained in the DEB from part 12?
   (14) Add the answer from parts 11 and 13. What is the significance of the result?
   (15) Add the answer from parts 8 and 13. What are the hex contents of the two bytes beginning at that address?
   (16) Convert the hex contents of the two bytes from part 15 to decimal.
   (17) Use the answer from part 16 to find a line in the TIOT table. Show how the TIOT entry relates to CARD-FILE.
   (18) Add the answer from parts 7 and 13. To what does this address refer? How do the contents of the 80 bytes beginning at this address support the conclusion from Chapter Eight, problem 7?
   (19) Add the answer from parts 9 and 13. What is contained at the two bytes beginning at that address? How does this relate to a COBOL FD?

(d) Using the DCB for PRINT-FILE:
   (20) Which DEB is associated with PRINT-FILE?
   (21) What is the DCB address contained in the DEB from part 20?
   (22) Add the answer from parts 11 and 21. What is the significance of the result?
   (23) Add the answer from parts 8 and 21. What are the hex contents of the two bytes beginning at that address?
   (24) Convert the hex contents of the two bytes from part 23 to decimal.
   (25) Use the answer from part 24 to find a line in the TIOT table. Show how the TIOT entry relates to PRINT-FILE.
   (26) Add the answers from parts 9 and 21. What is contained at the two bytes beginning at that address? How does this relate to a COBOL FD?

Figure 9.12 is a full-page system memory (TCB/DEB/TIOT) dump.

```
TCB  CCE5F8
 RBP    00CCFCF0   PIE      00000000   DEB   00CCE40C   TIO  00CCEAF8   CMP   800CB000   TRN   00000000
 MSS    00CCF5E8   PK-FLG   10850540   FLG   0003F3B    LLS  00CCE3D8   JLB   00CCE840   JPQ   00CCF140
 FSA    0120EF68   TCB      00000000   TME   00000000   JST  00CCE5F8   NTC   00000000   OTC   00CCEEF0
 LTC    00000000   IQE      00000000   ECB   00CCEAB4   TSF  20000000   D-PQE 00CCF760   AQE   00CCE108
 STAB   80CCE918   TCT      80CCEC60   USER  00000000   SDF  00000000   MDID  00000000   JSCB  00CCED8C
 RESV   00000000   IOBRC    00000000   DIAG  00000000   EXT  00000000   BITS  00000000   DAR   00000000
 EXT2   00CCE6F8   XTNT     001D04CC   TIRB  00CCEBF8   BAK  00CC8E6F0  LSQAP 00CCFFF8   IOTM  00000000
 TMSAV  00000000   ABCR     12000000   QECB  00000000   FOE  00000000   SWA   00CCFFE0   RESV  00000000
 GTF    00000000   RCMP     000CB000   RESV  00000000   RES  00000000


DEB
 CCE3E0                    00004FC0 01F37938   00004FC0 00000000   00004FC0 00000000   *................3..*
 CCE400  00000000 00002BE0 0F200003 04CCE5F8   10CCE57C C8000000   8F000000 01000000   *.......W..TY..V.H.V8*
 CCE420  3B000000 1F20E680 02CCE3E8 33002A34   00010001 00000000   00000000 0000007D   *..........V8..V.H.*
 CCE440  C2C2C2C1 C3D3C3C6 00000000 00000000   00000000 00000000   00000000 00000000   *BBBACLCF........*


DEB
 CCE540                    00004FC0 01F37938   00004FC0 00000000   00004FC0 00000000   *................3..*
 CCE560  10CCE8C4 C8000000 0F000000 01000000   0F200002 04CCE5F8   1F1D1230 02CCE558   *...YDH.........V...V8*
 CCE580  00010001 00000000 00000000 00000000   3B000000 33002BCC   C1D9C1C9 C3D3C3C6   *.ARAICLCF......V*
 CCE5C0  00000000 00000000 00000000 00000000   00000000 00000000   00000000 00000000   *................*


DEB
 CCE8A0  00004FC0 00000000 00004FC0 00000000   00004FC0 00000000   00010EE0 00000000   *................*
 CCE8C0  0F200001 03CCE5F8 10000000 C8000000   01000000 00000000   3B000000 1F1D117C   *......V8....H...V8*
 CCE8E0  02CCE8A0 33002734 00010001 00000050   C1D8C1C1 C3C30000   C1D8C1C3 C3C30000   *..Y......AQACC..AQACC..*
 CCE900  00000000 00000000 00000000 00000000   00000000 00000000   00000000 00000000   *................*


TIOT
 JOB  ARTJHM22  STEP  GO
 DD   14040140   PGM=*.DD     004F2D00   80000DCC
 DD   14040140   SYSUDUMP     007A1600   80002A34
 DD   14040140   SYSDBOUT     007A1D00   80002A64
 DD   14040140   STEPLIB      00E00E00   80000E4C
 DD   14040100   SYSTERM      00E01000   80002B9C
 DD   14040140   SYSUDUMP     00E01200   80002BB4
 DD   14040140   SYSOUT       00E01400   80002BCC
 DD   14040140   CARDS        00E01600   80002734
```

Figure 9.12 Material for Problem 1

```
1D1120  F0F0E2E3  C1E3C9E2  E3C9C3E2  C5C2C1E3  E6E240C5  D5C4E240  C8C5D9C5  87AE87B0  *00STATISTICSEBATWS ENDS HERE.....*
1D1140  87B287B4  00000000  00000000  00000000  00000000  051D3C9A  001D0D1E  00000001  *.................................*
1D1160  00000001  00000000  00000000  00410000  00000000  00000000  00000000  00000000  *.................................*
1D1180  00000000  00000000  0220EA00  00004000  0220EA00  00000001  461D19F2            *...............................2*
1D11A0  801D1144  00A44800  00CCE8C4  12F545A8  00F54400  06000001  00090050  28022828  *...............YD.5..5...........*
1D11C0  0020E888  0020EA58  0020EA08  00000050  00000001  00F5E0C8  00000000            *...........Y.............5.H.....*
1D11E0  00000000  00000000  00000000  00000000  00000001  00800000  00000000  00000000  *.................................*
1D1200  00000000  00000000  051D3C9A  001D0D1E  00000001  00000001  00000000  00000000  *.................................*
1D1220  00480000  0220E8E8  00000000  80000000  46000000  841D11F8  00900048  00CCE57C  *.............YY..................*
1D1240  92F67A90  00F67980  07000001  00090085  28022828  0020E818  0020E975  0020E975  *......6...6........8....Y..Z.....*
1D1260  00000085  00000000  00000000  00D4E618  05FF0700  00000000  00000000  0020E975  *.................MW...............*
1D1280  00000000  008400B8  001FA0F8  F0404040  00000000  40404040  40404040  40404040  *.................................*
1D12A0  C1E5C5D9  C1C7C57A  40F34BF0  F0404040  40404040  40404040  40404040  40404040  *AVERAGE. 3.00....................*
1D12C0  40404040  40404040  40404040  40404040  40404040  40404040  40404040  40404040  *.................................*
LINE 1D1300 SAME AS ABOVE
1D1320  40404040  40404040  40404040  40404040  4070B1EC  0030C4C2  0020EF68            *.................DB..*
1D1340  001D2798  501D185C  001D26E8  00CCE5F8  001D1588  00000005  001D0DE5            *.........Y..V8...........V*
1D1360  001D19F8  001D0D98  0020EA08  001D12B0  001D1B76  001D0CF8  001D15B8            *.........8.....8..8.*
1D1380  3462804B  00000000  00000000  00000005  001D0CF8  601D19C6  001D41E2            *.........8.......*
1D13A0  001D1B30  001D1588  001D0DE4  001D0CF8  001D0DE5  00000006  0020EA58            *.............U....V.......F..S*
1D13C0  001D12B0  001D1B76  001D0CF8  001FA238  001D15B8  000101F0  001FA228            *....8..8......0..9*
1D13E0  4780B2F2  4800A009  4C00D44A  4C00D44A  181E4C10  D44E1A10  41215B16  001FA228  *...2....M.........M...*
1D1400  F8112000  D216940F  2000960F  061D3568  001D2DA8  2000D214  001FA248            *8..K.........K....8.*
1D1420  E000D215  960FE002  41115B1B  50FFFA54  D2121000  F8441000  001FA288            *.K.....M...K..M....K*
1D1440  100407FF  48E0A007  4CE0D44E  D2011000  D498411E  5B26D202  001FA2A8            *.K.....M...K..M....K*
```

Figure 9.12 Material for Problem 1 (continued)

```
20E8A0  0020E8B0  00000000  0220EA58  C1E5C5D9  40404040   0220EA08  20000050  0020E8B0  0020E838  7F000000   *....Y.....Y.....Y.....Y....*
20E8C0  00000000  7F20E8BC  20000050  40F34BF0  40404040   001D117C  001D117C  0020E8E0  0020E8E0  00000000   *....Y.....Y....YY.....Y...Y*
20E8E0  0220EA58  20000050  00000000  40F5F5F5  40404040   F0404040  40404040  40404040  00020088  0C000000   *AVERAGE. 3.00.........0*
20E900  20000050  00000000  00020088  40404040  40404040   40404040  40U4U40   40404040  40404040  0020E838   *......................*
20E920  0020E838  0020E8E0  F0404040  F0404040  40404040   40404040  40404040  40404040  40404040  F0404040   *.....*

LINE 20E940 SAME AS ABOVE

20E960  40404040  40404040  40U4U40   40404040   40404040  40000000  40404040  40404040  40002400   *....555.........3*
20E980  40404040  40F5F5F5  40404040   40F34040   40404040  40404040  40404040  40404040   *.........3...*
20E9A0  40404040  40404040  40404040   40404040   40404040  40404040  40404040  40404040   *....B*

LINE 20E9C0 SAME AS ABOVE

20E9E0  40404040  40404040  40404040  40404040   40404040  40404040  404040F3  F9F6F0F0  F4F6F6F6  40002400   *.........SMITH. JOHN  39004666*
20EA00  00000000  00020050  E2D4C9E3  C86B40D1   D6C8D540  404040F3  F9F6F0F0  F4F6F6F6            *B0777B0888C0999C0*
20EA20  C2F0F7F7  F7C2F0F8  F8F8C3F4  F9F9F9C3   F0404040  40404040  C2D6D9D6  E66B40D1            *.....231.....BOROW. J*
20EA40  40404040  40404040  40404040  40404040   40F2F3F1  4B404040  F8F8C3F4  F9F9F9C3            *....39004666B 777B4888C4999C*
20EA60  F4404040  40404040  40404040  40404040   C240F7F7  F7C2F4F8  F8F8C3F4  40404040            *..........MAIN*
20EA80  40F2F3F2  4B404040  0020EB38  00000090   40404040  0020EB0C  0020EB0C  D4C1C9D5            *4.....232.*
20EAA0  D7D9D6C7  E2E4C2D9  E3D54040  40404040   0020EB34  0020EB0C  0020EB0C  D4C1C9D5            *PROGSUBRTN.....*
20EAC0  0001F440  00006400  00000000  00000000   40404040  04000100  03044001  004F2F00            *..4....*
20EAE0  004F2C03  00000000  0000000C  010000A4   00000009D  01000000A4 0100006E  01000006E           *....*
20EB00  02000000  00000037  02000000  00000037   02000037  004F2D00  00000070  00000070            *....*
20EB20  00000000  02000000  00000000  00000037   0020EBF8  801D4114  001D32E4  801D37DC            *....8....8*
20EB40  0000006E  0000186E0 00000000  00000037   0020EBB0  0020EAB0  0020EAB0  0020EB30            *........U*
20EB60  001D2798  0020EDEC  001D3CE0  0020EB40   00000000  0000055C  00000084  0020EAB0            *...U*
20EB80  00028000  0020EB0C  00000000  000003C0   00000000  0020E768  0020EBF8  401D383A            *...X....8*
20EBA0  001D32E4  00000000  00000000  0000006E   00000000  00083BDA  00000000  401D383A            *...U...W...X...Z.*
20EBC0  001D32E4  801D37DC  0000006E  0020EDEC   001D2DA8  401D356E  00000000  00CCE918            *...U...W...X...Z.*
20EBE0  0020E7B0  00CCE698  0020EF68  0020E7B0   001D2DA8  401D356E  00000000  0020EBB0            *...X....X.....6.*
20EC00  00000000  00000000  00000000  401D34FA   92F678A0  0020EDEC  0020EC40  0020EDEC            *.....*
```

Figure 9.12 Material for Problem 1 (continued)

JCL and Utilities for the COBOL Programmer

OS JCL

OVERVIEW

An operating system is a complex set of programs, supplied by the mainframe manufacturer, to improve the effectiveness of a computer. Communication with the operating system is accomplished through user-prepared control cards known as Job Control Language (JCL). This section is directed at the COBOL programmer who continually uses the facilities of an operating system but whose knowledge of JCL is typically below his COBOL capability. "Just give me the control cards" is a phrase heard far too often.

For some unfortunate reason, OS JCL retains a mystique which frequently makes both student and practitioner shy away. Admittedly, the multipage collection of /'s, X's, and so on, is somewhat foreboding, but given half a chance, it becomes thoroughly understandable. Our objective is simply to remove the apprehension associated with OS JCL. We begin with the basic job stream for the procedure COBUCLG. We next consider syntactical rules, elementary statements (JOB, EXEC, DD, /*, and //), keyword and positional parameters, and system output. We develop jobstreams

255

for sequential and nonsequential processing. We cover ISAM, VSAM, and the COBOL SORT. Finally, we present a brief discussion of MVS differences.

BASIC JOB STREAM

Figure 10.1 is a typical jobstream to compile, link edit, and execute a COBOL program. It also illustrates keyword and positional parameters, rules for continuation of JCL, and placement of comments.

Figure 10.1 contains five types of statements: JOB, EXEC, DD, /*, and //. Our entire discussion of OS JCL revolves around variations in the first three. The JOB, EXEC, and DD statements each consist of up to five parts in specified order: //, name, operation, parameter, and comments. If the name is supplied, it must begin in column

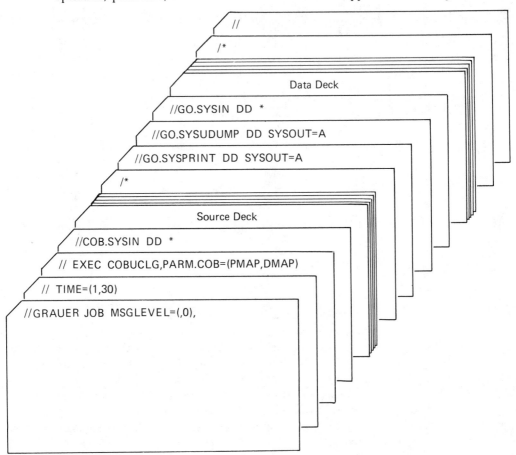

```
                                        //
                                    /*
                                Data Deck
                            //GO.SYSIN DD *
                          //GO.SYSUDUMP DD SYSOUT=A
                        //GO.SYSPRINT DD SYSOUT=A
                      /*
                    Source Deck
                  //COB.SYSIN DD *
                // EXEC COBUCLG,PARM.COB=(PMAP,DMAP)
              // TIME=(1,30)
            //GRAUER JOB MSGLEVEL=(,0),
```

Figure 10.1 OS Jobstream to Compile, Link Edit, and Execute a COBOL Program

three immediately following //. Whether or not a name is used depends on the type of statement and whether subsequent references are made back to the statement. In Figure 10.1, names are given to the JOB and four DD statements but not to the EXEC statement. The operation (i.e., JOB, EXEC, or DD) follows next. Optional parameters (e.g., MSGLEVEL or PARM) follow the operation. A blank separates the name, operation, and parameter fields. However, if the name is omitted, as in the EXEC statement, a blank separates the // and operation. A comma delineates individual parameters. Comments may follow the last parameter.

Parameters are of two types, keyword and positional. *Keyword parameters* may appear in any order within a statement; it is the keyword itself which conveys meaning to the system. *Positional parameters*, as the name implies, are required to appear in a specified order. If a positional parameter is omitted, its absence must be denoted by a comma, unless no additional positional parameters follow in the statement.

The JOB statement in Figure 10.1 contains both keyword and positional parameters. MSGLEVEL and TIME are *keywords* and their order could be reversed. However, the subparameters appearing in parentheses are *positional* and must appear in the order shown. (1,30) indicates one minute and 30 seconds. If the minutes parameter were omitted (i.e., if only 30 seconds were desired), the comma is still required (,30). This is further discussed under the JOB statement.

The JOB statement also illustrates the rules for continuation. Coding begins in column 1 and continues up to and including column 71. If additional space is needed, one stops somewhere before column 71 and continues on a second, third, . . ., card. The continued card (all cards but the first) require // in columns 1 and 2 and a blank in column 3. Coding on the continued card must begin between columns 4 and 16. The statement which was continued (i.e., the first card) must end with a comma. Earlier versions of OS also required that a nonblank character be inserted in column 72 of the first card, but this is not shown in Figure 10.1.

The EXEC statement of Figure 10.1 invokes the procedure COBUCLG, which will compile, link edit, and execute a COBOL program. (The procedure concept is explained in the next section.) The PARM parameter in this statement tells the compiler to generate Procedure and Data Division maps with the COBOL compilation.

There are four DD (Data Definition) statements in Figure 10.1, each of which supplies information about an input or output file. The * is a positional parameter which means that the file immediately follows in the jobstream. Thus, COBOL source and data decks follow the COB.SYSIN and GO.SYSIN DD cards, respectively. In the DD statement for SYSPRINT, SYSOUT=A means that the file is to appear on a class A output device (i.e., a printer). The DD statement for SYSUDUMP causes a dump to appear on a CLASS A output device (i.e., a printer) in the event of an ABEND. The /* denotes the end of a data set and appears after both the COBOL source deck and input data cards.

A COBOL program which merely goes "card to print" typically results in the series of messages shown in Figure 10.2. (Note that Figure 10.2 was *not* created by Figure 10.1, as can be seen by the different job names. However after reading this section, the reader should be able to determine the job stream which did produce Figure 10.2). The reaction of most beginners is to bypass Figure 10.2 as quickly as possible and turn immediately to the COBOL listing. We try to do better. We do, however, avoid line-by-line detailed explanations and aim instead at an overall level of conceptual understanding.

Figure 10.2 consists primarily of lines beginning with XX, //, or IEF. Statements beginning with // indicate that the line originated in the programmer-supplied JCL, whereas statements beginning with XX indicate a JCL statement pulled from a procedure. (It is also possible to have statements beginning with an X/, indicating that a JCL statement in a proc was overridden by an incoming JCL statement; more on this in Chapter Eleven.) The letters IEF are the first three characters in a system message, indicating a particular action the system has taken.

The programmer-supplied EXEC statement of Figure 10.2 specified execution of the procedure COBUCLG, which in turn consists of three job steps: compile (step name COB), link edit (step name LKED), and execute (step name GO). Subsequent JCL statements will reference these step names; for example, see the discussion of PARM.COB in the EXEC statement. Each job step is denoted by a XX EXEC (really // EXEC) statement, requesting execution of a program [e.g., IKFCBL00 for the compile (COB) step].

At the conclusion of each job step a completion message, perhaps of the form STEP WAS EXECUTED—COND CODE 0000 appears. The value of the condition code indicates the success encountered during that step. In the compile step, for example, a condition code of 0000 indicates no diagnostics, a code of 0004 indicates a warning was the most severe level of error, 0008 means a C-level diagnostic, and 0012 an E-level diagnostic. If a step is abnormally terminated (i.e., ABENDs), the condition code is replaced by a completion code stating the reason for the termination (e.g., COMPLETION CODE S0C7). In Figure 10.2 the three steps are executed with codes of 0004, 0000, and 0C7, respectively. Thus, by examining the system output, we can tell the highest severity error encountered during the execution of each job step. We can also tell how far the COBOL program went in the compile, link-edit, and execute sequence.

The DD statements of Figure 10.1 are also made clearer by a conceptual understanding of Figure 10.2. Consider the components of the statement //GO.SYSIN DD *. // is followed by the step-name.DDname (i.e., GO.SYSIN). GO is the step name for the execute step of COBUCLG, SYSIN indicates the file name and is tied to the COBOL select statement, DD indicates the operation, and * states that the file (i.e., data cards) follows immediately in the jobstream.

The concept of a procedure (or proc) is fundamental to OS. It is perfectly permissible, albeit impractical, for the COBOL programmer to submit the entire jobstream (i.e., procedure), with his program. Common practice is to catalog the necessary JCL into a procedure, and then invoke the procedure. In this way the job of the individual is simplified, and every programmer has convenient access to identical jobstreams. Installations usually establish a procedure library, with many of the actual procs supplied by IBM (e.g., COBUCLG).

```
//DANBB142 JOB   TIME=(1,30)                    ── Programmer supplied
// EXEC COBUCLG,PARM.COB=(PMAP,DMAP)              ── EXEC statement
XXCOBUCLG PROC SUT1=15,SOBJ=15,SLUT1=50,SLUT2=20,SLMOD1=50,SLMOD2=20,    00000100
XX             ADDLIB='SYS1.ADDLIB',STEPLIB='SYS1.ADDLIB'               00000200
XXCOB     EXEC PGM=IKFCBL00                                              00000300
XXSYSPRINT DD  SYSOUT=A,DCB=BLKSIZE=1936                                 00000400
XXSYSUT1   DD  UNIT=3330,SPACE=(TRK,(&SUT1,5))                           00000500
IEF653I SUBSTITUTION JCL - UNIT=3330,SPACE=(TRK,(15,5))
XXSYSUT2   DD  UNIT=3330,SPACE=(TRK,(&SUT1,5))                           00000600
IEF653I SUBSTITUTION JCL - UNIT=3330,SPACE=(TRK,(15,5))
XXSYSUT3   DD  UNIT=3330,SPACE=(TRK,(&SUT1,5))                           00000700
IEF653I SUBSTITUTION JCL - UNIT=3330,SPACE=(TRK,(15,5))
XXSYSUT4   DD  UNIT=3330,SPACE=(TRK,(&SUT1,5))                           00000800
IEF653I SUBSTITUTION JCL - UNIT=3330,SPACE=(TRK,(15,5))
XXSYSUT5   DD  UNIT=3330,SPACE=(TRK,(&SUT1,5)),DISP=(,PASS)              00000900
IEF653I SUBSTITUTION JCL - UNIT=3330,SPACE=(TRK,(15,5)),DISP=(,PASS)
XXSYSLIN   DD  DSNAME=&LOADSET,DCB=BLKSIZE=3120,DISP=(MOD,PASS),         00001000
XX             UNIT=3330,SPACE=(6400,(&SOBJ,10))                         00001100
IEF653I SUBSTITUTION JCL - UNIT=3330,SPACE=(6400,(15,10))
//COB.SYSIN DD *
IEF236I ALLOC. FOR DANBB142 COB
IEF237I 77E  ALLOCATED TO SYSPRINT      ── Step name — COB
IEF237I 268  ALLOCATED TO SYSUT1           (Beginning of compile step)
IEF237I 268  ALLOCATED TO SYSUT2
IEF237I 268  ALLOCATED TO SYSUT3
IEF237I 268  ALLOCATED TO SYSUT4
IEF237I 269  ALLOCATED TO SYSUT5
IEF237I 268  ALLOCATED TO SYSLIN
IEF237I 784  ALLOCATED TO SYSIN
IEF142I - STEP WAS EXECUTED - COND CODE 0004     ── End of compile step
IEF285I    SYS76273.T113030.RV001.DANBB142.ASP0A001     DELETED
IEF285I    VOL SER NOS= ASP77E.
IEF285I    SYS76273.T113030.RV001.DANBB142.R0002648     DELETED
IEF285I    VOL SER NOS= SCR001.
IEF285I    SYS76273.T113030.RV001.DANBB142.R0002649     DELETED
IEF285I    VOL SER NOS= SCR001.
IEF285I    SYS76273.T113030.RV001.DANBB142.R0002650     DELETED
IEF285I    VOL SER NOS= SCR001.
IEF285I    SYS76273.T113030.RV001.DANBB142.R0002651     DELETED
IEF285I    VOL SER NOS= SCR001.
IEF285I    SYS76273.T113030.RV001.DANBB142.R0002652     PASSED
IEF285I    VOL SER NOS= SCR002.
IEF285I    SYS76273.T113030.RV001.DANBB142.LOADSET      PASSED
IEF285I    VOL SER NOS= SCR001.
IEF285I    SYS76273.T113030.RV001.DANBB142.ASPI0001     DELETED
IEF285I    VOL SER NOS= 016948.

 ** START - STEP=COB        JOB=DANBB142    DATE= 9/29/76   CLOCK=11.30.40   PGM=IKFCBL00
 ** END -                                   DATE= 9/29/76   CLOCK=11.31.18   CPU=    0.81 SEC;
 ** EXCPS - DISK=   240,   CTC=    210,   TAPE=    0,   TOTAL=    450;   REGION USED=   120K

      DDNAME       EXCP COUNT    PCI COUNT
      LINK/SVC:        78          447
      SYSPRINT:        53
      SYSUT1  :        31
      SYSUT2  :        37
      SYSUT3  :        50
      SYSUT4  :        32
      SYSUT5  :         0
      SYSLIN  :        12          ── Condition parameter
      SYSIN   :       157             tests results of compile
XXLKED    EXEC PGM=IEWL,PARM='LIST,XREF,LET',COND=(5,LT,COB)    step   00001200
XXSYSLIN   DD  DSNAME=&LOADSET,DISP=(OLD,DELETE)                        00001300
XX         DD  DDNAME=SYSIN                                             00001400
XXSYSLMOD  DD  DSNAME=&&GOSET(GO),DISP=(NEW,PASS),UNIT=3330,            00001500
XX             SPACE=(1024,(&SLMOD1,&SLMOD2,1))                         00001600
IEF653I SUBSTITUTION JCL - SPACE=(1024,(50,20,1))
XXSYSLIB   DD  DSNAME=&ADDLIB,DISP=SHR                                  00001700
IEF653I SUBSTITUTION JCL - DSNAME=SYS1.ADDLIB,DISP=SHR
XX         DD  DSNAME=SYS1.COBLIB,DISP=SHR                              00001800
XXSYSUT1   DD  UNIT=(3330,SEP=(SYSLIN,SYSLMOD)),                        00001900
XX             SPACE=(1024,(&SLUT1,&SLUT2))                             00002000
IEF653I SUBSTITUTION JCL - SPACE=(1024,(50,20))
XXSYSPRINT DD  SYSOUT=A,DCB=BLKSIZE=1936                                00002100
```

Figure 10.2 System Output for COBUCLG Procedure

259

```
IEF236I ALLOC. FOR DANBB142 LKED
IEF237I 268    ALLOCATED TO SYSLIN
IEF237I 268    ALLOCATED TO SYSLMOD
IEF237I 251    ALLOCATED TO SYSLIB
IEF237I 251    ALLOCATED TO                    ┌─ End of linkage-editor step
IEF237I 269    ALLOCATED TO SYSUT1             │
IEF237I 77E    ALLOCATED TO SYSPRINT          │
┌──────────────────────────────────────────────────┐
│IEF142I - STEP WAS EXECUTED - COND CODE 0000      │
└──────────────────────────────────────────────────┘
IEF285I    SYS76273.T113030.RV001.DANBB142.LOADSET      DELETED
IEF285I    VOL SER NOS= SCR001.
IEF285I    SYS76273.T113030.RV001.DANBB142.GOSET        PASSED
IEF285I    VOL SER NOS= SCR001.
IEF285I    SYS1.ADDLIB                                  KEPT
IEF285I    VOL SER NOS= SYS002.
IEF285I    SYS1.COBLIB                                  KEPT
IEF285I    VOL SER NOS= SYS002.
IEF285I    SYS76273.T113030.RV001.DANBB142.R0002653     DELETED
IEF285I    VOL SER NOS= SCR002.
IEF285I    SYS76273.T113030.RV001.DANBB142.ASP0A002     DELETED
IEF285I    VOL SER NOS= ASP77E.

 ** START - STEP=LKED      JOB=DANBB142    DATE= 9/29/76    CLOCK=11.31.18    PGM=IEWL
 ** END   -                                DATE= 9/29/76    CLOCK=11.31.47    CPU=    0.15 SEC;
 ** EXCPS - DISK=   116,    CTC=    11,    TAPE=    0,    TOTAL=    127;    REGION USED=   128K

        DDNAME       EXCP COUNT     PCI COUNT
     LINK/SVC:          10            15
     SYSLIN  :          10
     SYSLMOD :          15
     SYSLIB  :          81
        "    :           0
     SYSUT1  :           0    ┌─ Step name — GO
     SYSPRINT:          11       (Beginning of execute step)

┌─────────┐
│XXGO     │  EXEC PGM=*.LKED.SYSLMOD,COND=((5,LT,COB),(5,LT,LKED))         00002200
└─────────┘
XXSTEPLIB  DD  DSNAME=SYS1.COBLIB,DISP=SHR                                 00002300
XX         DD  DSNAME=&STEPLIB,DISP=SHR                                    00002400
IEF653I SUBSTITUTION JCL - DSNAME=SYS1.ADDLIB,DISP=SHR
XXSYSUT5   DD  DSN=*.COB.SYSUT5,DISP=(OLD,DELETE)                          00002500
XXSYSDBOUT DD  SYSOUT=A,DCB=BLKSIZE=1936                                   00002600
XXDISPLAY  DD  SYSOUT=A,DCB=(RECFM=FA,LRECL=121,BLKSIZE=121,BUFNO=1)       00002700
XXDELETE   DD  DSN=&&GOSET,DISP=(OLD,DELETE,DELETE)                        00002800
//GO.SYSUDUMP DD SYSOUT=A
//GO.PRINT DD SYSOUT=A
//GO.SYSIN DD  *
//
IEF236I ALLOC. FOR DANBB142 GO
IEF237I 268    ALLOCATED TO PGM=*.DD
IEF237I 251    ALLOCATED TO STEPLIB
IEF237I 251    ALLOCATED TO
IEF237I 269    ALLOCATED TO SYSUT5
IEF237I 778    ALLOCATED TO SYSDBOUT
IEF237I 779    ALLOCATED TO DISPLAY
IEF237I 268    ALLOCATED TO DELETE         ┌─ Completion code for GO step
IEF237I 77B    ALLOCATED TO SYSUDUMP       │  indicates ABEND
IEF237I 77C    ALLOCATED TO PRINT          │
IEF237I 77D    ALLOCATED TO SYSIN          │
┌──────────────────────────────────────────────┐
│COMPLETION CODE - SYSTEM=0C7  USER=0000        │
└──────────────────────────────────────────────┘
IEF285I    SYS76273.T113030.RV001.DANBB142.GOSET        PASSED
IEF285I    VOL SER NOS= SCR001.
IEF285I    SYS1.COBLIB                                  KEPT
IEF285I    VOL SER NOS= SYS002.
IEF285I    SYS1.ADDLIB                                  KEPT
IEF285I    VOL SER NOS= SYS002.
IEF285I    SYS76273.T113030.RV001.DANBB142.R0002652     DELETED
IEF285I    VOL SER NOS= SCR002.
IEF285I    SYS76273.T113030.RV001.DANBB142.ASP0A003     DELETED
IEF285I    VOL SER NOS= ASP778.
IEF285I    SYS76273.T113030.RV001.DANBB142.GOSET        DELETED
IEF285I    VOL SER NOS= SCR001.
IEF285I    SYS76273.T113030.RV001.DANBB142.ASP0A005     DELETED
IEF285I    VOL SER NOS= ASP77B.
IEF285I    SYS76273.T113030.RV001.DANBB142.ASP0A006     DELETED
IEF285I    VOL SER NOS= ASP77C.
IEF285I    SYS76273.T113030.RV001.DANBB142.ASPI0002     DELETED
IEF285I    VOL SER NOS= 026948.
```

Figure 10.2 System Output for COBUCLG Procedure (continued)

JOB Statement

Format: //jobname JOB (Acct information), programmer-name,
  // keyword parameters
  Note: continuation on a second card may be required

Useful keywords: CLASS
  REGION
  MSGLEVEL
  TIME

Example: //GRAUER JOB MSGLEVEL=(,0),
  //   TIME=(1,30)

The JOB statement may contain some or all of the following information: job name, accounting information, programmer's name, indication of whether or not control statement and allocation messages are to be printed, priority, and region size.

It has two positional parameters—accounting information and programmer name. In addition, several of the keyword parameters have subparameters which are positional in nature.

The job name must begin with an alphabetic (A-Z) or national (#, @, $) character and may be up to eight alphanumeric characters in length.

If accounting information is supplied, it must be coded prior to any other parameters. It can consist of only an account number, or other additional parameters required by the installation's accounting system. If more than one account parameter is supplied, all such parameters are enclosed in parentheses. If there is only one parameter, parentheses are omitted.

The programmer name is a positional parameter which follows the accounting information. Since it is the last positional parameter, its omission does not require a comma. In Figure 10.1 both positional parameters (i.e., accounting information and programmer name) are omitted, hence no comma is used.

Keyword parameters are explained below:

REGION=NNNNK: NNNN specifies the amount of main storage [in units of 1024 bytes (1K = 1024 bytes)] that is to be allocated to the entire job

MSGLEVEL=(S,M): S = 0 if only the job statement is to be printed
  1 if all input job control and all cataloged procedure statements are to be printed
  2 if only input JCL is to be printed
  M = 0 if no allocation messages are to be printed
  1 if all allocation messages are to be printed

Note that S and M are positional subparameters; omission of S requires a comma as shown in Figure 10.1

TIME=(MM,SS): MM = CPU time in minutes
  SS = CPU time in seconds

These parameters need not be in parentheses if only minutes are specified; they are both positional subparameters

261

CLASS = X: where X indicates the class of a job; the meaning of each class is determined by the individual installation; job class specifies the region (MVT) or partition (MFT) in which the job will run.

EXEC Statement

Format: //stepname EXEC operands

Useful keywords: PARM
                 COND
                 REGION
                 TIME

Example: //STEP1 EXEC COBUCLG,PARM.COB='PMAP,DMAP'

The EXEC statement is used to execute either a single program or a procedure. If a program is to be executed, the keyword PGM must be specified (e.g., // EXEC PGM=IKFCBL00). If a procedure is to be executed, the keyword PROC can either be specified or omitted. Both statements below are valid:

```
// EXEC PROC=COBUCLG
// EXEC COBUCLG
```

The step name is optional in the EXEC statement. If used, it must begin in column 3 immediately following the //; if omitted, a space is required in column 3. Accordingly, both statements below are valid:

```
//STEP1 EXEC COBUCLG      (step name—STEP1)
// EXEC COBUCLG           (step name not supplied)
```

The PARM parameter requests options for a job step and overrides any defaults that were established at system generation. The keyword PARM is followed by a period and the step name for which the options are to apply. PARM.COB='PMAP, DMAP' supplies Procedure and Data Division maps for the step name COB (the compile step). Remember that the procedure COBUCLG consists of three separate steps: compile, link edit, and execute, with step names COB, LKED, and GO, respectively. Other compiler options are shown in Table 10.1. All options are established with a default value, depending on the installation.

The COND (condition) parameter avoids unnecessary usage of computer time by conditionally suppressing execution of specified job steps. Essentially, it ties execution of the present job step to the results of a previous step. Consider its use in the procedure COBUCLG shown in Figure 10.2.

```
//LKED EXEC PGM=IEWL,PARM='LIST,XREF,MAP',COND=(5,LT,COB)
```

The COND parameter permits execution of the link-edit step (step name LKED) if and only if the system return code of the compile step (COB) was not greater than 5. This makes considerable sense if we recall that a condition code of 4 indicates a

Table 10.1   Compilation Parameters

SOURCE: Prints the source listing (suppressed by NOSOURCE)

CLIST: Produces a condensed listing of the Procedure Division map in which only the address of the first machine instruction of every COBOL statement is shown (suppressed by NOCLIST—cannot be used simultaneously with PMAP)

DMAP: Produces a Data Division map (suppressed by NODMAP)

PMAP: Produces a Procedure Division map (suppressed by NOPMAP—cannot be used simultaneously with CLIST)

LIB: Indicates that a COPY statement appears in the COBOL program (NOLIB indicates that COPY statements are not present and also provides more efficient compilation)

VERB: Prints procedure and verb names on the Procedure Division map (suppressed by NOVERB)

LOAD: Stores object program on direct-access device for input to the linkage editor or loader programs (suppressed by NOLOAD)

DECK: Punches object deck (suppressed by NODECK)

SEQ: Checks incoming COBOL statements for proper sequence in columns 1-6 (suppressed by NOSEQ)

LINECNT=nn: Specifies the numbers of lines to be printed on each page of output listing (60 is default)

FLAGW: Prints all diagnostic messages

FLAGE: Prints C-, E-, and D-level diagnostics; suppresses W-level diagnostics

SUPMAP: Suppresses the PMAP option if an E-level diagnostic was present (suppressed by NOSUPMAP)

QUOTE: Specifies that quotation marks (") will enclose nonnumeric literals

APOST: Specifies that the apostrophe (') will enclose nonnumeric literals

XREF: Generates a cross-reference listing (suppressed by NOXREF)

SXREF: Generates a sorted reference listing (suppressed by NOSXREF)

STATE: Prints the statement number being executed at the time of an ABEND (see example in Chapter Eight)

FLOW=N: Lists the last n procedures that were executed prior to an ABEND (see example in Chapter Eight)

SYMDMP: Requests a formatted dump in the event of an ABEND and allows symbolic debugging statements to be used

---

warning, while higher condition codes indicate C- or E-level diagnostics. Subsequent execution would most likely be incorrect if either of the latter two were present; a warning need not necessarily cause incorrect execution, and therefore it is allowed.

The precise format of the COND parameter is:

COND=(code,operator,stepname)

Permissible operators are:

LT: Less than
LE: Less than or equal
EQ: Equal
NE: Not equal
GT: Greater than
GE: Greater than or equal

The operator specifies the comparison to be made between the specified code in the COND parameter and the system return code. The code in the COND parameter is compared to the system return code. If the relationship is true, the step is bypassed. Assume, for example, a return code of 8 after the compile step (i.e., a C-level diagnostic). The comparison is (5.LT.8), which is true, and hence the step LKED would be bypassed.

The REGION and TIME parameters are used in the EXEC statement in much the same way as in the JOB statement. The REGION parameter specifies the amount of core to be allowed to a particular job step, e.g.:

//STEP1 EXEC PGM=PROGA,REGION=128K

The TIME parameter specifies the maximum amount of CPU time (minutes, seconds) for a job step:

//STEP1 EXEC PGM=PROGA,TIME=(1,30)

Both REGION and TIME are keyword parameters and can appear in the same EXEC statement in any order.

DD Statement

Format: //DDname DD operands

Example: //GO.SYSIN DD *
           //GO.PRINT DD SYSOUT=A

The Data Definition (DD) statement appears more often than any other. Every data set requires its own DD statement, either as part of a proc, or in the programmer-supplied jobstream. The DD statement encompasses the functions of the DOS TLBL, DLBL, EXTENT, and LBLTYP statements (see Chapter Twelve). It may contain both keyword and positional parameters.

Recall that the procedure COBUCLG consists of three separate steps: compile, link edit, and execute. The DD statements of the execute (GO) step are tied to the COBOL SELECT statement. Consider:

COBOL: SELECT PRINT-FILE ASSIGN TO UT-S-PRINT.
            SELECT CARD-FILE ASSIGN TO UT-S-SYSIN.

JCL: //GO.PRINT DD SYSOUT=A
           //GO.SYSIN DD *

The COBOL SELECT links a programmer-defined file name to a system device; the DD statement provides information as to the location and disposition of that file. *The last entry in the SELECT must match the DD name, thus the appearance of PRINT and SYSIN in both SELECT and DD statements.* In the COBOL program, PRINT-FILE is tied to the system device PRINT. The corresponding DD statement causes PRINT to be assigned to a printer via SYSOUT=A. CARD-FILE is linked to SYSIN in COBOL. The * in the matching DD statement means that the data set for SYSIN follows in the jobstream (i.e., it is a card file).

SYSIN and PRINT are commonly used DD names for the card reader and printer, respectively. However, the programmer may supply any other suitable names as long as consistency is maintained. The DD name can be up to eight characters in length, the first of which must be alphabetic. Thus, the following pair is perfectly acceptable:

COBOL: SELECT CARD-FILE ASSIGN TO UT-S-INCARDS.

JCL: //GO.INCARDS DD *

More than one printer and/or card reader can be conceptually specified via multiple pairs of DD and SELECT statements. Suppose that we are processing a series of card transactions, several of which are in error. The erroneous transactions are randomly scattered throughout the input deck, but the requirements of the problem call for separate reports for the valid and invalid transactions. This is easily accomplished by creating two print files:

COBOL: SELECT VALID-FILE ASSIGN TO UT-S-PRINT.
            SELECT ERROR-FILE ASSIGN TO UT-S-ERROR.

JCL: //GO.PRINT DD SYSOUT=A
           //GO.ERROR DD SYSOUT=A

In the COBOL program, valid transactions are output to the file VALID-FILE. Invalid transactions are written to ERROR-FILE. The two DD statements specify that both PRINT and ERROR are assigned to a printer, and the reports will list separately.

DEVICE INDEPENDENCE AND THE
SELECT STATEMENT

Every file in a COBOL program requires a SELECT statement to tie a programmer-chosen file name to a system name. The general form of the SELECT statement is:

SELECT file-name ASSIGN TO system-name.

System-name, in turn, has the form

Class [-device] -organization-name.

Class may be one of three values: UR (unit-record), UT (utility), or DA (direct-access). Device type is optional and is often omitted to achieve device independence. Organization commonly assumes one of four values: S (sequential), D (direct), I (indexed), or R (relative). However, organization is *not* specified for key-sequenced VSAM data sets (see Figure 5.12).

Consider the system name UR-2540R-S-SYSIN. UR is the device class and denotes unit record, 2540R signifies a 2540 card reader, S denotes sequential organization, and SYSIN matches the DD name in a JCL statement. Since the device is optional in the SELECT statement, it is preferable to omit the device entirely and thereby obtain device independence. Thus, the preferred system name for a card file becomes UT-S-SYSIN. The system will know that SYSIN is to be a card file from a subsequent DD statement, //GO.SYSIN DD *.

The following are other examples of valid system names:

1. DA-3330-I-ISAM.

2. DA-D-DIRECT.

3. UT-2400-S-TAPE.

4. UT-S-TAPE.

The JCL needed for COBOL compilation and execution, using only card input and printed output, has been covered. Extension to tape and disk requires additional parameters for the DD statement. Table 10.2 summarizes these parameters, which are discussed further in the subsequent sections.

PROCESSING TAPE FILES

Standard tape labels consist of volume, header, and trailer labels. The volume label appears at the beginning of each reel and contains information to verify that the correct tape has been mounted. Header labels appear before each file on a volume; trailer

Table 10.2   Summary of Common DD Parameters

*:	Indicates that the file follows immediately in the jobstream
DATA:	Indicates that the file follows immediately in the jobstream. The difference between the DATA and * parameters is that the DATA parameter permits JCL cards, except a /*, to be included in the file (see Chapter Eleven for examples) The /* terminates the data set.
DUMMY:	Specifies that no operations are to be performed on a data set. Dummy status can be used to check program flow without processing actual data (see Chapter Eleven for examples)
SYSOUT:	Indicates a unit record (printer or punch) output device. SYSOUT=A and SYSOUT=B typically denote the printer (stock paper) and punch, respectively. Special forms are indicated by different letters established at the installation
DSNAME or DSN:	Indicates the name by which a data set is identified to the system
UNIT:	Specifies the device used by a data set
VOL=SER:	Specifies the volume serial number of a data set; causes a mount message to be printed if the volume is not already available
DISP:	Indicates whether the file already exists and its disposition in the event of a successful completion or abnormal termination of the job step
SPACE:	Requests a space allocation for a new file created on a direct-access device
DCB:	Specifies characteristics of a file, such as record length, blocking factor, fixed- or variable-length records, and so on. This parameter can supply information not contained in the COBOL FD and hence provide a higher degree of flexibility
LABEL:	Specifies the type of labels used (if any), the retention period for a new file, and the location of an existing file on a tape containing several files

labels appear after the file. These labels contain almost identical information to identify the data set, creation date, expiration date, and much more. In addition, the trailer label contains a block count field which contains the number of physical records recorded for the file. Label-processing routines ensure that the proper volume is mounted. They create new labels for output data sets and can prevent accidental overwriting of vital data sets. Installations also have the opportunity to develop their own label (user labels) and label-processing routines.

Information required for tape processing is supplied on a DD statement with additional parameters as shown in Figure 10.3.

```
//GO.ddname  DD  DISP=(current status,normal disposition,cond disposition),
//      VOL=SER=nnnnnn,DSN=dsname,
//      LABEL=(data-set-sequence-#,SL, ⎡EXPDT=yyddd⎤),
//                                     ⎣RETPD=DDDD⎦
//                    ⎧ unit-address ⎫
//      UNIT=         ⎨ device-type  ⎬
//                    ⎩ group-name   ⎭
```

Figure 10.3 DD Parameters

DISP (DISPosition) Parameter

The DISP parameter indicates the status of the data set at the start and conclusion of processing. It has three positional subparameters with possible values as follows:

$$
DISP = \left(\begin{bmatrix} NEW \\ OLD \\ SHR \\ MOD \end{bmatrix}, \begin{bmatrix} DELETE \\ KEEP \\ PASS \\ CATLG \\ UNCATLG \end{bmatrix}, \begin{bmatrix} DELETE \\ KEEP \\ CATLG \\ UNCATLG \end{bmatrix} \right)
$$

The first parameter indicates the status of a data set at the start of the job step. NEW specifies the data set is to be created, whereas OLD means it already exists. SHR means the data set already exists and may be used simultaneously (*shar*ed) with other jobs. MOD states that the data set is to be added to (*mod*ified) and causes the read/write mechanism to be positioned after the last record in the data set.

The second positional parameter specifies the disposition at the normal conclusion of the job step. KEEP means that the data set is to be retained. It causes the tape to be rewound, unloaded, and a message sent to the operator directing him to retain the tape. PASS causes the data set to be passed for use by a subsequent job step. (The final disposition of a passed data set should be indicated in the last DD statement referring to that data set.) It causes the tape to be rewound, but not unloaded. DELETE states that the data set is no longer needed and allows it to be scratched. CATLG causes the data set to be retained and establishes an entry in the system catalog pointing to the data set. UNCATLG also causes the data set to be retained, but removes the entry in the catalog. Omission of the second positional parameter causes new data sets to be deleted and existing (old) data sets to be retained. (However, data sets which were created in a previous step with disposition of (NEW, PASS) will not be retained, unless a disposition of KEEP is specified later in the jobstream.)

The third subparameter specifies disposition if the job terminates abnormally. If this parameter is omitted, disposition defaults to that specified for normal processing. Some examples:

1. DISP=(NEW,KEEP,DELETE)

Explanation—creates a new data set, keeps it if job step successfully executes, deletes it if the step ABENDS

268

2. DISP=(SHR)

Explanation—allows an existing data set to be used simultaneously by other jobs and retains it under all circumstances (i.e., KEEP is implied for both normal and abnormal termination)

3. DISP=OLD

Explanation—specifies an existing data set to be retained under both normal and abnormal termination; note that parentheses are not required, since only the first positional parameter was specified

4. DISP=(NEW,CATLG,DELETE)

Explanation—creates a new data set, catalogs it if job step executes successfully, deletes it if step ABENDS

UNIT Parameter

The UNIT parameter indicates the physical device on which the data set is to be processed. It is specified in one of three ways: unit address, device type, or group name. Specification of the unit address UNIT=185 explicitly specifies the device (i.e., tape drive 185). This is not a particularly good way of indicating the unit, since the system must wait for the particular tape drive, even if others are available. The device type indicates the class of tape drive (e.g., UNIT=2400), which calls for a series 2400 tape drive to be used. The system determines which 2400 units are available, selects one, and issues the appropriate message in conjunction with the VOL parameter. UNIT=TAPE illustrates how a group name is specified. This instructs the system to use any available tape device. Often this corresponds exactly to specification of a device type, as in the case where only 2400 series drives are present. However, the group name can provide greater flexibility if all sequential devices (tape and disk) are combined under SYSSQ and the request is for UNIT=SYSSQ. Of course, such specification is not always feasible.

VOL (VOLUME) Parameter

The VOL parameter specifies the tape volume which contains the data set. VOL=SER=123456 causes a message to be printed directing the operator to mount tape #123456. (The physical device is determined by the UNIT parameter.) In addition, when standard labels are used, the VOL parameter causes IOCS to verify that 123456 is the volume serial number present in the volume label of the mounted tape. When an output data set is created on tape, the VOL parameter is typically omitted. In that instance the system will tell the operator to mount a scratch tape (i.e., a tape with nothing of value on it). After the job is completed, the volume serial number of the scratch tape is noted for future reference. The VOL parameter is required for input data sets unless the data set has been previously cataloged. This enables the system to locate the specified files.

LABEL Parameter

The LABEL parameter uses two positional subparameters to specify the type of label processing and the location of a data set on a volume set. The first entry specifies the relative position of a data set on the reel. The second parameter indicates if labels are used, and the type of label processing (e.g., SL-standard labels, NL-no labels, etc.). Retention period is specified by a keyword subparameter in one of two ways. Either an explicit number of days is indicated with the keyword RETPD, or an explicit expiration date is specified via EXPDT. RETPD=1000 retains a file for 1000 days. EXPDT=99365 retains a file until the last day of 1999.

DSN (DSNAME or Data Set Name) Parameter

The DSN parameter specifies the actual name of the data set. It may be up to eight characters, the first of which is alphabetic (qualified names that may be longer than eight characters are discussed in conjunction with Figure 10.6). The parameter is required if the data set is to be cataloged. Its name is independent of all other names used in the program.

The information on tape processing is summarized in Figure 10.4. The JCL for a sequential update is shown, in which a new master is created from an existing master and transaction file. Both the old and new master files are contained on tape. The transaction file is contained on cards. Information for the COBOL files OLD-MASTER and NEW-MASTER is provided in the DD statements for OLD and NEW, respectively. Both files use standard labels. The OLD-MASTER file is the third data set on volume number 001234 (LABEL and VOL parameters). The NEW-MASTER file will be retained for 365 days after the job successfully completes execution, or else it will be deleted (see LABEL and DISP parameters). Note that the VOL parameter is omitted for the output data set, denoting that a scratch tape is used. A dump is printed in the event of an ABEND via the DD statement for SYSUDUMP.

PROCESSING SEQUENTIAL FILES ON DIRECT-ACCESS DEVICES

A major difference in the organization of direct-access volumes is that unlike tape, disk packs are not organized sequentially. The volume label of a direct-access device always appears on cylinder zero, track zero, and contains information similar to that in a tape volume label. In addition, it contains a pointer to the VTOC (*Volume Table Of Contents*), which is a separate data set, contained somewhere on the disk. The VTOC contains information about every data set on the volume, and it is through the VTOC that the system is able to locate data sets specified by the DSN parameter. The VTOC contains information analogous to the header and trailer labels of tape: creation date, expiration date, and so on.

OS JCL for sequential disk processing is essentially the same as that for tape processing, with one exception. Newly created direct-access data sets require a SPACE parameter in the DD statement to indicate the size of the file. In addition, changes in the UNIT parameter are discussed which cover direct-access devices and qualification in the DSNAME parameter. (Qualification is permitted for files stored on either tape or disk.)

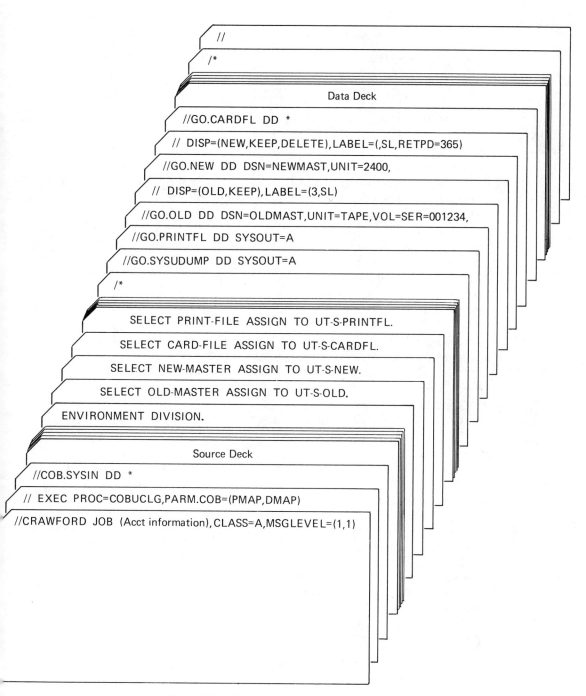

```
//
/*
                        Data Deck
//GO.CARDFL DD *
// DISP=(NEW,KEEP,DELETE),LABEL=(,SL,RETPD=365)
//GO.NEW DD DSN=NEWMAST,UNIT=2400,
// DISP=(OLD,KEEP),LABEL=(3,SL)
//GO.OLD DD DSN=OLDMAST,UNIT=TAPE,VOL=SER=001234,
//GO.PRINTFL DD SYSOUT=A
//GO.SYSUDUMP DD SYSOUT=A
/*
        SELECT PRINT-FILE ASSIGN TO UT-S-PRINTFL.
        SELECT CARD-FILE ASSIGN TO UT-S-CARDFL.
        SELECT NEW-MASTER ASSIGN TO UT-S-NEW.
        SELECT OLD-MASTER ASSIGN TO UT-S-OLD.
    ENVIRONMENT DIVISION.
                        Source Deck
//COB.SYSIN DD *
// EXEC PROC=COBUCLG,PARM.COB=(PMAP,DMAP)
//CRAWFORD JOB (Acct information),CLASS=A,MSGLEVEL=(1,1)
```

Figure 10.4 OS Jobstream for Tape Processing

271

SPACE Parameter

The SPACE parameter is required when creating data sets on direct-access devices. Its symbolic format is

$$\text{SPACE}=(\left\{\begin{matrix} \text{TRK} \\ \text{CYL} \\ \text{blocklength} \end{matrix}\right\}, \text{(primary-quantity,secondary-quantity)}, [\text{RLSE}], [\text{CONTIG}])$$

Subparameters, other than those above, are also available but beyond the scope of this discussion. The SPACE parameter indicates how much space is required for an output data set. It is not used for an input data set since the file already exists and such information would be superfluous.

The SPACE parameter requests space on a direct-access device in terms of tracks, cylinders, or blocks. SPACE=(TRK,400) requests 400 tracks, SPACE=(CYL,100) requests 100 cylinders, and SPACE=(1000,3000) specifies space for 3000 blocks, each 1000 bytes. The number of tracks or cylinders required for a given data set varies with the device. However, the number of blocks is a function of the file itself and is device-independent. Capacities of various IBM direct-access devices are shown in Table 10-3.

Table 10.3 is essential for determining the space requirements of a data set. Obviously, the same file requires fewer tracks on a 3330 than a 2311.

The SPACE parameter can also provide for a secondary allocation if the primary allocation is insufficient. SPACE=(TRK,(100,20)) specifies a primary allocation of 100 tracks, and secondary amount of 20 tracks. In this example, OS will add an additional 20 tracks to the data set if the primary allocation is insufficient. It will do this up to 15 times (total = 300 tracks), at which time the job step terminates if space is still inadequate.

Two additional subparameters, RLSE and CONTIG, are frequently specified.

Table 10.3 IBM Direct-Access Capacities

Device	Track Capacity	Tracks per Cylinder	Number of Cylinders
2311 disk	3,625	10	200
2314 disk	7,294	20	200
3330 disk	13,030	19	404 or 808
3340 disk	8,368	12	348 or 696
3350 disk	19,254	30	555
2301 drum	20,483	8	25
2303 drum	4,892	10	80
2321 data cell	2,000	20	980

RLSE returns any unused portion of the primary allocation, a highly desirable practice. The CONTIG subparameter requires that the primary allocation is contiguous. A contiguous allocation generally speeds up subsequent I/O since the access delay (seek time) is reduced. However, the programmer must be sure that sufficient contiguous space is available; else execution will be delayed and perhaps terminated. Thus, the CONTIG option should be specified with caution.

UNIT Parameter

The UNIT parameter serves the same purpose with direct-access devices as with tape. Reference may be by unit address, device type, or group name. Device types for disks include: 2311, 2314, 3330, 3340, and 3350. Other direct-access device types are drums (2301, 2302, and 2305) and the 2321 data cell. Group names are installation-dependent, but UNIT=DISK or UNIT=SYSDA are used almost universally to specify a disk device.

The information on sequential disk processing is summarized in Figure 10.5. Very little, except for the SPACE parameter, is different from the jobstream for tape processing in Figure 10.4. The EXEC statement invokes the procedure COBUCLG with Procedure and Data Division maps and a cross-reference listing (see Table 10.1). A dump is specified in the event of an ABEND via the DD statement for SYSUDUMP. Note the correspondence between the four COBOL SELECT statements and the JCL DD statements.

Note well that the COBOL SELECT statements in Figure 10.5 are identical to those in Figure 10.4. This is possible because the SELECT statements are coded to be device-independent. Hence, any COBOL program written for sequential files can access either card, tape, or disk with no COBOL modification whatsoever. The changes are entered in the JCL rather than the program itself.

The DD statements for the two disk files in Figure 10.5 do contain some new material. A SPACE parameter is provided for the COBOL file, NEW-MASTER. The primary allocation is 50 tracks, which must be contiguous. Any unused amount will be returned to the system due to the RLSE subparameter. The SPACE parameter is omitted for the COBOL file OLD-MASTER, since that file already exists (DISP=OLD). The newly created data set, MASTER.FEB01, will be deleted if the job ABENDS; else it will be retained until the last day of 1980.

The DSN parameter in the DD statements illustrates qualification. Qualification is used because a given installation may have hundreds or even thousands of data sets, each of which must have a unique name. When the DSN parameter was first introduced, we stated that it was limited to eight characters. Qualification helps to ensure uniqueness and also provides more meaningful names. A qualified data name consists of two or more levels, separated by a period, in much the same way the hyphen is used in ordinary COBOL data names. The entire qualified data name cannot exceed 44 characters, and the individual levels (i.e., entries between the periods) cannot exceed eight characters. MASTER.FEB01 and MASTER.JAN01 are examples of qualified data set names.

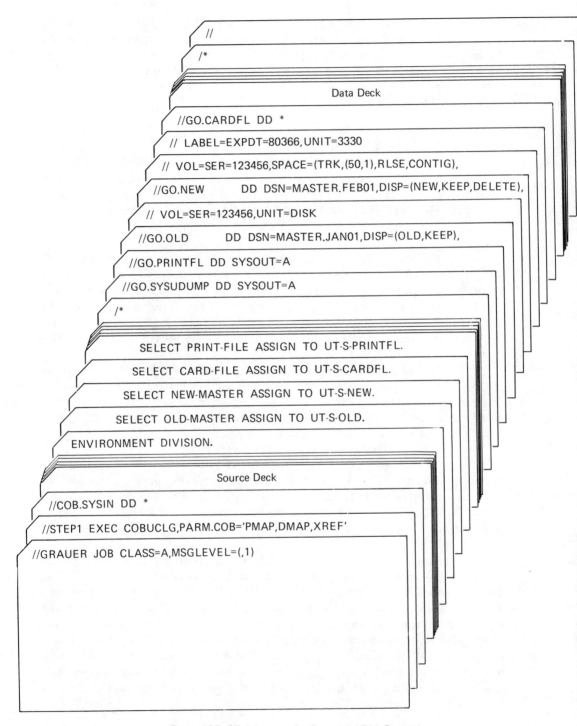

```
//
/*

                              Data Deck

//GO.CARDFL DD  *

// LABEL=EXPDT=80366,UNIT=3330

// VOL=SER=123456,SPACE=(TRK,(50,1),RLSE,CONTIG),

//GO.NEW          DD DSN=MASTER.FEB01,DISP=(NEW,KEEP,DELETE),

// VOL=SER=123456,UNIT=DISK

//GO.OLD          DD DSN=MASTER.JAN01,DISP=(OLD,KEEP),

//GO.PRINTFL DD SYSOUT=A

//GO.SYSUDUMP DD SYSOUT=A

/*

    SELECT PRINT-FILE ASSIGN TO UT-S-PRINTFL.

    SELECT CARD-FILE ASSIGN TO UT-S-CARDFL.

    SELECT NEW-MASTER ASSIGN TO UT-S-NEW.

    SELECT OLD-MASTER ASSIGN TO UT-S-OLD.

ENVIRONMENT DIVISION.

                              Source Deck

//COB.SYSIN DD  *

//STEP1 EXEC COBUCLG,PARM.COB='PMAP,DMAP,XREF'

//GRAUER JOB CLASS=A,MSGLEVEL=(,1)
```

Figure 10.5 OS Jobstream for Sequential Disk Processing

274

Generation Data Groups

The jobstream in Figure 10.5 poses one problem for subsequent updates—that the DD statements have to be changed each time the master file is updated. Consider, for example, a monthly cycle. On February 1, the old master file (i.e., DSN=MASTER. JAN01) is used with the transactions accumulated during January to produce a new master, DSN=MASTER.FEB01. However, when the job is rerun on March 1, the old master (i.e., the data set specified in the GO.OLD DD statement) is now DSN= MASTER.FEB01, whereas the new master (i.e., the data set for the GO.NEW DD statement) would be MASTER.MAR01. If this explanation is confusing here, it becomes almost unworkable in a production environment. The problem is solved through the use of generation data groups which permit several generations (e.g., months) of the same data set name to exist.

A generation data group is a collection of data sets which are chronologically related. Each successive data set in the group reflects the same file as its predecessor but with *newer* information. All data sets in a group have the identical data set name. The distinction between group members is made through a generation number. The current data set has a relative generation number of zero [e.g., MASTER.FILE(0)]. Its immediate predecessor is referenced as MASTER.FILE(−1), its immediate successor as MASTER.FILE(+1).

Only two changes are required in Figure 10.5 to utilize generation data groups. The DSN parameters in the DD statements for OLD and NEW are changed to MASTER(0) and MASTER(+1), respectively.

The advantage of generation data groups is that all data sets have the same name, and consequently production jobstreams can remain unchanged. The system automatically adds and deletes successive generations. Generation data groups are used like any other data set except for the appearance of the generation group in the DSN parameter. They can have either sequential or direct organization and reside on any device appropriate to their organization.

In order to use generation data groups, indexes must be established in the system catalog giving the name and number of generations to be retained. This is accomplished through the IBM utility IEHPROGM and is discussed in Chapter Eleven.

JCL FOR ISAM FILES

Indexed sequential files are a very common type of file because they permit both sequential and nonsequential processing. All the material to date is applicable. In addition, ISAM files require specification of a DCB parameter with various subparameters. The DCB parameter can also be used with sequential files, as discussed below.

DCB Parameter

Every file in a COBOL program requires its own DCB macro to be completed before execution can take place. The DCB macro contains information about file characteristics such as record length, block size, record format, file organization, and so on. The information may come from a combination of three sources: (1) the COBOL FD, (2) the DCB parameter on the DD statement, or (3) the data set header label. Further, there is a specified hierarchy for extracting information and building the DCB. The information in the COBOL FD has first priority, followed by the DCB parameter on the DD statement, and finally information on the header label. Consider the following code:

```
COBOL:     SELECT TAPE-FILE ASSIGN TO UT-S-TAPEFILE.
              .
                .
                  .
           FD  TAPE-FILE
               LABEL RECORDS ARE STANDARD
               BLOCK CONTAINS 0 RECORDS
               RECORD CONTAINS 100 CHARACTERS
               RECORDING MODE IS F
               DATA RECORD IS TAPE-INFORMATION.

JCL:       //GO.TAPEFILE   DD    DISP=(OLD,KEEP),UNIT=2400,
           //  LABEL=(3,SL),DCB=(BLKSIZE=500,RECFM=FB),
           //  VOL=SER=000123
```

The COBOL FD implies that TAPE-FILE has standard labels and fixed-length records of 100 bytes. It specifies that a block contains zero records, which is *not* a typographical error. Rather it is COBOL's way of informing the system that block size will be entered through the JCL. A similar capability is also possible with the RECORD CONTAINS clause. However, it is our preference to explicitly code record size within the FD so that the compiler will verify that individual picture clauses do sum to the proper record size. The reader is advised to consult the *OS Programmer's Guide* for a complete discussion of available DCB subparameters.

What is to be gained by using the DCB over the COBOL FD? The answer in a word is flexibility. Often the same COBOL program may be used to process different files. If block size is not specified in the COBOL FD, the only necessary modification is in the execution time JCL, but the program itself need not be recompiled. The DCB parameter can be specified for any file type (i.e., tape, card, etc.). It is *optional* in all cases except for ISAM files, which require the entry DCB=DSORG=IS (*D*ata *S*et *ORG*anization=*I*ndexed *S*equential). In addition, there are other subparameters of the DCB parameter used to elect certain file options. The most important of these is the OPTCD subparameter.

In discussing the OPTCD subparameter of the DCB parameter, we discuss terms which are perhaps unfamiliar to the reader. Accordingly, we first define some of these to maintain the reader's continued interest. The mechanics of ISAM processing were discussed in detail in Chapter Five and the reader is referred there for a more complete discussion.

The overflow area is the space allocated for records, forced from their original (prime) tracks by the addition of new records. Thus, records in an ISAM file are in *logically sequential*, but not necessarily *physically sequential*, order. Two types of overflow are commonly used: *cylinder* and *independent*. The programmer may freely select one or the other by specifying appropriate DCB parameters.

If cylinder overflow is chosen, a specified number of tracks on each cylinder are reserved to hold the overflow records for the tracks on that cylinder. An advantage of cylinder overflow is that additional seek operations are not required to locate overflow records. A disadvantage is that a large amount of the overflow area may be unused if records are distributed unevenly through the file.

Independent overflow specifies a common overflow area for the entire file. Additional seeks are required anytime the overflow area is accessed. However, less space need be reserved for the overflow area than under the cylinder approach.

A common technique is to specify *both* cylinder and independent overflow for the same file. The cylinder overflow area is made large enough to accommodate the average overflow for each cylinder. (It is not, however, as large as when cylinder overflow is used exclusively, in which case the overflow area must be large enough to handle all overflow.) The independent area will then be used as individual cylinder areas are filled.

Three types of indexes are associated with an ISAM file: *track index, cylinder index,* and *master index.* The first two are required, whereas a master index is optional.

Each cylinder of the prime data area has its own track index, stored on track 0 of the cylinder. The track index contains information only for the cylinder on which it resides. Each entry in a track index contains the key of the highest record residing on a particular track.

The cylinder index contains an entry for each cylinder in the file, specifying the key of the highest record stored on a given cylinder. The location of the cylinder index itself is specified through JCL when the file is loaded.

The master index is used for very large files when the cylinder index physically stretches over many tracks. It is the highest-level index and points to tracks within the cylinder index. Its function is to speed nonsequential processing.

We now discuss options of the OPTCD parameter.

OPTCD Parameter

This subparameter specifies that additional facilities are to be provided. Any combination can be requested. If more than one option is requested, the individual options are written together as a character string, with no intervening blanks or commas. Thus, OPTCD=WYL specifies three options: W, Y, and L. Explanation of the more common options follows:

OPTCD=W: Requests a write validity check in which data are read back from a direct-access data set immediately after being written. This ensures that the data were correctly transferred from core. It does, however, require an extra revolution of the direct-access device and is therefore time-consuming.

OPTCD=Y: Requests that a cylinder overflow area be created. Specification of this parameter requires that another DCB parameter, CYLOFL=XX, also be specified. The latter denotes the number of tracks on each cylinder devoted to overflow.

OPTCD=L: Requests that marked records (i.e., those with HIGH-VALUES in the first byte) be deleted when space is required for new records.

OPTCD=I: Requests that an independent overflow area be created. Use of this parameter requires specification of DSNAME=dsname(OVFLOW) in the DD statement for the ISAM file.

OPTCD=M: Requests that a master index be created in addition to the cylinder and track indexes. Specification of this parameter requires another DCB parameter, NTM=XX, denoting the number of tracks the cylinder index can contain prior to creating a master index. Thus, NTM=5 will cause a master index to be created when the number of tracks in the cylinder index exceeds 5.

Figure 10.6 is a jobstream to load an ISAM file from tape. The file, TEST. ISAM.CREATE, is the first file on reel 654321 (VOL=SER=654321). Specification of standard labels and position on the reel is accomplished by LABEL=(,SL). Note that the first subparameter is omitted in the LABEL parameter, and its absence is denoted by a comma. A default of one is assumed; the equivalent specification would be LABEL= (1,SL).

The DCB parameter for the ISAM file has three subparameters. DSORG=IS is required for all ISAM processing. The options W, Y, and L are requested by the OPTCD parameter. CYLOFL=2 specifies that two tracks of each ISAM cylinder are allocated for cylinder overflow. The presence of this subparameter is mandated by OPTCD=Y.

A primary allocation of five contiguous cylinders is requested. Requested space for an ISAM file must be contiguous, and further must be specified in terms of cylinders, rather than tracks or blocks.

Location of Prime, Index, and Overflow Areas

Figure 10.6 has only one DD statement for the ISAM file. Accordingly, the index area is automatically placed at the end of the prime area. Moreover, if there is space remaining on the last cylinder of the index area, it will automatically be allocated to an independent overflow area, even though such an area was not requested. It is also possible to explicitly specify other locations for the index and independent overflow areas. This is accomplished by a concatenated DD statement for the ISAM file and is illustrated in Figure 10.7.

In Figure 10.7, there are two DD statements without a DDname following the DD statement for GO.ISAMFILE. When a DD statement, without a DDname, follows a DD statement with a DDname, the two are said to be *concatenated*. The system treats a concatenated data set as one logical file.

The DSN parameters on the three DD statements specify NEWISAM(INDEX), NEWISAM(PRIME), and NEWISAM(OVFLOW), denoting index, prime, and independent overflow areas, respectively. Notice that the volume parameter for the index area is different from that of the other two, indicating that the three areas do not have to be stored on the same volume.

The DCB parameter is fully specified in the DD statement associated with the

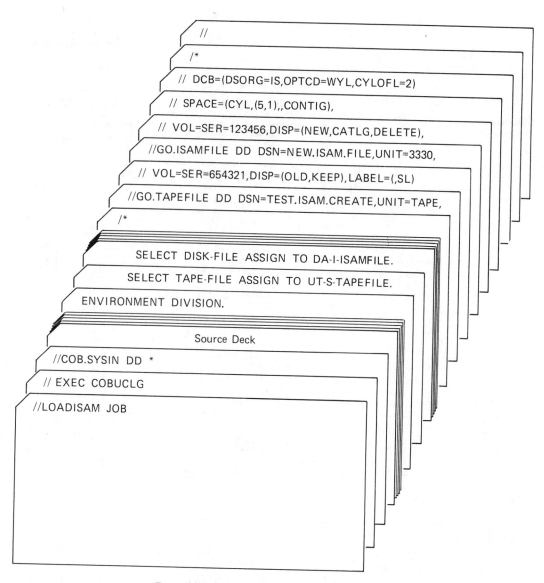

```
//
/*
// DCB=(DSORG=IS,OPTCD=WYL,CYLOFL=2)
// SPACE=(CYL,(5,1),,CONTIG),
// VOL=SER=123456,DISP=(NEW,CATLG,DELETE),
//GO.ISAMFILE DD DSN=NEW.ISAM.FILE,UNIT=3330,
// VOL=SER=654321,DISP=(OLD,KEEP),LABEL=(,SL)
//GO.TAPEFILE DD DSN=TEST.ISAM.CREATE,UNIT=TAPE,
/*
       SELECT DISK-FILE ASSIGN TO DA-I-ISAMFILE.
       SELECT TAPE-FILE ASSIGN TO UT-S-TAPEFILE.
   ENVIRONMENT DIVISION.

            Source Deck
//COB.SYSIN DD  *
// EXEC COBUCLG
//LOADISAM JOB
```

Figure 10.6 OS Jobstream to Load an ISAM File

index area [i.e., DCB=(DSORG=IS,OPTCD=LIMW,NTM=5)]. It is specified as a *refer-back parameter* in the DD statements for the prime and overflow areas (i.e., DCB=*.GO. ISAMFILE). (The asterisk specifies a reference to a previous DD statement. It is a convenient shorthand and specifies that the DCB parameter is the same as on the statement for GO.ISAMFILE.) Specifications in the OPTCD subparameter request: deletion of inactive records (L), independent overflow (I), creation of a master index (M), and a write validity check (W). Note that the CONTIG subparameter is preceded by two commas, indicating that a positional subparameter, RLSE, has been omitted.

279

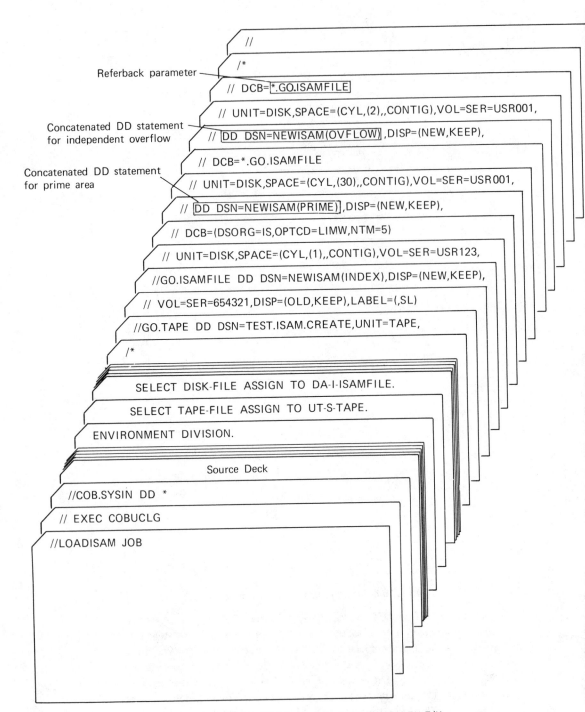

Referback parameter

`// DCB=*.GO.ISAMFILE`

`// UNIT=DISK,SPACE=(CYL,(2),,CONTIG),VOL=SER=USR001,`

Concatenated DD statement
for independent overflow

`// DD DSN=NEWISAM(OVFLOW),DISP=(NEW,KEEP),`

`// DCB=*.GO.ISAMFILE`

Concatenated DD statement
for prime area

`// UNIT=DISK,SPACE=(CYL,(30),,CONTIG),VOL=SER=USR001,`

`// DD DSN=NEWISAM(PRIME),DISP=(NEW,KEEP),`

`// DCB=(DSORG=IS,OPTCD=LIMW,NTM=5)`

`// UNIT=DISK,SPACE=(CYL,(1),,CONTIG),VOL=SER=USR123,`

`//GO.ISAMFILE DD DSN=NEWISAM(INDEX),DISP=(NEW,KEEP),`

`// VOL=SER=654321,DISP=(OLD,KEEP),LABEL=(,SL)`

`//GO.TAPE DD DSN=TEST.ISAM.CREATE,UNIT=TAPE,`

`/*`

`SELECT DISK-FILE ASSIGN TO DA-I-ISAMFILE.`

`SELECT TAPE-FILE ASSIGN TO UT-S-TAPE.`

`ENVIRONMENT DIVISION.`

Source Deck

`//COB.SYSIN DD *`

`// EXEC COBUCLG`

`//LOADISAM JOB`

Figure 10.7 OS Jobstream to Load an ISAM FILE/II

280

VSAM (Virtual Storage Access Method) is an entity unto itself. It was discussed conceptually in Chapter Five and contrasted to ISAM. Implementation of VSAM, from a JCL viewpoint, is far more complex than ISAM and much more than could ever be completely covered here. Accordingly, we give only a brief indication of VSAM JCL and direct the reader to the suitable IBM publications. These include *OS/VSAM Programmer's Guide* (GC26-3818-0) and *OS/VS Access Methods Services* (GC35-0009).

Most VSAM processing is accomplished through a multipurpose utility, Access Method Services. This utility is used to define a VSAM data set, to catalog it, to load records into it, to convert a sequential or indexed sequential data set to VSAM, to reorganize a data set, to provide a backup copy, and to make a data set portable from one operating system to another. In other words, Access Method Services is used for virtually every operation relating to VSAM.

Owing to the multiple functions of Access Methods Services, the functions of many DD parameters are changed or no longer apply for VSAM data sets. For example, the SPACE parameter is not specified in the jobstream associated with a COBOL program to create a VSAM data set. Rather, Access Methods Services is called in a prior step to allocate space for the data set. In other words, VSAM data sets will always be regarded (by the COBOL programmer) as existing data sets, and consequently the SPACE parameter is meaningless.

The DCB parameter, as well as all its subparameters, is not used with VSAM. A special control block, the access-method control block (rather than the DCB), describes VSAM data sets; hence, the DCB parameter is never used.

The DISP parameter has little meaning under VSAM, as these data sets are created, cataloged, and kept as a function of the Access Methods Services utility. If, for example, CATLG is coded, a message will be issued, but the data set will not be cataloged. Similarly, if DELETE is coded, a message will be issued, but the data set is not deleted. If DISP=NEW is specified, OS/VS will allocate space that will never be used by VSAM.

Temporary data set names cannot be assigned to VSAM data sets because the latter are built by Access Methods Services. Nor can members of partitioned data sets or generation data groups be specified in the DSN parameter; if they are, they are ignored.

VSAM appears to offer much in the way of improved file organization, as was shown in Chapter Five. However, considerable education in the use of the Access Methods Services utility is required. We present two illustrative jobstreams, but emphasize the need for additional education.

Our illustration describes how to define a VSAM data set and then to reference it in subsequent job steps. The first step in creating a VSAM file is to define the master VSAM catalog. However, unless you are the first one in your shop to use VSAM, the master catalog will have already been created. After a master catalog is established, many installations define user catalogs as well. Although these are not required, user catalogs speed up access by limiting the number of catalog entries in the master. In addition, they increase the portability of VSAM data sets because they may be copied with a file. (User catalogs require either a JOBCAT or STEPCAT DD statement to identify the particular user catalog in subsequent jobstreams accessing a data set. JOBCAT and STEP-CAT pertain to an entire job and single step, respectively; they are analogous to JOBLIB and STEPLIB DD statements. See Figure 11.22 for illustration of STEPLIB.)

After the user catalogs have been created, an additional job is needed to allocate space for VSAM data sets; again this is likely to be done by the installation. Finally, we come to the province of the COBOL programmer: defining a particular VSAM data set, as shown in Figure 10.8.

The jobstream in Figure 10.8 calls for execution of the program, IDCAMS (i.e., Access Methods Services). IDCAMS, in turn, calls for three DD statements: SYS-PRINT, SYSIN, and STEPCAT. The SYSPRINT DD statement specifies where the utility's messages should appear and is invariably a printer. The STEPCAT (or JOBCAT) DD statement provides the location of a user catalog if one is present. Finally, SYSIN is the DD name for the command file to IDCAMS and the commands themselves form the bulk of Figure 10.8. An intuitive description of these commands follows.

DEFINE CLUSTER is the command used to create a VSAM data set and its index, which are collectively called a *cluster*. The hyphen ending several of the lines in Figure 10.8 indicates that the DEFINE command is continued on a subsequent card. NAME identifies the DSN of the VSAM data set. KEYS (9,1) indicates that the VSAM key is nine bytes long, beginning in the second (no misprint) byte of the record. (VSAM considers the first byte in a record as byte zero.) VOLUME specifies the volume on which the data set is located. RECORDSIZE (41,41) calls for fixed-length records 41 bytes long; it specifies a minimum and maximum record size for each record. FREESPACE will be 20% of each control interval and 10% of each control area. Space is requested for 1000 records, and future allocations are in 100-record increments. DROPSRAC is the password for the user catalog, and is required because of the new entry made in the catalog.

After a VSAM set is created, it is referenced in subsequent jobs by simply specifying its DSN and a disposition of SHR. No other information is required on the DD statement for the VSAM data set; however, either a STEPCAT or JOBCAT DD statement is necessary to indicate the user catalog that contains the data set.

Figure 10.9 contains a jobstream to convert an existing ISAM data set to VSAM. Implicit in this JCL is the assumption that the VSAM data set, VSAM.EXAMPLE, has been entered in the user catalog, SRAC.VSAMCTLG. The EXEC statement is identical to the one in Figure 10.8, as are the functions of the STEPCAT, SYSPRINT, and SYSIN DD statements. This time, however, the SYSIN command is REPRO. It takes the incoming data set (specified in the DD statement for ISAMFILE) and converts it to a VSAM data set (specified in the DD statement for VSAMFILE). Note well that the only specifications for the VSAM data set, VSAM.EXAMPLE, are the DSN and DISP parameters. The STEPCAT DD statement provides the user catalog in which VSAM.EXAMPLE can be found. Note also that it is *not* necessary to specify the password for the user catalog, since we are merely referencing it, rather than adding to it, as was done in Figure 10.8.

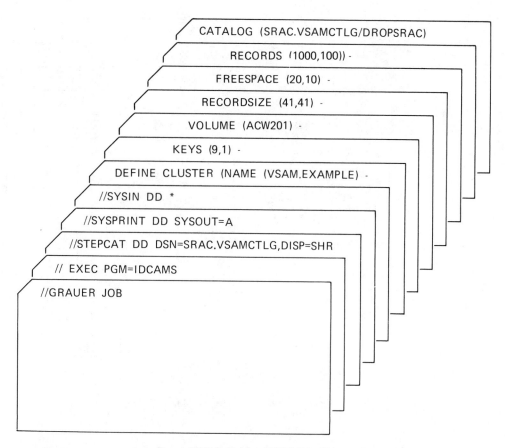

Figure 10.8 Defining a VSAM Data Set

USING THE COBOL SORT

Chapter Four contained a description of the SORT verb and its use within a COBOL program. The SELECT and SORT statements of Figure 4.2 are as follows:

```
SELECT SORT-FILE ASSIGN TO UT-S-SORTOUT.
      .
      .
      .
SORT    SORT-FILE
        ASCENDING KEY SR-LAST-AND-FIRST-NAME
        INPUT PROCEDURE B-INPUT-PROCEDURE
        OUTPUT PROCEDURE C-OUTPUT-PROCEDURE.
```

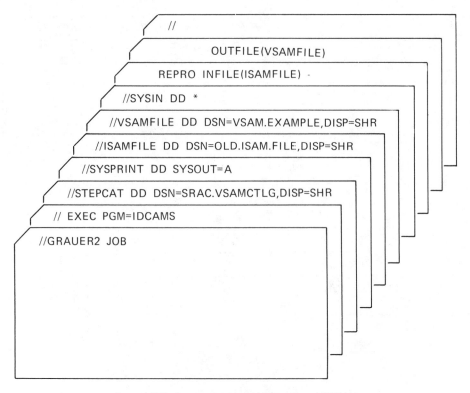

```
                    //
                        OUTFILE(VSAMFILE)
                REPRO INFILE(ISAMFILE) -
            //SYSIN DD  *
        //VSAMFILE DD  DSN=VSAM.EXAMPLE,DISP=SHR
      //ISAMFILE DD  DSN=OLD.ISAM.FILE,DISP=SHR
    //SYSPRINT DD  SYSOUT=A
   //STEPCAT DD  DSN=SRAC.VSAMCTLG,DISP=SHR
  // EXEC PGM=IDCAMS
 //GRAUER2 JOB
```

Figure 10.9 Converting an ISAM Data Set to VSAM

Additional JCL must be provided in the jobstream to accommodate the sort work areas, indicate where the sort program itself may be found, and provide a place for the messages created by the sort program. An example of a typical jobstream is shown in Figure 10.10.

The sort program requires at least three work areas, SORTWK01, SORTWK02, and SORTWK03. (Additional work space can be provided as specified in the IBM SORT/MERGE publication.) The space assigned to these work files *must be* contiguous under IBM's sort but not under Syncsort. (The latter is a software product of Whitlow Computer Systems and is installed at over 50% of the OS sites nationwide.) Note that there is no DD statement corresponding to the SELECT statement for SORT-FILE. An alternative would be to change the DDname in the SELECT statement for SORT-FILE to SORTWK01. A SORTLIB DD statement may be required to specify the location of modules called by the sort program. The disposition of this data set is SHR, and no other parameters are specified, since SYS1.SORTLIB is presumed to be a cataloged data set. Finally, a DD statement is provided for SYSOUT to accommodate the messages produced by the sort program.

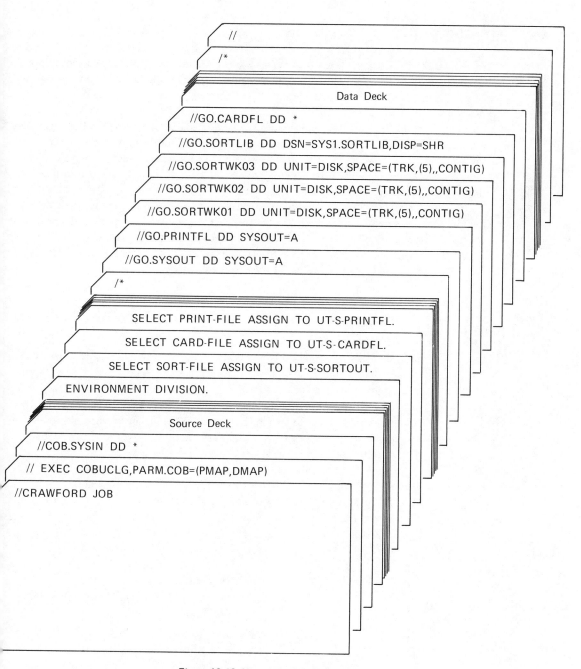

```
                                    //
                                    /*

                                    Data Deck

                    //GO.CARDFL DD *
                    //GO.SORTLIB DD DSN=SYS1.SORTLIB,DISP=SHR
                    //GO.SORTWK03 DD UNIT=DISK,SPACE=(TRK,(5),,CONTIG)
                    //GO.SORTWK02 DD UNIT=DISK,SPACE=(TRK,(5),,CONTIG)
                    //GO.SORTWK01 DD UNIT=DISK,SPACE=(TRK,(5),,CONTIG)
                    //GO.PRINTFL DD SYSOUT=A
                    //GO.SYSOUT DD SYSOUT=A
                    /*

                SELECT PRINT-FILE ASSIGN TO UT-S-PRINTFL.
                SELECT CARD-FILE ASSIGN TO UT-S-CARDFL.
                SELECT SORT-FILE ASSIGN TO UT-S-SORTOUT.
            ENVIRONMENT DIVISION.

                    Source Deck

        //COB.SYSIN DD *
        // EXEC COBUCLG,PARM.COB=(PMAP,DMAP)
//CRAWFORD JOB
```

Figure 10.10 Use of the COBOL SORT verb

MVS DIFFERENCES

Needless to say, there are subtle differences in OS JCL mandated by the conversion to MVS. However, these differences are for the most part minor and should pose no great concern to the applications programmer. Further, there are virtually *no* differences at our level of discussion in that all the material in this chapter and the next is directly applicable to MVS.

There is, however, one significant improvement under MVS which will be immediately obvious to the COBOL programmer. JCL diagnostics are grouped together on a separate page, which greatly facilitates identification and correction. Figure 10.11 illustrates how incoming JCL statements are listed first, followed by a separate page of diagnostics.

Observe in Figure 10.11 that there were 18 cards (not counting the final //) but only 17 statement numbers. This is because JCL statement 16 contained a continuation which went to a separate card. However, both cards comprise one statement.

Figure 10.11 also serves as an excellent review of the entire chapter in that it contains several JCL errors. It is left to the reader as an exercise.

SUMMARY

This chapter was intended to make OS JCL less intimidating. It began with the simplest of jobstreams (i.e., a COBOL program to go "card to print") and built from there. We included material on sequential processing for tape and disk, ISAM and VSAM, generation data groups, and use of the sort utility. We alluded to some differences required under MVS. In Chapter Eleven we cover additional JCL features such as temporary data sets, referbacks, concatenated data sets, partitioned data sets, and establishing and using procedures.

In conclusion, the JCL used by the COBOL programmer revolves around three basic statements, JOB, EXEC, and DD, with emphasis on the latter. The keyword and positional parameters which were discussed in the chapter are listed as a review:

1. JOB

CLASS:	Assigns a class to a job
REGION:	Assigns an amount of core for the job
MSGLEVEL:	Controls printing of system output and messages
TIME:	Assigns a maximum CPU time allocation to a job

Incoming statements

```
 1    //SSTBERN1 JOB (SAGS,0056),CTL978,BERNYS,CLASS=1,MSGCLASS=Q
 2    //  EXEC PGM=ERRORS
 3    //DD1 SYSOUT=A
 4    //DD2 DD DISP=(NEW,KEEP),DCB=(LREC=80,BLKSIZE=80)
 5    //DD3 DD DCB=LRECL=80,BLKSIZE=80
 6    //  STEP2 EXEC PGM=PROBLEMS
 7    //DD4 DD DSN=ABC,DEF,DISP=SHR
 8    //DD5 DD DISP=(NEW,PASS),SPACE(TRK,(1,1)),UNIT=DISK   ** TRICKY **
 9    //DD6 DD*
10    //DD7 DD SYSOUT=A                                     ** TRICKY **
11    //  EXEC PGM=WOES
12    //DD8 DD UNIT=DISK,SPACE=(TRK,(1,1),CONTIG),DISP=(NEW,CATLG),
13    //DD9 DD UNIT=DISK,SPACE=(TRK,(1,1),RLSE),DISP=OLD,KEEP
14    //DD10 DD UNIT=DISK,SPACE=(CYL,(2,2)
15    //DD11 SYSOUT=A
16    //DD12 DD DSN=NEW.DISK.FILE,UNIT=DISK,DISP=(NEW,KEEP),    ⎤ Two cards comprise one statement
      //  SPACE=(TRK,(1,1) )                                   ⎦
17    //DD13 DD DSN=NEW.FILE.ON.DISK12,UNIT=TAPE,LABEL=(,SL),VOL=SER=USR001,DISP=SHR
```

JCL diagnostics

```
STMT NO.  MESSAGE

 3   IEF605I  UNIDENTIFIED OPERATION FIELD
 4   IEF630I  UNIDENTIFIED KEYWORD IN THE DCB FIELD
 5   IEF630I  UNIDENTIFIED KEYWORD IN THE LRECL SUBPARAMETER OF THE DCB FIELD
 6   IEF605I  UNIDENTIFIED OPERATION FIELD
 7   IEF632I  FORMAT ERROR IN THE DSNAME FIELD
 8   IEF632I  FORMAT ERROR IN THE DISP FIELD
 9   IEF605I  UNIDENTIFIED OPERATION FIELD
10   IEF630I  UNIDENTIFIED KEYWORD ON THE DD STATEMENT
11   IEF605I  UNIDENTIFIED OPERATION FIELD
12   IEF621I  EXPECTED CONTINUATION NOT RECEIVED
13   IEF632I  FORMAT ERROR IN THE DISP FIELD
14   IEF622I  UNBALANCED PARENTHESIS ON THE DD STATEMENT
15   IEF605I  UNIDENTIFIED OPERATION FIELD
16   IEF622I  UNBALANCED PARENTHESIS ON THE DD STATEMENT
17   IEF621I  EXPECTED CONTINUATION NOT RECEIVED
```

Figure 10.11 JCL Error Listing Under MVS

2. EXEC

PARM:	Controls job-step parameters
COND:	Prevents unnecessary job steps from execution
REGION:	Assigns an amount of core for a job step (MVT only)
TIME:	Assigns a maximum CPU time for a job step

3. DD

*:	Indicates the file follows immediately in the jobstream
DATA:	Indicates the file follows immediately in the jobstream and that JCL statements, except for /*, may appear in the file
DUMMY:	Indicates a null data set
SYSOUT:	Directs an output data set to a printer or punch
DSN:	Specifies the data set name
UNIT:	Specifies the unit to process the data set
DCB:	Supplements the COBOL FD; supplies additional parameters for ISAM processing
DISP:	Specifies disposition of data sets
SPACE:	Assigns space for an output data set
VOLUME:	Directs the operator to mount a specified volume; also used in label checking
LABEL:	Specifies type of label processing, location of a data set on a volume (tape only), and retention period
OPTCD:	Used with ISAM files to select options

As often as not, a COBOL program fails in execution due to JCL-associated errors. Such mistakes are particularly irksome to the COBOL programmer, who may incorrectly feel that JCL is not his/her province. We have tried to make it clear that working knowledge of JCL is very definitely in the realm of responsibility and, further, that such knowledge is not difficult to achieve. As a pedagogic aid, we offer the following list of *errors to avoid*:

1. Improper format for EXEC statement. The syntactical rules for this statement are simple: // in columns 1 and 2 and a blank in column 3 if the job step is unnamed. If the step is named, the step name begins in column 3 and is followed by a blank, then the word EXEC. Valid and invalid statements are:

Valid: // EXEC COBUCLG
Valid: //STEP1 EXEC PGM=PROGA

Invalid: //EXEC COBUCLG
Invalid: // STEP1 EXEC PGM=PROGA

2. Improper format for JOB statement. The job name begins in column 3, followed by a blank and the word JOB. (Other information is installation dependent and follows JOB.) Examples are:

Valid: //JONES JOB
Invalid: // JONES JOB

3. Invalid continuation. The card to be continued (i.e., the first card) must end on a comma. Continued cards begin with // in columns 1 and 2, a space in 3, then continue anywhere in columns 4 through 16.

4. Misspelled procedure and/or program name. These names are chosen for uniqueness, not necessarily mnemonic significance. IBM utility program names are especially difficult to remember. Copy the name correctly and completely.

5. Misspelled keyword parameters. Misspellings, either through keypunch or programmer error, are far too common. BLKSIZE, LRECL, DSORG, LABEL, CATLG, SHR, and MSGLEVEL are *correct* spellings of frequently abused parameters.

6. Omission of // at end of jobstream. While not technically an error, it can have serious consequences. Omission of the null (//) statement means that subsequent cards can be taken as part of your jobstream. Thus, if the job after yours contains a JOB card JCL error, your job may "flush" through no fault of your own.

7. Omission of a positional parameter or associated comma. Positional parameters derive their meaning from a specified order. If omitted, their absence must be indicated by a comma.

8. Incorrect order of DD statements. Occurs frequently when adding or overriding statements in a proc. In COBUCLG, for example, the COB step precedes the GO step. Thus, all DD statements for the former (e.g., //COB.SYSIN DD *) must precede those of the latter (e.g., //GO.SYSIN DD *). Procedure overrides are discussed in Chapter Eleven.

9. Omission of a DD statement. Every file, in every job step, requires a DD statement. Make sure that you have them all.

10. Incorrect or omitted DSN for an input file. The purpose of the DSN parameter in the DD statement is to identify a data set. If this parameter is left out or misspelled, the system will not be able to locate the proper file on which to operate.

11. Incorrect or omitted VOL=SER parameter. This parameter causes a message to be printed informing the operator of the proper volume. Obviously, incorrect specification makes it difficult for the operator to comply with the request.

12. Inadvertent blank on a JCL statement. Comments may appear on *any* JCL statement and begin one space after the last operand. Frequently, one omits a comma, causing subsequent fields to be treated as comments. Consider the statement

```
// EXEC COBUCLG PARM.COB='LIB'
```

The probable intent is to specify the LIB option for the compiler. However, omission of the comma following COBUCLG causes the PARM information to be treated as comments. This is not a JCL error in the sense that syntax has been violated. However, it is extremely difficult to detect.

13. Going past column 72. This error can cause any of the above as well as a host of others. JCL statements must end before column 72. If one exceeds this limit, it is hard to catch because all 80 columns are listed, although not interpreted by the JCL reader.

REVIEW EXERCISES

true	*false*	1. A given DD statement may contain either positional or keyword parameters, but not both.
true	*false*	2. BLOCK CONTAINS 0 RECORDS is a valid clause within a COBOL FD.
true	*false*	3. The COBOL SELECT statement requires explicit specification of a physical device.
true	*false*	4. Every jobstream must contain one and only one /* statement.
true	*false*	5. A procedure may contain more than one EXEC statement.
true	*false*	6. The DD and EXEC statements must have a blank in column 3.
true	*false*	7. Comments are not permitted on JCL statements.
true	*false*	8. The /* statement is the last statement in a jobstream.
true	*false*	9. The omission of a positional parameter *always* requires a comma.
true	*false*	10. The EXEC statement does not require a step name.

true	*false*	**11.** The procedure COBUCLG will *always* attempt to execute the compiled program.
true	*false*	**12.** The same DD name may appear in two different steps of a procedure.
true	*false*	**13.** The SPACE parameter is required for input data sets.
true	*false*	**14.** The DISP parameter has three positional subparameters.
true	*false*	**15.** The SPACE parameter must specify required space in terms of tracks.
true	*false*	**16.** VOL=SER= is required if UNIT is specified.
true	*false*	**17.** The secondary space allocation in the SPACE parameter is attempted only once.
true	*false*	**18.** A card file must have an * on its DD statement.
true	*false*	**19.** DD statements precede the EXEC card.
true	*false*	**20.** Certain parameters may appear on either the JOB or EXEC statement.
true	*false*	**21.** The DCB parameter overrides information in the COBOL FD.
true	*false*	**22.** If the normal disposition of an existing data set is not specified, the data set is deleted at the end of the job step.
true	*false*	**23.** A data set name may consist of more than eight characters if it is qualified.
true	*false*	**24.** The same ISAM file may contain both cylinder and independent overflow areas.
true	*false*	**25.** The index, prime, and overflow areas of an ISAM file must all reside on the same volume.
true	*false*	**26.** DSN=MASTER.FILE(0) is an invalid data set specification.
true	*false*	**27.** DSN=MASTER.FILE(+1) refers to the current version of the data set MASTER.FILE.
true	*false*	**28.** Generation data groups can only be used for direct-access files.
true	*false*	**29.** Concatenated data sets omit the DD name on all DD statements after the first.
true	*false*	**30.** Work space for the sort program must be contiguous.
true	*false*	**31.** The number of work files provided for the sort program must be between 1 and 3.
true	*false*	**32.** A SYSLIB statement is required to provide the location of the sort program whenever the SORT verb is used.
true	*false*	**33.** It is not necessary to provide a DD statement for the sort messages.
true	*false*	**34.** VSAM data sets may be optionally cataloged.
true	*false*	**35.** The SPACE and DCB parameters function identically for ISAM and VSAM.
true	*false*	**36.** DISP=(NEW,CATLG) is applicable to VSAM.
true	*false*	**37.** Temporary data set names cannot be used with VSAM.
true	*false*	**38.** The DCB parameter is never used with a VSAM data set.

PROBLEMS

1. Given the DD specification

```
//GO.TAPEFILE DD DISP=(OLD,KEEP),LABEL=(2,SL),
// DSN=TESTFILE,VOL=SER=123456,UNIT=2400
```

answer true or false:

- (a) TAPEFILE is the entry on the COBOL SELECT statement.
- (b) TESTFILE is the first file on the tape.
- (c) The operator will be directed to mount the tape with an external label TESTFILE.
- (d) The tape will be scratched if the job ABENDs.
- (e) The tape will be mounted on any available 2400 tape drive.

2. Given the DD specifications

```
//GO.NEWFILE DD DISP=(NEW,KEEP),SPACE=(CYL,20),
// DSN=OUTPUT,UNIT=DISK,LABEL=EXPDT=79365,
// VOL=SER=123456
```

answer true or false:

- (a) OUTPUT is the entry in the COBOL SELECT statement.
- (b) The file will be retained indefinitely if the job executes successfully.
- (c) The file will be deleted if the job ABENDs
- (d) The job will terminate if more than 20 cylinders are required.
- (e) The file will be stored in contiguous cylinders.
- (f) Any available disk pack may be used.
- (g) A message to mount volume number 123456 will definitely be issued.

3. Complete the following table; indicate whether the job step is executed or bypassed:

Code in COND Parameter	Operation	System Return Code from Last Step	Executed or Bypassed
5	LT	4	
9	GT	8	
5	LT	(C-level diagnostic)	
5	LT	(W-level diagnostic)	
12	EQ	(E-level diagnostic)	
12	NE	12	

4. Complete the SPACE parameters for an output data set of 3300 blocks. Each block is 1000 bytes in length. (Assume that 3, 6, and 11 are the number of blocks per track for the 2311, 2314, and 3330, respectively). In each case provide a secondary allocation equal to 10% of the primary allocation:

(a) //GO.OUTDISK DD UNIT=2311,SPACE=(TRK,(   ))
(b) //GO.OUTDISK DD UNIT=2311,SPACE=(CYL,(   ))
(c) //GO.OUTDISK DD UNIT=2314,SPACE=(TRK,(   ))
(d) //GO.OUTDISK DD UNIT=2314,SPACE=(CYL,(   ))
(e) //GO.OUTDISK DD UNIT=3330,SPACE=(1000,(   ))

5. Write the necessary JCL to compile, link, and execute a "card to print" COBOL program. Your jobstream must:

(a) Produce Data and Procedure Division maps.
(b) Produce a dump in the event of an ABEND.
(c) Include all COBOL SELECT statements.

6. Write the necessary JCL to compile, link, and execute a COBOL program for sequential file maintenance. Your jobstream should accommodate:

(a) A condensed listing, the FLOW and STATE options, and a dump in the event of an ABEND.
(b) An old master file stored as the first file on tape number 123456, with DSN=OLD. MASTER.FILE.
(c) A transaction file coming from cards.
(d) A new master file going to tape number 654321. Use appropriate DSN and any other parameters.
(e) Show all COBOL SELECT statements.

7. Modify problem 6 so that the old and new master files are contained on disk. In addition:

(a) The block size of both the old and new master files is to be entered in the JCL. The blocking factor is 10 and the logical record size is 100 bytes.
(b) Allow 15 tracks as the primary allocation and two tracks as the secondary allocation. The output device is a 3330.
(c) Use identical COBOL SELECT statements as in problem 6.
(d) Use the data sets OLD.DISK.MASTER.FILE and NEW.DISK.MASTER.FILE for the old and new master, respectively. Both on VOL=SER=USR001.

8. Modify Problem 7 to use generation data groups.

9. Write the complete JCL to compile, link, and execute a COBOL program using the SORT verb. In particular:

(a) The INPUT PROCEDURE/OUTPUT PROCEDURE is used. The COBOL program will read incoming records from tape (use appropriate parameters) and output will consist only of a printed report.
(b) Show COBOL SELECT statements.

OS Utilities and the Linkage Editor

Chapter Ten discussed the fundamentals of OS JCL. Although such material goes a long way toward strengthening the capabilities of the individual, it is by no means all that one should know. Accordingly, this chapter motivates the need for utility programs and discusses the basics of five OS utilities: IEBGENER, IEBPTPCH, IEBUPDTE, IEHPROGM, and IEBISAM. It presents additional JCL features, such as temporary data sets and referbacks. It covers the establishment of procedures, the use of symbolic parameters, and how to add, nullify, or override parameters on existing DD statements. Finally, it covers the linkage-editor and shows how the applications programmer can make explicit use of this program to great advantage.

The emphasis of this chapter is on OS utilities. However, the authors in no way intend their material to be a substitute for the IBM manual on OS utilities. The reader is, in fact, referred to the reference manual (GT35-0005-2, *OS/VS2 Utilities*) for additional features of the utilities we cover, and for complete coverage of the many utilities we omit. The authors do believe, however, that this chapter is a solid introduction to the subject, and suggest that the uninitiated reader will have a far easier time with the reference manual *after* reading this chapter.

VOCABULARY

The words *data set* and *file* are synonymous. Chapter Ten dealt primarily with *sequential* data sets; it also included JCL features necessary for *indexed sequential* files. The discussion in this chapter concerns sequential data sets and also a new type of file, partitioned data sets (PDS).

A *partitioned data set* is composed of one or more sequential data sets known as *members*. There is a directory at the beginning of the partitioned data set which lists the members in the file and their location. A good analogy is a hotel; when a guest checks in, he signs the register (i.e., the directory) and is assigned the next available room. In order to find a particular guest, a visitor checks the directory. When the guest checks out, his name is removed from the directory, but no one can move directly into his room (i.e., the bed has to be made, linen changed, etc.). In similar fashion, when a member is deleted from a partitioned data set, the space used by that member *cannot* be allocated to a new member until the entire file has been compressed. Similarly, if a guest checks out of a hotel, then checks back in a week later, it is unlikely that he would be assigned the same room. The situation is shown schematically in Figure 11.1.

The empty space in Figure 11.1 between members 2 and 3 cannot be reused until the entire PDS has been compressed. Further, if a new version of member 2 were created prior to the reorganization, it would appear physically after member 3. The previous space taken up by member 2 becomes unusable until after the entire file is compressed. Finally, the directory would be altered to point to the proper version of member 2.

Partitioned data sets are used extensively with libraries, particularly those containing "small" members (e.g., procedure libraries). Partitioned data sets make more efficient use of disk space than do sequential data sets, in that many members can be stored on one track. Sequential data sets, however, are each required to begin on a separate track, which is the smallest unit of allocatable space.

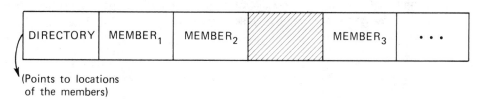

(Points to locations
of the members)

Figure 11.1 Schematic Illustration of a Partitioned Data Set

THE NEED FOR UTILITY PROGRAMS

A utility program performs a very basic function; in essence it is a program to do a routine job in a computer installation. Utilities can be used to copy files from one storage medium to another (e.g., card to disk, tape to print, etc.). Utilities can back up and restore disk packs, catalog, scratch, or rename files, copy and compress partitioned data sets, and so on. Installations may develop their own utility programs in house. They may also purchase utilities from independent software houses. In general, though, many installations are content to use the utilities supplied by the manufacturer. Our discussion therefore concerns some of the more common utility programs supplied by IBM.

There is no law requiring a programmer to use OS utilities. Programming managers, however, generally discourage their staff from reinventing the wheel. Accordingly, they frown on a programmer writing a COBOL "disk to print" program if one already exists in the form of an IBM-supplied utility.

The need for utility programs is tremendous, much greater than the beginning programmer would imagine. Consider for example, the COBOL program(s) of Chapter One to merge two files. A simple system flowchart for this application is shown in Figure 11.2.

Now consider what is actually involved in testing this program. The COBOL programmer requires access to two disk files as input to his program. In addition, he must be able to "see" the contents of those files as well as the contents of the merged file after it has been created. In essence, then, we are talking of five additional steps (two file creations and three file listings) to adequately test the merge program. A more complex flowchart, showing these additional steps, is shown in Figure 11.3.

In Figure 11.3, step 1 is a "card to disk" program, which creates the first disk file. Step 2 is a "disk to print" program, which prints the contents of the newly created file. Steps 3 and 4 perform these tasks for the second file. Step 5 is the COBOL merge. Step 6 is a "disk to print" program for the merged file. As can be seen from Figure 11.3, the COBOL programmer needs two additional programs merely to test his merge program. A "card to disk" program to create the files is run twice in steps 1 and 3. A "disk to print" program to list the contents of the disk files is run three times, in steps 2, 4, and 6.

There are two approaches to obtaining these additional programs. The first is for the programmer to write *and debug* his own programs in COBOL. A second and preferred approach is to use an existing program which is sufficiently general to accomplish the same task; that existing program is the IBM utility IEBGENER.

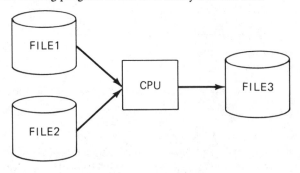

Figure 11.2 System Flowchart for a Simple Merge Program

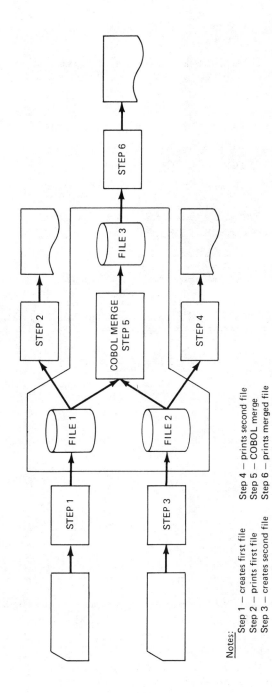

Figure 11.3 System Flowchart for Testing COBOL Merge

Notes:

Step 1 — creates first file
Step 2 — prints first file
Step 3 — creates second file

Step 4 — prints second file
Step 5 — COBOL merge
Step 6 — prints merged file

IEBGENER

IEBGENER is a program that copies a sequential data set or a partitioned member from one I/O device to another. Like many IBM utilities, it requires four DD statements as follows:

SYSPRINT: DDname for the IEBGENER messages (usually SYSOUT=A)

SYSUT1: DDname for the input file

SYSUT2: DDname for the output file

SYSIN: DDname for the control cards; very often a "dummy" file

The JCL to go "card to disk," using IEBGENER, requires specification of these four DD statements. Consider:

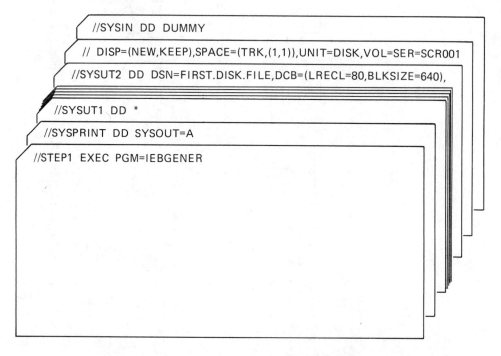

```
//SYSIN DD DUMMY
// DISP=(NEW,KEEP),SPACE=(TRK,(1,1)),UNIT=DISK,VOL=SER=SCR001
//SYSUT2 DD DSN=FIRST.DISK.FILE,DCB=(LRECL=80,BLKSIZE=640),
//SYSUT1 DD *
//SYSPRINT DD SYSOUT=A
//STEP1 EXEC PGM=IEBGENER
```

These control cards represent nothing new in the way of JCL. What is new are the DDnames for IEBGENER. Note in particular the use of the DUMMY parameter for SYSIN, which specifies that SYSIN is an empty file. IEBGENER does permit the use of control cards in the SYSIN file to give additional power (e.g., to copy only specified columns of the input file), but that is not covered here. The use of such control cards is illustrated for the utilities IEBPTPCH and IEBUPDTE.

Given the JCL to go "card to disk," let us construct the JCL to go "disk to print." Realize that the output file from step 1 (i.e., FIRST.DISK.FILE, which was specified as the data set name for SYSUT2) is now the input file for step 2. Thus, the

DD statements, for SYSUT2 in step 1 and SYSUT1 in step 2, pertain to the *same* file. The JCL to print the file, FIRST.DISK.FILE, would be:

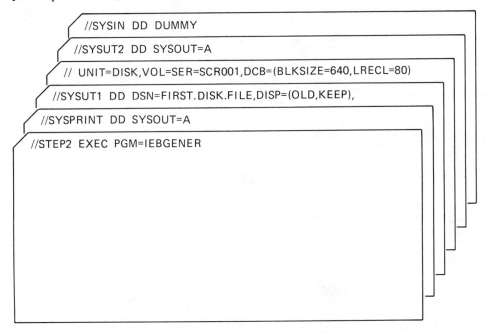

```
//SYSIN DD DUMMY
//SYSUT2 DD SYSOUT=A
// UNIT=DISK,VOL=SER=SCR001,DCB=(BLKSIZE=640,LRECL=80)
//SYSUT1 DD DSN=FIRST.DISK.FILE,DISP=(OLD,KEEP),
//SYSPRINT DD SYSOUT=A
//STEP2 EXEC PGM=IEBGENER
```

The entire jobstream corresponding to the system flowchart of Figure 11.3 appears in Figure 11.4. Realize that in order to match the DD statements of the GO step, the COBOL SELECT statements in the merge program itself must be in the form:

```
SELECT FIRST-FILE ASSIGN TO UT-S-INPUT1.
SELECT SECOND-FILE ASSIGN TO UT-S-INPUT2.
SELECT MERGED-FILE ASSIGN TO UT-S-OUTPUT.
```

Also note that in Figure 11.4 IEBGENER is executed a total of five times. Comments and step names appear on the EXEC cards.

Figure 11.5 is a second jobstream, which also corresponds to the system flow-chart of Figure 11.3. It accomplishes the identical functions as Figure 11.4 but introduces additional JCL features: temporary data sets and referback parameters.

A temporary data set exists *only* for the duration of the job. The temporary status is indicated by two ampersands preceding the data set name (e.g., &&TP1 in step 1). (The name of a temporary data set is restricted to eight characters and qualification is *not* permitted!) In step 1 of Figure 11.5, the temporary data set &&TP1 is created and passed to step 2 [i.e., DISP=(NEW,PASS)]. The subsequent DD statement for SYSUT1 in step 2 refers to &&TP1 by specifying DISP=(OLD,PASS). The volume of a temporary data set is not specified, as the system puts the data set wherever it chooses.

The DCB parameter for SYSUT1 in step 2 is specified as DCB=*.STEP1. SYSUT2. The asterisk denotes a referback parameter and means that the DCB character-

```
                                                    Comment
//STEP1 EXEC PGM=IEBGENER                       ** CREATE FIRST DISK-FILE
//SYSPRINT DD SYSOUT=A
//SYSUT1 DD *                         Output from STEP1 is input to STEP2
//SYSUT2 DD DSN=FIRST.DISK.FILE,DCB=(LRECL=80,BLKSIZE=640),
//    DISP=(NEW,KEEP),SPACE=(TRK,(1,1)),UNIT=DISK,VOL=SER=SCR001
//SYSIN DD DUMMY
//STEP2 EXEC PGM=IEBGENER                        ** PRINT FIRST DISK FILE
//SYSPRINT DD SYSOUT=A
//SYSUT1 DD DSN=FIRST.DISK.FILE,DISP=(OLD,KEEP),
//    UNIT=DISK,VOL=SER=SCR001,DCB=(BLKSIZE=640,LRECL=80)
//SYSUT2 DD SYSOUT=A
//SYSIN DD DUMMY
//STEP3 EXEC PGM=IEBGENER                        CREATE SECOND DISK FILE
//SYSPRINT DD SYSOUT=A
//SYSUT1 DD *
//SYSUT2 DD DSN=SECOND.DISK.FILE,DCB=(LRECL=80,BLKSIZE=640),
//    DISP=(NEW,KEEP),SPACE=(TRK,(1,1)),UNIT=DISK,VOL=SER=SCR001
//SYSIN DD DUMMY
//STEP4 EXEC PGM=IEBGENER                        ** PRINT SECOND DISK FILE
//SYSPRINT DD SYSOUT=A            Step name
//SYSUT1 DD DSN=SECOND.DISK.FILE,DISP=(OLD,KEEP),
//    UNIT=DISK,VOL=SER=SCR001,DCB=(LRECL=80,BLKSIZE=640)
//SYSUT2 DD SYSOUT=A
//SYSIN DD DUMMY
//STEP5 EXEC COBUCLG,PARM.COB='PMAP,DMAP'  ** COBOL MERGE
//COB.SYSIN DD *
/*
//GO.INPUT1 DD UNIT=DISK,DISP=(OLD,KEEP),DSN=FIRST.DISK.FILE,
//    VOL=SER=SCR001
//GO.INPUT2 DD UNIT=DISK,DISP=(OLD,KEEP),DSN=SECOND.DISK.FILE,
//    VOL=SER=SCR001
//GO.OUTPUT DD UNIT=DISK,DISP=(NEW,KEEP),DSN=MERGED.FILE,
//    SPACE=(TRK,(1,1)),VOL=SER=SCR001
/*                                                  Comment
//STEP6 EXEC PGM=IEBGENER                       ** PRINT MERGED FILE
//SYSUT1 DD UNIT=DISK,DISP=(OLD,KEEP),DSN=MERGED.FILE,
//    DCB=(BLKSIZE=640,LRECL=80),VOL=SER=SCR001
//SYSUT2 DD SYSOUT=A,DCB=(BLKSIZE=80,LRECL=80)
//SYSPRINT DD SYSOUT=A
//SYSIN DD DUMMY
/*
//
```

Figure 11.4 Illustration of IEBGENER

istics for SYSUT1 in step 2 are the same as for SYSUT2 in step 1. (The general form of the referback specification is *.STEPNAME.DDNAME. It is also possible to use referbacks within a job step, and this would be indicated by *.DDNAME.)

IEBPTPCH

IEBPTPCH is a widely used utility to print or punch a data set. Although IEBGENER can also be used to print a data set (as was done in Figures 11.4 and 11.5), IEBPTPCH offers much more flexibility and is discussed for that reason. As with IEBGENER, four DD statements are required. These are SYSPRINT, SYSUT1, SYSUT2, and SYSIN. SYSPRINT is the DDname for the utility messages. SYSUT1 and SYSUT2

```
//STEP1 EXEC PGM=IEBGENER                    ** CREATE FIRST DISK FILE
//SYSPRINT DD SYSOUT=A         Temporary Data Set
//SYSUT1 DD *
//SYSUT2 DD DSN=&&TP1,UNIT=DISK,DCB=(LRECL=80,BLKSIZE=640),
//     DISP=(NEW,PASS),SPACE=(TRK,(1,1))     Referback parameter
//SYSIN DD DUMMY
//STEP2 EXEC PGM=IEBGENER                     ** PRINT FIRST DISK FILE
//SYSPRINT DD SYSOUT=A
//SYSUT1 DD DSN=&&TP1,UNIT=DISK,DCB=*.STEP1.SYSUT2,DISP=(OLD,PASS)
//SYSUT2 DD SYSOUT=A
//SYSIN DD DUMMY
 /STEP3 EXEC PGM=IEBGENER                     ** CREATE SECOND DISK FILE
//SYSPRINT DD SYSOUT=A          Step name
//SYSUT1 DD *
//SYSUT2 DD DSN=&&TP2,UNIT=DISK,DCB=(LRECL=80,BLKSIZE=640),
//     DISP=(NEW,PASS),SPACE=(TRK,(1,1))                   Comments
//SYSIN DD DUMMY
//STEP4 EXEC PGM=IEBGENER                     ** PRINT SECOND DISK FILE
 /SYSPRINT DD SYSOUT=A
//SYSUT1 DD DSN=&&TP2,UNIT=DISK,DCB=*.STEP3.SYSUT2,DISP=(OLD,PASS)
//SYSUT2 DD SYSOUT=A
//SYSIN DD DUMMY
//STEP5 EXEC COBUCLG,PARM.COB='PMAP,DMAP'  ** COBOL MERGE
//COB.SYSIN DD *
/*                                                      Passing newly created
//GO.INPUT1 DD UNIT=DISK,DISP=(OLD,PASS),DSN=&&TP1     data set to next step
//GO.INPUT2 DD UNIT=DISK,DISP=(OLD,PASS),DSN=&&TP2
//GO.OUTPUT DD UNIT=DISK,DISP=(NEW,PASS),DSN=&&MERGED,
//      SPACE=(TRK,(1,1))
/*
 /STEP6 EXEC PGM=IEBGENER                     ** PRINT MERGED FILE
//SYSUT1 DD UNIT=DISK,DISP=(OLD,PASS),DSN=&&MERGED,
// DCB=(BLKSIZE=640,LRECL=80)
//SYSUT2 DD SYSOUT=A,DCB=(BLKSIZE=80,LRECL=80)
//SYSPRINT DD SYSOUT=A
//SYSIN DD DUMMY
/*
//
```

Figure 11.5 Illustration of IEBGENER/II

denote input and output files, respectively. SYSIN is the DDname for the command file; as such it can contain a variety of control cards, only four of which are discussed. These are PRINT, PUNCH, TITLE, and RECORD.

Control statements for the SYSIN file are coded free-form in columns 2-71. The operation (e.g., PRINT) is coded first. This is followed by the operands associated with the control card. Comments are permitted after the last operand. One or more spaces separate the operation from the first operand, and also the last operand from optional comments. [Additional rules; (i.e., for continuation and for naming the control statement) can be found in the OS utility manual.]

EXAMPLE 1
PRINT, TITLE, and RECORD Statements

Figure 11.6 contains the JCL and utility control cards to print the data set SESAME.STREET described in SYSUT1.

301

There are three IEBPTPCH control cards in Figure 11.6: PRINT, TITLE, and RECORD. PRINT specifies the operation (i.e., print or punch). The operand on this statement, MAXFLDS=1, denotes the maximum number of FIELD parameters appearing on subsequent RECORD statements. The TITLE card provides an output title and beginning column for that title.

The RECORD control card specifies which fields of the incoming records are to be printed, and their output columns. FIELD=(80) means that the first 80 columns of an input record are to appear in the first 80 columns of an output record. (A subsequent example covers this parameter in greater detail.)

Figure 11.7 shows output produced by Figure 11.6; there were 10 records in the incoming data set.

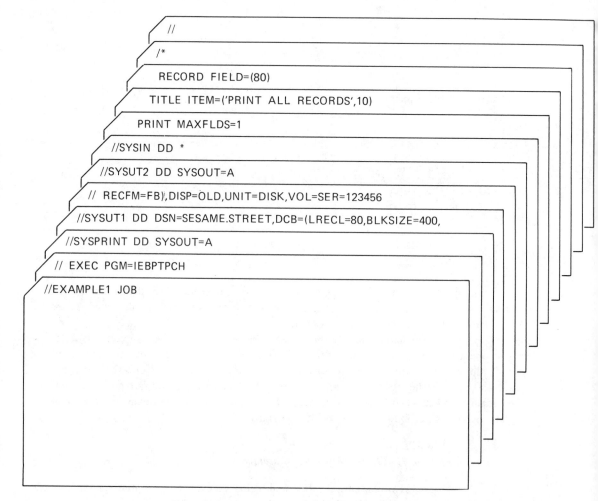

//

/*

RECORD FIELD=(80)

TITLE ITEM=('PRINT ALL RECORDS',10)

PRINT MAXFLDS=1

//SYSIN DD *

//SYSUT2 DD SYSOUT=A

// RECFM=FB),DISP=OLD,UNIT=DISK,VOL=SER=123456

//SYSUT1 DD DSN=SESAME.STREET,DCB=(LRECL=80,BLKSIZE=400,

//SYSPRINT DD SYSOUT=A

// EXEC PGM=IEBPTPCH

//EXAMPLE1 JOB

Figure 11.6 JCL and Control Cards for IEBPTPCH Example 1

```
                    PRINT ALL RECORDS
        000000000THE COUNT
        111111111ERNIE
        222222222BERT
        333333333OSCAR THE GROUCH
        444444444ROOSEVELT FRANKLIN
        555555555COOKIE MONSTER
        666666666BIG BIRD
        777777777GROVER
        888888888SHERLOCK HEMLOCK
        999999999KERMIT THE FROG
```

Figure 11.7 Output Produced by IEBPTPCH, Example 1

EXAMPLE 2
PUNCH and RECORD Statements

As a second example, assume the records in SESAME.STREET are to be punched rather than printed. Further assume that sequence numbers are to appear in columns 73-80 of the punched cards, and that only the first five records are to be punched. The control cards for IEBPTPCH are as follows:

```
PUNCH   STOPAFT=5,MAXFLDS=1,CDSEQ=100,CDINCR=10
RECORD  FIELD=(72)
```

The operand STOPAFT=5 specifies the number of records to be punched. (There is also an analogous operand, STRTAFT=n, which causes n records to be skipped before punching begins. Both STOPAFT and STRTAFT are available with the PRINT command as well.) CDSEQ=100 specifies the initial sequence number of the first output record. CDINCR=10 specifies the increment to be used in generating sequence numbers. Observe that the field parameter in the RECORD statement has been changed to 72, since the last eight columns will contain sequence numbers.

The OS JCL for these commands is not shown but is identical to that of Figure 11.6 except that SYSUT2 should specify SYSOUT=B to denote punched output. The output produced in this example is shown in Figure 11.8.

EXAMPLE 3
Reordering of Output Fields

The third example for IEBPTPCH focuses on the use of the RECORD control card and the selection and reordering of fields on the output record. The general form of the FIELD parameter is

```
FIELD = (length [,input-location] [,conversion] [,output-location] )
```

where length	= length (in bytes) of the input field
input-location	= starting byte of the input field (1 is assumed if input-location is not specified)
conversion	= two-byte code indicating the type of conversion (if any) to be performed before the field is printed or punched. For example, XE would cause alphanumeric data to be converted to hexadecimal data.
output-location	= starting location of the output field (1 is assumed if output-location is not specified)

303

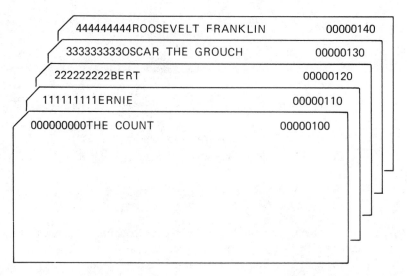

```
444444444ROOSEVELT  FRANKLIN              00000140
333333333OSCAR  THE  GROUCH              00000130
222222222BERT                            00000120
111111111ERNIE                           00000110
000000000THE  COUNT                      00000100
```

Figure 11.8 Output Produced by IEBPTCH, Example 2

Assume now that alternate records in the input file are to be printed. Further assume that columns 1-9 of an input record are to appear in columns 21-29 of the output record. In addition, columns 10-29 of the input record are to appear in columns 1-19 of the output record. The necessary commands are:

```
PRINT     MAXFLDS=2,SKIP=2
TITLE     ITEM=('ALTERNATE RECORDS WITH SWITCHED FIELDS',10)
RECORD    FIELD=(9,1,,21),FIELD=(20,10,,1)
```

The specification of MAXFLDS=2 indicates two FIELD operands on the RECORD statement. SKIP=2 says that every second record is to be printed (i.e., print the second, fourth, sixth, etc.). Output for the third example is shown in Figure 11.9.

```
          ALTERNATE RECORDS WITH SWITCHED FIELDS
ERNIE                 111111111
OSCAR THE GROUCH      333333333
COOKIE MONSTER        555555555
GROVER                777777777
KERMIT THE FROG       999999999
```

Figure 11.9 Output Produced by IEBPTCH, Example 3

EXAMPLE 4
Use with a Partitioned Data Set

IEBPTCH can be used for partitioned as well as sequential data sets. A partitioned data set (PDS) is indicated by the operand TYPORG=PO on either the PRINT or PUNCH control cards. (Omission of this parameter causes IEBPTPCH to assume a sequential data set as was done in the previous examples. It is also possible to explicitly specify a sequential data set via TYPORG=PS on the PRINT or PUNCH control card.)

    If an entire PDS is to be considered the input file, no further specification other than TYPORG=PO is necessary. If, however, a selected member(s) is the input file, a separate MEMBER statement is required for each. In addition, the operand MAXNAME=n is required on the PRINT or PUNCH statement, where *n* equals the number of subsequent MEMBER statements. The control statements

```
PRINT      TYPORG=PO,STOPAFT=5,MAXFLDS=1
TITLE      ITEM=('PRINT 5 RECORDS FROM EACH MEMBER')
RECORD     FIELD=80
```

will print five records from *each* member of a partitioned data set.

    The control statements

```
PRINT      TYPORG=PO,STOPAFT=5,MAXNAME=2,MAXFLDS=1
TITLE      ITEM=('PRINT 5 RECORD FROM TWO MEMBERS')
MEMBER     NAME=AAA
RECORD     FIELD=(80)
MEMBER     NAME=BBB
RECORD     FIELD=(40)
```

will print five records from two members, AAA and BBB, of the PDS specified in SYSUT1. Since individual RECORD statement(s) follow the MEMBER statements to which they refer, it is possible to print different members of a PDS under different specifications.

IEBUPDTE

    IEBUPDTE is a utility that changes (updates) information in a disk file. Specifically, it can add, delete, or change information in a sequential data set, or in a specified member of a partitioned data set. It can create a new member for an existing partitioned data set or create an entirely new partitioned data set.

    IEBUPDTE requires DD statements for SYSPRINT, SYSUT1, SYSUT2, and SYSIN. SYSUT1 and SYSUT2 point to the incoming and outgoing data sets respectively, and are usually one and the same for IEBUPDTE. SYSPRINT is the DDname for IEBUPDTE messages and SYSIN references the data set for the utility control cards. IEBUPDTE control cards begin with ./ in columns 1 and 2, followed by the operation and operands. Three control cards are discussed. These are ADD, to add a new member to an existing partitioned data set; REPL, to replace an existing member in its entirety; and ENDUP, to denote the end of input to SYSIN.

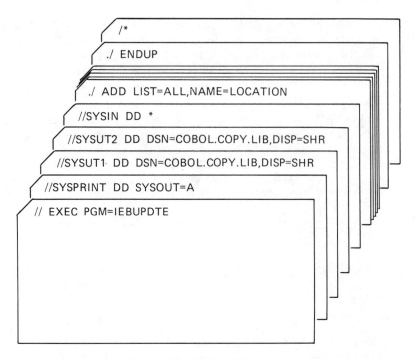

```
         /*
       ./ ENDUP
       ./ ADD  LIST=ALL,NAME=LOCATION
     //SYSIN DD  *
     //SYSUT2  DD  DSN=COBOL.COPY.LIB,DISP=SHR
     //SYSUT1  DD  DSN=COBOL.COPY.LIB,DISP=SHR
   //SYSPRINT  DD  SYSOUT=A
   // EXEC PGM=IEBUPDTE
```

Figure 11.10 IEBUPDTE Example 1

EXAMPLE 1
Adding to the COBOL Source Statement Library

IEBUPDTE is used by the COBOL programmer to add a new member to a source statement library for subsequent use in a COPY statement. Figure 11.10 contains the JCL to add a series of COBOL statement to the library, COBOL.COPY.LIB. The statements to be added, i.e., the new member, appear immediately after the ADD control card.

SYSUT1 and SYSUT2 both reference COBOL.COPY.LIB, a cataloged data set. Hence, there is no need to specify VOLUME, UNIT, and so on. Output produced by the utility is shown in Figure 11.11.

Figure 11.11 shows that a new member, LOCATION, has been created in the partitioned data set, COBOL.COPY.LIB. LOCATION in turn, may be copied into a COBOL program by the statement COPY LOCATION. Use of the COPY feature in COBOL requires specification of the LIB option as a parameter for the compiler and also mention of where the copied member can be found. The latter is accomplished via a SYSLIB card that is included in the jobstream for the COBOL compile. The necessary JCL statements to support use of the COPY feature in COBOL are

```
// EXEC COBUCLG,PARM.COB='LIB'
//SYSLIB DD DSN=COBOL.COPY.LIB,DISP=SHR
```

306

SYSIN   NEW MASTER

```
./ ADD LIST=ALL,NAME=LOCATION

       01  LOCATION-VALUE.
           05  FILLER        PIC X(16)    VALUE '010ATLANTA'.
           05  FILLER        PIC X(16)    VALUE '020BOSTON'.
           05  FILLER        PIC X(16)    VALUE '030CHICAGO'.
           05  FILLER        PIC X(16)    VALUE '040DETROIT'.
           05  FILLER        PIC X(16)    VALUE '050KANSAS CITY'.
           05  FILLER        PIC X(16)    VALUE '060LOS ANGELES'.
           05  FILLER        PIC X(16)    VALUE '070MINNEAPOLIS'.
           05  FILLER        PIC X(16)    VALUE '080NEW YORK'.
           05  FILLER        PIC X(16)    VALUE '090PHILADELPHIA'.
           05  FILLER        PIC X(16)    VALUE '100SAN FRANCISCO'.
       01  LOCATION-TABLE REDEFINES LOCATION-VALUE.
           05  LOCATIONS OCCURS 10 TIMES
                       INDEXED BY LOCATION-INDEX.
               10  LOCATION-CODE  PIC X(3).
               10  LOCATION-NAME  PIC X(13).

./ ENDUP
```

Figure 11.11 Output from IEBUPDTE

IEB817I MEMBER NAME (LOCATION) NOT FOUND IN NM DIRECTORY. STOWED WITH TTR.
IEB818I HIGHEST CONDITION CODE WAS 00000000
IEB819I END OF JOB IEBUPDTE.

The copied member appears in a COBOL program as though the programmer had coded it directly. The only difference is a C appearing in column 7 to indicate that a given statement was pulled from a library. Use of the COBOL COPY is shown in Figure 11.12.

```
00192              COPY LOCATION.  ——Invoking COPY
00193  C      01    LOCATION-VALUE.
00194  C             05    FILLER      PIC X(16)   VALUE '010ATLANTA'
00195  C             05    FILLER      PIC X(16)   VALUE '020BOSTON'.
00196  C             05    FILLER      PIC X(16)   VALUE '030CHICAGO'.
00197  C             05    FILLER      PIC X(16)   VALUE '040DETROIT'.
00198  C   Indicates 05   FILLER      PIC X(16)   VALUE '050KANSAS CITY'.
00199  C   copied    05   FILLER      PIC X(16)   VALUE '060LOS ANGELES'.
00200  C   entry     05   FILLER      PIC X(16)   VALUE '070MINNEAPOLIS'
00201  C             05    FILLER      PIC X(16)   VALUE '080NEW YORK'.
00202  C             05    FILLER      PIC X(16)   VALUE '090PHILADELPHIA'.
00203  C             05    FILLER      PIC X(16)   VALUE '100SAN FRANCISCO'.
00204  C      01    LOCATION-TABLE REDEFINES LOCATION-VALUE.
00205  C             05    LOCATIONS OCCURS 10 TIMES
00206  C                              INDEXED BY LOCATION-INDEX.
00207  C                  10   LOCATION-CODE   PIC X(3).
00208  C                  10   LOCATION-NAME   PIC X(13).
```

Figure 11.12 Use of the COPY Feature in COBOL

EXAMPLE 2
Altering the COBOL Source Statement Library

It may become necessary to alter the member LOCATION after it has been entered in the library. This can be accomplished in one of two ways: either through the CHANGE and DELETE control statements, which add, alter, or delete specific card images; or by the REPL statement, which replaces the entire member. Use of CHANGE and DELETE requires sequence numbers which will be subsequently copied into the COBOL module in conjunction with columns 1-72. Since the sequence numbers referenced by IEBUPDTE may be in conflict with those in the rest of the COBOL program, we prefer to replace the entire module. The necessary jobstream to replace the entire member LOCATION, including IEBUPDTE control cards, is shown in Figure 11.13.

Figure 11.13 is quite similar to Figure 11.10, which created the original version of LOCATION. The only mandatory change is in the IEBUPDTE control statement, which now requires REPL in lieu of ADD. A second change is in the DISP parameter for SYSUT1 and SYSUT2. Specification of DISP=OLD prevents other jobs from using the data set COBOL.COPY.LIB while the job is running. This is good practice since individuals should be locked out from LOCATION while it is being altered.

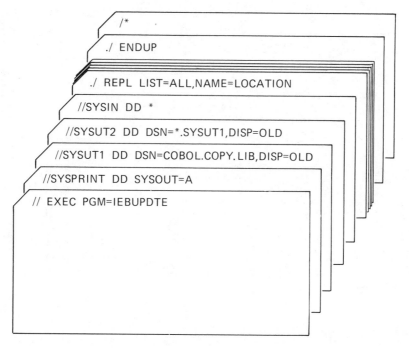

```
/*
        ./ ENDUP
            ./ REPL  LIST=ALL,NAME=LOCATION
          //SYSIN  DD  *
        //SYSUT2  DD  DSN=*.SYSUT1,DISP=OLD
      //SYSUT1  DD  DSN=COBOL.COPY.LIB,DISP=OLD
    //SYSPRINT  DD  SYSOUT=A
  //  EXEC  PGM=IEBUPDTE
```

Figure 11.13 IEBUPDTE Example 2

EXAMPLE 3
Adding and Testing New Procedures

Another frequent use of IEBUPDTE is to add new procedures to a library. While the beginner is content to use procs supplied by another (e.g., COBUCLG), the more sophisticated programmer will want to develop his own. A logical proc to develop is one that adds members to the partitioned data set, COBOL.COPY.LIB. A PROC statement is used as the first card of a cataloged procedure. The PROC statement may optionally have a name coded beginning in column 3 to identify the procedure. The PROC itself (i.e., the JCL to add a member to COBOL.COPY.LIB), must be added to the procedure library (e.g., SYS1.PROCLIB). This is accomplished by IEBUPDTE, as shown in Figure 11.14a.

In Figure 11.14, DATA is used in the DD statement for SYSIN. This instructs the system that there may be JCL cards in the jobstream which follows, and that these statements are to be treated as ordinary data. JCL will be treated as such after the first /* is encountered.

After the procedure ADMEMBER is created by the JCL of Figure 11.14, it may be called to add or replace other members in the PDS COBOL.COPY.LIB. The jobstream to invoke ADMEMBER is shown in Figure 11.14b.

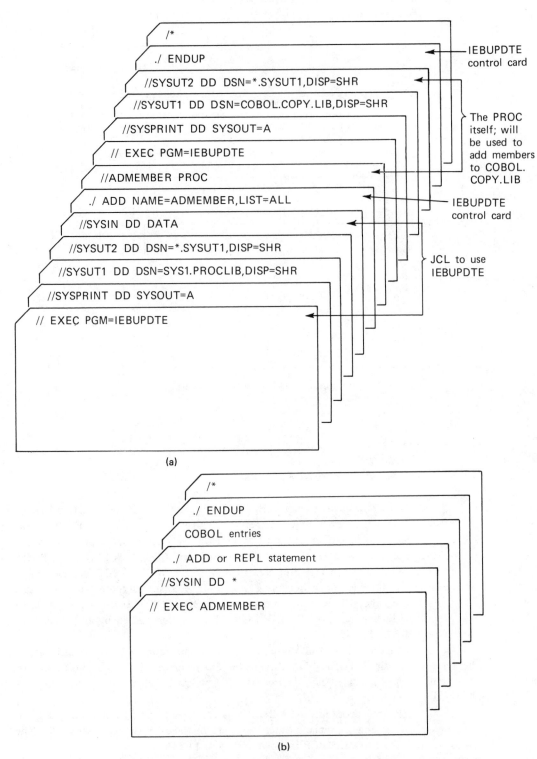

Figure 11.14(a) Use of IEBUPDTE to Enter a Procedure in SYS1.PROCLIB; (b) Calling a Procedure

310

When a procedure is first created, it is likely to contain errors. Hence, new procedures must be "debugged," in the same sense as programs are debugged. The jobstream of Figure 11.14 is a bit premature since the programmer should first test his proc *before* putting it in the procedure library. This is accomplished by creating an instream procedure through use of a PEND statement. Figure 11.15 contains the JCL to test the proc, ADMEMBER, *without* putting it in the system library.

The PEND statement denotes the end of the instream proc. The control cards that come after the PEND statement in Figure 11.15 are the same as those to invoke the proc when it is eventually added to the proc library. The advantage of an instream procedure is that the programmer can be sure his proc works before announcing it to the world. Once the programmer is satisfied that his proc is "clean," he will enter it in a library via the jobstream of Figure 11.14.

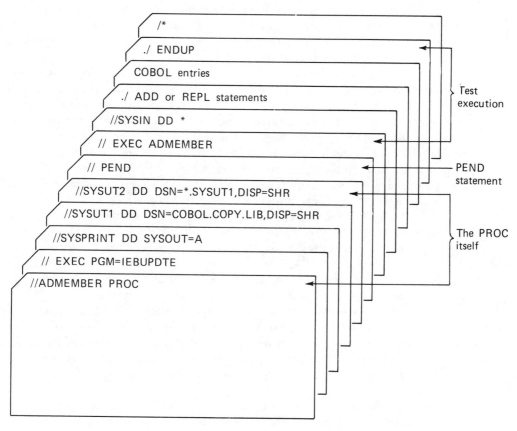

```
/*
./ ENDUP
COBOL entries
./ ADD or REPL statements
//SYSIN DD *
// EXEC ADMEMBER
// PEND
//SYSUT2 DD DSN=*.SYSUT1,DISP=SHR
//SYSUT1 DD DSN=COBOL.COPY.LIB,DISP=SHR
//SYSPRINT DD SYSOUT=A
// EXEC PGM=IEBUPDTE
//ADMEMBER PROC
```

Test execution

PEND statement

The PROC itself

Figure 11.15 Instream Procedure

USING CATALOGED PROCEDURES

While we are on the subject of developing, testing, and invoking procs, it is more than worthwhile to discuss how one alters the DD statements associated with a given procedure. The reader should be well aware that DD statements can be added to a proc in their entirety. For example, //COB.SYSIN DD * is invariably included in the jobstream to execute the proc COBUCLG, yet it is not part of the proc itself. (A DD * statement may never appear in any proc, since the * means data follows in the jobstream. Consequently, a DD * would require the proc to contain data, an impossible situation.) One can also add, nullify, or alter individual parameters on an existing DD statement. The rules for accomplishing these functions are quite simple.

If the DDname on a submitted card matches the DD name in a proc, parameters on the proc's DD statement will be overridden. The order of the DD parameters in a given statement does not matter. (This does not imply that the order of the DD statements is unimportant. Indeed, their order is *critical*, as explained in the next paragraph.) Parameters are overridden if they match. For example, if UNIT appears on both the proc and overriding DD statement, the value of the UNIT parameter on the submitted card will supersede the value on the proc statement. Parameters are added to the proc DD statement if they appear on the overriding card but not in the proc. Parameters in existing DD statements are nullified if they appear in the submitted jobstream followed by an equal sign and comma (e.g., UNIT=,).

DD statements must be overridden in the *order* in which they appear in the proc. Any additional (i.e., new) DD statements must appear *after* the overriding statements for that step. For example, COB.SYSIN DD * is a new DD statement for the COB step. It appears after any overriding DD statements for the COB step but *before* any overriding DD statements for the subsequent LKED and/or GO steps. (If the name of a new DD statement appears more than once, all occurrences but the first are ignored.) Note well that new DD statements are added in their entirety, whereas existing DD statements are modified parameter by parameter. Finally, all changes are temporary in that they apply only to the particular run and not to the proc in general.

Figure 11.16 should clarify these concepts. The submitted jobstream invokes the proc EXAMPLE. The effective JCL for the job SHOWOFF is obtained by combining the cataloged procedure with submitted JCL. In the effective jobstream, statements are shown to begin with either //, XX, or X/. This notation is consistent with OS messages and denotes statements originating in the submitted jobstream (//), statements originating in the procedure (XX), or a statement with an overridden parameter (X/).

The DD statement for ABC is unchanged and begins with XX, indicating that it was pulled directly from the proc. The DD statement for SYSIN, however, does not appear in the proc at all, and hence is shown with //. Finally, the DD statement for DEF illustrates the addition, nullification, and substitution of individual DD parameters. UNIT was changed from DISK (in the original proc) to TAPE, SPACE was nullified, and LABEL was added.

To further stress the importance of order in overriding DD statements, consider what would happen if the incoming JCL statements of Figure 11.16 were rearranged. Specifically, assume that the DD statement for STEP1.SYSIN appeared *before* STEP1.DEF in the submitted jobstream.

The first DD statement in the submitted JCL now has the name STEP1.SYSIN. Since the DDname SYSIN is not contained in STEP1 of the procedure, the system concludes that STEP1.SYSIN is a new DD statement and adds it to the effective JCL. The

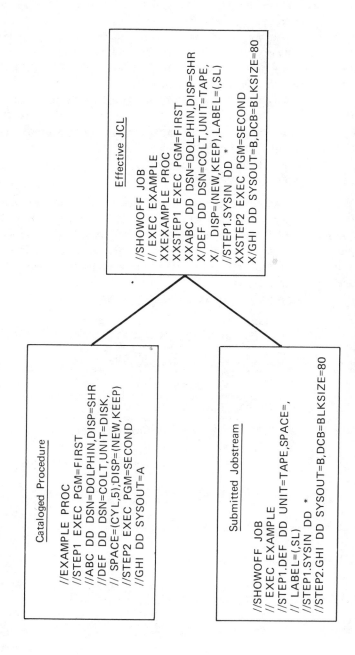

Figure 11.16 Overriding DD Statements in a Cataloged Procedure

Cataloged Procedure

```
//EXAMPLE PROC
//STEP1 EXEC PGM=FIRST
//ABC DD DSN=DOLPHIN,DISP=SHR
//DEF DD DSN=COLT,UNIT=DISK,
// SPACE=(CYL,5),DISP=(NEW,KEEP)
//STEP2 EXEC PGM=SECOND
//GHI DD SYSOUT=A
```

Submitted Jobstream

```
//SHOWOFF JOB
// EXEC EXAMPLE
//STEP1.DEF DD UNIT=TAPE,SPACE=,
// LABEL=(,SL)
//STEP1.SYSIN DD *
//STEP2.GHI DD SYSOUT=B,DCB=BLKSIZE=80
```

Effective JCL

```
//SHOWOFF JOB
// EXEC EXAMPLE
XXEXAMPLE PROC
XXSTEP1 EXEC PGM=FIRST
XXABC DD DSN=DOLPHIN,DISP=SHR
X/DEF DD DSN=COLT,UNIT=TAPE,
X/ DISP=(NEW,KEEP),LABEL=(,SL)
//STEP1.SYSIN DD *
XXSTEP2 EXEC PGM=SECOND
X/GHI DD SYSOUT=B,DCB=BLKSIZE=80
```

313

system next encounters STEP1.DEF in the submitted JCL and assumes that it, too, is a *new* DD statement. This is because overriding DD statements in a given step must precede new DD statements for that step, and that as soon as one new DD statement is reached, any subsequent DD statements are also considered new. Hence, *once a new DD statement is read from the submitted jobstream (e.g., STEP1.SYSIN), it is no longer possible to override DD statements in that step.*

The system now is confronted with two DD statements for DEF, one from the proc and one from the submitted JCL. In any case of duplicate DD names in the same step, all occurrences but the first are ignored. Consequently, the DD statement for STEP1.DEF in the submitted JCL has no effect.

Symbolic Parameters

Let us return to the proc of Figure 11.14 and assume that we want to add members to a partitioned data set other than COBOL.COPY.LIB. It is, of course, possible to override the DD statements for SYSUT1 and SYSUT2. However, that requires knowing the exact order of the DD statements within the proc. Symbolic parameters provide an alternative. A symbolic parameter is preceded by an ampersand and is one to seven alphanumeric characters in length, the first of which must be alphabetic. The ADMEMBER proc is rewritten to utilize a symbolic parameter.

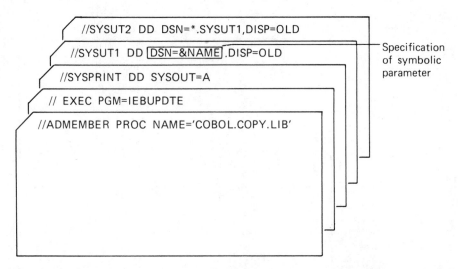

```
//SYSUT2 DD DSN=*.SYSUT1,DISP=OLD
//SYSUT1 DD DSN=&NAME.DISP=OLD          Specification
                                        of symbolic
//SYSPRINT DD SYSOUT=A                   parameter
// EXEC PGM=IEBUPDTE
//ADMEMBER PROC NAME='COBOL.COPY.LIB'
```

The DSN parameter now has a value of &NAME indicating that the value of NAME can be specified when the proc is later invoked. Note that the PROC statement supplies a default value of COBOL.COPY.LIB, so that the jobstream to add or replace members in COBOL.COPY.LIB is identical to what it was previously. However, the jobstream to add to another partitioned data set (e.g., SYS1.PROCLIB) must supply the name of the partitioned data set on the EXEC statement.

Thus, the jobstream to invoke ADMEMBER to add a proc to SYS1.PROCLIB is then

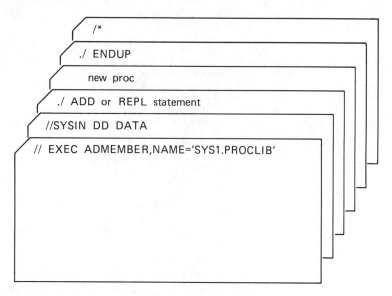

```
/*
./ ENDUP
    new proc
./ ADD or REPL statement
//SYSIN DD DATA
// EXEC ADMEMBER,NAME='SYS1.PROCLIB'
```

IEHPROGM

IEHPROGM is used to catalog or uncatalog a data set, and to scratch or rename a sequential or partitioned data set or member. It is also used to build the necessary indexes for generation data groups. Unlike the other utilities discussed so far, IEHPROGM typically requires only three DD statements. Two of these, SYSPRINT and SYSIN, are used for the utility messages and control statements, respectively. The third DD statement may have any name and specifies the data set to be cataloged, scratched, and so on. Three examples follow.

The first example, Figure 11.17, shows the jobstream to scratch the data set YOURFILE. There is a single control card, with the action word SCRATCH beginning in column 2 or beyond. Two parameters, DSNAME and VOL, specify the data set name, type of device, and volume serial number. Note that while these parameters give virtually the same information as the DD statement, they are required nevertheless. Moreover, DSNAME must be specified as DSNAME rather than DSN, which is permitted in JCL statements.

Additional parameters may be specified with the SCRATCH control card. Two such parameters, MEMBER and PURGE, are discussed. Inclusion of the former causes only a specified member of a partitioned data set to be scratched. Modification of Figure 11.17 to scratch only the member GOODBYE from the partitioned data set YOURFILE requires the statement

SCRATCH DSNAME=YOURFILE, VOL=3340=USR001, MEMBER=GOODBYE

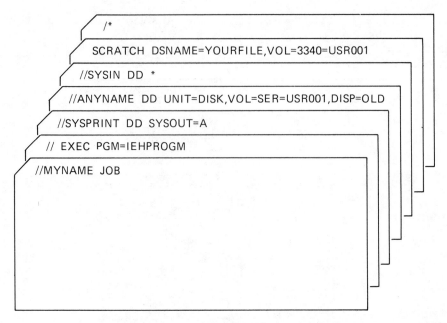

```
                    /*
              SCRATCH DSNAME=YOURFILE,VOL=3340=USR001
         //SYSIN DD *
       //ANYNAME DD UNIT=DISK,VOL=SER=USR001,DISP=OLD
     //SYSPRINT DD SYSOUT=A
   // EXEC PGM=IEHPROGM
 //MYNAME JOB
```

Figure 11.17 Use of IEHPROGM—Scratching a Data Set

The PURGE parameter will scratch a file prior to its expiration date. Every newly created data set is given an expiration date either by the EXPDT parameter in associated JCL or through a system default if the parameter is omitted. If one attempts to scratch a file prior to its expiration date without including the PURGE parameter, the system responds with an error message and the file will not be scratched. Inclusion of the PURGE parameter will eliminate the file regardless of its expiration date. Modification of Figure 11.17 to scratch the data set YOURFILE, without concern for the expiration date, is simply

SCRATCH DSNAME=YOURFILE, VOL=3340=USR001, PURGE

A second function of IEHPROGM is to rename a data set. The control statement to accomplish this function is RENAME. Figure 11.18 shows the necessary jobstream to rename a file from OLD to NEW. An individual member of a partitioned data set can be renamed by inclusion of the MEMBER parameter. (Realize, however, that if the new name is to be cataloged and/or the old name uncataloged, then additional control statements CATLG and UNCATLG are required.)

IEHPROGM is also used to create the necessary indexes for generation groups via the BLDG control statement. The data set information contained in the DD statement is associated with the generation data group. The jobstream to establish a generation data group of six levels is shown in Figure 11.19.

```
RENAME  VOL=3330=USR002,DSNAME=OLD,NEWNAME=NEW
//SYSIN  DD  *
//ANYDD  DD  UNIT=DISK,VOL=SER=USR002,DISP=OLD
//SYSPRINT  DD  SYSOUT=A
//  EXEC  PGM=IEHPROGM
//SMITH  JOB
```

Figure 11.18 Use of IEHPROGM—Renaming a Data Set

```
/*
BLDG  INDEX=YOUR.GEN.DATA.GROUP,ENTRIES=6,DELETE
//SYSIN  DD  *
//DD1  DD  UNIT=DISK,VOL=SER=SYSRES,DISP=SHR
//SYSPRINT  DD  SYSOUT=A
//STEP1  EXEC  PGM=IEHPROGM
//YOURNAME  JOB
```

Figure 11.19 Establishing a Generation Data Group

It is important to realize that ISAM files are stored in logical rather than physical sequential order. Accordingly, these files must be periodically reorganized as overflow areas become filled and processing slows. IEBISAM will copy an ISAM file from one direct access volume to another. In so doing it will delete those records marked for deletion (i.e., those with HIGH-VALUES in the first byte) and empty the overflow areas by copying those records to the prime area. In addition, the utility can create a sequential (unloaded) data set on a magnetic tape as backup. It can also restore an ISAM file on a direct-access device from an unloaded version. Figure 11.20 shows the jobstream to reorganize an ISAM file from one direct-access device to another.

Conspicuous by its absence in Figure 11.20 is the DD statement for SYSIN.

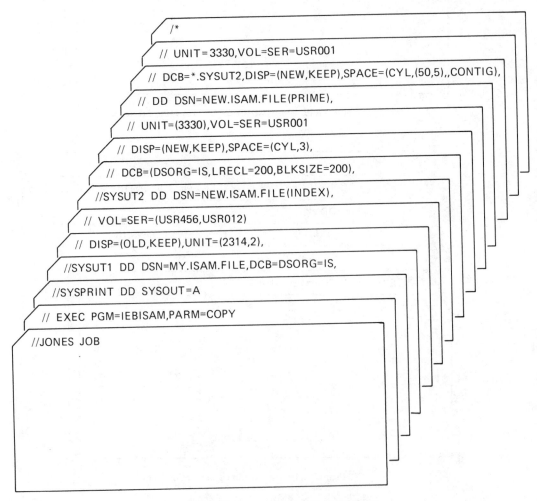

Figure 11.20 Reorganization of an ISAM File

318

The statement is unnecessary because IEBISAM is controlled completely by the PARM parameter of the execute statement. PARM=COPY specifies a copy (i.e., reorganization) operation. As with other utilities, SYSUT1 and SYSUT2 denote the input and output data sets respectively. Specification of the UNIT parameter for SYSUT1 [i.e., UNIT=(2314,2)] indicates that two 2314s are assigned for this data set. Note the correspondence in the VOL parameter, which contains two serial numbers. The presence of an unnamed DD statement following SYSUT2 indicates a concatenated data set, as was explained in Chapter Ten. IEBISAM can also be used to print an ISAM file if PARM= (PRINTL,N) is specified on the EXEC statement. SYSUT1 would still indicate the input file, but SYSUT2 would indicate a print file, e.g. SYSOUT=A.

THE LINKAGE EDITOR

The linkage editor is something most COBOL programmers take for granted and never use explicitly. They realize that the linkage editor is necessary for their programs to work, but unfortunately the knowledge of many programmers stops there. To better understand the function of this vital program, let us examine what happens when the procedure COBUCLG is invoked. Consider Figure 11.21, which illustrates execution of the proc COBUCLG.

The compiler accepts COBOL source statements (contained on cards, disk, etc.) and translates them to machine language. The output of the compiler is known as an *object module*.

The linkage editor accepts the object module passed to it by the compiler. (It may also accept other object modules from disk or previously punched object decks.) The linkage editor determines which external subprograms are necessary (e.g., IBM-supplied I/O routines to complete statements such as READ, WRITE, DISPLAY, etc.)

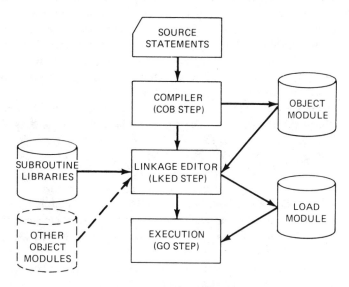

Figure 11.21 Execution of COBUCLG

and searches various libraries to locate these modules. Finally, it determines which programs call other programs and resolves all external references (i.e., symbols contained in one program which are referenced in another). The linkage editor combines all these programs into a complete program, known as a *load module*, for subsequent execution.

The linkage editor is automatically called when the programmer executes the proc, COBUCLG. A closer look at Figure 10.2 will reveal DD names for SYSLIN and SYSLMOD in the LKED step. The former is input to, while the latter is output from, the linkage editor. The data set names associated with SYSLIN and SYSLMOD are &LOADSET and &&GOSET(GO), respectively. (Either one or two ampersands can indicate a temporary data set under MVT. Two ampersands are more commonly used, since a single ampersand also denotes a symbolic parameter. Under MVS, however, two ampersands are required.)

Since &LOADSET, the DSN name for SYSLIN, is input to the linkage editor, it must be output from the compiler, and careful search of Figure 10.2 reveals its presence in the COB step. &&GOSET(GO) is the output from the linkage editor and should be input, therefore, to the GO step. Indeed, the EXEC statement of the GO step, //EXEC PGM=*.LKED.SYSLMOD, executes the module contained in the DD statement for SYSLMOD of the LKED step [i.e., &&GOSET(GO)]. Note the use of an asterisk to denote a referback parameter.

One major conclusion to be drawn from Figure 10.2 is that the load module, &&GOSET(GO), is a temporary data set. This is perfectly acceptable as long as we are restricted to the testing phase of a single program. It is obviously unacceptable for production, and also unacceptable for testing more than one program [e.g., a main and subprogram(s)]. The linkage editor can be used to make the latter process more efficient, as is done in Figure 11.22.

Figure 11.22 is a jobstream to compile, link, and execute a COBOL main and subprogram. It makes explicit use of the linkage editor in that the object modules produced by each of the two compiles are retained as members in the partitioned data set WYL.BB.RBG.LOADLIB. The advantage of this technique over the more straightforward "compile, link, and go" comes about as the main and subprograms are changed individually. For example, assume that the subprogram is completely debugged but that the main program is undergoing modification. It would be rather wasteful to continually recompile the subprogram when it is not changing. This is especially true in large systems developed under a modular concept where there may be a single main program with many independent subroutines. Obviously, each program should be compiled separately and retained in its object form for subsequent link editing and eventual execution.

There are four explicit steps in Figure 11.22. STEP1 invokes the procedure COBUCL for the main program. This procedure, in turn, consists of two substeps, COB and LKED. The compile step produces an object module for the main program. The link step produces a load module for the main program and permanently stores it as a member, MAINPROG, in the partitioned data set, WYL.BB.RBG.LOADLIB. STEP2 serves the identical function for the subroutine. STEP3 explicitly invokes the linkage editor and produces a single load module, COMPLETE, from the two individual modules. STEP4 executes the program COMPLETE.

There is much that is new in Figure 11.22. Both STEP 1 and STEP2 contain DD statements for SYSLMOD. These statements are necessary to permanently store the load modules produced for the main and subprograms. Notice that STEP1 also has a SYSLIB card mandated by the LIB option for the compile step.

STEP3 explicitly invokes the linkage editor to produce a single load module for execution in STEP4. The linkage editor requires a DD statement for SYSUT1, a scratch data set. It requires a DD statement for SYSPRINT, a print data set. It requires DD statements for SYSLIN and SYSLMOD, the functions of which were explained earlier. This time, however, SYSLIN is in card image format (as indicated by the asterisk in its DD statement) and consists of three linkage-editor control cards.

Control cards for the linkage editor begin in column 2 or beyond. The INCLUDE statement specifies a source of input to the linkage editor. The format is INCLUDE DDname(member). Thus, ANYNAME is the DDname for a DD statement in Figure 11.22. The two INCLUDE statements specify that the members MAINPROG and SUBRTN, referenced by the DD statement ANYNAME, are input to the linkage editor. ENTRY specifies the first instruction to be executed in the load module. In this instance it is the first instruction in MAINPROG. (For COBOL programs this *must* be the program-id name of the main program. The ENTRY statement may, however, be omitted if the main program is the first program and is optional in Figure 11.22.)

STEP4 executes the program COMPLETE, which is the load module produced in STEP3. It requires a STEPLIB DD statement, telling the system where to find

```
                                                     SYSLIB statement to
                                                     support COBOL COPY
//STEP1   EXEC COBUCL,PARM.COB='PMAP,DMAP,LIB'
//COB.SYSLIB DD DSN=WYL.BB.RBG.DUMMY.LIB,DISP=SHR
//COB.SYSIN DD *
/*
//LKED.SYSLMOD DD DSN=WYL.BB.RBG.LOADLIB(MAINPROG),
//       DISP=(SHR,KEEP),UNIT=DISK,VOL=SER=USR003
//STEP2   EXEC COBUCL,PARM.COB='PMAP,DMAP,LIB'    Load module for main program
//COB.SYSIN DD *
/*
//LKED.SYSLMOD DD DSN=WYL.BB.RBG.LOADLIB(SUBTRN),
//       DISP=(SHR,KEEP),UNIT=DISK,VOL=SER=USR003
//STEP3   EXEC PGM=IEWL,PARM='MAP'          Load module for subprogram
//SYSUT1 DD UNIT=SYSDA,SPACE=(6144,100)
//SYSPRINT DD SYSOUT=A,DCB=BLKSIZE=1694
//SYSLMOD DD DSN=WYL.BB.RBG.LOADLIB(COMPLETE),UNIT=3330,
//    VOL=SER=USR003,DISP=OLD
//ANYNAME DD DSN=WYL.BB.RBG.LOADLIB,UNIT=3330, Fully executable load module
//    VOL=SER=USR003,DISP=SHR
//SYSLIN DD *
  INCLUDE    ANYNAME(MAINPROG)
  INCLUDE    ANYNAME(SUBTRN)       Linkage editor control cards
  ENTRY MAINPROG
/*
//STEP4   EXEC  PGM=COMPLETE
//STEPLIB  DD   DISP=SHR,DSN=WYL.BB.RBG.LOADLIB
//GO.SYSUDUMP DD SYSOUT=A
//SYSOUT DD SYSOUT=A                STEPLIB statement
//CARDS DD *
//
```

Figure 11.22 Jobstream for a Main and Subprogram (Includes Linkage Editor and Control Cards)

the executable program. The UNIT and VOL parameters are omitted from the STEPLIB card, implying a cataloged data set. DISP=SHR allows other jobs to access WYL.BB. RBG.LOADLIB simultaneously.

Several variations are possible with the jobstream of Figure 11.22. Consider first the situation where changes are still being made to the main program but where the subprogram is debugged. The jobstream would consist of STEP1, STEP3, and STEP4 from Figure 11.22. The subprogram does not have to be compiled or linked, so STEP2 is eliminated. There is still the need to include the load module for the subroutine, and this is handled in STEP3. There is no problem in locating the load module SUBRTN, because it exists as a member of WYL.BB.RBG.LOADLIB. It should be obvious that this technique can be extended to large systems with several subroutines.

A second variation in Figure 11.22 occurs when the program goes into production. STEP4 is all that is required. There is no need for either a compile or link edit; rather the load module is executed immediately.

SUMMARY

OS utilities are a necessary tool for the competent applications programmer. In addition to the five covered in this chapter, there are several others, the functions of which should at least be known to the COBOL programmer. Indeed, the most difficult thing about using utilities is knowing which one to select. As a partial recap of this chapter, we list the primary functions of the utilities covered:

IEBGENER: Copies sequential files or members of partitioned data sets from one medium to another

IEBPTPCH: Prints or punches all, or selected portions of, sequential or partitioned data sets

IEBUPDTE: Creates or modifies card image data in sequential or partitioned data sets; adds members to source statement or procedure libraries

IEHPROGM: Catalogs or uncatalogs data sets; scratches or renames data sets and/or members; maintains data set passwords; necessary to build an index for a generation data group

IEBISAM: Copies an ISAM file from one direct-access device to another; can create sequential backup from an ISAM file; can print records from an ISAM file

In addition, the following three utilities, not covered in the text, are frequently used:

IEHMOVE: Backs up and restores partitioned data sets to or from tape

IEBCOPY: Copies one or more partioned data sets from one or more direct-access volumes to a single direct-access volume; compresses a partitioned data set

IEHLIST: Lists entries in the VTOC, or in the directory of one or more partitioned data sets, or in the catalog

Finally, the reader is referred to the IBM publication *OS/VS2 Utilities* (GT35-0035-2) for additional information.

As a final look at OS JCL, we return to the abundant system output initially introduced in Chapter Ten. Figure 11.23 shows a partial listing to compile and execute a main program and a subprogram. (The technique used in this listing is different from that of Figure 11.22 and will be explained shortly.) Figure 11.23 was produced under MVS, and as such may be contrasted to Figure 10.2, created under MVT.

Under MVS, JCL statements originating in either the jobstream or procedure are numbered. Observe, however, that statements rather than lines are numbered, and that several lines may comprise a single statement (e.g., statement 19 consists of 10 lines). Second, messages appear collectively at the conclusion of the JCL listing and the messages refer to individual statement numbers. (See the summary in Chapter Ten for additional examples.)

The jobstream that produced Figure 11.23 will compile a main and subprogram and then attempt execution. Two EXEC statements are present. The first, EXEC COBVC, precedes the main program. The second, EXEC COBVCLG, precedes the subprogram. Note well the reference to two different procs. COBVC consists of a single step, COB, whereas COBVCLG contains three: COB, LKED, and GO.

The output from the COB step in each procedure is specified in a DD statement for SYSLIN. Observe the identical DSN=&&LOADSET on both. Also note the disposition parameter (MOD,PASS). MOD states that a data set is to be *modified* and causes the read/write mechanism to be positioned after the last record in the data set. Hence, a modified data set may be created when it does not yet exist (as in the first EXEC statement), or if it already exists, merely added to.

The LKED step in COBVCLG has DD names for SYSLIN and SYSLMOD, denoting input to and output from, the linkage editor. The DSN specified for SYSLIN is &&LOADSET [i.e., the modified data set created in the preceding compile (i.e., COB) steps]. The disposition for this data set is (OLD,DELETE) (i.e., it exists prior to the LKED step but has no further use). The DISP for the data set specified on SYSLMOD is (MOD,PASS) (i.e., the output of the linkage editor is passed to the next step for execution).

The GO step specifies the program for execution. It refers to the program created in the LKED step (via the subsequent STEPLIB DD statement) that was specified in the DD statement for SYSLMOD (i.e., PGM=GO).

```
 1   //SGTEST  JOB  (WACS,0053),ENG999.COPE,MSGCLASS=S,MSGLEVEL=1      JOB 670    00000100
 2   // EXEC COBVC,PARM.COB=(NOPT,PMAP,NOCLIST,NOLIB,'FLOW=10',STATE)             00000200
 3   XXVSCOBOL  PROC CRGN=256K,                                                   00000300
     XX         CPRM=APOST,                                                       00000400
     XX         OPT='NOPT,',                                                      00000500
     XX         CLASS=T                                                           00000600
 4   XXCOB      EXEC PGM=CPXUPTSM,PARM='&OPT.&CPRM',REGION=&CRGN                   00000700
 5   XXSTEPLIB  DD DSN=VS.CAPEX.MODULES,DISP=SHR                                   00000800
 6   XX         DD DSN=VS.VSCOBOL.MODULES,DISP=SHR                                 00000900
 7   XXSYSIN1   DD DSN=&&SYSIN1,UNIT=SYSDA,SPACE=(605,(4640,580))                 00001000
 8   XXSYSIN2   DD DSN=&&SYSIN2,UNIT=SYSDA,SPACE=(400,(240,80))                   00001100
 9   XXSTATSDD  DD DUMMY                                                          00001300
10   XXSYSUT1   DD DSN=&&UT1,UNIT=SYSDA,SPACE=(460,(6000,1500))                   00001400
11   XXSYSUT2   DD DSN=&&UT2,UNIT=SYSDA,SPACE=(460,(700,100))                     00001500
12   XXSYSUT3   DD DSN=&&UT3,UNIT=SYSDA,SPACE=(460,(700,100))                     00001600
13   XXSYSUT4   DD DSN=&&UT4,UNIT=SYSDA,SPACE=(460,(700,100))                     00001700
14   XXSYSUT5   DD DSN=&&UT5,UNIT=SYSDA,SPACE=(460,(700,100))                     00001800
15   XXSYSLIN   DD DSN=&&LOADSET,DISP=(MOD,PASS),UNIT=SYSDA,
     XX            SPACE=(80,(500,100))
16   XXSYSPRINT DD SYSOUT=&CLASS
17   //COB.SYSIN DD *
18   // EXEC COBVCLG,PARM.COB=(NOPT,PMAP,NOCLIST,NOLIB,'FLOW=10',STATE)          00000010
19   XXVSCOBOL  PROC CRGN=256K,                                                  00000020
     XX         CPRM=APOST,                                                      00000030
     XX         OPT='NOPT,',                                                     00000040
     XX         LPRM='LIST,LET,XREF',                                            00000050
     XX         LRGN=128K,LPRM='LIST,LET,XREF',                                  00000060
     XX         SYSLIB1='VS.VSCOBOL.SUBLIB',                                     00000070
     XX         GRGN=,                                                           00000080
     XX         GPRM=,                                                           00000090
     XX         GTIME=,                                                          00000100
     XX         CLASS=T
```

Annotations:
- Main program
- Default value for symbolic parameter
- Use of symbolic parameter for REGION
- SPACE is requested in blocks, rather than tracks or cylinders
- Specification for compiler output
- EXEC statement for subprogram
- Several "cards" comprise one JCL statement

Figure 11.23 MVS Listing for a Main and Subprogram

324

```
20  XXCOB      EXEC PGM=CPXUPTSM,PARM='&OPT.&CPRM',REGION=&CRGN                      00000110
21  XXSTEPLIB  DD DSN=VS.CAPEX.MODULES,DISP=SHR                                      00000120
22  XX         DD DSN=VS.VSCOBOL.MODULES,DISP=SHR                                    00000130
23  XXSYSIN1   DD DSN=&&SYSIN1,UNIT=SYSDA,SPACE=(605,(4640,580))                     00000140
24  XXSYSIN2   DD DSN=&&SYSIN2,UNIT=SYSDA,SPACE=(400,(240,80))                       00000150
25  XXSTATSDD  DD DUMMY                                                              00000160
26  XXSYSUT1   DD DSN=&&UT1,UNIT=SYSDA,SPACE=(460,(6000,1500))                       00000170
27  XXSYSUT2   DD DSN=&&UT2,UNIT=SYSDA,SPACE=(460,(700,100))                         00000180
28  XXSYSUT3   DD DSN=&&UT3,UNIT=SYSDA,SPACE=(460,(700,100))                         00000190
29  XXSYSUT4   DD DSN=&&UT4,UNIT=SYSDA,SPACE=(460,(700,100))                         00000200
30  XXSYSUT5   DD DSN=&&UT5,UNIT=SYSDA,SPACE=(460,(700,100))                         00000210
31  XXSYSLIN   DD DSN=&&LOADSET,DISP=(MOD,PASS),UNIT=SYSDA,                          00000220
32  XX            SPACE=(80,(500,100))                                              00000230
33  XXSYSPRINT DD SYSOUT=&CLASS                                                      00000240
34  //COB.SYSIN DD *
35  XXLKED     EXEC PGM=HEWL,PARM='&LPRM',REGION=&LRGN,COND=(5,LT,COB)               00000250
36  XXSYSLIB   DD DISP=SHR,DSN=&SYSLIB1                                              00000260
37  XXSYSLMOD  DD DSN=&&GOSET(GO),DISP=(MOD,PASS),SPACE=(1024,(500,100,1)),          00000270
38  XX            UNIT=SYSDA                                                         00000280
39  XXSYSLIN   DD DSN=&&LOADSET,DISP=(OLD,DELETE)                                    00000290
40  XX         DD DDNAME=SYSIN                                                       00000300
41  XXSYSUT1   DD UNIT=SYSDA,SPACE=(1024,(500,100))                                  00000310
42  XXSYSPRINT DD SYSOUT=&CLASS                                                      00000320
43  XXGO       EXEC PGM=GO,                                                          00000330
44  XX            PARM=&GPRM,REGION=&GRGN,TIME=&GTIME                                00000340
45  XXSTEPLIB  DD DSN=*.LKED.SYSLMOD,DISP=(OLD,DELETE)                               00000350
46  XX         DD DSN=VS.VSCOBOL.SUBLIB,DISP=SHR                                     00000360
47  //GO.SYSUDUMP DD SYSOUT=S
    X/SYSUDUMP  DD SYSOUT=&CLASS                                                     00000370
    XXSYSDBOUT  DD SYSOUT=&CLASS                                                     00000380
    //GO.SYSOUT DD SYSOUT=S
    //GO.CARDS  DD *
```

Annotations:
- 00000240 — DDname for output from the compiler; note disposition of MOD
- 00000260 — Provided for COBOL COPY clause
- 00000290 — Input to the linkage editor
- 00000330 — Illustrates concatenated DD statement

Figure 11.23 MVS Listing for a Main and Subprogram (continued)

STMT NO. MESSAGE

Messages refer to specific JCL statements from previous page; this shows the effective value of the symbolic parameter REGION to be 256K

```
4        IEF653I SUBSTITUTION JCL  - PGM=CPXUPTSM,PARM='NOPT,APOST',REGION=256K
16       IEF653I SUBSTITUTION JCL  - SYSOUT=T
20       IEF653I SUBSTITUTION JCL  - PGM=CPXUPTSM,PARM='NOPT,APOST',REGION=256K
32       IEF653I SUBSTITUTION JCL  - SYSOUT=T
34       IEF653I SUBSTITUTION JCL  - PGM=HEWL,PARM='LIST,LET,XREF',REGION=128K,COND=(5,LT,COB)
35       IEF653I SUBSTITUTION JCL  - DISP=SHR,DSN=VS.VSCOBOL.SUBLIB
40       IEF653I SUBSTITUTION JCL  - SYSOUT=T
41       IEF653I SUBSTITUTION JCL  - PARM=,REGION=,TIME=
44       IEF653I SUBSTITUTION JCL  - SYSOUT=T
45       IEF653I SUBSTITUTION JCL  - SYSOUT=T

         IEF236I ALLOC. FOR SGTEST COB
         IEF237I 12E ALLOCATED TO STEPLIB
         IEF237I 12E ALLOCATED TO
         IEF237I 12B ALLOCATED TO SYS00004
         IEF237I 12A ALLOCATED TO SYSIN1
         IEF237I 12C ALLOCATED TO SYSIN2
         IEF237I DMY ALLOCATED TO STATSDD
         IEF237I 12C ALLOCATED TO SYSUT1
         IEF237I 12C ALLOCATED TO SYSUT2
         IEF237I 12A ALLOCATED TO SYSUT3
         IEF237I 12A ALLOCATED TO SYSUT4
         IEF237I 12A ALLOCATED TO SYSUT5
         IEF237I 12A ALLOCATED TO SYSLIN
         IEF237I JES ALLOCATED TO SYSPRINT
         IEF237I JES ALLOCATED TO SYSIN

         IEF142I SGTEST COB - STEP WAS EXECUTED - COND CODE 0000

         IEF285I   VS.CAPEX.MODULES                              KEPT
         IEF285I   VOL SER NOS= PRD534.
         IEF285I   VS.VSCOBOL.MODULES                            KEPT
         IEF285I   VOL SER NOS= PRD534.
         IEF285I   SYSCTLG.VPRD533                               KEPT
         IEF285I   VOL SER NOS= PRD533.
         IEF285I   SYS78099.T133739.RA000.SGTEST.SYSIN1          DELETED
         IEF285I   VOL SER NOS= AMX536.
         IEF285I   SYS78099.T133739.RA000.SGTEST.SYSIN2          DELETED
         IEF285I   VOL SER NOS= AMX534.
         IEF285I   SYS78099.T133739.RA000.SGTEST.UT1             DELETED
         IEF285I   VOL SER NOS= AMX534.
```

Result of first COB step

Figure 11.23 MVS Listing for a Main and Subprogram (continued)

```
IEF285I   SYS78099.T133739.RA000.SGTEST.UT2              DELETED
IEF285I   VOL SER NOS= AMX534.
IEF285I   SYS78099.T133739.RA000.SGTEST.UT3              DELETED
IEF285I   VOL SER NOS= AMX536.
IEF285I   SYS78099.T133739.RA000.SGTEST.UT4              DELETED
IEF285I   VOL SER NOS= AMX536.
IEF285I   SYS78099.T133739.RA000.SGTEST.UT5              DELETED
IEF285I   VOL SER NOS= AMX536.
IEF285I   SYS78099.T133739.RA000.SGTEST.LOADSET          PASSED
IEF285I   VOL SER NOS= AMX536.
IEF285I   JES2.JOB00670.SO0104                           SYSOUT
IEF285I   JES2.JOB00670.SIO101                           SYSIN
IEF373I STEP /COB     / START 78099.1337
IEF374I STEP /COB     / STOP  78099.1338 CPU    0MIN 07.28SEC SRB    0MIN 00.53SEC VIRT   256K SYS   216K
IEF236I ALLOC. FOR SGTEST COB
IEF237I 12E ALLOCATED TO STEPLIB
IEF237I 12E ALLOCATED TO
IEF237I 12B ALLOCATED TO SYS00006
IEF237I 12C ALLOCATED TO SYSIN1
IEF237I 12C ALLOCATED TO SYSIN2
```

Statistics for first COB step

Remainder of printed messages is not shown

Figure 11.23 MVS Listing for a Main and Subprogram (continued)

327

Figure 11.23 makes abundant use of symbolic parameters, which are indicated by a single ampersand. Consider, for example, the REGION parameter, REGION=&CRGN, on statement four. This means that the value of the REGION parameter can either be supplied on the EXEC statement, or taken as default from the procedure definition (i.e., CRGN=256K). Since no mention was made on the EXEC statement, the default was taken. Note well that the action taken is confirmed by the system messages showing substitution JCL.

Figure 11.23 illustrates a host of other JCL features. These include concatenated data sets, temporary data sets, nullification of parameters, use of the COND parameter, and of course referbacks and symbolic parameters. In short, the often-ignored system output can continually serve as a brief, but effective JCL review and reference.

REVIEW EXERCISES

true   *false*   1. Either IEBGENER or IEBPTPCH may be used to print a data set.

true   *false*   2. The statement //SYSIN DD DATA would permit JCL statements to be included in the incoming jobstream.

true   *false*   3. Symbolic parameters are denoted by two ampersands.

true   *false*   4. Temporary data sets may be denoted by one or two ampersands.

true   *false*   5. SYSLIN and SYSLOUT denote input to, and output from, the linkage editor.

true   *false*   6. ENTRY and INCLUDE are control statements for the linkage editor.

true   *false*   7. If a job contains more than one step, step names *are required* on each EXEC statement within the jobstream.

true   *false*   8. Comments are not permitted on JCL statements.

true   *false*   9. The statement //SYSIN DD DUMMY is syntactically invalid.

true   *false*   10. SYSUT1 and SYSUT2 denote input to, and output from, the COBOL compiler.

true   *false*   11. A SYSLIB card is required in the jobstream for a COBOL compile if the COPY clause is used.

true   *false*   12. A STEPLIB card is required in the jobstream for a COBOL compile if the COPY clause is used.

true   *false*   13. IEBUPDTE typically has equivalent DD statements for SYSUT1 and SYSUT2.

true   *false*   14. IEBUPDTE cannot reference a partitioned data set.

true   *false*   15. DSN=AAA(B) indicates that B is a member in the partitioned data set, AAA.

true   *false*   16. Output from the linkage editor must go to a temporary data set.

true   *false*   17. A procedure cannot be tested unless it is in a procedure library.

true   *false*   18. It is possible for a DD statement not to have a DD name.

true	*false*	19. IEBUPDTE is required to establish generation data groups.
true	*false*	20. IEHPROGM is used to scratch a data set.
true	*false*	21. IEBISAM can unload an ISAM file as a sequential data set on tape.
true	*false*	22. IEBISAM does not require a DD statement for SYSIN.
true	*false*	23. Utility control statements usually begin in column 1.
true	*false*	24. The order of DD statements in a submitted jobstream is not important when overriding DD statements in a cataloged procedure.
true	*false*	25. The order of individual DD parameters on an overriding DD statement is not important.
true	*false*	26. Once a DD parameter is entered in a cataloged procedure, it can never be nullified.

PROBLEMS

1. Indicate which of the following could *never* be considered a valid specification of the DSN parameter:

    (a) DSN=&&MYNAME
    (b) DSN=&&MYNAME.AND.YOURS
    (c) DSN=&ANYNAME
    (d) DSN=*.SYSUT1
    (e) DSN=*.STEP1. SYSUT1
    (f) DSN=A.B.C.D.E
    (g) DSN=PDS(MEMBER)
    (h) DSN=ANYNAME

2. Indicate which of the following are *invalid* JCL statements.

    (a) // EXEC COBUCLG
    (b) // EXEC IEBGENER
    (c) //STEPNAME EXEC COBUCLG,PARM.COB='LIB'   COPY OPTION
    (d) // EXEC PGM=IEBGENER
    (e) // STEP1 EXEC COBUCLG
    (f) // EXEC PROC=COBUCLG

3. Identify the utility (or utilities) in question:

    (a) Does not require a SYSIN DD statement.
    (b) Used to rename a partitioned data set.
    (c) Used to rename a member of a partitioned data set.
    (d) Used to print only a selected number of records from a file.
    (e) Does not require DD statements for SYSUT1 and SYSUT2.
    (f) Used to add members to a procedure library or COBOL source statement library.
    (g) Copies and/or reblocks a sequential file from tape to disk.
    (h) Copies an ISAM file from one direct-access volume to another.
    (i) Required to establish indexes for a generation data group.

4. Identify each of the following control statements as to function and associated utility. Indicate at least two parameters used with each control statement:

    (a) PRINT
    (b) REPL
    (c) SCRATCH
    (d) RENAME
    (e) PUNCH
    (f) ADD
    (g) RECORD
    (h) BLDG

5. Modify the jobstream of Figure 11.5 to use IEBPTPCH rather than IEBGENER in steps 2, 4, and 6. Specify appropriate control cards for IEBPTPCH to print only the first 20 columns of each record; also, print an appropriate heading before each file.

6. Modify the jobstream of Figure 11.4 to create sequential files on tape rather than disk. Specify volumes 111111 and 222222 for steps 1 and 3, respectively. In each case the newly created file is to be the first file on the tape. The merged file should be the first file on a tape with serial number 333333. Finally, the blocking factor for each file should be increased to 20.

7. Write a complete jobstream, consisting of several steps as follows:

    (a) Step 1—Create a disk file, with BLKSIZE=400, from cards.
    (b) Step 2—Print the newly created disk file, with an appropriate heading.
    (c) Step 3—Unblock the disk file created in step 1.
    (d) Step 4—Print only columns 1-10 of the unblocked file. Print only the first five records of the unblocked file.
    (e) Step 5—Rename the data set from step 1 to NEWDATA.
    (f) Step 6—Scratch the data set, NEWDATA.

8. Develop the necessary jobstream to put a COBOL table, COPYTAB, into the cataloged partitioned data set, TEST.RTG.SYSLIB. In particular:

    (a) The COBOL table is of the form

```
01   JOB-TITLE.
     05   FILLER   PIC X(20) VALUE '010ACCOUNTANT'.
     05   FILLER   PIC X(20) VALUE '020ADMINISTRATOR'.
     •

     •

     •
     etc.
01   JOB-TABLE REDEFINES JOB-TITLE.
     05   JOBS OCCURS 20 TIMES.
          10   JOB-CODE          PIC X(3).
          10   JOB-DESCRIPTION   PIC X(17).
```

(b) What change would be necessary if TEST.RTG.SYSLIB were not cataloged?

(c) Show the necessary modifications to add two additional job titles once the member COPYTAB is created.

(d) Show how the cataloged member would be called by a COBOL program; indicate both the COBOL COPY clause and any additional JCL required.

9. Develop the complete jobstream to compile and link two COBOL programs. Then in the third step invoke the linkage editor to produce an executable module. The first program in the jobstream has the ID PROGONE, which in turn calls for the second program, PROGTWO, as a subprogram. In step 4, call for the execution of the load module obtained in step 3. Accommodate the following:

(a) Store the load module obtained in step 3 as MYPROG in the partitioned data set TEST.RTG.PGMLIB.

(b) Assume that the main program has only one card and one print file; the subprogram has no files. Show associated SELECT statements.

10. Show the effective JCL produced by the cataloged procedure HOMEWORK and the submitted jobstream TRYIT.

```
//HOMEWORK PROC DATASET=YOURS
//STEP1 EXEC PGM=MINE
//DD1 DD DSN=FIRST,DISP=OLD,UNIT=SYSDA
//DD2 DD DSN=SECOND,DISP=(NEW,KEEP),
//    SPACE=(CYL,(10,1)),VOL=SER=USR001,
//    UNIT=DISK
//DD3 DD DSN=&DATASET,SPACE=(TRK,(10,2))

//TRYIT JOB
// EXEC HOMEWORK,DATASET=OUTPUT
//DD1 DD DSN=LAST,DISP=SHR,UNIT=,DCB=BLKSIZE=80
//DD3 DD DISP=(NEW,CATLG),UNIT=SYSDA,
//    SPACE=(TRK,(100,5))
//DD4 DD *
//DD2 DD *
```

11. Develop a jobstream to create and test instream a proc to go either "card to tape" or "card to disk." The proc should utilize IEBGENER and contain DD statements for SYSIN, SYSPRINT, and SYSUT2. It must *not* contain the DD statement for SYSUT1, //SYSUT1 DD *, since procedures may not contain DD statements with DD *. Instead, the DD statement for SYSUT1 will be included with the JCL to test the proc. In addition:

(a) Use symbolic parameters in the proc for output device and data set name.

(b) Specify specific DCB characteristics for SYSUT2 in the proc [e.g., DCB=(BLKSIZE=800,LRECL=80)]. Then override some or all of these when testing.

(c) Include a SPACE parameter for SYSUT2 in the proc. Show how to nullify this parameter if the output is tape.

DOS JCL

The COBOL programmer has definite need for working knowledge of an operating system. This chapter is designed to provide the individual in a DOS environment with sufficient information to make him comfortable with JCL. We cover typical jobstreams required by the COBOL programmer. We discuss how DITTO, a general utility program, is used by the applications programmer. We include material on newer features of DOS/VS such as generic assignments and procedures. Finally, we make a brief comparison between DOS and OS from the viewpoint of JCL.

BASIC JOBSTREAM

The JCL to compile, link edit, and execute a COBOL program to go "card to print" is shown in Figure 12.1. As can be seen from Figure 12.1, the necessary JCL consists of JOB, OPTION, EXEC, /*, and /& statements.

All JCL statements consist of up to four components, with blanks as the delimiters between components. Most statements begin with // in columns 1 and 2. There are some exceptions: /* denotes the end of a file, /+ denotes the end of a pro-

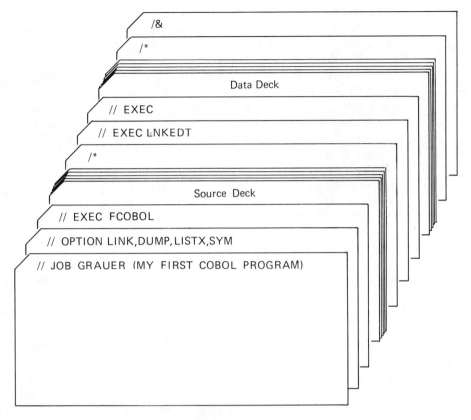

Figure 12.1 Basic DOS JCL

cedure, and /& denotes the end of a job. In addition, an * in column 1 denotes a comment, causing the information to appear with a listing of JCL, but otherwise having no effect. The second component on statements beginning with // indicates the operation (e.g., EXEC, OPTION, etc.) and may be up to eight characters long. Operands follow next. A statement may have none (e.g., the last EXEC card in Figure 12.1) or several, as in the OPTION statement. Comments are last and follow the last operand, as illustrated in the JOB statement of Figure 12.1.

Each of the JCL statements appearing in Figure 12.1 will subsequently be explained in detail. Prior to that, however, it is useful to discuss the relationship of each statement to various components of the operating system.

The Initial Program Loader, IPL, loads the supervisor into main storage when the system is initiated. It is used only at the start of operations or after a system crash, when the system has to be reinitiated. The job control program is loaded after the IPL procedure is complete. Job control reads and processes control statements. The first JCL statement, JOB, indicates the start of a job, gives it a name, and provides accounting information. OPTION LINK directs subsequent compiler output to be link-edited and then temporarily cataloged in the core image library. Any EXEC statement,

333

in this case EXEC FCOBOL, causes the job control program to relinquish control to the supervisor, which loads the desired program (e.g., the COBOL compiler). The latter, in turn, processes all statements up to the /*. Job control regains control, reads the EXEC LNKEDT statement, and relinquishes control to the supervisor, which loads the linkage editor. This program, in turn, resolves all external references, brings in the necessary I/O modules, and places an executable module in the core image library. Job control next processes the last EXEC statement, causing the supervisor to load the executable module from the core image library. The COBOL program, now in executable form, reads and processes data until the /*. Job control regains control for the last time and reads the /& signaling end of job.

Given this brief overview of JCL and the interaction of the various control programs, we proceed to a discussion of DOS JCL.

Notation

The presentation of JCL statements in the chapter is facilitated through standard COBOL notation. Thus:

Uppercase letters: Denote items that are required to appear in a JCL statement exactly as shown in the sample format

Lowercase letters: Denote generic terms that are replaced in the actual JCL statement

[ ] : Indicate an optional specification (i.e., the contents of the brackets appear at the discretion of the programmer in conjunction with his requirements)

{ } : Require that a choice be made among the items stacked within

··· : Denote repetition, at programmer discretion, of the last syntactical element

JOB Statement

Format: // JOB jobname

Example: // JOB GRAUER (MY FIRST COBOL PROGRAM)

The job name is a programmer-defined name consisting of one to eight alphanumeric characters. User comments may appear on the JOB card following the job name through column 72.

OPTION Statement

Format: // OPTION option1,option2,option3. . .

Example: // OPTION LINK

Default values for all options are established when the system is generated (SYSGEN time). The OPTION statement permits one to temporarily (i.e., for the duration of the job, override the standard options). Table 12.1 contains a partial list of DOS options, which are listed for the most part in mutually exclusive pairs (e.g., DUMP and NODUMP).

Table 12.1   Partial List of DOS Options

DUMP:	Causes a dump of main storage and registers to be printed in case of abnormal program termination (e.g., a data exception)
NODUMP:	Suppresses the DUMP option
LINK:	Indicates the object module is to be link-edited
NOLINK:	Suppresses the LINK option
DECK:	Causes the compiler to punch an object deck
NODECK:	Suppresses the DECK option
LISTX:	Generates a Procedure Division map; in addition, other information, such as register assignments and the literal pool, is also printed
NOLISTX:	Suppresses the LISTX option
XREF:	Provides a cross-reference list
NOXREF:	Suppresses the XREF option
SYM:	Generates a Data Division map; in addition, other information, such as register assignments and the literal pool, is also printed
NOSYM:	Suppresses the SYM option
ERRS:	Causes compiler diagnostics to be listed
NOERRS:	Suppresses the ERRS option
CATAL:	Causes the cataloging of the program in the core image library

Note: The LINK and CATAL options may not appear in the same statement.

The CATAL option does not appear in a mutually exclusive pair. This option will *catalog* a program in the core image library. If the option is not specified, no cataloging will take place; however, it is *incorrect* to say NOCATAL.

As an illustration, assume that we want Data and Procedure Division maps, a dump in the event of ABEND, and for the object module to be link-edited. All this is accomplished by the statement

// OPTION LISTX,SYM,DUMP,LINK

What about the options of Table 12.1 not specified in the option statement (i.e., which is, in effect, LIST or NOLIST, ERRS or NOERRS, etc.)? The answer depends on the options included in the system generation. Typically, LIST and ERRS are default options, and hence there is no reason to specify them explicitly. The purpose of the OPTION card is to *temporarily* override the default options. Common practice, therefore, is to specify only those options which differ from the SYSGEN, but it is certainly not incorrect to explicitly specify all options. Options may be listed in any order.

EXEC Statement

Format: // EXEC prog-name

Example: // EXEC FCOBOL

The EXEC statement causes the execution of a program. A given jobstream can contain several EXEC statements, each of which produces a job step. The program name field must be specified when the program to be executed is in the core image library (e.g., FCOBOL or LNKEDT). It is not specified if the COBOL program was freshly compiled and link-edited as in Figure 12.1.

/* (Slash Asterisk) Statement

The /* control card signifies that the end of data has been reached. It appears after the COBOL source deck in Figure 12.1, since the COBOL source deck is the data for the COBOL compiler. It also appears after the data cards.

/& (Slash Ampersand) Statement

This statement denotes the end of a job, and it is the last statement in a jobstream. A given job may contain several /* statements, but it must contain one and only one /& card.

DEVICE ASSIGNMENTS
(ASSGN and PAUSE statements)

A computer is connected to its I/O devices through a *channel*, which is a hardware device with limited logic circuitry. It permits overlap (i.e., simultaneous I/O and processing) and is therefore essential to maximize overall utilization of a system's resources. Each I/O device is attached to a channel through a control unit. There can be several control units hooked to one channel and several I/O devices tied to one control unit. Each type of I/O device, however, requires its own control unit. The functions of the control unit are indistinguishable to the user from the functions of the I/O device itself. Indeed, some control units (e.g., printer) are physically housed within the device itself; others (e.g., tape drives) require a separate piece of equipment in the machine room.

The JCL ASSGN statement ties an I/O device to a symbolic address. The COBOL SELECT statement links the programmer-defined file name to the symbolic address of an I/O device. The two statements in combination relate COBOL-defined file names to specific I/O devices. (Disk files require an additional JCL statement, the EXTENT statement covered in a later section in this chapter to specify the exact location of a file on the disk pack.)

A three-digit number of the form cuu is used in the ASSGN statement to specify the address of the I/O device; c denotes the channel number, the first u denotes the control unit, and the second u denotes the device. Figure 12.2 is a schematic diagram of an installation with four tape drives, four disk drives, a card reader and punch, a printer, and a keyboard. Note the boxes denoting the tape- and disk-drive control units. Further note that the tapes and disks are all on channel 1. There are two control units hooked to channel 1: one for the tape drives and one for the disk drives. The card reader, punch, printer, and keyboard are all on channel 0. The reader, punch, and printer share a common control unit; the control unit for the console is housed within the device itself.

The four tape drives are addressed by 181, 182, 183, and 184, respectively. Each of these drives is on channel 1. The disk drives are 191, 192, 193, and 194 and are

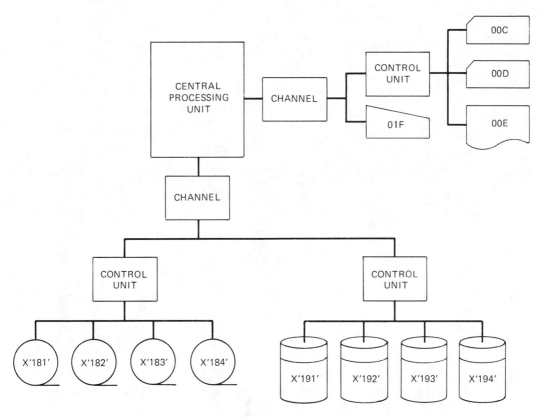

Figure 12.2 Schematic Illustration of a Typical Installation

all on channel 1: The card reader, punch, printer, and keyboard are 00C, 00D, 00E, and 01F, respectively.

The COBOL programmer does not refer to an I/O device by its address. Instead, he uses a symbolic name which causes programs to be dependent on a device type rather than a particular device. At execution time, the symbolic name is tied to the specific device by a table of permanent assignments established at SYSGEN or by individual ASSGN statements which override permanent assignments. Symbolic names are divided into system and programmer units as shown in Table 12.2.

We have discussed the symbolic addresses and permanent assignments of I/O devices. Both are tied to COBOL through the SELECT statement. Consider

SELECT INPUT-FILE ASSIGN TO SYS004-UR-2540R-S.

The programmer specifies that INPUT-FILE is to come from SYS004, and further that SYS004 is a card reader. According to Table 12.2, SYS004 is permanently assigned to the card reader and there is no need for further JCL. We could, however, optionally provide an ASSGN card, which temporarily (for the duration of the JOB or until another ASSGN card is read) overrides the permanent assignment of Table 12.2.

337

Table 12.2   Typical Permanent Device Assignments

	Symbolic Name	Address	Device Type
	SYS004	X'00C'	Card reader
	SYS005	X'00D'	Card punch
	SYS006	X'00E'	Printer
	SYS010	X'181'	Tape drive
Programmer	SYS011	X'182'	Tape drive
logical	SYS012	X'183'	Tape drive
units	SYS013	X'184'	Tape drive
	SYS014	X'191'	Disk drive
	SYS015	X'192'	Disk drive
	SYS016	X'193'	Disk drive
	SYS017	X'194'	Disk drive

	Symbolic Name	Address	Function
	SYSRDR	X'00C'	Input for JCL
	SYSIPT	X'00C'	Input for programs
System	SYSPCH	X'00D'	Punched output
logical	SYSLST	X'00E'	Printed output
units	SYSLOG	X'01F'	Operator messages
	SYSLNK	X'191'	Input to linkage editor
	SYSRES	X'192'	Contains operating system

Note: These assignments are representative of permanent assignments established at system generation. They will, of course, vary from installation to installation.

ASSGN Statement

Format: // ASSGN SYSnnn,X'cuu'

Example: // ASSGN SYS004,X'00C'

In this example SYS004 is assigned to the device whose address is 00C. Since the temporary and permanent assignments match, the ASSGN card has no effect. It is common practice, however, to explicitly specify all assignments in the JCL, to avoid any ambiguity. Moreover, in a majority of instances, ASSGN statements are mandatory rather than optional. Consider the COBOL statements:

SELECT OLD-TAPE-MASTERFILE ASSIGN TO SYS010-UT-2400-S

SELECT NEW-TAPE-MASTERFILE ASSIGN TO SYS011-UT-2400-S

The programmer specifies SYS010 and SYS011 for OLD-TAPE-MASTERFILE and NEW-TAPE-MASTERFILE, respectively. These symbolic names are permanently assigned to tape drives 181 and 182. Assume, however, that one of these drives, 181, is unavailable. Are we to wait until it becomes available before our program can be executed? That would hardly be practical. We bypass the problem by assigning SYS010 to an available drive via an ASSGN statement, // ASSGN SYS010,X'183'.

Generic Assignments

Generic assignments specify a device type rather than a particular device and are available only under DOS/VS. Consider the difference between

// ASSGN SYS010,X'180'

and

// ASSGN SYS011,TAPE,VOL=123456

The first example is the "old-fashioned" ASSGN statement which *requires* device 180 for SYS010. The second example assigns SYS011 to any tape drive which has a tape mounted with a volume number of 123456.

Generic assignments also make it possible to share a disk device across partitions (see Appendix A). Thus, programs executing concurrently in separate partitions can access the same physical device at the same time. This is accomplished via the SHR parameter as shown:

// ASSGN SYS012,DISK,VOL=WORK01,SHR

The generic assignment causes each disk in a ready status to be examined until a disk with a volume-id of WORK01 is found. SYS012 is then assigned to that device. Inclusion of the SHR parameter allows the unit to be simultaneously assigned to any other job. Accordingly, unless a private volume is required, SHR should be used with all generic assignments for disk. The parameter has no meaning for other device types (e.g., it is meaningless to share a tape or printer among two jobs).

Generic assignments for other kinds of devices are also permitted. Thus, the statements

// ASSGN SYS009,PRINTER
// ASSGN SYS010,READER
// ASSGN SYS011,PUNCH

would assign SYS009, SYS010, and SYS011 to any available printer, card reader, and punch, respectively.

One last form of the generic assignment ensures that two logical units will be assigned the same physical device. Consider

// ASSGN SYS015,DISK,VOL=WORK01,SHR
// ASSGN SYS016,SYS015

The second statement causes SYS016 to be assigned to the same physical device as SYS015.

Ignoring Assignments

It is possible to negate (ignore) I/O operations through the command // ASSGN SYSXXX,IGN. This causes logical IOCS commands to the specified SYS number to be ignored. The effect in COBOL is that an end-of-file condition is registered on the first read for an input file, and/or that output records are not written to any device. This capability is extremely useful as follows.

Assume that a new system is implemented with a master file in, a master file out, and transactions. No input master is available for the first cycle. However, if the input file is assigned to IGN, the problem of the missing master is solved quite easily.

On the output side, there are many instances where a file is required only under specific conditions. Creation of the file is controlled by the IGN parameter.

PAUSE Statement

Format: // PAUSE comments

Example: // PAUSE MOUNT TAPE REEL #123456

The PAUSE statement allows one to instruct the operator in between job steps. It is a convenient way to request that a particular reel of tape, disk pack, print form, and so on, be mounted. The preceding example requests the operator to mount reel #123456.

When a PAUSE statement is encountered by the operating system, its message prints on the keyboard and processing is suspended. The operator complies with the request, then hits the "end of block" key on the console, whereupon processing resumes. A variety of messages can be given via the PAUSE statement. Most commonly, instructions are given to mount specific volumes (tape reels or disk packs), and special forms for the printer (e.g., payroll checks, multiple-part paper, etc).

PROCESSING TAPE FILES
(TLBL and LBLTYP statements)

The tape library of a typical installation consists of hundreds or even thousands of reels. When the programmer requests a specific reel via a PAUSE statement or other instruction, he is referring to an *external* label (i.e., a piece of paper pasted on the reel of tape for visual identification). Unfortunately, it is far too easy to inadvertently mount the wrong reel, and the consequences of such an action could be disastrous. *Internal* labels, consisting of information written on the tape itself, are used as a precaution.

There are three standard DOS labels: volume, header, and trailer. The volume label appears at the beginning of each volume (i.e., reel) and contains a six-digit serial number to uniquely identify the volume. A header label is an 80-byte record which appears before each file on the tape. The trailer label, also 80 bytes, appears at the end of each file. The latter two labels contain identical information, with the exception of a block count field (in the trailer label) that indicates the number of records contained in the file.

Every volume contains one and only one volume label. It can contain several sets of header and trailer labels, depending on the number and size of the files on the reel. The COBOL programmer indicates that label processing is desired by the clause LABEL RECORDS ARE STANDARD in the FD for the file. If this clause is included for a tape file, supporting JCL—the LBLTYP and TLBL statements—are also required.

Volume, header, and trailer labels are illustrated schematically in Figure 12.3. Figure 12.3 is an example of a multifile volume [i.e., several files are contained on the same volume (reel)]. It is also possible to have a multivolume file in which the same file extends over several volumes.

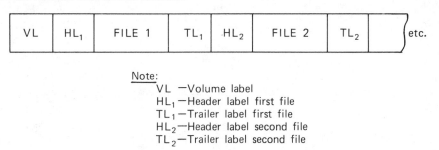

Note:
VL —Volume label
HL_1—Header label first file
TL_1—Trailer label first file
HL_2—Header label second file
TL_2—Trailer label second file

Figure 12.3 Volume, Header, and Trailer Labels

LBLTYP Statement

Format: // LBLTYP $\begin{cases} \text{TAPE} \\ \text{NSD(nn)} \end{cases}$

Example: // LBLTYP TAPE

The LBLTYP statement specifies that storage is to be allocated for label processing. The NSD (nonsequential disk) option is used only when processing nonsequential disk files and is discussed in that section. The LBLTYP statement must appear immediately before the // EXEC LNKEDT statement.

TLBL Statement

Format: // TLBL filename [,'file-identifier'] [,date]
           [,file-serial-number] [,volume-sequence-number]
           [,file-sequence-number] [,generation-number]
           [,version-number]

Example: // TLBL SYS010,,99/365,111111

The TLBL statement is used when tape label processing is desired. It is a complex statement in that a number of parameters may optionally be specified. Observe that only one parameter, the file name (derived from the COBOL SELECT statement) is mandatory. If a parameter is omitted and others follow, an extra comma is used. In the example above, file-identifier was skipped; thus, two commas follow filename. If, however, a parameter is omitted, and no further parameters appear to its right, the extra commas are not used. Since file-serial-number was the last specified parameter, all other commas were skipped. Each of the entries in the TLBL statement is explained below:

Filename: From one to seven characters in length. It identifies the file to the control program and is taken directly from the COBOL SELECT statement. If SELECT TAPE-FILE ASSIGN TO SYS010-UT-2400-S appears in the COBOL program, SYS010 must be the file name in the TLBL statement.

File-identifier: Consists of one to seventeen characters and is contained within apostrophes. If omitted on output files, the file name is used. If it is omitted on input files, no checking is done.

Date: Consists of one to six characters in the form yy/ddd, indicating the expiration date of the file. Output files may specify an alternative format, dddd, indicating the number of days the file is to be retained.

File-serial-number: Consists of one to six characters, indicating the volume serial number of the first (often only) reel of the file

Volume-sequence-number: Consists of one to four characters, indicating the sequence number of a multivolume file (i.e., a large file extending over several reels)

File-sequence-number: Consists of one to four characters, indicating the sequence number of the file on a multifile volume (i.e., several short files contained on one volume)

Generation-number: One to four digits, indicating the number of a particular edition of the file

Version-number: One or two digits, which modify the generation number

All parameters in the TLBL card correspond directly to entries in the standard tape labels shown in Figure 12.4. Header and trailer labels for a given file are identical except for the label identifier (indicating the type of label) and the block count field (showing the number of physical records in the file). If an output file is processed, then header and trailer labels are written on the tape according to specifications in the TLBL card. If an input file is processed, the label information on the tape is checked against the TLBL card to ensure that the proper reel has been mounted.

Information on tape processing is summarized via Figure 12.5. It shows JCL for a COBOL program to update an existing tape file from transactions punched

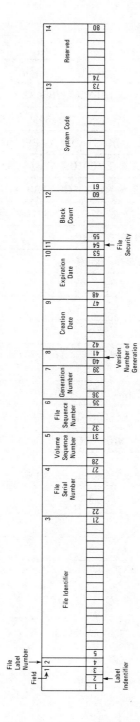

Figure 12.4 Standard Tape Label

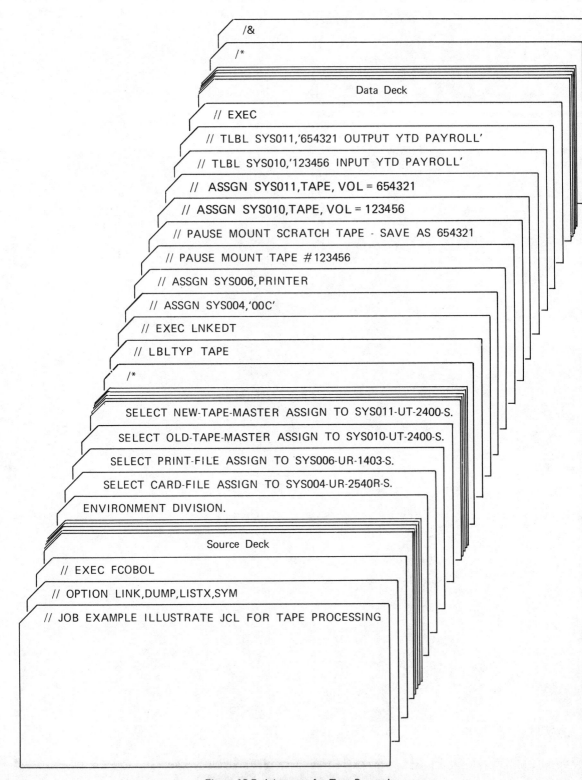

```
/&
/*
                    Data Deck
  // EXEC
  // TLBL SYS011,'654321 OUTPUT YTD PAYROLL'
  // TLBL SYS010,'123456 INPUT YTD PAYROLL'
  // ASSGN SYS011,TAPE, VOL = 654321
  // ASSGN SYS010,TAPE, VOL = 123456
  // PAUSE MOUNT SCRATCH TAPE - SAVE AS 654321
  // PAUSE MOUNT TAPE #123456
  // ASSGN SYS006,PRINTER
  // ASSGN SYS004,'00C'
  // EXEC LNKEDT
  // LBLTYP TAPE
  /*
    SELECT NEW-TAPE-MASTER ASSIGN TO SYS011-UT-2400-S.
    SELECT OLD-TAPE-MASTER ASSIGN TO SYS010-UT-2400-S.
    SELECT PRINT-FILE ASSIGN TO SYS006-UR-1403-S.
    SELECT CARD-FILE ASSIGN TO SYS004-UR-2540R-S.
  ENVIRONMENT DIVISION.
                    Source Deck
  // EXEC FCOBOL
  // OPTION LINK,DUMP,LISTX,SYM
  // JOB EXAMPLE ILLUSTRATE JCL FOR TAPE PROCESSING
```

Figure 12.5 Jobstream for Tape Processing

on cards. The program creates a new tape file and a printed exception report. Label processing is done for both input and output tapes. The OPTION card provides for the linkage editor, Procedure and Data Division maps, and a dump in the event of an ABEND. Label processing is called for by the phrase LABEL RECORDS ARE STANDARD in the COBOL program. Note the tie between the COBOL SELECT and the ASSGN and TLBL statements; also note the use of generic assignments which permit any available drive to be used. Finally, note the use of the PAUSE statement to provide instructions to the operator.

Some changes of technique are possible, and common, in connection with Figure 12.5. The first has to do with using multiple comment cards and a single PAUSE, rather than two PAUSE statements. As Figure 12.5 now stands, the operator is required to respond to two PAUSE statements (i.e., he must hit "end of block" twice for processing to continue). An alternative is to stack all instructions to the operator in comment statements, followed by a single PAUSE to give the operator a chance to respond. For example:

```
* MOUNT TAPE #123456
* MOUNT SCRATCH TAPE — SAVE AS 654321
// PAUSE
```

The advantage of a single pause is that the operator only has to respond once. This may not seem like much of a difference in Figure 12.5, but it does add up when stretched over a shift. The second change in technique has to do with altering the TLBL statements. As Figure 12.5 stands now, the use of unique label names for the input and output (i.e., old and new master) versions of the same file is not practical. This is because production jobstreams would have to change each cycle. Accordingly, the TLBL statements would most likely appear as

```
// TLBL SYS010,'PAYROLL YTD MAST'   INPUT
// TLBL SYS011,'PAYROLL YTD MAST'   OUTPUT
```

These statements would still offer some protection in that the file identifier would be checked for PAYROL YTD MAST. However, it would be an *external* control function to ensure that the correct version of the file was mounted for SYS010 and SYS011. Realize that instructions on which tape to mount would be specified by production control in a job sheet rather than on JCL statements; otherwise, we are back to ground zero (OS' circumvents this problem nicely through generation data groups; see Chapter Ten).

Some programmers have really become extreme and use TLBL statements of the form // TLBL SYS011. This statement, although functional, allows any tape to be read as input and effectively bypasses label processing. It may be useful at times, but in most cases it is *undesirable*.

PROCESSING DISK FILES
(DLBL and EXTENT statements)

The concepts of label processing are applicable to disk as well as tape. Just as there is a TLBL statement, there is a DLBL statement. There is also one major extension for disk files. Tape processing is strictly sequential, whereas disk processing may be either sequential or nonsequential. Thus, the DLBL statement contains an additional parameter indicating the type of file organization. In addition, the EXTENT statement, required for disk files, specifies the address of the file on the disk device by providing a cylinder and track number where the first record in the file may be found. The EXTENT statement also specifies the size (extent) of the file by stating the number of tracks allocated for its storage.

DLBL Statement

Format: // DLBL filename [, 'file-identifier'] [, date] [, codes]

Example: // DLBL SYS013,'THIS IS DISK FILE',99/365,SD

The DLBL statement provides the necessary information for processing disk labels. As with tape processing, if an input file is referenced, label checking is done to ensure that the proper volume was mounted. If an output file is specified, a disk label is created in accordance with Figure 12.6. Only the filename parameter is required on the DLBL card, and it is tied to the COBOL SELECT, as was the filename in the TLBL statement. All parameters are explained below:

Filename: One to seven characters in length and is tied directly to the SELECT statement (i.e., the SYS number matches in both statements). However, the symbolic address in the DLBL card need not match the symbolic address on the ASSGN or EXTENT statements (more on this in the next section).

File-identifier: File name as it appears in the volume label; consists of 1 to 44 characters

Date: One of two formats, as in the TLBL statement. Omission of this parameter causes the file to be retained for 7 days.

Codes: A two- or three-character field, indicating the type of file as follows:

        SD: Sequential disk
        DA: Direct access
        ISC: Create ISAM file
        ISE: Existing ISAM file

Omission of this parameter causes a default to sequential disk.

EXTENT Statement

Format: // EXTENT[symbolic-unit] [,serial-number] [,type]
        [,sequence-number] [,relative-track] [,number-of-tracks]
        [,split-cylinder-track] [,B-bins]

Example: // EXTENT SYS014,111111,8,,200,20

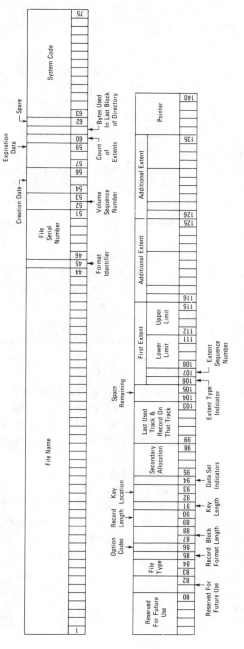

Figure 12.6 Standard Disk Label

347

The EXTENT statement specifies the exact location of a file, the number of tracks in the file, and other information associated with the file. One or more EXTENT statements *must* follow the corresponding DLBL card. Parameters are described below.

Symbolic-unit: SYS number of the device on which the file is physically located. It must match the symbolic name on the ASSGN card (or standard assignment) and may, but is not required to, match the SYS number on the COBOL SELECT and corresponding DLBL card. (Stay with us—we clarify the statement in ensuing examples.)

Serial-number: One to six characters specifying the volume serial number. If omitted, the volume serial number of the preceding EXTENT card is used. If omitted entirely, the serial number is not checked and the programmer runs the risk of processing the wrong volume.

Type: One-character field indicating the type of extent as follows:

1: Data area
2: Overflow area (ISAM)
4: Index area (ISAM)
8: Split cylinder data area (Split
Cylinders are not covered in the text)

Sequence-number: One to three digits indicating the sequence number of the extent within a multiextent file. Its use is optional for sequential (code= SD on DLBL) or direct-access (code=DA on DLBL) files, but mandatory for ISAM files.

Relative-track: One- to five-digit number indicating the sequential number of the track (relative to zero) where the file begins. A simple calculation is required to convert a cylinder and track address to a relative track. The calculation is device-dependent and is shown in Table 12.3.

Number-of-tracks: One- to five-digit number specifying the number of tracks allocated to the file

Split cylinder and bin parameters are not discussed further in the book. (The reader is referred to the *DOS Programmer's Guide* for information.)

Table 12.3   Conversion of Cylinder and Track Address to Relative Track

Device	Formula
2311	Relative track = 10 * cylinder + track
2314	Relative track = 20 * cylinder + track
3330	Relative track = 19 * cylinder + track
3340	Relative track = 12 * cylinder + track

Sometimes it is necessary to go in reverse (i.e., calculate a cylinder and track address given a relative track). Again, the formula is device-dependent:

Device	Formula	
2311	(relative track)/10	quotient = cylinder, remainder = track
2314	(relative track)/20	quotient = cylinder, remainder = track
3330	(relative track)/19	quotient = cylinder, remainder = track
3340	(relative track)/12	quotient = cylinder, remainder = track

SEQUENTIAL PROCESSING

Figure 12.7 shows JCL necessary to update a sequential disk file from card transactions. A new master file is created as is a printed exception report. Both disk files are stored on the same pack. Among other points, the example emphasizes relationships between the SELECT, ASSGN, DLBL, and EXTENT statements.

OLD-MASTER and NEW-MASTER are assigned to SYS014 and SYS016, respectively, via COBOL SELECT statements. There are corresponding DLBL statements for each of these filenames. Both DLBL cards are followed by EXTENT statements specifying the physical device where the file is located, in this instance SYS010 for both. Both files are on the same device, SYS010, which in turn is assigned to any available drive by the generic ASSGN statement. The file NEW-MASTER will be retained until the last day of 1999, as per the entry on its DLBL statement. It begins on relative track 1000 and continues for 100 tracks (EXTENT statement).

Label processing will be performed, but the LBLTYP card is omitted, as that statement is not used with sequential disk files. The ASSGN statements have been omitted for CARD-FILE and PRINT-FILE, since those SELECT statements match the permanent assignments in Table 12.2.

NONSEQUENTIAL PROCESSING

We have discussed sequential processing for both tape and disk. We now proceed to JCL for nonsequential processing, in particular ISAM reorganization. ISAM processing becomes less efficient as new records are added and old records are logically deleted (ISAM organization was discussed in Chapter Five). Accordingly, an ISAM file is periodically reorganized whereby the logically deleted records are physically dropped from the file, and the additions are transferred from the overflow to the prime data area. The decision of how often this is to be done is made by a systems analyst and is not discussed here.

Reorganization is generally a two-step process. First, the ISAM file is read sequentially and dumped on tape. Next, the newly created tape is used as input to a second COBOL (or utility) program, which restores the ISAM file on disk. The restored file is logically equivalent to the original; however, its records have been physically rearranged to make processing more efficient. Figure 12.8 shows the JCL needed for the first step.

Much of Figure 12.8 has already been reviewed in Figures 12.5 and 12.7 and

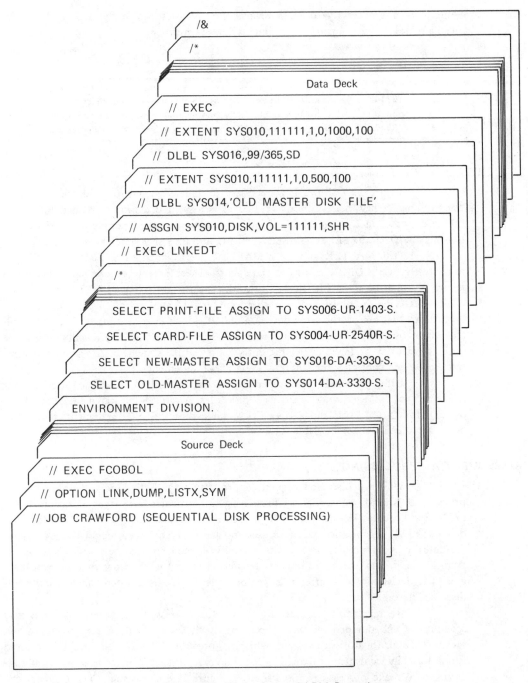

/&

/*

Data Deck

// EXEC

// EXTENT SYS010,111111,1,0,1000,100

// DLBL SYS016,,99/365,SD

// EXTENT SYS010,111111,1,0,500,100

// DLBL SYS014,'OLD MASTER DISK FILE'

// ASSGN SYS010,DISK,VOL=111111,SHR

// EXEC LNKEDT

/*

SELECT PRINT-FILE ASSIGN TO SYS006-UR-1403-S.

SELECT CARD-FILE ASSIGN TO SYS004-UR-2540R-S.

SELECT NEW-MASTER ASSIGN TO SYS016-DA-3330-S.

SELECT OLD-MASTER ASSIGN TO SYS014-DA-3330-S.

ENVIRONMENT DIVISION.

Source Deck

// EXEC FCOBOL

// OPTION LINK,DUMP,LISTX,SYM

// JOB CRAWFORD (SEQUENTIAL DISK PROCESSING)

Figure 12.7 JCL for Sequential Disk Processing

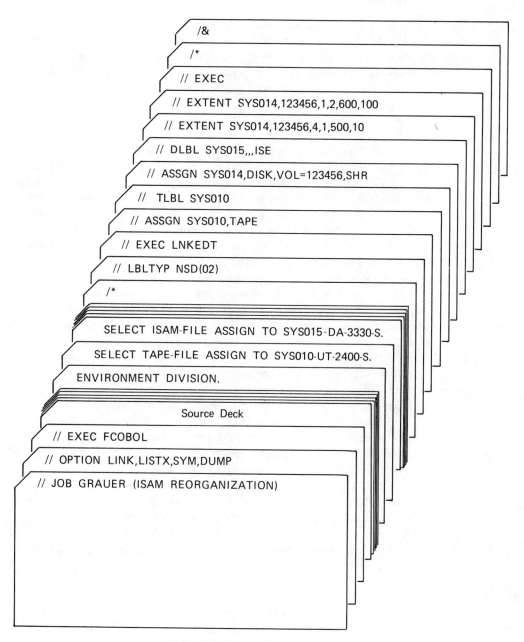

```
/&
/*
// EXEC
// EXTENT SYS014,123456,1,2,600,100
// EXTENT SYS014,123456,4,1,500,10
// DLBL SYS015,,,ISE
// ASSGN SYS014,DISK,VOL=123456,SHR
// TLBL SYS010
// ASSGN SYS010,TAPE
// EXEC LNKEDT
// LBLTYP NSD(02)
/*
    SELECT ISAM-FILE ASSIGN TO SYS015-DA-3330-S.
    SELECT TAPE-FILE ASSIGN TO SYS010-UT-2400-S.
ENVIRONMENT DIVISION.
            Source Deck
// EXEC FCOBOL
// OPTION LINK,LISTX,SYM,DUMP
// JOB GRAUER (ISAM REORGANIZATION)
```

Figure 12.8 JCL for ISAM Reorganization

that discussion is not repeated here. Note, however, the NSD parameter in the LBLTYP statement. The 02 in parentheses indicates the number of EXTENT cards associated with the nonsequential disk file. The type and sequence parameters in the EXTENT statements assume importance. In this example, the first EXTENT has a type of 4, indicating the EXTENT for the cylinder index. The second EXTENT has a type of 1 indicating EXTENTs for the prime data area.

USE OF PROCEDURES

DOS/VS has grown increasingly more powerful through use of multi-programming, private libraries, and so on. These additional features are not without their price, however. The COBOL programmer is required to provide more complex jobstreams, often with "unusual" EXTENTs and/or DLBL statements. An everyday occurrence is the interaction between COBOL and a private source library in which the COBOL program to be compiled is contained in the library rather than on cards. The simple jobstream of Figure 12.1 is no longer applicable, because the system must be told where to find the COBOL program. This involves some rather "strange-looking" control statements which can easily bother the applications programmer.

The solution is for a systems programmer to develop the necessary jobstream once and then catalog it as a procedure (i.e., a set of "canned" control statements). The procedure, or proc, is assigned a name (e.g., EASYCOB). The applications programmer in turn simply invokes the proc through a single execute statement, // EXEC PROC=EASYCOB.

Figure 12.9 shows how the procedure EASYCOB could be cataloged in the procedure library. Realize that the jobstream in Figure 12.9 is the province of the systems programmer rather than the applications programmer. It is *not* necessary for the COBOL programmer to know how to catalog a proc, nor even to fully understand it. What is required is for the reader to appreciate what a procedure is and how to call it.

The proc in Figure 12.9 consists of four statements: ASSGN, DLBL, EXTENT, and EXEC. It allows an incoming COBOL program to come from a private source statement library stored on a volume whose id is SYSPK1. To use this proc, one codes // EXEC PROC=EASYCOB. The system, in turn, goes to the procedure library and pulls in the remaining JCL. In this way the programmer is not concerned with DLBLs and EXTENTs, private libraries, work areas, and so on. Moreover, if the location of a file in the procedure is changed, only the proc is altered. Thus, the many established jobstreams which utilize the proc are unaffected.

DOS UTILITIES—DITTO

The arguments for utility programs, discussed in Chapter Eleven for OS, apply equally well to DOS. Although DOS has a variety of such programs, application programmers typically use only a single utility, DITTO. [Complete documentation for DITTO is obtained simply by executing the program (i.e., a list of all available functions and required parameters will appear on each DITTO listing). The ensuing discussion relates to the DOS/VS version.]

DITTO is a very flexible program with the generalized function of transferring a file from one medium to another. DITTO can block or unblock files, copy only

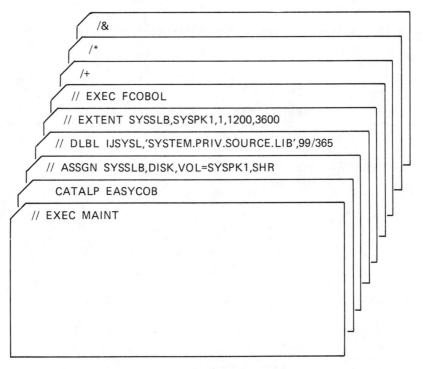

```
            /&
           /*
          /+
      // EXEC FCOBOL
      // EXTENT SYSSLB,SYSPK1,1,1200,3600
      // DLBL IJSYSL,'SYSTEM.PRIV.SOURCE.LIB',99/365
      // ASSGN SYSSLB,DISK,VOL=SYSPK1,SHR
        CATALP EASYCOB
   // EXEC MAINT
```

Figure 12.9 Cataloging a Procedure

a limited number of records from a file, append sequence numbers in columns 1-6 of a COBOL source deck, as well as a host of other functions. The complete list of DITTO functions is shown in Table 12.4

Each of the operations in Table 12.4 requires additional parameters to fully specify the command, as shown in Table 12.5. DITTO commands may be entered either within the jobstream or from the console.

The use of DITTO is best illustrated by example. Consider Figure 12.10, which shows the jobstream to copy a standard label tape and then print the first three blocks from the copied tape. Several statements merit explanation. // UPSI 1 is required when DITTO commands are entered in the jobstream rather than from the console. [The communications region of the supervisor contains a special byte, the UPSI byte, whose bits are frequently used as a program switch(es). At the beginning of every job, this byte contains all zero bits. // UPSI 1 resets the high-order bit in the UPSI byte to 1. DITTO, in turn, checks the UPSI byte to determine from where to read the commands (i.e., the console or jobstream).]

The two ASSGN statements tie the symbolic devices used in subsequent DITTO commands, SYS010 and SYS011, to specific tape drives, 181 and 182. The PAUSE statement is there only as a reminder as to which drive is input and output. The output tape, drive 181, requires a file protect ring for writing; the tape on drive 182, however, should have the ring removed as precaution against accidentally writing on an

Table 12.4 List of DITTO Functions

```
*******************************************************************************
*                                                                             *
* * * * * * * * * *          D O S / D I T T O          * * * * * * * * * *   *
*                                                                             *
*                        CARD FUNCTIONS                                       *
*     CC            CARD TO CARD                                              *
*     CCS           CARD TO CARD WITH SEQ. NUMBERS AND DECK NAME             *
*     CP            CARD TO PRINTER IN CHARACTER FORMAT                      *
*     CD            CARD TO PRINTER IN CHARACTER AND HEX DUMP FORMAT          *
*     CT            CARD TO TAPE BLOCKED 1 TO 400                            *
*     CTS           CARD TO TAPE RESEQUENCED                                 *
*                        TAPE FUNCTIONS                                       *
*     TC            TAPE TO CARD BLOCKED OR UNBLOCKED                        *
*     TP            TAPE TO PRINTER UNBLOCKED IN CHAR. FORMAT                *
*     TPD           TAPE TO PRINTER DEBLOCKED IN CHAR. FORMAT                *
*     TD            TAPE TO PRINTER UNBLOCKED IN CHAR. AND HEX DUMP          *
*     TDD           TAPE TO PRINTER DEBLOCKED IN CHAR. AND HEX DUMP          *
*     TPV           TAPE TO PRINTER VARIABLE RECDS CHAR. FORMAT              *
*     TDV           TAPE TO PRINTER VARIABLE RECDS CHAR. AND HEX DUMP        *
*     TFA           PRINT SYSLST TAPES TYPE A FORMS CONTROL, CCW CODE        *
*     TFD           PRINT SYSLST TAPES TYPE D FORMS CONTROL                  *
*     TRS           TAPE RECORD SCAN                                         *
*     TRL           TAPE RECORD LOAD                                         *
*     INT           INITIALIZE TAPE                                          *
*     TT            TAPE TO TAPE  (01 TO 99) FILES                           *
*     TTR           TAPE TO TAPE REBLOCKED                                   *
*     WTM           WRITE TAPE MARK                                          *
*     REW           REWIND TAPE                                              *
*     RUN           REWIND AND UNLOAD TAPE                                   *
*     FSR           FORWARD SPACE RECORD                                     *
*     BSR           BACK SPACE RECORD                                        *
*     FSF           FORWARD SPACE FILE                                       *
*     BSF           BACK SPACE FILE                                          *
*     ERT           ERASE TAPE  (DATA SECURITY ERASE 3410/3420 ONLY)        *
*                        DISK FUNCTIONS                                       *
*     DP            DISK TO PRINTER UNBLOCKED IN CHAR. FORMAT                *
*     DD            DISK TO PRINTER UNBLOCKED IN CHAR. AND HEX DUMP          *
*     DPD           DISK TO PRINTER DEBLOCKED IN CHAR. FORMAT                *
*     DDD           DISK TO PRINTER DEBLOCKED IN CHAR. AND HEX DUMP          *
*     DRL           DISK RECORD LOAD - KEY AND/OR DATA                       *
*     DRS           DISK RECORD SCAN - PARTIAL KEY OR DATA OR EOF            *
*     EOF           WRITE DISK EOF RECORD                                    *
*     DID           ALTER DISK IDENTIFICATION VOLUME NUMBER                 *
*                                                                             *
*     XXX           LIST FUNCTIONS ON SYSLST                                 *
*     EOJ           END OF JOB                                               *
*******************************************************************************
```

input tape; indeed, all reels containing live data should be stored without the file protect ring. The remainder of Figure 12.10 contains DITTO commands in accordance with Table 12.5. Note well the command syntax, $$DITTO in columns 1-7, the DITTO function beginning in column 10, and the operands starting in column 16.

The first two DITTO commands rewind the input and output tapes. The third command puts a tape mark on SYS011 (drive 181 via the ASSGN statement),

Table 12.5 Syntax of DITTO Commands Within a Jobstream

```
* * * * * * * * * *         FUNCTION CONTROL CARD FORMAT         * * * * * * * * * *


CC 1-7      FUNCTION         PARAMETERS

$$DITTO      CC
$$DITTO      CCS     DECKTYPE=XXX,DECKNAME=X...X
$$DITTO      CP
$$DITTO      CD
$$DITTO      CT      OUTPUT=SYSNNN,BLKFACTOR=N.N
$$DITTO      CTS     OUTPUT=SYSNNN,BLKFACTOR=N.N,DECKTYPE=XXX,DECKNAME=X...X
$$DITTO      TC      INPUT=SYSNNN
$$DITTO      TP      INPUT=SYSNNN,NBLKS=N..N
$$DITTO      TPD     INPUT=SYSNNN,RECSIZE=N...N,NBLKS=N..N
$$DITTO      TD      INPUT=SYSNNN,NBLKS=N..N
$$DITTO      TDD     INPUT=SYSNNN,RECSIZE=N...N,NBLKS=N..N
$$DITTO      TPV     INPUT=SYSNNN,NBLKS=N..N
$$DITTO      TDV     INPUT=SYSNNN,NBLKS=N..N
$$DITTO      TFA     INPUT=SYSNNN
$$DITTO      TFD     INPUT=SYSNNN
$$DITTO      TT      INPUT=SYSNNN,OUTPUT=SYSNNN
$$DITTO      TTR     INPUT=SYSNNN,OUTPUT=SYSNNN,RECSIZE=N...N,BLKFACTOR=N.N
$$DITTO      WTM     OUTPUT=SYSNNN
$$DITTO      REW     OUTPUT=SYSNNN
$$DITTO      RUN     OUTPUT=SYSNNN
$$DITTO      FSR     OUTPUT=SYSNNN,NBLKS=N..N
$$DITTO      BSR     OUTPUT=SYSNNN,NBLKS=N..N
$$DITTO      FSF     OUTPUT=SYSNNN
$$DITTO      BSF     OUTPUT=SYSNNN
$$DITTO      DP      INPUT=SYSNNN,BEGIN=CCCHH,END=CCCHH
$$DITTO      DD      INPUT=SYSNNN,BEGIN=CCCHH,END=CCCHH
$$DITTO      DPD     INPUT=SYSNNN,BEGIN=CCCHH,END=CCCHH,RECSIZE=N...N
$$DITTO      DDD     INPUT=SYSNNN,BEGIN=CCCHH,END=CCCHH,RECSIZE=N...N
$$DITTO      XXX
$$DITTO      EOJ




PARAMETER                       DESCRIPTION

INPUT=SYSNNN           PROGRAMMER LOGICAL INPUT DEVICE
OUTPUT=SYSNNN          PROGRAMMER LOGICAL OUTPUT DEVICE
BEGIN=CCCHH            LOWER DISK EXTENT
END=CCCHH             UPPER DISK EXTENT
NBLKS=N..N            NUMBER OF TAPE BLOCKS       1-9999
RECSIZE=N...N         LOGICAL RECORD SIZE         1-99999
DECKTYPE=XXX          DECKTYPE (BAL, RPG, COB)
DECKNAME=X...X        DECKNAME (0-3, 0-5, 0-8) CHAR.
BLKFACTOR=N.N         OUTPUT BLOCKING FACTOR       1-999


NOTE. SUBMIT (// UPSI 1) CARD TO DENOTE CONTROL CARD
OPERATION. LAST PARAMETER STATEMENT MUST BE EOJ.
NBLKS=N..N PARAMETER IS OPTIONAL.
```

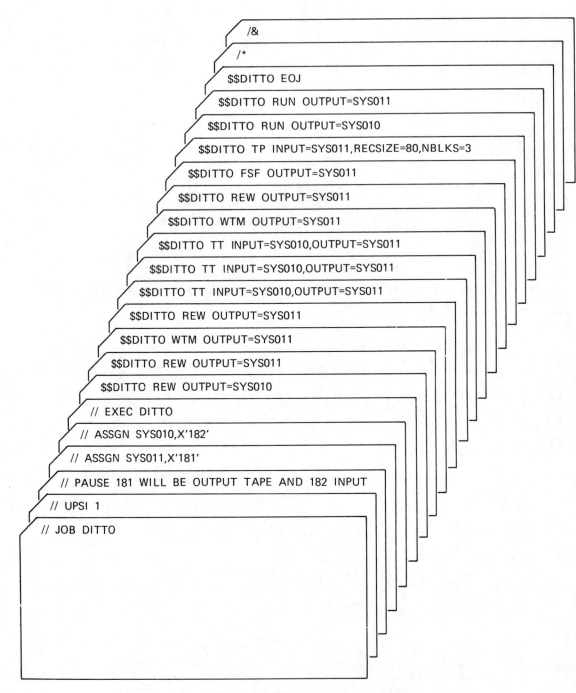

```
/&
/*
$$DITTO EOJ
$$DITTO RUN OUTPUT=SYS011
$$DITTO RUN OUTPUT=SYS010
$$DITTO TP INPUT=SYS011,RECSIZE=80,NBLKS=3
$$DITTO FSF OUTPUT=SYS011
$$DITTO REW OUTPUT=SYS011
$$DITTO WTM OUTPUT=SYS011
$$DITTO TT INPUT=SYS010,OUTPUT=SYS011
$$DITTO TT INPUT=SYS010,OUTPUT=SYS011
$$DITTO TT INPUT=SYS010,OUTPUT=SYS011
$$DITTO REW OUTPUT=SYS011
$$DITTO WTM OUTPUT=SYS011
$$DITTO REW OUTPUT=SYS011
$$DITTO REW OUTPUT=SYS010
// EXEC DITTO
// ASSGN SYS010,X'182'
// ASSGN SYS011,X'181'
// PAUSE 181 WILL BE OUTPUT TAPE AND 182 INPUT
// UPSI 1
// JOB DITTO
```

Figure 12.10 Use of DITTO to Copy a Standard Label Tape

and the fourth rewinds the output tape after the tape mark has been written. Each of the next three commands copy a file from one tape to another. Although this illustration is to copy one file from tape to tape, three TT commands were used. The reason is that the header and trailer labels are each considered a file, hence three "files" must be copied for each data file. Another tape mark is written after the files are copied and the output tape is rewound. The next commands print a portion of the copied tape to verify it was copied correctly. The first file (i.e., the header label) is skipped via the FSF (Forward Space File) command. The first three blocks are printed in character format. Finally, EOJ denotes end of job.

A second example (Figure 12.11) shows how DITTO commands may be entered directly from the console. A series of DITTO commands is supplied to go "card to tape" and then to print the newly created tape in various formats.

Of particular interest in Figure 12.11 is the series of prompting messages issued by the system. For example, the first command, ct (card to tape), requires specification of a blocking factor and output tape. The prompting messages can, however, be eliminated by supplying all required information with the command itself (e.g., CT, 282,10).

Printed output can assume a variety of formats as shown in Figure 12.12, which was produced from the commands in Figure 12.11. In Figure 12.12(a), all 27 records of the file are shown in three blocks, containing 10, 10, and 7 records, respectively. Figure 12.12(a) (DITTO Function TP) is in unblocked format (i.e., the blocks are separated), but the records within a block are not separated. Only the alphabetic interpretation of each character appears in Figure 12.12(a).

Figure 12.12(b) is in deblocked character format (DITTO Function TPD) (i.e., the blocks are separated and the records within each block are separated as well). Only the first block of 10 records is shown.

Figure 12.12(c) is also in deblocked format but shows hex as well as character representation (DITTO Function TDD). Only the first three records of the first block are shown. Inclusion of the hex dump reveals something not readily apparent in Figure 12.12(a) and (b). Note well that positions 25 through 29 of Figure 12.12(c) contain high values (FF in hex). The character interpretation for these positions in Figure 12.12(a) and (b) misleadingly implied that these columns contained blanks; in reality, they contained unprintable characters.

COMPARISON OF OS AND DOS

We conclude our discussion with a *brief* comparison of OS and DOS. In so doing, the background and biases of the authors must be known. We were both "raised" in a DOS environment but have worked in OS installations for several years. For us, DOS job control was simple to learn, whereas OS initially appeared overwhelming. However, after learning OS, we view its many optional parameters *as providing flexibility, rather than complexity*, and we would be hard-pressed to return to DOS.

Our comparison proceeds along the lines of JCL and is far from complete. There are many other items one would and should review when considering an upgrade to OS. Moreover, the advantages of OS should be carefully weighed against the cost of

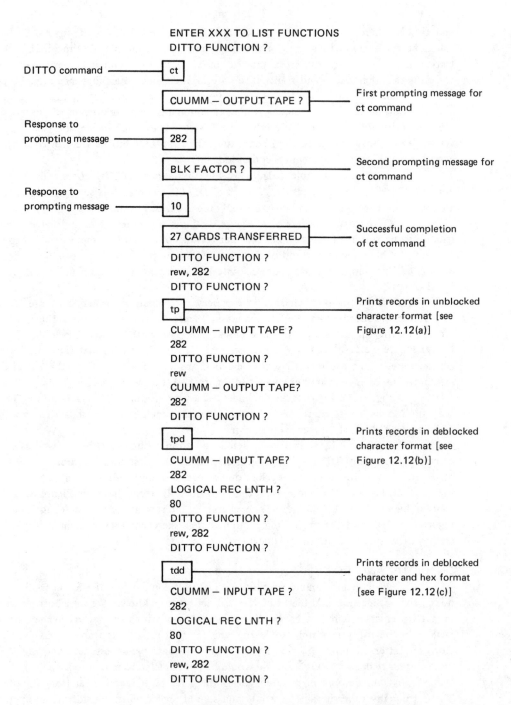

ENTER XXX TO LIST FUNCTIONS
DITTO FUNCTION ?

DITTO command ——— ct

CUUMM — OUTPUT TAPE ? ——— First prompting message for ct command

Response to
prompting message ——— 282

BLK FACTOR ? ——— Second prompting message for ct command

Response to
prompting message ——— 10

27 CARDS TRANSFERRED ——— Successful completion of ct command

DITTO FUNCTION ?
rew, 282
DITTO FUNCTION ?

tp ——— Prints records in unblocked character format [see Figure 12.12(a)]

CUUMM — INPUT TAPE ?
282
DITTO FUNCTION ?
rew
CUUMM — OUTPUT TAPE?
282
DITTO FUNCTION ?

tpd ——— Prints records in deblocked character format [see Figure 12.12(b)]

CUUMM — INPUT TAPE?
282
LOGICAL REC LNTH ?
80
DITTO FUNCTION ?
rew, 282
DITTO FUNCTION ?

tdd ——— Prints records in deblocked character and hex format [see Figure 12.12(c)]

CUUMM — INPUT TAPE ?
282
LOGICAL REC LNTH ?
80
DITTO FUNCTION ?
rew, 282
DITTO FUNCTION ?

Note: User responses are shown in lower case; DITTO Prompts are shown in upper case. Grouping responses (e.g. rew, 282) suppresses a prompt.

Figure 12.11 DITTO Commands from Console

Figure 12.12a TP (Tape to Printer Unblocked in Character Format)
note: Three blocks (i.e., all 27 records) are shown

```
REC   1   DATA   80
REC   2   DATA   80
REC   3   DATA   80
REC   4   DATA   80
REC   5   DATA   80
REC   6   DATA   60
REC   7   DATA   80
REC   8   DATA   80
REC   9   DATA   60
REC  10   DATA   60
```

```
DITTO SAMPLE DATA 000000   0000000000000000000000000000000000000000000000000001
DITTO SAMPLE DATA 000000   0000000000000000000000000000000000000000000000000002
DITTO SAMPLE DATA 000000   0000000000000000000000000000000000000000000000000003
DITTO SAMPLE DATA 000000   0000000000000000000000000000000000000000000000000004
DITTO SAMPLE DATA 000000   00000000000000000000000000000000000000000000000C0005
DITTO SAMPLE DATA 000000   0000000000000000000000000000000000000000000000000006
DITTO SAMPLE DATA 000000   0000000000000000000000000000000000000000000000000007
DITTO SAMPLE DATA 000000   0000000000000000000000000000000000000000000000000008
DITTO SAMPLE DATA 000000   0000000000000000000000000000000000000000000000000009
DITTO SAMPLE DATA 000000   0000000000000000000000000000000000000000000000000010
```

Figure 12.12b TPD (Tape to Printer Delocked in Character Format)
note: All 10 records from the first block are shown

```
                                                       Hex representations for columns 25 - 29
REC   1   DATA   80   CHAR   DITTO SAMPLE DATA 000000     000000000000000000000000000000000000000000000000001
                      ZONE   CCEED4ECDDDC4CCEC4FFFFFFFFFFFFFFFFFFFFFFFFFFFFFFFFFFFFFFFFFFFFFFFFFFFFFFFFFFFFFF
                      NUMR   493360214735041310000000FFFFF000000000000000000000000000000000000000000000000001
                             1...5...10...15...20...25...30...35...40...45...50...55...60...65...70...75...80
REC   2   DATA   80   CHAR   DITTO SAMPLE DATA 000000     000000000000000000000000000000000000000000000000002
                      ZONE   CCEED4ECDDDC4CCEC4FFFFFFFFFFFFFFFFFFFFFFFFFFFFFFFFFFFFFFFFFFFFFFFFFFFFFFFFFFFFFF
                      NUMR   493360214735041310000000FFFFF000000000000000000000000000000000000000000000000002
                             1...5...10...15...20...25...30...35...40...45...50...55...60...65...70...75...80
REC   3   DATA   80   CHAR   DITTO SAMPLE DATA 000000     000000000000000000000000000000000000000000000000003
                      ZONE   CCEED4ECDDDC4CCEC4FFFFFFFFFFFFFFFFFFFFFFFFFFFFFFFFFFFFFFFFFFFFFFFFFFFFFFFFFFFFFF
                      NUMR   493360214735041310000000FFFFF000000000000000000000000000000000000000000000000003
                             1...5...10...15...20...25...30...35...40...45...50...55...60...65...70...75...80
                      Indicates positions in record
```

Figure 12.12c TDD (Tape to Printer in Character Format and Hex Dump)
note: Only the first three records from the first block are shown

conversion and additional costs once the conversion is achieved (e.g., a larger supervisor and associated overhead). That, however, is not our purpose here. We wish merely to discuss various OS JCL parameters and their counterpart (or lack thereof) in DOS and/or DOS/VS.

OS JCL contains mainly DD statements (amidst a plethora of keywords), whereas DOS consists primarily of TLBL, DLBL, EXTENT, and ASSGN statements. The OS user requests space for an output file in terms of tracks, cylinders, or blocks *without caring where the file is located*. DOS requires the user to specify the starting track and cylinder (i.e., relative track), which mandates a knowledge of the pack's layout. Moreover, if the space requested is insufficient, the OS user can specify a secondary allocation in advance. No such feature exists in DOS except that the operator can allocate additional space (assuming he has a knowledge of the pack layout, which is an unrealistic requirement).

The OS user can specify, at execution time, certain file characteristics (e.g., block size). This is done through the DCB parameter with null entries in the COBOL FD (i.e., BLOCK CONTAINS 0 RECORDS). This feature provides added flexibility and may eliminate the need for additional compiles if data change. OS will also extract file information from the header label of an existing data set if that information is absent from both the COBOL program and the JCL, something DOS will not do.

Generation data sets are present in OS but absent in DOS. Thus, the OS user can use the *identical* jobstream for several generations of a file update. He merely specifies MASTER(−1), MASTER(0), or MASTER(+1) to indicate the previous, current, and next generation of a file. The DOS user must continually alter his JCL and is more susceptible to using the wrong version of a file. (The commonly chosen DOS alternative is to have the same name for both the input and output version of a file.)

DISP=(NEW,CATLG) presents a tremendous advantage for the OS user. The system catalog keeps track of the names, volumes, and locations of all data sets. In a DOS environment, however, this bookkeeping is done manually, although VSAM files do have their own catalog and hence offer a large improvement. There is, however, no corresponding feature for DOS tape management and/or other direct-access files.

Newer releases of DOS incorporate some OS-type features. DOS/VS users can avail themselves of a procedure library, although private procedure libraries do not exist in DOS. DOS/VS permits generic assignments which allow selection of a device type rather than a particular device. OS, however, has greater device independence in that an incoming sequential file can be contained on either tape or disk with one set of JCL; DOS has TLBL and DLBL statements for tape and disk, respectively.

A distinct disadvantage of DOS is that the user must specify, in advance, in which partition his job will run. This requires that sufficient I/O devices be allocated to the appropriate partition. (Indeed, prior to the availability of generic assign statements, the user had to specify the particular I/O device as well.) Moreover, since each DOS partition has its own queue, the situation can frequently arise where one or more partitions are idle, with resources going to waste. The OS user has no such concern. He never cares where his job runs or which devices to use. The system automatically allocates I/O devices and does it in an optimal manner. Thus, disk drives are allocated from an overall pool, as opposed to being dedicated to a single partition. An immediate benefit is that additional drives can be put to work immediately, whereas DOS jobstreams require considerable alteration of ASSGN statements.

SUMMARY

Job Control Language (JCL) is the means whereby the programmer communicates with an operating system. Sufficient JCL for DOS was presented to enable the programmer to do basic file processing. Newer features of DOS/VS were also covered. These included generic assignments and the use of procedures. DITTO, a general-purpose utility, was also discussed.

Finally, we suggest the following references to obtain additional information:

1. *DOS/VS System Control Statements* (GC33-5376).

2. *DOS/VS ANS COBOL Programmer's Guide* (SC28-6478).

A synopsis of the various JCL statements and their functions is listed:

JOB:	Indicates a new job and its job name
OPTION:	Specifies the options to be in effect for the duration of the job. Any options included in this statement override those established at SYSGEN. Any omitted options default to those of the SYSGEN.
EXEC:	Causes the execution of a program
/*:	Indicates the end of a file or data set (this statement appears at the end of a COBOL deck because the COBOL deck is the data for the program FCOBOL)
/&:	Indicates the end of a job
/+:	Indicates the end of a procedure
*:	Indicates a comment
ASSGN:	Links a symbolic device to a physical device; it is required only if the temporary assignment is different from the permanent assignment
PAUSE:	Temporarily suspends execution; it enables the programmer to to make requests of the operator, such as mounting a particular volume
LBLTYP:	Required for label processing of tape and nonsequential disk files; it is not used when processing sequential disk files
TLBL:	Contains information for label processing of tape files
DLBL:	Contains information for label processing of disk files
EXTENT:	Specifies the exact location(s) of a file on disk

The JOB statement is always the first in a jobstream. It is followed by an OPTION statement, if one is present. ASSGN, DLBL, and EXTENT cards *precede* their associated EXEC statement in the order listed. The LBLTYP statement is required before EXEC LNKEDT if label processing is requested for tape and nonsequential disk; it is *not* used with sequential disk processing.

The link between the TLBL, DLBL, and COBOL SELECT statements was discussed thoroughly. DOS JCL is relatively easy, and only a little practice is necessary to become thoroughly comfortable with it. You should expect, however, to make several errors, especially in the beginning. As a guide to understanding your mistakes, and also as a teaching aid, we offer a list of common JCL *errors to avoid*.

1. Incorrect format—*all* statements (except for /* and /&) require // in columns 1 and 2 and a space in column 3. Too often, this simple rule is violated as in //JOB.

2. Misspelling of key words—TLBL, DLBL, ASSGN, LNKEDT, and LBLTYP are correct spellings. Beginners, and accomplished programmers as well, are guilty of many variations.

3. Incomplete information for label processing—a TLBL or DLBL statement is required for label processing of tape and disk files, respectively. The LBLTYP card is also required for tape and nonsequential disk files. Finally, the phrase LABEL RECORDS ARE STANDARD must be present in the COBOL FD if label processing is desired.

4. Incorrect placement of LBLTYP—this statement, if present, must immediately precede the EXEC LNKEDT card.

5. Incorrect correspondence between COBOL SELECT and JCL—the SYS number in the COBOL SELECT must match with appropriate TLBL and DLBL statements.

6. Invalid extents—all disk files require one or more EXTENT statements, and frequently this information is incorrect or miscopied. This error may produce a cryptic message LOGICAL TRANSIENT AREA CANCELLED.

7. Incorrect volume (i.e., tape reel or disk pack)—this can result from several causes. The programmer might request the wrong volume, or the operator may fail to mount the volume requested by the programmer. Even if neither of these situations occurs, the system may still think it has the wrong volume because incorrect (i.e., nonmatching) label information was supplied in the TLBL or DLBL statement.

8. Omission of OPTION LINK with EXEC LNKEDT—NOLINK is usually established as the default option at SYSGEN. Thus, if a program is to be link-edited after compilation, OPTION LINK must be specified.

9. Omission of ASSGN statement(s)—an ASSGN statement is not necessary if the temporary assignment matches the permanent assignment. In the majority of instances, this is not the case and a separate ASSGN card is required for every device where the assignments do not match.

REVIEW EXERCISES

true	*false*	1. Every JCL statement begins with // in columns 1 and 2.
true	*false*	2. Every jobstream must contain one and only one /& card.
true	*false*	3. Every jobstream must contain one and only one /* card.
true	*false*	4. There may be more than one EXEC statement within a jobstream.
true	*false*	5. The /* statement is the last card in a deck.
true	*false*	6. Comments are not permitted on JCL statements.
true	*false*	7. The PAUSE statement suspends processing for 2 minutes.
true	*false*	8. The LBLTYP statement must be present whenever label processing is performed.
true	*false*	9. The ASSGN statement is required only when a permanent assignment matches a temporary assignment.
true	*false*	10. The COBOL SELECT statement matches the SYS number in a DLBL or TLBL card.
true	*false*	11. A TLBL card is mandatory whenever a tape file is processed.
true	*false*	12. The SYS number in the DLBL statement must match the SYS number in the EXTENT card that follows it.
true	*false*	13. A given file can have more than one EXTENT statement.
true	*false*	14. The formula to calculate the relative track from a cylinder and track address is device-dependent.
true	*false*	15. The expiration date of a file is specified on its EXTENT card.
true	*false*	16. The ASSGN statement equates a logical (symbolic) device to a physical device.
true	*false*	17. There is only one type of internal label.
true	*false*	18. The LBLTYP statement (if required) immediately follows the EXEC LNKEDT statement.
true	*false*	19. The code parameter in the DLBL card must always be specified.
true	*false*	20. The ASSGN statement *must* specify a particular device rather than a device type.
true	*false*	21. Generic assignments are not permitted for tape.
true	*false*	22. A disk drive may be simultaneously assigned to programs in different partitions.
true	*false*	23. A tape drive may be simultaneously assigned to programs in different partitions.

true	*false*	**24.** A generic assignment is a permanent assignment.
true	*false*	**25.** Parameters in the OPTION statement may be listed in any order.
true	*false*	**26.** Parameters in the TLBL statement may be listed in any order.
true	*false*	**27.** DITTO commands may be entered from either the console or the job-stream.
true	*false*	**28.** // UPSI 1 indicates that DITTO commands will be entered in the job-stream.
true	*false*	**29.** DITTO commands entered from cards are free-form (i.e., they do not require coding in any specific columns).
true	*false*	**30.** DITTO cannot be used to go "card to tape."

PROBLEMS

1. Show the DOS JCL to compile, link edit, and execute a COBOL program. The program reads a deck of cards (CARD-FILE) and writes them on tape (TAPE-FILE). Your JCL must accommodate all of the following:

    (a) Suppress Procedure and Data Division maps as well as the COBOL listing. A dump is required in the event of ABEND.

    (b) Perform label processing as follows:
        (1) Assign an expiration date of 1/1/80 to the tape file,
        (2) Assign file and volume identifiers of NEW TAPE MASTER and 123456, respectively.

    (c) Cause the operator to mount a scratch tape which will be saved as student tape #1 (external label).

    (d) Use 00C and 183 as the addresses of the card reader and tape drive, respectively.

    (e) Show appropriate COBOL SELECT statements.

2. Show the DOS JCL to compile, link edit, and execute a COBOL program that will create an ISAM file from cards. You are to accommodate all of the following:

    (a) Procedure Division and Data Division maps are required, as is a dump in the event of an unplanned termination.

    (b) An object deck is to be produced.

    (c) *Show* COBOL SELECTS for CARD-FILE, PRINT-FILE, and DISK-FILE; the latter is the ISAM file to be created.

    (d) The cylinder index is to be on the first five tracks of cylinder 60. Independent overflow is to take all of cylinders 61 and 62. Prime data area is to extend for all of cylinders 63-72. (Volume ID is 222222.) Assume a 2311.

    (e) 00C, 00F, and 191 are the addresses of the card reader, printer, and disk device, respectively.

    (f) Retain the newly created ISAM file for 2 weeks.

    (g) Create standard labels (supply necessary DLBL parameters).

3. Show the DOS JCL to execute a COBOL program UPDATE that has been cataloged in the core image library. The program UPDATE merges transactions from a tape file

(SYS010) and a sequential disk file (SYS014) to create a new sequential disk file (SYS015). Accommodate all of the following:

(a) Produce a dump in the event of an ABEND.
(b) Perform label processing:
    (1) Existing tape file—file serial number is 111111
    (2) Existing disk file—volume serial number is 222222
                  —file identifier is DISK-MASTER
    (3) New disk file—file identifier is NEW-FILE
            —retain 100 days
            —volume serial number is 222222
(c) Old disk file begins at cylinder 30, track 0, and goes for 100 tracks. New disk file begins at cylinder 60 and goes for 110 tracks. (Assume a 2314 device.)
(d) Use 181 and 281 as the tape and disk address, respectively.
(e) Instruct the operator to mount tape 000123 and disk pack 000456.

Appendices

Multiprogramming and Spooling

Multiprogramming is of paramount importance. The DOS/VS user, in particular, is constantly reminded of this by hearing terms such as POWER, Background, Foreground-1, and so on, on a daily basis. Although the COBOL programmer does not require any knowledge of systems programming, we believe that some basic understanding of multiprogramming is highly beneficial. Accordingly, we use this appendix to develop concepts of multiprogramming. We also allude to POWER, a program contained in DOS/VS, without which multiprogramming under DOS would be extremely difficult. Our discussion is by no means complete but is intended only as an introduction to the subject. IBM references are given at the end of the appendix.

This appendix can also be beneficial to the OS user who does not have a conceptual understanding of multiprogramming. Although the OS terms are different (e.g., region versus partition), the concepts are so basic as to have meaning in any environment. In addition, HASP is an OS counterpart to POWER, so a basic understanding of this important package can be gained as well.

371

OVERLAP

One of the most significant advances of third-generation computers (e.g., System 360) was the ability to overlap I/O operations with CPU processing. In other words, input, processing, and output were carried on *simultaneously* through the presence of hardware devices known as *channels*. These devices contain their own logic circuitry and are responsible for executing all instructions associated with I/O operations. Simultaneous I/O and processing is known as *overlap* and is illustrated in Figure A.1.

In Figure A.1 several events occur simultaneously. For example, record 3 is read, while record 2 is processed, while record 1 is output. In similar fashion, record 4 is read, record 3 is processed, and record 2 is output all at the same time. Note that at the end of 12 time intervals 10 records have been read, processed, and output. (The reader should realize that without overlap, a given time interval could accommodate only one operation; i.e. reading, or processing, or writing. Accordingly, only four records would complete all three operations after 12 intervals.)

Figure A.1 is overly simplistic because the input, processing, and output of one record are all depicted as taking identical amounts of time. In practice, I/O operations typically take longer than processing, although the reverse can also be true. Figures A.2 and A.3 depict more realistic situations.

Figure A.2 has the caption "I/O Bound Program," indicating that the time to completion of the entire job is constrained by the I/O devices rather than the CPU. In other words, increasing the speed of the I/O devices in Figure A.2 would decrease the completion time of the overall job. However, increasing the CPU speed in an I/O bound program would have no effect on the overall completion time. (During actual execution, the sequences depicted in this and subsequent illustrations vary slightly, depending on blocking and/or the use of buffers.)

A Process Bound program, shown in Figure A.3, is just the opposite. Increasing I/O speeds of a process bound program has no effect on the overall completion time. However, the availability of a faster CPU would decrease the overall completion time of a process bound job.

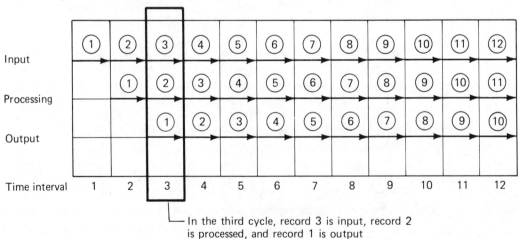

In the third cycle, record 3 is input, record 2 is processed, and record 1 is output

Figure A.1 Overlapped Processing

372

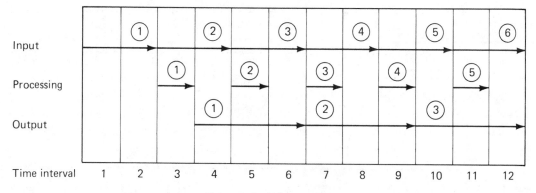

Figure A.2 I/O Bound Program

MULTIPROGRAMMING

Multiprogramming is a technique designed to increase the utilization of a system's resources. It is defined as the concurrent, not simultaneous, execution of two or more programs. Multiprogramming is accomplished by dividing main storage into two or more areas known as partitions. Each partition is assigned a priority which governs allocation of the CPU resource (i.e., if two or more partitions are in contention for the CPU, it will go to the one with the highest priority).

Figure A.4 illustrates multiprogramming in two partitions, foreground and background. The foreground partition is assigned the higher priority (i.e., the program executing in foreground will have the CPU whenever it needs it). The program executing in background has access to the CPU only when foreground does not require it. It is important to emphasize that at any given instant of time, the CPU is executing instructions from only one program (i.e., it executes only one instruction at a time).

Let us analyze Figure A.4. The program in the foreground has finished processing the first record at the end of the fourth interval. At that point, the supervisor initiates a write operation and determines which, if any, partitions require the CPU. Control is passed to the background partition which processes its first record.

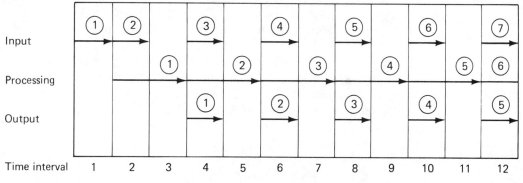

Figure A.3 Process Bound Program

373

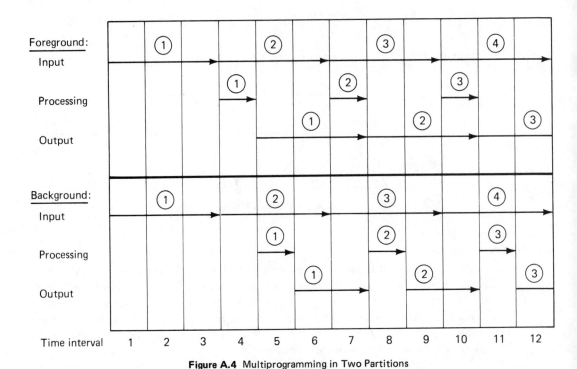

Figure A.4 Multiprogramming in Two Partitions

At the end of the fifth interval, the program in the background issues an I/O interrupt. The supervisor initiates the output operation for the first record in background and looks for another program to begin processing. However, since foreground is still waiting for the input operation of its second record to complete, the CPU is idle during the sixth interval. At the end of the sixth interval, an I/O interrupt is issued, signaling the end of the input operation for the second record in foreground. The CPU begins processing the second record and the cycle continues. In essence, multiprogramming enables work from two programs to be accomplished concurrently.

The success of multiprogramming is highly dependent on the program mix (i.e., which programs are run in which partitions). *As a general rule, I/O bound programs should run in partitions with high priority, whereas CPU bound programs should run in partitions with lower priority.* This is made readily apparent by analysis of Figure A.5(a) and (b).

Figure A.5(a) represents a typical multiprogramming situation in that the I/O bound program is assigned to the foreground partition. As the figure is drawn, the first record from background is processing during intervals 2 and 3. At the conclusion of the third interval, program A in the foreground partition issues an I/O interrupt signaling completion of an input operation. At that instant, both partitions are in contention for the CPU resource. Foreground, with the higher priority, gains control, and background is forced to suspend processing of its first record. At the end of the fourth interval, the foreground program completes processing and issues an I/O interrupt.

374

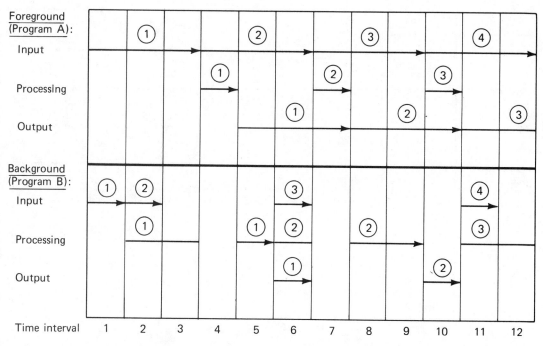

Figure A.5a Multiprogramming with I/O Bound Program in Foreground

Background then regains control and completes processing its first record. At the end of the sixth interval, foreground has completed another input operation, regains control of the CPU, and again forces background to suspend processing. The cycle continues and at the end of 12 time intervals, the program in the foreground partition has completed all operations for the first two records; has read, processed, and begun output for the third record; and has read the fourth. In addition, program B in the background partition has completed all operations for the first two records, has read and begun processing the third, and has read the fourth.

    Now consider the situation in Figure A.5(b), where the CPU bound program (program B) is assigned the foreground partition. The I/O bound program in the background partition (program A) is never able to gain control of the CPU. At the end of 12 cycles, the first three records of program B in the foreground partition have completed input, processing, and output. However, no records from program A, in the background partition, have been completely processed. Hence, to most observers, the overall throughput in Figure A.5(b) is less than in the previous case, Figure A.5(a).

    In practice, the situation is never as bleak as depicted in Figure A.5(b) because few, if any, programs are truly CPU bound. However, the program mix (i.e., the selection of which program to run in which partition) is *critical* to the overall level of throughput. This author can never forget the reaction of one student who worked as an operator on the graveyard shift for a large New York bank. "Dr. G.," he said "we do the opposite of

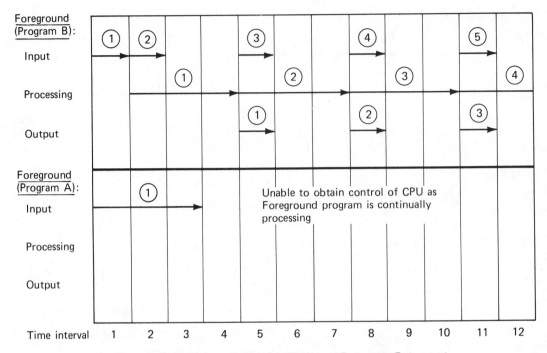

Figure A.5b Multiprogramming with CPU Bound Program in Foreground

what you suggest and run some I/O bound programs in background rather than fore-ground." After patiently suffering through the preceding lecture, he altered the program mix and excitedly reported finishing his night's work an hour and a half earlier than usual.

DOS/VS has an optional feature known as DOS/VS Advanced Function, which dynamically alters partition priorities while the system is running. For example, if the system senses an I/O bound job in the background, it would up the priority of the background partition. Commercial packages to accomplish "partition balancing" are commonly available from outside vendors with claims of 20% improvement on overall throughput.

POWER

Even with substantial multiprogramming the CPU is idle a considerable amount of time. This is due to the large discrepancy between CPU speeds, which are electronic and very high, versus unit record devices (card readers and printers), which are mechanical and rather slow. To further improve system performance, the DOS/VS user may take advantage of a service program, known as POWER, which is included in the operating system. (OS users may recognize HASP as a counterpart of POWER.)

Simply stated, *POWER is designed to increase throughput by reducing dependency on unit record I/O devices*. Punched-card input is read and stored in POWER input queues on a direct-access device before the actual start of a job. In similar fashion, a job's output is stored in an output queue, where it can be subsequently printed. Queueing

376

of input and output streams on a direct-access device is known as *spooling*; it is shown conceptually in Figure A.6.

In addition to increasing overall throughput, POWER eliminates the necessity of each partition having its own unit record I/O device (i.e., the I/O devices used by POWER can support the I/O requirements of all other partitions serviced by POWER). Another advantage of POWER is that the system can continue processing, even if a card reader, printer, or punch becomes inoperative. For example, if the card reader went down, the system could process those jobs already in the input queues on disk. Similarly, if a printer became inoperable, the system would continue to store output in the output queues until a printer became available.

This section is far from complete and intended only to introduce the reader to POWER, a DOS spooling package. The reader is referred to the *POWER/VS Work Station User's Guide* (GC33-6049-0) and/or the *DOS/VS POWER Installation Guide and Reference* (GC33-6048) for additional information.

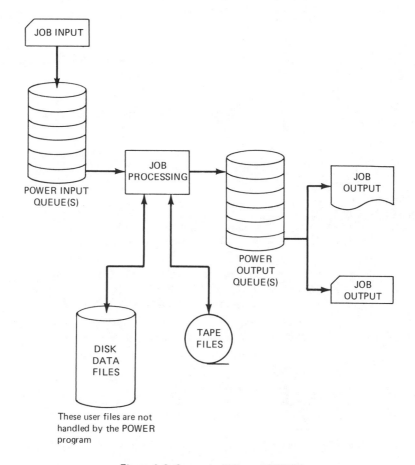

Figure A.6 Conceptual View of POWER
(Reprinted with permission of IBM)

COBOL Standards After the Fact

Few managers, if any, would argue against the desirability of coding standards in COBOL. Unfortunately, in many shops the standards manual has arrived recently, whereas the inventory of COBOL programs is several years old. Hence, the problem: How does one implement coding standards in existing COBOL programs? The authors believe they have achieved a dramatic solution in a recently released software package, known as the COBOL Structuring Aid (CSA). Additional information can be obtained from Marshal Crawford, CGA Computer Associates, 1370 Piccard Drive, Rockville, Maryland, 20850.

The COBOL Structuring Aid will realign new and/or existing COBOL programs according to installation standards. It is easy to use and *entirely* parameter driven. Specific capabilities include:

1. Record prefixing in DATA DIVISION.

2. Paragraph sequencing, unsequencing, or resequencing in PROCEDURE DIVISION.

3. Conversion to standard forms and columns for USAGE, PICTURE, and VALUE clauses.

4. Alphabetic listing of Working-Storage entries.

5. Replacement of nondescriptive data names with user-defined expanded data names.

6. Insertion or deletion of EJECTS, SKIPS, and blank lines as desired.

7. Ending, or beginning, lines on specified COBOL reserved words and/or punctuation.

8. Renumbering and indenting of level numbers.

9. Indentation of nested IFs, with relevant ELSE appearing under associated IF, to highlight possible logic errors.

10. Indentation of one reserved word under another (e.g., AT END under READ, INVALID KEY under WRITE, etc.).

11. Removal of commas in the PROCEDURE DIVISION.

12. Replacement of $>$, $<$, and $=$ symbols with expanded relational operators.

13. Multi-line stacking of OPEN filenames and CALL arguments.

Any and all of these capabilities are implemented through "English-like" commands. The purpose of this appendix is to give a *brief* overview of the COBOL Structuring Aid. This will be accomplished through a series of examples, each consisting of a COBOL listing "before and after," coupled with the necessary command(s). The comments accompanying each listing are brief, as the listings speak eloquently for themselves. Moreover, only a limited number of commands are illustrated in this appendix. Additional information is contained in the User's Manual and Reference Card (Figure B.11).

A series of examples follow:

EXAMPLE 1—Vertical Alignment of PICTURE, VALUE, and USAGE Clauses

The PICTURE, VALUE, and/or USAGE clauses can be reformatted to begin in user-specified columns. One must, however, exercise fore-thought in determining the desired action if a specified column is inappropriate. This is done through the FLOAT parameter, which indicates how far one is willing to go to the right and still retain the same line. Thus, the command PICTURE COLUMN 44 FLOAT 3 will attempt to begin all PICTURE clauses in column 44, and if impossible will go up to column 47 before dropping to a new line.

Use of the FLOAT parameter is illustrated in Figure B.1. Note the different action regarding the last two data names. The PICTURE clause for UN-ALTERNATE-CDE-B is floated three positions to the right and remains on the same line. However, the PICTURE clause for UN-ALTERNATE-CDE-BA would have to be floated four positions to remain on the same line. Since this exceeds the command specification, it is dropped to a new line.

```
COMMANDS
    PICTURE  COLUMN 44 FLOAT 3 ──── Determines how far one is
    USAGE    COLUMN 20 FLOAT 0      willing to go 'to the right'
    VALUE    COLUMN 58

INPUT:
    DATA DIVISION.
    01  UNIFORM-COLUMNS.
        05  UN-DESK-CODE      PIC S9(3)   VALUE 015     COMP-3.
        05  UN-ALTERNATE-CODES.
            10  UN-ALTERNATE-CDE-B   PIC S9(3)   VALUE 18.
            10  UN-ALTERNATE-CDE-BA  PIC S9(3)   VALUE 19.

OUTPUT:
                        USAGE clause forced to new line
                                                        PICTURE clause floated 3 columns to right
    DATA DIVISION.
    01  UNIFORM-COLUMNS.
        05  UN-DESK-CODE               PIC S9(3)     VALUE 015
            COMP-3.                                                  ── Vertical alignment of
        05  UN-ALTERNATE-CODES.                                        VALUE clause
            10  UN-ALTERNATE-CDE-B  PIC S9(3)   VALUE 18.
            10  UN-ALTERNATE-CDE-BA
                                    PIC S9(3)       VALUE 19.

                        PICTURE clause forced to new line since more
                        than 3 float positions are required
```

Figure B.1   Vertical Alignment of PICTURE, USAGE, and VALUE Clauses

EXAMPLE 2—*Standard Forms of PICTURE, USAGE, and VALUE Clauses*

PICTURE, USAGE, and VALUE clauses are converted to standard forms through the CONVERT command, as shown in Figure B.2. (Column alignment may require specification of additional commands, as shown in the previous example.)

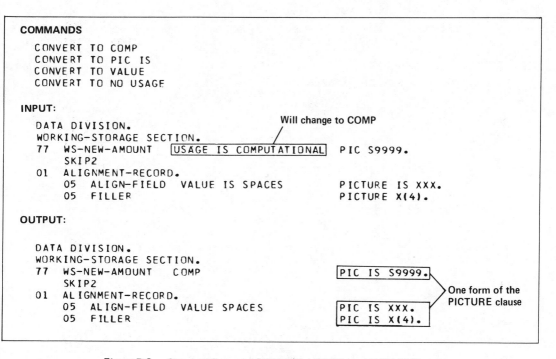

Figure B.2   Standard Forms of PICTURE, USAGE, and VALUE Clauses

EXAMPLE 3—Altering Level Numbers

The RENUMBER and INDENT commands are used to realign 01 records. Their sometimes dramatic effects are self-evident in Figure B.3.

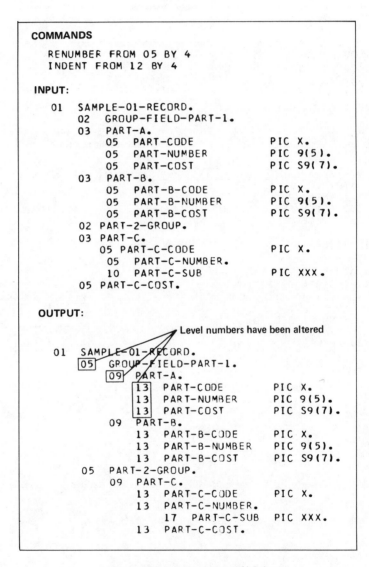

```
COMMANDS

  RENUMBER FROM 05 BY 4
  INDENT FROM 12 BY 4

INPUT:

  01   SAMPLE-01-RECORD.
       02  GROUP-FIELD-PART-1.
       03  PART-A.
           05   PART-CODE            PIC X.
           05   PART-NUMBER          PIC 9(5).
           05   PART-COST            PIC S9(7).
       03  PART-B.
           05   PART-B-CODE          PIC X.
           05   PART-B-NUMBER        PIC 9(5).
           05   PART-B-COST          PIC S9(7).
       02 PART-2-GROUP.
       03 PART-C.
          05 PART-C-CODE             PIC X.
           05   PART-C-NUMBER.
           10   PART-C-SUB           PIC XXX.
       05 PART-C-COST.

OUTPUT:

                              Level numbers have been altered

  01   SAMPLE-01-RECORD.
       05  GROUP-FIELD-PART-1.
           09  PART-A.
               13   PART-CODE        PIC X.
               13   PART-NUMBER      PIC 9(5).
               13   PART-COST        PIC S9(7).
           09  PART-B.
               13   PART-B-CODE      PIC X.
               13   PART-B-NUMBER    PIC 9(5).
               13   PART-B-COST      PIC S9(7).
       05  PART-2-GROUP.
           09   PART-C.
               13   PART-C-CODE      PIC X.
               13   PART-C-NUMBER.
                   17   PART-C-SUB   PIC XXX.
               13   PART-C-COST.
```

Figure B.3   Altering Level Numbers

382

EXAMPLE 4—Insertion of EJECTs, SKIPs, and/or Blank Lines

EJECTs, SKIPs, and blank lines can be inserted before or after COBOL reserved words, division and/or section headers, and/or paragraph names. Any such lines created by this command supersede similar lines in the original program (e.g., specification of blank lines before paragraph names will eliminate existing SKIPs before paragraph names). In addition, existing EJECTs, SKIPs, and/or blank lines may be removed by a DELETE command (not shown in illustration). Figure B.4 shows the necessary commands.

COMMANDS

```
   EJECT BEFORE DIVISION
   BLANK BEFORE PARAGRAPH
   SKIP1 BEFORE ACCEPT
```

INPUT:

```
   IDENTIFICATION DIVISION.
   PROGRAM-ID. SP0300.          ─── Replaced by EJECT in output
      SKIP1
   ENVIRONMENT DIVISION.
   CONFIGURATION SECTION.
   DATA DIVISION.
   WORKING-STORAGE SECTION.
   77  WS-TOTAL-AMT                  PIC S9(5)
   77  WS-ANOTHER-FIELD              PIC X.
   77  THIRD-ENTRY                   PIC XX.
   PROCEDURE DIVISION.
      SKIP1                ─── Replaced by blank line in output
   010-HSKPG.
      MOVE SPACES TO THIRD-ENTRY.
   020-CONTINUE.
      MOVE SPACES TO WS-ANOTHER-FIELD.
      MOVE 5 TO WS-TOTAL-AMT.
      IF WS-TOTAL-AMT = 5,
         ACCEPT THIRD-ENTRY.
      STOP RUN.
```

OUTPUT:

```
   IDENTIFICATION DIVISION.

   PROGRAM-ID. SP0300.
      EJECT
   ENVIRONMENT DIVISION.
   CONFIGURATION SECTION.
      EJECT
   DATA DIVISION.
```

Figure B.4 Insertion of EJECTs, SKIPs, and/or Blank Lines

```
WORKING-STORAGE SECTION.
77   WS-TOTAL-AMT                        PIC S9(5)
77   WS-ANOTHER-FIELD                    PIC X.
77   THIRD-ENTRY                         PIC XX.
     EJECT
PROCEDURE DIVISION.

010-HSKPG.
     MOVE SPACES TO THIRD-ENTRY.                Blank lines inserted before paragraph names

020-CONTINUE.
     MOVE SPACES TO WS-ANOTHER-FIELD.
     MOVE 5 TO WS-TOTAL-AMT.
     IF WS-TOTAL-AMT = 5,
     SKIP 1
         ACCEPT THIRD-ENTRY.
     STOP RUN.
```

Figure B.4   Insertion of EJECTs, SKIPs, and/or Blank Lines (continued)

EXAMPLE 5—Sorting Entries in Working-Storage

The SORT command rearranges 77 level entries in alphabetical order. As can be seen from Figure B.5, the user may specify that only a subset (or subsets) of 77 level entries is to be sorted. Thus, the first FILLER entry WS BEGINS HERE is unchanged as a result of the sort.

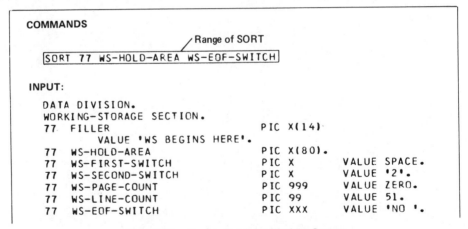

Figure B.5   Sorting Entries in Working-Storage

384

OUTPUT:

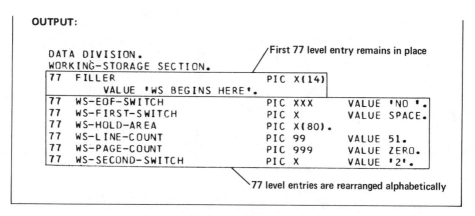

```
DATA DIVISION.                                    First 77 level entry remains in place
WORKING-STORAGE SECTION.
77   FILLER                      PIC X(14)
          VALUE 'WS BEGINS HERE'.
77   WS-EOF-SWITCH               PIC XXX      VALUE 'NO '.
77   WS-FIRST-SWITCH             PIC X        VALUE SPACE.
77   WS-HOLD-AREA                PIC X(80).
77   WS-LINE-COUNT               PIC 99       VALUE 51.
77   WS-PAGE-COUNT               PIC 999      VALUE ZERO.
77   WS-SECOND-SWITCH            PIC X        VALUE '2'.
```

77 level entries are rearranged alphabetically

Figure B.5   Sorting Entries in Working-Storage (continued)

EXAMPLE 6—Renaming

COBOL permits data names of up to 30 characters. Programmers, complaining of writer's cramp, typically use short, nondescriptive data names, and thereby defeat the self-documentation intent of COBOL. The RENAME command addresses this problem.

This command is a simple substitution—one character string for another. Renaming takes place in all divisions. Renaming may be used in conjunction with record prefixing and/or paragraph sequencing. Figure B.6 illustrates the RENAME command in isolation.

```
COMMANDS
    RENAME CD-FL TO CARD-FILE
    RENAME SW-A WS-PERFORMANCE-SWITCH
    R HSKP  010-HOUSE-KEEPING
              Alternate specification of RENAME command

INPUT:
    INPUT-OUTPUT SECTION.
    FILE-CONTROL.
        SELECT CD-FL ASSIGN TO UT-S-CARDFL.
    DATA DIVISION.
    FILE SECTION.
    FD  CD-FL
            LABEL RECORDS ARE OMITTED.
    01  CARD-RECORD                  PIC X(80).
    WORKING-STORAGE SECTION.
    77  SW-A                         PIC X      VALUE SPACE.

    PROCEDURE DIVISION.

    HSKP.
        MOVE '1' TO SW-A.
        OPEN INPUT CD-FL.
```

Figure B.6   Renaming

```
    INPUT-OUTPUT SECTION.
    FILE-CONTROL.
        SELECT CARD-FILE  ASSIGN TO UT-S-CARDFL.
    DATA DIVISION.
    FILE SECTION.                        CARD-FILE is renamed
    FD  CARD-FILE                        in 3 divisions
            LABEL RECORDS ARE OMITTED.
    01  CARD-RECORD                      PIC X(80).
    WORKING-STORAGE SECTION.
    77  WS-PERFORMANCE-SWITCH            PIC X        VALUE SPACE.

    PROCEDURE DIVISION.

    010-HOUSE-KEEPING.
        MOVE '1' TO WS-PERFORMANCE-SWITCH.
        OPEN INPUT CARD-FILE.
```

Figure B.6   Renaming (continued)

EXAMPLE 7—Record Prefixing

The PREFIX command makes feasible the addition of a common prefix to each data name in an 01 entry, and also to all 77-level entries. The Structuring Aid ensures that correct COBOL syntax is maintained by negating the prefix command on a particular data name if the newly prefixed data name exceeds 30 characters. The user can override the negation through the TRUNCATE option, which retains the prefix but removes the extra characters.

As can be seen from Figure B.7, omission of the TRUNCATE option negates the prefix if the newly prefixed data name exceeds 30 characters. Truncation is from right to left. Note that a data name will not be reprefixed if it already contains the prefix (see WS-ALREADY-PREFIXED). Naturally prefixing is carried through the procedure division.

```
COMMANDS
    PREFIX ALL-77 BY WS-
    PREFIX UNPREFIXED-RECORD BY UNION-   TRUNCATE
    PREFIX OTHER-RECORD BY RT-

INPUT:
    DATA DIVISION.
    WORKING-STORAGE SECTION.
    77  TOTAMT              Data-name will not be prefixed twice  PIC 9(6).
    77  CODE-AMOUNT                               PIC 99.
    77  WS-ALREADY-PREFIXED                       PIC X.

    01  UNPREFIXED-RECORD.
        05  TWENTY-FIVE-CHARACTERSX-X            PIC X.
        05  TWENTY-SIX-CHARACTERS-LONG           PIC XXX.
        05  SHORTER-FIELD                        PIC XX.
```

Figure B.7   Record Prefixing

```
01   OTHER-RECORD.
     05   SPECIAL-CODE                              PIC X.
     05   THIRTY-CHARACTERS-LONG-OVERALL            PIC X.
     05   SHORTER-NAMES.
          10   ABLE-TO-PREFIX                       PIC 99.
PROCEDURE DIVISION.
     MOVE SPEC-CDE TO TWENTY-FIVE-CHARACTERSX-X.
```

OUTPUT:

```
DATA DIVISION.                              77 level entries prefixed by WS-
WORKING-STORAGE SECTION.
77   WS-TOTAMT                                 PIC 9(6).
77   WS-CODE-AMOUNT                            PIC 99.
77   WS-ALREADY-PREFIXED                       PIC X.


01   UNION-UNPREFIXED-RECORD.
     05   UNION-TWENTY-FIVE-CHARACTERSX        PIC X.   ┐ Two characters were
     05   UNION-TWENTY-SIX-CHARACTERS-LO       PIC XXX. │ truncated to
     05   UNION-SHORTER-FIELD                  PIC XX.  ┘ accommodate prefix


01   RT-OTHER-RECORD.
     05   RT-SPECIAL-CODE                      PIC X.
     05   THIRTY-CHARACTERS-LONG-OVERALL       PIC X.   ┐ Prefix negated since
     05   RT-SHORTER-NAMES.                             │ TRUNCATE
          10   RT-ABLE-TO-PREFIX               PIC 99.  │ option was
PROCEDURE DIVISION.                                       not specified and data
     MOVE SPEC-CDE TO UNION-TWENTY-FIVE-CHARACTERSX.      name is already 30
                                                          characters
```

Figure B.7   Record Prefixing (continued)

EXAMPLE 8—Paragraph Sequencing

Paragraph names are easily sequenced, and multiple sequence commands may be applied to the same program, as shown in Figure B.8. The SEQUENCE and RENAME commands are compatible provided paragraphs mentioned in a SEQUENCE command are specified as they exist *after* the RENAME.

There is also an UNSEQUENCE command (not shown in this appendix), which permits paragraphs to be unsequenced and/or *resequenced*.

COMMANDS

```
SEQ BEGIN THRU END-MAINLINE FROM 100- BY 50
SEQ WRITE-ALL-RECORDS THRU END FROM A010- BY 10
RENAME HANDLE-INPUT TO A-HANDLE-INPUT
RENAME PROCESS TO PROCESS-ALL-RECORDS
```

INPUT:

```
PROCEDURE DIVISION.
HOUSEKEEPING.
     OPEN INPUT INPUT-FILE OUTPUT OUT-FILE.
READ-FIRST-RECORD.
     READ INPUT-FILE, AT END DISPLAY 'NO INPUT'.
```

Figure B.8   Paragraph Sequencing

387

```
┌─────────┐
│PROCESS.│
└─────────┘
      PERFORM HANDLE-INPUT ──────────── Paragraph name will be both
           UNTIL EOF-SWITCH = 'E'.     sequenced and renamed
  END-MAINLINE.
      CLOSE INPUT-FILE OUTPUT-FILE.
      STOP RUN.
  HANDLE-INPUT SECTION.
  WRITE-ALL-RECORDS.
      MOVE INPUT-RECORD TO OUTPUT-RECORD.
      ADD 1 TO INPUT-COUNT.
      WRITE-OUTPUT-RECORD.
  READ-NEXT-RECORD.
      READ INPUT-FILE AT END MOVE 'E' TO EOF-SWITCH.
```

OUTPUT:

```
  PROCEDURE DIVISION.
  100-HOUSEKEEPING.
      OPEN INPUT INPUT-FILE OUTPUT OUT-FILE.
  150-READ-FIRST-RECORD.
      READ INPUT-FILE, AT END DISPLAY 'NO INPUT'.
  ┌──────────────────────────┐
  │200-PROCESS-ALL-RECORDS.  │────── RENAME in conjunction
  └──────────────────────────┘        with SEQUENCE
      PERFORM A-HANDLE-INPUT
           UNTIL EOF-SWITCH = 'E'.
  250-END-MAINLINE.
      CLOSE INPUT-FILE OUTPUT-FILE.
      STOP RUN. ──────────────────── Simple RENAME
  ┌──────────────────────────┐
  │A-HANDLE-INPUT SECTION.   │
  ├──────────────────────────┤
  │A010-WRITE-ALL-RECORDS.   │
  └──────────────────────────┘
      MOVE INPUT-RECORD TO OUTPUT-RECORD.
      ADD 1 TO INPUT-COUNT. ──────────── Second set of sequenced
      WRITE-OUTPUT-RECORD.                paragraphs
  ┌──────────────────────────┐
  │A020-READ-NEXT-RECORD.    │
  └──────────────────────────┘
      READ INPUT-FILE AT END MOVE 'E' TO EOF-SWITCH.
```

Figure B.8   Paragraph Sequencing (continued)

EXAMPLE 9—IF/ELSE Alignment

The Structuring Aid provides the capability for IF/ELSE alignment according to compiler rather than programmer interpretation. The ALIGN command causes the ELSE clause to appear under its associated IF, and further to indent detail lines under both IF and ELSE. There is total flexibility as to the number of columns between successive IFs and also for the detail indentation. Blank lines are inserted before each IF in a nested IF, but this can be overridden.

The AFTER command is used to indent common pairs of verbs (e.g., AT END under READ, UNTIL under PERFORM, etc.). The AFTER and ALIGN commands are completely compatible and produce some astounding results, as shown in Figure B.9. Note well that alignment produced by the AFTER command is *subservient* to IF/ELSE indentations.

```
COMMANDS
    AFTER PERFORM GO OVER 2 ON VARYING
    AFTER PERFORM GO OVER 4 ON UNTIL
    AFTER PERFORM GO OVER 2 ON AFTER
    ALIGN IF FROM 12 BY 4 DETAIL OVER 4
    END LINE ON COMMA

INPUT:
    PROCEDURE DIVISION.
    INPUT-CODE-A.
        IF INPUT-CODE = 'A', MOVE INPUT-NAME TO HOLD-NAME
        IF INPUT-AMOUNT IS GREATER THAN 100
        PERFORM ADJUST-AMOUNT VARYING WS-SUB
        FROM 1 BY 1 UNTIL WS-SUB IS GREATER THAN 10
        AFTER HOLD-SUB FROM 1 BY 1 UNTIL HOLD-SUB IS EQUAL TO 8
        ELSE, NEXT SENTENCE ELSE, DISPLAY INPUT-NAME.

OUTPUT:
    PROCEDURE DIVISION.
    INPUT-CODE-A.
                                          VARYING indented 2 columns
                                          under PERFORM
        IF INPUT-CODE = 'A',
            MOVE INPUT-NAME TO HOLD-NAME

        IF INPUT-AMOUNT IS GREATER THAN 100
            PERFORM ADJUST-AMOUNT
              VARYING WS-SUB                  UNTIL indented 4 columns
              FROM 1 BY 1                      under PERFORM
                UNTIL WS-SUB IS GREATER THAN 10
              AFTER HOLD-SUB FROM 1 BY 1
                UNTIL HOLD-SUB IS EQUAL TO 8
        ELSE,
            NEXT SENTENCE
    ELSE,
        DISPLAY INPUT-NAME.

    IF/ELSE alignment
```

Figure B.9   IF/ELSE Alignment

EXAMPLE 10—Removal of Commas

The comma is treated as noise in COBOL (i.e., its presence in the procedure division has no effect on compiler interpretation). Initially, many programmers, the authors included, used commas to increase legibility. The trend today is to avoid commas because of the difficulty in distinguishing a comma from a period (see the guidelines in Chapter Three). The STRIP COMMA command eliminates all nonessential commas. [Please realize that elimination of commas could not be easily accomplished through a text editor because some commas are still required (e.g., between multiple subscripts, in literals, in PICTURE clauses, etc.).]

Figure B.10 shows the before and after listings associated with the STRIP COMMA command. Commas were eliminated in all nonessential places but remained where required. The presence of a second command, END LINE ON COMMA, causes

389

a Procedure Division statement to end where the comma used to be (e.g., the OPEN statement has been split into two lines by the END LINE command).

```
COMMANDS
   STRIP COMMA
   END LINE ON COMMA

INPUT:
   DATA DIVISION.
   FILE SECTION.
   FD  CARD-FILE,
           LABEL RECORDS ARE OMITTED,
           DATA RECORD IS CARD.
   01  CARD.
       05  CARD-CODE                PIC X.
           88  INVALID-CODES  VALUES ARE 'A', 'B', 'C', 'Z'.
       05  CARD-NAME                PIC X(13).
       05  CARD-INPUT-WTH-COMMA     PIC 999,999.
       05  FILLER                   PIC X(59).
   PROCEDURE DIVISION.
   HOUSEKEEPING.
       OPEN INPUT CARD-FILE, OUTPUT PRINT-FILE.
   READ-CARDS.
       READ CARD-FILE, AT END PERFORM END-OF-JOB-ROUTINE.

OUTPUT:
   DATA DIVISION.
   FILE SECTION.
   FD  CARD-FILE
           LABEL RECORDS ARE OMITTED
           DATA RECORD IS CARD.
   01  CARD.
       05  CARD-CODE                PIC X.
           88  INVALID-CODES  VALUES ARE 'A' 'B' 'C' 'Z'.    Commas have been eliminated
       05  CARD-NAME                PIC X(13).
       05  CARD-INPUT-WTH-COMMA     PIC 999,999.    Comma is retained in PICTURE
       05  FILLER                   PIC X(59).      clause
   PROCEDURE DIVISION.
   HOUSEKEEPING.
       OPEN INPUT CARD-FILE
           OUTPUT PRINT-FILE.     Comma has been stripped away,
   READ-CARDS.                    yet original line has ended
       READ CARD-FILE             where comma used to be
           AT END PERFORM END-OF-JOB-ROUTINE.
```

Figure B.10   Removal of Commas

SUMMARY

The importance of coding standards in COBOL cannot be overlooked. In this appendix, the authors presented a solution to the problem of achieving standards in existing programs. English-like commands are entered according to the syntax shown in the Reference card of Figure B.11.

2

CGA COMPUTER ASSOCIATES
1370 PICCARD DRIVE
ROCKVILLE, MARYLAND 20850
(301) 948-9600

CSA REFERENCE CARD

GENERAL COMMANDS

$$
\left\{ \begin{matrix} \text{BLANK} \\ \text{EJECT} \\ \text{SKIP1} \\ \text{SKIP2} \\ \text{SKIP3} \end{matrix} \right\}
\left\{ \begin{matrix} \text{AFTER} \\ \text{BEFORE} \end{matrix} \right\}
\left\{ \begin{matrix} \text{COPY} \\ \text{DIVISION} \\ \text{FD} \\ \text{PARAGRAPH} \\ \text{SECTION} \\ \text{01} \\ \text{COBOL verb or data name} \end{matrix} \right\}
$$

Function: Inserts a blank line, SKIP, or EJECT before or immediately after specified element.

$$
\text{DELETE} \quad \left\{ \begin{matrix} \text{ALL SKIP} \\ \text{BLANK} \\ \text{COMMENT} \\ \text{EJECT} \\ \text{SKIP1} \\ \text{SKIP2} \\ \text{SKIP3} \end{matrix} \right\} \quad \text{LINES}
$$

Function: Deletes all lines corresponding to the option chosen.

   Notes: 1. Comments are lines with an asterisk (*) in column 7.
           2. This command will not delete lines that are being added by the BLANK-SKIP-EJECT command.
           3. This command is not needed to delete an existing BLANK, SKIP or EJECT line when new ones are added by the BLANK-EJECT-SKIP command; e.g. EJECT BEFORE DIVISION replaces any blank lines, skip lines and eject lines that are currently in place before each DIVISION line

QUOTE IS "

Function: Indicates the use of double quotation mark in place of single apostrophe for entire program.

$$
\left\{ \begin{matrix} \text{RENAME} \\ \text{R} \\ \text{S} \end{matrix} \right\} \quad \text{data-name-1 TO data-name-2}
$$

Function: Replaces all occurrences of data-name-1 with data-name-2. As with all other commands, alignment on a new line is automatically handled when column 72 is exceeded.

   Notes: 1) Data-name-2 may contain one or more spaces, but total length may not exceed 30 characters. Thus, AP could be caused to expand to AFTER POSITIONING.

Figure B.11 (a)

RETAIN 73-80

Function: Retains columns 73-80 on each line of old program for use in newly aligned program.

   Notes: 1) If omitted, program name from program-id paragraph is used in 73-80 of new program.
           2) When RETAIN 73-80 is used, old lines with spaces in 73-80 and newly created lines, have program name inserted from program-id paragraph in columns 73-80.

SPECIAL OPTIONS list-of-number(s)

Function: Indicates special options over and above those specified in other commands.

   Option   1) Inserts a blank line before
   Numbers: the first IF in a nested IF. Does not insert a blank line before subsequent (nested) Ifs. Used in conjunction with the ALIGN command.
            2) Inserts a blank line after ending line of an IF statement.
            3) Same as EJECT BEFORE SECTION, except that only Procedure Division Sections are used.

STRIP COMMA

Function: Strips all commas found at the end of a data name in the Data Division or Procedure Division. Commas found embedded in PICTURE clauses are left alone.

$$
\text{SUPPRESS} \quad \left\{ \begin{matrix} \text{ALL} \\ \text{COMMANDS} \\ \text{INPUT} \\ \text{OUTPUT} \end{matrix} \right\}
$$

Function: Suppresses printing of commands, input program, newly aligned COBOL program, or all printing.

   Notes: 1) If SUPPRESS COMMANDS or SUPPRESS ALL is specified, all commands up to and including this SUPPRESS command are printed out.

DATA DIVISION COMMANDS

$$
\text{CONVERT TO} \quad \left\{ \begin{matrix} \text{COMP} \\ \text{COMPUTATIONAL} \end{matrix} \right\}
$$

$$
\text{CONVERT TO} \quad \left\{ \begin{matrix} \text{PIC} \\ \text{PIC IS} \\ \text{PICTURE} \\ \text{PICTURE IS} \end{matrix} \right\}
$$

$$
\text{CONVERT TO} \quad \left\{ \begin{matrix} \text{USAGE} \\ \text{USAGE IS} \\ \text{NO USAGE} \end{matrix} \right\}
$$

$$
\text{CONVERT TO} \quad \left\{ \begin{matrix} \text{VALUE} \\ \text{VALUE IS} \end{matrix} \right\}
$$

Function: Converts to a standard form of the COBOL reserved word(s) chosen.

   Notes: 1) CONVERT TO COMP requires CONVERT TO USAGE as well.
           2) NO USAGE specifies that USAGE and IS are to be stripped away.

Figure B.11 (b)

INDENT FROM COLUMN number-1 BY number-2

Function: Indents level numbers 02 thru 49 from a
starting column (number-1) by a standard
increment (number-2).

    Notes: 1) Number-1 must not be less than 12
or greater than 40.
2) Number-2 must not be greater than
28.

LEVEL 88 $\left\{\begin{array}{l}\text{BEGINS IN COLUMN}\\ \text{OVER}\end{array}\right\}$ number-1

Function: Forces a beginning column for 88 level
entries.

    Notes: 1) BEGINS IN COLUMN forces a uniform
column number for all 88 level
entries. (number-1 must be from
12 to 48.)
2) OVER specifies that 88 level
entry is to begin (number-1) columns from where the last level
number ends (i.e. last level number from 02-49 before the 88
level entry). Number-1 may be
zero.

LEVEL DETAIL OVER number-1

Function: Establishes an indentation of number-1 columns, relative to the existing level number's
starting column, for details starting on a
new line: e.g OCCURS, REDEFINES, INDEXED BY,
etc.

    Notes: 1. Number-1 may be either zero or a
positive number.
2. Entries belonging to a given
level entry, but starting on a
new line, begin number-1 columns
to the right of the level number.
3. 88 and/or 66 level entries are
not affected by this command.

$\left\{\begin{array}{l}\text{PICTURE}\\ \text{USAGE}\\ \text{VALUE}\end{array}\right\}$ COLUMN number-1 [FLOAT number-2]

Function: Forces a beginning column (number-1) for the
COBOL word indicated.

    Notes: 1) FLOAT specifies the number of
columns the entry can be moved
right (to retain the same line)
if it does not fit in the designated column.
2) Number-1 may be from 12 to 68.
3) Number-2 may be from 0 to 60.
4) IF FLOAT number-2 is not specified FLOAT 60 is assumed.
5) FLOAT 0 forces a new line when
the entry cannot start in the
column specified in number-1.
6) When floating is used to keep an
entry on the same line, the
entry is only floated the number
of positions needed to leave one
space between this and the previous entry.

Figure B.11 (c)

PREFIX $\left\{\begin{array}{l}\text{ALL-77}\\ \text{01-record-name}\end{array}\right\}$ BY character-string [TRUNCATE]

Function: Prefixes all 77 level entries or all data
names in an 01 record with the indicated
character-string. Prefixing on a given
entry is done throughout program.

    Notes: 1) Character-string must begin with
an alphabetic character.
2) The length of the string may not
exceed 10 positions.
3) If appropriate, put a dash (-)
as the last character for the
newly created data names.
4) If TRUNCATE is specified and the
length of the new data name with
prefix is over 30 characters,
then the new name is truncated
to 30 positions. If the 30th
position is a dash (-) it is
also truncated.
5) If TRUNCATE is not specified,
and a prefix would require that a
name over 30 positions be created,
then prefixing is not done on
that data name.
6) Any data name found having another identical data name elsewhere in the data division is not
prefixed, (i.e. names used in
qualification or as part of MOVE
CORRESPONDING are not prefixed).
7) 01-record-name in the PREFIX command must appear as it would
after renaming is done if a
RENAME command is present for
this name. No precaution is necessary if a RENAME command does
not exist for this 01-record-
name.
8) If the command is given to prefix 77 level entries or an 01
record, and a given entry already
has that prefix, then prefixing
is not done on that entry.

RENUMBER FROM number-1 BY number-2

Function: Renumbers level numbers 02 thru 49.
Number-1 specifies the starting level number (i.e. 02, 05, etc.) and number-2 specifies the increment between level numbers.

    Notes: 1) If renumbering is impossible on
any record due to exceeding 49
on an increment (e.g. RENUMBER
FROM 5 BY 5 and more than 9 different level numbers were found
in that record), renumbering is
not done on that 01 record and
a message is printed.
2) number-1 may be from 02 to 49.
3) number-2 may be from 02 to 47.

Figure B.11 (d)

$$\text{SORT} \begin{Bmatrix} 01 \\ 77 \end{Bmatrix} \begin{bmatrix} \text{name-1} & \text{name-2} \end{bmatrix}$$

Function: Sorts 77 level entries or 01 records in working-storage.

Notes: 1) name-1 is the beginning 77 level entry or 01 record name.

2) name-2 is the ending 77 level entry or 01 record name.

3) If name-1 and name-2 are omitted sorting is done on all 77 level entries or on all 01 records.

4) When sorting is done on 01 records, whole 01 records are sorted into sequence by the 01 record name. (This is useful if the 01 record name has the same prefix as the other data names in the record.) Redefinitions of 01 records (i.e. other 01 records with a redefines at the 01 level) remain with the parent 01 record that they belong to.

5) If name-1 is specified and name-2 is omitted then sorting starts at name-1 and continues for all remaining 77 or 01 entries.

6) name-1 and name-2 must not specify a data name used in a RENAME command (either as the before or after name).

PROCEDURE DIVISION COMMANDS

AFTER name-1 GO OVER number-1 ON name-2

Function: Highlights pairs of verbs; e.g. PERFORM/VARYING, READ/AT END, etc.

Notes: 1) name-1 specifies a COBOL verb (e.g. PERFORM). Name-2 specifies a second COBOL verb (e.g. VARYING). Number-1 specifies an increment in columns that name-2 will follow name-1 by.

2) Name-2 is forced to a new line if it is not already on a new line.

ALIGN IF FROM number-1 BY number-2 DETAIL OVER number-3

Function: Realigns IF statements with associated ELSE appearing directly under the corresponding IF according to compiler interpretation. Detail statements are moved over the number of columns specified in number-3.

Notes: 1) Number-1 specifies the column where the first IF of a nested IF starts.

2) Number-2 specifies the increment added to number-1 to calculate a column number for subsequent Ifs in a nested IF.

3) Number-3 specifies the increment the detail is moved from associated IF or ELSE (or OTHERWISE) column.

4) A blank line is inserted before each IF. (See SPECIAL OPTIONS, if this is not desired.)

5) Each IF and ELSE clause is automatically forced to a new line.

6) To put the word ELSE on a line by itself, see END LINE command.

7) Number-3 column can only be overridden by the AFTER command. If the latter is used, alignment of the IF statement is further enhanced.

BEGIN LINE IN COLUMNS number-1 AND number-2 ON name-1

Function: Forces a new line on selected names (name-1) and establishes two default columns (number-1 and number-2) for the COBOL word or data-name.

Notes: 1) Number-1 becomes the default column when the previous entry ended in a period.

2) Number-2 becomes the default column when the previous entry did not end in a period.

3) A new line is always forced by a BEGIN command.

4) Both Number-1 and Number-2 defaults are overridden by the detail column established in an IF statement as a result of the ALIGN command.

$$\text{END LINE ON} \begin{Bmatrix} \text{COMMA} \\ \text{ELSE} \\ \text{PERIOD} \\ \text{SEMI-COLON} \end{Bmatrix}$$

Function: Forces the end of a line after the selected punctuation or reserved word ELSE is found.

Notes: 1) When END LINE ON COMMA is used with the STRIP COMMA command, a new line is forced after a comma and then the comma is removed.

2) END LINE ON ELSE may be used to enhance IF statements in conjunction with the ALIGN command.

3) END LINE ON COMMA will not take effect if comma occurs between subscripts.

$$\text{EXPAND} \begin{Bmatrix} = \\ > \\ < \end{Bmatrix}$$

Function: Expands (=) to (EQUAL TO), (>) to (GREATER THAN), and (<) to (LESS THAN).

1) Expansion of an equal sign will not take place in a COMPUTE statement.

$$\text{FLAG} \begin{Bmatrix} \text{NESTED IFS} \\ \text{COBOL-verb} \\ \text{data-name} \end{Bmatrix}$$

Function: Flags all occurrences of Nested IFs, designated COBOL reserved word, or designated data-names.

Notes: 1) COBOL verbs and data names are limited to a length of 15 characters.

2) Element is flagged on right hand side of newly aligned COBOL listing.

Figure B.11 (e)

Figure B.11 (f)

HOLD LINE FOLLOWING name-1 [name-2] . . .

Function: Forces the two entries following name-1 to remain on the same line as name-1.

Notes: 1. More than one argument may be specified.
2. Name-1 may be either a COBOL verb or a data name; COBOL verbs are recommended.
3. Four commands cause entries to break to a new line when they might otherwise be held by the HOLD command. These are: END LINE, BEGIN LINE, AFTER (name-2), ALIGN (i.e. IF, ELSE, OTHERWISE).
4. If a held entry does not fit on one line, it will break to a new line.
5. A line can be held for more than two entries if names specified in a HOLD command are present in the entries being held.

SEQ [BEGIN / Paragraph-1] THRU [END / Paragraph-2] [WITH / FROM]

character-string [BY increment] [TRUNCATE]

Function: Sequences paragraph names with a character string with or without incrementing.

Notes: 1) ALL may be used to replace BEGIN THRU END.
2) When specifying a range of paragraphs care must be taken to specify paragraph-1 and paragraph-2 as they appear after renaming, if renaming was done with the RENAME command. If the RENAME command was not used on the begin or end paragraph, then no precaution is necessary.
3) The character-string must not exceed 10 characters in length.
4) Increment specifies a number, which is added to the number, found in the character string after the first new paragraph name is built. If two numbers are present in the character string (e.g. A02-100-) then the larger number (i.e. 100) is incremented. If incrementing is desired instead on the smaller number prefix the smaller number with a high-order asterisk (i.e. A*2-100-).
5) If TRUNCATE is specified and a data name exceeds 30 characters the name is truncated to 30 positions. If the 30th position is a dash (-), then it is truncated also.
6) If TRUNCATE is not specified and a data name exceeds 30 positions the paragraph name is left alone.

Figure B.11 (g)

394

STACK {OPEN / CLOSE / CALL}

Function: Stacks all entries in an OPEN, CLOSE and/or CALL statement.

Notes: 1) OPEN, CLOSE and CALL are started in column 12.
2) Other lines are started in column 16.
3) A new filename or call parameter is used to force a new line.
4) INPUT, OUTPUT, I-O, and USING are followed with one filename or call parameter.
5) Entries (WITH LOCK), (REVERSED), etc. remain on the line following their respective filename.
6) The STACK command is ignored for an OPEN, CLOSE, or CALL when the previous entry did not end in a period (e.g. an OPEN statement embedded in an IF statement).

UNSEQ string-1 [string-2] . . .

Function: Unsequences paragraph and section names in the Procedure Division. May be used in conjunction with SEQUENCE commands for resequencing.

Notes: 1. Each string is limited to 10 characters.
2. Letters, numbers, hyphens, and asterisks can be used in any order except that a dash may not be first in the string.
3. When letters, numbers or hyphens are specified, a paragraph must have identical letters, numbers, or hyphens in its corresponding positions for the paragraph name to be unsequenced.
4. If an asterisk is specified in a position, an existing paragraph name must have a valid digit from 0-9 in that corresponding position for the paragraph to be unsequenced.
5. Any paragraph or section name that meets the criteria in any of the UNSEQ commands is unsequenced.
6. If a paragraph has a leftmost hyphen after being unsequenced, the hyphen is also removed. If UNSEQ BB is specified the paragraph BB-TOTALS-ROUTINE becomes TOTALS-ROUTINE.
7. Do not use the unsequenced name when specifying a SEQUENCE command to resequence paragraph names. Use the paragraph as it appears before unsequencing is done.

RULES FOR CODING

1) Commands are free form and may be coded anywhere in columns 1-72.
2) To continue a command to the next line, leave a blank in column 71, and code C in column 72 of the first card.
3) Input to CSA must not contain C or E level diagnostics.
4) OUTPUT from CSA must be directed through COBOL complier to insure no errors have been introduced.

© Copyright 1977 CRAWFORD & GRAUER ASSOCIATES, INC.

Figure B.11 (h)

Report Writer

OVERVIEW

Report Writer is one of the most powerful, yet least used, facilities in COBOL. It is always interesting to hear reasons from practitioners on why it is avoided. The following responses are typical:

1. I never learned it.

2. I tried to use it, but the documentation was impossible to understand.

3. I used it once and it didn't work.

4. My program 'blew out' in Report Writer and I couldn't debug it.

The authors believe that the heart of the problem is in the documentation or lack thereof. The vendor's reference manual is often devoid of clear examples. Moreover, it is not designed to teach the subject, but rather to answer "nitty gritty" questions from users already familiar with the material. To compound the education problem, many academic curricula consider Report Writer as an extra and omit coverage entirely, or discuss it only briefly. In any event, reasons one to four above can be traced, directly or indirectly, to poor documentation and/or lack of academic coverage.

The purpose of this appendix is to provide the reader with an appreciation for the capabilities of Report Writer and an introduction to its use. We believe Report Writer is a convenient technique for many types of report formatting and almost indispensable for programs using multilevel control breaks.

The objective of Report Writer is to assume tedious tasks of programming from the programmer. These include: page headings, proper spacing, and most important, calculating totals and subtotals involving control breaks. The programmer describes in detail the physical appearance of a report in the Data Division and invokes the facility in the Procedure Division. In order to understand how this is accomplished, we must first define *control break* and *report group*.

VOCABULARY

A *control break* is a change in a designated field. For example, if an incoming file is sorted by employee location and location is the control field, a control break occurs every time location changes. If the file is sorted by location, and department within location, it is possible to designate two control fields, department and location.

Let us assume a given file has been sorted on location, and department within location. Hence, all employees in department 100 in the Atlanta office precede the Atlanta employees in department 200, who precede those in department 300, etc. Next come the employees in department 100 in Boston, followed by department 200 in Boston and so forth. A single control break occurs as we change departments within the same location; e.g., from department 100 in Atlanta to department 200 in Atlanta. A double control break, on location and department, arises when we go from department 300 in Atlanta to department 100 in Boston.

Our second definition has to do with the way Report Writer generates output. The facility classifies every line appearing in any report as belonging to one of seven kinds of *report groups*. It is not necessary that a given report contain all seven report groups, and further, any of the seven report groups can consist of one or more lines, i.e., a group of lines. The seven categories are:

1. *Report Heading*: one or more lines appearing only once at the beginning (initiation) of a report

2. *Report Footing*: one or more lines appearing only once at the conclusion (termination) of a report

3. *Page Heading*: one or more lines appearing at the beginning of each page after the report heading

4. *Page Footing*: one or more lines appearing at the end of each page

5. *Control Heading*: a group of lines appearing prior to each control break; i.e., when the contents of a designated field change

6. *Control Footing*: a group of lines appearing after each control break

7. *Detail*: one or more lines for each record in the file

EXAMPLE 1—A Double Control Break Program

In order to better understand these terms and Report Writer in general, we develop a complete COBOL program with objectives similar to the program of Chapter Two. The purpose there was to illustrate the technique of top down program development for a program requiring two control breaks. The purpose here is to demonstrate the ease with which Report Writer can produce similar results. Specifications are as follows. The management of World Wide Widgets requires monthly reports on sales activity. Detailed information on every salesman is to be provided showing all transactions for that salesman. The salesmen are to be listed by location, and alphabetically within location. Summary totals are required for each location and for the company at large.

Input consists of transaction records, one record per transaction. Each transaction contains the name of the salesman responsible, his (her) location, and the transaction amount. Transaction records have been validated and sorted in a previous run. Thus we can accept input to the program as being in sequence by location, and by salesman within location. Further, each transaction record can be assumed to contain complete and valid data.

Figure C.1 shows two pages from a report produced by the COBOL program developed later in the appendix to conform to these specifications. Note in particular, the presence of a page heading, control heading on a location change, and control footings on both salesman and location change.

DATA DIVISION REQUIREMENTS

The use of Report Writer is best explained through Figure C.2, the COBOL program which produced the output of Figure C.1. At first, its Data Division may appear unduly long and complex. In reality it is no longer than that of any meaningful COBOL program, with or without Report Writer.

A report is written to a file defined in a SELECT statement. The FD for this file contains an additional entry, REPORT IS (line 25 in Figure C.2), which specifies the name of the report. Note that there are no 01 entries for this FD since the description of the file is handled in the Report Section. (Multiple reports can be written to the same output file and/or from the same input file, but that is not covered here.) The entry in the REPORT IS clause has a corresponding RD (Report Description) in the Report Section (line 50) of the Data Division. The RD describes the structure and organization of the report and has the form:

```
RD      report-name

[WITH CODE mnemonic-name]
```

$$\left[\begin{Bmatrix} \underline{CONTROL} \ IS \\ \underline{CONTROLS} \ ARE \end{Bmatrix} \begin{Bmatrix} \underline{FINAL} \\ [\underline{FINAL}] \end{Bmatrix} identifier\text{-}1 \ [identifier\text{-}2] \ ... \right]$$

$$\left[\underline{PAGE} \begin{bmatrix} \underline{LIMIT} \ IS \\ \underline{LIMITS} \ ARE \end{bmatrix} integer\text{-}1 \begin{Bmatrix} \underline{LINE} \\ \underline{LINES} \end{Bmatrix} \right.$$

```
            [HEADING        integer-2]
            [FIRST DETAIL   integer-3]
            [LAST DETAIL    integer-4]
            [FOOTING        integer-5]  ].
```

The CODE clause of the RD specifies an identifying character placed at the beginning of each report line and has meaning only when multiple reports are written.

The CONTROL clause (line 51 in Figure C.2) identifies the control breaks. These are FINAL, TR-SALESMAN-LOCATION, and TR-SALESMAN-NAME in Figure C.2. Subsequent specification of control headings and/or control footings will cause information to print before and/or after control breaks in these fields. Specification of CONTROL IS FINAL causes a control break at the end of the report. Note well that the identifier(s) in the CONTROL clause, i.e., TR-SALESMAN-LOCATION and TR-SALES-MAN-NAME, must exist in each incoming record.

The remaining clauses of the RD physically describe the pages of the report. One can specify the maximum number of lines per page (PAGE LIMIT), the first line on which anything may be printed (HEADING), the first line for a detail (FIRST DETAIL), the last line for a control heading or detail (LAST DETAIL), and the last line for a footing (FOOTING).

The RD is followed by several 01 entries to describe report groups within that report, (just as an FD is followed by 01 entries to describe records within a file). Recall there are seven types of report groups, and that a given report need not contain all seven, but could contain multiple entries for the same type report group. Figure C.2 for example, does not contain either a page or report footing, but does contain three control footings (lines 98, 107 and 119).

A report group is described in an 01 entry and its associated subentries. The programmer specifies the physical and logical characteristics of the report group by

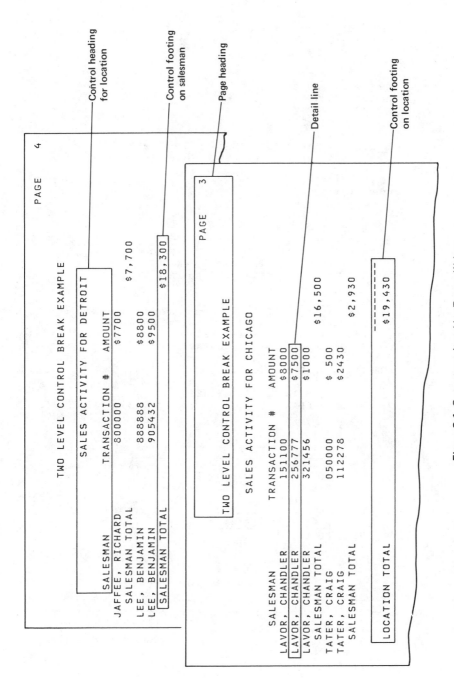

Figure C.1 Output produced by Report Writer

399

```
00001          IDENTIFICATION DIVISION.
00002          PROGRAM-ID.    TWOLEVEL.
00003          AUTHOR.        R GRAUER.

00005          ENVIRONMENT DIVISION.
00006          CONFIGURATION SECTION.
00007          SOURCE-COMPUTER.        IBM-370.
00008          OBJECT-COMPUTER.        IBM-370.
00009          INPUT-OUTPUT SECTION.
00010          FILE-CONTROL.
00011              SELECT SALES-FILE ASSIGN TO UT-S-SYSIN.
00012              SELECT PRINT-FILE ASSIGN TO UT-S-SYSOUT.

00014          DATA DIVISION.
00015          FILE SECTION.

00017          FD  SALES-FILE
00018              RECORDING MODE IS F
00019              LABEL RECORDS ARE OMITTED              ─── No 01 entry for
00020              RECORD CONTAINS 80 CHARACTERS               this file
00021              DATA RECORD IS TRANSACTION-RECORD.
00022          01  TRANSACTION-RECORD          PIC X(80).

00024          FD  PRINT-FILE
00025              REPORT IS CONTROL-BREAK    ─── Identifies report name in
00026              RECORDING MODE IS F             subsequent RD
00027              LABEL RECORDS ARE OMITTED
00028              RECORD CONTAINS 133 CHARACTERS.

00030          WORKING-STORAGE SECTION.
00031          77  FILLER                      PIC X(14)
00032                  VALUE 'WS BEGINS HERE'.
00033          77  WS-DATA-FLAG                PIC X(3)   VALUE SPACES.
00034              88  NO-MORE-DATA                       VALUE 'NO'.

00036          01  TRANSACTION-AREA.
00037              05   TR-SALESMAN-NAME       PIC X(20).
00038              05   TR-AMOUNT              PIC S9(4).
00039              05   FILLER                 PIC XX.          Fields designated as
00040              05   TR-NUMBER              PIC X(6).        control breaks in
00041              05   TR-TYPE                PIC X(1).        report section.
00042              05   TR-SALESMAN-REGION     PIC X(17).
00043              05   TR-SALESMAN-LOCATION   PIC X(20).
00044              05   FILLER                 PIC X(10).

00046          01  FILLER                      PIC X(12)
00047                  VALUE 'WS ENDS HERE'.
00049          REPORT SECTION.    ─── Beginning of report section
00050          RD  CONTROL-BREAK  ─── Report name matches entry in line 25
00051              CONTROLS ARE FINAL TR-SALESMAN-LOCATION TR-SALESMAN-NAME
00052              PAGE LIMIT 50 LINES
00053              HEADING 1                  ── Establishes control breaks
00054              FIRST DETAIL 5
00055              LAST DETAIL 45
00056              FOOTING 48.
00057          01  TYPE IS PAGE HEADING.    Indicates absolute line
00058              05  LINE NUMBER 1.            number
00059                  10   COLUMN NUMBER 61
00060                       PIC A(4)
```

Figure C.2 Report Writer—Example 1

```
00061                          VALUE 'PAGE'.
00062              10    COLUMN NUMBER 66
00063                    PIC ZZZ9
00064                    SOURCE PAGE-COUNTER.
00065         05   LINE NUMBER PLUS 2.          Indicates relative
00066              10    COLUMN NUMBER 22       line number
00067                    PIC X(31)
00068                    VALUE 'TWO LEVEL CONTROL BREAK EXAMPLE'.
00069      01   TYPE IS CONTROL HEADING TR-SALESMAN-LOCATION.
00070         05   LINE NUMBER 5.
00071              10    COLUMN NUMBER 25
00072                    PIC X(18)                Description of
00073                    VALUE 'SALES ACTIVITY FOR'.   two fields
00074              10    COLUMN NUMBER 44         appearing on
00075                    PIC X(10)                line 5
00076                    SOURCE TR-SALESMAN-LOCATION.
00077         05   LINE NUMBER 7.
00078              10    COLUMN NUMBER 6
00079                    PIC X(8)
00080                    VALUE 'SALESMAN'.
00081              10    COLUMN NUMBER 24
00082                    PIC X(13)
00083                    VALUE 'TRANSACTION #'.
00084              10    COLUMN NUMBER 40
00085                    PIC X(7)
00086                    VALUE 'AMOUNT'.
00087      01   TRANSACTION-LINE TYPE IS DETAIL.    Detail report group is
00088         05   LINE NUMBER PLUS 1.             referenced in subsequent
00089              10    COLUMN NUMBER 2           GENERATE statement
00090                    PIC X(20)
00091                    SOURCE TR-SALESMAN-NAME.
00092              10    COLUMN NUMBER 27          Control footing-
00093                    PIC X(6)                  prints whenever
00094                    SOURCE TR-NUMBER.         there is a break on
00095              10    COLUMN NUMBER 41          TR-SALESMAN-NAME
00096                    PIC $ZZZ9
00097                    SOURCE TR-AMOUNT.
00098      01   TYPE IS CONTROL FOOTING TR-SALESMAN-NAME.
00099         05   LINE NUMBER PLUS 1.
00100              10    COLUMN NUMBER 4
00101                    PIC X(15)
00102                    VALUE 'SALESMAN TOTAL'.
00103              10    SALESMAN-TOTAL
00104                    COLUMN NUMBER 48
00105                    PIC $$$$,999
00106                    SUM TR-AMOUNT.
00107      01   TYPE IS CONTROL FOOTING TR-SALESMAN-LOCATION.
00108         05   LINE NUMBER PLUS 2.
00109              10    COLUMN NUMBER 48
00110                    PIC X(10)
00111                    VALUE ALL '-'.
00112         05   LINE NUMBER PLUS 1.
00113              10    COLUMN NUMBER 4
00114                    PIC X(14)
00115                    VALUE 'LOCATION TOTAL'.
00116              10    COLUMN NUMBER 48
00117                    PIC $$$$,999
```

Figure C.2 Report Writer—Example 1 (continued)

```
00118                        SUM SALESMAN-TOTAL.
00119        01   TYPE IS CONTROL FOOTING FINAL.
00120             05   LINE NUMBER IS PLUS 5.
00121                  10   COLUMN NUMBER 10
00122                       PIC X(28)
00123                       VALUE '***FINAL TOTAL ALL LOCATIONS'.
00124                  10   COLUMN NUMBER 40
00125                       PIC $ZZZ,999
00126                       SUM SALESMAN-TOTAL.
```

Final control break; prints at report termination

```
00128        PROCEDURE DIVISION.
00129        0010-CREATE-REPORTS.
00130             OPEN INPUT SALES-FILE
00131                  OUTPUT PRINT-FILE.
00132             INITIATE CONTROL-BREAK.
00133             READ SALES-FILE INTO TRANSACTION-AREA
00134                  AT END MOVE 'NO' TO WS-DATA-FLAG.
00135             PERFORM 0020-PROCESS-ALL-TRANSACTIONS UNTIL NO-MORE-DATA.
00136             TERMINATE CONTROL-BREAK.
00137             CLOSE SALES-FILE
00138                   PRINT-FILE.
00139             STOP RUN.

00141        0020-PROCESS-ALL-TRANSACTIONS.
00142             GENERATE TRANSACTION-LINE.
00143             READ SALES-FILE INTO TRANSACTION-AREA
00144                  AT END MOVE 'NO' TO WS-DATA-FLAG.
```

INITIATE statement

TERMINATE statement

GENERATE statement to reference TRANSACTION-LINE report group

Figure C.2 Report Writer—Example 1 (continued)

including information on its:

function - accomplished through the TYPE clause specified at the 01 level. This indicates the nature of the report group; i.e., control heading, control footing, etc.

vertical spacing - accomplished through the LINE clause. It can be specified as absolute; e.g., begin on line 5, or relative; e.g., begin 2 lines past the last entry.

horizontal spacing - specified through the COLUMN clause, and

contents - determines how the value of a report entry is obtained and is specified in one of three ways. The VALUE clause specifies a constant; i.e., a literal. The SOURCE clause identifies a data name outside the Report Section whose current value is moved to the report entry. The SUM clause specifies that the entry is to be obtained by adding the specified field in detail records.

The COBOL syntax for specifying 01 and/or other subentries has four possible formats as shown in Figure C.3. The most unusual aspect of all four formats is that the data name is *optional*. Hence, when reading a Report Section for the first time, it may be somewhat startling to find level numbers followed immediately by clauses other than data names. For example, there are six 01 entries in the Report Section of Figure C.2, but

402

General Format 1—level-01 Group Entry

01   [data-name]
     TYPE Clause
     [LINE Clause]
     [NEXT GROUP Clause]
     [USAGE Clause].

General Format 2—Group Entry

level-number [data-name]
     [LINE Clause]
     [USAGE Clause].

General Format 3—Elementary Entry

level-number [data-name]
     [COLUMN NUMBER IS integer]

     [GROUP INDICATE]

     [LINE Clause]

$$
\left\{
\begin{array}{l}
\underline{SOURCE}\ IS\ identifier \\[4pt]
\underline{SUM}\ identifier\text{-}1\ [identifier\text{-}2]\ \ldots\ [\underline{UPON}\ data\text{-}name\text{-}2] \\[4pt]
\quad [\underline{RESET}\ ON\ \left\{
\begin{array}{l}
\underline{FINAL} \\
identifier\text{-}3
\end{array}
\right\}\ ] \\[4pt]
\underline{VALUE}\ IS\ literal
\end{array}
\right\}
$$

    PICTURE Clause
    [USAGE Clause]
    [BLANK WHEN ZERO Clause]
    [JUSTIFIED Clause]

General Format 4—level-01 Elementary Entry

01   [data-name]
     TYPE Clause
     [LINE Clause]
     [NEXT GROUP Clause]
     [COLUMN Clause]
     [GROUP INDICATE Clause]

$$
\left\{
\begin{array}{l}
SOURCE\ Clause \\
SUM\ Clause \\
VALUE\ Clause
\end{array}
\right\}
$$

    PICTURE Clause
    [USAGE Clause]
    [BLANK WHEN ZERO Clause]
    [JUSTIFIED Clause].

Figure C.3 COBOL Syntax of Report Groups

403

only one includes a data name, TRANSACTION-LINE (line 87), and that is because of a requirement in a subsequent Procedure Division statement (GENERATE in line 142). Our distinct preference is to omit data names in the Report Section where possible.

We now turn our attention to describing in detail some of the entries in Figure C.3, with reference to the COBOL program in Figure C.2. The TYPE clause specifies the type of report group and has the general form:

$$
\text{TYPE IS}
\left\{
\begin{array}{ll}
\left\{ \begin{array}{l} \underline{\text{REPORT}}\ \text{HEADING} \\ \underline{\text{RH}} \end{array} \right\} & \\[2ex]
\left\{ \begin{array}{l} \underline{\text{PAGE}}\ \text{HEADING} \\ \underline{\text{PH}} \end{array} \right\} & \\[2ex]
\left\{ \begin{array}{l} \underline{\text{CONTROL}}\ \text{HEADING} \\ \underline{\text{CH}} \end{array} \right\}
\left\{ \begin{array}{l} \underline{\text{FINAL}} \\ \text{identifier-n} \end{array} \right\} \\[2ex]
\left\{ \begin{array}{l} \underline{\text{DETAIL}} \\ \underline{\text{DE}} \end{array} \right\} & \\[2ex]
\left\{ \begin{array}{l} \underline{\text{CONTROL}}\ \text{FOOTING} \\ \underline{\text{CF}} \end{array} \right\}
\left\{ \begin{array}{l} \text{identifier-n} \\ \underline{\text{FINAL}} \end{array} \right\} \\[2ex]
\left\{ \begin{array}{l} \underline{\text{PAGE}}\ \text{FOOTING} \\ \underline{\text{PF}} \end{array} \right\} & \\[2ex]
\left\{ \begin{array}{l} \underline{\text{REPORT}}\ \text{FOOTING} \\ \underline{\text{RF}} \end{array} \right\} &
\end{array}
\right\}
$$

The TYPE clause is required for an 01 entry and cannot be specified at any other level. Figure C.2 contains six TYPE clauses, one for each report group.

General format 2 of Figure C.3 describes a group entry, e.g., a single report line which has several elementary items, i.e., fields, under it. Consider for example the control heading for TR-SALESMAN-LOCATION (COBOL lines 69-86). This report group, consisting of two lines, will print every time there is a control break on TR-SALESMAN-LOCATION. The first line will appear on line 5 of the page. This in turn is a group entry, as per general format 2, consisting of two fields beginning in columns 25 and 44 respectively. The second group item of the control heading specifies line 7 and in turn has 3 elementary items, i.e., fields, beginning in columns 6, 24, and 40 respectively.

General format 3 describes an elementary item as evidenced by the mandatory PICTURE clause. It specifies both a beginning column (COLUMN) for the field and also how the value of the field is determined; i.e., either through SOURCE, VALUE, or SUM.

Specification of SOURCE; e.g., SOURCE IS TR-SALESMAN-LOCATION (in line 76) says that the current value of the identifier TR-SALESMAN-LOCATION is to be moved to the output field. Specification of VALUE, e.g., VALUE 'SALESMAN' (in line 80) causes a literal to be moved to the output field. Finally, specification of SUM, e.g., SUM TR-AMOUNT (line 106) causes Report Writer to total the field TR-AMOUNT for each incoming record and print its value at the appropriate time. The sum is automatically reset to zero each time a break on TR-SALESMAN-NAME is encountered. (The RESET clause, which does not appear in Figure C.2, makes it possible to reset a total to zero at times other than the control break.) In this way, various totals and subtotals can be computed throughout a report.

PROCEDURE DIVISION REQUIREMENTS

The Procedure Division of Figure C.2 is remarkably short and contains three new verbs: INITIATE, GENERATE, and TERMINATE, all uniquely associated with Report Writer.

INITIATE is used to begin processing of a given report. Execution of this statement initializes counters, totals, etc. Its syntax is simply

<u>INITIATE</u> report-name-1 [report-name-2] . . .

Note that the report name CONTROL-BREAK of the INITIATE statement in line 132, appears in the REPORT clause of the FD for REPORT-FILE (line 25). It appears again in the RD entry on the REPORT SECTION (line 50) in the Data Division.

The GENERATE statement (line 142) causes Report Writer to automatically produce any of the seven report groups where and when they are needed. It has the general syntax:

$$\underline{\text{GENERATE}} \quad \left\{ \begin{array}{l} \text{report-name} \\ \text{data-name} \end{array} \right\}$$

Two types of reporting are possible: *summary reporting* in which only heading and footing groups are produced and *detail reporting* in which the detail report group named in the GENERATE statement is produced each time the statement is executed.

The GENERATE statement in Figure C.2 calls for detail reporting by specifying the data name of a report group, i.e., TRANSACTION-LINE. (Note the latter was designated as a DETAIL report group in line 87.) Figure C.4, shown later in this appendix, illustrates summary reporting.

The TERMINATE statement (line 136) completes report processing as if a control break at the highest level occurred. All footing groups up to the highest level are produced, all counters are reset, and report processing is ended. The statement has the syntax:

<u>TERMINATE</u> report-name-1 [report-name-2] . . .

EXAMPLE 2—Three Control Breaks

The COBOL program of Figure C.2 requires that incoming records be previously sorted. It is, however, possible to use Report Writer in conjunction with the SORT verb as shown in Figure C.4. This time, three control breaks (on region, location, and salesman), are specified (COBOL lines 63-66). The incoming file must have its records in proper order prior to the report generation. Sorting is accomplished *within* the program through the SORT statement of lines 162-165:

```
SORT    SORT-FILE
        ASCENDING KEY SORT-REGION SORT-LOCATION SORT-NAME
        USING SALES-FILE
        OUTPUT PROCEDURE 0010-CREATE-REPORTS.
```

Three sort keys are indicated with SORT-REGION as the major (i.e., most important) and SORT-NAME as the minor (i.e., least important). The clause, USING SALES-FILE, indicates that SALES-FILE contains the records to be sorted and causes the SORT verb to do the necessary I/O. Hence, SALES-FILE is opened, its records are released to sort, and the file is closed, all without programmer action. (This is in contrast to the technique employed in Chapter 4, Figure 4.12, in which the programmer selected the records to be 'released' to sort.)

After the sort is completed, control passes to the *section* specified as the OUTPUT PROCEDURE. This in turn reads, (i.e., returns) records from the sorted file and invokes Report Writer via INITIATE, GENERATE, and TERMINATE.

A second objective of Figure C.4 is to demonstrate the ease with which changes can be made using Report Writer. In particular, the specifications for the program of Figure C.2 have been amended to include a third control break on region. Secondly, it is no longer necessary to show all transactions for a given salesman, but only his (her) total. Finally, the report format has been altered to reflect these changes.

The modifications in Figure C.4 begin with specification of a control break on region (COBOL line 64). A control heading on region (line 84) has been added to effect a page break on region, and the control heading on location from Figure C.2 was eliminated. A control footing on region (line 138) was also added to achieve region totals. Finally, note that GENERATE statement (line 179) reflects summary reporting by specifying the report name, CONTROL-BREAK, rather than a detail report group as was done in Figure C.2.

A single page of output is shown in Figure C.5 for the MID-WEST region. The data reflected on this page are consistent with that of Figure C.1. Note, however, some changes. The three detail lines for LAVOR, CHANDLER of Figure C.1 have been replaced by a single summary line in Figure C.5. Secondly, the two location totals from Figure C.1 have been grouped into a regional total in Figure C.5. Finally, the page break is no longer on location (as was done in Figure C.1) but on region.

406

```
00001          IDENTIFICATION DIVISION.
00002          PROGRAM-ID.    THREELEV.
00003          AUTHOR.      R GRAUER.

00005          ENVIRONMENT DIVISION.
00006          CONFIGURATION SECTION.
00007          SOURCE-COMPUTER.        IBM-370.
00008          OBJECT-COMPUTER.        IBM-370.
00009          INPUT-OUTPUT SECTION.
00010          FILE-CONTROL.
00011              SELECT SALES-FILE ASSIGN TO UT-S-SYSIN.
00012              SELECT PRINT-FILE ASSIGN TO UT-S-SYSOUT.
00013              SELECT SORT-FILE ASSIGN TO UT-S-SORTWORK.

00015          DATA DIVISION.                    SELECT statement for
00016          FILE SECTION.                     sort file

00018          FD   SALES-FILE
00019               RECORDING MODE IS F
00020               LABEL RECORDS ARE OMITTED
00021               RECORD CONTAINS 80 CHARACTERS
00022               DATA RECORD IS SALES-RECORD.
00023          01   SALES-RECORD                 PIC X(80).

00025          FD   PRINT-FILE                   ─Identifies report name
00026               REPORT IS CONTROL-BREAK
00027               RECORDING MODE IS F
00028               LABEL RECORDS ARE OMITTED
00029               RECORD CONTAINS 133 CHARACTERS.

00031          SD   SORT-FILE
00032               RECORDING MODE IS F                  ─SD for sort file
00033               RECORD CONTAINS 80 CHARACTERS
00034               DATA RECORD IS SORT-RECORD.
00035          01   SORT-RECORD.
00036               05   SORT-NAME          PIC X(20).
00037               05   FILLER             PIC X(13).     ─Sort keys
00038               05   SORT-REGION        PIC X(17).      appearing
00039               05   SORT-LOCATION      PIC X(20).      in sort verb
00040               05   FILLER             PIC X(10).

00042          WORKING-STORAGE SECTION.
00043          77   FILLER                       PIC X(14)
00044                   VALUE 'WS BEGINS HERE'.
00045          77   WS-DATA-FLAG                  PIC X(3)    VALUE SPACES.
00046               88   NO-MORE-DATA                        VALUE 'NO'.

00048          01   TRANSACTION-AREA.
00049               05   TR-SALESMAN-NAME      PIC X(20).
00050               05   TR-AMOUNT             PIC S9(4).
00051               05   FILLER                PIC XX.
00052               05   TR-NUMBER             PIC X(6).
00053               05   TR-TYPE               PIC X(1).
00054               05   TR-SALESMAN-REGION    PIC X(17).
00055               05   TR-SALESMAN-LOCATION  PIC X(20).
00056               05   FILLER                PIC X(10).

00058          01   FILLER                       PIC X(12)
00059                   VALUE 'WS ENDS HERE'.
```

Figure C.4 Report Writer—Example 2

407

```
00061          REPORT SECTION.
00062          RD   CONTROL-BREAK
00063               CONTROLS ARE FINAL
00064                            TR-SALESMAN-REGION          Specification of
00065                            TR-SALESMAN-LOCATION        control breaks
00066                            TR-SALESMAN-NAME
00067               PAGE LIMIT 50 LINES
00068               HEADING 1
00069               FIRST DETAIL 5
00070               LAST DETAIL 45                          Page heading report group
00071               FOOTING 48.
00072          01   TYPE IS PAGE HEADING.
00073               05   LINE NUMBER 1.
00074                    10   COLUMN NUMBER 61
00075                         PIC A(4)
00076                         VALUE 'PAGE'.
00077                    10   COLUMN NUMBER 66
00078                         PIC ZZZ9
00079                         SOURCE PAGE-COUNTER.
0008C               05   LINE NUMBER PLUS 2.
00081                    10   COLUMN NUMBER 22
00082                         PIC X(33)
00083                         VALUE 'THREE LEVEL CONTROL BREAK EXAMPLE'.
00084          01   TYPE IS CONTROL HEADING TR-SALESMAN-REGION.
00085               05   LINE NUMBER 5.
00086                    10   COLUMN NUMBER 21
00087                         PIC X(27)
00088                         VALUE 'REGIONAL SALES ACTIVITY FOR'.
00089                    10   COLUMN NUMBER 54
00090                         PIC X(10)
00091                         SOURCE TR-SALESMAN-REGION.
00092               05   LINE NUMBER 7.
00093                    10   COLUMN NUMBER 6
00094                         PIC X(8)
00095                         VALUE 'LOCATION'.
00096                    10   COLUMN NUMBER 28
00097                         PIC X(15)
00098                         VALUE 'SALESMAN'.
00099                    10   COLUMN NUMBER 50
00100                         PIC X(7)
00101                         VALUE 'AMOUNT'.
00102          01   TRANSACTION-LINE TYPE IS DETAIL.
00103               05   LINE NUMBER PLUS 1.
00104                    10   COLUMN NUMBER 2
00105                         PIC X(20)
00106                         SOURCE TR-SALESMAN-NAME.
00107                    10   COLUMN NUMBER 27
00108                         PIC X(6)
00109                         SOURCE TR-NUMBER.
00110                    10   COLUMN NUMBER 41
00111                         PIC $ZZZ9
00112                         SOURCE TR-AMOUNT.
00113          01   TYPE IS CONTROL FOOTING TR-SALESMAN-NAME.
00114               05   LINE NUMBER PLUS 1.                Control footing on
00115                    10   COLUMN NUMBER 2               salesman break
00116                         PIC X(15)
00117                         SOURCE TR-SALESMAN-LOCATION.
00118                    10   COLUMN NUMBER 26
00119                         PIC X(20)
00120                         SOURCE TR-SALESMAN-NAME.
00121                    10   SALESMAN-TOTAL
00122                         COLUMN NUMBER 48
```

Figure C.4 Report Writer—Example 2 (continued)

408

```
00123                      PIC $$$$,999
00124                      SUM TR-AMOUNT.
00125          01   TYPE IS CONTROL FOOTING TR-SALESMAN-LOCATION.
00126              05   LINE NUMBER PLUS 1.
00127                  10   COLUMN NUMBER 48
00128                      PIC X(10)
00129                      VALUE ALL '-'.                    ⎬ Control footing on location break
00130              05   LINE NUMBER PLUS 1.
00131                  10   COLUMN NUMBER 4
00132                      PIC X(14)
00133                      VALUE 'LOCATION TOTAL'.
00134                  10   LOCATION-TOTAL
00135                      COLUMN NUMBER 58
00136                      PIC $$$$,999
00137                      SUM SALESMAN-TOTAL.
00138          01   TYPE IS CONTROL FOOTING TR-SALESMAN-REGION.
00139              05   LINE NUMBER IS PLUS 2.
00140                  10   COLUMN NUMBER 58
00141                      PIC X(10)                         ⎬ Control footing on region break
00142                      VALUE ALL '-'.
00143                  10   COLUMN NUMBER 4
00144                      PIC X(14)
00145                      VALUE 'REGIONAL TOTAL'.
00146              05   LINE NUMBER PLUS 1.
00147                  10   COLUMN NUMBER 58
00148                      PIC $$$$,999
00149                      SUM LOCATION-TOTAL.              ⎬ Final control footing
00150          01   TYPE IS CONTROL FOOTING FINAL.
00151              05   LINE NUMBER IS PLUS 5.
00152                  10   COLUMN NUMBER 10
00153                      PIC X(28)
00154                      VALUE '***FINAL TOTAL ALL LOCATIONS'.
00155                  10   COLUMN NUMBER 40
00156                      PIC $ZZZ,999
00157                      SUM SALESMAN-TOTAL.

00159          PROCEDURE DIVISION.
                                                    SALES-FILE is opened, read,
00161          0005-SORT.                           and closed by sort routine
00162              SORT SORT-FILE
00163                  ASCENDING KEY SORT-REGION SORT-LOCATION SORT-NAME
00164                  USING SALES-FILE
00165                  OUTPUT PROCEDURE 0010-CREATE-REPORTS.
00166              STOP RUN.

00168          0010-CREATE-REPORTS SECTION.          ⎬ Output procedure must be
00169              OPEN OUTPUT PRINT-FILE.              a section
00170              INITIATE CONTROL-BREAK.
00171              RETURN SORT-FILE INTO TRANSACTION-AREA
00172                  AT END MOVE 'NO' TO WS-DATA-FLAG.
00173              PERFORM 0020-PROCESS-ALL-TRANSACTIONS UNTIL NO-MORE-DATA.
00174              TERMINATE CONTROL-BREAK.
00175              CLOSE PRINT-FILE.
00176              GO TO 0030-SORT-EXIT.

00178          0020-PROCESS-ALL-TRANSACTIONS.         ⎬ Summary reporting
00179              GENERATE CONTROL-BREAK.
00180              RETURN SORT-FILE INTO TRANSACTION-AREA
00181                  AT END MOVE 'NO' TO WS-DATA-FLAG.
                                                    Records are returned, i.e. read
00183          0030-SORT-EXIT.                      from the sorted file
00184              EXIT.
```

Figure C.4 Report Writer—Example 2 (continued)

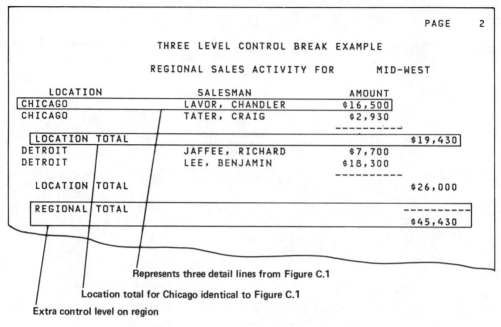

```
                                                    PAGE    2
                THREE LEVEL CONTROL BREAK EXAMPLE

                REGIONAL SALES ACTIVITY FOR        MID-WEST

        LOCATION              SALESMAN          AMOUNT
   CHICAGO                LAVOR, CHANDLER       $16,500
   CHICAGO                TATER, CRAIG           $2,930
                                               ----------
     LOCATION  TOTAL                                      $19,430
   DETROIT                JAFFEE, RICHARD        $7,700
   DETROIT                LEE, BENJAMIN         $18,300
                                               ----------
     LOCATION  TOTAL                                      $26,000

    REGIONAL  TOTAL                            ----------
                                                         $45,430
```

Represents three detail lines from Figure C.1

Location total for Chicago identical to Figure C.1

Extra control level on region

Figure C.5 Output From Three Control Break Program

SUMMARY

Two examples were presented illustrating the use of Report Writer. This powerful, but often neglected, COBOL feature is well suited to 'straightforward' reports; i.e., those with few or no exceptions. It is ideal for handling multilevel control breaks. However, situations requiring varied page headings, unusual formats, e.g., totals before detail lines, are best handled in other ways.

In essence, Report Writer produces a report by describing its physical characteristics in the Data Division, rather than by specifying detailed instructions in the Procedure Division. This philosophy simplifies the involved logic in computing subtotals and rolling them forward. Moreover, because the Report Section is divided into distinct report groups which specify control headings, footings, etc., it is easy to add (or remove) additional control breaks.

Since Report Writer performs its operations automatically, debugging may be difficult if results do not come out as expected. It is not possible to insert debugging statements to trace program flow and print intermediate results. Hence, the often heard complaint, "I blew out in Report Writer!" In spite of this objection, Report Writer is entirely consistent with a logic and beauty all its own. It is a powerful tool and should be in the realm of any COBOL programmer.

IBM OS/VS COBOL
Reference Format Summary

Reference Data

Operating System

IBM
OS/VS
COBOL

IBM OS/VS COBOL
Reference Format Summary

The general format of a COBOL source program is illustrated in these format summaries.

The first section, COBOL Program Outline, gives a general outline of the order in which COBOL Divisions, Sections, and Paragraphs must be written.

The following sections give detailed format summaries for each Division of a COBOL program and for the COBOL Special Features.

IBM extensions to American National Standard COBOL, X3.23=1974, are shown within boxes.

All of these formats are more fully documented in the text of this publication: IBM VS COBOL for OS/VS, Order No. GC26-3857-0.

COBOL Program Structure

```
{ IDENTIFICATION DIVISION.
{ [ ID DIVISION. ]
```

PROGRAM-ID. program-name.

```
[AUTHOR. [comment-entry] ... ]
[INSTALLATION. [comment-entry] ... ]
[DATE-WRITTEN. [comment-entry] ... ]
[DATE-COMPILED. [comment-entry] ... ]
[SECURITY. [comment-entry] ... ]
```

ENVIRONMENT DIVISION.

```
{ CONFIGURATION SECTION.
{ [ CONFIGURATION SECTION. ]
```

```
SOURCE-COMPUTER. entry
OBJECT-COMPUTER. entry
```

```
{ [SPECIAL-NAMES. entry]
{ [ [SPECIAL-NAMES. entry] ]
```

```
[INPUT-OUTPUT SECTION.
FILE-CONTROL. entry
[I-O-CONTROL. entry] ]
```

DATA DIVISION.

```
[FILE SECTION.
[file-description entry
[record-description entry] ... ] ... ]
```

```
[WORKING-STORAGE SECTION.
[data item description entry]
[record-description entry     ] ... ]
```

```
[LINKAGE SECTION.
[data item description entry]
[record-description entry     ] ... ]
```

1

2

Figure D.1

412

[COMMUNICATION SECTION.

[communication description entry
[record-description entry] ...] ...]

```
┌─────────────────────────────────────────────────────┐
│ [REPORT SECTION.                                      │
│ [report description entry                             │
│ [report-group description entry } ... ] ... ]         │
└─────────────────────────────────────────────────────┘
```

Procedure Division – Format 1

PROCEDURE DIVISION [USING identifier-1 [identifier-2]...].

[DECLARATIVES.

{ section-name SECTION [priority-number]. USE Sentence.

[paragraph-name. [sentence] ...] ... } ...
END DECLARATIVES.]
{ section-name SECTION [priority-number].
[paragraph-name. [sentence] ...] ... } ...

Procedure Division – Format 2

PROCEDURE DIVISION [USING identifier-1 [identifier-2]...].
{ paragraph-name. [sentence] ... } ...

Identification Division Formats

```
{ IDENTIFICATION DIVISION.  }
{ ┌─────────────┐           }
{ │ ID DIVISION.│           }
{ └─────────────┘           }
```

PROGRAM-ID. program-name.
[AUTHOR. [comment-entry] ...]
[INSTALLATION. [comment-entry] ...]
[DATE-WRITTEN. [comment-entry] ...]
[DATE-COMPILED. [comment-entry] ...]
[SECURITY. [comment-entry] ...]

ENVIRONMENT DIVISION.

```
{ [CONFIGURATION SECTION.  }
{ ┌────────────────────────┐}
{ │[CONFIGURATION SECTION. │}
{ └────────────────────────┘}
```

SOURCE-COMPUTER. computer-name [WITH DEBUGGING MODE].

OBJECT-COMPUTER. computer-name

```
                     { WORDS      }
  [MEMORY SIZE integer { CHARACTERS } ]
                     { MODULES    }
```

[PROGRAM COLLATING SEQUENCE IS alphabet-name]
[SEGMENT-LIMIT IS priority-number].
[SPECIAL-NAMES.
[function-name-1 IS mnemonic-name] ...
[function-name-2 [IS mnemonic-name]

```
{ ON STATUS IS condition-name-1]          }
{    [OFF STATUS IS condition-name-2]     } ] ...
{ OFF STATUS IS condition-name-2          }
{    [ON STATUS IS condition-name-1]      }
```

[alphabet-name IS

```
{ STANDARD-1                                              }
{ NATIVE                                                  }
{           { THROUGH }                                   }
{ literal-1 {         } literal-2                         } ]...
{           { THRU    }                                   }
{           ALSO literal-3                                }
{              [ALSO literal-4] ...]                      }
{                                                         }
{           { THROUGH }                                   }
{ [literal-5 {        } literal-6 ]..                     }
{            { THRU   }                                   }
{           ALSO literal-7                                }
{              [ALSO literal-8] ..]                       }
```

[CURRENCY SIGN IS literal-9]

```
{ [DECIMAL-POINT IS COMMA].]     }
{ ┌──────────────────────────┐   }
{ │[DECIMAL-POINT IS COMMA].]]│   }
{ └──────────────────────────┘   }
```

Figure D.2

Note: The key word FILE-CONTROL appears only once, at the beginning of the paragraph before the first File-Control entry.

FILE-CONTROL Paragraph – Sequential Files

```
FILE-CONTROL.

    SELECT [OPTIONAL] file-name
    ASSIGN TO assignment-name-1 [assignment-name-2] ...

    [RESERVE integer ⎡AREA  ⎤ ]
                     ⎣AREAS ⎦

    [ORGANIZATION IS SEQUENTIAL]
    [ACCESS MODE IS SEQUENTIAL]
    [PASSWORD IS data-name-1]

    [FILE STATUS IS data-name-2].
```

FILE-CONTROL Entry - Indexed Files

```
FILE-CONTROL.

    SELECT file-name
    ASSIGN TO assignment-name-1 [assignment-name-2] ...

    [RESERVE integer ⎡AREA  ⎤ ]
                     ⎣AREAS ⎦

    ORGANIZATION IS INDEXED

                        ⎧SEQUENTIAL⎫
    [ACCESS MODE IS     ⎨RANDOM    ⎬ ]
                        ⎩DYNAMIC   ⎭

    RECORD KEY IS data-name-3
        [PASSWORD IS data-name-1]

    [ALTERNATE RECORD KEY IS data-name-4
        [PASSWORD IS data-name-5]

        [WITH DUPLICATES] ] ...

    [FILE STATUS IS data-name-2].
```

FILE-CONTROL Entry – Relative Files

```
FILE-CONTROL.

    SELECT file-name
    ASSIGN TO assignment-name-1 [assignment-name-2] ...

    [RESERVE integer ⎡AREA  ⎤ ]
                     ⎣AREAS ⎦

    ORGANIZATION IS RELATIVE
    [ACCESS MODE IS

        ⎧SEQUENTIAL [RELATIVE KEY IS data-name-6]⎫
        ⎨RANDOM     ⎬                             ⎬ ]
        ⎩DYNAMIC    ⎭ RELATIVE KEY IS data-name-7 ⎭

    [PASSWORD IS data-name-1]

    [FILE STATUS IS data-name-2].
```

Note: The key word I-O-CONTROL appears only once, at the beginning of the paragraph before the first I-O-Control entry.

I-O-CONTROL Paragraph – Physical Sequential Files

```
I-O-CONTROL.

    [RERUN ON assignment-name
                ⎧integer-1 RECORDS⎫
        EVERY   ⎨         ⎧REEL⎫  ⎬ OF file-name-1] ...
                ⎩[END OF] ⎩UNIT⎭  ⎭

           ⎡RECORD     ⎤
    [SAME  ⎢SORT       ⎥ AREA
           ⎣SORT-MERGE ⎦
       FOR file-name-2 {file-name-3} ... ] ...

    [MULTIPLE FILE TAPE CONTAINS

        file-name-4 [POSITION integer-2]
        [file-name-5 [POSITION integer-3]] ... ] ... .
```

5

6

Figure D.3

414

I-O-CONTROL.

  [RERUN ON assignment-name

     EVERY integer-1 RECORDS OF file-name-1] ...

  [SAME $\begin{bmatrix} \text{RECORD} \\ \underline{\text{SORT}} \\ \underline{\text{SORT-MERGE}} \end{bmatrix}$ AREA

     FOR file-name-2 {file-name-3} ...] ... .

Data Division Formats

File Section Formats

Format 1 – Physical Sequential Files

FILE SECTION.

FD file-name

  [BLOCK CONTAINS [integer-1 TO] integer-2 $\begin{Bmatrix} \text{CHARACTERS} \\ \underline{\text{RECORDS}} \end{Bmatrix}$]

  [RECORD CONTAINS [integer-3 TO] integer-4 CHARACTERS]

  LABEL $\begin{Bmatrix} \underline{\text{RECORD}} \text{ IS} \\ \underline{\text{RECORDS}} \text{ ARE} \end{Bmatrix}$ $\begin{Bmatrix} \text{STANDARD} \\ \text{OMITTED} \end{Bmatrix}$

  [VALUE OF system-name-1 IS $\begin{Bmatrix} \text{data-name-1} \\ \text{literal-1} \end{Bmatrix}$

    [system-name-2 IS $\begin{Bmatrix} \text{data-name-2} \\ \text{literal-2} \end{Bmatrix}$] ...]

  [DATA $\begin{Bmatrix} \underline{\text{RECORD}} \text{ IS} \\ \underline{\text{RECORDS}} \text{ ARE} \end{Bmatrix}$ data-name-3 [data-name-4] ...]

  [LINAGE IS $\begin{Bmatrix} \text{data-name-5} \\ \text{integer-5} \end{Bmatrix}$ LINES

    [WITH FOOTING AT $\begin{Bmatrix} \text{data-name-6} \\ \text{integer-6} \end{Bmatrix}$]

    [LINES AT TOP $\begin{Bmatrix} \text{date-name-7} \\ \text{integer-7} \end{Bmatrix}$]

    [LINES AT BOTTOM $\begin{Bmatrix} \text{data-name-8} \\ \text{integer-8} \end{Bmatrix}$]

[$\begin{Bmatrix} \text{REPORT IS} \\ \underline{\text{REPORTS}} \text{ ARE} \end{Bmatrix}$ report-name-1 [report-name-2] ...]

[CODE-SET IS alphabet-name].

Format 2 – VSAM Files (Sequential, Indexed, Relative)

FILE SECTION.

FD file-name

  [BLOCK CONTAINS [integer-1 TO] integer-2 $\begin{Bmatrix} \text{CHARACTERS} \\ \underline{\text{RECORDS}} \end{Bmatrix}$]

  [RECORD CONTAINS [integer-3 TO] integer-4 CHARACTERS]

  LABEL $\begin{Bmatrix} \underline{\text{RECORD}} \text{ IS} \\ \underline{\text{RECORDS}} \text{ ARE} \end{Bmatrix}$ $\begin{Bmatrix} \text{STANDARD} \\ \text{OMITTED} \end{Bmatrix}$

  [VALUE OF system name-1 IS $\begin{Bmatrix} \text{data-name-1} \\ \text{literal-1} \end{Bmatrix}$

    [system-name-2 IS $\begin{Bmatrix} \text{data-name-2} \\ \text{literal-2} \end{Bmatrix}$] ...]

  [DATA $\begin{Bmatrix} \underline{\text{RECORD}} \text{ IS} \\ \underline{\text{RECORDS}} \text{ ARE} \end{Bmatrix}$ data-name-3 [data-name-4] ...].

01-49 data-name/FILLER Clause

  [REDEFINES Clause]

  [BLANK WHEN ZERO Clause]

  [JUSTIFIED Clause]

  [OCCURS Clause]

  [PICTURE Clause]

  [SIGN Clause]

  [SYNCHRONIZED Clause]

  [USAGE Clause].

[88 condition-name VALUE Clause.]

[66 RENAMES Clause.]

Note: Details of the above data description clauses are given in the following WORKING-STORAGE SECTION formats.

7

8

Figure D.4

415

WORKING-STORAGE SECTION.

$\left\{\begin{matrix} 77 \\ 01-49 \end{matrix}\right\}$ $\left\{\begin{matrix} \text{data-name-1} \\ \text{FILLER} \end{matrix}\right\}$

[REDEFINES data-name-2]

[BLANK WHEN ZERO]

[$\left\{\begin{matrix} \text{JUSTIFIED} \\ \text{JUST} \end{matrix}\right\}$ RIGHT]

[OCCURS Clause -- See Table Handling formats]

[$\left\{\begin{matrix} \text{PICTURE} \\ \text{PIC} \end{matrix}\right\}$ IS character-string]

[[SIGN IS] $\left\{\begin{matrix} \text{LEADING} \\ \text{TRAILING} \end{matrix}\right\}$ [SEPARATE CHARACTER]]

[$\left\{\begin{matrix} \text{SYNCHRONIZED} \\ \text{SYNC} \end{matrix}\right\}$ $\left[\begin{matrix} \text{LEFT} \\ \text{RIGHT} \end{matrix}\right]$]

[[USAGE IS]$\left\{\begin{matrix} \text{DISPLAY} \\ \text{INDEX} \\ \text{COMPUTATIONAL} \\ \underline{\text{COMP}} \\ \text{COMPUTATIONAL-3} \\ \underline{\text{COMP-3}} \\ \text{COMPUTATIONAL-4} \\ \underline{\text{COMP-4}} \end{matrix}\right\}$]

[VALUE IS literal].

[88 condition-name $\left\{\begin{matrix} \text{VALUE IS} \\ \text{VALUES ARE} \end{matrix}\right\}$

literal-1 [$\left\{\begin{matrix} \text{THROUGH} \\ \text{THRU} \end{matrix}\right\}$ literal-2]

[literal-3 [$\left\{\begin{matrix} \text{THROUGH} \\ \text{THRU} \end{matrix}\right\}$ literal-4]] ... .]

[66 data-name-1 RENAMES data-name-2

[$\left\{\begin{matrix} \text{THROUGH} \\ \text{THRU} \end{matrix}\right\}$ data-name-3].]

9

Note: Valid clauses in the LINKAGE SECTION are given with the formats for the Subprogram Linkage feature. Valid clauses in the COMMUNICATION SECTION are given with the formats for the Communication Feature.

Valid formats for the REPORT SECTION are given with the formats for the Report Writer Feature.

Procedure Division Formats

Conditional Expressions

Class Condition

identifier IS [NOT] $\left\{\begin{matrix} \text{NUMERIC} \\ \text{ALPHABETIC} \end{matrix}\right\}$

Condition – Name Condition

condition-name

Relation Condition

operand-1 IS [NOT] $\left\{\begin{matrix} \text{GREATER THAN} \\ > \\ \text{LESS THAN} \\ < \\ \text{EQUAL TO} \\ = \end{matrix}\right\}$ operand-2

Note: Operand-1 and operand-2 may each be an identifier, a literal, or an arithmetic expression. There must be at least one reference to an indentifier.

Sign Condition

operand IS [NOT] $\left\{\begin{matrix} \text{POSITIVE} \\ \text{NEGATIVE} \\ \text{ZERO} \end{matrix}\right\}$

Note: Operand must be a numeric identifier or an arithmetic expression.

Switch – Status Condition

condition-name

Negated Simple Condition

NOT simple-condition

10

Figure D.5

416

Combined Condition

condition $\left\{\begin{array}{c}\underline{AND}\\ \underline{OR}\end{array}\right\}$ condition ...

Abbreviated Combined Relation Condition

relation-condition $\left\{\ \left\{\begin{array}{c}\underline{AND}\\ \underline{OR}\end{array}\right\}\ [\underline{NOT}]\right.$

[relational-operator] object } ...

Procedure Division Header

<u>PROCEDURE</u> <u>DIVISION</u> [<u>USING</u> identifier-1 [identifier-2]...].

ACCEPT Statement (for Data Transfer)

<u>ACCEPT</u> identifier [<u>FROM</u> $\left\{\begin{array}{c}\text{mnemonic-name}\\ \boxed{\text{function-name}}\end{array}\right\}$]

ACCEPT Statement (for System Information Transfer)

<u>ACCEPT</u> identifier <u>FROM</u> $\left\{\begin{array}{c}\underline{DATE}\\ \underline{DAY}\\ \underline{TIME}\end{array}\right\}$

ADD Statement – Format 1

<u>ADD</u> $\left\{\begin{array}{c}\text{identifier-1}\\ \text{literal-1}\end{array}\right\}$ $\left[\begin{array}{c}\text{identifier-2}\\ \text{literal-2}\end{array}\right]$ ...

    <u>TO</u> identifier-m [<u>ROUNDED</u>]
       [identifier-n [<u>ROUNDED</u>]] ...

    [ON <u>SIZE</u> <u>ERROR</u> imperative-statement]

ADD Statement – Format 2

<u>ADD</u> $\left\{\begin{array}{c}\text{identifier-1}\\ \text{literal-1}\end{array}\right\}$ $\left\{\begin{array}{c}\text{identifier-2}\\ \text{literal-2}\end{array}\right\}$ $\left[\begin{array}{c}\text{identifier-3}\\ \text{literal-3}\end{array}\right]$ ...

    <u>GIVING</u> identifier-m [<u>ROUNDED</u>]
       [identifier-n [<u>ROUNDED</u>]] ...

    [ON <u>SIZE</u> <u>ERROR</u> imperative-statement]

ADD Statement – Format 3

<u>ADD</u> $\left\{\begin{array}{c}\underline{CORRESPONDING}\\ \underline{CORR}\end{array}\right\}$

    identifier-1 <u>TO</u> identifier-2 [<u>ROUNDED</u>]
    [ON <u>SIZE</u> <u>ERROR</u> imperative-statment]

ALTER Statement

<u>ALTER</u> procedure-name-1
        <u>TO</u> [<u>PROCEED</u> <u>TO</u>] procedure-name-2
    [procedure-name-3
        <u>TO</u> [<u>PROCEED</u> <u>TO</u>] procedure-name-4] ...

CLOSE Statement – Physical Sequential Files

<u>CLOSE</u> file-name-1 $\left[\begin{array}{c}\left\{\begin{array}{c}\underline{REEL}\\ \underline{UNIT}\end{array}\right\}\ \left[\begin{array}{c}\text{WITH NO }\underline{REWIND}\\ \text{FOR }\underline{REMOVAL}\end{array}\right]\\ \text{WITH }\left\{\begin{array}{c}\text{NO }\underline{REWIND}\\ \underline{LOCK}\end{array}\right\}\end{array}\right]$

    [file-name-2 $\left[\begin{array}{c}\left\{\begin{array}{c}\underline{REEL}\\ \underline{UNIT}\end{array}\right\}\ \left[\begin{array}{c}\text{WITH NO }\underline{REWIND}\\ \text{FOR }\underline{REMOVAL}\end{array}\right]\\ \text{WITH }\left\{\begin{array}{c}\text{NO }\underline{REWIND}\\ \underline{LOCK}\end{array}\right\}\end{array}\right]$] ...

CLOSE Statement – VSAM Files

<u>CLOSE</u> file-name-1 [WITH <u>LOCK</u>]
      [file-name-2 [WITH <u>LOCK</u>]] ...

COMPUTE Statement

<u>COMPUTE</u> identifier-1 [<u>ROUNDED</u>]
      [identifier-2 [<u>ROUNDED</u>]] ...
    = arithmetic-expression
    [ON <u>SIZE</u> <u>ERROR</u> imperative-statement]

11

12

Figure D.6

417

DECLARATIVES Procedures

<u>PROCEDURE</u> <u>DIVISION</u> [<u>USING</u> identifier-1 [identifier-2]...].

<u>DECLARATIVES</u>.
{section-name <u>SECTION</u> [priority-number]. <u>USE</u> sentence.

[paragraph-name. [sentence.] ...] ...] ...}
<u>END</u> <u>DECLARATIVES</u>.

DELETE Statement

<u>DELETE</u> file-name RECORD
　　[<u>INVALID</u> KEY imperative-statement]

DISPLAY Statement

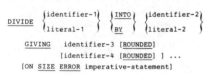

<u>DISPLAY</u> {identifier-1 / literal-1} [identifier-2 / literal-2] ...

　　[<u>UPON</u> {mnemonic-name / function-name}]

DIVIDE Statement – Format 1

<u>DIVIDE</u> {identifier-1 / literal-1}

　　<u>INTO</u>　identifier-2 [<u>ROUNDED</u>]
　　　　[identifier-3 [<u>ROUNDED</u>]] ...
　　[ON <u>SIZE</u> <u>ERROR</u> imperative-statement]

DIVIDE Statement – Format 2

<u>DIVIDE</u> {identifier-1 / literal-1} {<u>INTO</u> / <u>BY</u>} {identifier-2 / literal-2}

　　<u>GIVING</u>　identifier-3 [<u>ROUNDED</u>]
　　　　[identifier-4 [<u>ROUNDED</u>]] ...
　　[ON <u>SIZE</u> <u>ERROR</u> imperative-statement]

DIVIDE Statement – Format 3

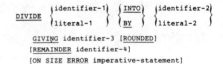

<u>DIVIDE</u> {identifier-1 / literal-1} {<u>INTO</u> / <u>BY</u>} {identifier-2 / literal-2}

　　<u>GIVING</u> identifier-3 [<u>ROUNDED</u>]
　　[<u>REMAINDER</u> identifier-4]
　　[ON <u>SIZE</u> <u>ERROR</u> imperative-statement]

ENTER Statement

　　<u>ENTER</u> language-name [routine-name].

EXIT Statement

paragraph-name. <u>EXIT</u> [<u>PROGRAM</u>].

<u>Note</u>:　The paragraph-name is not part of the EXIT statement format; however, it is always required preceding an EXIT statement.

GO TO Statement – Unconditional

　　<u>GO</u> TO procedure-name-1

GO TO Statement – Conditional

　　<u>GO</u> TO procedure-name-1 [procedure-name-2] ...
　　　　procedure-name-n <u>DEPENDING</u> ON identifier

GO TO Statement – Altered

　　<u>GO</u> TO.

IF Statement

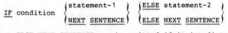

　　<u>IF</u> condition {statement-1 / <u>NEXT</u> <u>SENTENCE</u>} {<u>ELSE</u> statement-2 / <u>ELSE</u> <u>NEXT</u> <u>SENTENCE</u>}

<u>Note</u>:　ELSE NEXT SENTENCE may be omitted if it immediately precedes the period for the conditional statement.

13

14

Figure D.7

418

INSPECT Statement

```
INSPECT identifier-1
  [TALLYING {identifier-2
     FOR { {ALL      }  {identifier-3} }
         { {LEADING  }  {literal-1   } }
         {  CHARACTERS                  }
        [ {BEFORE} INITIAL {identifier-4} ])... } ... ]
        [ {AFTER }         {literal-2   }

  [REPLACING
   {                                                        }
   { CHARACTERS BY {identifier-6}                           }
   {              {literal-4   }                            }
   {                                                        }
   {    [ {BEFORE} INITIAL {identifier-7} ]                 ]
   {      {AFTER }         {literal-5   }                   }
   { {ALL    }  {identifier-5}    {identifier-6}            }
   { {LEADING}  {literal-3   } BY {literal-4   }            }
   { {FIRST  }                                              }
   {    [ {BEFORE} INITIAL {identifier-7} ] } ... } ...     }
   {      {AFTER }         {literal-3   }                   }
```

Note: Either the TALLYING option or the REPLACING option must be specified; both may be specified.

MOVE Statement — Format 1

```
MOVE {identifier-1} TO identifier-2 [identifier-3] ...
     {literal     }
```

MULTIPLY Statement — Format 1

```
MOVE {CORRESPONDING} identifier-1 TO identifier-2
     {CORR         }
```

MULTIPLY Statement — Format 1

```
MULTIPLY {identifier-1} BY identifier-2 [ROUNDED]
         {literal-1   }

         [identifier-3 [ROUNDED] ] ...
         [ON SIZE ERROR imperative-statement]
```

MULTIPLY Statement — Format 2

```
MULTIPLY {identifier-1} BY {identifier-2}
         {literal-1   }    {literal-2   }

   GIVING identifier-3 [ROUNDED]
          [identifier-4 [ROUNDED] ] ...
   [ON SIZE ERROR imperative-statement]
```

OPEN Statement — Sequential Files

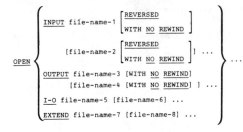

```
      { INPUT file-name-1 [REVERSED        ]            }
      {                   [WITH NO REWIND  ]            }
      {                                                 }
      {        [file-name-2 [REVERSED       ] ] ...     }
      {                     [WITH NO REWIND ]           }
OPEN  {                                                 } ...
      { OUTPUT file-name-3 [WITH NO REWIND]             }
      {        [file-name-4 [WITH NO REWIND] ] ...      }
      {                                                 }
      { I-O file-name-5 [file-name-6] ...               }
      {                                                 }
      { EXTEND file-name-7 [file-name-8] ...            }
```

OPEN Statement — Indexed Files

```
      { INPUT file-name-1 [file-name-2] ...   }
      { OUTPUT file-name-3 [file-name-4] ...  }
OPEN  { I-O file-name-5 [file-name-6] ...     }
      { EXTEND file-name-7 [file-name-8] ...  }
```

15

16

Figure D.8

OPEN Statement – Relative Files

$$\underline{OPEN} \quad \left\{ \begin{array}{l} \underline{INPUT}\ \text{file-name-1}\ [\text{file-name-2}]\ \dots \\ \underline{OUTPUT}\ \text{file-name-3}\ [\text{file-name-4}]\ \dots \\ \text{I-O}\ \text{file-name-5}\ [\text{file-name-6}]\ \dots \end{array} \right\} \ \dots$$

PERFORM Statement – Basic PERFORM

$$\underline{PERFORM}\ \text{procedure-name-1}\ [\ \left\{ \begin{array}{l} \underline{THROUGH} \\ \underline{THRU} \end{array} \right\} \ \text{procedure-name-2}]$$

PERFORM Statement – TIMES Option

$$\underline{PERFORM}\ \text{procedure-name-1}\ [\ \left\{ \begin{array}{l} \underline{THROUGH} \\ \underline{THRU} \end{array} \right\} \ \text{procedure-name-2}]$$

$$\left\{ \begin{array}{l} \text{identifier-1} \\ \text{integer-1} \end{array} \right\} \ \underline{TIMES}$$

PERFORM Statement – Conditional PERFORM

$$\underline{PERFORM}\ \text{procedure-name-1}\ [\ \left\{ \begin{array}{l} \underline{THROUGH} \\ \underline{THRU} \end{array} \right\} \ \text{procedure-name-2}]$$

$$\underline{UNTIL}\ \text{condition-1}$$

PERFORM Statement – VARYING Option

$$\underline{PERFORM}\ \text{procedure-name-1}\ [\ \left\{ \begin{array}{l} \underline{THROUGH} \\ \underline{THRU} \end{array} \right\} \ \text{procedure-name-2}]$$

$$\underline{VARYING} \ \left\{ \begin{array}{l} \text{index-name-1} \\ \text{identifier-1} \end{array} \right\} \ \underline{FROM} \ \left\{ \begin{array}{l} \text{index-name-2} \\ \text{literal-2} \\ \text{identifier-2} \end{array} \right\}$$

$$\underline{BY} \ \left\{ \begin{array}{l} \text{literal-3} \\ \text{identifier-3} \end{array} \right\} \ \underline{UNTIL}\ \text{condition-1}$$

$$[\underline{AFTER} \ \left\{ \begin{array}{l} \text{index-name-4} \\ \text{identifier-4} \end{array} \right\} \ \underline{FROM} \ \left\{ \begin{array}{l} \text{index-name-5} \\ \text{literal-5} \\ \text{identifier-5} \end{array} \right\}$$

$$\underline{BY} \ \left\{ \begin{array}{l} \text{literal-6} \\ \text{identifier-6} \end{array} \right\} \ \underline{UNTIL}\ \text{condition-2}$$

$$[\underline{AFTER} \ \left\{ \begin{array}{l} \text{index-name-7} \\ \text{identifier-7} \end{array} \right\} \ \underline{FROM} \ \left\{ \begin{array}{l} \text{index-name-8} \\ \text{literal-8} \\ \text{identifier-8} \end{array} \right\}$$

$$\underline{BY} \ \left\{ \begin{array}{l} \text{literal-9} \\ \text{identifier-9} \end{array} \right\} \ \underline{UNTIL}\ \text{condition-3]}\ ]$$

READ Statement – Sequential Retrieval

$$\underline{READ}\ \text{file-name}\ [\underline{NEXT}]\ \text{RECORD}\ [\underline{INTO}\ \text{identifier}]$$
$$[\text{AT}\ \underline{END}\ \text{imperative-statment}]$$

READ Statement – Random Retrieval

$$\underline{READ}\ \text{file-name}\ \text{RECORD}\ [\underline{INTO}\ \text{identifier}]$$
$$[\underline{KEY}\ \text{IS}\ \text{data-name}]$$
$$[\underline{INVALID}\ \text{KEY}\ \text{imperative-statemnt}]$$

REWRITE Statement

$$\underline{REWRITE}\ \text{record-name}\ [\underline{FROM}\ \text{identifier}]$$
$$[\underline{INVALID}\ \text{KEY}\ \text{imperative-statement}]$$

START Statement

$$\text{START}\ \text{file-name}\ [\text{KEY}\ \text{IS} \ \left\{ \begin{array}{l} \underline{EQUAL}\ \text{TO} \\ = \\ \underline{GREATER}\ \text{THAN} \\ > \\ \underline{NOT}\ \underline{LESS}\ \text{THAN} \\ \underline{NOT}\ < \end{array} \right\} \text{data-name}]$$

$$[\underline{INVALID}\ \text{KEY}\ \text{imperative-statement}]$$

17

Figure D.9

420

STOP Statement

$$\underline{STOP} \quad \begin{Bmatrix} RUN \\ literal \end{Bmatrix}$$

STRING Statement

$$\underline{STRING} \quad \begin{Bmatrix} identifier-1 \\ literal-1 \end{Bmatrix} \begin{bmatrix} identifier-2 \\ literal-2 \end{bmatrix} \dots$$

$$\underline{DELIMITED} \ BY \begin{Bmatrix} identifier-3 \\ literal-3 \\ \underline{SIZE} \end{Bmatrix}$$

$$\begin{bmatrix} \begin{Bmatrix} identifier-4 \\ literal-4 \end{Bmatrix} \begin{Bmatrix} identifier-5 \\ literal-5 \end{Bmatrix} \dots$$

$$\underline{DELIMITED} \ BY \begin{Bmatrix} identifier-6 \\ literal-6 \\ \underline{SIZE} \end{Bmatrix} \ ] \dots$$

INTO identifier-7

[WITH POINTER identifier-8]

[ON OVERFLOW imperative-statment]

SUBTRACT Statement – Format 1

$$\underline{SUBTRACT} \begin{Bmatrix} identifier-1 \\ literal-1 \end{Bmatrix} \begin{bmatrix} identifier-2 \\ literal-2 \end{bmatrix} \dots$$

FROM identifier-m [ROUNDED]

[identifier-n [ROUNDED]] ...

[ON SIZE ERROR imperative-statement]

SUBTRACT Statement – Format 2

$$\underline{SUBTRACT} \begin{Bmatrix} identifier-1 \\ literal-1 \end{Bmatrix} \begin{bmatrix} identifier-2 \\ literal-2 \end{bmatrix} \dots$$

$$\underline{FROM} \begin{Bmatrix} identifier-m \\ literal-m \end{Bmatrix}$$

GIVING identifier-n [ROUNDED]

[identifier-o [ROUNDED]] ...

[ON SIZE ERROR imperative-statement]

SUBTRACT Statement – Format 3

$$\underline{SUBTRACT} \begin{Bmatrix} \underline{CORRESPONDING} \\ \underline{CORR} \end{Bmatrix}$$

identifier-1 FROM identifier-2 [ROUNDED]

[ON SIZE ERROR imperative-statement]

TRANSFORM Statement

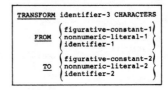

UNSTRING Statement

USE Sentence – EXCEPTION/ERROR Procedures

Figure D.10

WRITE Statement – Physical Sequential Files

```
WRITE record-name [FROM identifier]

  [ {BEFORE} ADVANCING { {identifier-2} [LINE ] } ]
    {AFTER }            { {integer    } [LINES] }
                        {                        }
                        { {mnemonic-name}        }
                        { {PAGE         }        }

  [AT {END-OF-PAGE} imperative-statement]
      {EOP        }
```

WRITE Statement – VSAM Sequential Files

```
WRITE record-name [FROM identifier]
```

WRITE Statement – VSAM Indexed and Relative Files

```
WRITE record-name [FROM identifier]
      [INVALID KEY imperative-statement]
```

Data Reference Formats

Qualification

Data Item References

```
{data-name-1   } [ {OF} data-name-2 ] ...
{condition-name}   {IN}
```

Procedure Name References

```
paragraph-name [ {OF} section-name]
                 {IN}
```

COPY Library References

```
text-name [ {OF} library-name]
            {IN}
```

Subscripting

```
{data-name-1   } [ {OF} data-name-2] ...
{condition-name}   {IN}

    (subscript [subscript [subscript]])
```

Indexing

```
{data-name-1   } [ {OF} data-name-2] ...
{condition-name}   {IN}

( {index-name-1 [ {±} literal-2]}
  {literal-1                    }

  [ {index-name-2 [ {±} literal-4]}
    {literal-3                    }
    {                             }
    {index-name-3 [ {±} literal-6]} ] ])
    {literal-5                    }
```

Table Handling Formats

Table Handling Data Division

OCCURS Clause – Fixed Length Tables

```
OCCURS integer-2 TIMES

  [ {ASCENDING } KEY IS data-name-2 [data-name-3]...]...
    {DESCENDING}

  [INDEXED BY index-name-1 [index-name-2]...]
```

OCCURS Clause – Variable Length Tables

```
OCCURS integer-1 TO integer-2 TIMES

  DEPENDING ON data-name-1

  [ {ASCENDING } KEY IS data-name-2 [data-name-3]...]...
    {DESCENDING}

  [INDEXED BY index-name-1 [index-name-2]... ]
```

USAGE IS INDEX Clause

```
[USAGE IS] INDEX
```

21

22

Figure D.11

422

23

Table Handling Procedure Division

SEARCH Statement — Sequential Search

SEARCH identifier-1 [VARYING $\begin{Bmatrix} \text{identifier-2} \\ \text{index-name-1} \end{Bmatrix}$]

    [AT END imperative-statement-1]

    WHEN condition-1 $\begin{Bmatrix} \text{imperative-statement-2} \\ \underline{\text{NEXT}}\ \underline{\text{SENTENCE}} \end{Bmatrix}$

    [WHEN condition-2 $\begin{Bmatrix} \text{imperative-statement-3} \\ \underline{\text{NEXT}}\ \underline{\text{SENTENCE}} \end{Bmatrix}$] ...

SEARCH Statement — Binary Search

    SEARCH ALL identifier-1

      [AT END imperative-statement-1]

      WHEN $\begin{Bmatrix} \text{relation-condition-1} \\ \text{condition-name-1} \end{Bmatrix}$

        [AND $\begin{Bmatrix} \text{relation-condition-2} \\ \text{condition-name-2} \end{Bmatrix}$] ...

      $\begin{bmatrix} \text{imperative-statement-2} \\ \underline{\text{NEXT}}\ \underline{\text{SENTENCE}} \end{bmatrix}$

Note: In Format 2, each relation-condition must be an
EQUAL TO (=) condition with an ASCENDING/DESCENDING KEY
data item for this table element as the subject.

SET Statement — Direct Indexing

    SET $\begin{Bmatrix} \text{index-name-1 [index-name-2]} \dots \\ \text{identifier-1 [identifier-2]} \dots \end{Bmatrix}$ TO $\begin{Bmatrix} \text{index-name-3} \\ \text{identifier-3} \\ \text{literal-1} \end{Bmatrix}$

SET Statement — Relative Indexing

    SET index-name-4 [index-name-5] ...

    $\begin{Bmatrix} \underline{\text{UP}}\ \underline{\text{BY}} \\ \underline{\text{DOWN}}\ \underline{\text{BY}} \end{Bmatrix}$ $\begin{Bmatrix} \text{identifier-4} \\ \text{literal-2} \end{Bmatrix}$

Sort Merge Formats

Sort/Merge Environment Division

FILE-CONTROL Entry

    SELECT file-name
    ASSIGN TO assignment-name-1 [assignment-name-2] ...

I-O-CONTROL Entry

    [SAME $\begin{Bmatrix} \underline{\text{RECORD}} \\ \underline{\text{SORT}} \\ \underline{\text{SORT-MERGE}} \end{Bmatrix}$ AREA

      FOR file-name-1 [file-name-2] ...].

Sort/Merge Data Division

SD Entry

SD file-name
    [RECORD CONTAINS [integer-1 TO] integer-2 CHARACTERS]

    [DATA $\begin{Bmatrix} \underline{\text{RECORD}}\ \text{IS} \\ \underline{\text{RECORDS}}\ \text{ARE} \end{Bmatrix}$ data-name-1 [data-name-2] ...].

24

Figure D.12

MERGE Statement

```
MERGE file-name-1

         ⎧ ASCENDING  ⎫
   ON    ⎨            ⎬  KEY data-name-1 [data-name-2]...
         ⎩ DESCENDING ⎭

         ⎧ ASCENDING  ⎫
  [ON    ⎨            ⎬  KEY data-name-3 [data-name-4]...]...
         ⎩ DESCENDING ⎭

  [COLLATING SEQUENCE IS alphabet-name]
   USING file-name-2 file-name-3 [file-name-4]...

  ⎧ GIVING file-name-5                              ⎫
  ⎪ OUTPUT PROCEDURE                                ⎪
  ⎨                      ⎧ THROUGH ⎫                ⎬
  ⎪ IS section-name-1 [  ⎨         ⎬  section-name-2]⎪
  ⎩                      ⎩ THRU    ⎭                ⎭
```

RELEASE Statement (SORT Feature only)

```
   RELEASE record-name [FROM identifier]
```

RETURN Statement

```
   RETURN file-name RECORD [INTO identifier]
        AT END imperative-statement
```

SORT Statement

```
   SORT file-name-1

         ⎧ ASCENDING  ⎫
   ON    ⎨            ⎬  KEY data-name-1 [data-name-2]...
         ⎩ DESCENDING ⎭

         ⎧ ASCENDING  ⎫
  [ON    ⎨            ⎬  KEY data-name-3 [data-name-4]...]...
         ⎩ DESCENDING ⎭
```

```
  [COLLATING SEQUENCE IS alphabet-name]

  ⎧ USING file-name-2 [file-name-3]...                   ⎫
  ⎪ INPUT PROCEDURE                                      ⎪
  ⎪                      ⎧ THROUGH ⎫                     ⎪
  ⎪ IS section-name-1 [  ⎨         ⎬  section-name-2]     ⎬
  ⎪                      ⎩ THRU    ⎭                     ⎪
  ⎪ GIVING file-name-4                                   ⎪
  ⎪ OUTPUT PROCEDURE                                     ⎪
  ⎨                      ⎧ THROUGH ⎫                     ⎬
  ⎪ IS section-name-3 [  ⎨         ⎬  section-name-4]     ⎪
  ⎩                      ⎩ THRU    ⎭                     ⎭
```

Report Writer Formats

Report Writer Environment Division

```
SPECIAL-NAMES.
   [function-name-1 IS mnemonic-name] ...
```

Report Writer Data Division

File Section – FD Entry

```
FD  file-name

    ⎧ REPORT IS   ⎫
    ⎨             ⎬  report-name-1 [report-name-2] ...
    ⎩ REPORTS ARE ⎭

    [RECORD CONTAINS [integer-1 TO] integer-2 CHARACTERS]

    [BLOCK CONTAINS Clause]
    LABEL RECORDS Clause
    [DATA RECORDS Clause]
    [VALUE OF Clause].
```

Report Section – RD Entry

```
RD  report-name
    [WITH CODE mnemonic-name]

     ⎧ CONTROL IS   ⎫ ⎧ FINAL   ⎫
   [ ⎨              ⎬ ⎨         ⎬ identifier-1 [identifier-2]... ]
     ⎩ CONTROLS ARE ⎭ ⎩ [FINAL] ⎭

           ⎡ LIMIT IS   ⎤            ⎧ LINE  ⎫
    [PAGE  ⎢            ⎥  integer-1 ⎨       ⎬
           ⎣ LIMITS ARE ⎦            ⎩ LINES ⎭

       [HEADING       integer-2]
       [FIRST DETAIL  integer-3]
       [LAST DETAIL   integer-4]
       [FOOTING       integer-5] ].
```

25   26

Figure D.13

424

Report Group Description Entry – Format 1

```
01 [data-name]

                  ⎧REPORT HEADING⎫
                  ⎨RH           ⎬
                  ⎩             ⎭

                  ⎧PAGE HEADING⎫
                  ⎨PH          ⎬
                  ⎩            ⎭

                  ⎧CONTROL HEADING⎫  ⎧FINAL      ⎫
                  ⎨CH             ⎬  ⎨identifier-n⎬
                  ⎩               ⎭  ⎩           ⎭
    TYPE IS       ⎧DETAIL⎫
                  ⎨DE    ⎬
                  ⎩      ⎭

                  ⎧CONTROL FOOTING⎫  ⎧identifier-n⎫
                  ⎨CF             ⎬  ⎨FINAL      ⎬
                  ⎩               ⎭  ⎩           ⎭

                  ⎧PAGE FOOTING⎫
                  ⎨PF          ⎬
                  ⎩            ⎭

                  ⎧REPORT FOOTING⎫
                  ⎨RF            ⎬
                  ⎩              ⎭

                          ⎧integer-1     ⎫
    [LINE NUMBER IS       ⎨PLUS integer-2⎬  ]
                          ⎩NEXT PAGE     ⎭

                          ⎧integer-1     ⎫
    [NEXT GROUP IS        ⎨PLUS integer-2⎬  ]
                          ⎩NEXT PAGE     ⎭

    [USAGE Clause].
```

Report Group Description Entry – Format 2

```
    level-number [data-name]
       [LINE Clause]
       [USAGE Clause].
```

Report Group Description Entry – Format 3

```
    level-number [data-name]
       [COLUMN NUMBER IS integer]
       [GROUP INDICATE]
       [LINE Clause]

       ⎧SOURCE IS identifier                                    ⎫
       ⎪SUM identifier-1 [identifier-2] ... [UPON data-name-2]  ⎪
       ⎨                      ⎧FINAL      ⎫                      ⎬
       ⎪         [RESET ON    ⎨identifier-3⎬  ]                 ⎪
       ⎪                      ⎩           ⎭                      ⎪
       ⎩VALUE IS literal                                        ⎭

        PICTURE Clause
       [USAGE Clause]
       [BLANK WHEN ZERO Clause]
       [JUSTIFIED Clause].
```

Report Group Description Entry – Format 4

```
01 [data-name]
    TYPE Clause
    [LINE Clause]
    [NEXT GROUP Clause]
    [COLUMN Clause]
    [GROUP INDICATE Clause]

    ⎧SOURCE Clause⎫
    ⎨SUM Clause   ⎬
    ⎩VALUE Clause ⎭

    PICTURE Clause
    [USAGE Clause]
    [BLANK WHEN ZERO Clause]
    [JUSTIFIED Clause].
```

27

28

Figure D.14

425

```
┌─────────────────────────────────────────────────────┐
│  Report Writer Procedure Division                     │
│                                                       │
│  GENERATE Statement                                   │
│                                                       │
│                        ⎧ data-name  ⎫                 │
│         GENERATE       ⎨            ⎬                 │
│                        ⎩ report-name ⎭                │
│                                                       │
│  INITIATE Statement                                   │
│                                                       │
│      INITIATE report-name-1 [report-name-2] ...       │
│                                                       │
│                                                       │
│  PRINT-SWITCH Statement                               │
│                                                       │
│      MOVE 1 TO PRINT-SWITCH                            │
│                                                       │
│  TERMINATE Statement                                  │
│                                                       │
│      TERMINATE report-name-1 [report-name-2] ...      │
│                                                       │
│                                                       │
│  USE BEFORE REPORTING Sentence                        │
│                                                       │
│      USE BEFORE REPORTING data-name.                  │
│                                                       │
└─────────────────────────────────────────────────────┘

Segmentation Formats

SEGMENT-LIMIT Clause — Environment Division

    SEGMENT-LIMIT IS priority-number

Priority-numbers – Procedure Division

section-name SECTION [priority-number].
```

Source Program Library Formats

COPY Statement

```
                       ⎧ OF ⎫
COPY text-name [       ⎨ ── ⎬ library-name]
                       ⎩ IN ⎭

        [SUPPRESS]

                      ⎧ ==pseudo-text-1== ⎫
                      ⎪ identifier-1       ⎪
        [REPLACING    ⎨                    ⎬
                      ⎪ literal-1          ⎪
                      ⎩ word-1             ⎭

                      ⎧ ==pseudo-text-2== ⎫
                      ⎪ identifier-1       ⎪
           BY         ⎨                    ⎬  ... ].
                      ⎪ literal-2          ⎪
                      ⎩ word-2             ⎭
```

```
┌─────────────────────────────────────────────────────┐
│  Extended Source Program Library Formats (IBM Extension) │
│  BASIS Statement                                      │
│  [sequence-number] BASIS basis-name                   │
│                                                       │
│  INSERT/DELETE Statements                             │
│                       ⎧ INSERT ⎫                      │
│  [sequence-number]    ⎨        ⎬ sequence-number-field │
│                       ⎩ DELETE ⎭                      │
│                                                       │
└─────────────────────────────────────────────────────┘
```

Subprogram Linkage Formats

LINKAGE SECTION – Data Division

LINKAGE SECTION.

```
   ⎧ 77    ⎫
[ ⎨        ⎬   data-name/FILLER Clause
   ⎩ 01-49 ⎭

    [REDEFINES Clause]
    [BLANK WHEN ZERO Clause]
    [JUSTIFIED Clause]
    [OCCURS Clause]
    [PICTURE Clause]
    [SIGN Clause]
    [SYNCHRONIZED Clause]
    [USAGE Clause].
[88  condition-name VALUE Clause.]
[66  RENAMES Clause.]]...
```

Figure D.15

31

Subprogram Linkage – Procedure Division

CALL Statement – Static Linkage

```
CALL literal-1 [USING identifier-1 [identifier-2] ...]
```

CALL Statement – Dynamic Linkage

```
CALL  {literal-2    }
      {identifier-3 }
      [USING identifier-1 [identifier-2] ... ]
      [ON OVERFLOW imperative-statement]
```

CANCEL Statement

```
CANCEL  {literal-1    }  [literal-2    ]  ...
        {identifier-1 }  [identifier-2 ]
```

ENTRY Statement

```
ENTRY literal [USING identifier-1 [identifier-2]...]
```

EXIT PROGRAM Statement

```
paragraph-name. EXIT PROGRAM.
```

Note: The paragraph-name is not part of the EXIT statement format; however, it is always required preceding an EXIT statement.

GOBACK Statement

```
GOBACK.
```

Procedure Division Header – Called Program

```
PROCEDURE DIVISION [USING identifier-1 [identifier-2]...].
```

STOP RUN Statement

```
STOP RUN.
```

Communication Feature Formats

Communication Feature Data Division

Input CD Entry – Option 1

```
CD  cd-name FOR [INITIAL] INPUT
        [SYMBOLIC QUEUE IS       data-name-1]
        [SYMBOLIC SUB-QUEUE-1 IS data-name-2]
        [SYMBOLIC SUB-QUEUE-2 IS data-name-3]
        [SYMBOLIC SUB-QUEUE-3 IS data-name-4]
        [MESSAGE DATE IS         data-name-5]
        [MESSAGE TIME IS         data-name-6]
        [SYMBOLIC SOURCE IS      data-name-7]
        [TEXT LENGTH IS          data-name-8]
        [END KEY IS              data-name-9]
        [STATUS KEY IS           data-name-10]
        [MESSAGE COUNT IS        data-name-11].
```

Input CD Entry – Option 2

```
CD  cd-name FOR [INITIAL] INPUT
        [data-name-1 data-name-2 ... data-name-11].
```

Output CD Entry

```
CD  cd-name FOR OUTPUT
        [DESTINATION COUNT IS    data-name-1]
        [TEXT LENGTH IS          data-name-2]
        [STATUS KEY IS           data-name-3]
        [DESTINATION TABLE OCCURS integer-2 TIMES
            [INDEXED BY index-name-1 [index-name-2] ... ] ]
        [ERROR KEY IS            data-name-4]
        [SYMBOLIC DESTINATION IS data-name-5].
```

Communication Feature Procedure Division

ACCEPT MESSAGE COUNT Statement

```
ACCEPT cd-name MESSAGE COUNT
```

32

Figure D.16

DISABLE Statement

$$\underline{\text{DISABLE}} \left\{ \begin{array}{l} \underline{\text{INPUT}}\ [\underline{\text{TERMINAL}}] \\ \underline{\text{OUTPUT}} \end{array} \right\} \text{cd-name}$$

$$\text{WITH } \underline{\text{KEY}} \left\{ \begin{array}{l} \text{identifier} \\ \text{literal} \end{array} \right\}$$

ENABLE Statement

$$\underline{\text{ENABLE}} \left\{ \begin{array}{l} \underline{\text{INPUT}}\ [\underline{\text{TERMINAL}}] \\ \underline{\text{OUTPUT}} \end{array} \right\} \text{cd-name}$$

$$\text{WITH } \underline{\text{KEY}} \left\{ \begin{array}{l} \text{identifier} \\ \text{literal} \end{array} \right\}$$

RECEIVE Statement

$$\underline{\text{RECEIVE}} \text{ cd-name} \left\{ \begin{array}{l} \underline{\text{MESSAGE}} \\ \underline{\text{SEGMENT}} \end{array} \right\} \underline{\text{INTO}} \text{ identifier}$$

$$[\underline{\text{NO}}\ \underline{\text{DATA}} \text{ imperative-statement}]$$

SEND Statement – Format 1

$$\underline{\text{SEND}} \text{ cd-name } \underline{\text{FROM}} \text{ identifier-1}$$

SEND Statement – Format 2

$$\underline{\text{SEND}} \text{ cd-name } [\underline{\text{FROM}} \text{ identifier-1}] \text{ WITH } \left\{ \begin{array}{l} \text{identifier-2} \\ \underline{\text{ESI}} \\ \underline{\text{EMI}} \\ \underline{\text{EGI}} \end{array} \right\}$$

$$\left[\left\{ \begin{array}{l} \underline{\text{BEFORE}} \\ \underline{\text{AFTER}} \end{array} \right\} \text{ADVANCING} \left\{ \begin{array}{ll} \left\{ \begin{array}{l} \text{identifier-3} \\ \text{integer} \end{array} \right\} & \left[\begin{array}{l} \text{LINE} \\ \text{LINES} \end{array} \right] \\ \left\{ \begin{array}{l} \text{mnemonic-name} \\ \underline{\text{PAGE}} \end{array} \right\} & \end{array} \right\} \right]$$

Debugging Feature Formats

Debugging Feature Environment Division

SOURCE-COMPUTER Paragraph

$$\underline{\text{SOURCE-COMPUTER}}. \text{ computer-name}$$

$$[\text{WITH } \underline{\text{DEBUGGING}}\ \underline{\text{MODE}}].$$

Debugging Feature Procedure Division

USE FOR DEBUGGING Sentence

$$\text{section-name } \underline{\text{SECTION}} \text{ [priority-number]}.$$

$$\underline{\text{USE}} \text{ FOR } \underline{\text{DEBUGGING}}$$

$$\text{ON} \left\{ \begin{array}{l} \text{cd-name-1} \\ [\text{ALL } \underline{\text{REFERENCES}} \text{ OF}] \text{ identifier-1} \\ \text{file-name-1} \\ \text{procedure-name-1} \\ \underline{\text{ALL}}\ \underline{\text{PROCEDURES}} \end{array} \right\}$$

$$\left[\begin{array}{l} \text{cd-name-2} \\ [\text{ALL } \underline{\text{REFERENCES}} \text{ OF}] \text{ identifier-2} \\ \text{file-name-2} \\ \text{procedure-name-2} \\ \underline{\text{ALL}}\ \underline{\text{PROCEDURES}} \end{array} \right] \cdots .$$

33

34

Figure D.17

428

IBM OS/VS COBOL
Reserved Words Summary

IBM Reference Data

Operating System

IBM
OS/VS
COBOL

IBM OS/VS COBOL
Reserved Words Summary

The following reserved word list identifies all reserved words in:

- IBM OS/VS COBOL
- American National Standard COBOL, X3.23-1974
- CODASYL COBOL (from *CODASYL COBOL Journal of Development*, dated January 1976)
- IBM COBOL implementations other than OS/VS COBOL

Each word in the list is preceded by an identification code that specifies the source of the reserved word. The codes and their meanings are listed in the figure below.

Any reserved word not identified as an OS/VS COBOL reserved word can be used in an OS/VS COBOL program; however, if CODASYL compatibility or IBM compatibility is important to an installation, these words should not be used.

Code	Meaning
(blank)	An OS/VS COBOL reserved word from the 1974 standard.
ans-o	An OS/VS COBOL reserved word from the 1968 standard.
ans-f	An OS/VS COBOL reserved word that is an IBM function-name conforming to the 1974 standard.
ans-n	A reserved word from the 1974 standard not used by OS/VS COBOL.
ibm-a	An OS/VS COBOL reserved word that is an extension to the 1974 standard.
ibm-c	An OS/VS COBOL reserved word that is an extension both to the 1974 standard and to CODASYL COBOL.
ibm-n	A reserved word not used by OS/VS COBOL, but used by another IBM COBOL.
cod	A CODASYL COBOL reserved word not used by OS/VS COBOL.

Figure: Codes Used in Reserved Word List

Figure E.1

Code	Word
	ACCEPT
	ACCESS
ibm-c	ACTUAL
	ADD
cod	ADDRESS
	ADVANCING
	AFTER
	ALL
cod	ALPHABET
	ALPHABETIC
cod	ALPHANUMERIC
cod	ALPHANUMERIC-EDITED
	ALSO
	ALTER
	ALTERNATE
	AND
cod	ANY
ibm-a	APPLY
	ARE
	AREA
	AREAS
	ASCENDING
	ASSIGN
	AT
	AUTHOR
ibm-c	BASIS
	BEFORE
ibm-a	BEGINNING
cod	BIT
cod	BITS
	BLANK
	BLOCK
cod	BOOLEAN
	BOTTOM
	BY
	CALL
	CANCEL
ibm-c	CBL
	CD
	CF
	CH
ibm-c	CHANGED
	CHARACTER
	CHARACTERS
ans-n	CLOCK-UNITS
	CLOSE
ans-n	COBOL
	CODE
	CODE-SET
	COLLATING
	COLUMN
ibm-n	COM-REG
	COMMA
	COMMUNICATION
	COMP
ibm-a	COMP-1
ibm-a	COMP-2
ibm-a	COMP-3
ibm-a	COMP-4
	COMPUTATIONAL
ibm-a	COMPUTATIONAL-1
ibm-a	COMPUTATIONAL-2
ibm-a	COMPUTATIONAL-3
ibm-a	COMPUTATIONAL-4
	COMPUTE
	CONFIGURATION

Code	Word	Code	Word	Code	Word
cod	CONNECT			ibm-c	ID
ans-f	CONSOLE	ibm-n	DEPTH		IDENTIFICATION
	CONTAINS		DESCENDING		IF
	CONTROL		DESTINATION		IN
	CONTROLS		DETAIL	cod	INCLUDING
cod	CONVERSION		DISABLE		INDEX
cod	CONVERTING	cod	DISCONNECT	cod	INDEX-n
	COPY	ibm-c	DISP		INDEXED
ibm-c	CORE-INDEX		DISPLAY		INDICATE
	CORR	ibm-c	DISPLAY-ST		INITIAL
	CORRESPONDING		DIVIDE	cod	INITIALIZE
	COUNT		DIVISION		INITIATE
ans-f	CSP		DOWN		INPUT
	CURRENCY	cod	DUPLICATE		INPUT-OUTPUT
cod	CURRENT		DUPLICATES	ibm-c	INSERT
ibm-c	CURRENT-DATE		DYNAMIC		INSPECT
ibm-n	CYL-INDEX		EGI		INSTALLATION
ibm-n	CYL-OVERFLOW	ibm-c	EJECT		INTO
ans-f	C01		ELSE		INVALID
ans-f	C02		EMI		IS
ans-f	C03	cod	EMPTY		JUST
ans-f	C04		ENABLE		JUSTIFIED
ans-f	C05		END	cod	KEEP
ans-f	C06		END-OF-PAGE		KEY
ans-f	C07	ibm-a	ENDING		LABEL
ans-f	C08		ENTER	ibm-n	LABEL-RETURN
ans-f	C09	ibm-c	ENTRY		LAST
ans-f	C10		ENVIRONMENT		LEADING
ans-f	C11		EOP	ibm-c	LEAVE
ans-f	C12		EQUAL		LEFT
	DATA	cod	EQUALS		LENGTH
	DATE	cod	ERASE		LESS
	DATE-COMPILED		ERROR		LIMIT
	DATE-WRITTEN		ESI		LIMITS
	DAY		EVERY		LINAGE
cod	DAY-OF-WEEK	ans-o	EXAMINE		LINAGE-COUNTER
cod	DB	cod	EXCEEDS		LINE
cod	DB-CONFLICT		EXCEPTION		LINE-COUNTER
cod	DB-EXCEPTION	cod	EXCLUSIVE		LINES
cod	DB-KEY	ibm-c	EXHIBIT		LINKAGE
cod	DB-PRIVACY-KEY		EXIT	cod	LOCALLY
cod	DB-REALM-NAME	cod	EXOR		LOCK
cod	DB-RECORD-NAME		EXTEND		LOW-VALUE
cod	DB-SET-NAME	ibm-n	EXTENDED-SEARCH		LOW-VALUES
cod	DB-STATUS		FD	ibm-n	MASTER-INDEX
	DE		FILE	cod	MEMBER
ibm-c	DEBUG		FILE-CONTROL	cod	MEMBERS
	DEBUG-CONTENTS	ans-o	FILE-LIMIT	cod	MEMBERSHIP
	DEBUG-ITEM	ans-o	FILE-LIMITS		MEMORY
cod	DEBUG-LENGTH	cod	FILES		MERGE
	DEBUG-LINE		FILLER		MESSAGE
	DEBUG-NAME		FINAL		MODE
cod	DEBUG-NUMERIC-CONTENTS	cod	FIND	cod	MODIFY
cod	DEBUG-SIZE	cod	FINISH	cod	MODULES
cod	DEBUG-START		FIRST	ibm-c	MORE-LABELS
cod	DEBUG-SUB		FOOTING		MOVE
cod	DEBUG-SUB-ITEM		FOR		MULTIPLE
cod	DEBUG-SUB-N		FREE		MULTIPLY
cod	DEBUG-SUB-NUM	cod	FROM	ibm-c	NAMED
	DEBUG-SUB-1		GENERATE		NATIVE
	DEBUG-SUB-2	cod	GET		NEGATIVE
	DEBUG-SUB-3		GIVING		NEXT
	DEBUGGING		GO		NO
	DECIMAL-POINT		GREATER	ibm-c	NOMINAL
	DECLARATIVES		GROUP	cod	NON-NULL
	DELETE		HEADING		NOT
	DELIMITED		HIGH-VALUE	ans-o	NOTE
	DELIMITER		HIGH-VALUES	ibm-n	NSTD-REELS
	DEPENDING		I-O	cod	NULL
			I-O-CONTROL		NUMBER
					NUMERIC

Figure E.2

431

Code	Word
cod	NUMERIC-EDITED
	OBJECT-COMPUTER
	OCCURS
cod	OF
	OFF
	OMITTED
	ON
cod	ONLY
	OPEN
	OPTIONAL
	OR
cod	ORDER
	ORGANIZATION
cod	OTHER
ibm-c	OTHERWISE
	OUTPUT
	OVERFLOW
cod	OWNER
cod	PADDING
	PAGE
	PAGE-COUNTER
ibm-c	PASSWORD
	PERFORM
cod	PERMANENT
	PF
	PH
	PIC
	PICTURE
	PLUS
	POINTER
	POSITION
ibm-c	POSITIONING
	POSITIVE
ibm-c	PRINT-SWITCH
ans-n	PRINTING
cod	PRIOR
cod	PRIVACY
	PROCEDURE
	PROCEDURES
	PROCEED
cod	PROCESS
ans-o	PROCESSING
	PROGRAM
	PROGRAM-ID
cod	PROTECTED
cod	PURGE
	QUEUE
	QUOTE
	QUOTES
	RANDOM
	RD
	READ
ibm-a	READY
cod	REALM
cod	REALMS
cod	REALM-NAME
	RECEIVE
	RECORD
cod	RECORD-NAME
ibm-c	RECORD-OVERFLOW
	RECORDS
	REDEFINES
	REEL
cod	REFERENCE-MODIFIER
	REFERENCES
	RELATIVE
	RELEASE
ibm-c	RELOAD
	REMAINDER
ans-o	REMARKS

Code	Word
cod	REMONITOR
	REMOVAL
	RENAMES
ibm-c	REORG-CRITERIA
	REPLACING
	REPORT
	REPORTING
	REPORTS
ibm-c'	REREAD
	RERUN
	RESERVE
	RESET
cod	RETAINING
cod	RETRIEVAL
	RETURN
ibm-c	RETURN-CODE
	REVERSED
	REWIND
	REWRITE
	RF
	RH
	RIGHT
	ROUNDED
	RUN
	SAME
	SD
	SEARCH
	SECTION
	SECURITY
ans-o	SEEK
	SEGMENT
	SEGMENT-LIMIT
	SELECT
cod	SELECTIVE
	SEND
	SENTENCE
	SEPARATE
	SEQUENCE
	SEQUENTIAL
ibm-c	SERVICE
	SET
	SIGN
	SIZE
ibm-c	SKIP1
ibm-c	SKIP2
ibm-c	SKIP3
	SORT
ibm-c	SORT-CORE-SIZE
ibm-c	SORT-FILE-SIZE
	SORT-MERGE
ibm-c	SORT-MESSAGE
ibm-c	SORT-MODE-SIZE
ibm-n	SORT-OPTION
ibm-c	SORT-RETURN
	SOURCE
	SOURCE-COMPUTER
	SPACE
	SPACES
	SPECIAL-NAMES
	STANDARD
	STANDARD-1
cod	STANDARD-2
	START
	STATUS
	STOP
cod	STORE
	STRING
	SUB-QUEUE-1
	SUB-QUEUE-2
	SUB-QUEUE-3

Code	Word
cod	SUB-SCHEMA
	SUBTRACT
	SUM
	SUPPRESS
cod	SUSPEND
	SYMBOLIC
	SYNC
	SYNCHRONIZED
ans-f	SYSIN
ibm-n	SYSIPT
ibm-n	SYSLST
ans-f	SYSOUT
ibm-n	SYSPCH
ans-f	SYSPUNCH
ibm-c	S01
ibm-c	S02
ibm-n	S03
ibm-n	S04
ibm-n	S05
	TABLE
ans-o	TALLY
	TALLYING
	TAPE
cod	TENANT
	TERMINAL
	TERMINATE
	TEXT
	THAN
ibm-a	THEN
	THROUGH
	THRU
	TIME
ibm-c	TIME-OF-DAY
	TIMES
	TO
	TOP
ibm-c	TOTALED
ibm-c	TOTALING
ibm-c	TRACE
ibm-c	TRACK
ibm-c	TRACK-AREA
ibm-c	TRACK-LIMIT
ibm-c	TRACKS
	TRAILING
ibm-c	TRANSFORM
	TYPE
cod	UNEQUAL
	UNIT
	UNSTRING
	UNTIL
	UP
cod	UPDATE
	UPON
ans-f	UPSI-0
ans-f	UPSI-1
ans-f	UPSI-2
ans-f	UPSI-3
ans-f	UPSI-4
ans-f	UPSI-5
ans-f	UPSI-6
ans-f	UPSI-7
	USAGE
cod	USAGE-MODE
	USE
	USING
	VALUE
	VALUES
	VARYING
	WHEN
ibm-c	WHEN-COMPILED
	WITH
cod	WITHIN
	WORDS
	WORKING-STORAGE
	WRITE
ibm-c	WRITE-ONLY
ibm-n	WRITE-VERIFY
	ZERO
	ZEROES
	ZEROS
	<
	+
	*
	**
	–
	/
	>
	=

Figure E.3

Assembler Formats

MACHINE INSTRUCTIONS

NAME	MNEMONIC	OP CODE	FOR-MAT	OPERANDS
Add (c)	AR	1A	RR	R1,R2
Add (c)	A	5A	RX	R1,D2(X2,B2)
Add Decimal (c)	AP	FA	SS	D1(L1,B1),D2(L2,B2)
Add Halfword (c)	AH	4A	RX	R1,D2(X2,B2)
Add Logical (c)	ALR	1E	RR	R1,R2
Add Logical (c)	AL	5E	RX	R1,D2(X2,B2)
AND (c)	NR	14	RR	R1,R2
AND (c)	N	54	RX	R1,D2(X2,B2)
AND (c)	NI	94	SI	D1(B1),I2
AND (c)	NC	D4	SS	D1(L,B1),D2(B2)
Branch and Link	BALR	05	RR	R1,R2
Branch and Link	BAL	45	RX	R1,D2(X2,B2)
Branch on Condition	BCR	07	RR	M1,R2
Branch on Condition	BC	47	RX	M1,D2(X2,B2)
Branch on Count	BCTR	06	RR	R1,R2
Branch on Count	BCT	46	RX	R1,D2(X2,B2)
Branch on Index High	BXH	86	RS	R1,R3,D2(B2)
Branch on Index Low or Equal	BXLE	87	RS	R1,R3,D2(B2)
Clear I/O (c,p)	CLRIO	9D01	S	D2(B2)
Compare (c)	CR	19	RR	R1,R2
Compare (c)	C	59	RX	R1,D2(X2,B2)
Compare and Swap (c)	CS	BA	RS	R1,R3,D2(B2)
Compare Decimal (c)	CP	F9	SS	D1(L1,B1),D2(L2,B2)
Compare Double and Swap (c)	CDS	BB	RS	R1,R3,D2(B2)
Compare Halfword (c)	CH	49	RX	R1,D2(X2,B2)
Compare Logical (c)	CLR	15	RR	R1,R2
Compare Logical (c)	CL	55	RX	R1,D2(X2,B2)
Compare Logical (c)	CLC	D5	SS	D1(L,B1),D2(B2)
Compare Logical (c)	CLI	95	SI	D1(B1),I2
Compare Logical Characters under Mask (c)	CLM	BD	RS	R1,M3,D2(B2)
Compare Logical Long (c)	CLCL	0F	RR	R1,R2
Convert to Binary	CVB	4F	RX	R1,D2(X2,B2)
Convert to Decimal	CVD	4E	RX	R1,D2(X2,B2)
Diagnose (p)		83		Model-dependent
Divide	DR	1D	RR	R1,R2
Divide	D	5D	RX	R1,D2(X2,B2)
Divide Decimal	DP	FD	SS	D1(L1,B1),D2(L2,B2)
Edit (c)	ED	DE	SS	D1(L,B1),D2(B2)
Edit and Mark (c)	EDMK	DF	SS	D1(L,B1),D2(B2)
Exclusive OR (c)	XR	17	RR	R1,R2
Exclusive OR (c)	X	57	RX	R1,D2(X2,B2)
Exclusive OR (c)	XI	97	SI	D1(B1),I2
Exclusive OR (c)	XC	D7	SS	D1(L,B1),D2(B2)
Execute	EX	44	RX	R1,D2(X2,B2)
Halt I/O (c,p)	HIO	9E00	S	D2(B2)
Halt Device (c,p)	HDV	9E01	S	D2(B2)
Insert Character	IC	43	RX	R1,D2(X2,B2)
Insert Characters under Mask (c)	ICM	BF	RS	R1,M3,D2(B2)
Insert PSW Key (p)	IPK	B20B	S	
Insert Storage Key (p)	ISK	09	RR	R1,R2
Load	LR	18	RR	R1,R2
Load	L	58	RX	R1,D2(X2,B2)
Load Address	LA	41	RX	R1,D2(X2,B2)
Load and Test (c)	LTR	12	RR	R1,R2
Load Complement (c)	LCR	13	RR	R1,R2
Load Control (p)	LCTL	B7	RS	R1,R3,D2(B2)
Load Halfword	LH	48	RX	R1,D2(X2,B2)
Load Multiple	LM	98	RS	R1,R3,D2(B2)
Load Negative (c)	LNR	11	RR	R1,R2
Load Positive (c)	LPR	10	RR	R1,R2
Load PSW (n,p)	LPSW	82	S	D2(B2)
Load Real Address (c,p)	LRA	B1	RX	R1,D2(X2,B2)
Monitor Call	MC	AF	SI	D1(B1),I2
Move	MVI	92	SI	D1(B1),I2
Move	MVC	D2	SS	D1(L,B1),D2(B2)
Move Long (c)	MVCL	0E	RR	R1,R2
Move Numerics	MVN	D1	SS	D1(L,B1),D2(B2)
Move with Offset	MVO	F1	SS	D1(L1,B1),D2(L2,B2)

MACHINE INSTRUCTIONS (Contd)

NAME	MNEMONIC	OP CODE	FORMAT	OPERANDS
Move Zones	MVZ	D3	SS	D1(L,B1),D2(B2)
Multiply	MR	1C	RR	R1,R2
Multiply	M	5C	RX	R1,D2(X2,B2)
Multiply Decimal	MP	FC	SS	D1(L1,B1),D2(L2,B2)
Multiply Halfword	MH	4C	RX	R1,D2(X2,B2)
OR (c)	OR	16	RR	R1,R2
OR (c)	O	56	RX	R1,D2(X2,B2)
OR (c)	OI	96	SI	D1(B1),I2
OR (c)	OC	D6	SS	D1(L,B1),D2(B2)
Pack	PACK	F2	SS	D1(L1,B1),D2(L2,B2)
Purge TLB (p)	PTLB	B20D	S	
Read Direct (p)	RDD	85	SI	D1(B1),I2
Reset Reference Bit (c,p)	RRB	B213	S	D2(B2)
Set Clock (c,p)	SCK	B204	S	D2(B2)
Set Clock Comparator (p)	SCKC	B206	S	D2(B2)
Set CPU Timer (p)	SPT	B208	S	D2(B2)
Set Prefix (p)	SPX	B210	S	D2(B2)
Set Program Mask (n)	SPM	04	RR	R1
Set PSW Key from Address (p)	SPKA	B20A	S	D2(B2)
Set Storage Key (p)	SSK	08	RR	R1,R2
Set System Mask (p)	SSM	80	S	D2(B2)
Shift and Round Decimal (c)	SRP	F0	SS	D1(L1,B1),D2(B2),I3
Shift Left Double (c)	SLDA	8F	RS	R1,D2(B2)
Shift Left Double Logical	SLDL	8D	RS	R1,D2(B2)
Shift Left Single (c)	SLA	8B	RS	R1,D2(B2)
Shift Left Single Logical	SLL	89	RS	R1,D2(B2)
Shift Right Double (c)	SRDA	8E	RS	R1,D2(B2)
Shift Right Double Logical	SRDL	8C	RS	R1,D2(B2)
Shift Right Single (c)	SRA	8A	RS	R1,D2(B2)
Shift Right Single Logical	SRL	88	RS	R1,D2(B2)
Signal Processor (c,p)	SIGP	AE	RS	R1,R3,D2(B2)
Start I/O (c,p)	SIO	9C00	S	D2(B2)
Start I/O Fast Release (c,p)	SIOF	9C01	S	D2(B2)
Store	ST	50	RX	R1,D2(X2,B2)
Store Channel ID (c,p)	STIDC	B203	S	D2(B2)
Store Character	STC	42	RX	R1,D2(X2,B2)
Store Characters under Mask	STCM	BE	RS	R1,M3,D2(B2)
Store Clock (c)	STCK	B205	S	D2(B2)
Store Clock Comparator (p)	STCKC	B207	S	D2(B2)
Store Control (p)	STCTL	B6	RS	R1,R3,D2(B2)
Store CPU Address (p)	STAP	B212	S	D2(B2)
Store CPU ID (p)	STIDP	B202	S	D2(B2)
Store CPU Timer (p)	STPT	B209	S	D2(B2)
Store Halfword	STH	40	RX	R1,D2(X2,B2)
Store Multiple	STM	90	RS	R1,R3,D2(B2)
Store Prefix (p)	STPX	B211	S	D2(B2)
Store Then AND System Mask (p)	STNSM	AC	SI	D1(B1),I2
Store Then OR System Mask (p)	STOSM	AD	SI	D1(B1),I2
Subtract (c)	SR	1B	RR	R1,R2
Subtract (c)	S	5B	RX	R1,D2(X2,B2)
Subtract Decimal (c)	SP	FB	SS	D1(L1,B1),D2(L2,B2)
Subtract Halfword (c)	SH	4B	RX	R1,D2(X2,B2)
Subtract Logical (c)	SLR	1F	RR	R1,R2
Subtract Logical (c)	SL	5F	RX	R1,D2(X2,B2)
Supervisor Call	SVC	0A	RR	I
Test and Set (c)	TS	93	S	D2(B2)
Test Channel (c,p)	TCH	9F00	S	D2(B2)
Test I/O (c,p)	TIO	9D00	S	D2(B2)
Test under Mask (c)	TM	91	SI	D1(B1),I2
Translate	TR	DC	SS	D1(L,B1),D2(B2)
Translate and Test (c)	TRT	DD	SS	D1(L,B1),D2(B2)
Unpack	UNPK	F3	SS	D1(L1,B1),D2(L2,B2)
Write Direct (p)	WRD	84	SI	D1(B1),I2
Zero and Add Decimal (c)	ZAP	F8	SS	D1(L1,B1),D2(L2,B2)

c. Condition code is set.
n. New condition code is loaded.
p. Privileged instruction.
x. Extended precision floating-point.

435

Floating-Point Instructions

NAME	MNEMONIC	OP CODE	FORMAT	OPERANDS
Add Normalized, Extended (c,x)	AXR	36	RR	R1,R2
Add Normalized, Long (c)	ADR	2A	RR	R1,R2
Add Normalized, Long (c)	AD	6A	RX	R1,D2(X2,B2)
Add Normalized, Short (c)	AER	3A	RR	R1,R2
Add Normalized, Short (c)	AE	7A	RX	R1,D2(X2,B2)
Add Unnormalized, Long (c)	AWR	2E	RR	R1,R2
Add Unnormalized, Long (c)	AW	6E	RX	R1,D2(X2,B2)
Add Unnormalized, Short (c)	AUR	3E	RR	R1,R2
Add Unnormalized, Short (c)	AU	7E	RX	R1,D2(X2,B2)
Compare, Long (c)	CDR	29	RR	R1,R2
Compare, Long (c)	CD	69	RX	R1,D2(X2,B2)
Compare, Short (c)	CER	39	RR	R1,R2
Compare, Short (c)	CE	79	RX	R1,D2(X2,B2)
Divide, Long	DDR	2D	RR	R1,R2
Divide, Long	DD	6D	RX	R1,D2(X2,B2)
Divide, Short	DER	3D	RR	R1,R2
Divide, Short	DE	7D	RX	R1,D2(X2,B2)
Halve, Long	HDR	24	RR	R1,R2
Halve, Short	HER	34	RR	R1,R2
Load and Test, Long (c)	LTDR	22	RR	R1,R2
Load and Test, Short (c)	LTER	32	RR	R1,R2
Load Complement, Long (c)	LCDR	23	RR	R1,R2
Load Complement, Short (c)	LCER	33	RR	R1,R2
Load, Long	LDR	28	RR	R1,R2
Load, Long	LD	68	RX	R1,D2(X2,B2)
Load Negative, Long (c)	LNDR	21	RR	R1,R2
Load Negative, Short (c)	LNER	31	RR	R1,R2
Load Positive, Long (c)	LPDR	20	RR	R1,R2
Load Positive, Short (c)	LPER	30	RR	R1,R2
Load Rounded, Extended to Long (x)	LRDR	25	RR	R1,R2
Load Rounded, Long to Short (x)	LRER	35	RR	R1,R2
Load, Short	LER	38	RR	R1,R2
Load, Short	LE	78	RX	R1,D2(X2,B2)
Multiply, Extended (x)	MXR	26	RR	R1,R2
Multiply, Long	MDR	2C	RR	R1,R2
Multiply, Long	MD	6C	RX	R1,D2(X2,B2)
Multiply, Long/Extended (x)	MXDR	27	RR	R1,R2
Multiply, Long/Extended (x)	MXD	67	RX	R1,D2(X2,B2)
Multiply, Short	MER	3C	RR	R1,R2
Multiply, Short	ME	7C	RX	R1,D2(X2,B2)
Store, Long	STD	60	RX	R1,D2(X2,B2)
Store, Short	STE	70	RX	R1,D2(X2,B2)
Subtract Normalized, Extended (c,x)	SXR	37	RR	R1,R2
Subtract Normalized, Long (c)	SDR	2B	RR	R1,R2
Subtract Normalized, Long (c)	SD	6B	RX	R1,D2(X2,B2)
Subtract Normalized, Short (c)	SER	3B	RR	R1,R2
Subtract Normalized, Short (c)	SE	7B	RX	R1,D2(X2,B2)
Subtract Unnormalized, Long (c)	SWR	2F	RR	R1,R2
Subtract Unnormalized, Long (c)	SW	6F	RX	R1,D2(X2,B2)
Subtract Unnormalized, Short (c)	SUR	3F	RR	R1,R2
Subtract Unnormalized, Short (c)	SU	7F	RX	R1,D2(X2,B2)

JCL Reference for MVS

The JOB Statement

//Name	Operation	Operand	P/K	Comments
//jobname	JOB	([account number] [,additional accounting information,...])	P	Identifies accounting information. Can be made mandatory.
		$\left[\text{ADDRSPC} = \left\{ \begin{matrix} \text{VIRT} \\ \text{REAL} \end{matrix} \right\} \right]$	K	Requests storage type.
		[CLASS=jobclass]	K	Assigns a job class to each job.
		[COND=((code,operator),...)]	K	Specifies test for a return code.
		[GROUP=group name]	K	Specifies a group associated with a RACF-defined user.
		[MSGCLASS=output class]	K	Assigns an output class for the job.
		$\left[\text{MSGLEVEL} = \left(\begin{bmatrix} 0 \\ 1 \\ 2 \end{bmatrix} \begin{bmatrix} ,0 \\ ,1 \end{bmatrix} \right) \right]$	K	Specifies what job output is to be written.
		[NOTIFY=user identification]	K	Requests a message be sent to a time-sharing terminal.
		[PASSWORD=(password [,new password])]	K	Specifies a password for a RACF-defined user.
		[PERFORM=n]	K	Specifies the performance group a job belongs to.
		[programmer's name]	P	Identifies programmer. Can be made mandatory.
		[PRTY=priority]	K	Specifies a job's priority.
		$\left[\text{RD} = \left\{ \begin{matrix} \text{R} \\ \text{RNC} \\ \text{NC} \\ \text{NR} \end{matrix} \right\} \right]$	K	Specifies restart facilities to be used.
		[REGION=valueK]	K	Specifies amount of storage space.
		$\left[\text{RESTART} = \left(\left\{ \begin{matrix} * \\ \text{stepname} \\ \text{stepname.procstepname} \end{matrix} \right\} [,\text{checkid}] \right) \right]$	K	Specifies restart facilities for deferred restart.
		$\left[\text{TIME} = \left\{ \begin{matrix} ([\text{minutes}] [,\text{seconds}]) \\ 1440 \end{matrix} \right\} \right]$	K	Assigns a job a CPU time limit.
		$\left[\text{TYPRUN} = \left\{ \begin{matrix} \text{HOLD} \\ \text{JCLHOLD} \\ \text{SCAN} \\ \text{COPY} \end{matrix} \right\} \right]$	K	Holds a job in job queue, scans JCL for syntax errors, or copies the input deck to SYSOUT.
		[USER=userid]	K	Identifies a RACF-defined user.

Legend:

P   Positional parameter.
K   Keyword parameter
{ }   Choose one.
[ ]   Optional; if more than one line is enclosed, choose one or none.

Figure G.1

The EXEC Statement

//Name	Operation	Operand	P/K	Comments
//[stepname]	EXEC	[ACCT [.procstepname] = (accounting information, ...)]	K	Accounting information for step.
		[ADDRSPC [.procstepname] = $\left\{ \begin{matrix} VIRT \\ REAL \end{matrix} \right\}$]	K	Requests storage type.
		[COND [.procstepname] = ($\left\{ \begin{matrix} (code,operator) \\ (code,operator,stepname) \\ (code,operator,stepname.procstepname) \end{matrix} \right\}$, ... [,] $\left[\begin{matrix} EVEN \\ ONLY \end{matrix} \right]$)]	K	Specifies a test for a return code.
		[DPRTY [.procstepname] =([value1] [,value2])]	K	Specifies dispatching priority for a job step.
		[DYNAMNBR [.procstepname] =n]	K	Specifies dynamic allocation.
		[PARM [.procstepname] =value]	K	Passes variable information to a program at execution time.
		[PERFORM [.procstepname] =n]	K	Specifies a performance group for a job.
		[PGM= $\left\{ \begin{matrix} program\ name \\ *.stepname.ddname \\ *.stepname.procstepname.ddname \end{matrix} \right\}$]	P	Identifies program.
		[[PROC=] procedure name]	P	Identifies a cataloged or instream procedure.
		[RD [.procstepname] = $\left\{ \begin{matrix} R \\ RNC \\ NC \\ NR \end{matrix} \right\}$]	K	Specifies restart facilities to be used.
		[REGION [.procstepname] =valueK]	K	Specifies amount of storage space.
		[TIME [.procstepname] = $\left\{ \begin{matrix} ([minutes] [,seconds]) \\ 1440 \end{matrix} \right\}$]	K	Assigns step CPU time limit.

Legend:

K Keyword parameter.
P Positional parameter.
{} Choose one.
[] Optional; if more than one line is enclosed, choose one or none.

Figure G.2

The DD Statement

//Name	Oper-ation	Operand	P/K	Comments
//⌈ddname⌉ ⌊procstepname. ddname⌋,	DD	[*]	P	Defines data set in the input stream.
		AMP={ AMORG ,'BUFND=number' ,'BUFNI=number' ,'BUFSP=number' ,'CROPS= {RCK' / NCK' / NRE' / NRC'} ,'OPTCD= {I' / L' / IL'} ,'RECFM= {F' / FB' / V' / VB'} ,'STRNO=number' ,'SYNAD=modulename' ,TRACE }	K	Completes the access method control block (ACB) for VSAM data sets.
		[BURST={Y / N}]	K	Specifies whether or not paper output is to go to the Burster-Trimmer-Stacker of the 3800.
		[CHARS=(table name [,table name . . .])]	K	Specifies character arrangement table(s) to be used when printing on the 3800.
		[CHKPT=EOV]	K	For checkpoint at end of volume.
		[COPIES=(nnn [, (group value,group value . . .)])]	K	Requests multiple copies (and grouping, for the 3800 only) of the output data set.
		[DATA]	P	Defines data set in the input stream.
		DCB=(list of attributes) DCB=({ dsname *.ddname *.stepname.ddname *.stepname.procstepname.ddname } [, list of attributes])	K	Completes the data control block (used for all data sets except VSAM).
		[DDNAME=ddname]	K	Postpones the definition of a data set.
		[DEST=destination]	K	Specifies a destination for the output data set.
		DISP=([NEW / OLD / SHR / MOD / ,] [,DELETE / ,KEEP / ,PASS / ,CATLG / ,UNCATLG / ,] [,DELETE / ,KEEP / ,CATLG / ,UNCATLG])	K	Assigns a status, disposition, and conditional disposition to the data set.
		[DLM=delimiter]	K	Assigns delimiter other than /*.

Figure G.3

440

The DD Statement (con't)

//Name	Oper-ation	Operand	P/K	Comments
//[ddname procstepname. ddname]	DD	[DSID=(id[,V])]	K	Indicates to a diskette reader that data is to be merged into the JCL stream at this point or specifies the name to be given to a SYSOUT data set written on a diskette.
		$\left[\begin{Bmatrix} DSNAME \\ DSN \end{Bmatrix} = \begin{Bmatrix} dsname \\ dsname(member\ name) \\ dsname(generation\ number) \\ dsname(area\ name) \\ \&\&dsname \\ \&\&dsname(member\ name) \\ \&\&dsname(area\ name) \\ *.ddname \\ *.stepname.ddname \\ *.stepname.procstepname.ddname \end{Bmatrix}\right]$	K	Assigns a name to a new data set or to identify an existing data set.
		[DUMMY]	P	Bypasses I/O operations on a data set (BSAM and QSAM).
		[DYNAM]	P	Specifies dynamic allocation.
		$\left[FCB=(image\text{-}id \begin{bmatrix} ,ALIGN \\ ,VERIFY \end{bmatrix}) \right]$	K	Specifies forms control information. The FCB parameter is ignored if the data set is not written to a 3211 or 1403 printer.
		[FLASH=(overlay name[,count])]	K	Identifies the forms overlay to be used on the 3800.
		$\left[FREE= \begin{Bmatrix} END \\ CLOSE \end{Bmatrix} \right]$	K	Specifies dynamic deallocation.
		$\left[HOLD= \begin{Bmatrix} YES \\ NO \end{Bmatrix} \right]$	K	Specifies whether output processing is to be deferred or processed normally.
		$\left[LABEL=\left(\begin{bmatrix} data\ set\ seq\ \# \end{bmatrix} \begin{bmatrix} ,SL \\ ,SUL \\ ,AL \\ ,AUL \\ ,NSL \\ ,NL \\ ,BLP \\ ,LTM \\ , \end{bmatrix} \begin{bmatrix} ,PASSWORD \\ ,NOPWREAD \\ , \end{bmatrix} \begin{bmatrix} ,IN \\ ,OUT \end{bmatrix} \begin{bmatrix} ,EXPDT=yyddd \\ ,RETPD=nnnn \end{bmatrix}\right) \right]$	K	Supplies label information.
		[MODIFY=(module name[,trc])]	K	Specifies a copy modification module that is to be loaded into the 3800.
		[MSVGP=(id[,ddname])]	K	Identifies a mass storage group for a mass storage system (MSS) device.
		[OUTLIM=number]	K	Limits the number of logical records you want included in the output data set.

Figure G.4

441

The DD Statement (con't)

//Name	Oper-ation	Operand	P/K	Comments
// [ddname / procstepname. / ddname]	DD	[PROTECT=YES]	K	Requests RACF protection for tape volumes or for direct access data sets.
		[QNAME=process name]	K	Specifies the name of a TPROCESS macro which defines a destination queue for messages received by means of TCAM.
		SPACE=({ TRK / CYL / blocklength },(primary quantity [,secondary quantity][,directory / ,index]) [,RLSE][,CONTIG / ,MXIG / ,ALX][,ROUND])	K	Assigns space on a direct access volume for a new data set.
		SPACE=(ABSTR,(primary quantity,address [,directory / ,index]))	K	Assigns specific tracks on a direct access volume for a new data set.
		[SUBSYS = (subsystem name [,parm1 [,parm2] ... [,parm254]])]	K	Specifies the subsystem that will process both the data set and the specified parameters.
		[SYSOUT=(class name [,program name][,form name / ,code name])]	K	Assigns an output class to an output data set.
		[TERM=TS]	K	Identifies a time-sharing user.
		[UCS=(character set code [,FOLD][,VERIFY])]	K	Requests a special character set for a 3211 or a 1403 printer.
		[{UNIT=([unit address / device type / user-assigned group name] [,unit count / ,P][,DEFER]) / UNIT=AFF=ddname}]	K	Provides the system with unit information.
		[{VOLUME / VOL}=([PRIVATE][,RETAIN][,volume seq number][,volume count][,] [SER=(serial number,...) / REF=dsname / REF=*.ddname / REF=*.stepname.ddname / REF=*.stepname.procstepname.ddname])]	K	Provides the system with volume information.

Legend:

P   Positional parameter.
K   Keyword parameter.
{}   Choose one.

[ ]   Enclosing subparameter, indicates that subparameter is optional; if more than one line is enclosed, choose one or more.

Figure G.5

442

Answers to Selected Exercises

CHAPTER 3

PROBLEMS

1. The 12 pairs of values are given below. Each set in parentheses represents (FIRST, SECOND).

$$(1,1), \ (1,2), \ (2,1), \ (2,2), \ (3,1), \ (3,2)$$
$$(4,1), \ (4,2), \ (5,1), \ (5,2), \ (6,1), \ (6,2)$$

2. The 24 sets of values are given below. Each set in parentheses represents (FIRST, SECOND, THIRD).

$$(1,1,1), \ (2,1,1), \ (1,2,1), \ (2,2,1), \ (1,3,1), \ (2,3,1)$$
$$(1,1,2), \ (2,1,2), \ (1,2,2), \ (2,2,2), \ (1,3,2), \ (2,3,2)$$
$$(1,1,3), \ (2,1,3), \ (1,2,3), \ (2,2,3), \ (1,3,3), \ (2,3,3)$$
$$(1,1,4), \ (2,1,4), \ (1,2,4), \ (2,2,4), \ (1,3,4), \ (2,3,4)$$

3. (a) Same
   (b) Different—the AND function will be performed first when parentheses are omitted.
   (c) Same
   (d) Different—substitution of AND for OR would make them equivalent.

4. (a) THIRD-ROUTINE
   (b) SECOND-ROUTINE
   (c) FIRST-ROUTINE
   (d) SECOND-ROUTINE
   (e) FIRST-ROUTINE
   (f) THIRD-ROUTINE

5. (a) IF A $>$ B
           IF C $>$ D
                MOVE E TO F
           ELSE
                MOVE G TO H.

   (b) IF A $>$ B
           IF C $>$ D
                MOVE E TO F
           ELSE
                MOVE G TO H
       ELSE
           MOVE X TO Y.

(c) IF A > B
    IF C > D
        MOVE E TO F
        ADD 1 TO E
    ELSE
        MOVE G TO H
        ADD 1 TO G.

(d) IF A > B
    MOVE X TO Y
    MOVE Z TO W
  ELSE
    IF C > D
        MOVE 1 TO N
    ELSE
        MOVE 2 TO Y
        ADD 3 TO Z.

6. (a) Once
    (b) Five times
    (c) Four times
    (d) None—comparison is made *prior* to performing the routine.

7. (a) Control would pass to the paragraph, FRESHMAN, then fall through to SOPHOMORE, JUNIOR, etc.
    (b) Control would pass to GRAD-SCHOOL.
    (c) Insert the statement

DIVIDE INCOMING-YEAR-CODE BY 10
GIVING INCOMING-YEAR-CODE

immediately before the GO TO DEPENDING.
    (d) IF INCOMING-YEAR-CODE = 11
        PERFORM FRESHMAN
    ELSE
        IF INCOMING-YEAR-CODE = 17
            PERFORM SOPHOMORE
        ELSE . . .

CHAPTER 4

TRUE/FALSE

1. False; COPY is permitted virtually anywhere in a COBOL program.
2. False; a table can occur at the elementary level and consequently require a picture.
3. False; it appears in the called program.

4. False; the difference is subtle and has to do with a CALL being active; see discussion in chapter.
5. False; a called program can have several entry points.
6. False; the order is critical.
7. False; it can contain several CALL statements, either to the same subprogram or to many different subprograms.
8. False; it has all four divisions.
9. False; indexing is more efficient than subscripting.
10. True
11. True
12. False; SEARCH denotes a sequential search; SEARCH ALL denotes a binary search.
13. True
14. True
15. False; only if SEARCH ALL is specified
16. True
17. False; it could require as many as 500!
18. True
19. False; it can be used if INPUT PROCEDURE is specified
20. True
21. True
22. True
23. True
24. False; it can contain several.
25. False; it must specify USING and either GIVING or OUTPUT PROCEDURE.
26. True
27. True
28. False; it is specified in an SD.
29. False; a COPY may never appear within a COPY.

PROBLEMS

1. (a)

STATE - TABLE					
STATE - NAME (1)		STATE - NAME (50)	POP (1)		POP (50)

(b)

STATE - TABLE					
NAME - POPULATION (1)			NAME - POPULATION (50)		
STATE - NAME (1)	POP (1)		STATE - NAME (50)	POP (50)	

...

(c)

ENROLLMENTS

COLLEGE (1)

COLLEGE (2)

SCHOOL (1)

SCHOOL (5) SCHOOL (1)

YR1   YR4   YR1   YR4 YR1

...   .

(d)

ENROLLMENTS

COLLEGE (1)

COLLEGE (2)

SCH1   SCH2 YR1   YR4 SCH1

...   .

447

2. (a) EMPLOYEE-LOCATION
   (b) EMPLOYEE-NAME
   (c) SORT-FILE
   (d) FILE-TWO
   (e) FILE-ONE, FILE-TWO, SORT-FILE
   (f) SORT-FILE

3. (a) WORKFILE
   (b) JANUARY-SALES, FEBRUARY-SALES, MARCH-SALES, and FIRST-QUARTER-SALES
   (c) WORKFILE
   (d) ACCOUNT-NUMBER
   (e) AMOUNT-OF-SALE
   (f) The record with the higher AMOUNT-OF-SALE
   (g) The record with the lower ACCOUNT-NUMBER
   (h) The record from JANUARY-SALES

4. If several programs utilize the same table and the table changes, each program has to change to reflect the new table. If a COPY is used, changes to the table are made only once, in the COPY member. Although the source code of each program would remain the same, each program still has to be recompiled.

   If however, values are read from a file and the table changes, individual programs need *not* be recompiled. Moreover, changes to the table are still made in one place (i.e., the file containing the table codes).

CHAPTER 5

TRUE/FALSE

1. False; HIGH-VALUES are moved to the first byte.
2. True
3. False; they are in physical order only when the file is initially created; as records are added, they go into overflow areas.
4. True
5. True
6. True
7. True
8. False; any record in a VSAM file is active as inactive records are immediately deleted; HIGH-VALUES denote inactive records under ISAM.
9. False; it contains one or the other, or neither (if DECLARATIVES is used).
10. False; REWRITE is used only to change an existing record.
11. True
12. True
13. False; NOMINAL KEY is required for nonsequential access of an ISAM file.

14. True
15. True
16. False; the file must be opened as I-O.
17. True
18. False; ISAM files can be processed under VS, although VSAM is preferred.
19. True
20. False; they must be in sequential order; else the INVALID KEY condition will be raised.

CHAPTER 6

PROBLEMS

1. (a) Insert a period after MOVE E TO F.
   (b) Remove the period after MOVE 'YES' TO READ-SWITCH.
   (c) Remove the period after ADD 1 TO COUNT-FIELD.
   (d) Remove the period after MOVE C TO D.
   (e) Remove the period after MOVE 'YES' TO INVALID-SWITCH.

2. (a) READ CARD-FILE
           AT END MOVE 'YES' TO END-OF-FILE.
        ADD 1 TO RECORDS-READ.

   (b) IF A > B
           IF C > D
               ADD 1 TO X
           ELSE
               IF E > F
                   ADD 1 TO Y
               ELSE
                   ADD 1 TO Z.

   (c) IF A > B
           IF C > D
               MOVE 1 TO X
           ELSE
               MOVE 1 TO Y
        ELSE
           MOVE 1 TO Z.

   (d) IF A > B
           MOVE X TO Y.
        MOVE A TO B.
        MOVE C TO D.
        MOVE E TO F.

(e) COMPUTE AA = BB + CC
        ON SIZE ERROR ADD 1 TO ERROR-COUNTER.
     PERFORM ERROR-ROUTINE.

(f) WRITE ISAM-RECORD
        INVALID KEY PERFORM ERROR-ROUTINE.
     PERFORM PROCESS-TRANSACTION.
     PERFORM WRITE-EXCEPTION-REPORT.

3. (a) No
   (b) Any group move is treated as an alphanumeric move; hence, the "wrong" kind of zeros are moved (see Figure 7.4).
   (c) Same answer as part b, except a data exception will occur.

4. The period after the AT END clause is in column 73. Hence, the next statement, MOVE 'YES' . . . , is interpreted as part of the AT END and executed *only* at the end of file.

CHAPTER 7

PROBLEMS

2. (a) | F0 | F0 | F2 | F0 |

   (b) | F0 | F0 | F2 | F0 |

   (c) | 00 | 14 |

   (d) | 00 | 14 |

   (e) | 00 | 00 | 00 | 14 |

   (f) | 00 | 00 | 00 | 00 | 00 | 00 | 00 | 14 |

   (g) | 00 | 00 | 00 | 00 | 02 | 0F |

   (h) | 00 | 02 | 0F |

   (i) | 00 | 00 | 00 | 02 | 0F |

3.

	(a)	*(b)*
(1)	1490	05 D2
(2)	−1	FF FF
(3)	32,767	7F FF
(4)	−32,768	80 00

4. (a) 12,345
   (b) 12,345
   (c) −54,321

9. (a) BE01
   (b) 1A69B
   (c) 9999
   (d) 4F01

10. (a) SI
    (b) RX
    (c) SS
    (d) SS
    (e) RR
    (f) RR
    (g) SS
    (h) SS

11. (a) 5B78
    (b) 1357
    (c) Packs what is in the three bytes beginning at 5B78 in the two bytes 1357 and 1358.

CHAPTER 8

PROBLEMS

3. A data exception occurs if and only if one tries to do arithmetic on invalid decimal data (e.g., an invalid sign). When a counter is not initialized, the computer uses whatever happens to be in that storage location. Hence, if by chance a valid decimal number were contained in the storage location for WS-TOTAL-STUDENTS, a data exception will not occur. The resulting sum, however, would be *incorrect*.

4. (a) A data exception would *not* occur. Consider, for example, an incoming four-position field with 7 in the low-order byte and preceded by high-order blanks (e.g. | 40 | 40 | 40 | F7 |). After packing, the field would appear as | 00 | 00 | 7F | . The packing operation "strips" the sign portion of each byte (i.e., the 4 from each blank), leaving a valid field.

   (b) Consider an incoming three-byte field, 7.0, as shown: | F7 | 4B | F0 | . After packing the field would appear as | 7B | 0F | . (Remember that packing switches the sign and digit of the low-order byte and strips the sign of the high-order digits.) B is an invalid decimal digit and would cause a data exception.

5. Since TOTAL-COUNTER was defined as a binary (i.e., COMPUTATIONAL) field, the generated machine instructions will specify binary arithmetic. *Any* combination of bits is *valid* as a binary number and hence a data exception will never occur. The value of TOTAL-COUNTER will be incorrect since it will pick up whatever was there as an initial value.

6. (a) There is no difference.
   (b) There is all the difference in the world. As the subprogram stands now, WS-QUALITY-POINTS and WS-TOTAL-CREDITS are initialized to zero (via MOVE statements) everytime SUBRTN is entered. If a value clause were used instead, they would be initialized only once (i.e., when the program is first loaded). In effect, WS-TOTAL-CREDITS and WS-QUALITY-POINTS would become running counters from student to student.

7. (1) 0CB
   (2) Attempt to divide by zero.
   (3) ID2AD8
   (4) ID0CF8
   (5) IDE0
   (6) No
   (7) 19F0
   (8) 3F0
   (9) SUBRTN
   (10) F8 73 D 200 D 202
   (11) 1D2AD8
   (12) COMPUTE statement in line 50 of SUBRTN
   (13) The instruction 3EA (i.e., FD 51 D 202 D 1FE)
   (14) FD (Divide Packed)
   (15) D (register 13)
   (16) 202
   (17) 1D299A (1D2798 + 202)
   (18) 6
   (19) 00000000000C; yes
   (20) D (register 13)
   (21) 1FE
   (22) 2
   (23) 000F; yes (in locations 1D2996 and 7)
   (24) The ABEND occurred because an attempt was made to divide by zero.
   (25) WS-STUDENT-RECORD
   (26) BL=3
   (27) 834
   (28) 1D152C
   (29) 0020EA08 (the value of BL=1)
   (30) 1D0D98 [found in the third word from 1D152C (i.e., beginning at location 1D1534)]

(31) SMITH, J (Beginning at location 1D0DB8, which is the value of BL=3, 1D0D98, plus the displacement of 020)

(32) DATA-PASSED-FROM-MAIN

(33) BLL=4

(34) 2B8

(35) 1D29A0 (1D0CF8 + 19F0 + 2B8)

(36) 00000000 (The value of BLL=1)

(37) 1D0DB8

(38) Both are used to point to the record in question. WS-STUDENT-RECORD is found at BL=3 plus its displacement of 020; DATA-PASSED-FROM-MAIN is found at BLL=4 plus its displacement of 000.

(39) Register 14 points to the return address in the calling program; register 15 points to the entry point in the called program.

(40) 1D0CF8

(41) 1D185C

(42) B64—the instruction at B64 in the main program is within the COBOL CALL of line 112. It is the place where processing resumes after a return from the subprogram. Note well the instruction immediately above BALR 14,15.

CHAPTER 9

PROBLEMS

1. (1) CCE5F8

    (2) CCE40C

    (3) CCE5F8 (i.e., the address of the TCB)

    (4) CCE57C

    (5) CCE8C4

    (6) Binary zeros in the address portion of the second word of the third DEB.

    (7) 4D

    (8) 28

    (9) 52

    (10) 3E

    (11) 2D

    (12) The last (i.e., third) DEB [DEBs are listed in the inverse order in which files were opened (i.e., the first file open has the last DEB)].

    (13) 1D117C (found in the seventh word)

    (14) 1D11A9 (the contents of the three bytes beginning at this location are CCE8C4, the DEB address)

    (15) 1D11A4; 00A4

    (16) 164

    (17) 164 − 24 = 140 ÷ 20 = 7; hence, the eighth line in TIOT. The DDname on the eighth line is CARDS, which corresponds to the SELECT statement for CARD-FILE.

(18) 1D117C + 4D = 1D11C9; this is the address where the address of last record can be found. The address in the three bytes beginning at 1D11C9 is 20EA08. The contents of the 80 bytes beginning at 20EA08 show that SMITH, JOHN was the last record read.

(19) 1D117C + 52 = 1D11CE; contents of the two bytes beginning at 1D11CE = $(0050)_{16} = (80)_{10}$. This is the record length associated with CARD-FILE, obtained from the COBOL FD.

(20) The second DEB in the chain, beginning at location CCE57C.

(21) 1D1230 (found in the seventh word)

(22) 1D1230 + 2D = 1D125D; this contains the address of the DEB for this DCB. The contents of the three bytes beginning at 1D125D are CCE57C, which match the answer obtained in part 4.

(23) 1D1230 + 28 = 1D1258; contents are 0090.

(24) 144

(25) $144 - 24 = 120 \div 20 = 6$; hence, the seventh line in TIOT. The DDname in the TIOT is SYSOUT, which corresponds to the SELECT statement for PRINT-FILE.

(26) 1D1230 + 52 = 1D1282; contents are $(85)_{16} = (133)_{10}$. This is the record length for PRINT-FILE, as specified in the COBOL FD.

CHAPTER 10

TRUE/FALSE

1. False; a DD statement may contain both keyword and positional parameters.
2. True
3. False; it is preferable to omit explicit specification to achieve device independence.
4. False; /* indicates the end of a data set and consequently may appear several times with a jobstream.
5. True
6. False; a blank in column 3 indicates that the statement is unnamed. All DD statements, with the exception of concatenated data sets, require a name. Moreover, it is good practice to name EXEC statements when a jobstream has more than one.
7. False; comments may follow after a blank.
8. False; // is the last statement.
9. False; no comma is required if no other positional parameters follow.
10. True
11. False; execution is controlled by the COND parameter. It will not be attempted if either the COB or LKED step return a code greater than 4.
12. True
13. False; it is required for *output* data sets on mass storage only.
14. True

15. False; cylinders or blocks can be specified also.
16. False; the system will choose its own volume if omitted.
17. False; it is attempted a maximum of 15 times.
18. False; DATA is also permitted.
19. False; they follow the EXEC statement.
20. True
21. False; the COBOL FD has precedence.
22. False; the data set is kept.
23. True
24. True
25. False; they can reside on different volumes.
26. False; it indicates the current version of a generation data group.
27. False; it indicates the next version.
28. False; they can be used for tape files also.
29. True
30. True for IBM; false for SYNCSORT
31. False; it must be at least three.
32. False; SYSLIB is used in conjunction with a COPY clause.
33. False; a DD statement for SYSOUT should be provided.
34. False; all VSAM data sets are cataloged.
35. False; the functions of these parameters are handled by Access Methods Services for VSAM.
36. False; VSAM data sets are created by Access Methods Services.
37. True
38. True

PROBLEMS

1. (a) True
   (b) False; it is the second file, as indicated by the LABEL parameter.
   (c) False; he will be directed to mount a volume with serial number 123456.
   (d) False; the default for the third subparameter of DISP is KEEP for an existing data set.
   (e) True

2. (a) False; NEWFILE appears in a COBOL SELECT.
   (b) False; the file will be retained until the last day of 1979.
   (c) True
   (d) True
   (e) False; CONTIG was not specified.
   (f) False; only the pack with serial number 123456
   (g) False; a mount message will be issued only if the pack is not currently available.

3. Executed
   Bypassed
   Bypassed
   Executed
   Bypassed
   Executed
   Note: The code in the COND parameter is compared to the system return code. If the relationship is *true*, execution is *bypassed*.

4. The 2311 holds three blocks per track; hence, 1100 (3300/3) tracks or 110 (1100/10) cylinders are required. The 2314 holds six blocks per track; hence 550 tracks, or 28 cylinders, are required.

   (a) //GO.OUTDISK DD UNIT=2311,SPACE=(TRK,(1100,110))
   (b) //GO.OUTDISK DD UNIT=2311,SPACE=(CYL,(110,11))
   (c) //GO.OUTDISK DD UNIT=2314,SPACE=(TRK,(550,55))
   (d) //GO.OUTDISK DD UNIT=2314,SPACE=(CYL,(28,3))
   (e) //GO.OUTDISK DD UNIT=3330,SPACE=(1000,(3300,330))

CHAPTER 11

TRUE/FALSE

1. True
2. True
3. False; symbolic operands are denoted by a single ampersand; a double ampersand denotes a temporary data set.
4. True under MVT; false under MVS.
5. False; SYSLIN and SYSLMOD
6. True
7. False; step names are not required but are decidedly good practice.
8. False; they are permitted on any JCL statement and follow the first blank after the operands.
9. False; it indicates that SYSIN is an empty data set.
10. False; SYSUT1 and SYSUT2 typically denote input and output for utilities.
11. True
12. False; a STEPLIB statement indicates where a particular program (or module) may be found.
13. True
14. False; it frequently references a PDS, as when referencing a procedure or source statement library.
15. True
16. False; it is often useful to save the load module.
17. False; it may be tested instream.
18. True

19. False; IEHPROGM is used.
20. True
21. True
22. True
23. False; they typically begin in column 2 or beyond.
24. False; the order is critical.
25. True
26. False; it is nullified by following the parameter with an equal sign and comma.

PROBLEMS

1. &&MYNAME.AND.YOURS [part (b)] is the only invalid entry. Temporary data sets cannot be qualified and cannot contain more than eight characters.

2. Part (b) is invalid and should read // EXEC *PGM*=IEBGENER.
   Part (e) is invalid because a blank was left in column 3 before the step name.

3. (a) IEBISAM   (f) IEBUPDTE
   (b) IEHPROGM   (g) IEBGENER
   (c) IEHPROGM   (h) IEBISAM
   (d) IEBPTPCH   (i) IEHPROGM
   (e) IEHPROGM

CHAPTER 12

TRUE/FALSE

1. False; What about /*, /&, or /+?
2. True
3. False; /* denotes end of file and may appear several times.
4. True
5. False; /& is the last statement.
6. False; comments may follow the last operand.
7. False; it suspends processing until the operator hits "end of block."
8. False; it is not required for sequential disk.
9. False; it is required when the permanent assignment does *not* match.
10. True
11. False; it is required if label processing is specified.
12. False; the SYS number in the DLBL corresponds to a COBOL SELECT; the EXTENT statement matches an ASSGN.
13. True
14. True
15. False; it is specified on a DLBL or TLBL statement.
16. True

17. False; there are three kinds: volume, header, and trailer.
18. False; it precedes the EXEC LNKEDT.
19. False; it defaults to sequential disk if omitted.
20. False; generic assignments are possible under DOS/VS.
21. False; they are permitted for tape.
22. True
23. False; a tape drive can be assigned to only one partition at a time.
24. False; it is a temporary assignment.
25. True
26. False; order is critical.
27. True
28. True
29. False; specific columns are necessary.
30. False; DITTO has CT and CTS functions.

Index